What They Said
in 1988

To

The Newsmakers of the World . . .

May they never be at a loss for words

What They Said
In 1988

The Yearbook Of World Opinion

Compiled and Edited by
ALAN F. PATER
and
JASON R. PATER

MONITOR BOOK COMPANY

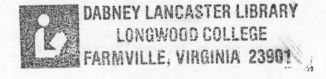

Preface to the First Edition (1969)

Words can be powerful or subtle, humorous or maddening. They can be vigorous or feeble, lucid or obscure, inspiring or despairing, wise or foolish, hopeful or pessimistic . . . they can be fearful or confident, timid or articulate, persuasive or perverse, honest or deceitful. As tools at a speaker's command, words can be used to reason, argue, discuss, cajole, plead, debate, declaim, threaten, infuriate, or appease; they can harangue, flourish, recite, preach, discourse, stab to the quick, or gently sermonize.

When casually spoken by a stage or film star, words can go beyond the press-agentry and make-up facade and reveal the inner man or woman. When purposefully uttered in the considered phrasing of a head of state, words can determine the destiny of millions of people, resolve peace or war, or chart the course of a nation on whose direction the fate of the entire world may depend.

Until now, the *copia verborum* of well-known and renowned public figures—the doctors and diplomats, the governors and generals, the potentates and presidents, the entertainers and educators, the bishops and baseball players, the jurists and journalists, the authors and attorneys, the congressmen and chairmen-of-the-board—whether enunciated in speeches, lectures, interviews, radio and television addresses, news conferences, forums, symposiums, town meetings, committee hearings, random remarks to the press, or delivered on the floors of the United States Senate and House of Representatives or in the parliaments and palaces of the world—have been dutifully reported in the media, then filed away and, for the most part, forgotten.

The editors of *WHAT THEY SAID* believe that consigning such a wealth of thoughts, ideas, doctrines, opinions and philosophies to interment in the morgues and archives of the Fourth Estate is lamentable and unnecessary. Yet the media, in all their forms, are constantly engulfing us in a profusion of endless and increasingly voluminous news reports. One is easily disposed to disregard or forget the stimulating discussion of critical issues embodied in so many of the utterances of those who make the news and, in their respective fields, shape the events throughout the world. The conclusion is therefore a natural and compelling one: the educator, the public official, the business executive, the statesman, the philosopher—everyone who has a stake in the complex, often confusing trends of our times—should have material of this kind readily available.

These, then, are the circumstances under which *WHAT THEY SAID* was conceived. It is the culmination of a year of listening to the people in the public eye; a year of scrutinizing, monitoring, reviewing, judging, deciding—a year during which the editors resurrected from almost certain oblivion those quintessential elements of the year's *spoken* opinion which, in their judgment, demanded preservation in book form.

WHAT THEY SAID is a pioneer in its field. Its *raison d'etre* is the firm conviction that presenting, each year, the highlights of vital and interesting views from the lips of prominent people on virtually every aspect of contemporary civilization fulfills the need to give the *spoken* word the permanence and lasting value of the *written* word. For, if it is true that a picture is worth 10,000 words, it is equally true that a verbal conclusion, an apt quote or a candid comment by a person of fame or influence can have more significance and can provide more understanding than an entire page of summary in a standard work of reference.

The editors of *WHAT THEY SAID* did not, however, design their book for researchers and scholars alone. One of the failings of the conventional reference work is that it is blandly written and referred to primarily for facts and figures, lacking inherent "interest value." *WHAT THEY SAID*, on the other hand, was planned for sheer enjoyment and pleasure, for searching glimpses into the lives and thoughts of the world's celebrities, as well as for serious study, intellectual reflection and the philosophical contemplation of our multifaceted life and mores. Furthermore, those pressed for time, yet anxious to know what the newsmakers have been saying, will welcome the short excerpts which will make for quick, intermittent reading—and rereading. And, of course, the topical classifications, the speakers' index, the subject index, the place and date information—documented and authenticated and easily located—will supply a rich fund of hitherto not readily obtainable reference and statistical material.

Finally, the reader will find that the editors have eschewed trite comments and cliches, tedious and boring. The selected quotations, each standing on its own, are pertinent, significant, stimulating—above all, relevant to today's world, expressed in the speakers' own words. And they will, the editors feel, be even more relevant tomorrow. They will be re-examined and reflected upon in the future by men and women eager to learn from the past. The prophecies, the promises, the "golden dreams," the boastings and rantings, the bluster, the bravado, the pleadings and representations of those whose voices echo in these pages (and in those to come) should provide a rare and unique history lesson. The positions held by these luminaries, in their respective callings, are such that what they say today may profoundly affect the future as well as the present, and so will be of lasting importance and meaning.

ALAN F. PATER

JASON R. PATER

Beverly Hills, California

Table of Contents

Preface to the First Edition (1969)   *v*

Editorial Treatment   *ix*

Abbreviations   *xiii*

The Quote of the Year   *xv*

PART ONE: NATIONAL AFFAIRS

The State of the Union Address   3
The American Scene   13
Civil Rights / Women's Rights   19
Commerce / Industry / Finance   34
Crime / Law Enforcement   51
Defense / The Military   68
The Economy / Labor   90
Education   117
The Environment / Energy   133
Foreign Affairs   142
Government   174
Law / The Judiciary   199
Politics   206
Social Welfare   253
Transportation   263
Urban Affairs   266

PART TWO: INTERNATIONAL AFFAIRS

Africa   271
The Americas   281
Asia and the Pacific   309
Europe   329
The Middle East   358
War and Peace   393

PART THREE: GENERAL

The Arts   399
Journalism   406
Literature   413
Medicine and Health   425

The Performing Arts
  Broadcasting   437
  Motion Pictures   442
  Music   455
  The Stage   463

Philosophy   470
Religion   483
Science and Technology   489
Sports   498

Index to Speakers   519
Index to Subjects   533

Editorial Treatment

ORGANIZATION OF MATERIAL

Special attention has been given to the arrangement of the book—from the major divisions down to the individual categories and speakers—the objective being a logical progression of related material, as follows:

(A) The categories are arranged alphabetically within each of three major sections:

Part One:	"National Affairs"
Part Two:	"International Affairs"
Part Three:	"General"

In this manner, the reader can quickly locate quotations pertaining to particular fields of interest (see also *Indexing*). It should be noted that some quotations contain a number of thoughts or ideas—sometimes on different subjects—while some are vague as to exact subject matter and thus do not fit clearly into a specific topic classification. In such cases, the judgment of the Editors has determined the most appropriate category.

(B) Within each category the speakers are in alphabetical order by surname, following alphabetization practices used in the speaker's country of origin.

(C) Where there are two or more quotations by one speaker within the same category, they appear chronologically by date spoken or date of source.

SPEAKER IDENTIFICATION

(A) The occupation, profession, rank, position or title of the speaker is given as it was *at the time the statement was made* (except when the speaker's relevant identification is in the past, in which case he is shown as "former"). Thus, due to possible changes in status during the year, a speaker may be shown with different identifications in various parts of the book, or even within the same category.

(B) In the case of a speaker who holds more than one position simultaneously, the judgment of the Editors has determined the most appropriate identification to use with a specific quotation.

(C) The nationality of a speaker is given when it will help in identifying the speaker or when it is relevant to the quotation.

THE QUOTATIONS

The quoted material selected for inclusion in this book is shown as it appeared in the source, except as follows:

(A) *Ellipses* have been inserted wherever the Editors have deleted extraneous words or overly long passages within the quoted material used. In no way has the meaning or intention of the quotations been altered. *Ellipses* are also used where they appeared in the source.

(B) *Punctuation and spelling* have been altered by the Editors where they were obviously incorrect in the source, or to make the quotations more intelligible, or to conform to the general style used throughout this book. Again, meaning and intention of the quotations have not been changed.

(C) *Brackets* ([ ]) indicate material inserted by the Editors or by the source to either correct obvious errors or to explain or clarify what the speaker is saying. In some instances, bracketed material may replace quoted material for sake of clarity.

(D) *Italics* either appeared in the original source or were added by the Editors where emphasis is clearly desirable.

Except for the above instances, the quoted material used has been printed verbatim, as reported by the source (even if the speaker made factual errors or was awkward in his choice of words).

Special care has been exercised to make certain that each quotation stands on its own and is not taken "out of context." The Editors, however, cannot be responsible for errors made by the original source, i.e., incorrect reporting, mis-quotations, or errors in interpretation.

DOCUMENTATION AND SOURCES

Documentation (circumstance, place, date) of each quotation is provided as fully as could be obtained, and the sources are furnished for all quotations. In some instances, no documentation details were available; in those cases, only the source is given. Following are the sequence and style used for this information:

Circumstance of quotation, place, date/Name of source, date:section (if applicable), page number.

Example: *Before the Senate, Washington, Dec. 4/The Washington Post, 12-5:(A)13.*

The above example indicates that the quotation was delivered before the Senate in Washington on December 4. It was taken for *WHAT THEY SAID* from *The Washington Post*, issue of December 5, section A, page 13. (When a newspaper publishes more than one edition on the same date, it should be noted that page numbers may vary from edition to edition.)

(A) When the source is a television or radio broadcast, the name of the network or local station is indicated, along with the date of the broadcast (obviously, page and section information does not apply).

(B) An asterisk (*) before the (/) in the documentation indicates that the quoted material was written rather than spoken. Although the basic policy of *WHAT THEY SAID* is to use only *spoken* statements, there are occasions when written statements are considered by the Editors to be important enough to be included. These occasions are rare and usually involve Presidential messages and statements released to the press and other such documents attributed to persons in high government office.

INDEXING

(A) The *Index to Speakers* is keyed to the page number. (For alphabetization practices, see *Organization of Material*, paragraph B.)

(B) The *Index to Subjects* is keyed to both the page number and the quotation number on the page (thus, 210:3 indicates quotation number 3 on page 210); the quotation number appears at the right corner of each quotation.

(C) To locate quotations on a particular subject, regardless of the speaker, turn to the appropriate category (see *Table of Contents*) or use the detailed *Index to Subjects*.

(D) To locate all quotations by a particular speaker, regardless of subject, use the *Index to Speakers*.

(E) To locate quotations by a particular speaker on a particular subject, turn to the appropriate category and then to that person's quotations within the category.

(F) The reader will find that the basic categorization format of *WHAT THEY SAID* is itself a useful subject index, inasmuch as related quotations are grouped together by their respective categories. All aspects of journalism, for example, are relevant to each other; thus, the section *Journalism* embraces all phases of the news media. Similarly, quotations pertaining to the U.S. President, Congress, etc., are in the section *Government*.

MISCELLANEOUS

(A) Except where otherwise indicated or obviously to the contrary, all universities, organizations and business firms mentioned in this book are in the United States; similarly, references made to "national," "Federal," "this country," "the nation," etc., refer to the United States.

(B) In most cases, organizations whose names end with "of the United States" are Federal government agencies.

SELECTION OF CATEGORIES

The selected categories reflect, in the Editors' opinion, the most widely discussed public-interest subjects, those which readily fall into the over-all sphere of "current events." They represent topics continuously covered by the mass media because of their inherent importance to the changing world scene. Most of the categories are permanent; they appear in each annual edition of *WHAT THEY SAID*. However, because of the transient character of some subjects, there may be categories which appear one year and may not be repeated the next.

SELECTION OF SPEAKERS

The following persons are always considered eligible for inclusion in *WHAT THEY SAID*: top-level officials of all branches of national, state and local governments (both U.S. and foreign), including all United States Senators and Representatives; top-echelon military officers; college and university presidents, chancellors and professors; chairmen and presidents of major corporations; heads of national public-oriented organizations and associations; national and internationally known diplomats; recognized celebrities from the entertainment and literary spheres and the arts generally; sports figures of national stature; commentators on the world scene who are recognized as such and who command the attention of the mass media.

The determination of what and who are "major" and "recognized" must, necessarily, be made by the Editors of *WHAT THEY SAID* based on objective personal judgment.

Also, some persons, while not generally recognized as prominent or newsworthy, may have nevertheless attracted an unusual amount of attention in connection with an important issue or event. These people, too, are considered for inclusion, depending upon the specific circumstance.

SELECTION OF QUOTATIONS

The quotations selected for inclusion in *WHAT THEY SAID* obviously represent a decided minority of the seemingly endless volume of quoted material appearing in the media each year. The process of selecting is scrupulously objective insofar as the partisan views of the Editors are concerned (see *About Fairness*, below). However, it is clear that the Editors must decide which quotations *per se* are suitable for inclusion, and in doing so look for comments that are aptly stated, offer insight into the subject being discussed, or into the speaker, and provide—for today as well as for future reference—a thought which readers will find useful for understanding the issues and the personalities that make up a year on this planet.

ABOUT FAIRNESS

The Editors of *WHAT THEY SAID* understand the necessity of being impartial when compiling a book of this kind. As a result, there has been no bias in the selection of the quotations, the choice of speakers or the manner of editing. Relevance of the statements and the status of the speakers are the exclusive criteria for inclusion, without any regard whatsoever to the personal beliefs and views of the Editors. Furthermore, every effort has been made to include a multiplicity of opinions and ideas from a wide cross-section of speakers on each topic. Nevertheless, should there appear to be, on some controversial issues, a majority of material favoring one point of view over another, it is simply the result of there having been more of those views expressed during the year, reported by the media and objectively considered suitable by the Editors of *WHAT THEY SAID* (see *Selection of Quotations*, above). Also, since persons in politics and government account for a large percentage of the speakers in *WHAT THEY SAID*, there may exist a heavier weight of opinion favoring the philosophy of those in office at the time, whether in the United States Congress, the Administration, or in foreign capitals. This is natural and to be expected and should not be construed as a reflection of agreement or disagreement with that philosophy on the part of the Editors of *WHAT THEY SAID*.

Abbreviations

The following are abbreviations used by the speakers in this volume. Rather than defining them each time they appear in the quotations, this list will facilitate reading and avoid unnecessary repetition.

ABM: Anti-ballistic missile
ACLU: American Civil Liberties Union
AFL-CIO: American Federation of Labor-Congress of Industrial Organizations
AIDS: acquired immune deficiency syndrome
ANC: African National Congress
AWACS: Airborne Warning and Command aircraft
BBC: British Broadcasting Corporation
CEO: chief executive officer
CIA: Central Intelligence Agency
DEA: Drug Enforcement Administration
DNA: deoxyribonucleic acid
DOD: Department of Defense
EC: European Community
ERA: Equal Rights Amendment
FAA: Federal Aviation Administration
FBI: Federal Bureau of Investigation
FCC: Federal Communications Commission
F.D.R.:   Franklin Delano Roosevelt
FHA: Federal Housing Administration
GDR: German Democratic Republic (East Germany)
GE: General Electric Company
GM: General Motors Corporation
GNP: gross national product
HUD: Department of Housing and Urban Development
ICBM: intercontinental ballistic missile
INF: intermediate-range nuclear forces
IRA: Irish Republican Army
IRS: Internal Revenue Service
I.Q.:   intelligence quotient
J.F.K.:   John Fitzgerald Kennedy

LBO:	leveraged buyout
LDR:	Liberal Democratic Party (Japan)
NASA:	National Aeronautics and Space Administration
NATO:	North Atlantic Treaty Organization
NBC:	National Broadcasting Company
NCAA:	National Collegiate Athletic Association
NRA:	National Rifle Association
NSC:	National Security Council
OAS:	Organization of American States
OAU:	Organization of African Unity
OPEC:	Organization of Petroleum Exporting Countries
PAC:	political action committee
PBX:	private branch exchange
PLO:	Palestine Liberation Organization
PNC:	Palestine National Congress
p.r.:	public relations
RCA:	Radio Corporation of America (RCA Corp.)
R&D:	research and development
SALT:	strategic arms limitation talks
SDI:	strategic defense initiative
START:	strategic arms reduction talks
SWAPO:	South-West Africa People's Organization
TV:	television
TWA:	Trans World Airlines
UN:	United Nations
UNESCO:	United Nations Educational, Scientific and Cultural Organization
UNITA:	National Union for the Total Independence of Angola
U.S.:	United States
U.S.A.:	United States of America
U.S.S.R.:	Union of Soviet Socialist Republics
VA:	Veterans Administration
VCR:	videocassette recorder
VFW:	Veterans of Foreign Wars
YMCA:	Young Men's Christian Association

The Quote of the Year

The exercise of political power in Washington is so extraordinarily complex that the only way one can understand or describe it is through a metaphor. . . Imagine R. F. K. Stadium—only imagine also that the field is magnetic. Each player is an atom or unit and carries an electrical charge. All the particles are moving about, seemingly at random. Some particles have more power than others, but all have some. Some particles attract; others repel. The field is full of players, hundreds of them, thousands of them. Several teams take the field at a time. Several kinds of games are in play at once. Players from one team, without changing uniform, sometimes play for another. There are no referees. The cheerleaders, dressed in power suits and Gucci loafers, send in plays from the sidelines. Political-action committees, dressed as trainers, dispense the steroids of modern politics—money—to the players on all sides. Meanwhile, the crowd's attention is riveted not on the field but on the media. The media sometimes declare what happens on the field, and sometimes they play their own games. Well, who are these particles? The President, the Cabinet, the 4,000 or so political appointments made directly by him, the 350,000 Federal civil servants, the 535 members of Congress, the 18,000 Congressional staffers, the 47,834 lawyers, the employees of the 11,000 associations, the 75 think tanks, the 4,196 political-action committees, the 9,127 lobbyists who registered in the last year, the 18,348 lobbyists who have not registered in the last two years and, last but not least, the 4,326 journalists—a cozy community of, some say, half a million, all shooting off electrical power charges.

—ALLAN E. GOTLIEB
Canadian Ambassador to the United States.
At National Press Club luncheon,
Washington, Dec. 20.

The State of the Union Address

Delivered by Ronald Reagan, President of the United States, at the Capitol, Washington, January 25, 1988.

Mr. Speaker, Mr. President, distinguished members of the House and Senate: When we first met here 7 years ago—many of us for the first time—it was with the hope of beginning something new for America. We meet here tonight in this historic chamber to continue that work. If anyone expects just a proud recitation of the accomplishments of my Administration, I say let's leave that to history; we're not finished yet. So my message to you tonight is: Put on your work shoes—we're still on the job.

Power of Ideas

History records the power of the ideas that brought us here those seven years ago. Ideas like: the individual's right to reach as far and as high as his or her talents will permit; the free market as the engine of economic progress; and as an ancient Chinese philosopher, Lao-Tzu, said: Govern a great nation as you would cook a small fish; do not overdo it.

These ideas were part of a larger notion—a vision, if you will, of America herself. An America not only right in opportunity for the individual but an America, too, of strong families and vibrant neighborhoods; an America whose divergent but harmonizing communities were a reflection of a deeper community of values—the value of work, of family, of religion—and of the love of freedom that God places in each of us and whose defense He has entrusted in a special way to this nation.

All of this was made possible by an idea I spoke of when Mr. Gorbachev was here: the belief that the most exciting revolution ever known to humankind began with three simple words: "We the people"—the revolutionary notion that the people grant government its rights, and not the other way around.

And there is one lesson that has come home powerfully to me, which I would offer to you now: just as those who created this republic pledged to each other their lives, their fortunes, and their sacred honor; so, too, America's leaders today must pledge to each other that we will keep foremost in our hearts and minds not what is best for ourselves or for our party, but what is best for America. In the spirit of Jefferson, let us affirm that, in this chamber tonight, there are no Republicans, no Democrats, just Americans.

Yes, we will have our differences. But, let us always remember: What unites us far outweighs whatever divides us. Those who sent us here to serve them—the millions of Americans watching and listening tonight—expect this of us. Let's prove to them and to ourselves that democracy works even in an election year.

Accomplishments

We have done this before. And as we have worked together to bring down spending, tax rates and inflation, employment has climbed to record heights; America has created more jobs and better, higher-paying jobs; family income has risen for four straight years, and America's poor climbed out of poverty at the fastest rate in more than 10 years. Our record is not just the longest peacetime expansion in history but an economic and social revolution of hope, based on work, incentives, growth and opportunity; a revolution of compassion that led to private sector initiatives and a 77 percent increase in charitable giving; a revolution that—at a critical moment in world history—reclaimed and restored the American dream.

In international relations, too, there is only one description for what, together, we have achieved: complete turnabout, a revolution. Seven years ago, America was weak and freedom everywhere was under siege; today, America is strong and democracy is everywhere on the move. From Central America to East Asia, ideas, like free markets and democratic reforms and human rights, are taking hold. We've replaced "Blame America" with "Look up to America." We've rebuilt our defenses; and, of all our accomplishments, none can give us more satisfaction than knowing that our young people are again proud to wear our country's uniform. And, in a few moments, I'm going to talk about three developments—arms reduction, the strategic defense initiative, and the global democratic revolution—that, when taken together, offer a chance none of us would have dared imagine seven years ago, a chance to rid the world of the two great nightmares of the postwar era. I speak of the startling hope of giving our children a future free of both totalitarianism and nuclear terror.

Tonight, then, we are strong. Prosperous. At peace. And we are free. This is the state of our union. And if we will work together this year, I believe we can give a future President and a future Congress the chance to make that prosperity, that peace, that freedom, not just the state of our union, but the state of our world.

Basic Objectives

Toward this end, we have four basic objectives tonight. First, steps we can take this year to keep our economy strong and growing, to give our children a future of low inflation and full employment. Second, let's check our progress in attacking social problems where important gains have been made but which still need critical attention. I mean schools that work; economic independence for the poor; restoring respect for family life and family values. Our third objective tonight is global: continuing the exciting economic and democratic revolutions we've seen around the world. Fourth and finally: Our nation has remained at peace for nearly a decade and a half; as we move toward our goals of world prosperity and world freedom, we must protect that peace and deter war by making sure the next President inherits what you and I have a moral obligation to give that President: a national

security that is unassailable and a national defense that takes full advantage of new technology, and is fully funded.

This is a full agenda. It's meant to be. You see, my thinking on the next year is quite simple: Let's make this the best of eight. And that means: It's all out, right to the finish line. I don't buy the idea that this is the last year of anything; because we're not talking here tonight about registering temporary gains, but ways of making permanent our successes.

That's why our focus is the values, principles and ideas that made America great. Let's be clear on this point: We're for limited government because we understand, as the founding fathers did, that it is the best way of insuring personal liberty and empowering the individual so that every American of every race and region shares fully in the flowering of American prosperity and freedom.

One other thing: We Americans like the future; like the sound of it, the idea of it, the hope of it. Where others fear trade and economic growth, we see opportunities for creating new wealth and undreamed-of opportunities for millions in our own land and beyond. Where others seek to throw up barriers, we seek to bring them down; where others take counsel of their fears, we follow our hopes. Yes, we Americans like the future and like making the most of it. Let's do that now.

The Deficit

And let's begin by discussing how to maintain economic growth by controlling and eventually eliminating the problem of Federal deficits. We have had a balanced budget only eight times in the last 57 years. For the first time in 14 years, the Federal Government spent less, in real terms, last year than the year before. We took $73 billion off last year's deficit compared to the year before. The deficit itself has moved from 6.3 percent of the G.N.P. to only 3.4 percent. And perhaps the most important sign of progress has been the change in our view of deficits. You know, a few of us can remember when, not too many years ago, those who created the deficits said they would make us prosperous and not to worry about the debt—"We owe it to ourselves." Well, at last there is an agreement that we can't spend ourselves rich.

Our recent budget agreement, designed to reduce Federal deficits by $76 billion over the next 2 years, builds on this consensus. But this agreement must be adhered to without slipping into the errors of the past—more broken promises and more unchecked spending. As I indicated in my first State of the Union, what ails us can be simply put: the Federal Government is too big and it spends too much money. I can assure you, the bipartisan leadership of Congress, of my help in fighting off any attempt to bust our budget agreement. And this includes the swift and certain use of the veto power.

Now, it is also time for some plain talk about the most immediate obstacle to controlling Federal deficits. The simple but frustrating problem of making expenses match revenues—something American families do and the Federal Government can't—has caused crisis after crisis in this city. Mr. Speaker, Mr. President, I will say to you tonight what I have said before—and will continue to say: the budget process has broken down, it needs a drastic overhaul. With each ensuing year, the spectacle before the American people is the same as it was this Christmas: budget deadlines delayed or missed completely, monstrous continuing resolutions that pack hundreds of billions of dollars worth of spending into one bill—and a Federal Government on the brink of default.

I know I'm echoing what you here in the Congress have said because you suffered so directly—but let's recall that in seven years, of 91 appropriations bills scheduled to arrive on my desk by a certain date, only 10 made it on time.

Last year, of the 13 appropriations bills due by Oct. 1, none of them made it. Instead, we had four continuing resolutions lasting 41 days, then 36 days, 2 days, and 3 days, respectively.

And then, along came those two behemoths—a reconciliation bill, six months late, that was 1,186 pages long, weighing 15 pounds, and the long-term continuing resolution, two months late, that was 1,057 pages long, weighing 14 pounds. Not to mention the 1,053-page conference report weighing 14 pounds. That was a

total of 43 pounds of paper and ink. You had three hours, yes, three hours to consider each, and it took 300 people at my Office of Management and Budget just to read the bill so the Government wouldn't shut down.

Congress shouldn't send another one of these. And if you do, I will not sign it.

Let's change all this; instead of a Presidential budget that gets discarded and a congressional budget that gets discarded and a Congressional budget resolution that is not enforced, why not a simple partnership, a joint agreement that sets out the spending priorities within the available revenues? And let's remember our deadline is Oct. 1, not Christmas; let's get the people's work done in time to avoid a footrace with Santa Claus. Yes, this year—to coin a phrase—a new beginning. Thirteen individual bills, on time and fully reviewed by Congress.

I am also certain you join me in saying: Let's help insure our future of prosperity by giving the President a tool that—though I will not get to use it—is one I know future Presidents of either party must have. Give the President the same authority that 43 Governors use in their states, the right to reach into massive appropriations bills, pare away the waste, and enforce budget discipline. Let's approve the line-item veto.

And let's take a partial step in this direction. Most of you in this chamber didn't know what was in this catch-all bill and report. Over the past few weeks, we have all learned what was tucked away behind a little comma here and there. For example, there's millions for items such as cranberry research, blueberry research, the study of crawfish, and the commercialization of wild flowers. And that's not to mention the $.5 million so that people from developing nations could come here to watch Congress at work. I won't even touch that. So, tonight, I offer you this challenge. In 30 days, I will send back to you those items, as rescissions, which if I had the authority to line them out, I would do so.

Review this multibillion-dollar package; that will not undercut our bipartisan budget agreement. As a matter of fact, if adopted, it will improve our deficit reduction goals. And what an example we can set: that we are serious about getting our financial accounts in order. By acting and approving this plan, you have the opportunity to override a Congressional process that is out of control.

There is another vital reform. Yes, Gramm-Rudman-Hollings has been profoundly helpful, but let us take its goal of a balanced budget and make it permanent. Let us do now what so many states do to hold down spending and what 32 state legislatures have asked us to do: let us heed the wishes of an overwhelming plurality of Americans and pass a constitutional amendment that mandates a balanced budget and forces the Federal Government to live within its means.

Reform of the budget process—including the line-item veto and balanced budget amendment—will, together with real restraint on Government spending, prevent the Federal budget from ever again ravaging the family budget.

Let's insure that the Federal Government never again legislates against the family and the home. Last September, I signed an Executive Order on the family requiring that every department and agency review its activities in light of seven standards designed to promote and not harm the family. But let us make certain that the family is always at the center of the public policy process, not just in this Administration but in all future Administrations. It is time for Congress to consider—at the beginning—a statement of the impact that legislation will have on the basic unit of American society, the family.

Education

And speaking of the family, let's turn to a matter on the mind of every American parent tonight—education. We all know the sorry story of the 60's and 70's—soaring spending, plummeting test scores—and that hopeful trend of the 80's, when we replaced an obsession with dollars with a commitment to quality, and test scores starting going back up. There is a lesson here that we all should write on the blackboard a hundred times—in a child's education, money can never take the place of basics like discipline, hard work, and, yes, homework.

As a nation we do, of course, spend heavily on education—more than we spend on defense—yet across the country, governors like New Jersey's

Tom Kean are giving classroom demonstrations that show how we spend is as important as how much we spend. Opening up the teaching profession to all qualified candidates; merit pay, so that good teachers get A's as well as apples; and stronger curriculum, as Secretary Bennett has proposed for high schools—these imaginative reforms are making common sense the most popular new kid in America's schools.

How can we help? Well, we can talk about and push for these reforms. But the most important thing we can do is to reaffirm that control of our schools belongs to the states, local communities and, most of all, to the parents and teachers.

Welfare Reform

My friends, some years ago, the Federal Government declared war on poverty, and poverty won. Today, the Federal Government has 59 major welfare programs and spends more than $100 billion a year on them. What has all this money done?

Too often it has only made poverty harder to escape. Federal welfare programs have created a massive social problem. With the best of intentions, government created a poverty trap that wreaks havoc on the very support system the poor need most to lift themselves out of poverty—the family. Dependency has become the one enduring heirloom, passed from one generation to the next, of too many fragmented families.

It is time—this may be the most radical thing I've said in seven years in this office—it is time for Washington to show a little humility. There are a thousand sparks of genius in 50 states and a thousand communities around the nation. It is time to nurture them and see which ones can catch fire and become guiding lights.

States have begun to show us the way. They have demonstrated that successful welfare programs can be built around more effective child-support enforcement practices and innovative programs requiring welfare recipients to work or prepare for work.

Let us give the states even more flexibility and encourage more reforms. Let's start making our welfare system the first rung on America's ladder of opportunity—a boost up from dependency; not a graveyard, but a birthplace of hope.

War Against Drugs

Now let me turn to three other matters vital to family values and the quality of family life. The first is an untold American success story . . . Recently, we released our annual survey of what graduating high school seniors have to say about drugs. Cocaine use is declining and marijuana use was the lowest since surveying began. We can be proud that our students are just saying "no" to drugs. But let's remember that ending this menace requires commitment from every part of America and every single American—a commitment to a drug-free America. The war against drugs is a war of individual battles, a crusade with many heroes—including America's young people, and also someone very special to me. She has helped so many of our young people to say "no" to drugs. Nancy, much credit belongs to you, and I want to express to you your husband's pride and your country's thanks.

Abortion

Now, we come to a family issue that we must have the courage to confront. Tonight, I call America—a good nation, a moral people—to charitable but realistic consideration of the terrible cost of abortion on demand. To those who say this violates a woman's right to control of her own body—can they deny that now medical evidence confirms the unborn child is a living human being entitled to life, liberty and the pursuit of happiness?

Let us unite as a nation and protect the unborn with legislation that would stop all Federal funding for abortion—and with a human life amendment making, of course, an exception where the unborn child threatens the life of the mother. Our Judeo-Christian tradition recognizes that right of taking a life in self-defense.

But with that one exception, let us look to those others in our land who cry out for children to adopt. I pledge to you tonight, I will work to remove barriers to adoption and extend full sharing in family life to millions of Americans, so that children who need homes can be welcomed to families who want them and love them.

School Prayer

And let me add here: So many of our greatest statesmen have reminded us that spiritual values alone are essential to our nation's health and vigor. This Congress opens its proceedings each day, as does the Supreme Court, with an acknowledgment of the Supreme Being—yet we are denied the right to set aside in our schools a moment each day for those who wish to pray. I believe Congress should pass our school prayer amendment.

Now, to make sure there is a full nine-member Supreme Court to interpret the law, to protect the rights of all Americans, I urge the Senate to move quickly and decisively in confirming Judge Anthony Kennedy to the highest court in the land and to also confirm 27 nominees now waiting to fill vacancies in the Federal judiciary.

Here then are our domestic priorities; yet if the Congress and the Administration work together, even greater opportunities lie ahead to expand a growing world economy; to continue to reduce the threat of nuclear arms and to extend the frontiers of freedom and the growth of democratic institutions.

Our policies consistently received the strong support of the late Congressman Dan Daniel of Virginia. I'm sure all of you join me in expressing heartfelt condolences on his passing.

Global Economy

One of the greatest contributions the United States can make to the world is to promote freedom as the key to economic growth. A creative, competitive America is the answer to a changing world, not trade wars that would close doors, create greater barriers and destroy millions of jobs. We should always remember: protectionism is destructionism; America's jobs, America's growth, America's future depend on trade—trade that is free, open and fair.

This year, we have it within our power to take a major step toward a growing global economy and an expanding cycle of prosperity that reaches to all the free nations of this earth. I'm speaking of the historic free trade agreement negotiated between our country and Canada. And I can also tell you that we're determined to expand this

7

concept, south as well as north. Next month I will be traveling to Mexico where trade matters will be of foremost concern. And, over the next several months, our Congress and the Canadian Parliament can make the start of such a North American accord a reality. Our goal must be a day when the free flow of trade—from the tip of Tierra del Fuego to the Arctic Circle—unites the people of the Western Hemisphere in a bond of mutually beneficial exchange; when all borders become what the U.S.-Canadian border so long has been—a meeting place, rather than a dividing line.

World Democracy

This movement we see in so many places toward economic freedom is indivisible from the worldwide movement toward political freedom—and against totalitarian rule. This global democratic revolution has removed the specter—so frightening a decade ago—of democracy doomed to a permanent minority status in the world. In South and Central America, only a third of the people enjoyed democratic rule in 1976. Today, over 90 percent of Latin Americans live in nations committed to democratic principles.

Nicaragua

And the resurgence of democracy is owed to those courageous people on almost every continent who have struggled to take control of their own destiny. In Nicaragua, the struggle has extra meaning because that nation is so near our own borders. The recent revelations of a former high-level Sandinista, Maj. Roger Miranda, show us that, even as they talk peace, the Communist Sandinista Government of Nicaragua has established plans for a large 600,000-man army. Yet even as these plans are made, the Sandinista regime knows the tide is turning and the cause of Nicaraguan freedom is riding at its crest. Because of the freedom fighters, who are resisting Communist rule, the Sandinistas have been forced to extend some democratic rights, negotiate with church authorities, and release a few political prisoners.

The focus is on the Sandinistas, their promises and their actions. There is a consensus among the four Central American democratic Presidents that the Sandinistas have not complied with the plan to bring peace and democracy to all of Central America. The Sandinistas again have promised reforms; their challenge is to take irreversible steps toward Democracy.

On Wednesday, my request to sustain the freedom fighters will be submitted which reflects our mutual desire for peace, freedom, and democracy in Nicaragua. I ask Congress to pass this request; let us be for the people of Nicaragua what Lafayette, Pulaski and Von Steuben were for our forefathers and the cause of American independence.

Afghanistan

So, too, in Afghanistan, the freedom fighters are the key to peace. We support the Mujahidin. There can be no settlement unless all Soviet troops are removed and the Afghan people are allowed genuine self-determination. I have made my views on this matter known to Mr. Gorbachev. But not just Nicaragua or Afghanistan; yes, everywhere, we see a swelling freedom tide around the world—freedom fighters rising up in Cambodia and Angola, fighting and dying for the same Democratic liberties we hold sacred. Their cause is our cause. Freedom.

Defense and Arms Reduction

Yet, even as we work to expand world freedom, we must build a safer peace and reduce the danger of nuclear war, but let's have no illusions. Three years of steady decline in the value of our annual defense investment have increased the risk of our most basic security interests, jeopardizing earlier hard-won goals. We must face squarely the implications of this negative trend and make adequate, stable defense spending a top goal both this year and in the future. This same concern applies to economic and security assistance programs as well.

But the resolve of America and its NATO allies has opened the way for unprecedented achievement in arms reduction. Our recently signed I.N.F. treaty is historic because it reduces nuclear arms and establishes the most stringent verification regime in arms control history, including several forms of short-notice, on-site inspection. I submitted the treaty today, and I urge the Senate to give its advice and consent to ratification of this landmark agreement.

In addition to the I.N.F. treaty, we are within reach of an even more significant START agreement that will reduce U.S. and Soviet long-range missile or strategic arsenals by half.

But let me be clear: our approach is not to seek agreement for agreement's sake, but to settle only for agreements that truly enhance our national security and that of our allies. We will never put our security at risk—or that of our allies—just to reach an agreement with the Soviets. No agreement is better than a bad agreement.

S.D.I.

As I mentioned earlier, our efforts are to give future generations what we never had; a future free of nuclear terror. Reduction of strategic offensive arms is one step. S.D.I. another. Our funding request for our strategic defense initiative is less than 2 percent of the total defense budget. S.D.I. funding is money wisely appropriated and money well spent. S.D.I. has the same purpose and supports the same goals of arms reduction. It reduces the risk of war and the threat of nuclear weapons to all mankind. Strategic defenses that threaten no one could offer the world a safer, more stable basis for deterrence. We must also remember that S.D.I. is also our insurance policy against a nuclear accident—a Chernobyl of the sky—or an accidental launch or some madman who might come along.

America as Leader

We have seen such changes in the world in seven years: As totalitarianism struggles to avoid being overwhelmed by the forces of economic advance and the aspiration for human freedom, it is the free nations that are resilient and resurgent. As the global democratic revolution has put totalitarianism on the defensive, we have left behind the days of retreat—America is again a vigorous leader of the free world, a nation that acts decisively and firmly in the furtherance of her principles and vital interests. No legacy would make me more proud than leaving in place a bipartisan consensus for the cause of world freedom, a consensus that prevents a paralysis of American power from ever occurring again.

But my thoughts tonight go beyond this. And I hope you will let me end this evening with a personal reflection. You know, the world could never be quite the same again after Jacob Shallus, a trustworthy and dependable clerk of the Pennsylvania General Assembly, took his pen and engrossed those words about representative government in the Preamble of our Constitution. And in a quiet but final way, the course of human events was forever altered when, on a ridge overlooking the Emmitsburg Pike in an obscure Pennsylvania town called Gettysburg, Lincoln spoke of our duty to government of and by the people and never letting it perish from the earth.

At the start of this decade, I suggested that we lived in equally momentous times—that it was up to us now to decide whether our form of government would endure and whether history still had a place of greatness for a quiet, pleasant greening land called America. Not everything has been made perfect in seven years—nor will it be made perfect in seven times 70 years—but before us, this year and beyond, are great prospects for the cause of peace and world freedom.

It means, too, that the young Americans I spoke of seven years ago—as well as those who might be coming along the Virginia or Maryland shores this night and seeing for the first time the lights of this capital city, the lights that cast their glow on our great halls of government and the monuments to the memory of our great men—it means those young Americans will find a city of hope in a land that is free.

We can be proud that for them, and for us, those lights along the Potomac are still seen this night—signaling, as they have for nearly two centuries and as we pray God they always will, that another generation of Americans has protected and passed on lovingly this place called America, this shining city on a hill, this government of, by, and for the people.

Thank you and God bless you.

National Affairs

The American Scene

Allan Bloom
Professor of political philosophy,
University of Chicago

1

You hear all the talk that this is a very large and diversified country. But precisely because we are diverse, we have to remind ourselves what we have in common all the time—what is America, what is a human being—in order that we not just break down into a set of atoms that cannot cohere to a greater whole. That was always the characteristic of the immigrants, who understood that. They became Americans not by growing up in old roots or maintaining ethnic diversity or accepting American myths, but by learning certain common principles. I'm a son of such immigrants, a Jewish boy, but one who could be raised in Indianapolis, the American Midwest.

Interview/Time, 10-17:74.

George Bush
Vice President of the United States;
Candidate for the 1988 Republican
Presidential nomination

2

I feel strongly about the innate decency and honor of the United States. We are the freest, we are the fairest, we are the most decent nation that ever existed on the face of the earth, and we have no higher calling than to work for peace and freedom and human rights. If we don't lead the free world, nobody else can, nobody else will, because they're not strong enough, they're not committed enough.

Campaign speech/
The Washington Post, 3-5:(A)12.

3

Ethnic pride, as I think of it, really rejoices, celebrates, not only the diversity of America, but the good things about America. It is the ethnic America that says, "Look, we are free, we appre-

ciate it more than others"; and our Administration has made a significant contribution to this concept of standing for freedom.

Campaigning, Milwaukee, July 22/
The New York Times, 7-23:9.

George Bush
Vice President of the
United States; 1988
Republican Presidential nominee

4

This has been called the American century, because in it we were the dominant force for good in the world. We saved Europe, cured polio, went to the moon and lit the world with our culture. And now we're on the verge of a new century, and what country's name will it bear? I say it will be another American century. Our work is not done; our force is not spent.

Accepting the nomination, at Republican
National Convention, New Orleans, Aug. 18/
The New York Times, 8-19:8.

5

[The U.S. is] the country of the little guy—the country where, no matter what the circumstances of your birth or background, you can go anywhere and do anything. In fact, it's so much the country of the little guy that people rarely use that phrase, because in a true democracy there are no little guys, only fellow citizens equal in the eyes of the law and the eyes of God.

Addressing U.S. Olympic team, Anaheim, Calif.,
Sept. 5/The New York Times, 9-6:10.

6

The flag is back. Today America is flag city, and we can never let that change again. I saluted it going to war; I salute it now in peace. I've seen it wave proudly. I've thrilled to the sight of that flag. I've seen it burned by our enemies abroad. I've seen it scorned by the misguided in our own country in times past, and I've seen it lowered to half-mast to mourn the passing of leaders, and I've seen it wrapped around the coffins of young

13

(GEORGE BUSH)

men. I've seen it given to their grieving widows and children.

Campaigning, Findlay, Ohio, Sept. 16/
The New York Times, 9-17:8.

1

What's the end purpose of this economic growth? Is it just to be rich? What a shallow ambition! The Americans of the 18th century were a revolutionary people—they invented a great nation. The Americans of the 19th century were a fearless people; they built that nation. The Americans of the latter part of the 20th century—what will they say of us? That we were fat and happy?

Campaign speech,
Bloomfield, N.J.,
Sept. 20/The New York Times, 9-21:10.

2

Think of the children you know. For the most part, they're not the hollow-eyed children of the ghetto. They live in warm, well-lit homes and they have clothes to wear and more good food than they choose to eat. Some, perhaps many, have these $40 jeans and $50 sneakers. We've showered our children with material things, and still we have a sense of unease. Do they know they're fortunate? Do they know it wasn't always like this for America, or for mankind in general? Do they have a sense of thanks? Of citizenship? Do they realize that perhaps they ought to be thinking of giving something back? Or are they cut off by their affluence, removed from the cares and concerns of others?

Before Comstock Club,
Sacramento, Calif.,
Oct. 4/The New York Times, 10-5:(A)17.

3

I have spoke in the past of a "thousand points of light" . . . I was using the phrase as shorthand for the fact—and people know this—that we are a nation of communities, of thousands of business and professional and religious and ethnic and regional communities. And in this diversity and pluralism is our salvation. That's where America will be saved—in our communities, which are spread like stars, like a thousand points of light in a broad and peaceful sky.

Before Comstock Club, Sacramento, Calif.,
Oct. 4/The Washington Post, 10-5:(A)16.

4

We have engaged in a wide range of social experimentation over the past 25 years. Marriage as a life-long commitment was marked as passe and old-fashioned; permissiveness moved on to promiscuity, open classrooms to open marriage. It just has not worked. But, even worse, it has destroyed our family structure. I am pleased that we are now moving into a resurgence of traditional values that derive from our broad Judeo-Christian heritage, not overtly religious, but rather "common sense."

Interview/Christianity Today, 9-16:40.

Fidel Castro
President of Cuba

5

We're getting closer to you [the U.S.] in sports, medicine, and from a social point of view we're ahead of you. We don't have people sleeping in the streets, begging. We don't have drugs or alcoholism. Economically, there are others ahead of you. You have been left behind in the chemical, steel, automotive and electronic industries. You are no longer Number 1.

Interview/USA Today, 2-22:(A)7.

Henry Steele Commager
Historian

6

We have lost . . . that inventiveness, that resourcefulness which we had beyond any other people in recorded history at the beginning of our history . . . Every major political institution we have was invented before the year 1800. [The U.S.] is going through a bad period. Maybe it's going through its adolescence . . . before maturity.

Broadcast interview/
"Bill Moyers' World of Ideas," PBS-TV, 9-15.

Carl N. Degler
Professor of history, Stanford University

7

Few historians of the United States believe that the culture of this country has been seriously

(CARL N. DEGLER)

influenced by ideas from Africa, China, Japan or indigenous North America ... That the people from those origins have shaped in profound ways the culture of this country, no historian could deny. [But] we are part of the West, not because this country received Italians, Scots, Germans, Greeks, Irish, Poles and Scandinavians within its borders, but because the language, religions, institutions, laws, customs, literature and, yes, the prejudices of this country were drawn overwhelmingly from Europe.

At debate, Stanford University/
The Christian Science Monitor, 4-8:20.

Michael S. Dukakis
Governor of Massachusetts (D);
Candidate for the 1988 Democratic
Presidential nomination

1

The two remaining candidates for the Democratic nomination for the Presidency are the son of immigrants from Massachusetts [himself] and a black man who grew up poor in South Carolina [Jesse Jackson]. I think that says everything that needs to be said about America.

At debate at University of Pennsylvania,
April 22/The New York Times, 4-23:8.

2

[On the American dream]: Every child who has ambition is its heir. Every worker who demands dignity keeps its flame. Every farmer who works the land is its ally ... Every barrier of race, sex and class we shatter is its strength. And every soul around the world who swells with hope at the sight of our flag is its truth.

Speech upon winning
California Democratic primary,
Los Angeles, June 7/Los Angeles Times, 6-8:(I)10.

Frances D. Fergusson
President, Vassar College

3

Two weeks ago, people listened to films of [the late] President [John] Kennedy exhorting the

nation [in the 1960s] "to ask what you can do for your country." Those words today sound surprisingly quaint, a meaningless piece of rhetoric rather than the fundamental call to service and leadership my generation heard with such excitement.

At The New York Times Presidents
Forum, New York, Dec.6/
The New York Times, 12-7:(B)9.

Alexander M. Haig, Jr.
Candidate for the 1988
Republican Presidential nomination;
Former Secretary of State
of the United States

4

A more perfect state of the union for the '90s demands that we do good, not just feel good. Excellence must become the standard of our schools, our personal behavior and our government.

Interview/USA Today, 1-25:(A)11.

Gary Hart
Candidate for the 1988
Democratic Presidential nomination;
Former United States Senator,
D-Colorado

5

I don't want to be President of a country that thinks like [President] Ronald Reagan does—a greedy, materialistic and superficial country. We have honored the Harvard Law School graduate who walked into a six-figure job. That has been our national goal. I want to encourage a shift from being like [convicted insider stock-trader] Ivan Boesky to being the way my generation was under [the late President] John Kennedy.

Interview, New Hampshire, Jan.6/
The New York Times, 1-7:9.

Jesse L. Jackson
Civil-rights leader; Candidate for
the 1988 Democratic Presidential
nomination

6

When we were cold in Greenville [S.C.], my grandmother couldn't afford to buy a blanket. So

(JESSE JACKSON)

she would reach in the closet for old pieces of coat and dress and slip and whatever she could find. Just patches and pieces. And she would lay them out on the cot. They were all different colors—red and yellow and black and brown; different textures—cotton, wool, silk, burlap. And while they were apart, they were just patches, just rags. You had to take strong cord and a steady hand and pull them together to make a quilt—a thing of unity, a thing of culture, a thing of hope. And that's what our nation needs now. A strong seamstress, a quilt-maker. Somebody who can pull our patches together into a thing of unity, a thing of power.

Campaign speech/
The Washington Post, 4-18:(A)10.

Anthony M. Kennedy
Associate Justice, Supreme Court
of the United States

1

The Constitution of the United States is the single idea, the single fact, the single reality, the single moral principle that sets the United States apart from other nations, now and throughout history.

At his swearing-in,
Washington, Feb. 18/
Los Angeles Times, 2-19:(I)4.

Paul Kennedy
Professor of history,
Yale University

2

I often think that a country's particular weaknesses are the obverse side of its strengths. The American strength has been its wonderful optimism, its "can do" attitude. That has given the United States great energy. But it also brought to belief that sheer optimism and resolve would by themselves always carry the day. This is a view that can prevent its holders from taking a critical stance with respect to their own situation. Historical self-confidence carries a price at those times when re-examination and fresh stock-taking may be the order of the day.

Interview/American Heritage, Sept.-Oct.:98.

David Kertzer
Professor of anthropology,
Bowdoin College

3

Pledges of allegiance and oaths of allegiance are marks of totalitarian states, not Western democracies. I cannot think of a single democracy except the United States that has a pledge of allegiance.

Los Angeles Times,
9-3:(I)22.

H. Ross Perot
Industrialist

4

We're like the inheritors of great wealth in this country. We've forgotten all the sacrifices that the people who've gone before us made to give us this wonderful life that we have. We accept it, we take it for granted, we think it's our birthright. The facts are, it's precious, it's fragile, it can disappear on us in a moment. It's like quicksilver. If this is going to be a country that's owned by its people, then the owners have got to be active in the management of the country. It's that simple. The wimps are us.

Interview/
Esquire, June:112.

Donald E. Petersen
Chairman,
Ford Motor Company

5

To be successful, you have to believe that your team, your society, is every bit as good as any other team, any other society. You have the ingredients to be successful if you have the desire to lay your plans and work together toward a common goal. We [Americans] always used to have that. We always used to believe that we could be winners, and I think there are at least some segments of our society that aren't so sure about that any more. They've lost their confidence in our ability, as a nation, to compete. I have not.

Interview/
Esquire, June:138.

David Puttnam
Motion-picture producer; Former
chairman, Columbia Pictures

1

As I see it, the United States is in genuine danger of becoming a lost land, at least of my youthful dreams, and in some cases, almost certainly yours. There is disillusionment wafting through the heady winds of the American dream.

At law symposium,
University of Southern California/
Daily Variety, 5-25:18.

Dan Quayle
United States Senator, R-Indiana;
1988 Republican Vice-Presidential
nominee

2

A great American novelist, the late Thomas Wolfe, once wrote that this is a fabulous country, the only fabulous country, the one where miracles not only happen, they happen all the time. Miracles do happen all the time in America because we live in freedom and because the energy and imagination of our people make their dreams come true every day.

Accepting the nomination, at
Republican National Convention, New Orleans,
Aug. 18/The New York Times, 8-19:11.

Ronald Reagan
President of the United States

3

Something that seems to be popular of late is suggesting that greed has characterized the 1980s in America. Well, I don't happen to believe that pejorative word is appropriate. We should applaud people who are trying to better their lot, not put them down.

To group of political appointees,
Washington, Jan 19/
Los Angeles Times, 1-20:(I)13.

4

We Americans make no secret of our belief in freedom. In fact, it's something of a national pastime. Every four years, the American people choose a new President, and 1988 is one of those years. . . . About 1,000 local television stations, 8,500 radio stations and 1,700 daily newspapers, each one an independent private enterprise, fiercely independent of the government, report on the candidates, grill them in interviews and bring them together for debates. In the end, the people vote. They decide who will be the next President.

At Moscow (U.S.S.R.) State
University, May 31/
USA Today, 6-1:(A)13.

5

This land, its people, the dreams that unfold here and the freedom to bring it all together, well, these are what make America soar, up where you can see hope billowing in those freedom winds. . . . When I pack my bags in Washington, don't expect me to be happy to hear all this talk about the twilight of my life. Twilight? Not in America. Here, it's a sunrise every day. Fresh new opportunities. Dreams to build. . . . You see, there's no sweeter day than each new one, because here in our country it means something wonderful can happen to you.

At Republican National Convention,
New Orleans, Aug. 15/
The Washington Post,
8-16:(A)21.

6

[On the controversy about whether the Pledge of Allegiance should be recited in public schools]: [I do not] see any reason why [students] should not learn the various customs, and so forth, that have to do with things of that kind. I've seen many children today who don't know what they're supposed to do when the national anthem is played or when the flag goes by. I remember that I learned all that in school. Why shouldn't they? . . . That's what [teachers are] there for. Their job is to teach something.

To reporters,
Washington, Sept. 21/
The New York Times, 9-22:14.

WHAT THEY SAID IN 1988

Andrei D. Sakharov
Dissident Soviet physicist

1

I respect in America her democracy, her hard work. I respect her dynamism. I respect her self-criticism. It's a rare quality in the world arena. The phrase you often hear in the U.S. is, "Can I help you?" That appears on the street, in interpersonal relations, but it also appears on the international stage.

News conference, Boston, Nov. 7/
USA Today, 11-8:(A)8.

Adam Smith
Author, Economist

2

I have a skepticism about America as a political country and an optimism about Americans. I have two different views of our country as it is run politically and how it runs itself. When I look at the challenges ahead and what's meeting the challenges, I think it would be a lot easier if we were meeting these challenges more rationally.

Interview/Los Angeles Times, 11-27:(IV)3.

Studs Terkel
Author

3

America won't be blown up. It'll suffocate. Polluted air, polluted water—it's going to be death by strangulation. The over-all detrius of banality will overwhelm us. Like *Waiting for Godot*. Deliquescence... There's got to be a change. I think it's happening. I hope. If you could coalesce all those little groups. Goliath has the networks and channels and certain newspapers. But we got the slingshots!

Interview, Washington/
The Washington Post, 9-22:(C)1.

Ralph Whitehead
Professor of public policy,
University of Massachusetts

4

[On Republican Presidential nominee George Bush's use of the Pledge of Allegiance as a campaign issue]: There are a lot of people who worry that the idea of American exceptionalism—which is at the very core of our national experience—may be slipping away. And because of that concern, people want a unifying creed. They want their President to give voice to that creed, and they want the creed to be a fusion of secular and religious values. The pledge is something that stands at the fusion point—it's a secular prayer.

The Washington Post, 10-4:(A)15.

Jim Wright
United States Representative,
D-Texas

5

I think all of us and each of us in his heart of hearts would subscribe to the belief that patriotism knows no political party... And surely nothing would be more reprehensible than for any of us to suggest that another member or another citizen, simply by reason of adhering to the principles of the other political party, was less patriotic than ourselves. Judge Learned Hand said it well. He said that "society is already in the process of dissolution where neighbors begin to view one another with suspicion or where nonconformity with accepted creed becomes a mark of disaffection." Let that not be the epitaph of this civilization.

Washington, Sept. 9/
The Washington Post, 9-13:(A)25.

Wilbur Zelinsky
Professor of geography, Pennsylvania
State University

6

Once upon a time, the Fourth of July was an extremely popular day to get married. It was a time of spontaneous nationalism. You didn't have to belong to the American Legion or any patriotic organization. People named their kids George or Thomas Jefferson or Benjamin Franklin.... [But] our faith in the nation is now imposed from above, in the form of museums, monuments and television events.

The Washington Post, 7-4:(A)18.

Civil Rights • Women's Rights

Ralph David Abernathy
Former president,
Southern Christian
Leadership Conference

1

[The late civil-rights leader] Martin Luther King, Jr., was the best thing that ever happened to America. If George Washington was the father of the nation, Martin Luther King will go down in history as the savior of the nation. He saved the nation through non-violence. He saved both oppressed and oppressor. An eye for an eye and a tooth for a tooth will end up with a blind generation and toothless people.

Interview/USA Today, 1-18:(A)11.

Lloyd Bentsen
United States Senator,
D-Texas;
1988 Democratic
Vice-Presidential nominee

2

Ask them about equality of opportunity [for women], and the Republicans will say, "We're for it." Ask them what they have done to *promote* equal opportunity, and the silence will be deafening.

Before National Federation of
Business and Professional Women's
Clubs, Albuquerque, July 27/
Los Angeles Times, 7-28:(I)14.

Zoya Boguslavskaya
Soviet author and critic

3

[After meeting more than 50 successful U.S. women from many fields]: Such remarkable women with such high achievements, and still they want more. More women lawyers, more women doctors. Here [in the U.S.], women are always trying to establish themselves and prove something. They always have to prove they're the same as men.

Interview, New York/
The Wall Street Journal, 6-22:20.

Robert H. Bork
Former Judge, United States
Court of Appeals for the
District of Columbia

4

[Criticizing Senator Edward Kennedy for rallying blacks against Bork's nomination to the U.S. Supreme Court, which was rejected by the Senate, during last year's confirmation hearings]: Even for a political campaign, [Kennedy's behavior] set record lows in mendacity, brutality and intellectual vulgarity . . . I won't take time to spell out my civil-rights record as Solicitor General and as a judge, but it is a very good one. That fact was obscured, and millions of black Americans were told that I was their enemy. The claim that I am hostile to black civil rights was a lie.

Before litigation section,
American Bar Association,
Rancho Mirage, Calif., Feb. 12/
Los Angeles Times, 2-13:(I)37.

George Bush
Vice President
of the United States;
Candidate for the 1988
Republican Presidential
nomination

5

[Saying he is opposed to legislation that would extend Federal-aid regulations on discrimination to all phases of an institution's activities, not just to that area where the discrimination exists]: Let me be very frank with you. The legislation on Grove City [College, which is the specific case at hand,] is imperfect and the imperfections should be corrected. Having said that, however, the Federal government must require that organizations that get tax dollars comply with our civil-rights laws. That's fundamental.

To group of his black supporters,
Washington, March 21/
The New York Times, 3-22:1.

(GEORGE BUSH)

1

We have had women in the Cabinet of the President of the United States, and we have had black Americans. We have had other minorities. If I become President, my Cabinet will be composed of the very best men and women—at least one of whom, finally, will be a Hispanic American. It's time, it's time . . . and that is a solemn pledge.

*Before League of United
Latin American Citizens,
Dallas, July 6/
The Washington Post,
7-7:(A)6.*

2

I guarantee you, I will be personally involved in protecting the civil rights of all Americans. This effort will be at the top of the agenda of my Attorney General, and he or she will be directly accountable to me for results. I intend to stand for a new harmony among the races. We are on a journey to a new century and we must finally leave the tired old baggage of bigotry behind us. Wherever racism rears its ugly head . . . we must be there to cut it off.

*At NAACP convention,
Washington, July 12/
Los Angeles Times,
7-13:(I)10.*

3

Today, women working full-time earn 70 cents for every dollar earned by men. There is only one amount that women should earn for every dollar earned by a man, and that is one dollar. Equal pay for equal work is not a slogan, not an opinion, not an interesting idea. It is a right.

*Before National Federation of
Business and Professional
Women's Clubs,
Albuquerque, July 24/
The New York Times,
7-25:11.*

George Bush
*Vice President
of the United States;
1988 Republican
Presidential nominee*

4

I believe abortion is wrong. We should work to change *Roe v. Wade* [the Supreme Court ruling permitting abortion]. Abortion on demand should not be legal. And it won't be—but only if we persevere. I believe we need a human-life amendment. I favor exceptions for rape, incest and those cases in which the life of the mother is in danger. I know that not all of us agree on those exceptions. But we *do* agree on the principle. Our Constitution is and should be designed to protect human life.

*Interview/
Christianity Today, 9-16:40.*

5

. . . I oppose abortion, and I favor adoption, and if we can get this law [permitting abortions] changed where everybody should make the extraordinary effort to take these kids that are unwanted and sometimes aborted, let them come to birth, and then put them in a family where there will be love . . . I've seen abortion sometimes used as a birth-control device, for heaven's sakes, see the millions of these killings accumulate, and this is one where you can have an honest difference of opinion . . . I'm for the sanctity of life, and once that illegality [of abortion] is established, then we can come to grips with the penalty side; and, of course, there's got to be some penalties to enforce the law, whatever they may be.

*At Presidential debate,
Winston-Salem, N.C.,
Sept. 25/The New York Times,
9-26:11.*

6

I don't agree with most of the positions of the ACLU[1]. I simply don't want to see the ratings on movies [eliminated]—I don't want my 10-year-old grandchild to go to an X-rated movie. I like those rating systems. I don't think they're right to

(GEORGE BUSH)

try to take the tax exemption away from the Catholic Church. I don't want to see the kiddie pornographic laws repealed. I don't want to see "under God" come out from our currency. Now, these are all positions of the ACLU, and I don't agree with them.

At Presidential debate,
Winston-Salem, N.C.,
Sept. 25/The New York Times,
9-26:11.

George Bush
Vice President,
and President-elect,
of the United States

1

When you look back at the history of the United States of America, I think there are far fewer incidents built on bigotry [today] than there have been [in the past]. But I would certainly do my level best to make very clear that bigotry has no place in America.

News conference, Nov. 9/
The Christian Science Monitor,
11-17:5.

Jimmy Carter
Former President
of the United States

2

[On civil-rights leader Jesse Jackson's quest for the 1988 Democratic Presidential nomination, which he lost to Michael Dukakis]: There have been many people in the country who have not accepted until now the proposition that blacks have a legitimate role within the councils of government. I think what Jesse has done in his extraordinary campaign is to let moderate and even many conservative Democrats see that the issues that are important to Jesse's narrowly defined constituency also apply to them. To me, this may be not the final but at least the penultimate peak in the acceptance of blacks within the American political system.

Interview, Atlanta/Time, 8-1:19.

Rosalynn Carter
Wife of former President
of the United States
Jimmy Carter

3

I really believe [abortion] should be a religious issue. I couldn't do it because of my religious beliefs, but who am I to impose my feelings on someone else? Some religions are not that strict about it. Also, the Constitution calls for separation of church and state. How can you impose through law a religious belief on all people?

Interview, L. B. J. Ranch,
Texas/Good Housekeeping,
February:172.

Shirley Chisholm
Former United States
Representative, D-New York

4

Women's-rights advocates had better be prepared to accommodate the conservative views of Southern women if they expect to maintain national influence and power. Compromise is not a dirty word.

Before National Organization
for Women, Buffalo, N.Y.,
June 26/USA Today, 6-27:(A)9.

Michael S. Dukakis
Governor of Massachusetts (D);
Candidate for the 1988
Democratic Presidential
nomination

5

I think there is a Constitutional distinction between political [free] speech and obscenity. That is, I think we can regulate Constitutional obscenity. I think it's got to be limited and restrained. I think if somebody wants to put a pornographic bookstore in the middle of downtown Stoughton, Massachusetts, the people of downtown Stoughton have the right to say: "Sorry, we don't want that bookstore" . . . Look, I'm a card-carrying member of the American Civil Liberties Union and I think you have to be

(MICHAEL S. DUKAKIS)

very restrained, but I'm not somebody who takes the position that under no circumstances can society impose restrictions on material that by any standard is clearly pornographic.

Interview/
Los Angeles Times,
5-26:(I)24.

Michael S. Dukakis
Governor of Massachusetts (D);
1988 Democratic
Presidential nominee

1

[Supporting the right to have an abortion]: It's the woman, in the exercise of her own conscience and her own religious beliefs, who has to make that judgment. This doesn't mean that [I] support abortion, or like it, or think it's a good thing. The question is who makes the decision, and do we go back to the days when we branded a woman a criminal for making that decision.

News conference,
St. Louis, July 24/
The New York Times,
7-25:11.

Mervyn Dymally
United States Representative,
D-California

2

We need a [U.S.] Civil Rights Commission that supports civil rights, that obeys the law . . . Let the [current] Commission fade away on its current budget, then reorganize it next year. Under a new Republican Administration it will operate in behalf of civil rights more than it has under the present [Reagan] Administration. If a Democratic Administration is elected, it will definitely be an advocate of the cause of civil rights. The present commission is now an apologist for an anti-affirmative-action policy. It's an embarrassment for those of us who knew it in the 1960s and '70s.

The Christian Science Monitor,
3-11:7.

Jerry Falwell
Evangelist

3

I think the abortion thing [the current legality of abortions] is not going to change until our people, the pro-life people, look on the unborn as a disenfranchised minority, make it a civil-rights issue [and] go to the same level of commitment the civil-rights people did—civil disobedience. It's just beginning . . . I think we can—with sit-ins, pray-ins—shut down [abortion] clinics . . . get a human-life amendment . . . probably with rape, incest and the life of the mother as exceptions.

Interview, New Orleans/
Newsweek, 8-29:5.

Geraldine Ferraro
1984 Democratic
Vice Presidential nominee;
Former United States
Representative,
D-New York

4

Every time a woman runs for any elective office, it's like throwing a stone in a lake. The ripple effect is felt far beyond the immediate point of impact. [But] if you don't run, you can't win.

At "Women and the Constitution:
A Bicentennial Perspective"
symposium, Atlanta/
The Christian Science Monitor,
2-16:5.

Linda D. Fienberg
Executive Assistant to
U.S. Security and
Exchange Commission Chairman
David Ruder

5

It is helpful [for women] to have a mentor, when you are new at a place, who is interested in your success. More mentors are men than women. If every time there is a male-female mentor relationship people draw unfair conclusions, it will make it harder for women to succeed. I'm concerned that due to fears developing among men and women, those kinds of relationships

(LINDA D. FIENBERG)

could be discouraged. It would be sad if men and women couldn't have professional relationships without people forming conclusions there were sexual undertones.

Interview/
The Washington Post, 11-7:(A)21.

Beatrice Fitzpatrick
President, American
Woman's Economic
Development Corporation

1

Women are deciding that the answer to their socio-economic problems is to go into their own businesses. Minority women feel that's the only way they're going to get a fair shake. Women single heads of households are starting firms in their houses where they can keep one eye on the kids and one eye on the business. Older women, who've been out of the workforce for a long time because they were raising a family, start businesses because they can't get jobs commensurate with their skills. Women in large corporations are deciding that they can't reach the level in the corporation that they want to within the time frame they want to, and the only way they're going to get the authority and responsibility they want is to go into their own business.

Interview/USA Today, 5-19:(A)15.

Abraham Foxman
National director,
Anti-Defamation League
of B'nai B'rith

2

There are lots of reasons for anti-Semitism. It is an irrational disease. A lot of psychoanalysts have said that the reason adolescents act this out is because they have frustrations, anxieties, anger against parents, the establishment . . . They've heard anti-Semitism in the home, in the school. It's something that they know in history people have done. And as long as they do not perceive that it is a crime, a serious offense against society, it will continue. Our job is to educate,

and this is why I think it is important to tell young people that every time you call somebody a dirty name because of his religion or race or color, you're building toward that. The next time somebody calls you a dirty name because of your origins or color, you say, "Hey, don't do that, because that's hatred. That's hatred that hurts. That's hatred that can burn a synagogue or church."

Interview/USA Today, 9-27:(A)7.

Mary Hatwood Futrell
President, National
Education Association

3

[On the current march to Washington by 55,000 people to commemorate the civil-rights march on Washington in 1963 led by Martin Luther King, Jr.]: I believe the fact that so many people have turned out for this march is saying to America that while we have made progress [in race relations], we still have much to do, and we're not going to stop until everyone has an opportunity to achieve his or her full potential. I think the marching is basically to send a message to the officials and to the people of this country that there are a lot of people who still care about equality and, if necessary, we're willing to take to the streets to demonstrate that commitment. It's a symbolic effort, but it sends a very strong message that the civil-rights movement is alive. It sends a message that the people care about equal opportunity, and it sends a message that we are going to continue to fight for justice.

Interview/USA Today, 8-29:(A)9.

Ellen Futter
President, Barnard College

4

Women are absolutely mired in middle management in business. There have been a lot of articles about the fact that there's no woman in the fast track to becoming a chief executive officer of a *Fortune* 500 company. Even in academia, we are very unusual in having over 50 per cent of our faculty being women. There's almost nobody who touches that statistic. In cer-

23

(ELLEN FUTTER)

tain fields, women are nearly invisible. International relations, for example. There are exceptions, but very, very few, so that there are both enormous strides within specific fields to be made and some fields that need to be invaded.

Interview/USA Today, 9-7:(A)11.

Albert Gore, Jr.
United States Senator,
D-Tennessee;
Candidate for the 1988
Democratic Presidential
nomination

1

The tremendous progress we [in the South] have made in civil rights has given us perhaps a keener appreciation than the rest of the country for how much work remains to be done in putting prejudice behind us and creating a better society. I think that those of us who live in what's sometimes called the New South are eager to help build a new America.

Interview, Washington/
U.S. News & World Report,
2-15:17.

2

[On affirmative-action programs]: There is an inevitable tension between goals in our society that sometimes come into conflict. I do not agree with the application of a quota in an individual case in a way that says to one person, you will have this job because of your race or sex and another will not have it because they are of a different race or sex. I do, however, favor the use of guidelines that will over time result in a more inclusive policy of hiring to enable individuals who have been discriminated against to find an easier time gaining employment. And I recognize that that tension sometimes produces real conflicts. I nevertheless stand by my support of affirmative action if it is sensitively implemented so as to minimize the kinds of manifestly unjust choices that disadvantage members of a majority group. There's no easy answer.

Interview/
The New York Times, 4-11:12.

William H. Gray III
United States Representative,
D-Pennsylvania

3

[On civil-rights leader Jesse Jackson's quest for the 1988 Democratic Presidential nomination]: Has Jackson been successful to a great degree at heightening the consciousness of blacks for the need for political participation? Absolutely. That's the great symbolism of his candidacy, which I don't think Michael Dukakis [who won the Party's nomination for President] understands and most whites can never fathom. I mean, you cannot understand being down there on that floor last night [at the Party convention in Atlanta], being black in the United States of America. Who cares whether the guy [Jackson] came in second? Right over there is [the late civil-rights leader] Martin Luther King's grave. Right over there is Ebenezer Baptist Church. Right over there is the old YMCA where the black leadership in the '40s and '50s used to meet because they couldn't meet in hotels like this to plot strategy. And the emotional feeling that, God, we are making progress. Most people can't understand that.

Interview, Atlanta/
Newsweek, 8-1:4.

Jesse Helms
United States Senator,
R-North Carolina

4

[Arguing against a bill that would pay $20,000 to Americans of Japanese descent who were put in detention camps in the U.S. during World War II]: We all have 20-20 vision on Monday morning . . . It's easy to criticize what happened. But I can't buy this business of kicking our government around at a time when the horrible destruction of Pearl Harbor had happened.

Los Angeles Times, 4-21:(I)1.

Daniel K. Inouye
United States Senator,
D-Hawaii

5

[Approving of the Senate decision to make $20,000 payments to Americans of Japanese

(DANIEL K. INOUYE)

descent who were put in detention camps in the U.S. during World War II]: There is a debt here. These Japanese-Americans were unfairly branded as disloyal during wartime, solely on the ground of racial ancestry. Their internment was unprecedented in the history of American civil-rights deprivation.

Washington, April 20/
Los Angeles Times, 4-21:(I)1.

Jesse L. Jackson
Civil-rights leader;
Candidate for the 1988
Democratic Presidential
nomination

1

[As black students,] our minds were segregated; our ambitions were segregated. It affected our dreams. We dreamed segregated dreams. No one should negotiate their dreams. Dreams must be free to flee and fly high. No government, no legislature, has a right to limit your dreams. You should never agree to surrender your dreams. There are no more impossible dreams. I am taking the lid off of dreams.

At North Carolina A&T State
University commencement, May 8/
The New York Times, 5-9:10.

2

[Criticizing anti-abortionists who are not concerned with what happens to a baby after it is born]: I'm just as concerned about those who are absolutely obsessed with the fetus from conception through nine months and then have no commitment to the baby from birth to death.

At debate among Democratic
Presidential candidates,
Des Moines, Iowa, Jan. 15/
Los Angeles Times, 1-16:(I)22.

3

[On how the media treats minorities, particularly blacks and Latinos]: It projects us as less intelligent than we are, as less hard-working than we work, as less patriotic than we are, as less universal than we are and as more violent than we are—in ways designed to poison the minds of the common people.

At fund-raising luncheon,
Sacramento, Calif., Jan. 19/
Los Angeles Times, 1-20:(I)17.

Jesse L. Jackson
Civil-rights leader;
Former candidate for
the 1988 Democratic
Presidential
nomination

4

It seems to me that prejudice means to prejudge, to assume that people are not something, cannot *be* something, because they are black, or female, or Jewish, or Hispanic. We may prejudge them because of their lack of experience. Well, I've been exposed, so I *post*judge. And my postjudgment is that every human right, every right of respect, every right of expectation available to a man should be available to a woman.

Interview/
Lear's, Nov.-Dec.:131.

John E. Jacob
President, National
Urban League

5

While America was riding an economic boom [over the last decade], black poverty rose and we've slipped further back from our goal of parity with white citizens . . . [The Reagan Administration] liberated people to be discriminatory in their behavior as well as in their attitudes and, therefore, I think they have had a profound negative impact on the progression that had taken place.

Upon making public the annual
State of Black America Report,
Washington, Jan. 14/
The New York Times,
1-15:7.

25

Kay James
Director of public affairs,
National Right to Life Committee

1

[On the 1973 *Roe vs. Wade* Supreme Court case legalizing abortions]: The most profound impact of *Roe vs. Wade* on our culture was to usher out the *value*-of-life ethic in our country and usher in a *quality*-of-life ethic, where life-and-death decisions are made based on someone's perceived quality of life. That's very scary . . . It's very callous. That's why, in 1973, there were those pro-life [anti-abortion] activists who talked about how we were ushering in an age which was opening the door for acceptance of infanticide and euthanasia. As we go into 1988, we see that they were not bizarre at all, and that's where the whole pro-life struggle is headed, to protect all human life.

Interview/USA Today, 1-22:(A)11.

Barbara Jordan
Professor of public values and ethics,
University of Texas, Austin;
Former United States Representative,
D-Texas

2

All women do not support the Equal Rights Amendment. Those who do must respect the right of others to choose not to support ERA. [But ERA would] end all ambiguity and obfuscation and place women squarely within the letter of the Constitution.

At "Women and the Constitution:
A Bicentennial Perspective"
symposium, Atlanta/
The Christian Science Monitor,
2-16:5.

Thomas H. Kean
Governor of New Jersey (R)

3

Republicans will make it clear: We will search out bigotry and racism; we will drag it into the sunshine of understanding and make it wither and die.

At Republican National Convention,
New Orleans, Aug. 16/
Los Angeles Times, 8-17:(I)10.

Edward M. Kennedy
United States Senator,
D-Massachusetts

4

[Saying the Reagan Administration has retreated from civil-rights]: They piously pretend that they hear no racism, see no racism and speak no racism in America. But I ask, "Who among us would choose to live in Howard Beach [N.Y.] or move to [Georgia's] Forsyth County [places where there have been recent racial clashes] if our skin were black?

Boston, Jan. 18/
The New York Times, 1-19:11.

Arthur Lelyveld
Rabbi; former president,
American Jewish Congress

5

The American dedication to human equality and opportunity not only persists but has persisted in strength in large measure because of [the late black civil-rights leader] Martin Luther King. He said that he had a dream that our nation would someday rise up and live out the true meaning of its creed. The dream was inclusive. It was not just a dream for black liberation. He knew that black liberation would bring about white liberation.

Interview/USA Today, 1-18:(A)11.

C. Eric Lincoln
Professor of sociology of religion,
Graduate School,
Duke University

6

Yesterday, the black person who tried to make it out of the black community moved tentatively to the white neighborhood, which I call the hallowed heights. But he or she had to go back home four times a week: on Friday to get his hair cut, on Saturday to party, on Sunday for some good soul preaching and on Monday to get his clothes washed. Today's middle-class [black] professionals, sons and daughters of these same people, have gone to schools like Duke and Vanderbilt [Universities] and their young white counterparts tell them, "You're just like us; we

(C. ERIC LINCOLN)

went to school together. You don't have to go home on Friday to get your hair done; you can get it done at my salon. On Saturday you can party with us, and on Sunday no one goes to church anyway."

The Washington Post, 8-20:(A)6.

Wilma Mankiller
Principal Chief, Cherokee
(American Indian) Nation

1

There are so many forces working against Indian tribes. There are people in Tulsa and Oklahoma City who don't realize our communities exist as they do today, that we have a language that is alive, that we have a tribal government that is thriving. Most people like to deal with us as though we were in a museum or a history book... Relocation was yet another answer from the Federal government to the continuing dilemma of what to do with us. We are a people with many, many social indicators of decline and an awful lot of problems, so in the '50s they decided to mainstream us, to try to take us away from the tribal landbase and the tribal culture, get us into the cities. It was supposed to be a better life.

Interview/"Ms.," January:69.

Thurgood Marshall
Associate Justice,
Supreme Court of
the United States

2

A recent survey shows that racism is broader and stronger than before. We're not gaining ground, my friends. We might be losing. But one thing I'm sure of: This is no time to stop. What is important is a goal toward which we are moving, a goal that is the basis of true democracy, which is over and above the law. And it's something that won't happen. But you must pray for it and work for it, and that goal is very simple. That goal is that if a child, a Negro child, is born to a black mother in a state like Mississippi, or any other

state like that, born to the dumbest, poorest sharecropper, if by merely drawing its first breath in the democracy, there and without any more, he is born with the exact same rights as a similar child born to a white parent of the wealthiest person in the United States. No, it's not true. It never will be true. but I challenge anybody to take the position that that is not the goal that we should be shooting for. And stop talking about how far we've come, and stop talking about how close we are.

Before National Bar Association,
Aug. 10/The New York Times,
8-11:10.

Frank Matthews
Professor of law,
George Mason University

3

The environment created by the Reagan Administration is largely responsible [for the resurgence of racism on college campuses]. Students have read the Administration's attacks on affirmative action and civil rights as license to act in a heretofore unacceptable fashion. The students get their cues from the top, and when you have a President and an Attorney General saying it's okay to act out your racism, this is what happens.

Ebony, December:130.

Robert H. Michel
United States Representative,
R-Illinois

4

We used to have minstrel shows when I was in grade school. Of course, today you can't do that, everybody blackfaced-up. I think it's too bad, you know, some of these things. I used to love to imitate, for example, Kingfish [of] *Amos 'n' Andy*. We never thought of it in [racially] disparaging terms. It was just a part of life and it was fun. I get to thinking, we're seeing [today] the Russians rewrite their history again. They rewrote it initially, and now they're coming back to maybe recognizing some of it for what it really was. Well, we find ourselves in that same boat, or

WHAT THEY SAID IN 1988

same mold, trying to rewrite history. That doesn't wash well with me.

Broadcast interview/
The Washington Post, 11-17:(A)8.

Kate Michelman
Executive director, National
Abortion Rights Action League

1

[On the 1973 *Roe vs. Wade* Supreme Court case legalizing abortions]: It is solely responsible for saving women's lives, saving women's health, and saving women from shame and degradation. It is an important milestone in the quest for equality and liberty . . . Had *Roe* not happened, we would have continued in the long process of state by state, law by law, establishing the right of a woman to choose an abortion, and in some states we would not have the right established . . . The anti-abortion movement has captured the public forum. They've been successful in casting the pro-choice proponents as people thoughtless about children and life, and that women who have abortions are selfish and immoral. But they have not been able to move this country at all to embracing the notion that abortion should be illegal. The most fascinating thing about our study is that even among those who are the most anti-abortion groups in the country, you have this demonstrated opposition to government intrusion into private life.

Interview/USA Today, 1-22:(A)11.

2

Even though polls show that most Americans support the right to abortion, the anti-abortion side has in some way won the public debate, captured the terms and framed the issues. There is very little discussion these days about how every dimension of a woman's life is influenced by the right to reproductive freedom. We have to remind people that abortion is the guarantor of a woman's full right to choose and her right to participate fully in the social and political life of society.

The New York Times, 5-10:8.

Norman Y. Mineta
United States Representative,
D-California

3

[On the House's approval of a bill granting $20,000 to Japanese-Americans who were put in internment camps in the U.S. during World War II]: This is a deeply personal issue for a small number of us. But this legislation touches all of us because it goes to the very core of our nation. Does our Constitution protect all of us—regardless of race or culture? Do our rights remain inalienable even in times of stress—and especially in times of stress? Passage of this legislation answers these questions—a resounding "yes." I am deeply honored to serve in this body as it takes the great step of admitting and redressing a monumental injustice.

Before the House, Washington,
Aug. 4/Los Angeles Times,
8-5:(I)1.

Charles Moody
Vice provost for minority
affairs, University of Michigan

4

There's a national tolerance for racism created by the Reagan Administration and that tolerance is being reflected on the nation's college campuses. But we can't close our eyes to it and pretend it will go away. It won't. Institutions have a responsibility to all students to admit it is there and take whatever steps are necessary to change it.

Ebony, December:130.

Charles Morgan
Lawyer; Former director,
Southern Christian
Leadership Conference

5

[On the late civil-rights leader Martin Luther King, Jr.]: He resurrected a society. No one else did that. No one except [Franklin] Roosevelt. King made every day election day in America. He forced American citizens to watch. He forced the Congress to act. The courts responded prop-

(CHARLES MORGAN)

erly, and together they vindicated the Constitution of the United States.

Los Angeles Times, 3-29:(I)1.

Milton Morris
Research director,
Joint Center for
Political Studies

1

The good news is the extent of the mobilization of the black electorate in the South. The bad news is that the races are as polarized as much as they have been at any time in the last two decades. What you have is a white electorate and a black electorate, and they are not crossing very much. If you look at the 6,600 black elected officials in the country, the overwhelming majority of them are elected by black voters. What we have very often is not a non-racial electorate, but a highly racial cleavage.

Los Angeles Times, 3-29:(I)12.

Ralph G. Neas
Executive director,
Leadership Conference on
Civil Rights

2

[President] Reagan has compiled the worst civil-rights record of any Administration in more than half a century. He seized every opportunity to weaken civil-rights laws and repudiate the enforcement policies of previous Democratic and Republican Administrations—in housing, voting, education and employment.

The Christian Science Monitor,
1-18:18.

Eleanor Holmes Norton
Professor of law,
Georgetown University;
Former Chairman, Federal
Equal Employment
Opportunity Commission

3

[On the late civil-rights leader Martin Luther King, Jr.]: His legacy is much larger than an opening up of the American political process. He addressed the much deeper malady of racism. We had lived with racism for our entire history. It is our oldest social scourge, and he made the country think about it.

Los Angeles Times, 3-29:(I)1.

Sandra Day O'Connor
Associate Justice,
Supreme Court of
the United States

4

There is no question that the [Supreme] Court has now made clear that it will no longer view as benign archaic and stereotypic notions concerning the roles and abilities of males and females. Despite the encouraging and wonderful gains and the changes for women which have occurred in my lifetime, there is still room to advance and to promote correction of the remaining deficiencies and imbalances.

At conference sponsored by
Emory University and
Georgia State University, Atlanta,
Feb. 11/The New York Times,
2-12:28.

Jack O'Dell
Member, National
Rainbow Coalition

5

Today, the struggle [for blacks] is not for equality before the law and to clean up the remnants of injustice, but to establish equality in our standing in the life and political economy of this country. Civil equality would mean if we have 11 per cent of the U.S. population, we would have 11 per cent, at least, of the national income, . . . 47 Congresspersons, not 23, and 11 U.S. Senators, not zero. Civil equality would mean that we would be as prominent in the government structure, in television and radio corporations and major banks and academic institutions as we are among workers in the cafeteria . . . We would be 11 per cent of the poor, if poor is considered a status, not 25 per cent of all the poor.

At Smithsonian Institution seminar/
Los Angeles Times, 3-29:(I)12.

Norman J. Ornstein
Resident scholar,
American Enterprise Institute

1

[On President-elect George Bush's stand against abortion]: By having a Democratic [Presidential] candidate [Michael Dukakis] who was emphatically pro choice, and using rhetoric that appealed to the pro-life people, George Bush did mobilize people that might not otherwise have voted for him. He is going to think twice before he acts to alienate that base. I think there is almost no question that, in making Supreme Court appointments, abortion will be among the top three questions the White House will ask.

The New Your Times,
11-14:(A)12.

Dolly Parton
Singer

2

I remember, myself, that I didn't like to hear a lot of women singers on the radio, or women deejays. Back then, it was sort of like listening to a woman preacher—hard to accept because you're not used to it. Now I love them, because I'm familiar with them. They just sort of saturated the market, and some of them had a great deal of talent. I'm not one of those people out there kicking and cussing for women, but women deserve the opportunity to be whatever they can be. And especially in creative things, women should have the respect they deserve, and I'm happy to see the new breed come along. Whatever part I've played in that, I'm proud of.

Interview/
TV Guide, 10-8:40.

Clarence M. Pendleton, Jr.
Former Chairman,
United States Commission
on Civil Rights

3

Affirmative action was to achieve equal opportunity but has turned into preferential treatment.

USA Today, 8-26:(A)8.

Charles Peters
Editor, "The Washington
Monthly"

4

The great mistake of the women's movement was the extent to which they got involved in imitating the worst in men instead of having men imitate the best in women. The women of my generation have fewer chips on their shoulders. They had much less macho silliness than men did. They were much less likely to get us into a war, and they were much less likely to waste time posturing.

Interview/
The Washington Post, 6-9:(B)3.

Dan Quayle
United States Senator,
R-Indiana;
1988 Republican
Vice-Presidential nominee

5

There is no doubt that the Republicans missed the boat somewhat on trying to advance civil rights. The problem we have is: Where are you going to use the Federal government? Conservatives are very reluctant to use government regulations, which makes them seem anti-civil rights. Yet they would use the government to outlaw abortion. There are stark inconsistencies.

Interview/Time, 8-29:25.

Maureen Reagan
Co-chairman, Republican
National Committee

6

I will feel that equality has arrived when we can afford to elect women to [public] office who can prove themselves to be as unqualified as some of the men who are already there.

Denver, June/
The Washington Post, 8-16:(E)4.

Ronald Reagan
President of the United States

7

[Saying he is anti-abortion]: We're told about a woman's right to control her own body, but

(RONALD REAGAN)

doesn't an unborn child have a higher right? And that is to life, liberty and the pursuit of happiness. Are we to forget the entire moral mission of our country through history? Well, my answer is no.

Speaking by telephone to
anti-abortion demonstration,
Washington, Jan. 22/
The New York Times, 1-23:10.

Alan Reitman
Associate director,
American Civil
Liberties Union

1

Throughout its history, the ACLU has defended rights. But just because you defend a person's rights does not mean you should be tarred with the substance of their cause. When we defend the right of an individual, you don't automatically agree with his point of view.

The Christian Science Monitor,
10-3:4.

William Bradford Reynolds
Assistant Attorney General,
Civil Rights Division,
Department of Justice
of the United States

2

[Criticizing Congress for exempting itself from a number of civil-rights laws]: It is almost laughable to sit here and listen to these grand protestations by members of Congress about this [Reagan] Administration's civil-rights record. [As for complaints from liberals that the Administration is trying to turn back the clock on civil rights], this chamber has not seen fit in over 200 years to reach out and even once wind the civil-rights clock that watches in forced silence over its activities.

Before Senate Judiciary
Committee, Washington, May 26/
The New York Times,
5-28:10.

Frank H. T. Rhodes
President, Cornell
University; Chairman,
Commission on Minority
Participation in Education
and American Life

3

[On the findings of the commission he headed, which was formed by the American Council on Education and the Education Commission of the States]: After examining all the available evidence, we have reached this disturbing conclusion: We're moving backward, not forward, in our efforts to achieve the full participation of minority citizens in the life and prosperity of the nation.

News conference,
Washington, May 23/
The Washington Post,
5-24:(A)4.

Roy S. Roberts
Vice president, personnel
administration and
development, General Motors
Corporation

4

Like it or not, companies that fail to make the connection between a minority work force and the bottom line will be companies that lose the competitive race, and you can take that to the bank.

Before American Newspaper
Publishers Association, Honolulu/
The New York Times,
4-27:44.

Nawal Saadawi
Egyptian women's-rights
activist

5

There are [many] women here [in Egypt] who wear the veil, but they go to work. There are women in the U.S. who don't work. It's the veiling of the brain that's dangerous.

Interview/
USA Today, 9-16:(A)9.

31

Eleanor Smeal
*President, Fund for
the Feminist Majority;
Former president, National
Organization for Women*

1

I think that a substantial number of men, and a majority of women, are for equality [for women]. But I think that the key to gaining equality is that those who have been denied must seek it. Our first job is to organize those who have been discriminated against. Women in themselves have power. We are the majority. As Eleanor Roosevelt said, it takes the consent of the governed for government to work. And we should not consent to inequality.

*Interview/
USA Today, 11-22:(A)13.*

Olympia Snowe
*United States Representative,
R-Maine*

2

Our laws will have to change to conform to the fact that the only people who carry and bear children [women] are indispensable in the workforce. From the standpoint of fairness, that which makes women different from men should not be a disadvantage in the workplace.

*At "Women and the Constitution:
A Bicentennial Perspective"
symposium, Atlanta/
The Christian Science Monitor, 2-16:5.*

Lowell P. Weicker, Jr.
*United States Senator,
R-Connecticut*

3

During the last decade, we have seen a systematic dismantling of civil-rights laws. And action by the courts combined with inaction by Congress have allowed discrimination to continue and discriminators to get the advantage of tax dollars.

*At memorial service
for the late civil-rights leader
Martin Luther King, Jr.,
Atlanta, Jan. 18/
The New York Times, 1-19:11.*

Molly Yard
*President, National
Organization for Women*

4

Every Republican candidate who ran [for the 1988 Republican Presidential nomination], including [frontrunner, Vice President] George Bush, is opposed to the Equal Rights Amendment and supports the Human Life Amendment. For Bush, it's a total switch. He used to be the other way around. But the right wing has totally bamboozled him and he has caved in, and we'd [women] never support him.

*Interview/
USA Today, 6-27:(A)9.*

5

Women can't just drop everything and run [for political office]. And what have we seen all our lives? All-male legislatures, all-male Congress, all-male this, all-male that. And women have not seen themselves as leaders in making public policy because that's the way they've been brought up.

*Interview/
USA Today, 6-27:(A)9.*

Raul Yzaguirre
*President,
National Council
of La Raza*

6

[On Hispanics in the U.S.]: We never managed to capture the media attention. Our issues are much more complicated than simply being segregated on the basis of color. The [black] race issue, particularly in the South, lent itself to the graphics of television and the evening news. You could portray the discrimination, the egregious nature of segregation, by taking a picture of dogs behind sheriffs attacking blacks who wanted to eat at the lunch counter. With the Hispanic community, where issues are pluralism, bilingual education, the lack of education and dead-end-jobs—these things are much more complicated.

*Interview/
USA Today, 9-14:(A)9.*

Andrew Young
Mayor of Atlanta

1

Georgia is more liberal than Massachusetts on issues of race. Georgia has a large black population. It has 20 years of black people and white people living and working together in a desegregated society . . . I believe the people are ready to move and vote beyond race. It doesn't mean they will elect me [a black] Governor, but they might.

Interview, Boston/
The Christian Science Monitor, 11-30:3.

Commerce • Industry • Finance

C. Michael Aho
*Authority on trade, Council on
Foreign Relations*

1

We [the U.S.] are no longer the major actor in the world, but only the biggest kid on the block. The United States is in the competitive fight of its 200-year history, fighting not only for markets, but to sustain high living standards. If it wants to remain Number 1, the United States is going to have to work for it. The competition can no longer be taken lightly. Others may be striving harder.

*The Christian Science Monitor,
11-14:1.*

Vedat Akgiray
*Assistant professor of finance,
Clarkson University*

2

The [stock] market is not a gambling casino as some people claim. In the short term, the stock market can be quite risky for the small investor who can't follow it day to day. For the long term, it turns out to be a good investment.

Los Angeles Times, 11-20:(IV)2.

Bruce Babbitt
*Candidate for the
1988 Democratic
Presidential nomination;
Former Governor
of Arizona (D)*

3

I watched the stock market drop a hundred and forty-something points . . . and I asked, why is it that our leaders are turning Wall Street into a casino, where the lives and jobs of Americans are being traded like so many poker chips. And I asked, why is it that our corporate leaders are setting an example that says we're going to give workers pink slips at the same time that we're taking "golden parachutes" . . . lifetime security.

I think that stuff has a terribly corrosive kind of quality about it. It sets an example which says to Americans—you don't need to work. You don't need to do an honest day's labor. You get ahead by getting rich quick, by speculating. That's the moral deficit. And it's time that all of us stand up and say there's a better way.

*Campaign speech/
The New York Times, 1-21:10.*

Ravi Batra
Author; Economist

4

Most business executives are over-paid. Workers' compensation has been lagging behind inflation; executive compensation has been sky-rocketing even in industries where profits have fallen or losses have occurred. The worst excesses occur, I think, among the brokerage firms.

*Interview/
Los Angeles Times, 5-22: (IV)3.*

Karl D. Bays
Chairman, IC Industries

5

I believe in making strategic acquisitions when they lead to better products, lower production and distribution costs and increased sales. But . . . I'm against the takeover artists who buy companies, sell off the pieces, pocket the cash and then walk away.

*Before Financial Executives
Institute, Chicago/
Nation's Business, May:16.*

Lloyd Bentsen
*United States Senator,
D-Texas; 1988
Democratic Vice-
Presidential nominee*

6

We [Democrats] passed a trade bill that has this premise: that any country that has full access

(LLOYD BENTSEN)

to our markets—we're entitled to have full access to their markets. Now, that means that we're going to stand tough for America and we're going to protect those jobs and we're going to push American products. And we're going to open up markets around the world. We'll show leadership in that respect, and turn this deficit in trade around.

At Vice-Presidential debate,
Omaha, Neb., Oct. 5/
The New York Times, 10-7:(A)12.

1

I feel very strongly that we ought to be doing more for the American farmer, and what we've seen under this [Reagan] Administration is neglect of that farmer. We've seen them drive 220,000 farmers off the farm. They seem to think the answer is move them to town. But we ought not be doing that . . . We've seen an Administration that has lost much of our market abroad because they have not had a trade policy. We saw our market lost by some 40 percent, and that's one of the reasons that we've seen the cost of the farm program, which was only about $2.5-billion when they took office, now go about $25-billion. Now we can bring that kind of a cost down and get more to market prices if we'll have a good trade policy.

At Vice-Presidential debate,
Omaha, Neb., Oct. 5/
The New York Times, 10-7:(A)13.

James Bere
Chairman,
Borg-Warner Corporation

2

[On the multi-billion-dollar take-over effort for RJR Nabisco]: In its own way, the deal has been typically American, where nothing is in moderation, including the enormous selfishness of management. It's touched a nerve. Sometimes we have to do things in extremes before we can put the total in perspective.

Time, 12-5:70.

Daniel J. Boorstin
Historian;
Former Librarian of
Congress of the
United States

3

Designer labels have the aura of celebrity that distinguishes them from other labels, and the celebrity value is likely to overshadow the functional value of the product. But celebrity value is also a function. It gives psychological and emotional income to the purchaser . . . I think it is a mistake to assume that the main value from a product is its actual physical functioning value. We buy things for all sorts of reasons. When I buy a [Pierre] Cardin pan, I'm counting on the fact that you're going to be impressed I bought it. Maybe it's worth something to tell others that I've got the money, the taste and prestige hunger to buy a PC frying pan . . . Economists have long said that psychological satisfaction has to be counted into a product's market value. The appeal of a designer product is much vaguer, but no less valid. That's not bad, getting more satisfaction.

Interview/Forbes, 5-2:95.

Nicholas F. Brady
Investment banker;
Chairman, Presidential panel
investigating the
1987 stock-market crash

4

Look at the nature of securities firms today. They are dealing all over the world, in different currencies. The worry is that you do have a domino effect . . . we have a financial system that is based on the idea of many marketplaces, rather than one. That just is no longer possible. You do take a chance with the total system by taking that approach. Part of the worry is that a bank that lends to a securities firm in New York based on its holdings of New York Stock Exchange securities may not have any idea what kind of exposure the firm has in Chicago in the futures markets. That's why I think our conclusions, and really our strongest one, is that we ought to have a unified clearing system. A unified clearing

(NICHOLAS F. BRADY)

system gives you a better picture of what is going on in the system.

Interview, New York/
The New York Times, 1-12:29.

Nicholas F. Brady
Secretary of the Treasury
of the United States

1

I was always taught that the best loan that you could make was a character loan—one that looked beyond the hard numbers and took a leap of faith and counted on the character and strength of the individual involved. That principle applies to countries as well. The Treasury Department will . . . do the pick-and-shovel work to make sure the numbers are right, but we will always be guided by your faith that character is at the root of all human endeavor.

To President Reagan
after being sworn in as
Treasury Secretary,
Washington, Sept. 16/
Los Angeles Times,
9-17:(I)14.

2

If [the countries of the world] embark on a course that involves the transfer of [financial] risk from the private to the public sector, a true and lasting solution to the restoration of sustained growth among debtor nations will have escaped. And then, when official resources have been exhausted, as they will be, when our international institutions have been made static and vulnerable, and they will be, when private lenders have long since withdrawn from the financing of development, we will still face exactly the same problems we see today.

At meeting of International
Monetary Fund and World Bank,
West Berlin, Sept. 27/
The New York Times,
9-28:46.

James Burke
President, Merrill
Lynch Capital Partners

3

[On leveraged buyouts of companies]: The most positive thing is that they put ownership back in the hands of managers. Typically, management winds up with 20 per cent of the firm, and as the new owners find ways to cut the fat, most companies become more efficient and profitable. Moreover, these deals make special sense for a maturing economy like ours in which many firms are highly profitable but slow growing. In the 1960s and '70s, managers took excess cash and diversified into something they didn't know. Now people realize that they are much better off if they stick to their knitting . . . Right now, most public companies are owned by faceless institutions that don't hold managers strictly accountable. So if a manager walks out of the office and leaves the light on, he still gets paid. In the aftermath of an LBO, when 20 cents of every dollar saved goes into his pocket, he is much more likely to turn off that light.

Interview/
U.S. News & World Report,
12-12:73.

George Bush
Vice President of the United
States; Candidate for the
1988 Republican
Presidential nomination

4

A Bush Administration will help farmers export more crops, not force farmers to produce less. That is the major difference [between himself and Democratic Presidential candidate Michael Dukakis]. Those who advocate stringent supply controls have been proven wrong before and they are just as wrong today. If I am elected President, and I really do believe I will be, the top agricultural priority of my Administration will be to expand farm markets, both domestic and foreign.

Before Agricultural
Communicators Congress,
Washington, July 11/
The New York Times, 7-12:10.

George Bush
Vice President
of the United States;
1988 Republican
Presidential nominee

1

[Criticizing Democratic Presidential nominee Michael Dukakis for expressing concern about too much foreign investment and ownership in the U.S.]: Now, 30 days before the election, the last couple of days ago, for political reasons, he sees advantage in stoking fears about foreign influence. Never mind that we have an increasingly interdependent economy in this world. Never mind record American investment abroad. Never mind that foreign investment in the United States . . . helps to create jobs. And never mind that booming American exports are fueling our continued growth and cutting the trade deficit. My opponent desperately needs an issue, and he's willing to scare people to find it.

Campaign speech at
Seattle University Business School,
Oct. 11/The New York Times, 10-12:(A)10.

2

[On Democratic Presidential nominee Michael Dukakis' criticism of Bush's proposal to lower capital-gains taxes]: Unfortunately, my opponent's only experience with business is regulating it and taxing it. He's never run a business. He's never started a business. He's never met a payroll. He doesn't understand how, when you're starting out, you need people to join you in taking risks. So he paints my proposal as an effort to help the rich. Wrong. The majority of capital-gains recipients earn less than $50,000. And the cut will create jobs—and that will help everyone.

Before Economic Club of Detroit/
The Washington Post,
10-27:(A)20.

Robert C. Byrd
United States Senator
D-West Virginia

3

It's a shock to be told that America is no longer Number 1 around the world—that our products are increasingly outsold, that our manufacturing jobs are shipped overseas. Regaining our leadership rank among nations presents our people with an enormous challenge. And government has a big role—not to subsidize industry, but to give American producers and exporters the best advantage we can. To improve our highways and our ports. To encourage productive investment.

Broadcast address to the nation,
Jan. 25/USA Today, 1-26:(A)9.

Beverly Chain
Director,
office of communication,
United Church of Christ

4

Everybody knows that the free-market concept does not work to protect consumers. It works only to protect the seller. Markets are not free for more than 10 minutes. That's why we have antitrust laws.

Emmy Magazine, Jan-Feb.:41.

Kumar Chittipeddi
Assistant professor
of management,
University of Dayton

5

[Saying big business may be generating worker and shareholder antagonism due to generous perks given to its top executives]: Even though we define American society in egalitarian terms, when it comes to corporate management philosophy, we have tended to be more authoritarian and dictatorial. And this attitude is extended to perks.

Los Angeles Times, 11-27:(IV)2.

Robert L. Clarke
Comptroller of the Currency
of the United States

6

While poor economic conditions certainly make banking more difficult, the efforts of [bank] management have greater influence on success or failure. The capability, experience and integ-

(ROBERT L. CLARKE)

rity of [a bank's] chief executive officer is probably the most important determinant.

June 20/
The Washington Post, 6-21:(E)1.

Stephen L. Cooney
Director of international
investment and finance,
National Association of
Manufacturers

1

[On new legislation that would give the President authority to stop foreign acquisitions of U.S. companies if he believes the national security is threatened by such acquisitions]: We expect they will look only at take-overs that have been flagged by a particular [government] department. The new legislation gives them the power to go to court and stop the investment, or alter it. At the same time it gives the foreign investor some protection that he doesn't have now. The government has to make a determination within 90 days whether or not it will seek to block the merger. Before, the foreign company never knew where it stood. There were no rules. It was more like a star chamber.

Interview, Washington, March 28/
The New York Times, 3-29:30.

Robert J. Dole
United States Senator,
R-Kansas; Candidate for the
1988 Republican
Presidential nomination

2

[Criticizing those who say tougher U.S. trade protection would cause other countries to retaliate]: Every time I hear the word retaliation I am reminded that Japan and South Korea and Taiwan already block Florida oranges and Georgia peaches and Alabama melons [from being sold in their countries] . . . Let's be realistic. We're talking about American jobs, not protectionism.

Campaign debate,
Atlanta, Feb. 28/
Los Angeles Times, 2-29:(I)19.

Michael S. Dukakis
Governor of Massachusetts (D);
Candidate for the 1988 Democratic
Presidential nomination

3

The next American frontier is in the marketplace of our international competition. The next President of the United States must lead the fight for jobs and economic opportunity for all of our people. Instead of honoring corporate raiders and economic buccaneers, he should be honoring businesses that retrain workers and retool factories and rebuild their communities. He should insist on products that can compete anywhere in the world. He should demand that the international benchmark of quality be the label, "Made in the U.S.A."

Campaign speech/
The New York Times, 1-4:9.

4

I think there is enormous energy, creativity and entrepreneurship in this country. I'm not surprised by the comeback in manufacturing. I'd like to enlarge it and stimulate it . . . We've got to go to work on it, we've got to [get] a much closer relationship between government and our basic industries.

Interview, Tinton Falls, N.J./
The Washington Post, 6-1:(A)19.

5

This [Reagan] Administration has mortgaged our future to a bunch of defense contractors and merger maniacs and sharp operators on Wall Street. They've turned Main Street America into a shopping mall for foreign investors. And now they want a new four-year contract from the American people. Who do they think *they* are and how dumb do they think *we* are?

Campaign speech, Milwaukee,
March 31/Los Angeles Times,
4-1:(I)12.

6

[As President,] I'll help basic industries rebuild and retool. We ought to say to industries

(MICHAEL S. DUKAKIS)

that are in trouble: "We'll provide you with some protection [from imports] for a limited period of time, if you agree, in advance, to use that time to invest and modernize ... When I say invest, I don't just mean investments in new technology and equipment; I mean investments in your workers and in the quality of your workplace as well."

Speech/
The Washington Post, 6-18:(A)7.

Michael S. Dukakis
Governor of Massachusetts (D);
1988 Democratic
Presidential nominee

1

[On Vice President and 1988 Republican Presidential nominee George Bush]: In 1983, the Vice President was put in charge of managing our trade problems with Japan, and the trade deficit with Japan was $22-billion. After visiting Japan and meeting with Japanese government officials, he came home and declared that U.S.-Japanese trade relations were, in his words, "superb." Since then, our trade deficit with Japan has tripled.

Campaigning, Aug. 24/
The New York Times, 8-25:10.

2

Foreign investors own 10 percent of our manufacturing base, 20 percent of our banking industry and a third of the commercial real estate in our nation's capital. We have a choice. Will we keep running in place, or will we forge ahead? Will our future belong to our competitors, or to us? Will we sell off more and more of our land, our factories and our banks, or will we take charge of our future? ... I'm not against foreign ownership. I'm against the policies that make us dependent. I'm against the fire sale of America ... That's why I think we need a second Declaration of Independence in this country: independence from the budget deficit that has made us the world's greatest borrower; independence

from the trade deficit that's now making America a shopping mall for foreign investors ...

Campaign speech at
Tufts University, Oct. 11/
The New York Times, 10-12:(A)10.

Frances D. Fergusson
President, Vassar College

3

So much of economic activity today is nonproductive; there is, too often, profit without a product. The focus today is not on the welfare of the consumer but on that of the individual dealmaker. There is little sense of how a "deal" of economic interchange can, will or should work for the betterment of the company, the product or society. In short, we have often today forsaken the focus which gave America its competitive edge, namely, the emphasis on a product developed through creative thinking, innovative spirit, a global outlook, an awareness of the long-term effects on one's actions, and a developed sense of societal responsibility.

At The New York Times
Presidents Forum,
New York, Dec. 6/
The New York Times, 12-7:(B)9.

John Kenneth Galbraith
Professor emeritus of economics,
Harvard University

4

The stock market is but a mirror which ... provides an image of the underlying or *fundamental* economic situation.

USA Today, 1-4:(A)6.

Richard A. Gephardt
United States Representative,
D-Missouri; Candidate for
the 1988 Democratic
Presidential nomination

5

[Calling for U.S. trade measures to retaliate against unfair trade practices in foreign countries such as South Korea that make U.S. goods

(RICHARD A. GEPHARDT)

so costly there is almost no market for them there]: A $10,000 Chrysler K car costs $48,000 in Korea by the time they slap on nine separate taxes and tariffs. We're not selling many of our cars in a market like that, and I'm tired of hearing our workers blamed for that . . . If I am President and we have to walk away from the [trade] negotiating table, the Koreans will know two things. We'll still honor our treaties to defend them, because that's the kind of country we are. But they'll also be left asking themselves how many Americans are going to pay $48,000 for a [South Korean] Hyundai [automobile, after the U.S. adds on new taxes and tariffs].

Campaigning in Fort Dodge, Iowa/
The New York Times,
1-18:13.

George Gould
Under Secretary of the
Treasury of the United States

1

If you can give me a world without a trade deficit, without a domestic [budget] deficit, with non-inflationary growth, with low interest rates, and throw in for good measure peace in the Middle East, I would suggest to you there would be less volatility in the [financial] markets. I cannot cure all of those things for the small investor.

Before House Telecommunications
and Finance Subcommittee,
Washington, May 19/
Los Angeles Times,
5-20:(IV)2.

Alan Greenspan
Chairman,
Federal Reserve Board

2

We cannot provide an ironclad guarantee that there will not be another October 19 [1987 stock-market crash] in our future. If, however, we succeed in fully addressing the structural inadequacies of our financial markets, we can at

least reduce . . . the even now very small probability of a replay of last October.

Before House Telecommunications
and Finance Subcommittee,
Washington, May 19/
Los Angeles Times,
5-20:(IV)2.

3

[Saying the Federal government should not over-regulate the U.S. financial markets]: We must be careful not to impose undue burdens on our home markets lest investors shift their trading to other, less costly, centers [in other countries]. The advanced state of computer and telecommunications technology makes the choice of where to execute a trade little more than a phone call away. We must focus on policies that will strengthen our securities system and that concomitantly will increase, not reduce, their attractiveness to investors here and abroad.

Before Securities Industry
Association, Boca Raton, Fla.,
Nov. 30/
The New York Times,
12-1:(C)2.

William Greider
Author; Former editor,
"The Washington Post"

4

[On Paul Volcker, former Chairman of the Federal Reserve Board, about which Greider recently authored a book]: I know there will be a tendency to say I'm making Volcker the villain of the story, but that's not my intention at all. He didn't have any good choices, that's true, but what I'm saying is that there is something wrong in a system that allows the credit-expanding system to get out of control and then tends to single out the weakest, most vulnerable players— farmers, home builders, small business and manufacturers in general—for punishment to bring it back under control.

Interview/
Los Angeles Times,
1-18:(V)3.

WHAT THEY SAID IN 1988

James M. Guinan
Vice chairman,
Consolidated Stores
Corporation

1

Retailing is knowing your customer, finding a market niche, pricing appropriately and making money.

The New York Times, 8-24:29.

Richard J. Haayen
Chairman, Allstate
Insurance Company

2

There is something sick about a person whose only interest is money. And the same can be said, I think, for the company whose sole goal is profit. That kind of mentality shrinks a corporation's spirit and narrows its vision.

At Allstate Forum
on Public Issues/
Nation's Business, March:16.

Lord Hanson
Chairman,
Hanson PLC (Britain)

3

The best thing that government can do is get out of business. When governments interfere less, managers can do their job better.

Interview/
U.S. News & World Report,
6-20:46.

Robert Hawke
Prime Minister of Australia

4

... we live in a world where the principle of free trade between nations is at risk because of the increasingly complex economic environment. There are pressures, particularly where massive trade imbalances have built up between nations, to take the easy road of protectionism—which is a recipe for disaster.

Interview, Canberra/
USA Today, 5-6:(A)13.

James Hohorst
Head of foreign-exchange
trading in North America,
Manufacturers Hanover
Trust Company, New York

5

[On foreign-exchange trading]: Ninety per cent of what we do is based on perception. It doesn't matter if that perception is right or wrong or real. It only matters that other people in the market believe it. I may know it's crazy, I may think it's wrong. But I lose my shirt by ignoring it. This business turns on decisions made in seconds. If you wait a minute to reflect on things, you're lost. I can't afford to be five steps ahead of everybody else in the market. That's suicide.

Interview/
The Wall Street Journal,
9-23:(R)27.

Robert Hormats
Vice chairman, Goldman,
Sachs International

6

On the economic front, [President] Reagan did restore faith in the importance of the market and market forces. But in so doing, he led people to believe that the market could cure all our ills. We know it can help produce growth, but it has not been able to deal with the social infrastructure.

The Christian Science Monitor,
11-15:16.

Lee A. Iacocca
Chairman,
Chrysler Corporation

7

Japanese kids figure that being on the factory floor is like being a hero at the front during a war. They're educated to know there is nothing wrong with getting their hands dirty and building something. I wonder if everyone on Wall Street making millions is as happy. They may be richer, but they don't produce much of anything.

Interview/
Fortune, 8-29:40.

WHAT THEY SAID IN 1988

(LEE A. IACOCCA)

1

I often think if there were a [government] job that would be of some interest to me and [for which] the world may need a tough-nosed business attitude, it would be the [President's] trade negotiator's job. I don't think [other] countries would like me in that position, because I am an unabashed patriot. I would come home with the bacon for the U.S. more often than not.

At Foreign Correspondents Club,
Tokyo, Oct. 19/
Los Angeles Times, 10-20:(IV)3.

Jesse L. Jackson
Civil-rights leader;
Candidate for the 1988
Democratic Presidential
nomination

2

The Number 1 exporter from Taiwan is not Taiwan. It's General Electric. Which owns RCA. Which owns NBC. Which says, "Buy American," while NBC workers are forced to strike and make concessions. The first four years of the Reagan Administration, GE made $10-billion. That's all right. But as profits went up, wages and jobs went down. They paid zero taxes. That's not all. They got a $100-million tax rebate, while workers on unemployment compensation had to pay taxes. That is economic violence.

Campaign speech/
Los Angeles Times, 4-2:(I)19.

William S. Kanaga
Chairman, United States
Chamber of Commerce

3

The vast majority of business people are honest. The few who are not create problems for all of business. It is up to each business leader to set a conspicuous example of integrity and to make certain that their subordinates know that exemplary behavior will be demanded and required at every level of the enterprise . . . The key

is the CEO, with strong backing from the board of directors, determined to establish and enforce strict ethical behavior throughout the organization. I have a deep concern with the lack of impact in our daily business life of the deep roots our country has inherited from its Judeo-Christian beginnings. What I see is a breakdown in the home and in family training—in community life and in many of the positive aspects of peer pressure. Our young men and women entering the business world are fed with a large dosage of cynicism about how to succeed. That cynicism comes not alone from disclosures in the media and from some blase peers ahead of them, but also from the teachings they receive on, and the influence of, the university campus.

Nation's Business, June:65.

Jack Kemp
United States Representative,
R-New York;
Candidate for the 1988
Republican Presidential nomination

4

[Holding up a U.S. currency note]: See this little piece of paper? This is an IOU. It says Federal Reserve on here, but there is absolutely nothing guaranteeing that the purchasing power of this piece of paper will not collapse tomorrow other than our faith, and our hard work, and our muscle, and our might, and our capital and labor. I am a radical believer in the idea that the dollar should be so honest, so sound, so trustworthy, so good, so predictable, so lasting in value, that it's as good as gold.

Campaign speech/
The New York Times, 1-12:11.

Arthur Levitt, Jr.
Chairman,
American Stock Exchange

5

I'm into sounds. I love the sound of a crowd right before the opening bell at a heavyweight championship fight, or right before the first pitch of the baseball season or the kickoff at the Super Bowl. But of all the sounds anywhere, nothing

(ARTHUR LEVITT, JR)

compares to the sounds on the floor of the stock exchange every day. There's no sound like it; I never get tired of it and it always chills me. I mean, always.

USA Today, 2-29:(D)2.

Martin Lipton
Take-over lawyer, Wachtell,
Lipton, Rosen & Katz

1

[Saying leveraged buyouts of companies have gone too far]: You can't ignore history. The junk-bond financing in vogue today is going to create a bust comparable to the Florida land bust of the 1920s or the real-estate investment-trust bust of the 1970s—not necessarily a world-wide depression or a market crash, but a bust. Sure, there are some very successful LBOs, but now we have hundreds of them. I just don't believe there's that much talent for the activity; it has become another fad. You get $25-billion invested in these partnerships that chase deals, and you can be sure a lot of bad deals are going to be done.

Interview/
U.S. News & World Report,
12-12:73.

Richard E. Lyng
Secretary of Agriculture of the
United States

2

We now have an aggressive trade policy—don't call it "predatory," I allow our competitors to call it predatory . . . [But] I've been saying over and over, if we have a world in which there are no subsidies that affect trade and if we don't have these barriers to trade, and non-tariff barriers, . . . if we can get rid of those and if farmers can compete with one another on the basis of comparative advantage, the world would be a vastly better place for consumers and farmers as well.

Interview/
The Washington Post,
2-12:(A)1,14.

Akio Morita
Chairman,
Sony Corporation (Japan)

3

Americans and Europeans do import more Japanese goods than they export to Japan. But that has nothing to do with unfairness [by the Japanese]; it is simply the result of the free play of the market. To treat us like a closed country is scandalous. Consider the automobile industry: American companies manufactured 250,000 cars in Japan last year, only to sell them to customers in the U.S. They have never really tried to sell us their cars. And the recent agreement to increase Japanese imports of American agricultural goods is not going to bridge the gap. To do that, every Japanese would have to eat several tons of beef and oranges a year. No; the Americans are responsible for the imbalance.

Interview/
World Press Review, October:31.

E. James Morton
Chairman, John Hancock
Mutual Life Insurance
Company

4

[On whether deregulation of banking would result in an increase in bank failures]: Something like that would happen. There would be some decrease in the number of banks. But I am not sure how much. What I don't worry about is an over-concentration of economic power. The same kind of shakeout happened in the securities industry, and there are still an awful lot of securities firms. To survive today you just have to be much smarter than before. I think the same thing will happen in banking. Personally, I think it would be a good thing. There would be fewer banks, but in the long run they would be stronger.

Interview, Washington/
The New York Times, 8-2:30.

Rupert Murdoch
Media entrepreneur

5

I'm no believer in the theory that a manager is a manager is a manager—that someone who can

43

(RUPERT MURDOCH)

run a department store can run a newspaper. In corporate America, people move around, often with disastrous results.

Interview/
U.S. News & World Report, 3-7:56.

James J. Needham
Former chairman,
New York Stock Exchange

1

Computer-directed [stock] trading has been characterized as a demon and as a saint. It is neither. It is neutral. It is the product of the accumulated knowledge of various sciences made useful by creative people. The proposals to ban this method of modern-day arbitrage is nonsensical. What must be done is to adapt the trading mechanisms to this new practice. Apparently, this will require time. So, for the short run, I reluctantly concede it is in everyone's interest to institute temporary fail-safe procedures, provided that the "circuit-breaker" concept is not in reality a renaming of a dangerous expedient practice of the pre-high-tech era of inserting a penny in the fuse box, which I believe it will be proven to be.

Congressional testimony,
Washington, May 11/
The Wall Street Journal, 6-22:22.

H. Ross Perot
Industrialist

2

[On what he looks for when he hires people]: We don't care who you are. We don't care where you come from. We don't care where you went to school. We don't care what color you are, what race, what sex, what religion. Young people will say, "Do you care about anything?" And I'll say, "You bet. I care about what you can do. I care about what you've done lately. Because this is a cross-country run, it's not a 100-yard dash; one quick race is not a business career. So I'm interested in what you can do and what you've done."

Interview/USA Today, 6-29:(A)9.

3

There are only two places a 28-year-old can make a half million dollars—Wall Street and dealing dope.

Newsweek, 7-11:13.

Peter Peterson
Investment banker

4

The hardest subject today, I guess, is the foreign buying up of America. I'd like to turn that question around. What I am for is reducing our deficits and increasing our net national savings so we don't have to rely on foreign capital. I think that relying on this much foreign capital is very dangerous to our economic and our political health.

Interview, New York/
Time, 10-31:68.

Theo H. Pitt, Jr.
Chairman,
United States League
of Savings Institutions

5

The savings-and-loan business is not in crisis . . . The business is comprised of nearly 3,200 institutions, the overwhelming majority of which are earning profits. But you don't read or hear about those institutions. What you read and hear about is aggregate first-quarter losses for our business amounted to $3.8-billion. What you don't read about is that $3.7-billion of the $3.8-billion in net losses is attributable to a mere 50 institutions . . . The self-appointed experts on our business conveniently ignore the positives, preferring instead to use the negative numbers to smear us all.

Nation's Business, September:16.

Karl Otto Poehl
President, Central Bank
of West Germany

6

The [U.S.] dollar is still the world's most important currency. About 80 per cent of all

(KARL OTTO POEHL)

international assets are denominated in dollars. What is necessary is to create enough confidence in financial markets to convince dollar holders and potential dollar holders to remain invested in dollars.

Interview, Frankfurt, Feb. 5/
The Washington Post, 2-6:(A)17.

Clyde Prestowitz
Former Japan specialist,
Department of Commerce
of the United States

1

[On the concern in the U.S. about increasing foreign investment in, and ownership of, American property and business]: The Japanese long have had a very sophisticated system for encouraging [foreign] investment which they thought would encourage a flow of technology into their economy, and screening out investment they thought would do nothing but raise domestic real-estate prices. I think we should have a similar system.

The Christian Science Monitor,
11-22:3.

William Proxmire
United States Senator,
D-Wisconsin

2

[Addressing Federal Reserve Board Chairman Alan Greenspan]: [I am] troubled by the extent of the political pressure being put on the Fed [-eral Reserve] by the Reagan Administration in this Presidential-election year. I think it is both deplorable and counter-productive for the Reagan Administration to pressure you as much as they have in recent months. Ironically, when the Administration badgers the Federal Reserve they may make it harder for you to ease monetary policy than would be the case if they were silent. Even if you have eased money for sound technical reasons, you will certainly be accused of bending to political pressure. Insinuations of political manipulation harm both your reputa-

tion as Chairman and the reputation of the Federal Reserve.

At Senate Banking Committee
hearing, Washington, Feb. 24/
The Washington Post, 2-25:(B)1.

Dan Quayle
United States Senator,
R-Indiana;
1988 Republican
Vice-Presidential nominee

3

A lot of younger Republicans like me are not terribly comfortable with Big Business. I'm talking about Big Business that doesn't want competition. Big Business did not care about the plant-closing bill; it already gives 60 days' notice [to employees]. The ones who are going to be hit by that legislation are the smaller firms. Big Business would love government-mandated benefits because they don't want some guy to come in there and compete with them and not give as much health care or pensions to employees as the big firms do.

Interview/Time, 8-29:25.

4

[On Democratic Presidential nominee Michael Dukakis]: The Governor of Massachusetts, he has a farm program. He went to the farmers in the Midwest and told them not to grow corn, not to grow soybeans, but to grow Belgium endive. That's what he and his Harvard buddies think of the American farmer: grow Belgium endive; to come in and to tell our farmers not to grow corn, not to grow soybeans. That's the kind of farm policy you'll get under a Dukakis Administration, and one I think the American farmer rightfully will reject.

At Vice-Presidential debate,
Omaha, Neb., Oct. 5/
The New York Times, 10-7:(A)13.

Ronald Reagan
President of the United States

5

[On last year's stock-market crash]: First of all, I don't believe that the dollar or anything

(RONALD REAGAN)

outside Wall Street had anything to do with the great debacle in October . . . So I don't anticipate a recession unless some of the doom-criers scare the people into one . . . what took place was a panic as a result of, well, there were no more than . . . about 15 firms that were involved in the great change that was taking place in the marketplace, but that it was induced within the marketplace, and not from something, some factor, outside.

Before City Club,
Cleveland, Jan. 11/
The Washington Post, 1-12:(A)3.

1

The United States, which has been the engine keeping the world economy moving forward, has a trade deficit because our growing economy enables us to buy their goods. Over time, however, these imbalances should be reduced, and there are two ways to do it. We can become more like them, or they can become more like us. We can raise taxes, re-regulate our economy, and adopt protectionist legislation of the kind now being considered in Congress, that will effectively slow growth in this nation and stifle international trade. We won't be able to buy their goods, and certainly no one will want to invest in the United States. The world can all shrink together, and we can all look forward to hearing the experts once again pontificate about convergence and the limits to growth. The other solution is for them to become more like us, to adopt low-tax, pro-growth policies; to encourage trade, not discourage it; to make it freer, fairer and more plentiful; to join with other nations in a cooperative upward growth cycle in which all participate; to embrace possibilities of the new world economy.

Before City Club, Cleveland,
Jan. 11/USA Today, 1-12:(A)11.

2

[Arguing against protectionist trade legislation in the U.S.]: If enacted, [it] could weaken the international trading system and could require the President to start trade wars. It's a bad proposal under any circumstances. But it's particularly bad now that American exports are soaring and American manufacturers are exporting as never before, so are vulnerable to retaliation as never before . . . Protectionism isn't just bad economics—it's bad politics. I think the American people have decided that one Great Depression is enough and they aren't going to give the trade demagogues a second chance.

To employees of
Reynolds Metals Co.,
Richmond, Va., March 28/
Los Angeles Times,
3-29:(I)18.

Donald T. Regan
Former Secretary of the
Treasury of the
United States

3

[On program-trading and other questionable stock-market practices]: The public has every reason to believe the present [stock-market] game is rigged. It is. Many would be better off in the casinos . . . I don't think it's too extreme to say that over-all confidence in our free-market system is threatened by this sort of scandal.

Before Senate
Banking Committee,
Washington, May 11/
Los Angeles Times, 5-12:(IV)2.

Robert B. Reich
Lecturer in public policy,
John F. Kennedy School
of Government,
Harvard University

4

[On the multi-billion-dollar take-over effort for RJR Nabisco]: This is the sort of excess that investment bankers have worried about for years, because it so clearly exposes the greed and rapaciousness of so many of the take-overs.

Time, 12-5:67.

David S. Ruder
Chairman, Securities
and Exchange Commission
of the United States

1

[On the October, 1987, stock crash]: I think if you follow the last 50 years, you will find that the stock market has moved up and down, in some cases dramatically. Anybody who's an average investor who reads the stories ought to recognize that between August of 1982 and August, 1987, the market increased from 750 points on the Dow Jones industrial average to 2,700 points on the Dow. And that even at the [October, 1987] low, which was about 1,750, the market was still up 1,000 points over its August, 1982, level. Let's assume you went to Africa or some remote place on the first of January, 1987, and came back on the first of January, 1988. You would say, "Well, it wasn't a very good year—stocks only went up 5 per cent." And that's what happened. I think a small investor needs to take a longer-term view of the market.

Interview/
Los Angeles Times, 10-11:(IV)21.

2

I do not believe that it is easy to determine the economic consequences of [corporate] take-overs and LBOs and various restructuring activities. Since I think it is so difficult to determine those economic consequences, I believe that they should be allowed to go forward, based upon the market evaluation of the environment.

At Congressional hearing,
Washington, Dec. 22/
The New York Times, 12-23(C)1.

Charles F. Rule
Assistant Attorney General,
Antitrust Division,
Department of Justice of
the United States

3

[Calling for wider authority for the government to use wiretapping in antitrust investigations]: The next Administration should seek legislation enabling courts to authorize wiretaps to assist in antitrust investigations . . . Changing the law would eliminate any uncertainty. Antitrust investigations would, as a result, be more effective. In addition, I think every price-fixer and bid-rigger ought to have some question when they are planning their crime that maybe the FBI is listening in.

At New England Antitrust Conference,
Harvard Law School, Oct. 28/
Los Angeles Times, 10-28:(I)25.

Helmut Schmidt
Publisher, "Die Zeit"
(West Germany);
Former Chancellor
of West Germany

4

By 1989, the foreign debt of the U.S. will exceed half a trillion dollars. At an interest rate of 8 per cent, you would need to transfer $40-billion to the rest of the world on top of your trade deficit. There are two dangers here: First, those who hold American IOUs will try to swap them by buying up American factories, real estate and shares. Americans will resent this, with political repercussions—more regarding the Japanese than the Germans. However, if the swap does not occur and you have to pay the interest, there is no other way than to broaden the money supply—that is, print the interest. Therefore, I expect new dollar inflation as well as a world recession. So 1989 will be a dramatic year for the new [U.S.] President. Whether he's a Republican or a Democrat makes no great difference.

Interview, Bonn/
U.S. News & World Report,
1-11:39.

Jeffrey L. Schott
Research analyst, Institute
for International Economics,
Washington

5

[On why the monthly trade-deficit reports affect the securities markets]: The reason the markets react to it is that, despite its relative

(JEFFREY L. SCHOTT)

inaccuracy, it's a constant monthly reminder that we don't have our house in order.

Los Angeles Times, 1-13:(I)16.

George P. Shultz
Secretary of State
of the United States

1

[Arguing against further U.S. protectionist legislation]: We have seen over the past, say, 10 years, a gradual increase in protection of our markets . . . We are the biggest exporter in the world. Our exports, right now, are in a very strong upward thrust. All of the moonshine about how we're flat on our backs, and not able to do anything, is shown to be just that.

At luncheon honoring
U.S. career diplomats,
Washington, May 6/
Los Angeles Times, 5-7:(I)2.

2

When the economic history of the 1980s is written, it will be recognized that the growth of the U.S. trade deficit, with all of its potentially troubling implications, was a mutually beneficial development—enabling world trade to expand, while helping our own economic growth to proceed without inflation.

Before Indonesian Economists
Association, Jakarta, July 11/
Los Angeles Times,
7-12:(I)5.

3

Sometimes it seems to us that everyone [in the world] wants the U.S. market to be open, and that's as far as it goes . . . You think we don't have farmers that notice when they can't penetrate other people's markets, and that they don't raise Cain? . . . So it's got to be both ways.

Before Korean Newspaper Editors
Association, Seoul, July 18/
Los Angeles Times, 7-18:(I)1.

Adam Smith
Author, Economist

4

If I could make up an axiom, it's that in the '80s the markets are bigger than the governments . . . The head of the Japanese Life Insurance Association—and it's the Japanese life companies that lend us [the U.S.] the money to run the Post Office and pay the nation—said that [U.S.] interest rates are going to be dictated in Tokyo, and so will American stock prices.

Interview/
Los Angeles Times, 11-27:(IV)3.

Jeffrey Sonnenfeld
Associate professor,
Harvard Business School

5

The chief executive's departure is a significant event, not only in human terms but because of the impact it leaves on a company. There's a good deal of focus on the grooming process and succession plans for future leaders. Yet the other half of the equation—how the incumbent departs—has an enormous influence both on the integrity of that succession process and on the strategic direction of the firm. In interviews I did with 50 corporate leaders and in a survey of another 300, not a single one ever accepted the word "retirement." They had signed on to the companies' pension plans and announced to shareholders in their annual reports that they were leaving. Yet almost all wrote on their survey form, "Well, I'm not really retired." For many CEOs, retirement is closely linked with death. In his suicide note, George Eastman, the founder and head of Eastman Kodak for 52 years, wrote: "My work is done. What else is there to do?"

Interview/
U.S. News & World Report, 11-14:54.

Thomas Sweitzer
Media adviser to
Senator Albert Gore,
candidate for the 1988
Democratic Presidential nomination

6

[On a TV campaign ad he produced attacking Chrysler Corporation chairman Lee Iacocca]:

(THOMAS SWEITZER)

There is a real sense that corporations just don't have any loyalty to America anymore, and corporate greed is becoming a potent issue—that's what that spot was about.

Los Angeles Times, 5-3:(I)15.

Steven D. Symms
United States Senator,
R-Idaho

1

There is an amendment in the House version of the trade bill . . . to require all sorts of disclosure of information by anyone who wants to bring capital investments into the United States. The supporters of this provision will tell you it is harmless, because it only requires disclosure. But . . . it has a much more far-reaching and possible sinister effect that could be very negative to markets in the United States . . . It is not merely a disclosure of information. It does not look harmless to people around the world. It looks dangerous to them—and appearances are all that count in the world of investment . . . We think we have a big budget deficit now. If you create a situation where we have an enormous flight of capital from the United States, the deficit problem will grow much worse. That is what happens in banana republics—the flight of capital from those kinds of unstable countries. We are, after all, the bastion of stability in the world-wide economy, and we are the best place to invest money.

Before the Senate, March 28/
The Washington Post, 3-30:(A)16.

Meir Tamari
Chief economist,
Governor's Office,
Bank of Israel

2

The free-market economy is the most effective means of providing goods and services. But at the same time, the economy may have to be distorted or regulated in order to protect the weak, in order to prevent immoral abuse . . .

Market efficiency is very important, but I don't think we want it to be more important than morality . . . The whole concept of "let the buyer beware," for example—putting the onus on the buyer . . . The onus is on the seller. The seller is always obligated to point out any defects in a product he's selling.

Los Angeles Times, 11-15:(IV)11.

Alvin Toffler
Futurist

3

Unfortunately, in corporate America, sometimes there is conflict between "strategic *planning*" and "strategic *thinking*." Too often strategic planning consists of simple linear extrapolation or mechanical models. I believe that most managers were trained to be the thing they most despise—bureaucrats. They were taught that they should fit into and help operate an organizational machine. The problem is, machines don't do well in crisis; people do better. So managers should stop thinking like machines. A machine can do linear extrapolation, but people have the creative power to think the "unthinkable." And they should use it.

Interview/Newsweek, 4-4:14.

Susan Tolchin
Professor of public
administration, George
Washington University

4

Foreign investors [in the U.S.] have brought 3 million jobs to America. They've revitalized certain sections of the economy and buoyed the stock market, certainly propped up the deficit. They've revitalized regions where American investors have not wanted to invest. But it's not a totally free lunch . . . We're so anxious for foreign investment that we offer hundreds of millions of dollars in incentives for foreign investors to come and invest in this country. Kentucky gave Toyota $125-million in tax incentives, low-cost bonds, new roads, sewers, etc., in order to lure Toyota. And this is true of Governors and Mayors all over the country who want to bring foreign investment into their states.

Interview/USA Today, 3-24:(A)11.

Alexander Trowbridge
President, National
Association of Manufacturers

1

[On the benefits of foreign investment in the U.S.]: One, it brings new jobs and new manufacturing and service capacity to our economy. Secondly, it helps us pay our trade and Federal budget deficits. And thirdly, if we restrict unduly the foreign-investment flow, we invite retaliation against American investment overseas, which is a very important asset that earns funds that come back to not only buy American exports but to help us in our balance of payments.

Interview/
USA Today, 3-24:(A)11.

C. William Verity, Jr.
Secretary of Commerce
of the United States

2

I think that in order to do well in the future, we're going to have to change our educational system, teach geography and language at an earlier age, so that Americans realize that it's the world market that's important, not just the American market. We have had such a big market that American manufacturers have never had to worry about anything other than this one. Now they do. Now it's a different ballgame. Americans are going to have to talk a foreign language, learn one.

Interview/USA Today, 4-11:(A)11.

3

I think the long-term measure of success for America is that "Made in the U.S.A." is going to have to once again mean highest quality. I think that's what many companies are striving for. In fact, I *know* many companies are striving for it . . . And now I think most manufacturers, most industries, are striving for world-class quality.

Interview/
USA Today, 4-11:(A)11.

William V. Weithas
Chairman, Lintas:
Worldwide

4

It is the goal of good advertising to add the aura of a diamond to whatever it is you wish to market . . . In the 1950s, the Volkswagen was just a $900 ugly German car when [advertising man] Bill Bernbach decided to call it the "Beetle" and endear it to the American public. Rice Krispies was just another cereal from Battle Creek until "Snap, Crackle and Pop" made it part of America's breakfast. And diet colas remained marginal until my agency told people that they could drink Diet Coke "just for the taste of it."

Nation's Business, August:12.

Jim Wright
United States Representative,
D-Texas

5

In spite of what the President [Reagan] says, the trade gap has risen sharply every year for the past seven years, and was higher last year than ever in our history. This has made America the Number 1 debtor country in the world. That isn't a sign of strength.

Broadcast address to the nation,
Washington, Jan. 25/
Los Angeles Times, 1-26:(I)16.

Jim Wright
United States Representative,
D-Texas

6

Antitrust laws have been blithely and dangerously ignored [during the Reagan Administration] . . . [Reagan's policies have] made the rich richer and the poor poorer. There has been a tidal shift to fewer and larger farms and ranches, fewer and larger banks, fewer and larger airlines, fewer and larger corporations. I view that with great misgivings.

To reporters,
Washington, Nov. 23/
The New York Times, 11-24:(C)1.

Crime • Law Enforcement

James Austin
Director of research,
National Council on
Crime and Delinquency

1

[On over-crowding in the U.S. prison system]: The problem has a tremendous impact on state services. California has a prison budget of $1.6-billion a year. When the prison population reaches 100,000, as it figures to do in the next five or six years, the cost will be $3-billion. That will take its toll on other state services, including education and medical care, both of which might have a greater impact on the crime problem. In addition, the bulk of the growth will be among blacks and Hispanics, both disproportionately involved in street drug activity, and that will create additional problems. And finally, as the prison population gets older—an inevitable result of longer sentences—we will find not only that prisons will need to provide special geriatric services but also that imprisonment will become much less effective in dealing with crime. Crime is a young man's game. But when older offenders, who are not that big a threat any more, take up more and more prison space, you run out of space for the younger men who are feeding the crime statistics, particularly members of the under-class . . . Trying to solve the crime problem by building more prison cells is like trying to solve the problem of AIDS by building more hospitals.

Interview/
The Washington Post, 4-14:(A)23.

Georgette Bennett
Criminologist

2

There is no question we have a very big drug problem in this country. The question is, is our current policy the best way to deal with it? My answer is no: By making drugs a criminal matter, we have in fact made the problem worse. If we decriminalize, at least we would only have a massive public-health problem on our hands, instead

of a massive crime problem, a massive corruption problem and a massive foreign-policy problem.

Newsweek, 5-30:37

Joseph R. Biden, Jr.
United States Senator,
D-Delaware

3

[Supporting the creation of a government drug czar to oversee the fight against illegal drugs]: Just as we would never send an army into battle to fight the enemy without a good plan and a good general, we cannot begin the war on drugs without a national strategy and a single Cabinet officer with the authority to implement the strategy.

Los Angeles Times, 10-21:(I)4.

Otis R. Bowen
Secretary of Health and Human
Services of the United States

4

One of the two remaining Democratic candidates [for the 1988 nomination for President, Jesse Jackson,] is getting some of his highest marks for his passionate and creative oratory on the drug epidemic and is poised to steal from our [Republican] Party what has been a traditional Republican issue—law enforcement. I believe as we approach the end of this second term [of President Reagan], we need to take a fresh look at what we're doing to secure a lasting end to the demand for illicit drugs. On the topic of treatment, we also need to talk turkey with big-city Mayors, councils and suburban jurisdictions as well, who often knuckle under to pressure from those who are, quote-unquote, "all for treatment, as long as it's not in my backyard."

At meeting of
National Drug Policy Board,
Washington, April 28/
The New York Times, 4-30:7.

51

WHAT THEY SAID IN 1988

Allen F. Breed
*Criminologist, National
Council on
Crime and Delinquency*

1

[On prison over-crowding]: There's beginning to be a recognition that we can't build our way out of this. Nation-wide, we're still putting about 750 more inmates in prison each week than we're releasing. Fifty per cent of the people in prison are there for property crimes. How many of these people do we want to lock up and for what periods of time? There's a kind of hate that comes forth from inmates that you didn't see before. All they talk about is getting even. If all you do is lock them up for long periods of time with terrible idleness, over-crowding, tension gang activity, they truly become hateful animals. We breed them, and we develop them, and society is some day going to have to learn to deal with them.

The New York Times, 4-25:11.

George Bush
*Vice President of the United
States; Candidate for
the 1988 Republican
Presidential nomination*

2

The flow of [illegal] drugs continues and the reason is obvious—the problem is demand, not just supply-side. As long as Americans are willing to pay billions of dollars for illegal narcotics, somebody somewhere in the world is going to provide it, and it's just as simple as that.

*At Marquette High School,
Milwaukee, March/
The New York Times, 3-19:7.*

3

Drug dealers are domestic terrorists, killing kids and cops, and they should be treated as such. I won't bargain with terrorists, and I won't bargain with drug dealers either, whether they're on U.S. or foreign soil.

*At Los Angeles Policy Academy,
May 18/The Washington Post,
5-19:(A)16.*

4

[On the war against illegal drugs]: If we're going to move from holding our own in this war to winning it, we must turn our attention from the middle of the drug flow—the dealers—to the beginning and the end—the producers and users, because this is not a pipeline we're talking about, controlled by a single shutoff valve. It is a flood, cascading through our thousands of miles of open border, by land, sea and air, sucked in by the prospect of enormous financial reward. Some propose that we seal off our borders. We can do better there. But do you know the biggest single problem at New York's Attica state prison, heavily fortified Attica prison? Illegal drugs. If we can't keep drugs out of Attica, that shows you . . . the severity of the problem. The logic is simple. The cheapest and safest way to eradicate narcotics is to destroy them at their source.

*Before Chamber of Commerce,
Hackensack, N.J., May 26/
The Washington Post,
5-27:(A)16.*

5

There are those who say that drug testing is an invasion of individual rights. But the use of drugs is not just a personal matter, like buying a dress or a car; it's a matter that you see affects the health and safety of others. We've run out of patience; the country's run out of pity. And it's time to say, "We've had enough."

*Before Meadowlands Chamber of
Commerce, Newark, N.J., May 26/
The New York Times,
5-27:10.*

6

For too many years we've been held hostage by well-meaning and misguided politicians and judges who get their legal views from the ACLU. The rights accorded criminals must never overshadow the wrongs done to the victims.

*Before National Sheriffs' Association,
Louisville, Ky., June 22/
The New York Times, 6-23:10.*

(GEORGE BUSH)

1

[Criticizing Democratic Presidential nominee Governor Michael Dukakis of Massachusetts]: Let's get the facts straight. Until March of this year, Massachusetts had the most liberal weekend [prison] release program in the nation, the only state program permitting inmates sentenced to life without parole to take unsupervised leave from prison grounds. A weekend pass for first-degree murderers.

Campaigning, Cincinnati/
The Christian Science Monitor,
8-8:6.

2

There are those, like the ACLU, whose first concerns are the protection of criminals' rights and the potential abuse of power by police. My first concerns are the protection of law-abiding citizens and the abuse of our systems of Constitutional protections by thugs who can hire smart lawyers and find rights judges to set them free.

Before Fraternal Order of Police,
Erie, Pa., Aug. 9/
The New York Times,
8-10:9.

George Bush
Vice President of the United
States; 1988 Republican
Presidential nominee

3

[Criticizing Democratic Presidential nominee Michael Dukakis for saying the Reagan Administration's anti-drug policies are "criminal" and "absurd"]: He should not use the words "criminal" and "absurd" when it comes to that kind of action, for he is the Governor who vetoed mandatory sentencing for drug dealers. He opposed capital punishment for drug kingpins and he fought, tooth and nail, to keep that outrageous furlough program [in Massachusetts] that let murderers, rapists and drug dealers out of jail.

Campaigning in Texas, Aug. 26/
The New York Times,
8-27:6.

4

[On the drug problem in the U.S.]: I think we've seen a deterioration of values. I think for a while as a nation we condoned those things we should have condemned. For a while, as I recall, it even seems to me that there was talk of legalizing, or decriminalizing, marijuana and other drugs. And I think that's all wrong. So we've seen a deterioration in values. And one of the things that I think we should do about it in terms of cause is to instill values into the young people in our schools. We got away, we got into this feeling that a value-free education was the thing. And I don't believe that at all. I do believe there are fundamental rights and wrongs as far as [drug] use.

At Presidential debate,
Winston-Salem, N.C., Sept. 25/
The New York Times, 9-26:10.

5

I favor the death penalty [for drug-related murders]. I know it's tough, and honest people can disagree, but when a narcotics wrapped-up guy goes in and murders a police officer, I think they ought to pay with their life. And I do believe it would be inhibiting [a deterrent].

At Presidential debate,
Winston-Salem, N.C., Sept. 25/
The New York Times,
9-26:11.

6

For many years, liberal thinkers—and I use the term loosely—thought it was compassionate to lighten up on sentencing [of criminals], to allow early releases and furloughs ... there is something very wrong when there is so much sympathy for criminals and very little left over for victims. We still have too many liberal, permissive judges in this country. I will appoint judges that apply the law rather than make the law, and who will mete out tough sentences our laws call for.

Campaign speech,
Trenton, N.J., Oct. 10/
The Washington Post, 10-11:(A)6.

(GEORGE BUSH)

1

I see violent crime as a great civil-rights question of our time, that the victims of crime are not the rich and the well-connected, but the working poor and the young and the old—and that an old woman who is afraid to go out for bread after dark is every bit as oppressed as a political prisoner in some totalitarian country.

At University of Notre Dame,
Nov. 1/
The Washington Post, 11-2:(A)25.

2

I respect the tradition of Harry Truman for a liberalism that is committed abroad and concerned at home. But some of today's liberals do not see as clearly as their forefathers. A civil-rights infraction is still a crime to them, but street crime is somehow beneath their notice; it doesn't register. And if you bring it up, they'll call you insensitive or backward.

At University of Notre Dame,
Nov. 1/
The Washington Post,
11-2:(A)25.

3

I have always opposed Federal gun registration or licensing of gun owners, [but] we must balance the legitimate interests of gun owners with the rights of society . . . We must do all we can to keep guns out of the hands of convicted criminals.

The New York Times,
11-4:(A)11.

George Bush
Vice President, and
President-elect, of the
United States

4

We must, as many of you have done at the state level, increase the number of prison cells if we are to prevent the unacceptable spectacle of hardened criminals being turned loose for lack of space . . .

More prison cells is the backbone of a tough anti-crime program.

Before Republican Governors Association,
Point Clear, Alabama, Nov. 22/
The Washington Post, 11-23:(A)4.

John Climaco
General counsel, International
Brotherhood of Teamsters

5

[Criticizing the U.S. Justice Department's decision to have the government oversee the Teamsters Union because of alleged criminal activities of its leadership]: I think it's completely contrary to the established principles of labor relations and trade unions in our country. Because, unlike Communist countries, there has been a basic principle in this country of limited government interference in any private organization . . . I do not believe that organized crime holds the Teamsters captive. I do not believe that there is even the influence that the government likes to indicate exists . . . There is no valid law-enforcement justification for intricate and contrived stratagems whose purpose is to make it easy for the government to take control of unions composed of thousands of honest, hard-working trade unionists. And there can be no doubt that government supervision is synonymous with the destruction of free trade unions, not with their salvation.

Interview/
USA Today, 7-5:(A)9.

William S. Cohen
United States Senator,
R-Maine

6

[Questioning recent legislation calling for increased involvement of the military in anti-drug operations]: I'm beginning to believe that in its attempt to pass legislation about the drug problem, Congress rushed off and came up with a purely emotional response to a deep-seated social problem. It seems we reached a political solution to a social problem. Political solutions are bound to fail.

The Washington Post, 6-15:(A)21.

David Conover
Federal liaison, National
Rifle Association

1

[Criticizing a proposed national seven-day waiting period on sales of handguns to individuals]: The idea of having to ask permission from the police to purchase a pistol for self-defense is repugnant. Waiting periods [while the backgrounds of prospective purchasers are checked] don't work: Criminals don't fill out forms and certainly don't give their correct names and addresses and wait for the police to find out their criminal activity. This is the only issue before Congress that affects every gun owner, and we'll make this our top priority.

Interview, June 30/
Los Angeles Times, 7-1:(I)1.

Alan Cranston
United States Senator,
D-California

2

[Arguing against giving the military power to make arrests for drug trafficking]: When we give the military the authority to arrest civilians, we are using a tool of the police state. Too many nations that have taken that first step . . . have eventually found themselves subject to military domination of their politics.

Los Angeles Times,
5-14:(I)18.

Alfonse M. D'Amato
United States Senator,
R-New York

3

[Supporting a Federal death penalty for drug-related killings]: The death-dealing drug lords fear no one . . . The only thing they fear is death itself . . . Let them be on the end of that fear for a change.

Before the Senate, Washington/
The Washington Post,
5-17:(A)6.

Butler Derrick
United States Representative,
D-South Carolina

4

[Criticizing proposed Federal legislation that would require a seven-day waiting period for purchasing handguns]: It's the nose of the [Federal] camel under the tent. The next time it will be a year [waiting period]; the next time it will be three years; the next time it will be no ownership of guns at all in this country.

Before the House,
Washington, Sept. 15/
The Washington Post, 9-16:(A)12.

Alan Dershowitz
Professor of law,
Harvard University

5

We've already decriminalized two drugs, alcohol and tobacco. Now it's time to decriminalize a third, heroin.

Time, 5-30:15.

Michael S. Dukakis
Governor of Massachusetts (D);
1988 Democratic Presidential
nominee

6

Today, there are 11 Cabinet departments and almost three dozen Federal agencies involved in the drug war. No one person is responsible; no one is accountable; no one is in charge. Now, the Vice President [George Bush] says that, if elected [President], he's going to put his Vice President in charge of the war against drugs. President Reagan tried that, and it didn't work.

Campaigning, Cleveland, Aug. 25/
The Washington Post, 8-26:(A)6.

7

I think hunters and sportsmen should have the right to have weapons and hunt and engage in activities. I think people have a right to protect themselves in their homes subject to state law. [But] I'm concerned about teen-agers roaming

55

(MICHAEL S. DUKAKIS)

around our cities with Uzis [submachine guns] and Saturday night specials. I'm concerned about felons and people who have histories of mental instability who walk into a store and buy a gun without at least having somebody check on them.

Campaign speech,
West Yellowstone, Mont., Sept. 15/
The New York Times, 9-16:11.

1

The streets of America do not belong to drug peddlers and crack gangs; they belong to us. And we're going to take them back . . . As far as Mike Dukakis is concerned, there's nowhere you can run; there's nowhere you can sail; there's nowhere you can fly; there's nowhere you can hide; there will be no safe haven for dope peddlers and drug profits anywhere on this Earth.

At Los Angeles Police Academy,
Sept. 16/The New York Times,
9-17:9.

2

[On the drug problem in the U.S.]: . . . values are important, but it's important that our leaders demonstrate those values from the top. That means those of us who are elected to positions of political leadership will have to reflect those values ourselves. Here we are with a government [the Reagan Administration] that's been dealing with a drug-running Panamanian director [Manuel Noriega]; we've been dealing with him, he's been dealing drugs to our kids. And Governors like me and others have been trying to deal with the consequences . . . I want to be a President of the United States who makes sure that we never again do business with a drug-running Panamanian dictator, that we never again funnel aid to the contras [Nicaraguan rebels] who are convicted drug dealers. Values begin at the top, in the White House.

At Presidential debate,
Winston-Salem, N.C., Sept. 25/
The New York Times, 9-26:10.

3

I'm opposed to the death penalty. I think everybody knows that. I'm also very tough on violent crime. And that's one of the reasons my state has cut crime by more than any other industrial state in America, one of the reasons why we have the lowest murder rate of any industrial state in the country, one of the reasons why we have a drug education and prevention program that is reaching out and helping youngsters all over our state—the kind of thing I want to do as President of the United States.

At Presidential debate,
Winston-Salem, N.C., Sept. 25/
The New York Times,
9-26:11.

4

When a law-enforcement official is killed in the line of duty, we all die a little bit. And when drugs are the cause, that grief must be matched by determination. Determination to fight. Determination to wage war. Determination to beat the drug peddlers and thugs who are terrorizing our people and poisoning our kids. Our grief is above politics. And our determination to win this war should know no bounds.

At First African Methodist
Episcopal Church,
New York, Oct. 21/
Los Angeles Times, 10-22:(I)23.

5

[Criticizing Republican Presidential nominee George Bush for not vowing to cut U.S. aid to any country not cooperating with U.S. efforts to fight drug trafficking]: I'll be damned if I'll let those countries send their poison into the United States of America to poison our kids. Maybe he [Bush] thinks there are other things more important than the future of our children, more important than the stuff that is pouring into our cities and destroying our families. I say you have to draw the line somewhere.

At rally, Chicago, Nov. 2/
Los Angeles Times,
11-3:(I)1.

Arthur Coleman Eads
Chairman, National District
Attorneys Association

1

[Opponents of capital punishment have concluded that] the best way in this country to defeat it is to delay it until finally you get to a point where you throw up your hands and say, "Well, we can't do anything with it, therefore, let's abolish it." I don't think the prosecutors in this country will ever accept that proposition.

The New York Times, 8-8:8.

Mickey Edwards
United States Representative,
R-Oklahoma

2

[On the House's voting for heavy fines for casual drug users]: Today we're sending a message to weekend cocaine users and occasional pot smokers. We're saying they must be accountable for their selfish indulgence . . . People who use cocaine and marijuana may think they have little in common with heroin addicts, but they all depend on a network of criminals, murderers and smugglers to keep them supplied with drugs. If people get caught, they should pay the price.

Washington, Sept. 14/
Los Angeles Times, 9-15:(I)1,28.

Glenn English
United States Representative,
D-Oklahoma

3

[On the possibility of the U.S. military being used in the war against illegal drugs]: The military wants no part of this war, and given their experience in Vietnam I don't blame them. This is another war of containment. It's not a war to win.

Newsweek, 5-30:38.

Daniel J. Evans
United States Senator,
R-Washington

4

[Arguing against imposing the death penalty for drug-related murders]: Do we respond to the brutalization of society by criminals with a legal brutalization of society by imposing the death penalty? We'll score an election-year slam-dunk . . . but it won't even slow down the drug problem in this country.

The Washington Post, 6-10:(A)8.

Milton Friedman
Economist

5

The harm that is done by drugs is predominantly caused by the fact that they are illegal. You would not have had the crack epidemic if it was legal.

Time, 5-30:14.

Isaac Fulwood
Assistant Chief of Police of
Washington, D.C.

6

[On young people who are involved in drug trafficking]: We may think about marriage, families, planning for retirement, owning a home. But these kids don't think about that. They think their lives are going to be short, so they figure they're going to have some fun while they're here. They live only for today.

To reporters, Oct. 31/
The Washington Post, 11-2:(A)21.

Daryl Gates
Chief of Police of Los Angeles

7

[On Democratic Presidential nominee Michael Dukakis]: One thing I would do if I were him, and I would say this to his face, I'd burn that ACLU card so fast. You can't be strong on law and order and be a member of the ACLU.

To reporters,
Los Angeles, Sept. 16/
The New York Times, 7-17:9.

Rudolph W. Giuliani
United States Attorney for the
Southern District of New York

8

The [U.S.] State Department has an elitist attitude toward the drug problem. They don't

57

WHAT THEY SAID IN 1988

(RUDOLPH W. GIULIANI)

want to deal with it. Yet it is just as important as our relations with the Soviet Union or the Middle East.

Time, 3-14:20.

Norma B. Gluckstern
Director, Patuxent Institution
(Maryland)

1

[Defending her prison's program of granting unsupervised leaves to inmates convicted of violent crimes]: I think there's very little in corrections that works, but I think Patuxent does work. It works for a certain group of inmates who can come back out as productive citizens. I think it's a hope. And to give up this hope, what you're really doing is saying that you're giving up hope on corrections in general.

News conference, Nov. 18/
The Washington Post, 11-19:(A)12.

Ronald Goldstock
Director, New York State
Organized Crime Task Force

2

[On the U.S. Justice Department's decision to have the government oversee the Teamsters Union because of alleged criminal activities of its leadership]: . . . the way we've dealt with organized crime and labor racketeering in the past is to use simple criminal convictions as a means of getting rid of the racketeers, whether they be in syndicate operations or running a particular union. And we've found empirically that that doesn't solve the problem. Perhaps the Teamsters offer the best example . . . [The government's overseeing that Union is] not something that's desirable, but it's something that's necessary. When there has been a history of the Union members having their rights taken away from them and not being allowed to vote in their own leaders who would represent them, then it's appropriate. In fact, I think it's obligatory for the government to take some means to re-establish democratic practices. And if other means are not

successful, and have not been successful, then the trusteeship is something that ought to be employed.

Interview/
USA Today, 7-5:(A)9.

Lester Grinspoon
Psychiatrist,
Harvard University

3

[If the sale of narcotics is permitted,] there won't be the tremendous encroachment on our civil liberties. Are we willing to sacrifice our freedom for the small increase in the number of people who may use the drugs under a legalized system?

Time, 5-30:15.

Alexander M. Haig, Jr.
Candidate for the
1988 Republican
Presidential nomination;
Former Secretary of State
of the United States

4

The drug culture in America, that despite all the hoopla continues to increase in its severity, is an ugly rebuke to our entire society. Today, we are spending about 40 billions of dollars at state, Federal and local levels in three essential programs: one designed to educate our young people about the dangers of drugs, another to enhance our law-enforcement capability, and the third to rehabilitate those who are already caught in the web of this dreadful scourge. Let me tell you, as important as those programs are, it's time we turned our attention to the foreign source of the drug epidemic in America—those nations in this hemisphere who permit, willingly or unwillingly, the production of these illicit substances. To borrow an expression of mine from another context, we've got to "go to the source." This is a concept that worked before and it can work again.

Campaign speech/
The New York Times,
1-15:8.

Margaret Hambrick
Warden, Metropolitan (Federal)
Detention Center, Los Angeles

1

It is possible for prisoners to rehabilitate themselves. That's an important distinction. We can provide programs and opportunities . . . Inmates may participate in these programs, take advantage of these opportunities, while they're in prison. But whether or not they take that skill that they have learned, that trade, that improved reading and writing ability, and put it to use when they leave the institution, is really up to them.

Interview/
USA Today, 12-5:(A)11.

2

[On prison furloughs]: They can be helpful. The Federal prison system generally grants furloughs to people within one year of release. These are people who have been locked away in an unnatural environment, even though we try to make it more like the outside world. I believe that furloughs do help them to have some phased process of reintegration into the community.

Interview/
USA Today, 12-5:(A)11.

Orrin G. Hatch
United States Senator,
R-Utah

3

Capital punishment is our society's ultimate recognition of the sanctity of human life.

Los Angeles Times, 5-17:(I)4.

Mark O. Hatfield
United States Senator,
R-Oregon

4

[Criticizing a Senate vote to permit capital punishment for killings by drug "kingpins"]: In our disgust and outrage [at drug killings], we must not grow numb to the principles which are called into question by this provision. The desire for vengeance, for eye-for-eye justice, is a principle and a mentality unworthy of civilized government and of this body.

Before the Senate, Washington,
Oct. 13/The Washington Post,
10-14:(A)4.

Jesse Helms
United States Senator,
R-North Carolina

5

[Criticizing pending legislation that would easily permit U.S. and foreign law-enforcement agencies to swap evidence about individuals to be used in criminal prosecutions, a move he says could infringe on the rights of American citizens]: Whenever anybody in the State Department and the Justice Department says it's unwise to write in Constitutional protections for our people, then I say, to hell with the State Department, to hell with the Justice Department.

Washington, Sept. 22/
The Washington Post, 9-23:(A)4.

Lois Herrington
Chairman, White House
Conference for a
Drug Free America

6

A real concern is that we are not being tough enough on the drug traffickers and that a lot of people are getting by with very minor sentences, which means there's no deterrent . . . Many of the laws are in place, but the judges have used discretion on sentencing. Or, if they do sentence, then you get the parole boards that never look to the protection of the public when they're paroling. We have strengthened the Federal laws. There's a lot to be done with some of the state laws and in having the judges understand how many people are victimized by this crime.

Interview/USA Today, 3-1:(A)11.

7

The user is one who drives the [illegal-drug] demand, who makes the profit for the people bringing the drugs into this country. The people

59

who corrupt governments and catch innocent people in the crossfire are driven by the demands of the users. This is a good place to begin a national focus.

Interview/USA Today, 3-1:(A)11.

Stephen E. Higgins
Director, Federal Bureau of Alcohol,
Tobacco and Firearms

1

I know we're [his Bureau] doing about right when we get a little bit of criticism from both the people who would be called anti-gun, and from those who would be called pro-gun. When we're somewhere in the middle of those groups, we know we're probably doing what we're paid to do, which is enforce the existing laws, without getting out and telling people there ought to be more or different laws.

The New York Times, 2-1:12.

Bill Honig
California State Superintendent
of Public Instruction

2

You want to know where prison reform starts? I'll tell you. It's the third grade. We know the high-risk groups who will drop out of school. We know individuals from these groups make up a disproportionate share of prison inmates. Give me part of the $20,000 a year we now spend [in California] on these kids as adults, give it to me now, and we can make sure they won't wind up in prison, costing the state money not only to lock them up, but for the crimes they've committed, and for the welfare payments, if they have a family.

The Christian Science Monitor,
7-28:14.

John Hospers
Professor of philosophy,
University of
Southern California

3

[On people who would pick up and keep large amounts of cash found in the street, fallen from armored cars or from lost wallets]: There are people who feel that they have been had by society, so if they can get back at society by taking whatever they find in the street, it's strictly retaliation.

Time, 4-4:68.

Dan Howard
Spokesman for the
Department of Defense
of the United States

4

[On the interdiction of illegal drugs coming into the U.S.]: If the demand [for the drugs] is there, the stuff is going to come in. The drug interdiction efforts at sea have been working ordinarily well. But drugs are like quicksilver: They flow to wherever else there is an opening... The country has got to get serious about turning off the demand right here at home.

News briefing, May 12/
The Washington Post, 5-13:(A)4.

Jesse L. Jackson
Civil-rights leader;
Candidate for the 1988
Democratic Presidential nomination

5

The Number 1 threat to this nation is drugs—cocaine, crack, heroin, PCP. We're consuming $150-billion worth of drugs a year. The Number 1 tax-free industry in America is drugs. Drugs are corrupting leaders, killing our children. But don't just focus on children and ballplayers. Children do not buy $150-billion worth of drugs a year. And ballplayers do not launder $150-billion in drug money through banks. We must get serious about ending [drugs] in this country. Stop the cocaine, the crack, the heroine. Ban the drugs. Ban the handguns. Make our streets secure and safe again.

Campaign speech/Los Angeles Times, 4-2:(I)19.

John Paul II
Pope

6

Drug commerce has become an authentic traffic in liberty, in that it leads to the most

(JOHN PAUL II)

terrible form of slavery and sows your soil with corruption and death. Therefore, it is urgent not only to protect youths from drug consumption but also to combat the traffic itself, as it is an infamous activity by all lights.

Homily, Santa Cruz, Bolivia,
May 13/Los Angeles Times,
5-14:(I)3.

Lloyd D. Johnston
Social psychologist, Institute
for Social Research,
University of Michigan

1

[On the drug-abuse problem]: Supply reduction has been an abject failure. The supply of cocaine has never been greater on the streets, the price has never been lower, the drug has never been purer. We've basically lost on the supply battlefield, and in my opinion will continue to lose even if we pour a quarter of the treasury into it.

The New York Times, 4-12:1.

Mark Kleiman
Authority on law enforcement,
Kennedy School,
Harvard University

2

[On the U.S. war on illegal drugs]: You can't fight a war without any maps . . . Until the U.S. government knows as much about the market for cocaine as Procter & Gamble knows about the soap-flakes market, it is hard to take seriously the notion of a "war" on drugs.

The Christian Science Monitor,
11-28:32.

Edward I. Koch
Mayor of New York

3

[On the illegal-drug problem]: It's sad. There has to be greater attention on every level—prosecutors, courts, police, Mayor, Governor,

President—greater intensity everywhere. If you can't solve this issue, nothing else can be solved, because it's destroying the country.

The New York Times, 6-24:12.

David E. Kyvig
Professor of history,
University of Akron (Ohio)

4

People all across the political spectrum [are] looking at the history of the temperance movement and saying this government intervention into social behavior [the Prohibition period of the 1920s] was not only probably a good idea but was a more successful idea than it was given credit for . . . If there were a handgun prohibition, the prohibition-of-alcohol experience suggests it might not be totally effective, but I would suggest that the whole category of handgun fatalities would be significantly reduced because, frankly, most people would obey the law.

The Christian Science Monitor,
10-13:17.

John Lawn
Administrator, Drug
Enforcement Administration
of the United States

5

Drugs are not bad because they're illegal. They're illegal because they're bad. Anyone who talks in terms of legalizing [now-illegal] drugs is willing to write the death warrants for people in the lower socio-economic classes.

Time, 5-30:16.

Carl Levin
United States Senator,
D-Michigan

6

Over and over again, we have convicted the wrong people of crimes. I oppose capital punishment because you can't correct your mistakes.

Los Angeles Times, 5-17:(I)4.

61

Neil Malamuth
Professor of psychology,
University of California,
Los Angeles

1

I don't know that we have any real basis for saying sexual violence against women is increasing any more so than other crimes. But there's greater willingness to talk about it, a greater awareness of the seriousness of the problem and the seriousness of the long-term effects of being victimized, not only by the madman jumping out of the bushes but more so in date rape and various kinds of behavior by "normal" people in the context of socially acceptable relations.

Interview/
USA Today, 4-20:(A)11.

Stephen Markman
Assistant Attorney General
of the United States

2

[Criticizing legal regulations the police must adhere to, such as the Miranda rule]: The issue is not whether the police have learned to live with the rules, but whether society has learned to live with unprecedentedly high crime rates.

Newsweek, 7-18:53.

Bill McCollum
United States Representative,
R-Florida

3

If we're really going to be serious about deterrence [of drug-related crime], let's once and for all pass the death penalty [for major drug traffickers] and put the laws on the books to truly deter the drug kingpin. Education and rehabilitation are not enough [to stop demand for drugs]. If we don't have a deterrent, we won't win the war on the demand side. And if we don't win on the demand side, we won't win the war, period.

Los Angeles Times,
9-9:(I)40.

Edwin Meese III
Attorney General of
the United States

4

While we have succeeded in committing additional resources to law enforcement and prosecution, corrections has not received the same treatment . . . Court-imposed "caps" [on prison capacity] at the Federal level could potentially require the government to release prisoners earlier than current incarceration policies—and common sense—dictate. We would be unable, in all likelihood, to follow our current enforcement, detention, sentencing and incarceration policies. We may be forced to decline to prosecute many types of cases simply because there would be no place to incarcerate those convicted.

Before American Correctional
Association, Phoenix, Jan. 12/
Los Angeles Times,
1-13:(I)14.

5

Overwhelming evidence now exists that links drug use to criminal activity. Drug abuse by criminal suspects far exceeds the estimated use in the general population where it appears to be leveling off. Among criminal defendants, however, it seems to be increasing.

Statement*/
The New York Times,
1-22:9.

James P. Moran
Mayor of Alexandria, Va.

6

Every day, drug dealers are fighting turf battles in our neighborhoods with automatic weapons and huge payoffs. The war we are fighting . . . is over the hearts and souls of our young people . . . Drugs are killing our young people.

At conference sponsored by
Metropolitan Washington Council
of Governments, April 27/
The Washington Post,
4-28:(A)19.

Norval Morris
*Professor of law and
criminology,
University of Chicago*

1

The criminal-justice system does not have much to do with crime rates. It's more an expression of public disapproval of behavior and a sense of society collectively trying to protect its own.

The New York Times, 4-25:11.

Charles Orasin
President, Handgun Control

2

[Supporting the Congressional vote to control the manufacture of plastic handguns, which can escape detection more easily than metal ones]: This is a tremendous victory for law enforcement and all those citizens who want to keep handguns out of the wrong hands. The NRA fought this legislation, but then they threw in the towel when they realized that not only law enforcement but Congress and the Administration supported the bill. It shows a growing recognition in Congress that something must be done about these issues.

*Oct. 20/
Los Angeles Times, 10-21:(I)15.*

Enrique Parejo Gonzalez
*Former Minister of Justice
of Colombia*

3

It is absurd to say that certain countries benefit and others are hurt by [the international] narcotics [trade] . . . Equally wrong would be those tempted to distinguish between producer and consumer countries. Experience has shown that every producer country ultimately turns into a consumer country and that the opposite situation is equally true. They are all victims without exception—victims of the greedy transnational organizations that seek to increase their gains and power, taking advantage of conditions that enable them to produce, process and distribute their deadly product and to induce large numbers to consume it; victims also of the huge power to corrupt men and institutions at all levels in order to guarantee the success of this dirty trade.

*At PRIDE International
Conference on Youth and Drugs,
Atlanta, April 15/
The Washington Post, 4-22:(A)22.*

Lewis F. Powell, Jr.
*Associate Justice, Supreme
Court of the United States*

4

If capital punishment cannot be enforced even where innocence is not an issue and the fairness of the trial is not seriously questioned, perhaps Congress and the state legislatures should take a serious look at whether retention of a punishment that is not being enforced is in the public interest.

*Before American Bar Association,
Toronto, Aug. 7/
The New York Times, 8-8:8.*

5

In this country, opinion remains sharply divided on the subject of gun control. Much scholarly debate has centered on the extent to which the Second Amendment [to the Constitution] applies to private ownership of arms, or is restricted to the need for a "well-regulated militia." With respect to handguns, however—as opposed to sporting rifles and shotguns—it is not easy to understand why the Second Amendment, or the notion of liberty, should be viewed as creating a right to own and carry a weapon that contributes so directly to the shocking number of murders.

*Before American Bar Association,
Toronto, Aug. 7/
USA Today, 8-9:(A)10.*

Dan Quayle
*United States Senator,
R-Indiana;
1988 Republican
Vice-Presidential nominee*

6

[Criticizing Democratic Presidential nominee Michael Dukakis' stand favoring gun control]: It

63

(DAN QUAYLE)

seems very clear to me that Mr. Dukakis believes that you should supervise law-abiding citizens who want to Constitutionally bear arms, but not supervise first-degree murderers who roam the countryside on the weekend furloughs [as occurs in Massachusetts, the state of which Dukakis is Governor]. The man at the top of our ticket, George Bush, is a life member of the National Rifle Association while Mr. Dukakis boasts that he is a card-carrying member of the American Civil Liberties Union.

The New York Times, 8-27:6.

1

The drug problem is the Number 1 issue. The military aspect of the drug problem [using the military more in an effort to curtail drugs] is being addressed. As a matter of fact, we are using the Department of Defense in a coordinated effort in reconnaissance. But I don't believe that we're going to turn the Department of Defense into a police organization . . . We need to focus on another part of this problem, and that problem is law enforcement. And here's where we have a major disagreement with the Governor of Massachusetts [Democratic Presidential nominee Michael Dukakis]. He is opposed to the death penalty for drug kingpins. We believe people convicted of that crime deserve the death penalty. You cannot have a war on drugs, you cannot be tough on drugs—and weak on crime.

At Vice-Presidential debate,
Omaha, Neb., Oct. 5/
USA Today, 10-6:(A)11.

Nancy Reagan
Wife of President
of the United States
Ronald Reagan

2

The casual [illegal-drug] user may think, as he takes a line of cocaine or smokes a joint in the privacy of his nice condo, listening to his expensive stereo, that he's somehow not bothering any-

one. But there's a trail of death and destruction that leads directly to his door.

At White House conference
on a drug-free America,
Washington, Feb. 29/
The Christian Science Monitor,
3-1:25.

Ronald Reagan
President of the United States

3

Now, I've heard critics say employers have no business looking for drug abuse in the workplace. But when you pin the critics down, too often they seem to be among the handful who still believe that drug abuse is a "victimless" crime. [However,] the drug user is a victim. His employer is a victim. His fellow employees are victims. The family that depends on his wages are victims. And America, which is only as strong and as competitive as all of us together, America is the victim. It would be hard to find any crime with more victims than drug abuse.

At drug-abuse forum,
Duke University, Feb. 8/
Los Angeles Times, 2-9:(I)17.

4

It is time to back up the rhetoric on the drug problem with action, and I call on the House and Senate to vote promptly on my bill providing for capital punishment when a death results from drug dealing and when a Drug Enforcement Administration or other law-enforcement officer is murdered. When drug syndicates commit murder, our sympathy should be with the victims, not the killers.

At memorial ceremony for those
killed investigating drug trafficking,
Washington, April 19/
Los Angeles Times, 4-20:(I)4.

Ann Richards
State Treasurer of Texas

5

[The Republican Administration tells] us that they're fighting a war on drugs, and then people

(ANN RICHARDS)

come on TV and testify that the CIA and the DEA knew they were flying drugs into America all along. And they're negotiating with a [Panamanian] dictator who is shoveling cocaine into this country like crazy. I guess that's their Central American strategy.

At Democratic National Convention,
Atlanta, July 18/
The New York Times, 7-19:10.

Mitchell Rosenthal
President, Phoenix House,
New York

1

To legalize [now-illegal] drugs would give us a vast army of people who would be out of control. People say only 10 per cent of those who drink are problem drinkers, so they assume that only 10 per cent of the people who take drugs will become addicts. But there is no reason to believe that if we made crack available in little crack shops, that only 10 per cent would be addicted; the number would probably be more like 75 per cent.

Time, 5-30:16.

Paul N. Samuels
Executive vice president,
Legal Action Center,
New York

2

[On the increasing involvement of drug use by those charged with crimes]: When you have a situation where you are putting all your money into law enforcement, it is a revolving door that just spins faster. I think that increasing drug treatment has to go hand-in-hand with any strategies designed to fight drug abuse and crime.

The New York Times, 1-22:9.

William Donald Schaefer
Governor of Maryland (D)

3

All of you know about prisons. They are jammed in. There's nothing to do with the people

that are there. It's just put them in, and out they come after five years, 10 years, whatever it might be. That's wrong, that's wrong.

State of the State address,
Annapolis, Jan. 14/
The Washington Post, 1-15:(A)16.

Kurt Schmoke
Mayor of Baltimore

4

[Proposing legalization of now-illegal drugs]: If you take the profit out of drug trafficking, you won't have young children hiding drugs [on behalf of pushers] for $100 a night or wearing beepers to school because it makes more sense to run drugs for someone than to take some of the jobs that are available. I don't know of any kid who is making money by running booze.

Time, 5-30:14.

William S. Sessions
Director, Federal Bureau
of Investigation

5

[Saying the FBI should recruit more women and minorities and that any discrimination within the Bureau be eliminated]: [If] you don't have those kind of people, then you're disabled. If you need to infiltrate an organization characterized by a particular nationality and you don't have that nationality of person available in a trained, ready status, then you're disabled . . . It's absolutely essential we do not have discriminatory conduct or activities on the part of anybody anywhere in the Bureau—period. I think it's debilitating . . . it's contrary to law . . . My belief is now that the Bureau as a Bureau reflects that. And if there are unfortunate circumstances, they are truly unfortunate.

Interview, Washington, Jan. 6/
Los Angeles Times, 1-7:(I)15.

Wayne Sheets
Director of education and training,
National Rifle Association

6

[On accidental shootings of children with guns owned by individuals]: The key to the whole

(WAYNE SHEETS)

thing is education. In this country people have freedom of choice, and if a person chooses to have a gun in the home, that's a choice he makes for himself. The issue is if he does make that choice he has to take responsibility for it, and that responsibility begins with educating himself and whoever might come in contact with that gun.

The New York Times, 1-13:7.

George P. Shultz
Secretary of State
of the United States

1

[On the fight against drugs entering the U.S. from South America]: The fact is that despite the money spent, the laws passed and the lives lost, there is more cocaine entering the United States and Europe from South America than ever before. We have failed to stop the enemy. We [in the U.S.] are responsible because the demand for drugs still exists; and you [in South America] are responsible because the drugs are still being produced and shipped northward.

Speech, La Paz, Bolivia, Aug. 8/
The Washington Post, 8-9:(A)18.

Arlen Specter
United States Senator,
R-Pennsylvania

2

Aside from the Presidency, there is no post more important in our government than that of Attorney General. It is the symbol of justice for all Americans.

Before the Senate, Washington,
Aug. 11/
Los Angeles Times, 8-12:(I)4.

James K. Stewart
Director, National Institute
of Justice of the United States

3

Public debate has mistakenly focused on the cost of imprisonment compared with the cost of

probation. The correct way to look at the issue is to compare the costs of imprisonment to probation costs, plus the costs of crime to the individual victim and to the community . . . Confinement is not too expensive when weighed against the price of crimes that would otherwise be prevented by incapacitation.

July 3/
The Washington Post, 7-4:(A)22.

Preble Stolz
Professor of law,
University of California,
Berkeley

4

There's no question that [capital-case] backlog is having an adverse impact [on the court system]—but that's the price you pay for having a death penalty. Death cases are unique—they involve a complex review process—and they're going to prove costly and time-consuming in that respect. The best argument there is for abolishing the death penalty is the effect it has on the system as a whole.

Los Angeles Times, 7-24:(I)1.

Dick Thornburgh
Attorney General
of the United States

5

[On legislation to impose penalties on illegal-drug users]: Anyone using drugs had better look over your shoulder, because there might be a law-enforcement official there to present you with your share of the bill of the cost of drug abuse and trafficking in this country.

Interview/
Los Angeles Times, 11-22:(I)16.

Anthony P. Travisono
Executive director,
American Correctional
Association

6

We're stuck with the wrong visions [of prisons]. The public has no idea what it means to work and live in one of these facilities for any length of time. People just don't visualize what it means to

(ANTHONY P. TRAVISONO)

operate a prison with 800 to 1,000 men in it when it was built to accommodate 500. In the desire to put somebody someplace, they just don't visualize what that is on a daily basis.

The Christian Science Monitor,
7-26:17.

1

[On criticism of prison furlough programs by which prisoners are let out on weekend passes]: Furlough programs are good programs. Mistakes are made [when inmates commit crimes or escape while on furlough], but with a 98 per cent success rate, we don't want the baby thrown out with the wash water.

USA Today, 10-14:(A)10.

Maurice T. Turner, Jr.
Chief of Police of
Washington, D.C.

2

The police alone cannot solve the drug problem. Any society whose appetite for illicit narcotics cannot be satisfied must suffer the consequences of eroding morality and deteriorating values which result in alarming increases in violent crime. Until . . . society can curb that

hunger, we will not experience a reversal in this alarming spiral of drug-related homicides.

News conference,
Washington, Oct. 26/
The Washington Post, 10-27:(A)29.

William von Raab
Commissioner, United
States Customs Service

3

[On the fight against illegal drugs]: You must treat it like a war—total mobilization, total commitment . . . When you fight a war, every man, woman and child should be mobilized to that effort. Before Munich, all the diplomats hoped around the world that Hitler was a nice guy and we would be able to deal with him. I believe that in this [drug war] there's going to have to be a basic difference in attitude adopted.

Interview, Washington, May 24/
The Washington Post, 5-25:(A)17.

Benjamin Ward
Police Commissioner of
New York City

4

[On walks he takes in his neighborhood]: Sometimes I walk with a gun, sometimes a machine gun, always with something, and rarely ever in the same place.

Newsweek, 10-10:21.

Defense • The Military

Allan Adler
Legislative counsel,
American Civil
Liberties Union

1

Over the years, the decisions of the Supreme Court, furthered by acts of Congress, have insulated the military from many of the Constitutional protections that civilians enjoy. Altogether, the measures allow the military to meet what it considers its paramount needs—to maintain discipline and protect the chain of command.

Los Angeles Times, 3-20:(I)1.

Sergei F. Akhromeyev
Chief, Soviet Armed Forces
General Staff

2

Perestroika [reform] has made Soviet military doctrine purely defensive in form and content. It was defensive before . . . but the concrete ways of answering enemy aggression could be either defensive or offensive. Now we are restructuring precisely this, so that our military doctrine and military strategy will be only defensive.

Interview, Moscow/
Newsweek, 7-11:36.

3

I often caught myself thinking [when inspecting U.S. military forces as part of recent reciprocal U.S.-Soviet inspections], as I looked at U.S. armaments and equipment, that almost all of what the Americans showed us is comparable—and sometimes absolutely identical—to what we have. That is the logic of weapons development. The arms race means, unfortunately, that countries always upgrade their weapons.

Interview/
World Press Review,
October:46.

Edward C. Aldridge
Secretary of the Air Force
of the United States

4

[On the high cost of the new U.S. *Stealth* bomber]: Whatever it costs, it's worth it. How much is deterrence worth? This thing is a significant contributor to the strategic deterrence of our country. The Soviets know it. They know the capabilities this aircraft can provide.

New conference,
Washington, Dec. 16/
The New York Times, 12-17:10.

Oscar Arias
President of Costa Rica

5

You have to choose between rifles and bread; between army helicopters and hospitals; between tanks and schools. Spending money on arms is incompatible with economic and social growth.

Interview/USA Today, 9-9:(A)2.

Les Aspin
United States Representative,
D-Wisconsin

6

[On the scandal involving fraud in defense-industry contract procurement]: We're looking at a serious potential gridlock over national-security issues regarding what you do with tainted contracts . . . It seems to me we're looking for some kind of a solution that falls between the two extremes: One is to say, "*C'est la vie,* that's life," and go ahead and produce the planes and whatever else. And the other extreme is to say, "By God, you've broken the law. We're going to take your contract away and damn the taxpayer and the security of the country."

At House Armed Services
Committee hearing,
Washington, June 29/
Los Angeles Times, 6-30:(I)18.

(LES ASPIN)

1

[On Soviet leader Mikhail Gorbachev's recent speech at the UN in which he outlined plans to reduce and reorganize Soviet military forces in Europe]: We don't fight wars by the numbers. Perhaps the most significant segment of Gorbachev's speech was his promise to reorganize Soviet forces in Eastern Europe so they are "clearly defensive" ... A reorganization that removes the Soviet offensive capability declaws the Russian bear and is far more important than numbers on a chart.

Washington, Dec. 7/
Los Angeles Times, 12-8:(I)28.

James R. Blaker
Former Director, Special
Regional Studies Division,
Department of Defense
of the United States

2

There's a growing disparity between what the United States sees as the importance of its bases [overseas] and what foreign governments believe is the value to them. As the over-all number of American bases has declined, the value of each one to the United States increases, and this gives each foreign government great leverage in negotiations [for renewing base leases]. The issue for the future is this: What happens if we're not willing or able to accept the costs being asked for our bases?

Los Angeles Times, 5-15:(I)1.

David Boren
United States Senator,
D-Oklahoma

3

I don't know that we can afford to avoid research on the Strategic Defense Initiative, or "Star Wars" [space defense system]. We have to keep pace with research in case the other [Soviet] side scores some major breakout. But at the same time, spending on "Spy Wars," improving our satellite [intelligence] systems and our national technical means is money very well spent. One dollar spent there can save you $10 in your military budget, because you can find out what are the new systems they're developing. The more information you have, the more you can learn how to counter those new systems. Therefore, you can target your money.

Interview/USA Today, 10-26:(A)7.

Harold Brown
Former Secretary of Defense
of the United States

4

The [U.S.-Soviet talks on] START verification provisions are going to be horrendous to work out, much more difficult than INF, and the expectations the [U.S. Reagan] Administration has generated are just not going to be fulfilled.

Newsweek, 5-23:26.

George Bush
Vice President of
the United States;
Candidate for the 1988
Republican Presidential
nomination

5

[Democratic Presidential candidate Michael Dukakis opposes] virtually every step we are taking to keep our defenses at the technological edge. Dukakis opposes the MX [missile]. He opposes testing of nuclear weapons. He opposes flight testing of ballistic missiles. He opposes the ... Strategic Defense Initiative [the space defense system] ... The Dukakis Doctrine is a doctrine of wishful thinking. Even [former Democratic President] Jimmy Carter and [former Democratic Vice President] Walter Mondale supported systems that Governor Dukakis opposes.

Campaign speech, Fullerton, Calif.,
May 13/
Los Angeles Times, 5-14:(I)20.

6

The liberal elite do not understand [defense issues]. I do not think they mean to do harm. I think they simply don't understand that reducing

(GEORGE BUSH)

our defense will erode our security. Maybe they don't understand that simply pulling back on our global responsibilities, without thinking it through and preparing the ground, will make the world more dangerous. I'm sure they would claim it isn't so and they're all in favor of a strong defense. But what are we to think when they say they're for a strong defense but they oppose every new weapons system that would preserve our strength? Against a space shield, against the MX [missile], against the 600-ship Navy, against *Midgetman* [missile], B-1 [bomber], *Stealth* [bomber], against any increase whatsoever in the defense of the United States . . . They act as if they believe that strength is the preoccupation of bullies, as if they believe that our desire to remain strong is proof that we are the aggressor. They are so blinded by ideology that they cannot see what Americans have understood for 40 years: that peace flows from strength.

At U.S. Military Academy
commencement, May 25/
The New York Times, 5-26:10;
Los Angeles Times, 5-26:(I)20.

1

[On those guilty in the arms-procurement scandal involving the Pentagon and defense contractors]: They will be prosecuted to the full extent of the law, and, if guilty, we will throw the book at them. We cannot tolerate lawlessness, in the Congress, in the Pentagon, the Executive Branch or on the streets . . . [But] the first reaction in Congress to the scandals, to increase the regulatory bureaucracy at Defense, though understandable, that's only going to add to the complexity and worsen the problem. The answer is to reduce, cut and simplify, including staff and executive overhead.

Before World Affairs Council,
San Francisco, June 29/
The New York Times, 6-30:14.

2

[On probable Democratic Presidential nominee Michael Dukakis' Conventional Defense Initiative, CDI, which would concentrate on modernizing conventional, rather than nuclear, forces]: What troubles me about CDI is it seems to move away from our own strategic deterrence . . . You see, I have a feeling . . . that my opponent really is anti-nuclear-weapons to the degree that he'd . . . [try] to keep the peace through conventional deterrence alone. That is perhaps an over-statement because I don't think he's proposing elimination [of strategic nuclear weapons], but it moves us to a very different form of deterrence.

News conference, Atlanta, July 8/
The Washington Post, 7-9:(A)4.

3

Already the first phase of a space-based SDI technology is ready to come out of the lab and begin demonstration. The technology isn't the problem—that's progressing faster than its most ardent supporters ever dreamed—it's the Democrats in Congress that are dragging their feet, for instance, cutting the space-based interceptor appropriations from over $300-million to $85-million and boasting they've "taken the stars out of Star Wars." I am committed to deployment of SDI as soon as feasible, and will determine the exact architecture of the system in my first term as [President] as the technologies are tested, some rejected, some accepted, some proven. As President, I will not leave America defenseless against ballistic missiles.

Before Mid-America Committee,
Chicago, Aug. 2/
The Washington Post, 8-3:(A)6.

4

[Supporting the proposed U.S. space defense system]: There are few developments more frightening than that of unstable, sometimes irrational, Third World regimes being able to press a button and deliver weapons of terror across great distances . . . That fact is that Chicago, this city, just like every other city in the United States, has absolutely no defense against an attack today.

Before Mid-America Committee,
Chicago, Aug. 2/
The New York Times, 8-3:8.

(GEORGE BUSH)

1

[On Democratic Presidential nominee Michael Dukakis]: At first, he favored a nuclear freeze that would have made our arms-reduction talks with the Soviets impossible. And last week, at first he said he was still in favor of the freeze, and then he changed his mind. Such vacillation may be riskless in a campaign, but in a dangerous world it could prove to be disastrous. Except for opposition to virtually every weapons system that would insure our security, my opponent's policies are invisible. He's the "stealth" candidate. For, while he can't decide about the *Stealth* bomber, he favors stealth policies, and they can be neither seen nor heard. His campaign jets from place to place, but no issues show up on the radar screen.

Before Republican platform committee,
New Orleans, Aug. 8/
The New York Times, 8-9:1.

George Bush
Vice President
of the United States;
1988 Republican
Presidential nominee

2

[Despite recent U.S.-Soviet arms-control agreements,] we're not out of the woods yet. The Soviets are now deploying two new ICBMs: the SS-24 and SS-25. So even with *perestroika*—reform—Soviet military modernization, including their own research into strategic defense, has not slackened. Soviet military spending continues to rise. Only a [U.S.] willingness to modernize [our own forces] gives the Soviet Union the incentive to negotiate real arms reduction.

Before American Legion,
Louisville, Ky., Sept. 7/
The New York Times, 9-8:12.

3

[On the first destruction of U.S. nuclear missiles in accordance with the recent U.S.-Soviet INF treaty]: We are witnessing today one of those unique moments in the career of man—a moment when the tides of history turned, that a new future dawned. It's a moment we will be able to tell our children and grandchildren about. This was the day when we began destroying the weapons of destruction.

Karnack, Texas, Sept. 8/
Los Angeles Times, 9-9:(I)14.

4

We're in the serious stages of negotiation with the Soviet Union now in the strategic-arms control talks . . . The Soviets are modernizing. They continue to modernize. And we can't simply say we've got enough nuclear weapons, let's freeze. We can't do that. We have to have modernization, especially if we achieve the 50 per cent reduction in strategic weapons that our President [Reagan] is taking the leadership to attain.

At Presidential debate,
Los Angeles, Oct. 13/
The New York Times, 10-15:11.

5

If I'm elected President, if I'm remembered for anything, it would be this: a complete and total ban on chemical weapons. Their destruction forever. That's my solemn mission . . . I thought we had relegated the horrors of chemical warfare to the history books. I thought we had banished forever what we saw only a few months ago [in the Iran-Iraq war]: a picture of that mother trying to protect her child, waving her arms against the invisible winds of death: chemical weapons.

At University of Toledo, Oct. 21/
The Washington Post, 10-22:(A)7.

George Bush
Vice President,
and President-elect,
of the United States

6

The first duty of the President specified by the Constitution is that the President shall serve as the Commander-in-Chief of the armed forces. And I certainly regard no duty of the President as

71

(GEORGE BUSH)

more important than maintaining a strong national defense. Protecting our security and promoting peace are the groundwork upon which all other national progress is laid. And they're the prerequisites for a prosperous and forward-looking nation. And if we've proven anything in the last eight years, it is that peace through strength works.

News conference, Washington,
Dec. 16/The New York Times,
12-17:8.

Robert C. Byrd
United States Senator,
D-West Virginia

1

No President has ever effectively consulted on a regular basis with the Congress [about the commitment of U.S. forces in a war situation]. Instead, the Congress has almost always been treated to after-the-fact consultation, which is no consultation at all.

The New York Times,
5-20:3.

Frank C. Carlucci
Secretary of Defense of the
United States

2

[Saying the Soviets have built sophisticated underground shelters for their leaders that would allow them to wage a protracted nuclear war]: There can only be one purpose for these shelters—to provide the Soviet leadership the ability to fight a protracted nuclear conflict. These facilities contradict in steel and concrete Soviet protestations that they share [U.S.] President Reagan's view that nuclear war can never be won and must never be fought. These facilities reveal that they are preparing themselves for just the opposite.

News conference,
Washington, April 29/
Los Angeles Times, 4-30:(I)16.

3

[On Soviet leader Mikhail Gorbachev's reform program in the Soviet Union]: He is not, so to speak, changing the fundamental structure of society; he is just trying to make the system more efficient. If the end result of that is a Soviet Union that is less expansionist, that stops its human-rights violations ... and is more open to a dialogue with the West, then we will all be better off. But if the end result is that the Western alliance relaxes its defense effort and the Soviet Union modernizes its industrial and technological base and ... ends up as a society that can produce enormous quantities of weapons even more effectively than it does today, then we will have made an enormous miscalculation.

Tokyo/
The Washington Post, 6-13:(A)2.

4

[On scandals involving defense contractors and former Defense Department workers]: I'm not sure we need more laws. You've got to be very careful with blanket prohibitions so you don't drive out of DOD the talent it needs. If you say somebody can't go into industry after they leave DOD, is a nuclear physicist going to leave his job, go into DOD, and then know he can't go back to work for his company? There has to be a balance.

Interview/USA Today, 7-26:(A)9.

5

We recognize that the Soviet Union has legitimate defense needs and we are aware of the suffering your country has endured in the past. No one begrudges you the need for a strong and capable army. What troubles us is when the Soviet Union continues to develop forces far in excess of what it needs for purposes of its own defense—and especially when that newly added strength focuses on forces designed for massive offensive operations to seize and hold territory.

At Voroshilov Military Academy
of the Soviet General Staff,
Moscow, Aug. 1/
The New York Times, 8-2:4.

(FRANK C. CARLUCCI)

1

[On criticism of public air shows put on by military flying teams in the wake of several fatal accidents abroad recently, resulting in many civilian deaths]: You have to accept the fact that a significant element of any fighting force is its morale. You could make the same argument about bands, or marching. It's part of morale and discipline. The inspirational element, if you will, of demonstrating your capabilities is a very useful recruiting tool, and it is part of the muscle and sinew of military forces.

To reporters, Washington, Sept. 1/
The New York Times, 9-2:8.

Alan Cranston
United States Senator,
D-California

2

[On the Senate's approval of the U.S.-Soviet INF treaty]: We are making a breakthrough. It is not a substantially significant treaty . . . But it lays the foundation [for future treaties] that can substantially reduce the scale, cost and dangers of this arms race.

May 27/Los Angeles Times,
5-29:(I)1.

3

[On Soviet leader Mikhail Gorbachev's recent speech at the UN in which he outlined plans for a Soviet cutback in arms and a desire for better relations with the West]: Gorbachev's speech could be the end of the cold war, the end of the arms race, the end of the danger of nuclear war and the end of the burdens that we and they carry on military preparedness . . . I don't think we can discuss American troop reductions in Europe until we see exactly what the Soviets do. But this could lead to the possibility of less of a burden for the United States and its allies in Europe, because if the Soviets make significant reductions, perhaps we could also make some matching reductions.

To reporters, Washington, Dec. 7/
Los Angeles Times, 12-8:(I)28.

William J. Crowe, Jr.
Admiral, United States Navy;
Chairman, Joint Chiefs
of Staff

4

[Endorsing the U.S.-Soviet INF Treaty]: [To keep the NATO Alliance strong] at reasonable levels of investment . . . we must exploit key areas where we enjoy potential long-term technological advantages . . . The United States did make certain that the INF Treaty would leave the door open for NATO to exploit fully emergent technologies in the modernization of strategic nuclear, theatre nuclear and conventional forces . . . It is imperative for the Alliance to take stock of its military posture and to reassess the way it is preparing for the long haul.

Before Senate Armed Services
Committee, Washington, Jan. 27/
The Washington Post, 1-28:(A)4.

5

There are no solely military solutions. So we need warriors who can operate in the policy world as well. It's the same within the military. We need broad-based fighters. We need managers, too. The Pentagon spends huge sums developing and producing new weapons systems. That has to be done well. Our challenge is to develop leaders who can fight and manage, and fighters who can contribute to policy-making. We have to develop a promotion system that recognizes all those talents. A man can be a first-class warrior, but if he can't function in the policy arena, that's a serious deficiency in higher commands.

Interview, Washington/
Time, 12-26:73.

Ronald V. Dellums
United States Representative,
D-California

6

[Criticizing Democrats who call for strengthening U.S. conventional forces if U.S.-Soviet agreements are reached limiting nuclear forces]: Why are we talking about expanding our conven-

(RONALD V. DELLUMS)

tional capabilities? Either we are a party advocating peace or we are a party advocating war.

*At debate sponsored by Democratic
Party platform committee,
Alexandria, Va., May 20/
The New York Times, 5-21:8.*

William L. Dickinson
*United States Representative,
R-Alabama*

1

The B-1B [bomber] does work. It flies fast. It flies low—below enemy radar. And it has a radar cross-section that is 100 times smaller than the B-52, which it was meant to replace. It can employ a variety of weapons and ... deliver them with great accuracy ... The B-1 bomber has had a long and, at times, tortuous path to development, but it is now a critical part of our force structure. We on the Armed Services Committee have identified the problems, but must also acknowledge the successes of the program. The B-1B is ready, on alert, and represents a credible signal to all of this nation's military strength and strategic deterrent.

*Before the House,
Washington, May 4/
The Washington Post, 5-13:(A)22.*

Robert J. Dole
*United States Senator,
R-Kansas;
Candidate for the 1988
Republican Presidential
nomination*

2

[On START talks between the U.S. and the Soviet Union]: We have to be absolutely sure that the agreement leaves us with a credible nuclear deterrent. Any START agreement from the ongoing Geneva talks must meet this vital standard ... Indeed, if the residual forces on each side are misaligned, if ours are left more vulnerable to attack by theirs, or if we fail to adequately fund programs which insure the sur-

vivability and utility of our deterrent forces—under any of those circumstances, the effectiveness of our deterrence would be reduced, even though the Soviets would have fewer weapons. And under those circumstances, it would be better we have no START agreement at all.

*At University of Iowa, Jan. 19/
The Washington Post,
1-20:(A)15.*

Robert J. Dole
*United States Senator,
R-Kansas;
Former candidate for the
1988 Republican
Presidential nomination*

3

We have all kinds of demands to scrutinize Pentagon programs. We have all these tainted programs. There have always been all kinds of hearings and the public is led to believe, and properly so in some cases, that the Pentagon does not have much control, that the consultants have taken over, and we are spending a lot of tax money that should not be spent. So far as I understand it, most of this is based on personal greed. It is not widespread but it is something that has to be dealt with.

*Before the Senate,
Washington, July 14/
The Washington Post,
7-25:(A)9.*

Joseph Douglass, Jr.
*Former Deputy Director,
Defense Advanced Research
Projects Agency of
the United States*

4

In the case of arms control, cheating and deception [by the Soviets] are in the planning process even before negotiations [with the West] begin.

*Before Senate Foreign Relations Committee,
Washington, Feb. 18/
Los Angeles Times, 2-19:(I)12.*

Michael S. Dukakis
Governor of Massachusetts (D);
Candidate for the 1988
Democratic Presidential nomination

1

In the future we want, there will be a difference between a defense budget that keeps growing bigger, and real defenses that keep growing better. It will not be unpatriotic to question Pentagon mismanagement—or a multi-billion-dollar fantasy called "Star Wars" [the proposed space defense system] that is unworkable and unnecessary and that happens to violate the ABM treaty.

Campaign speech/
The New York Times, 1-4:9.

2

I'm for a policy of no early first use [of nuclear weapons]. But our present strategy in Europe assumes that if the Soviets were to invade, and conventional forces couldn't stop them, that we'd reserve the right to use nuclear force. I don't think that's going to happen and, in fact, I see the opposite happening. I see a real opportunity now to bring down the level of conventional forces with the Soviets. I think [Soviet leader Mikhail] Gorbachev is serious about his need to significantly reduce his commitment of conventional forces. So, I don't think it's going to happen. But until that happens we've got to be prepared to use nuclear force—obviously with great restraint and only when there seems to be no other alternative.

Interview/
Los Angeles Times, 4-14:(I)20.

3

We need a strong and survivable nuclear deterrent; and we have a strong and survivable nuclear deterrent. But we continue to have serious deficiencies in our conventional forces. The commanders of our armed forces have repeatedly warned us of the dangers we face. Maintenance backlogs are growing. We have serious shortfalls in airlift and sea lift, in spare parts and ammunition. In the words of one senior Air Force commander: "At the end of this year,

we are going to see airplanes without engines." We don't need SDI [the proposed space defense system]; we need CDI [conventional defense initiative]. We need . . . to apply advanced technology to the challenge of fighting—and winning—a conventional war.

Before Atlantic Council,
Washington, June 14/
Los Angeles Times, 6-15:(I)16.

4

[On revelations about defense contract fraud]: The basic problem . . . goes back to these massive increases in the defense budget at a time when neither the [Reagan] Administration nor the Pentagon were ready for them, and when money was flowing so freely and so lavishly that people simply couldn't control it.

Campaigning,
New Orleans, June 17/
Los Angeles Times, 6-18:(I)22.

Michael S. Dukakis
Governor of Massachusetts (D);
1988 Democratic
Presidential nominee

5

We must be, we are, and we will be militarily strong. But we must back that military strength with economic strength. We must give the men and women of our armed forces weapons that work. We must have a Secretary of Defense who will manage—and not be managed by—the Pentagon. And we must have a foreign policy that reflects the decency and the principles and the values of the American people. President Reagan has set the stage for deep cuts in nuclear arms—and I salute him for that. He has said that we should judge the Soviet Union not by what it says, but by what it does—and I agree, I agree with that. But we can do a lot more to stop the spread of nuclear and chemical arms in this world.

Accepting the nomination at
Democratic National Convention,
Atlanta, July 21/
The New York Times, 7-22:8.

(MICHAEL S. DUKAKIS)

1

Deterrence requires vigilance and determination, and it requires leadership. But it does not require the seemingly endless development of new and more expensive nuclear weapons systems—particularly when, thanks to President Reagan and [Soviet leader] Gorbachev, we may have the best opportunity in our lifetime to build a safer world.

At New York University, Aug. 11/
The Washington Post, 8-12:(A)8.

2

[On the proposed U.S. space defense system]: I'm not opposed to [it]. But before we commit billions or trillions of dollars to "Star Wars," we've got to do the research that will tell us whether or not the system can work and whether or not it's essential to our national defense . . . If I [as President] made the judgment and if Congress made the judgment that it was essential to our national security, then, obviously, we'd proceed with it . . . [But] obviously, we're not going to test and deploy it if it's a violation of the [U.S.-Soviet ABM] treaty.

News conference,
Louisville, Ky., Sept. 8/
The New York Times, 9-9:8.

3

We must have—and in a Dukakis Administration we will have—strategic forces that are strong and modern and versatile. Strategic forces that will convince any potential adversary that they have nothing to gain and everything to lose by attacking the United States and our allies and friends. And we must do whatever is necessary through modernization, and, if possible, through arms control, to insure an effective, credible deterrent. What does that mean in specifics? It means I support, and I intend to go forward as planned, with the *Trident 2* sea-based missile to offset the Soviet Union's highly accurate missiles, and with the *Stealth* bomber and the advanced cruise missile to counter improvements in Soviet air defense . . . And what about

"Star Wars" [the proposed U.S. space defense system]? My friends, if we're going to keep America strong; if we're going to increase, rather than undermine, the stability of the nuclear balance; if we're going to make our defense dollars count, we've got to stop pouring billions and billions into this program and do some hard thinking about what we're trying to achieve.

At Georgetown University, Sept. 14/
The New York Times, 9-15:14.

4

[Republican Presidential nominee] George Bush and his running mate [Dan Quayle] have opposed virtually every single effort aimed at Pentagon reform. They opposed the creation of an independent Inspector General to investigate defense fraud. They opposed establishing an organization in the Pentagon to test weapons before we buy them. They opposed putting restrictions on the revolving door between the Pentagon and the defense industry. And they opposed giving our field commanders more authority over what types of weapons we buy. In fact, there is what you might call a new Republican triad: waste, duplication and fraud.

At Georgetown University, Sept. 14/
The New York Times, 9-15:14.

5

We are not going to spend the billions and trillions that [Republican Presidential nominee George] Bush wants to spend on "Star Wars" [the proposed U.S. space defense system]. We're not going to spend billions on MX's [missiles] on railroad cars, which is a weapons system we don't need, can't afford and won't help our defense posture at all. We're not going to spend hundreds of millions on the space plane from Washington to Tokyo. Those are decisions that the Chief Executive has to make. Yes, we're going to have a strong and credible and effective nuclear deterrent. We're going to go forward with the *Stealth* [bomber], the D-5 and the advanced cruise missile, and good conventional forces. But the next President of the United States will have to make some tough and difficult decisions.

At Presidential debate, Los Angeles,
Oct. 13/The New York Times, 10-15:11.

(MICHAEL S. DUKAKIS)

1

We have 13,000 strategic nuclear warheads on land, on air and in the sea. That's an incredibly powerful nuclear deterrent. I don't rule out modernization . . . but there are limits to what we can spend . . . How can we build a strong America militarily that's teeter-tottering on a mountain of debt?

At Presidential debate,
Los Angeles, Oct. 13/
USA Today, 10-14:(A)6.

2

I would cut "Star Wars" [the proposed U.S. space defense system] back to where it was in 1983. I would not spend money on MX missiles on railroad cars. I don't think the *Midgetman* missile really adds much to our national security. I think it's highly questionable building two more supercarrier task forces at a cost of $18-billion apiece, with $1-billion a year in operating expenses, given our deficit.

Interview/
Reader's Digest, October:65.

3

You've got to pick a Secretary of Defense who can manage the Pentagon. If you have somebody who thinks throwing money at problems gives you national security—and that's what we've had for seven years—you're going to have a disaster. [Also,] you've got to be able to make some tough choices. There's no way that we can build all of these weapons systems that are currently on the shelf with the amount of money that the President and the Congress agreed they are going to spend. No matter who the next President is, in real terms the defense budget is not going to increase. We cannot buy every weapons system in the defense candy store.

Interview/
Reader's Digest, October:71.

4

[On arms-control negotiations with the Soviet Union]: I think we have an extraordinary oppor-tunity here: step by step, carefully, always with verification and inspection, now, to build on the work that's been done for strategic-arms reduction, for a comprehensive [nuclear] test-ban treaty—which I strongly favor, the [Reagan] Administration does not. This [Reagan Administration] is the first Administration since Dwight Eisenhower not to favor comprehensive test-ban treaty, and for negotiations leading to reductions in conventional forces in Europe, with deeper cuts on the Soviet side.

Interview/USA Today, 11-1:(A)6.

John R. Galvin
General, United States Army;
Supreme Allied
Commander/Europe

5

[Saying it takes more than a "bean count" of each side's weapons to determine the balance of power]: From the bean count it has to go to capabilities: the capabilities to get a warning, to mobilize, to deploy, to reinforce, to sustain, to maneuver, firepower . . . There's some other countries in the world besides NATO. What are they going to do? And there's geography, indus-trial capabilities of nations.

To reporters, Washington, Jan. 22/
The Washington Post, 1-23:(A)21.

Makhmut A. Gareyev
Deputy Chief, Soviet
Armed Forces General Staff

6

[Saying the Soviet Union will be more open about its military forces]: Broader *glasnost* [openness] makes it possible to better acquaint the public with the activities of the armed forces and to establish a constructive dialogue between the Soviet Union and the United States and between the Warsaw Treaty Organization and NATO at various levels, including at top mili-tary level . . . As confidence-building measures [with NATO] grow wider in scope, further declassification of the activities of various [Soviet] military departments will be considered, and more information on the Soviet armed forces

(MAKHMUT A. GAREYEV)

will be provided. Information on the quantitative and qualitative composition of the Soviet strategic nuclear forces has been made public; all nuclear tests are promptly reported; more and more often we exchange military delegations and invite foreign military observers to exercises, and Western and Soviet newsmen to garrisons and special facilities of the Soviet armed forces.

Interview/Los Angeles Times, 9-26:(I)1,8.

Mikhail S. Gorbachev
General Secretary, Communist
Party of the Soviet Union

1

I think that he who pushes for an arms race in space is committing a crime against the people—his own people, and others. Such an approach, such an idea, is a road to destabilization, to unpredictability on matters of security. This must be condemned, the initiator of such an approach must be pilloried.

Interview/Newsweek, 5-30:32.

2

I cannot agree with those who think that the drive for a nuclear-free world is hopeless. I have argued more than once with representatives of the West over their case that without nuclear weapons we would never have survived for 40 years without another world war. This is just a conjecture . . . The so-called "balance of fear" . . . has given us nothing but unheard-of militarization of foreign policies, economies and even intellectual life . . . I am convinced that strategic military parity can be maintained at a low level and without nuclear weapons.

Interview/Newsweek, 5-30:32.

Albert Gore, Jr.
United States Senator,
D-Tennessee;
Candidate for the 1988
Democratic Presidential
nomination

3

As the absolute numbers of weapons on both sides gets lower, the interrelationship between

the arsenals becomes more important. What I mean when I refer to the pattern of reductions is actually very simple. I want to change the relationship between the arsenals as they are reduced in order to make it absolutely impossible for either side to gain any sort of advantage, even a hypothetical advantage, even a prospective advantage, from a first strike. The warhead-to-target ratio is one of the key measures in determining whether or not either superpower might prospectively gain a first-strike advantage. Even more specifically, that ratio should be lower than two accurate warheads for each strategically important target on the other side.

Interview/
The New York Times, 4-11:12.

4

The uncertainty [about U.S. use of nuclear weapons] in the minds of Soviet leaders is itself a strategic asset. We have always regarded it as such, NATO has always regarded it as such, and that is why we have never said to the Soviet Union, "We will launch a first strike under these circumstances or under those circumstances."

News conference/
The Christian Science Monitor,
4-19:3.

Alfred M. Gray
General, and Commandant,
United States Marine Corps

5

I don't think [Marine Corps] boot camp is tough enough; I think we pamper them too much. [And] careerism is rampant throughout the Corps; I'm going to stamp it out.

Speech, Cherry Point (N.C.)
Marine Corps Air Station/
Newsweek, 1-11:17.

6

[Saying spending for the armed forces should not be cut]: We must continue to impress upon Congress that a professional force costs money, and request their continued support to keep our

(ALFRED M. GRAY)

quality force . . . We must avoid repeating the costly mistake of the 1970s, when compensation and other military-personnel programs were squeezed to the point that the more talented, ambitious and hard-working youth of the country choose alternatives to military service.

The New York Times, 11-30:(A)15.

Alexander M. Haig, Jr.
Candidate for the 1988
Republican Presidential
nomination; Former
Secretary of State of
the United States

1

Right now, everyone is focusing on arms control. But the real issue of arms control with the U.S.S.R. is not how many missiles we destroy or how many violations we can detect, but how many wars we can prevent. And deterrence of war goes far beyond the counting of arsenals. It concerns international behavior.

Campaign speech/
The New York Times, 1-15:8.

2

With all of the heinous character of the nuclear weapon, it cannot be disinvented. And if one looks back to the troubled conclusion of World War II, it has been that nuclear weapon that has preserved the peace over those almost 50 years.

Interview, McLean, Va./
U.S. News & World Report, 2-8:12.

Gary Hart
Candidate for the 1988
Democratic Presidential
nomination; Former
United States Senator,
D-Colorado

3

. . . since [the U.S. war with] Vietnam, my party, the Democrats, have come close to being irrelevant on the issue of defense and national security. Most of us have opposed growth in nuclear weapons. We've opposed just about every use of military force, and—except for conservative Democrats—we've generally opposed increases in the Pentagon's budget and its spending. But we have also lost four out of the last five national elections, in part, at least, because a lot of voters didn't think we had anything positive to say about the defense of this country, and I think they were basically right. On the other hand, part of the mess that I think this country's in today, at home and abroad, is caused by kind of a traditional mindless mentality that says give the military everything it wants and use it anytime you can't think of anything else to do.

Campaign speech/
The New York Times, 1-26:13.

Jesse Helms
United States Senator,
R-North Carolina

4

[Criticizing the proposed U.S.-Soviet INF treaty which would need the signature of Soviet leader Mikhail Gorbachev as well as that of U.S. President Reagan]: [Gorbachev] is the boss of the Communist Party, nothing more, nothing less. Accepting his signature would be comparable to allowing the chairman of the [U.S.] Republican National Committee to sign a treaty on behalf of the United States and thereby have him pretend to bind the country and future Administrations.

Before the Senate,
Washington, May 18/
The New York Times, 5-19:8.

Jeanne Holm
Major General, United States
Air Force (Ret.);
Former Director, Women
in the Air Force

5

I do not view the issue of women in the military as an equal-opportunity issue, but as an issue of manpower and necessity, providing quality people for the forces. That's always got to

79

(JEANNE HOLM)

be the driving consideration . . . They're serving as missile-launch officers now. They could wipe out an enemy city. That's pretty combative. It's the hand-to-hand combat that is the muddiest, the nitty-grittiest problem. Women are already flying tanker aircraft that refuel fighters on the way to combat missions. We have women serving all over the world in jobs that, if war were to break out, they would be coming home in body bags. So it's really kind of academic as to whether you call them combatants or not . . . I also believe that if we have the occasion to reconsider the draft in the future, it will have to include women.

Interview/USA Today, 4-28:(A)9.

Fred C. Ikle
*Under Secretary of Defense
of the United States*

1

In the 1970s, it was inconceivable that the country would make a major effort to build ballistic-missile defenses. Now it is inconceivable that we could not at least continue research and development of anti-ballistic missile defenses. People no longer use the language of "mutual assured destruction."

*Interview, Washington, Jan. 18/
The New York Times, 1-20:10.*

Jesse L. Jackson
*Civil-rights leader;
Candidate for the 1988
Democratic Presidential
nomination*

2

[President] Reagan put out the deal that we are weak militarily. That's not true. We're the strongest military in the world. Our boys got killed in Lebanon. We have strong military, weak policy. Our boys are vulnerable in the Persian Gulf, going up and down that river every day being looked at down the gun-barrel of American-made guns, sold to the Ayatollah [Khomeini of Iran] illegally. We've got a strong military and a weak Commander-in-Chief. We can cut *Midgetman* missiles, $45-billion; we don't need it and can't afford it. We got 13 aircraft carriers. Russia's got one. Reagan wants to make two more. It will cost $40-billion. You could wipe out poverty for every woman, infant and child in America for $36-billion. I choose to wipe out poverty for every woman, infant and child rather than two [military] systems we do not need.

*Campaign speech/
The New York Times, 1-19:12.*

3

We have guided missiles, but unguided minds . . . Our leadership has to come from the power of our ideas and the force of our example, not from the size of our arsenal.

*The Christian Science Monitor,
4-1:6.*

4

I am opposed to first use of nuclear weapons . . . It doesn't make any sense to defend Europe with a pledge to blow up the world. As [former Secretary of State] Henry Kissinger said, "Mutual suicide cannot be made into a rational option."

*Interview/
Los Angeles Times, 5-27:(I)1.*

Jesse L. Jackson
*Civil-rights leader;
Former candidate for the
1988 Democratic
Presidential nomination*

5

We are spending over $150-billion a year defending Europe and Japan 43 years after the war is over. We have more troops today in Europe than we had seven years ago. Yet the threat of war is ever more remote. Germany and Japan are now creditor nations; we are a debtor nation. Let them share more of the burden of their own defense.

*At Democratic National Convention,
Atlanta, July 19/
The New York Times, 7-20:12.*

Lawrence J. Korb
*Former Assistant Secretary
for Manpower and Logistics,
Department of Defense
of the United States*

1

[Saying the new Bush Administration's Secretary of Defense will have a good opportunity for reforming Pentagon operations]: It's an unprecedented opportunity to take control of policy, process and the budget, and get them together. The new Secretary will have a tremendous opportunity, because he won't run into the usual roadblocks of Congress and the Chiefs [of Staff] which faced other Secretaries, [since everyone today seems to be of a mind to reform the Defense Department]. You really have to rethink the whole policy and strategy: Who is the enemy? What kind of weapons should you build? You don't want to build the same kind of strategic weapons we are building today if you're going to have a START [treaty].

*The Washington Post,
11-12:(A)12.*

Anatoly Kuntsevich
*Lieutenant General, Soviet
Ministry of Defense;
Deputy Chief, Soviet
Army Chemical Corps*

2

[On chemical weapons]: These are invisible weapons. A human being does not know where the danger lies. If I see a bomb dropping, or a tank, I can protect myself. But this is a very treacherous weapon—a kind of aerosol that moves noiselessly, without warning, and hurts everyone in its way. [Chemical warfare] is a very peculiar way of killing people.

*Interview, Moscow/
The Christian Science Monitor,
12-14:(B)1.*

Patrick J. Leahy
*United States Senator,
D-Vermont*

3

Scandals, cost overruns, mismanagement on a vast scale, inefficiency and incompetence have justifiably and understandably shaken public support for defense spending. Something must be done to get the Pentagon's house in order.

*Press briefing,
Washington, Dec. 19/
Los Angeles Times, 12-20:(I)4.*

Alexei D. Lizichev
*General, Soviet armed forces;
Member, Soviet Communist
Party Central Committee*

4

People who propose unilateral [Soviet] disarmament can only be either naive or who are singing a foreign line. [The Soviet Union must have sufficient defense so] if some madman wants to attack us, he receives a worthy answer.

*Interview, June 28/
The Christian Science Monitor,
6-30:14.*

Edward Luttwak
*Authority on war and
military affairs,
Center for Strategic
and International Studies,
Georgetown University*

5

The permanent problem for military organizations is that they're supposed to be ready for war in peacetime. That's tremendously difficult. It's like trying to operate a whole hospital and have it ready to run when it actually has no patients. It has doctors, nurses, lab technicians, cleaners, whatever, everybody on duty day after day, year after year, and no patients; and then they're supposed to be ready when the patients start flooding in. Of course, if that happens, there are liable to be problems. A thousand things could have gone wrong unobserved.

*Interview/American Heritage,
July-Aug:80.*

Michael A. Mahoney
*Major, United States Marine
Corps*

6

Unconditional obedience and loyalty [of military personnel] is dangerous because under-

(MICHAEL A. MAHONEY)

standing of the ends and means and their proper relationship, which is essential to moral conduct, is either not present or is somehow suspended . . . I may, for instance, act for the welfare of my service; but if I lie, cheat or steal in order to accomplish this, then my action is not praiseworthy. [An officer] must keep in mind that he is first of all a servant of the Constitution and the American people. [But an implicit condition in obeying orders is that] your superiors are acting as responsible, moral executives of the United States . . . We should be careful not to delude ourselves. We should not believe that we can fall short in our moral obligations without compromising our integrity.

At conference on loyalty and obedience,
National Defense University/
The New York Times, 1-19:10.

George J. Mitchell
United States Senator,
D-Maine

1

[Criticizing the War Powers Act]: It was . . . an attempt to reassert Congress's authority to decide when the United States would become involved with war. But it has not worked . . . [It] severely undercuts the President by encouraging our enemies to simply wait for U.S. law to remove the threat of further American military action. [It] could have debilitating effects on our military policy by prompting Presidents to think in terms of short-term military action regardless of purpose, and by encouraging political actions that may not be strategically sound.

The Christian Science Monitor,
5-20:3.

Francois Mitterrand
President of France

2

As for disarmament, it complements deterrence. Deterrents are made to prevent war; the object of disarmament is to reduce the risks of war. It all converges.

Interview/
U.S. News & World Report, 3-7:43.

3

. . . though security is based on deterrence, that does not mean either constant over-bidding or redundancy, and a reduction of the arms race is the logical complement of this strategy.

Interview/Time, 5-16:50.

Richard M. Nixon
Former President of the
United States

4

The Soviet [military] buildup continues, slowly but inexorably. We [the U.S.] are cutting down our defense budget this year. We're cutting back on "Star Wars" [the proposed space defense system]. But the Soviets continue to build up. The military-industrial complex here is very vulnerable to the criticism it gets in the media among political leaders. It doesn't have a life of its own.

Interview/USA Today, 4-5:(A)11.

Sam Nunn
United States Senator,
D-Georgia

5

[Criticizing the War Powers Resolution]: Time deadlines for completing military action are precisely the wrong way to commit American forces. [The automatic-withdrawal provision] gives foreign governments and terrorist groups a level for influencing U.S. policy debate.

The New York Times, 5-20:3.

Robert Orton
Colonel, United States Army;
Chief, Army's chemical-
weapons modernization program

6

[On critics of chemical warfare]: People say that coughing your lungs out in 3 minutes because of a nerve agent is an immoral way of dying, while bleeding to death in 12 because your leg has been shot off is somehow better. Those arguments leave me cold.

The Christian Science Monitor,
12-13:(B)2.

David Packard
Former Under Secretary of
Defense of the United States

1

[Criticizing the Pentagon's weapons-procurement system]: One could do just as good a job in awarding the major contracts by putting the names of qualified bidders on the wall and throwing darts. This would also save a lot of time and money . . . [The contracting process involves] literally tons of paper work, describing how the bidder would meet a bunch of Mickey Mouse requirements that have absolutely nothing to do with doing the job right.

Before Senate Armed Services
Committee, Washington, July 27/
Los Angeles Times, 7-28:(I)1.

Richard N. Perle
Former Assistant Secretary
for International Security
Policy, Department of
Defense of the United States

2

Agreement for agreement's sake has become the principal motive behind [current U.S.-Soviet] arms-control negotiations.

USA Today, 6-2:(A) 8.

Ronald Reagan
President of the United States

3

[On the proposed space defense system]: Today, both America and the Soviet Union have an opportunity to develop a defensive shield against ballistic missiles, a defensive shield that will threaten no one. For the sake of a safer peace, I am committed to pursuing the possibility that technology offers.

Broadcast address to Soviet people,
Jan. 1/The Washington Post, 1-2:(A)16.

4

[On his proposed space defense system]: [If the Soviets] had now an almost foolproof defense against our nuclear missiles at the same time they've got their nuclear missiles, they would

have the ability for a first strike. They could hit us and, when we fired back, we couldn't hit them. They see the same thing for us. If we get SDI . . . and we still have these missiles that we have, they see a first-strike capability. Now, the difference is—and it's almost impossible to convince them—we don't have any intention of a first strike . . . There's no one in America [who] wants to go to war with them.

Interview, Washington, Feb. 25/
The Washington Post, 2-26:(A)18.

5

If our [NATO's] common approach to the East over the years has given coherence to our message of peace and world freedom, it has been our unwavering commitment to defend ourselves that has given it credibility.

Speech, Washington, March 1/
The New York Times, 3-2:8.

6

[On the proposed U.S. space defense system]: SDI in my mind—maybe some of my people wouldn't agree with me—but the whole thing was my idea, to see if there could not be developed a defensive weapon that would make it virtually impossible for nuclear missiles to get through to their targets in another country. And from the very beginning, I have said that if and when such a system can be developed, I would support the idea of making it available world-wide, because since we all know how to make nuclear missiles, sometime there could be a madman come along, as a Hitler came along, who could then make those missiles.

News conference, Moscow, June 1/
The New York Times, 6-2:6.

7

. . . nations do not distrust each other because they are armed; they are armed because they distrust each other.

News conference, Moscow, June 1/
The Washington Post, 6-2:(A)26.

8

The history of our time will undoubtedly include a footnote about how, during this decade

(RONALD REAGAN)

and the last, the voices of retreat and hopelessness reached a crescendo in the West, insisting the only way to peace was unilateral disarmament, proposing nuclear freezes, opposing deployment of counter-balancing weapons such as intermediate-range missiles or the more recent concept of strategic defense systems... And when the Soviets left the negotiating in Geneva for 15 months, [the voices] proclaimed disaster. And yet, it was our double-zero option, much maligned when first proposed, that provided the basis for the INF treaty, the first treaty ever that did not just control offensive weapons, but reduced them... And that's why although history will duly note that we, too, heard voices of denial and doubt, it is those who spoke with hope and strength who will be best remembered.

Before Royal Institute of
International Affairs,
London, June 3/
The Washington Post, 6-4:(A)18.

1

[On revelations of fraud in Defense Department procurement]: We are accountable [to the public, but] on the other hand, I think there's some things that you can see in something as complex as that whole process and the number of corporations and all. Corporate heads probably are surprised at what they're learning, also... You can't be down there watching several million people in the total of all of the companies and of the Defense Department every day and what they're doing or what phone calls they're making. And I'm quite sure that no one would think that we should be tapping all of those phones and listening in on conversations of everybody just on the suspicion that someone might be out of line.

News conference,
Toronto, June 21/
USA Today, 6-22:(A)9.

2

Even as diplomatic and technological progress holds out the hope of at last diminishing the awful cloud of nuclear terror we have lived under in the post-war era, even at this moment another ominous terror is loose once again in the world ... Poison gas. Chemical warfare. Mr. Secretary General, distinguished delegates, the terror of it. The horror of it. We condemn it. The use of chemical weapons in the Iran-Iraq war—beyond its tragic human toll—jeopardizes the moral and legal strictures that have held those weapons in check since World War I. Let this tragedy spark reaffirmation of the Geneva protocol outlawing the use of chemical weapons.

At United Nations,
New York, Sept. 26/
The New York Times, 9-27:6.

3

The liberals would break faith with anti-Communist freedom fighters. They oppose a strategic defense against nuclear missiles. They would cancel essential defense systems and receive nothing in return. They're against the B-1 bomber, and they would wipe out two carrier battle groups... Let's remember, the Soviets did business [with the U.S. on arms limitation] because they saw that we meant business.

Speech, Detroit, Oct. 7/
The Washington Post, 10-8:(A)13.

Jeremy Rifkin
President, Foundation on
Economic Trends

4

[On biological weapons]: Microbes are the foot soldiers of the 21st century... We're talking about the possibility of powerful new genetic weapons that could rival nuclear weapons in the future. People think AIDS [disease] is dangerous? Imagine what could happen if military establishments set out to deliberately create a virus that has no cure.

The Christian Science Monitor, 12-15:(B)4.

William P. Rogers
Former Secretary of State
of the United States

5

[On the U.S.-Soviet INF treaty]: I can't think of a more serious setback to American foreign

(WILLIAM P. ROGERS)

policy and to American interests throughout the world than to have this treaty fail—either fail by vote or die in the crib from being smothered because it never gets to a vote. I think it would be a calamity to have that happen . . . To my mind, the most significant feature of the treaty may be the provision for on-site inspection. I believe that a precedent has been established that holds out great promise for mankind.

Before Senate Foreign Relations
Committee, Washington, Jan. 27/
The New York Times, 1-28:6.

William V. Roth, Jr.
United States Senator,
R-Delaware

1

[Calling for closing no-longer-needed military bases in the U.S.]: We no longer need to guard the Pony Express routes to the Wild West. We no longer need to maintain moated forts to guard against assault by British sailing ships. We all know why these unnecessary bases have been kept open. They have been maintained for selfish political reasons in order to maintain a flow of defense dollars into our states. But the budgetary good times are gone. We simply cannot justify throwing money away.

Los Angeles Times, 5-22:(I)2.

Edward L. Rowny
Special Adviser to President
of the United States Ronald
Reagan for Arms Control

2

[On the pending U.S.-Soviet INF treaty]: We worked out the verification [of compliance] issues pretty well, and the [U.S.] Senate needs to satisfy itself that this treaty is verifiable. Once they look at it, they'll find out that it is. It's not perfect. But, on balance, it's the first treaty that eliminates an entire class of weapons. It's the first treaty that has on-site inspection. It will have a couple of hundred Soviets living in Magna, Utah, for the next 13 years, and a couple of

hundred of our people are going to live in Votkinsk. It's revolutionary.

Interview/
USA Today, 5-25:(A)11.

Andrei D. Sakharov
Dissident Soviet physicist

3

[On the proposed U.S. space defense system]: There's a lack of understanding about what this system is good for, and about which system would be created by one country or the other country. This could push both sides [the U.S. and the Soviet Union] into dangerous action. Underestimation and overestimation of SDI—both directions are dangerous.

News conference, Boston, Nov. 7/
USA Today, 11-8:(A)8.

4

We all now know that a large-scale thermonuclear war is not simply a calamity for humankind—it would be a total disaster for humankind. And we also know that if we drop the scale to an intermediary-scale war, or a local thermonuclear war, that kind of event would very quickly escalate into a large-scale nuclear war . . . As a counterweight to conventional arms, nuclear weapons do not provide a balance or alternative. Moreover, nuclear weapons undercut security, because they throw out of balance the whole system of military balances.

Accepting Albert Einstein Peace
Prize Award, Nov. 15/
The Washington Post, 11-23:(A)20.

James R. Sasser
United States Senator,
D-Tennessee

5

[On Soviet leader Mikhail Gorbachev's pledge to cut Soviet weapons and troops in Eastern Europe and at home]: With this initiative on the part of Gorbachev, it's going to make it almost impossible for those [in the U.S.] who argue for an increase in defense spending. It's going to

(JAMES R. SASSER)

make it very difficult even for those who want to hold the line at the present level.

Dec. 8/
The New York Times, 12-9:(A)7.

James R. Schlesinger
Former Secretary of Defense
of the United States

1

[On the verification process agreed upon between the U.S. and the Soviet Union for the INF treaty]: I think, basically, this is a satisfactory verification regime, given the weakness of Soviet incentives to cheat and our desire not to allow the Soviets to intrude into the United States. What I am concerned about is that this verification regime be regarded as a talisman that makes us complacent about the outcome. The real problem lies in the START area. In the START area we are going to have to have much greater rights of intrusion in order to deal with presumed violations.

Before Senate Foreign Relations
Committee, Washington, Feb. 2/
Los Angeles Times, 2-3:(I)6.

2

It has frequently been observed both by those who are cautiously sympathetic to arms control and those who are hostile to arms control that the greatest danger in an arms-control agreement, even one as attractive as the [new U.S.-Soviet] INF agreement, is that it will create euphoria and cause us to let down our guard. The fear is that a well-founded agreement will sweep us along in a torrent of good feeling and cause us to embrace other agreements that are ill-advised. Regrettably, I must conclude on this somber note: Such apprehension is amply justified. As we proceed with further arms-control discussions, we must be cold-eyed if not cold-blooded, regarding the terms of any prospective agreement.

Before Senate Armed Services
Committee, Washington/
The Wall Street Journal, 2-5:14.

3

The biggest problem that we've had in recent years has been a failure of confidence amongst Congress, the Administration, the Pentagon and the defense industry. Unless we are able to restore some degree of mutual trust, we are not going to be able to get out of the defense budget what we should.

Panel discussion/
The Washington Post, 11-21:(A)11.

Nikolai V. Shishlin
Spokesman, Central
Committee, Communist
Party of the Soviet Union

4

I don't think that constant adherence to . . . dealing from military strength furthers the reduction of military budgets . . . I cannot say the Soviet military doctrine is perfect at this point, but there is no doubt it is defensive in nature.

Interview, Moscow/
Newsweek, 11-28:56.

George P. Shultz
Secretary of State of the
United States

5

The [U.S.-Soviet] INF treaty strengthens U.S. and allied security. It enhances international stability. It may be opening a new chapter in arms control—the beginning of reductions. It reduces nuclear weapons, rather than setting guidelines for their future growth. It achieves U.S.-Soviet equality by eliminating substantially more Soviet weapons than American ones.

Before Senate Foreign Relations
Committee, Washington, Jan. 25/
The Washington Post, 1-26:(A)4.

6

[On the pending U.S.-Soviet INF treaty]: There is no such thing as absolute, 100 per cent verification [that the treaty will be complied with by the Soviets]. But it is our judgment that this treaty, through its successive layers of proce-

(GEORGE P. SHULTZ)

dures, contains the measures needed for effective verification ... The bottom line is that the verification provisions of this treaty get the job done.

Before Senate Foreign Relations
Committee, Washington, May 16/
The Washington Post, 5-17:(A)19.

1

It is ironic that just as the major powers are making progress in getting their arms competition under some control, the developing world is increasingly burdened by [the] flow of advanced weaponry. The international community as a whole must find ways to stanch this arms traffic.

At banquet in his honor,
Peking, July 14/
The Washington Post, 7-15:(A)15.

Nicholas Sims
Lecturer in international
relations, London School
of Economics (England)

2

At the simplest level, a lot of people are very frightened at being attacked with chemical weapons. The simplest way to get rid of that fear is to get rid of the enemy's [chemical] weapons. And you're not going to get that without getting rid of your own. Hence, multilateral disarmament. It seems to me we're a lot closer to disarmament in this area than in any other.

The Christian Science Monitor,
12-16:(B)2.

Yevgeny Sverdlov
Director, Laboratory of
Nucleic Acids Biotechnology,
Shemyakin Institute
of Bio-organic Chemistry
(U.S.S.R.)

3

[On biological weapons]: We're living through the time of a certain revolution in biotechnology

in general. And any revolution has two sets of consequences. One is usually used to raise up the welfare of the people. The other can be used for annihilation.

The Christian Science Monitor,
12-15:(B)2.

Steven D. Symms
United States Senator,
R-Idaho

4

[Saying the U.S. should require the Soviet Union to comply with past arms treaties before signing a new missile-reduction agreement with them].: What is wrong with asking the Soviet Union, if they are to become our new partners in peace, to get in compliance with other treaties? If we don't have the political will to ask them to get in line, what is the point of this new verification system so highly touted in this treaty?

Before the Senate, Washington/
The New York Times, 5-21:3.

William H. Taft IV
Deputy Secretary of Defense
of the United States

5

The European countries, Japan as well, can afford to invest more in their defense programs than they are doing today. They should do this; the requirement is there, the ability to pay is there ... The way we have addressed this is not as an opportunity for the United States to do less than it is doing. Our view is, and we have been emphatic about this throughout the discussion, is that the United States needs to do at least as much as it is doing, that it can afford to do what it is doing.

News conference,
Washington, Dec. 28/
The Washington Post, 12-29:(A)11.

John G. Tower
Secretary of Defense-designate
of the United States

6

The bottom line is that we must provide at least as much if not more defense for less money. And

(JOHN G. TOWER)

to meet that challenge we must do several things: We must rationalize our force structure; we must refine and reform our management and procurement procedures; we must have biennial budgeting. All of this is going to require very close cooperation with the Congress.

News conference,
Washington, Dec. 16/
The New York Times, 12-17:8.

1

Fifty per cent of our [defense] budget goes for people. Hopefully, by going to less manpower-intensive systems we can make some economies ... We're going to have to face some tough choices. A smart hawk recognizes that he must operate within the parameters of restraint sometimes. The next war is going to be a come-as-you-are party. You go with what you've got.

Broadcast interview/
"Face the Nation," CBS-TV,
12-25.

Cyrus R. Vance
Former Secretary of State
of the United States

2

[On the U.S.-Soviet INF treaty]: The political effects within the [Atlantic] Alliance of our being unable to go forward at this time [with the treaty] would be absolutely disastrous. Having watched and seen that we were unable to be constant enough to continue with SALT II, and then to see, after 10 years of negotiations, that the United States is unprepared at the last moment to go forward, would have dire political effects within the Alliance. In addition, I think it would have very grave consequences for any arms-control negotiations in the future, and to me that would a very sad, and indeed a very disastrous, consequence.

Before Senate Foreign Relations
Committee, Washington, Jan. 27/
The New York Times,
1-28:6.

Carl E. Vuono
General and Chief of Staff,
United States Army

3

[The Army War College] must clarify the strategic context in which the Army, its sister services and coalition partners must operate in peace, transition to war, conflict and conflict termination. Ethics and military history—cornerstones of the profession of arms—must be woven throughout the curriculum.

Before House Armed Services
Committee Panel on Military Education/
The New York Times, 8-13:5.

John W. Warner
United States Senator,
R-Virginia

4

The next President has got to break the mold and compel an examination of roles and missions [among the Army, Navy, Air Force and Marine Corps] and eliminate duplications. Today, each has its own helicopter training. Each has its own aviation branch. Each has this. Each has that. That's a luxury we're not able to afford any longer. We're basically locked into the same organizational structure that was laid down in 1947. The next President, or somebody, has to have the courage to break the mold.

The Washington Post,
4-25:(A)4.

James H. Webb, Jr.
Secretary of the Navy
of the United States

5

It would seem illogical to reduce the size of our sea services at the very moment in history when they should be assuming an even greater role ... unless our leaders wish to consciously acknowledge that we will be unable to meet the contingencies of the future.

Before National Press Club,
Washington, Jan. 13/
Los Angeles Times,
2-23:(I)17.

(JAMES H. WEBB, JR.)

1

This building [the Pentagon] needs to be led. It needs leadership; it needs vision. I'm saying that if I had a piece of advice to give to [Defense] Secretary Carlucci, it would be to spend a lot more time with the top leaders in this building. He's been spending a lot of time with the State Department and a lot of time on [Capitol] Hill. I think they [Pentagon officials] need to feel his vision and to understand what he believes in.

To reporters, announcing his
resignation as Navy Secretary,
Washington, Feb. 22/
The Washington Post, 2-23:(A)1.

2

Since I became Navy Secretary last year, I have stated . . . frequently my belief that the force levels of our sea services remain minimal and must not be reduced. Since recommendations to that effect were rejected by your Secretary of Defense, I am unable to support him personally or to defend this amended budget . . . I can only conclude that the decision to reduce the level of our fleet to a point that it may never reach the 600-ship goal was motivated by other than military and strategic reasoning.

Letter to President Reagan
announcing his decision to
resign as Navy Secretary, Feb. 22/
Los Angeles Times, 2-23:(I)1;
The New York Times, 2-23:1.

Albert Wohlstetter
Former director, Rand
Corporation study of
strategic military bases

3

It's very hard to protect our interests if we don't have a [military base] presence overseas . . . Some advances in modern technology enable you to reduce your reliance on overseas bases, but they sure don't replace them. [For military purposes], it's just a lot easier if you have some place where you're based nearby [to where your foreign interests lie].

Los Angeles Times, 5-15:(I)6,7.

The Economy • Labor

Abel Aganbegyan
Director, economic section,
Soviet Academy of Sciences;
Chief economic adviser
to Soviet leader
Mikhail S. Gorbachev

1

We are trying to combat egalitarianism. The principle is: Those who work harder should earn more. There are not many people who still support egalitarianism. The people content with egalitarianism were those who worked little and earned a lot. Now these people will have to work differently to justify their salary—but they constitute a minority. Salaries must increase because all prices will be changed, and we do not want price reform to diminish the quality of our people's lives. Price is the principal economic regulator, and *perestroika* [reform] aims to substitute economic fluctuations for administrative methods of price management. Prices should correspond to production costs; they should be related to efficiency and product quality; they should reflect supply and demand; they should respect world price levels.

Interview/
World Press Review, January:17.

John F. Akers
Chairman, International
Business Machines Corporation

2

After the war, our non-farm business productivity grew at an annual rate of nearly 3 per cent. After 1966, it dropped to 2 per cent, then to less than 1 per cent. And in the past six years it has recovered, but only to 1.5 per cent . . . Now the demographics have caught up to us. Increasing our goods and services by simply increasing our employment just isn't in the cards any more. If we want to raise the country's standard of living, from now on we have only one choice—beef up our productivity; cut the Federal deficit; get the savings rate up from less than 4 per cent—our lowest in 40 years—to a rate closer to Germany's 12 per cent or Japan's 17 per cent; and put more of those savings into new tools of production, not the 10 per cent of our GNP we've been investing, but more like that of Taiwan and Japan—16 per cent.

Washington, May 11/
The Washington Post, 5-20:(A)20.

John D. Ashcroft
Governor of Missouri (R)

3

Unless we have a competitive set of workers, and a work-place that is productive and efficient, we won't be able to provide people with jobs and the standard of living that we have become accustomed to. Also, transitions in the work-place are coming at an accelerated pace. It used to be that a person had a single career of doing a single job. Now it's estimated that people will go through six or seven career changes.

Interview/
USA Today, 8-10:(A)9.

Bruce Babbitt
Candidate for the 1988
Democratic Presidential
nomination; Former
Governor of Arizona (D)

4

[Republican Vice President George Bush said], "I'm running for President of the United States. I recognize that the [Federal budget] deficit is a problem and I'm going to deal with it by cutting taxes." Would you believe that? I tried that out on my fifth-grader. I said, "What happens when you have a deficit and you subtract from it?" And he said, "Well, that means you have a bigger deficit." I said, "Yeah, go tell that to George Bush." [Candidate Jack Kemp] says, "Elect me President and we'll solve our problems by going to the gold standard." The gold standard—and I think, "Yeah, the gold stan-

(BRUCE BABBITT)

dard gives the power to those that have the gold—that's the Soviet Union, South Africans, the American Dental Association." And then, I dare say, in all honesty, I listened to the Democrats [who are running for President]. I listened to Senator [Paul] Simon saying, "I'm going to deal with the deficit by putting up the biggest public-works program since the Egyptian pyramids." He says, "Well, I don't think we need taxes, but if we do, we'll tax the richest 1 per cent by raising the tax rates 1 per cent." I hear [candidate] Mike Dukakis said it—"We don't need to do any of the hard choices. I know that all over America people have money hidden under their mattresses, and I'm going to hire 30,000 revenue collectors to go get it" . . . Let's act like we're worthy of the trust of the American people. Let's simply acknowledge one simple fact—that deficit can destroy our future . . . And won't you all stand up and join me, not in endorsing Bruce Babbitt, but in acknowledging what we all know, and that is that we must cut expenditures and raise taxes.

Campaign speech/
The New York Times, 1-21:10.

1

[On how to cure the Federal budget deficit]: I don't think we need mortgage-interest deductions for ski condos and beach houses: savings, $1.3-billion. I don't think we need subsidies for corporate mega-farms: $1.2-billion. I don't think we need to pay for parking lots for big hotels: $300-million. I don't think we have to give the same tax-free Social Security benefit to the Vanderbilts as we give a widow in a cold-water flat: $4-billion.

Interview/
USA Today, 2-5:(A)8.

James A. Baker III
Secretary of the Treasury
of the United States

2

I've been up there [Capitol Hill] now for 7½ years, and it's been my experience that if you

raise taxes—and we have raised some taxes; even though on net we have cut taxes, we have raised some—the Congress uses that money on additional spending programs because, as you say, politicians like to get re-elected.

Broadcast interview/
"This Week With David Brinkley,"
ABC-TV, 5-15.

Ravi Batra
Economist

3

[The] rising wealth concentration [in the U.S.] in the end will bring about a depression. This is exactly what happened in the 1920s. If there is a depression in the near future . . . the blame will have to fall on the greed and conceit of the rich people in America.

Interview/
Los Angeles Times, 5-22:(IV)3.

Richard Belous
Labor economist,
The Conference Board

4

I think what workers are getting [in terms of paid vacation time] is fair, and, given the forces of international competition and the pressures that many employers are under, workers can't expect to be given too many more paid days of vacation and still have these organizations be internationally competitive. On average, American workers are getting around 11 paid days off, which has been a tremendous growth since the 1940s. The other thing which our economy is offering is many alternatives to the 9-to-5, 52-week-a-year job. Now we have many, many more options. We're seeing the growth of contingent workers—part-timers, temporaries, life-of-project people, consultants and even something called leased employees. There are many more people now who can call the tune as to when they work. If they want to go away and take a long vacation, they can do that.

Interview/
Los Angeles Times, 7-3:(IV)3.

Lloyd Bentsen
United States Senator,
D-Texas; 1988
Democratic Vice-Presidential
nominee

1

[Saying the American people do not like the burgeoning national debt]: I think they're ready for a change from a situation where you've seen this country more than double the national debt. They say that doesn't make any difference to people. It does make a difference. They want a change from a situation where we're, in effect, spending about 104 per cent and we're producing about 100 per cent. You can't keep doing that without ultimately lowering the standard of living of the people. And they understand that.

Interview/
U.S. News & World Report, 7-25:23.

2

[Criticizing Reagan Administration economic policies, even though they have resulted in lower interest rates, lower inflation and lower unemployment]: You know, if you let me write $200-billion worth of hot checks every year, I could give you an illusion of prosperity, too. This is an Administration that has more than doubled the national debt, and they've done that in less than eight years. They have taken this country from the Number 1 lender nation in the world to the Number 1 debtor nation in the world. And the interest on that debt next year, on this Reagan-Bush debt of the nation, is going to be $640 for every man, woman and child in America, because of this kind of a credit-card mentality.

At Vice-Presidential debate, Omaha, Neb.,
Oct. 5/The New York Times, 10-7:(A)13.

3

It will profit America little to gain the whole world of military superiority if we lost the soul of our economic capacity. It will profit us little to be military hawks if the [international] competition is between economic eagles and we are sitting ducks.

Before Los Angeles World Affairs
Council, Oct. 27/
Los Angeles Times, 10-28:(I)22.

Alan S. Blinder
Professor of economics,
Princeton University

4

Any [new] President who does something serious about the [Federal budget] deficit would automatically give the Fed more leeway to expand money and credit to keep the economy on a stable growth path. But if little is done about closing the deficit, the danger is that the Fed would feel compelled to tighten up after the [forthcoming] election to prevent the economy from growing at an excessive rate.

Los Angeles Times, 10-8:(I)16.

Michael J. Boskin
Professor of economics,
Stanford University

5

Sure, you could reduce the [Federal budget] deficit by simply raising taxes, but you would undermine the incentives to work and invest. Unless we get spending under control, you won't be able to ease monetary policy at all.

Los Angeles Times, 10-8:(I)16.

Bill Bradley
United States Senator,
D-New Jersey

6

[Criticizing President Reagan's recent proposal to reinstate a tax break for capital gains]: Ronald Reagan should not make a proposal such as this. A cut in the capital-gains rate will create tremendous pressure to raise tax rates, [meaning] loopholes for the rich and the special interests and high tax rates for all of us.

Jan. 25/
The Washington Post, 1-26:(A)11.

Roger E. Brinner
Senior economist,
Data Resources, Inc.

7

Monetary policy has succeeded since 1983 in braking the economy without breaking it. By

(ROGER E. BRINNER)

preventing booms, the Fed has also averted busts.

Los Angeles Times, 4-6:(IV)5.

William E. Brock
Former Secretary of Labor
of the United States

1

This nation is living beyond its [economic] means, borrowing long-term in order to satisfy short-term demands, and imposing as a consequence huge new obligations each week, each month, each year on our children. Like some confused Robin Hood, we rob from those who have no voice or vote to satisfy our every whim.

USA Today, 11-21:(A)10.

George Bush
Vice President of the United
States; Candidate for the
1988 Republican
Presidential nomination

2

Looking to Congress for leadership [in controlling spending] is simply hopeless . . . The Congress cannot control spending. The answer is to give the President what 43 Governors have—the line-item veto. And let the President control spending if Congress can't do it.

Campaigning, New Hampshire/
The New York Times, 2-3:11.

3

If we raise taxes to close the [Federal budget] deficit, Congress won't close the deficit. Congress will spend more money and make the deficit worse.

Campaign speech,
Chicago, March 10/
Los Angeles Times, 3-11:(I)1.

4

[Democratic Presidential candidate Michael] Dukakis [was] talking the other night about pink slips and plant closings. I want to talk about the fact that there is a greater percentage of the work force at work today than at any time in the history of this country.

The Washington Post, 4-30:(A)6.

5

[Comparing his experience in economics with that of Democratic Presidential candidate Michael Dukakis]: When I wanted to learn the ways of the world, I didn't go to the Kennedy School [where Dukakis taught], I came to Texas. I didn't go to a symposium on job creation, I started a business. I didn't study a monograph on the effects of economic growth, I met a payroll.

At Texas state Republican
convention, Houston, June 9/
Los Angeles Times, 6-10:(I)4.

6

For the past 7½ years, [the Democrats] have pounded away relentlessly at our proposals and our prospects, proclaiming, "Misery is just around the corner." In the last eight years, we've taken America from double-digit inflation to double-barreled recovery . . . Last year alone, black teen employment grew almost as much as it did in the entire five-year expansion from 1975 to 1980. More than half of the new jobs have gone to women, and the unemployment rate for women is now as low as it is for men—a milestone in our economic history.

At Republican Party fund-raising
luncheon, New York, June 30/
The New York Times, 7-1:8.

George Bush
Vice President of the United
States; 1988 Republican
Presidential nominee

7

Eight years ago this economy was flat on its back—intensive care. And we came in and gave it emergency treatment—got the temperature down by lowering regulation, and got the blood pressure down when we lowered taxes. And

(GEORGE BUSH)

pretty soon the patient was up, back on his feet and stronger than ever. And now who do we hear knocking on the door but the same doctors [the Democrats] who made him sick. And they're telling us to put them in charge of the case again. My friends, they're lucky we don't hit them with a malpractice suit! We've created 17 million new jobs the past five years, more than twice as many as Europe and Japan combined. And they're good jobs. The majority of them created in the past six years paid an average of more than $22,000 a year. And someone better take "a message to Michael" [Dukakis, the Democratic Presidential nominee]: Tell him that we have been creating good jobs at good wages. The fact is, they talk and we deliver. They promise and we perform.

Accepting the nomination,
at Republican National Convention,
New Orleans, Aug. 18/
The New York Times, 8-19:8.

1

My opponent [in the Presidential election, Democratic nominee Michael Dukakis] now says he'll raise [taxes] as a last resort, or a third resort. But when a politician talks like that, you know that's one resort he'll be checking into. My opponent won't rule out raising taxes. But I will [rule it out], and the Congress will push me to raise taxes, and I'll say no, and they'll push, and I'll say no, and they'll push again. And I'll say to them: Read my lips, no new taxes.

Accepting the nomination,
at Republican National Convention,
New Orleans, Aug. 18/
The New York Times, 8-19:8.

2

When economists and politicians and others speak of jobs only in terms of GNP and statistics, they miss the point. They miss the point that jobs are the best social program—because they supply more than income. They supply pride.

Campaign speech,
San Diego, Sept. 5/
The Washington Post, 9-6:(A)16.

3

[On how, if elected President, he would go about producing good jobs]: We go about it with the three lows—low tax, low regulation and low spending; and these are the lows that make the highs—high employment, high growth, high expectations. What will my opponent [Democratic Presidential nominee Michael Dukakis] do? Well, he comes from a wing of the [Democratic] Party—the left liberal wing—that has a historic tendency to impose high taxes. And they make the highs that end up making the lows—high taxes and high spending and high regulation and the resulting low growth, low job creation and low hopes.

Campaign speech,
Orange county, Calif., Sept. 14/
The Washington Post,
9-15:(A)11.

4

[On Democratic Presidential nominee Michael Dukakis]: Lately, as the campaign heats up, he's pursued a strategy of emphasizing differences between rich and poor, between one region of the country and another. I understand his motivation—he won't win unless he convinces the electorate that everything is bad in America—but I am dismayed by this "divide and conquer" strategy. You can't strengthen the weak by weakening the strong; you can't help small men by tearing down big men; you can't help the poor by destroying the rich; you can't lift the wage earner by pulling down the wage payer.

Before Bucks County Chamber of
Commerce, Bensalem, Pa.,
Sept. 19/The New York Times,
9-20:10.

5

We cut taxes, and revenues are up by 25 per cent in three years. So the problem is, it's not that the working man is being taxed too little, it is that we are continuing to spend too much [in government]. So my formula says grow with the rate of inflation, permit the President to set the priorities on where we do the spending, and remem-

(GEORGE BUSH)

ber, the Federal deficit has come down $70-billion in one year, 1987.

At Presidential debate,
Winston-Salem, N.C., Sept. 25/
The New York Times, 9-26:10.

1

Today, the economy is strong. A greater percentage of the work force is at work than ever before in history. I can't let [Democratic Presidential nominee Michael] Dukakis talk about plant closings. I should get the emphasis on plant *openings* and job creation and opportunity and education and hope. I think that will be the determining factor [in the forthcoming Presidential election], just as it has been in '84 and in other years. It is the economy that is fundamental.

Interview/
Reader's Digest, October:73.

2

[Saying the Reagan Administration should not be entirely blamed for the large Federal budget deficit]: The American people are pretty smart. They know who writes out the checks. And they know who appropriates the money. It is the United States Congress. And by 2 to 1, Congress is blamed for these deficits. And the answer is to discipline both the Executive Branch and the Congressional Branch by holding the line on taxes.

At Presidential debate,
Los Angeles, Oct. 13/
The New York Times, 10-15:10.

3

My opponent [Democratic Presidential nominee Michael Dukakis] talks about the squeeze on the middle class, but he called our 25 per cent tax cut—and here's the words—one of the worst bills Congress could have ever passed. And that tax cut is saving the average man $2,200 a year, and I'm not going to let him take that away from you, the taxpayers of this country . . . But the Gover-

nor of Massachusetts, his answer is to unleash a new conventional force army of IRS agents into the homes of the American people. It used to be a chicken in every pot; now it's an IRS agent in every kitchen. We don't want that; we don't need that. The IRS ought to work for us and not the other way around.

Campaign speech, Illinois/
The New York Times, 10-24:(A)10.

4

[On Democratic Presidential nominee Michael Dukakis]: [His economic policies] cannot be understood as a rational approach to economic growth and the creation of jobs. It is my belief, and I've said it before in a nice, kind and gentle way, that my opponent—and I'll phrase this properly—is far outside the mainstream of economic thinking and has broken with the American traditions of entrepreneurship and free enterprise.

Before Ohio Association of
Broadcasters, Columbus, Oct. 25/
The Washington Post, 10-26:(A)11.

Robert C. Byrd
United States Senator,
D-West Virginia

5

The dark side of the [President] Reagan years has only begun to loom. Instead of a balanced budget, he has presided over a doubling of the national debt in seven years. Our record budget and trade deficits—once just abstract numbers—have now forced the government to default on its most fundamental promises, like education and health. We have surrendered economic leadership in markets around the world.

Broadcast address to the nation,
Washington, Jan. 25/
The New York Times, 1-26:11.

Anthony Carnevale
Economist, American Society for
Training and Development

6

People with less schooling and lower levels of skills, if they haven't got enough seniority to be

(ANTHONY CARNEVALE)

protected, are going to be losers [in the future job market]. Many of them are likely to be minorities. And unless we get down to real labor shortages—that means 5 per cent unemployment or less—many of those people are going to be a lost generation.

Los Angeles Times, 9-6:(I)17.

John H. Chafee
United States Senator,
R-Rhode Island

1

[Supporting a bill that requires 60-day notice to employees if a major plant is to be shut down or workers laid off]: This will help soften the blow, to ease the transition to unemployment. It is fair and right for companies to inform workers when their jobs are to be eliminated. Because they will know of an important closing or layoff, workers will be able to plan, to utilize job training and placement services and to make financial arrangements. Corporate executives often get fabulous deals and benefits when they lose their jobs. Why shouldn't workers get fair treatment?

The New York Times, 8-3:9.

Lawton Chiles
United States Senator,
D-Florida

2

. . . the share of middle-wage jobs has decreased significantly during the last decade. Although there is a greater share of high-wage jobs now than eight years ago, the share of low-wage jobs has increased by twice as much. Since 1979, over 50 per cent of the net increase in employment was paying below poverty-level wages. The sad truth is that jobs paying below the poverty level are growing faster than any other kind. [If this trend exists in a time of economic growth,] I fear what a more uncertain economic future might bring the American worker.

Before the Senate, Washington,
Sept. 26/
Los Angeles Times, 9-27:(I)4.

Bill Clinton
Governor of Arkansas (D)

3

There's a lot of evidence you can sell people on tax increases if they think it's an investment. Interestingly enough, the thing people are least willing to do is to have their taxes raised to pay the debt off or have their taxes raised to expand a program they think is already failing, or a failing government.

Interview/Newsweek, 8-1:5.

Edward Cornish
President, World Future
Society, Washington

4

You see different figures on how often people will change careers [in the future]. I think the fact is that the technology is changing very rapidly and people have to try to keep up. The year 2000 is not very far away. I believe that the good jobs will increasingly involve high tech and a high degree of education and, in general, considerable advanced training. For those who can keep up, I think the rewards will be great.

Interview/
Los Angeles Times, 9-5:(V)2.

Mario M. Cuomo
Governor of New York (D)

5

President Reagan and Reaganomics were not absurd, conceptually. If you had spent a little less money for defense, but still increased defense spending; if you had spent less money in tax cuts but had a tax cut; if you said you don't have to balance the budget in three years, you have to balance the budget in 10 or 13 years—Reaganomics would have been fine.

Interview, Albany, N.Y./
The New York Times, 1-6:9.

Richard G. Darman
Director-designate,
Federal Office of
Management and Budget

6

I agree as to the importance of [Federal budget] deficit reduction. It represents an ob-

(RICHARD G. DARMAN)

vious and major challenge. And I agree, also, that in reducing the deficit, we must have an eye toward some of the underlying problems, so that the way in which we reduce the deficit is consistent with our longer-term interest in raising our savings rate, increasing investment, increasing productivity and assuring that our economic growth continues.

News conference,
Washington, Nov.21/
The New York Times, 11-22:(A)8.

Sandor Demjan
Chairman, Hungarian
Credit Bank

1

Marx would have been satisfied with modern-day Sweden; he would accept that as socialism. In fact, I think he would accept the United States . . . There must be a historic compromise between Communism and social democracy. In the field of the economy, it is we [Communists] who should make bigger concessions.

The Wall Street Journal, 7-18:18.

Geoffrey Dicks
Economist, London
Business School (England)

2

[On U.S. Vice President George Bush's victory in the recent Presidential election]: The first thing that all economic analysts are looking for from the new President is serious measures to tackle the [Federal] budget deficit. And unfortunately, as far as everyone can tell, that means putting up taxes in one form or another.

Nov. 9/
The Christian Science Monitor, 11-10:10.

Robert J. Dole
United States Senator,
R-Kansas; Candidate for the
1988 Republican
Presidential nomination

3

When I'm sworn in [as President] in January, 1989, I'm going to tell the Congress we're going

to spend this year what we spent in '88. No more, except maybe for low-income, vulnerable groups . . . What the American people want is a fair program with no exceptions, except for low-income Americans . . . Just a one-year freeze will save, over three years, about $150-billion. It would have a positive impact on the deficit. It would send a signal around the country and the world that the President and Congress want to deal with the deficit. One has to do more, but this is a start.

Campaigning in Iowa, January/
The New York Times, 1-15:9.

4

[On the Federal budget deficit]: That's the single biggest threat. Either we're going to have to sacrifice or we're going to have to continue to ask our children to sacrifice. And the only problem with that is: Many of them aren't even old enough to vote.

Interview/
The Christian Science Monitor,
1-15:15.

5

[Criticizing those who say tougher U.S. trade protection would cause other countries to retaliate]: Every time I hear the word retaliation I am reminded that Japan and South Korea and Taiwan already block Florida oranges and Georgia peaches and Alabama melons [from being sold in their countries] . . . Let's be realistic. We're talking about American jobs, not protectionism.

Campaign debate,
Atlanta, Feb. 28/
Los Angeles Times, 2-29:(I)19.

Barney Frank
United States Representative,
D-Massachusetts

6

In the cities . . . they have learned the economic progress in some cases, without govern-

(BARNEY FRANK)

ment concern, can be damaging to the most vulnerable members of our society, who can in a time of general prosperity find themselves priced out of housing, forced out of the jobs they used to work at; the jobs they used to work at in the inner-city areas may now be forced out. Some of our cities have started to zone ... because they are going to be losing the light manufacturing that provides jobs to working people and people of lower income to jobs in the service industry and in the financial industry, which will not hire them. We should be working to promote a thriving private sector, but the notion that the President [Reagan] has promulgated and that guides too many of our colleagues here, that that is enough to bring about the kind of society we want is wrong.

Before the House, Washington,
March 23/
The Washington Post, 3-25:(A)24.

Michael S. Dukakis
Governor of Massachusetts (D);
Candidate for the 1988
Democratic Presidential nomination

1

I'm running for President because, during the past seven years, I've seen too many people thrown out into the streets after decades on the job. I've listened to too many women whose husbands have had to leave town in order to find a good job; to too many people who work hard from dawn to midnight every day and still can't pay their bills. I've talked to too many students who have the skills and the energy and the ambition to go to college, but not the money. I've talked to too many local leaders who've seen their communities become ghost towns of boarded-up hopes and foreclosed dreams.

Campaign speech,
Milwaukee, March 31/
The Washington Post, 4-1:(A)8.

2

I've read too many stories about how America is supposed to be in decline, about how our children will have to settle for a second-rate economy and a second-class future. I don't buy that. We Americans aren't about to write off a whole generation of young people. We're not about to sit on the sidelines while our neighbors are thrown out of work and America's home towns are boarded up and left to die.

Campaign speech, Ohio, April 29/
The New York Times, 4-30:8.

3

You know, every tax is an income tax. This notion that a sales tax is a consumption tax, in my judgment, is nonsense. It all comes out of your pocket. The way you impose taxes will have to be on the basis of ability to pay. Those who have more ought to pay more.

USA Today, 5-3:(A)11.

4

What I think is needed is a credible [Federal budget] reduction plan agreed to by the Congress and the President that brings our deficit down steadily—whether it may be $20-billion, $25-billion, $30-billion a year. Every year [it should be] coming down steadily. I would think that over a four- or five-year period, barring some unforeseen circumstance, we ought to be able to bring that budget into balance. I hope without [a tax increase], but I'm not going to rule it out.

Interview, Tinton Falls, N.J./
The Washington Post, 6-1:(A)19.

5

Yes, I know that today there are more Americans working than at any time in our history. But average family income in America is right where it was 20 years ago, even though there's been a tremendous increase in the number of families where both parents work ... Some economists are saying that the young people of today will be the first generation of Americans since World War II to have a lower standard of living than their parents. Well, I don't buy that, and neither should you.

Campaign speech,
McCook, Ill., June 30/
The New York Times, 7-1:8.

Michael S. Dukakis
Governor of Massachusetts (D);
1988 Democratic
Presidential nominee

1

In nine years, I've balanced nine more budgets than this [Reagan] Administration has, and I've just balanced a tenth. And I've worked with the citizens of my state—worked hard to create hundreds of thousands of new jobs—and I mean good jobs, jobs you can raise a family on, jobs you can build a future on, jobs you can count on. And I'm very proud of our progress. But I'm even prouder of the way we've made that progress— by working together, by excluding no one and including everyone, business and labor, educators and community leaders and just plain citizens—sharing responsibility, exchanging ideas, building confidence about the future.

Accepting the nomination,
at Democratic National Convention,
Atlanta, July 21/
Los Angeles Times, 7-22:(I)6.

2

[On the recent increase in the prime rate]: Frankly, given the latest developments on the economic side of the country, I think we deserve an explanation from the Republicans at [their forthcoming national convention] as to just what they are doing to the American people, what they're doing to our economic future, and why the prime rate today has reached 10 per cent . . . When that prime rate goes up by a percentage point, the Federal budget deficit goes up by another $15-billion, the cost to young families buying and owning their homes goes up by hundreds of dollars, and the cost to our farmers, in the loans that they've got to take out to support themselves and their families, goes up to 14 or 15 per cent. Americans are ready for a change.

Campaigning,
Richmond, Va., Aug. 12/
The New York Times, 8-13:9.

3

[On Vice President George Bush, the 1988 Republican Presidential nominee]: [He is] for cutting taxes for the wealthy. He's also for spending money on all these very expensive weapons systems. And he wants to give every family with less than $20,000 a year a thousand bucks [for child care]—no guarantee that they're going to use it for child care, no guarantee that the child care they get is going to be quality child care. And by the way, he says he's not going to raise taxes. The Vice President is in a kind of a fiscal cloud cuckooland if he thinks the American people are going to buy the notion that you can spend billions on all of these weapons systems, provide real support to our conventional forces, give millions of families a thousand bucks whether it goes to child care or not, and cut taxes for the wealthy by billions of dollars. And he says no raising taxes. It's a fairy tale and it isn't going to sell.

Interview/Newsweek, 8-29:28.

4

[On the Reagan Administration's economic record]: High-paying jobs being replaced by low-paying jobs, average weekly wages down over the past eight years, benefits down over the past eight years. Can we afford four more years of that [by electing Reagan Administration Vice President George Bush as President]?

Sept. 5/USA Today, 9-6:(A)1.

5

[Criticizing Republican Presidential nominee George Bush's economic policy]: What he's proposing after over a trillion dollars in new debt—which has been added to the Federal debt in the course of the past eight years, an IOU that our children and grandchildren will be paying for years—is a tax cut for the wealthiest 1 per cent of the people in this country. An average of about $30,000 that we're going to give to people making $200,000 a year [via a lower capital-gains tax rate]. Why, that's more than the average teacher makes. We've had enough of that, ladies and gentlemen. We've run up more debt in the last eight years than under all of the Presidents from George Washington and Jimmy Carter combined.

At Presidential debate, Winston-Salem, N.C.,
Sept. 25/The New York Times, 9-26:10.

(MICHAEL S. DUKAKIS)

1

[On whether, if he is elected President, he would raise taxes]: No serious candidate for the Presidency can guarantee the American people he will not ask for new revenues from Congress. But it's a last resort, not a first resort.

Interview/
Reader's Digest, October:64.

2

[Republican Presidential nominee George Bush] wants to spend billions on virtually every weapon system around, says he's not going to raise taxes though he has broken that pledge repeatedly. He says he wants to give the wealthiest 1 per cent of the people in this country a five-year, $40-billion tax break and we're going to pay for it. And he's been proposing all kinds of programs for new spending costing billions. Now, if we continue with these policies, this trillion and a half dollars worth of new debt that's already been added on the backs of the American taxpayers is going to increase even more; and if we continue with this for another four years, then I'm worried about the next generation, whether we can ever turn this situation around.

At Presidential debate,
Los Angeles, Oct. 13/
The New York Times, 10-15:10.

3

... to suggest that an answer to this country's economic problems at a time when we're struggling with this massive [Federal budget] deficit— and borrowing billions from abroad from foreign bankers to finance it—is another tax cut for the wealthy [a cut in capital-gains taxes suggested by Republican Presidential nominee George Bush], is the worst kind of economic policy. If we're going to invest in communities like Detroit, if we're going to invest in communities like Rockford, Illinois, if we're going to invest in South Texas, where the unemployment rate is 30 and 35 per cent, where are you going to get the resources?

Interview/USA Today, 11-4:(A)6.

S. Norman Feingold
Clinical psychologist;
Specialist in career counseling

4

We're creating new jobs and casting off old ones at an unprecedented rate ... We all have jobs that are in transition. It's a dynamic situation today in which the rules keep changing. We can no longer think in terms of 30-year service to the company, and the gold watch.

Interview/
Los Angeles Times, 9-5:(V)1.

Mervin Field
Public-opinion analyst

5

The pendulum [on taxes] has swung back, but not all the way back. What you have is a pragmatic view: that we need taxes and that people are willing to tax themselves for particular purposes. But people still aren't ready for general tax increases. They want to maintain some control.

The New York Times, 5-31:13.

Douglas A. Fraser
Former president,
United Automobile Workers
of America

6

Too often, rather than give vacation time, [workers] are paid in lieu of vacation—so they don't get the time off. It would be more satisfying and rewarding if they actually took the time off to spend some time with their families. Employers wouldn't want to give you *any* vacation at all if it was up to them.

Interview/
Los Angeles Times, 7-3:(IV)5.

Richard A. Gephardt
United States Representative,
D-Missouri; Candidate for the
1988 Democratic
Presidential nomination

7

[Criticizing the 1981 Reaganomics tax cut]: In seven years, that one mistake transformed our

(RICHARD A. GEPHARDT)

nation from the world's largest creditor into the world's largest debtor. Reaganomics isn't an economic theory; it's theft from our children. It's a felony against the future and it has played the hard-working, tax-paying families of middle America for fools.

*Speech, Johnson School of
Public Affairs, Austin, Tex.,
Feb. 26/Los Angeles Times,
2-27:(I)22.*

1

The central issue of this [Presidential] campaign is whether Americans will regain control of our economic destiny. In recent years, that control has been lost to foreign powers and private interests ... First, we lost much of our steel industry; now we are losing whole segments of the computer industry. First, we were told that free trade permitted our farmers to sell abroad; now they are being locked out of the European market. We devalue the dollar, hoping to sell our goods cheaper abroad, and then trade barriers still bar the way—and the trade deficit with Japan roars on ... Americans now understand that for Americans to be strong from a security standpoint, to be strong from an environmental standpoint, to be strong from a social-policy standpoint, to be strong from a fairness standpoint, America's economy has to work again.

*Campaigning/
The Washington Post,
3-3:(A)16.*

Lou Gerstner
*President, American
Express Company*

2

I lie awake at night wondering where I'm going to find well-qualified employees for the future ... If you don't have the human capital to equal or exceed your competitors, you will fall behind.

Time, 12-19:57.

Willis D. Gradison, Jr.
*United States Representative,
R-Ohio*

3

Far from being a drag on the economy, a policy of generating [Federal] budget surpluses would be beneficial. As long as the surplus was achieved in a way that didn't reduce private savings, the main effect would be to reduce the amount we have to borrow from abroad. We'd make Uncle Sam the master of our ship of state again instead of rattling a tin cup in our hand for the rest of the world to fill.

Los Angeles Times, 5-22:(I)28.

Alan Greenspan
*Chairman, Federal
Reserve Board*

4

Entitlement programs offer substantial opportunities for long-term budgetary savings, since they currently account for nearly half of total [government] outlays. And with the base of expenditures certain to expand in conjunction with the increase in the beneficiary population during the next few decades, the deficit-reduction benefits of changes in the law today will accumulate over time, leading to much larger savings in the year 1995 and beyond than in, say, 1990 or 1991.

*Before Senate Budget Committee,
Washington/
Nation's Business, May:16.*

5

[On the large Federal budget deficit]: It is difficult to convince people that we have a problem when we unquestionably have a very vigorous economy, one which is by most indicators doing exceptionally well. That could very readily lead to a degree of euphoria and an unwillingness to come to grips with difficult problems. We will find that when the problem hits, it will be very late in the game and very difficult to deal with ... It is very crucial that we resolve that deficit issue while the economy is doing well.

*Before House Banking subcommittee,
Washington, July 28/
The Washington Post, 7-29:(G)1.*

(ALAN GREENSPAN)

1

It is beguiling to contemplate the strong economy of recent years in the context of very large deficits and to conclude that the concerns about the adverse effects of the [Federal budget] deficit on the economy have been misplaced. But this argument is fanciful. The deficit has already begun to eat away at the foundations of our economic strength.

Before National Economic Commission,
Washington, Nov. 16/
The New York Times, 11-17:(A)10.

Lawrence A. Guest
Senior vice president,
Marriott Hotels and Resorts

2

It's clear our company, like others, faces two challenges: First, we want to get our fair share of the youth component of the population [as employees]. Second, we need to change our ideas about what [employee] components we can draw on. We've been giving very close thought to our job requirements. For example, we're recruiting the handicapped for jobs we know they can do. A blind person may not be able to work as a bellhop, but there's no reason a blind person can't run a PBX or telephone system. A mentally handicapped person can work in a dish-washing room. We're hiring from other non-traditional groups, too—housewives, for part-time work, retirees, the economically disadvantaged, minorities, recent immigrants, inner-city residents, laid-off workers from other industries. One of our facilities is almost entirely staffed with dependents of military personnel.

Interview/
Nation's Business, February:20.

Alexander M. Haig, Jr.
Candidate for the 1988
Republican Presidential
nomination; Former
Secretary of State of
the United States

3

This [Federal budget] deficit is a Republican deficit, and any candidate [for the Presidency] who suggests it's the fault of the liberal left-wing Democrats in the House—who do have a major contributory role—is wrong. We [Republicans] were in the White House, and we had control of the U.S. Senate, and the men involved in this deficit have some questions to answer to the Republican Party and the American people.

The Christian Science Monitor,
1-8:14.

4

In 1981, we launched two schools of economic theory simultaneously. The first was the great supply-side mania and the conviction that deregulation and tax rebates alone would be enough to get our economic engine started again. The other was a directly contrary school of economic theory applied by Paul Volcker, the Chairman of the Fed [-eral Reserve Board], who knew that 13 per cent double-digit runaway inflation had to be stopped. So he introduced classic monetarism: a constraint theory with tight money and high interest designed to squeeze inflation out of the economy. It was like putting the automobile in first gear and reverse at the same time. And the grinding you heard was the mounting national debt.

Campaign speech/
The New York Times, 1-15:8.

Alexander M. Haig, Jr.
Former candidate for the
1988 Republican
Presidential nomination;
Former Secretary of State
of the United States

5

[Let] me remind you that if free [labor] unions ever disappear in this country, that will mark the beginning of the end of democracy.

The New York Times, 7-4:9.

Orrin G. Hatch
United States Senator,
R-Utah

6

[Criticizing the U.S. taking control over the Teamsters Union[: This is not Poland; this is not

(ORRIN G. HATCH)

the Soviet Union. Our Constitution and Bill of Rights guarantee institutions the right of association, and guarantee institutions the right to exist in our democratic society. To place an institution like the Teamsters under government control flies in the face of those Constitutional guarantees and makes us no better than the Soviets or the Poles.

The New York Times, 7-4:9.

Robert Hawke
Prime Minister of Australia

1

The U.S. has to tackle the problem of its twin deficits. It's no good to only talk about its external imbalances. It has to tackle the problem of its internal deficit, because it will distort economic decision-making in the U.S. and, because of the size of the U.S. economy, it will affect the rest of the world.

Interview, Canberra/
USA Today, 5-6:(A)13.

Constance Horner
Director, Federal Office of
Personnel Management

2

There is more to work performance than just knowledge about the task. Strong job performance has both an intellectual and moral component. Smarter people perform better on jobs, but smartness is not just cognitive, it is also a function of personal qualities like drive, ambition and ability to be generous and work cooperatively with people.

The Washington Post, 6-23:(A)9.

John J. Hudiburg
Chief executive officer,
Florida Power & Light
Company

3

In addressing quality and the need to improve our business performance as a nation, we cannot

overlook the service industries of America. The service sector provides the muscle to keep things moving in the manufacturing sector . . . And if we can do a better quality job in service, we'll find ourselves doing a better quality job in manufacturing.

At press briefing announcing
"Malcolm Baldrige National
Quality Award"/
Nation's Business, July:12.

Lee A. Iacocoa
Chairman,
Chrysler Corporation

4

One of our most expensive and highly automated plants gives us the most trouble. Maybe it is lousy management, maybe a lousy work-force, maybe a combination of the two. It may be personality clashes, whatever, but it permeates down, and the guys don't do their job right. Neither labor nor management is always right or wrong. It takes two to screw it up royally. On the other hand, it appears that our plant with the least automation and least investment is turning out the best quality. You ask, "What's going on?" Well, it has to be the people in the plant—management and labor. It is how the people approach their jobs that does it. Everybody talks about quality circles, worker involvement, wearing the same uniform, and eating in the same cafeteria. I think that is all nice, but it is not the answer. The answer is to make a guy—any guy—feel that when he comes to work, he does something and contributes something, so that he can't wait to come back tomorrow.

Interview/Fortune, 8-29:41.

Jesse L. Jackson
Civil-rights leader;
Candidate for the 1988
Democratic Presidential
Nomination

5

Workers of America must have a right to a job and get paid, with security, for the work that you do. The American worker is not asking for

(JESSE L. JACKSON)

welfare; he's asking for a fair share—not for charity but for parity. There's something wrong when corporate owners make exhorbitant profits while workers lose their jobs, and then get "golden parachutes" and land in tall grass while workers are put on skateboards without ball bearings.

*Campaign speech/
The New York Times, 1-19:12.*

1

Every generation has a challenge. Our challenge is to end economic violence. You know something has gone awry when profits go up and wages go down, and 600,000 farms are foreclosed, and plants are closed and workers are abandoned. It's called reverse Robin Hood. It's taking from the poor and giving to the rich. And that is not fair. Now the top 1 per cent of wage earners 10 years later pay 20 per cent less in taxes, instead of paying 20 per cent more. Government [has been] used as a lever to take from working people and the poor and to give to the rich.

*Campaign speech/
Los Angeles Times, 4-2:(I)19.*

2

South Koreans did not take jobs from us; GM took jobs to them—with government incentives. They close down a plant in America, they get a tax break. They take a job to South Korea, they get another tax break. I would shift the incentives. Right now, Congress can merge and then purge workers and then submerge the economy . . . That must shift. The incentive must be to re-invest in America, retrain our workers, reindustrialize our nation, research the benefits and the reconversion during peacetime economy.

USA Today, 5-3:(A)11.

J. Bennett Johnston
*United States Senator,
D-Louisiana*

3

The [Federal budget] deficit is a time bomb with a lighted fuse. [President-elect George]

Bush's tendered solution, his "flexible freeze," is deja voodoo all over again. The idea that we can "grow" our way out of this mess is absolute nonsense. If Bush really believes he can do what has to be done without cutting into entitlements and defense and without raising at least some taxes, then he's smoking something. And if he thinks we Democrats are going to drag him kicking and screaming into taxland and take all the heat alone, then he's dreaming as well as smoking.

Time, 11-28:23.

Victor Kamber
*Labor-union lobbyist and
consultant*

4

[On charges that various labor unions are involved in organized crime]: I'm not ashamed of the work we've done for any international union. If someone is a crook, if someone is bad, if someone is embezzling, stealing, robbing or whatever, those people should be prosecuted and put in jail, whether it's in labor, or business, or in church office, because we don't need crooks in this society. I equally believe that everyone is innocent until proven guilty of something, and if I have the ability to serve an institution I believe in—and I happen to believe in the free trade-union movement in this country—then I'm going to serve the institution, whether it be the airplane pilots, or the sheet-metal workers, or the laborers.

*Interview/
The New York Times,
1-8:24.*

Thomas H. Kean
Governor of New Jersey (R)

5

[On Democratic Presidential nominee Michael Dukakis]: What does the name of Dukakis sound to you like? More taxes . . . The liberal Democrats want to take money out of the pockets of working men and women because, you see, they think that Washington can spend it better. Now, I know those Democrats like to insist they under-

(THOMAS H. KEAN)

stand the average person, but the average people I know don't want to pay higher taxes.

At Republican National Convention,
New Orleans, Aug. 16/
The New York Times, 8-17:13.

Jack Kemp
United States Representative,
R-New York; Candidate for
the 1988 Republican
Presidential nomination

1

Have you noticed every time the interest rate comes down, the American auto sales go up? Every time interest rates go down, housing starts to go up? Every time interest rates go down, farmers are able to restructure debt, refinance debt, roll over debt, grow out from underneath their debt, commodity prices can recover? Every time interest rates go down, Third World countries who want to buy something from Detroit, or Buffalo, or Iowa, or New Hampshire, to pick a couple of states, can start to pay off New York City banks and can buy more from America? The answer to the trade deficit: Get interest rates down to help those economies, so they can begin to grow again.

Campaign speech/
The New York Times, 1-12:11.

Edward M. Kennedy
United States Senator,
D-Massachusetts

2

[On the large Federal budget and trade deficits]: It is fair to say that our present crisis is not a uniquely Republican failing. For the past 20 years, in Democratic and Republican Administrations alike, we have sown the seeds of neglect and economic mismanagement. Now we are reaping the whirlwind.

Before Woman's National
Democratic Club, Washington,
Jan. 20/The Washington Post,
1-21:(A)8.

3

No matter how you manipulate the figures that are passed over from the Commerce Department or the Labor Department, every working family in this country, every young family, knows that it is virtually impossible to buy a home in the United States of America today.

Sept. 13/
The Washington Post, 9-14:(A)10.

Paul Kennedy
Professor of history,
Yale University

4

There's no blinking the fact that the United States has lost its *relative* place in the sun. After World War II, this country was the steel-maker to the world, the breadbasket of the world, the auto manufacturer for the world. America's predominance in manufacturing and in agriculture—a mighty combination, you must admit—was without peer. Not surprisingly, the American dollar was also the strongest currency in the world. All these elements of economic superiority have been eroded. The United States is still the largest economic entity on the planet, but it is not any longer the entity whose performance puts it in a class by itself, hopelessly beyond the reach of any would-be competitor. On the contrary, we have seen the most astonishing "invasion" of this economy by foreign products. What is perhaps even more significant is the rapidity with which the American sense of its economic superiority has given way to a feeling of its having lost its bearings—of not knowing how to compete or where to compete.

Interview/American Heritage,
Sept.-Oct.:97.

Lane Kirkland
President, American
Federation of Labor-Congress
of Industrial Organizations

5

The labor movement has a long, well-documented record of fighting for the rights and the standard of living of working Americans but, in

105

(LANE KIRKLAND)

spite of that, there are still many Americans who have serious misconceptions about what unions do and about whether or not they are necessary in today's workplace.

Los Angeles Times, 5-12:(VI)5.

Richard L. Lesher
President, Chamber of
Commerce of the United States

1

In the modern era of rapid technological change, the advantages of free enterprise are more conspicuous than ever. If it were not so, the Soviet Union and China would not be groping their way toward more open economies. Thus, we must recognize our basic strength and build upon it. That means keeping taxes down and government interference in the economy to a minimum.

Before National Press Club/
Nation's Business, March:16.

Thomas E. Mann
Director of governmental studies,
Brookings Institution

2

Members of Congress are sick and tired of the [Federal] budget; it never goes away. The more they wrestle with it, and in their terms bite the bullet on hard decisions, the more it comes back to haunt them. They make politically painful spending cuts that are supposed to reduce the deficit, only to see them eaten up a few months later by changes in economic conditions.

The New York Times, 2-18:24.

Ann Dore McLaughlin
Secretary of Labor
of the United States

3

The most joy [about being Labor Secretary] is the very real personal aspect that every day we're touching the life of a Hispanic person coming into this country who wants to have the language skills to get a job. A young teen-age drop-out who

finally got into a Job Corps program, and is learning a trade, and can get a job. An older worker who comes in and says, "I've retired, but I have some other ideas about how I can contribute." They're very real. It's your neighbor, your cousin, your brother, your sister—that's what we're talking about every day, and I dare say the [Labor] Department's the largest regulatory department in government. We touch everybody.

Interview/USA Today, 3-22:(A)9.

4

The dividing line between work life and family life can no longer be so easily separated. So a key consideration for business will be the degree of corporate involvement outside the work-place—in schools, families and community programs, and in problems ranging from teen pregnancy to substance abuse. Because the problems of the employee are the problems of the employer, more involvement by business will be a strategic necessity, in areas as basic as teaching literacy skills, training and retraining as jobs change and providing child care and flexible benefits. Business will simply have to get serious about investing in its work force. The effort will not be born of altruism, but out of strenuous competition for employees, and the need to maintain a high level of productivity.

April 25/
The Washington Post, 5-4:(A)22.

5

Two-thirds of the new entrances to the work force by the year 2000 will be women. The rest will be minorities and immigrants. A small number will be white males. Do you know what that says about opportunity [for women]? There has been a 253 per cent increase of managerial roles for women; 80 per cent of insurance, real estate and other professional fields are women. When a statistic gets to be 50 per cent, it's no longer a statistic—it's a way of life; and the way of life is that women are taking jobs across the board.

Interview, New Orleans/
The Washington Post, 8-16:(E)1.

Robert E. Mercer
Chairman, Goodyear Tire &
Rubber Company

1

I would say [President-elect George Bush has] got to raise taxes, but he has already pledged not to. I see the need for a tax increase, but I don't see how he can do that; I see a need for his credibility to remain intact more than for a tax increase. George can say he's not for a tax increase, but if you had a responsible Congress, they would shove something through. They ought to do the tax increase even over a veto to get us out of this thing [the Federal budget deficit].

Nov. 9/
Los Angeles Times, 11-10:(IV)1.

George Miller
United States Representative,
D-California

2

We are creating [an economic] dumbbell. The poor are poorer, and there are more of them. The rich are richer, and there are more of them.

Time, 10-10:28.

Francois Mitterrand
President of France

3

[The U.S. budget deficit] creates general disorder beyond the American border and impedes the smooth running of Western economies and those of the Third World. In particular, it gives rise to real interest rates, which are too high. Europe sees its capital filling in for the U.S. deficits rather than being used for investment at home.

Interview/
U.S. News & World Report, 3-7:45.

Franco Modigliani
Economist, Massachusetts Institute
of Technology

4

[Criticizing the Reagan Administration for allowing too much foreign investment in the

U.S.]: [It demonstrates] a profound misunderstanding of the role of borrowing abroad. It's perfectly true this borrowing abroad for the purpose of increasing one's capital may be an indication that you have good investment opportunities. But when you have capital imports resulting from and produced by a $200-billion fiscal deficit, then that is a sign of weakness in, and madness in, the government that allows that to happen.

Interview, Jan. 11/
Los Angeles Times, 1-12:(I)16.

Ken Moroi
Chairman, Chichibu Cement Company
(Japan)

5

Today, the economy is increasingly dominated by service and information-related industries, and the mass production of standardized products is becoming anachronistic. Corporations no longer need to hire large numbers of think-alike recruits each year. The "organization man" has outlived his usefulness. At Chichibu Cement, we have to go outside the company for young talent, as we diversify. We need self-starters, individuals who can think for themselves. There's no more room for the corporate clone.

World Press Review,
September:50.

Frank Morris
President, Federal Reserve
Bank of Boston

6

We really have an economy that is getting pretty stretched out, in terms of manpower and industrial capacity. It is in this sort of environment that inflation begins to sprout . . . We can't permit the economy to grow in excess of 3 per cent for terribly long without doing something about it. We have to be cautious . . . We could end up with a situation where we have a choice of having accelerating inflation or having a recession.

Interview, Boston/
The Christian Science Monitor, 8-9:10.

Daniel Patrick Moynihan
United States Senator,
D-New York

1

[Saying the Reagan Administration deliberately created high Federal budget deficits in order to force reduced domestic spending]: [They] set about creating a fiscal crisis which they hoped would produce a political transformation. When it did not, the crisis only deepened, and now it is with us in protean and unnerving manifestations.

The New York Times, 2-16:12.

Rupert Murdoch
Media entrepreneur

2

I see a continuing lessening of roles [for labor unions]. People are more attuned to changing jobs, less fearful of unemployment. And when you remove that fear, there's less point in unions. The union that over-bargains for its member usually ends up putting him out of work—in a world of free trade.

Interview/
U.S. News & World Report, 3-7:56.

Paul F. Oreffice
Chairman, Dow Chemical
Company

3

The main thing business pines for is stability ... The key is that this so-called [economic] recovery over the last six years has been very gradual. And it could continue at 2.5 per cent growth a year if we don't give the system any shocks, like a tightening at the Fed or great legislative changes.

Interview, Nov. 9/
The New York Times, 10-10:(C)1.

Bob Packwood
United States Senator,
R-Oregon

4

[On the Tax Reform Act of 1986]: The system is fairer because it will require people of great income, corporations of great income, to pay taxes when, in the past, some of them paid no taxes at all. It is fairer because it will encourage people to invest in things that they know and that they hope they can make money on. I don't know why in a capitalist society you should have to emphasize that, but they will invest to make money rather than in tax shelters. And that is both fair and good for the economy.

Interview/USA Today, 4-14:(A)11.

Karl Otto Poehl
President, Central Bank
of West Germany

5

I'm very positive on the prospects for the U.S. economy. Things are not all bad. The United States is a very vital and dynamic economy. Its interest rates are high, and the exchange rate is now more realistic. It has enormous long-term growth potential.

Interview, Frankfurt, Feb.5/
The Washington Post, 2-6:(A)17.

William Proxmire
United States Senator,
D-Wisconsin

6

[Forecasting a severe recession]: You will not get one in 100 to admit it, but the best thing that could happen to the Democrats might be to lose the [forthcoming] Presidential election.

Newsweek, 7-25:15.

David H. Pryor
United States Senator,
D-Arkansas

7

The IRS is the creature of the Congress. In fact, it was created by Abraham Lincoln 126 years ago, in the basement of the Capitol with six employees. But it's 110,000 employees now. Today, we see the development of "the bounty-hunter mentality," especially in the collection, levy and seizure areas. The taxpayer literally has no rights ... The IRS does not care how long it

(DAVID H. PRYOR)

takes; it will eventually wear you down and beat you financially into the ground.

Interview/USA Today, 4-12:(A)9.

Dan Quayle
United States Senator,
R-Indiana; 1988 Republican
Vice-Presidential nominee

1

The one thing [Democratic Vice-Presidential nominee Lloyd Bentsen] tried to point out about [Democratic Presidential nominee Governor Michael] Dukakis is that he's cut taxes [in his state]. The fact of the matter is, Senator Bentsen, he's raised taxes five times. He just raised taxes this last year. And that's why a lot of people refer to him as Tax Hike Mike. That's why they refer to the state of Massachusetts as Taxachusetts. Because every time there's a problem, the liberal Governor from Massachusetts raises taxes.

At Vice-Presidential debate,
Omaha, Neb., Oct. 5/
The New York Times, 10-7:(A)12.

2

[On criticism that the U.S. is now a debtor nation]: . . . you have got to see why we are a debtor and what is attracting the foreign investment into our country today, whether it's Japanese or others. I would rather have people come over here and to make investments in this country, rather than going elsewhere. Because by coming over here and making investments in this country, we are seeing jobs. Do you realize that today we are producing [Japanese] Hondas and exporting Hondas to Japan? We are the envy of the world. The United States. Some of [Democratic Vice-Presidential nominee Lloyd] Bentsen's supporters laugh at that. They laugh at that because they don't believe that the United States of America is the envy of the world. Well, I can tell you the American people think the United States of America *is* the envy of the world.

At Vice-Presidential debate,
Omaha, Neb., Oct. 5/
The New York Times, 10-7:(A)14.

3

We're going to need all the tools possible to bring this Federal budget deficit down. We need the tools of a line-item veto. A line-item veto that 43 Governors in this country have, but not the President of the United States. The President of the United States needs to have a line-item veto when Congress goes ahead and puts into appropriations bills unrequested and unnecessary spending. Let the President put a line through that, send it back to the Congress and let the Congress vote on it again. Congress has got to help out in reducing this budget deficit as much as the Executive Branch.

At Vice-Presidential debate,
Omaha, Neb., Oct. 5/
The New York Times, 10-7:(A)15.

Pierce Quinlan
Executive vice president,
National Alliance of Business

4

Businessmen in more and more cities are getting involved in the [school] dropout problem these days because there's a manpower crisis out there. The business community is now saying that the dropout problem is not just a social issue but also an economic, bottom-line issue. Jobs today require more literacy, more math, more social flexibility than in the days of an industrial economy.

The New York Times, 8-24:22.

Richard Rahn
Vice president and chief
economist, United States
Chamber of Commerce

5

There are no limits to the duration of [the current] economic expansion as long as markets remain open and government remains limited to its properly assigned tasks . . . The record demonstrates that far from consuming our seed corn over the past 6½ years, we have been husbanding resources well and stand prepared to reap the harvest of our investment in higher output, which benefits all Americans.

Nation's Business, August:10.

(RICHARD RAHN)

1

Daily, we are subjected to news stories stating that taxes will have to go up [because of the Federal budget deficit], or the economy will founder. [But] a fair and flexible [spending] freeze is eminently doable. The deficit persists not because revenues are growing too slowly but because Federal spending has been increasing too rapidly.

USA Today, 11-21:(A)10.

Ronald Reagan
President of the United States

2

I'm not saying there aren't problems [in the U.S. economy]. The one that sticks out like a sore thumb is that United States budget deficit. It's an embarrassment and a shame, most dangerous, perhaps, because it signals a complete breakdown of the most basic function of the United States government.

Before City Club,
Cleveland, Jan.11/
The Washington Post, 1-12:(A)3.

3

Everywhere in the democratic world we are seeing the emergence of a new consensus that growth and opportunity go hand in hand. I don't need to tell you that the United States has led the way, or that the remarkable performance of our economy is the driving force behind the new consensus that has brought the economies of America, Britain, Canada and so many countries roaring back.

Before Atlantic Council,
Washington/
The New York Times, 6-20:7.

4

[Criticizing expected Democratic Presidential nominee Massachusetts Governor Michael Dukakis]: Should we expect that if the Democrats' all-but-certain Presidential candidate is elected, that he would raise taxes? Yep. In fact, he just did. Not only has he hiked taxes as Governor of Massachusetts, but in the last five years he has increased Massachusetts' state spending at double the rate of Federal spending. So, yes, the man expected to head up the Democratic ticket . . . is a true liberal who, instead of controlling government spending, raises taxes . . . We can either have an economy that puts the private citizen at the center . . . or we can put the government at the center of the economy and let bureaucrats and politicians call the balls and strikes, decide who's out—who's out of work, who's out of business—or who will get the big contract and be home free.

At Republican fund-raising
luncheon, Miami,
June 29/Los Angeles Times,
6-30:(I)20.

5

[There have been] those who called for more government planning, more regulations and even more taxes. [But] in a nation, as in a man or a woman, economic success is not a matter of bricks, mortar, balance sheets or subsidies. No, if a national economy is to soar, first the inventive, enterprising, pioneering, dreaming entrepreneurial spirit of the nation's people must soar. And that meant not more regulations, but fewer. Not more government direction, but less. And yes, not higher taxes, but lower taxes.

Before U.S. Chamber of Commerce,
Washington/
Nation's Business, July:63.

6

[Criticizing the Democratic Party for saying the U.S. needs a change away from the Republican Party in this Presidential-election year]: Some people are telling you to take for granted the economic growth of today and of the last seven years. Their message is "you can take prosperity for granted; it's time for a change; take a chance on us." That's sort of like someone telling you that you've stored up all the cold beer you could want, so now you can unplug the refrigerator. But, no more than with a refrig-

(RONALD REAGAN)

erator, you can't unplug our pro-growth economic policies and expect things to stay the same.

Before employees of
U.S. Precision Lens Co., Cincinnati,
Aug. 8/Los Angeles Times, 8-9:(I)14.

1

It's time for some more straight talk. This time it's about the [Federal] budget deficit. Yes, it's much too high. But the President doesn't vote for a budget, and the President can't spend a dime. Only the Congress can do that . . . Every single year I've been in office, I have supported and called for a balanced-budget amendment to the Constitution, and the liberals have said no. Every year, I called for the line-item veto, which 43 [state] Governors have, to cut fat in the budget, and the liberals have said no. Every year, I have attempted to limit their wild spending sprees, and they have said no. They would have us believe that runaway budget deficits began in 1981 when we took office. The fact is, beginning with their war on poverty in the middle '60s—from 1965 through 1980, just 15 years—the budgets increased to five times what they had been, and the deficits went up to 52 times what they had been.

At Republican National Convention,
New Orleans, Aug. 15/
The Washington Post, 8-16:(A)21.

2

[When the Reagan Administration took office,] we said something shocking: Taxes ought to be reduced, not raised. We cut the tax rates for the working folks of America. We indexed taxes, and that stopped bracket creep, which kicked average wage-earners into higher tax brackets when they had only received a cost-of-living pay raise. And we initiated reform of the unfairness in our tax system. And what do you know? The top 5 per cent of earners are paying a higher percentage of the total tax revenue than they ever had before, and millions of earners at the bottom of the scale have been freed from paying any income tax at all.

At Republican National Convention,
New Orleans, Aug. 15/
The Washington Post, 8-16:(A)21.

Robert B. Reich
Lecturer in public policy,
John F. Kennedy School
of Government,
Harvard University

3

Traditionally, liberals didn't pay a great deal of attention to productivity, and liberalism was perceived to be saying that economic growth is bad for flowers and other living things. The Democrats need to announce a public philosophy that connects social justice with prosperity.

The New York Times, 7-6:14.

Ann Richards
State Treasurer of Texas

4

I don't really think that people think the economy feels better now. We've got the largest [Federal budget] deficit in the history of the nation—larger than all of the deficits since George Washington combined. And the American people know that they are going to pay it, and their children are going to pay it. The American people also know that our trade deficit is of real concern. We're seeing foreign interests come in and buy our property, buy our companies, and they are unaccustomed to having this nation owned by foreigners.

Interview/USA Today, 7-18:(A)11.

5

[The Republican Administration tells] us that employment rates are great and that they're for equal opportunity, but we know it takes two paychecks to make ends meet today, when it used to take one, and the opportunity they're so proud of is low-wage, dead-end jobs.

At Democratic National Convention,
Atlanta, July 18/
The New York Times, 7-19:10.

Charles S. Robb
Chairman, Democratic
Leadership Council;
Former Governor of Virginia (D)

6

[On the nomination of Massachusetts Governor Michael Dukakis as the Democratic Party's

(CHARLES S. ROBB)

candidate for President]: I think that this ticket is more likely to take quick, decisive [budget] action than almost any ticket we could have nominated. Others might chart better with my views on some of the other issues, but in terms of fiscal discipline, Mike may be the only other Governor that I know of that I would yield a spot [to] in the Cheapy Hall of Fame.

Interview/Newsweek, 8-1:4.

Clayton Roberts
Vice president, National
Right to Work Committee

1

In light of the poor representation provided by the [labor-] union hierarchy, it would certainly appear that a great many union officials are overpaid. The rank and file of American workers has no say in determining what the salary of a union official shall be. You are compelled as a condition of employment to pay dues to the union officials, and that money may be used for a variety of causes that many of the workers might disagree with: anything from political, social and ideological campaigns, to loaded salaries for union officials. I am not saying that [AFL-CIO president] Lane Kirkland isn't worth his six-figure salary, but that question should be determined by the union rank and file. Unfortunately, it is determined by the union hierarchy.

Interview/Los Angeles Times, 5-22:(IV)7.

James D. Robinson III
Chairman, American
Express Company

2

[Criticizing a bill to provide workers with advance notice of plant closings]: The plant-closing feature has been largely misunderstood. It gets into issues of layoffs, in fact how you can run your very business. It's got 10 sections, 56 subsections and inconsistent language. A bill with that particular provision in there is not a desirable thing.

At meeting of business leaders,
Hot Springs, Va./
The Washington Post, 5-25:(A)12.

Felix G. Rohatyn
Senior partner, Lazard
Freres & Company;
Chairman, Municipal
Assistance Corporation
of New York

3

Neglect of our internal needs is undermining our future. The role of government and the behavior of a great, modern world power consists of more than just presiding over [Federal budget] deficit reduction. It consists in investing for the future to be competitive and to provide opportunity for all its citizens.

At Wharton School commencement,
University of Pennsylvania/
The Christian Science Monitor,
11-15:16.

Jerome Rosow
President, Work in
America Institute

4

We are tied to an obsolete system of determining vacations [from work]. It's time for American business to re-examine vacation policy and to make more provisions for increased leisure and for the recognition that vacation time is a tremendous reward—particularly with the feminization of the labor force . . . Companies don't use vacations as a reward. It's a major oversight in existing personnel policy. They think of giving people cash bonuses or stock options, but they wouldn't think of saying we're going to give you a month's vacation with full pay because of the great job you did last year. So vacations could also be a tremendous incentive that I would urge American business to look at.

Interview/
Los Angeles Times, 7-3:(IV)3.

Dan Rostenkowski
United States Representative,
D-Illinois

5

[On the Tax Reform Act of 1986]: It appears that we succeeded in taking millions of poor

(DAN ROSTENKOWSKI)

people off the rolls, and tens of millions of others got tax cuts. I believe that the system is a lot fairer for everyone now than it used to be. I hear a lot of complaints from people. Well, when you change anything, everybody complains. You always hear complaints about taxes.

Interview/
USA Today, 4-14:(A)11.

Allen Schick
Professor of public policy,
University of Maryland

1

We think of the 1980s as the age of the [Federal] budget. The irony is that we are consumed by the budget process not because it is strong, but because it is paralyzed.

The New York Times,
2-18:24.

Helmut Schmidt
Publisher, "Die Zeit" (West
Germany); Former Chancellor
of West Germany

2

In my judgment, the world is heading for recession in 1988. The three governments mainly responsible—in Washington, Bonn and Tokyo—do not understand how enormously important their behavior is for the world economy and how to act accordingly. I have not seen effective steps by [the U.S.] Congress, for example, to cut the budget—only steps indicating intent. Will recession turn into depression? I think not. People in North America and Europe at least know what governments must do. The political class remembers 1929 to 1931. So a depression isn't likely. But I do not exclude it, because the stupidity of government should never be underestimated. In neither America nor Germany is there the urgent debate we ought to have about what should be done.

Interview, Bonn/
U.S. News & World Report,
1-11:38.

Paul Simon
United States Senator,
D-Illinois; Candidate for
the 1988 Democratic
Presidential nomination

3

[President] Reagan asks us to spend $36-billion on a nuclear aircraft flotilla, and nobody seems to get very excited about it. I want to spend a few billion dollars on jobs and education, which really is going to help the future of this country, and I get labeled a big spender.

April 1/
Los Angeles Times, 4-2:(I)19.

Allen Sinai
Chief economist,
The Boston Company

4

[The U.S. economy] is moving into a world different from what we have seen in the past seven or eight years. In the labor markets, in manufacturing, we are moving into boom-like times. We are in a strong industrial economy such as we have not seen at least since 1980 . . . This is terrific news for a lot of Americans. More of them are working and more of them are getting more wages. The cost is higher inflation and higher interest rates, but for the time being that will seem a small price to pay.

May 6/
Los Angeles Times, 5-8:(I)10.

John R. Stepp
Associate Deputy Secretary
for Labor Management Relations,
Department of Labor
of the United States

5

It's a myth that our manufacturing base is eroding and that we are becoming a nation of service providers. We're producing as much as we ever did and the skill level of manufacturing labor has been enhanced. The quality of jobs is higher. Reasoning skills, higher language skills, math and analytic skills are fundamental for the new jobs . . . Take your average machinist on a pro-

(JOHN R. STEPP)

duction line. He used to be surrounded by people all doing pretty much what he was doing, over and over. The main skills called for [were] eye-hand coordination and the ability to repeat the same operation. Now in these restructured plants, robots and other advanced machinery intervene to do the repetitive work. They can do it more consistently and more accurately. So the worker becomes a machine operator, a production inspector, even a manager. He is doing several jobs at once and the skill requirements increase. All these workers have to be trained to integrate a whole range of duties during the course of a production operation. These can be very subtle skills, hard to learn and hard to train.

Los Angeles Times, 9-6:(I)17.

David A. Stockman
Economist; Former Director,
Federal Office of
Management and Budget

1

In terms of what [President] Ronald Reagan used to flail away at, in terms of an out-of-control "welfare state," the Reagan legacy is not contraction but consolidation. What Reagan did, essentially, despite his declared agenda, was to pick up the 1981 Democratic budget and complete the job of consolidation, winnowing out minor programs. But the consolidation, combined with the deep tax cuts, leaves an untenable and unsustainable fiscal structure and financial burden.

The New York Times, 2-16:12.

2

The first thing the next President will have to do is level with the American public and tell them that we have cut domestic spending about as far any kind of political consensus will permit . . . and that there is no way to [control the Federal budget deficit] without a significant tax increase . . . The math is overwhelming. There is literally nothing significant left in the budget . . . that could be cut in any realistic way that would

make more than a billion dollars' worth of difference. The [Presidential] candidates have implicitly pledged themselves to taxes. They simply need to acknowledge it publicly, I think.

Broadcast interview/
"Face the Nation," CBS-TV, 8-29.

Robert S. Strauss
Co-chairman, National
Economic Commission;
Former chairman, Democratic
National Committee

3

People who think we can balance the [Federal] budget with budget cuts don't understand that 75-80 per cent of the budget is Social Security, defense and interest. You don't have to be a genius to understand that.

To reporters, Washington/
The Christian Science Monitor,
11-10:3.

Clyde Summers
Professor of law,
University of Pennsylvania

4

It will be very difficult to clean up the Teamsters [union] and get the union on a democratic footing unless you change the whole structure of the election of national officers. As long as you have the national officers elected by the national convention, you will never clean up that union because, in the very nature of union conventions, the national officers have enormous influence over its operation.

Los Angeles Times, 6-29:(I)18.

John H. Sununu
Governor of
New Hampshire (R)

5

[On Democratic Presidential candidate Governor Michael Dukakis]: Mike Dukakis'

(JOHN H. SUNUNU)

"Massachusetts miracle" is a Massachusetts mirage . . . If the job rate of growth of the country were the same as the job rate of growth of Massachusetts, we would have 10 million fewer jobs in this country. Mike Dukakis has threatened to do to America what he did to Massachusetts.

The Christian Science Monitor,
6-29:3.

Arthur A. Taylor
Dean,
Graduate School of Business,
Fordham University

1

We rationalize that we are a nation of service industries; we let other nations manufacture. But no economy can thrive serving McDonald's hamburgers. The most important thing is that we need trained young people to cope with an America that no longer is sitting on the top. They must learn to be competitive and to understand that it will be tougher to continue our standard of living. They probably will need a lot of retraining later.

Interview/
The New York Times, 3-29:45.

John Van de Kamp
Attorney General
of California

2

[Criticizing the U.S. taking control over the Teamsters Union]: Just to pose one of the most obvious questions: to whom would those placed in command owe their allegiance? Would they respond to the working men and women or to the political administration from which the request for trusteeship came? We have rarely faced such dilemmas in the United States because, unlike many countries, we have insisted that the day-to-day management of unions should be free from government control.

The New York Times, 7-4:9.

Alfred S. Warren, Jr.
Vice president of industrial
relations, General Motors
Corporation

3

A better-educated, better-trained work force leads to better-quality products. These products generate higher sales, here and abroad. And that means stable employment which gives our workers greater spending power. Those ingredients strengthen the U.S. economy, from international trade right down to the corner grocery store.

Interview/USA Today, 9-2:(A)8.

Michio Watanabe
Chairman, policy research
council, Liberal-Democratic
Party of Japan;
Former Minister of Finance
and Trade of Japan

4

[Americans] use credit cards a lot. They have no savings, so they go bankrupt. If Japanese become bankrupt, they think it serious enough to escape into the night or commit family suicide. But among those guys over there [in the U.S.] are so many blacks and so on, who would think nonchalantly: "We're bankrupt, but from tomorrow on we don't have to pay anything back. We just can't use credit cards any more."

Speech at Liberal-Democratic
Party conference,
Karuizawa, Japan, July 23/
The New York Times, 7-26:4.

Pat Williams
United States Representative,
D-Montana

5

[Supporting an increase in the minimum wage]: We've got to protect the woman who cleans the toilets if we are going to protect the boys in the board room.

USA Today, 3-4:(A)7.

WHAT THEY SAID IN 1988

William Winpisinger
President, International
Association of Machinists
and Aerospace Workers

1

The U.S. is last among industrialized nations in the amount of paid vacation workers get for various lengths of service. Most of our trade competitors close up shop for a month in the summertime. I'm not saying that that is the magic answer, but it doesn't seem to me that a month is too long ... Each industry has its own particular problems based on order cycles or various production emergencies and so on. Each industry has to schedule it to fit its own peculiar circumstances ... I think extended vacations or sabbaticals are a heck of an idea. We've been unable to advance it over nearly a decade now. I think it's a good idea and I'd like to see it tried in some expanding industry.

Interview/Los Angeles Times, 7-3:(IV)5.

Jim Wright
United States Representative,
D-Texas

2

Nobody can deny that today it is harder for a 30-year-old couple to buy a house than it was 10 years ago. That is social retrogression. It is harder, not easier, for a 40-year-old couple to set aside money to send a child to college ... There will be 5,000 to 6,000 home foreclosures this year in the Dallas-Fort Worth area. It is attributable to the erosion of our industrial base through the trade deficit and the loss of good-paying jobs. Sure there are more jobs [than when the Reagan Administration first took power]—the population has increased—but there are two people in a family working at lesser-paying jobs.

To reporters,
Washington, Nov. 23/
The New York Times,
11-24:(C)15.

John D. Ashcroft
Governor of Missouri (R);
Chairman, Education
Commission of the States

1

One reason [why Japanese students outperform their U.S. counterparts] is that Japan has a 240-day school year, and their commitment to education has had that element of seriousness to it that ours simply hasn't had. We are also behind a number of other countries in terms of reading literacy and skills. That's one of the reasons we've got to act quickly, because we have enjoyed a standard of living that cannot persist in the face of an illiterate population.

Interview/USA Today, 8-10:(A)9.

2

Schools . . . will be more effective if we fully motivate the direct, immediate consumers of education—students and their parents—to increase their demands for education and to raise their expectations about what a good education really means. When parents are involved in the learning process, whole schools get better. When schools get better, children learn more. As children learn more, they value education more. As they value it more, they learn even more and pass it on to their own kids.

Before Education Commission
of the States, Baltimore/
The New York Times, 8-17:26.

Alexander W. Astin
Professor of education,
University of California,
Los Angeles

3

When one thinks of the hierarchy of a university, there might be some dispute over what to put at the top: law, medicine, physics. But there is little dispute over what goes at the bottom: nursing and education. Education departments

and schools of education do not have the largest budgets; they have the smallest. And they do not attract the best people. The teachers who teach teachers and the students who become teachers are, by and large, thought to be the worst in the university.

Los Angeles Times, 3-14:(I)1.

4

[On education-research funding]: One way to look at how dismal the situation is is to compare how much we spend on research for education with how much we spend on research on health care. For every dollar we spend in education research, we spend about $1,000 in health research. This creates a kind of vicious circle. It is said that education research is not very good, therefore it is not funded. But when it is not funded, this drives many of the good researchers out of the field.

Los Angeles Times, 3-16:(I)3.

Terrel H. Bell
Professor of educational administration,
University of Utah;
Former Secretary of Education
of the United States

5

No school can compensate for failure in the home. The home and the parent, those are crucial elements in the success of schools, and that's why I believe that we should be pressing hard for more involvement, more parental responsibility for the education of their children. We have to have a deliberate strategy for getting the home involved with the school so that we have that support system that we must have.

Interview/USA Today, 4-26:(A)11.

William J. Bennett
Secretary of Education
of the United States

6

Surround children with as many responsible adults as you can and give them the message,

117

(WILLIAM J. BENNETT)

"Stay in school; it's important to study, and here's why." Our studies show kids don't leave school because demands are made of them. Kids tend much more often to leave school because demands *aren't* made of them. Nobody knows their name, nobody cares, and it doesn't make a whole hell of a lot of difference whether they're there or not.

Interview/USA Today, 1-11:(A)11.

1

Education reform really has two stages. One, to convince the public of the need for reform. Surveys tell us that the American people put our schools somewhere between a "C" and a "B." The second stage requires action by the people whose job it is to improve our schools: teachers, principals, superintendents, state legislatures, state boards. Among many people in the schools, the perception of school performance is a good deal rosier then the general public's—too rosy.

Interview/USA Today, 2-29:(A)7.

2

The most important educational institution in our society is still the family, not the school. Good schools can overcome the deficits that children bring to schools. We know of schools where children come from poverty, from broken homes; but those schools still succeed in getting those children up to reasonable levels of achievement, because they do not take the child's background as an excuse for not educating that child. Just because kids come from desperate circumstances is no reason to give up on them.

Interview/USA Today, 2-29:(A)7.

3

Too often, a quiet but insidious "deal" is struck in American classrooms—minimal demand from teachers in exchange for minimal disruption by students.

Report to President Reagan,
April 26*/USA Today, 4-26:(A)11.

4

Some states are now showing us that maybe some of the problems of schooling aren't as intractable as we thought. Maybe we don't have to re-invent the wheel, re-create the world every five years. Corporations say the problem isn't that kids can't follow complexity, it's that they can't read, can't follow instructions, don't show up on time. I wish we could defancify some of this. There's a need for basic basics.

Interview, Washington/
The Christian Science Monitor,
8-8:17.

5

...Americans know what they want from their elementary schools. We want our children—by the end of the eighth grade—to read well, to write and speak clear and grammatical English, and to be acquainted with the varieties and qualities of fiction and non-fiction literature. . . If new laws or textbooks seem advisable, we should get them. If more and better teachers or principals are called for, we should find them.

Publishers Weekly, 9-16:11.

Lloyd Bentsen
United States Senator,
D-Texas;
1988 Democratic
Vice-Presidential nominee

6

A college education is slipping beyond the reach of millions of hard-working Americans. If you have a child that's born today, plan on having $60,000 in the bank when that child reaches the age of 18 in the hopes of sending that child to a public university. And if the Republicans have their way, you won't have any college loan program to help work it out for you.

Accepting the nomination,
at Democratic National
Convention, Atlanta, July 21/
Los Angeles Times, 7-22:(I)7.

7

For eight years now we've watched as the Reagan-Bush Administration trashed educa-

(LLOYD BENTSEN)

tional opportunity in America. They led the assault on the college loans and grants that, for millions of our people, are the only avenue to higher education. We know that, if America loses the battle for educational excellence, we lose the contest for world leadership. It's that simple and that important.

At Virginia Polytechnic
Institute and State University,
Sept. 6/Los Angeles Times,
9-7:(I)22.

1

Every year 700,000 children drop out of school before graduating. It is estimated that the decision to drop out will cost them about $220-billion in earnings, and it will cost the Federal government $68-billion in lost revenue. Here we've got American business struggling to modernize, to compete in world markets, and they have to spend $10-billion a year to train their employees in the basic skills they could and should be learning in school.

Before National Education
Association, Washington, Sept. 30/
The New York Times, 10-1:9.

Allan Bloom
Professor of political philosophy,
University of Chicago

2

[Criticizing American education]: I do partly blame the universities. One of the reasons for students' not reading seriously is their belief that they can't learn important things from books. They believe books are just ideologies, mythologies or political tools of different parties. If the peaks of learning offered some shining goal in the distance, it would be very attractive to an awful lot of people—people with very diverse backgrounds. The golden thread of all education is in the first questions: How should I live? What's the good life? What can I hope for? What must I do? What would be the terrible consequences if we knew the truth?

Interview/Time, 10-17:74.

Ernest L. Boyer
President, Carnegie
Foundation for the
Advancement of Teaching

3

An incompetent teacher is worse than an incompetent surgeon, because a surgeon can only cut up one person at a time.

At Trinity University
commencement/Time, 6-13:74.

Anthony Burgess
British author

4

[On his lectures to U.S. students]: These American students don't want to learn things that aren't useful. You see, the American education system may be rigorous, but it doesn't foster creativity or curiosity.

Interview, New York/
TWA Ambassador, October:47.

George Bush
Vice President of the
United States;
Candidate for the 1988
Republican Presidential
nomination

5

We got too far away in this country from education with values. I think we can stand up for values in our schools, while maintaining the proper separation of church and state. We can agree on common values—decency, honor, kindness, whatever it is. I want to emphasize, and see emphasized, those four Rs—reading, writing, arithmetic and respect—and get those back in these schools and then watch these kids perform. So I'm convinced that we can do a better job in education, and I'm convinced that it is the best answer to poverty and hope.

Campaign speech/
The New York Times, 2-4:10.

6

Good education is good policy, and it is good politics. In the years ahead, education can be our

(GEORGE BUSH)

most powerful economic program, our most important trade program, our most effective urban program, our best program for producing jobs and bringing people out of poverty. The best investment we can make is in our children.

U.S. News & World Report,
6-13:19.

1

I have visited schools all over the country, and it is clear to me that the Federal government cannot hope to duplicate the variety of approaches that I have seen. But I want to take a moment today to discuss a few of the steps we should take at the Federal level to promote excellence in our schools . . . First, there must be an emphasis on accountability—setting goals, objectively measuring progress toward those goals, changing what doesn't work and rewarding what does. It seems like common sense, but it is too seldom done. Let me say right away, I am for teachers. The sacrifice they make and the dedication they show for relatively low pay are overwhelming. We should give them the support they need to control their own classrooms and concentrate on teaching. . . I propose that we give awards to individual schools that significantly improve their performance. Let the states determine the criteria for improvement. Each school meeting the criteria would be recognized as a "National Merit School" [and receive a Federal financial reward] . . . [And there is] my proposal last year to create a College Savings Bond. In order to encourage parents to save for their children's college costs, such a bond would enjoy tax-free growth if used for college education.

Speech, Washington, June 6/
The New York Times, 8-17:29.

George Bush
Vice President
of the United States;
1988 Republican
Presidential nominee

2

The surest way to win the war against poverty is to win the battle against ignorance. Even though we spend more on education than any other nation on earth, we just don't measure up. People who earn high-school diplomas are only one-third as likely to be poor as those who drop out. The challenge of the future is not just to make education more available, but to make it more worthwhile, with more choices for parents and students in the public-school system.

Interview/
Christianity Today, 9-16:40.

3

[Criticizing Democratic Presidential nominee Michael Dukakis' plan for tuition aid for students wishing to go to college, which calls for payback through a salary-withholding system after college graduation]: We have got a big difference on how to handle college costs. His approach would create a complicated government program, a brand new tax that, if you are successful in life, you would keep on paying for the rest of your life. We do not need to put the IRS on your tail for the rest of your life as the reward for a college education.

At Illinois State University,
Bloomington, Sept. 28/
The New York Times, 9-29:15.

Bruce M. Carnes
Deputy Under Secretary
for Planning, Budget and
Evaluation, Department of
Education of the United States

4

College costs are going up two and three times the rate of inflation, and Federal student grants can't keep up. Colleges are filthy stinking rich and they are rolling in dough and they are going to be getting buckets of the stuff.

Interview/
The New York Times, 2-3:14.

5

[Many colleges] choose to increase tuition because they can get away with it, and they can get away with it because inflation is down.

(BRUCE M. CARNES)

They've decided they can go ahead and pig out . . . [but] it's not a function of money. It's what goes on at the school. There's no substitute for discipline, good curriculum and hard work, and I don't think you can buy those things.

The New York Times, 3-23:18.

Lauro F. Cavazos
Secretary of Education
of the United States

1

[On his appointment as Education Secretary]: I see this as a window of opportunity. I'm trying to raise the awareness of this nation concerning the problems of lack of education. We hear so much about positioning America to compete. How can we achieve what we want to achieve if our citizens are not educated to their fullest potential?

Interview, Washington/
The New York Times, 10-20:(A)16.

2

We've got three major deficits in this country— budget deficits, trade deficits and an educational deficit. The third is just as dangerous as the other two, but Americans don't understand this. If they did, we would be seeing a marshaling of resources comparable to what we saw with the effort to conquer polio or put a man on the moon.

Interview, Washington/
The New York Times, 12-7:(B)9.

William M. Chase
Professor of English,
Stanford University

3

[Criticizing proposed changes in Stanford's curriculum that would give more emphasis to contributions to American culture by minorities]: It's a version of academic populism, and populism is always dangerous for a university. Education is not a democracy. Students don't come here thinking that they know as much as their professors. There is a system of deference, and if the system breaks down, we're in real trouble. We owe it to our students to tell them, "Here's the kind of thing you will find of long-term value. These are the things that thousands of people have lived their lives by." To relegate them to the status of "white male writing" may be factually true, but it's of low significance.

The New York Times, 1-19:8.

John Chubb
Senior fellow and specialist
in education,
Brookings Institution

4

[Public] schools generally are worrying about budgets first, and performance second. If they can hire [a teacher] who is less expensive, they will.

The Christian Science Monitor,
7-18:3.

James P. Comer
Professor of child psychiatry,
Yale University Child Study
Center; Associate dean,
Yale School of Medicine

5

Children in bad environments eventually face choosing between the school and the home or neighborhood—and usually choose the latter. We need schools that bond children to the idea of education. Academic learning isn't enough, because there's no home reinforcement. *We* have to supply that.

Interview, New Haven, Conn./
The Christian Science Monitor,
12-9:23.

Robert Corrigan
Chancellor, University of
Massachusetts, Boston

6

We still see teachers as if they were members of a blue-collar profession. They have no control of the classroom, the curriculum or their working

(ROBERT CORRIGAN)

conditions. They are treated like people in a factory milieu.

Before American Council on
Education, Washington/
The New York Times, 1-20:16.

Michael S. Dukakis
Governor of Massachusetts (D);
Candidate for the
1988 Democratic
Presidential nomination

1

Last year, we celebrated the 200th anniversary of our nation's Constitution. And yet today there are 25 million adult Americans who can't read the Preamble to the Constitution. Make no mistake about it: Illiteracy is a curable disease—if we get business and government and labor and community groups working together; if we build on existing state programs and use new technology to make it easier for adults to become literate; and if we work with the Congress to implement the innovative literacy programs that are in the trade bill.

Speech,
Long Beach, Calif., May 13/
The New York Times,
8-17:29.

2

I believe very strongly that our country must commit itself to one basic principle: that no youngster in this country who completes high school, is qualified to do college work and is admitted to college, should ever be denied that opportunity because of financial need... I'll put a team of the smartest investment bankers and college administrators in America to work with states to create college opportunity funds—funds that will allow families to set aside enough today to meet the cost of college tuition tomorrow.

Speech,
Long Beach, Calif., May 13/
The New York Times,
8-17:29.

Michael S. Dukakis
Governor of Massachusetts (D);
1988 Democratic
Presidential nominee

3

[Vice-Presidential nominee] Lloyd Bentsen and I do not need an election-year conversion on the subject of education. While [the Reagan Administration] led an assault on college loans and grants, we've quadrupled scholarship assistance to low- and middle-income students. While they've invested billions in "Star Wars" [space defense system], we've developed a regional network of Star Schools that is putting the latest in new technology to work to helping our youngsters master the science and math skills they need to compete—and to win—in the 1990s and the 21st century.

Campaign speech, Oakland, Calif.,
Sept. 1/The New York Times, 9-2:9.

4

[On his college-tuition finance plan that involves Federally guaranteed loans to students that would be paid back through Federal withholding on income earned after college]: It's going to reach out to millions of youngsters from middle-income families who are not eligible for grants and loans today, or who choose not to take advantage of loans because they don't want to start out in life burdened by tens of thousands of dollars of debt... For our families, we'll be helping to bring college within the reach of all our children, and helping to bring prosperity home to millions who now find themselves being pushed to the economic margins of the American dream. For our taxpayers, we'll be providing a reliable, self-financing new mechanism for making and enforcing the collection of student loans.

At Kean College, Sept. 7/
The New York Times, 9-8:1.

Chester E. Finn, Jr.
Assistant Secretary for
Research, Department of
Education of the United States

5

[Lowering school class size has become] an ersatz reform goal around the country. There are

(CHESTER E. FINN, JR.)

a lot better and less costly things you can do and get results. There's no question that good teachers in tiny classes are one of the reasons people pay for expensive private schools. But it's not a very prudent investment strategy if you're trying to improve the vast enterprise of American education.

Interview/
Los Angeles Times, 3-31:(I)24.

Chester E. Finn, Jr.
Former Assistant Secretary
for Research, Department of
Education of the United States

1

After five years of reform, nobody has yet described the product schools are supposed to produce—what kids should know to enter adulthood, and how to make schools accountable for teaching it. The organized forces of American education flee from the responsibility for outcomes.

The Christian Science Monitor,
12-16:21.

William Fitzsimmons
Director of admissions,
Harvard University and
Radcliffe College

2

[Saying colleges have stepped up their recruitment of black students]: I think you would find a consensus among top universities that things are starting to happen. At Ivy League colleges, and similar colleges, we are reaching an enormous percentage of top minority students through direct mail, receptions for minorities and a whole series of special events. There really aren't many that are being overlooked.

The New York Times, 5-19:9.

Mary Hatwood Futrell
President, National
Education Association

3

When [Secretary of Education William] Bennett talks about accountability in education, I

wonder if he understands that includes the Federal government. Who holds it accountable? The [Reagan] Administration refuses to be an active participant in reform; it's sitting on the sidelines and is totally unaware of what it is supposed to do to help us. . . The money issue is critical. They've abdicated their responsibility to guarantee every child in this country the right to receive a quality education.

Interview/USA Today, 4-26:(A)11.

4

I'm a Washington *Redskins* [football] fan, and I see a linebacker, Wilbur Marshall, just signed a contract for $6-million. Or take Dave Winfield, a New York *Yankees* [baseball] outfielder, who has a contract worth $22-million. Then, teachers in this country, who educate everyone, have a beginning pay of about $18,000. After 15 years of experience and earning a master's degree, the average pay for 1987-88 is $28,000. When I look at what teachers have to do and what some other people have to do, it seems that things are grossly out of whack. Athletes have to put in enough hours to develop their skills and be able to play the game and win. But teachers put in an average of about 56½ hours a week. We don't have a season that goes from August to January; our season is from September to June.

Interview/
Los Angeles Times, 5-22:(IV)7.

Ellen Futter
President, Barnard College

5

Education is empowerment—individual and national. . . For the United States of America to be populated by a citizenry that is uneducated is a prescription for disaster and a sentence to everlasting mediocrity.

At Barnard College commencement/
Time, 6-13:74.

6

We know that at women's colleges, the women students are the ones who occupy the leadership positions—president of student government,

(ELLEN FUTTER)

editor of the paper. We know that the students are much more likely to pursue study in the so-called non-traditional fields, such as the sciences, and not just while they're in college, but as graduate students. . . There's an interesting study called *The Classroom Climate: A Chilly One For Women*, which says that at the co-ed schools, the women are invited in and take the same classes and the like, but there are some subtle and some not-so-subtle means of discrimination—they don't get the same attention in the classroom, the same counseling, the same amount of professional time, office-hour time. They don't get encouraged to go on in certain fields. All the data show that the women who go to women's colleges have dramatically better outcomes.

Interview/USA Today, 9-7:(A)11.

A. Bartlett Giamatti
*President, National
(baseball) League;
Former president,
Yale University*

1

The enemy of the university is not dissent, not disagreement, not disagreeableness. Gentility is the mark of a great finishing school, not a university.

*At Massachusetts Institute of
Technology commencement/
Time, 6-13:74.*

2

[Former Education Secretary] Bill Bennett has been flailing the colleges for the last few years. . . I don't think information and education are the same; that's a notion that Bennett has exploited. He's on a mission to reform our souls. I don't have any problems with reformation, but these neo-Puritans make me very nervous. . . The Renaissance drew upon the ancient view that the purpose of education is to create a good citizen. That is not a theme any less vital now than it was 500 years ago. The purpose was intellectual training for civic goals and a broadly

educated mind—almost to toughen the mind as a muscle. This would prepare you for the problems that the world would confront you with.

*Interview, New York/
The New York Times, 12-28:(B)3.*

Gerald Grant
*Chairman, department of
sociology, Syracuse University*

3

School reform has real meaning only in the construction of a particular world. Federal and state lawmakers can prescribe change, but it has to happen in the life and operation of a school.

*Interview/
The Christian Science Monitor,
7-11:19.*

Richard R. Green
*Chancellor, New York City
Public School System*

4

Education is the most important thing that a person can have. It's the most important gift that we can give, and we need to value those who are successful. I need to make sure that a child knows that the choice between the "boom box" and the "Reeboks" and a good education is what the Chancellor of the New York public schools stands for.

*Interview/
USA Today, 1-11:(A)11.*

5

Obviously there are people with varying degrees of mental and physical handicaps, but education has demonstrated that, regardless of your condition, there's something you can learn. If there is a desire to learn—and on occasion, when there is not a desire—we still have been able to show that all children can learn. I don't believe that people have to stay in their station in life simply because that's where they started, and those who choose to believe that there aren't opportunities are wrong.

Interview/Esquire, June:189.

(RICHARD R. GREEN)

1

There must be a sense that we will *not* promote failure through the school system. If that means intervening in a child's education as young as age five or six or seven, if that means saying that they must have some prerequisite skills in order to take advantage of the next step of their education, then these are decisions that have to be made. Because by socially promoting students who do not have the necessary skills, we are really promoting failure. And that is something that neither society nor the children can afford.

Interview/Ebony, August:72.

2

I want to make the people—teachers and principals—who dedicate their lives to working with kids seem valued for doing that. We're at a time in history where that kind of professional staff has been devalued, when it no longer is perceived as valuable to be working in a public-school system. What is more valuable, I ask? The future of the nation is on the shoulders of teachers and how they teach kids; the future of the world is in the classroom where the teachers are. And if we have any chance to guarantee a positive bridge to the 21st century, it is how we educate the children in the classrooms today.

Interview/Ebony, August:74.

3

For 20 years we have been told that public schools cannot operate in place of parents, but in urban centers we have no choice. Teachers may already be the most important adult in the lives of many of our children. We already function *in loco parentis,* and I accept that role.

Interview/
The New York Times, 8-22:12.

Gilbert M. Grosvenor
Chairman and president,
National Geographic Society

4

[Announcing his Society's gift of $20-million for a foundation to aid in the teaching of geog-

raphy in schools]: Our kids don't know where they are. And if you don't know where you are, you're nowhere. . . We want to train these teachers to teach geography. Since World War II, geography has disappeared from the school system. . . Our youngsters today are geographically illiterate.

Los Angeles Times, 1-18:(II)5.

Lawrence A. Groves
Associate dean of admissions,
University of Virginia

5

Students in the past might have been satisfied going to a perfectly fine regional school that is not well known outside that geographic region. [Today's] students feel, "If I'm going to get ahead in this world, I can't with a local, state school; I've got to do it at Duke, Stanford or the Ivy Leagues."

The Washington Post, 5-23:(A)5.

Alexander M. Haig, Jr.
Candidate for the 1988
Republican Presidential
nomination; Former
Secretary of State
of the United States

6

Education is the key to America's future. But the graduates of American grade schools, high schools, colleges and universities are on a declining curve of capability when compared with the graduates of other Western industrialized societies and Japan. For too long, we've measured the quality of America's education by the quantity of Federal bucks that we have dumped into our higher institutions of learning. The failures of American education are not in our colleges and universities, although they, too, must strive for excellence. They are in the grade schools and the high schools in America, where we have failed to teach reading, writing, arithmetic and the analytical skills associated with those basics of rudimentary education. We have paid too little attention to education in democracy—the values that make this country great. And it's not exactly a matter of national pride

(ALEXANDER M. HAIG, JR.)

that our high-school and grade-school teachers to whom we turn over our most precious legacy— our children—are among the lowest paid of our professions.

Campaign speech/
The New York Times, 1-15:8.

Roald Hoffmann
Professor of physical science,
Cornell University; Winner,
1981 Nobel Prize for chemistry

1

To today's science students, I would say this: "Sure, push ahead in science as much as you can. But in college you have the first and best opportunity to absorb the great ideas of civilization— the literature, the philosophy, the art, the music— without which we cannot be complete human beings. Don't let yourself be captured just by science. The world is there to be perceived. If you can fulfill an English requirement by reading Chaucer or by reading science fiction, for God's sake, take the Chaucer."

Interview/
U.S. News & World Report,
3-14:58.

Jesse L. Jackson
Civil-rights leader;
Candidate for the 1988
Democratic Presidential
nomination

2

Education is not a dispensable social program. It is a defense act. Any nation that spends 55 cents of every Federal income-tax dollar for the military, and only 2 cents for education, has to re-order its priorities.

The Christian Science Monitor,
4-1:6.

Richard Jungkuntz
Provost, Pacific
Lutheran University

3

What would you say was the quality of elementary and secondary schooling in the first

quarter of our century, and before that? I think it was an age in which the quality was superior. What were the incentives to going into teaching in those days? Lousy. Salaries were worse than the worst salaries are now. But what was the communities' perception of the teaching profession? Relatively high. My father in 1921 was addressed as professor by people. He was a grade-school teacher and a good one and he was regarded highly, at the same level as the clergy in town and perhaps somewhat higher than the Mayor. . . But remember, you can't make a silk purse out of a sow's ear. No methodology will make a good teacher out of someone who doesn't have the motivation. So how do you get the silk? Enhance the image of the profession. Get educated teachers worthy to be called professionals. Is that old-fashioned? I'm afraid it is.

Before National Council on
Education, Washington/
The New York Times, 1-20:16.

Barry M. Katz
Historian,
Stanford University

4

[On contemplated changes in Stanford's curriculum to give more emphasis to contributions to American culture by minorities]: Plato will not be banned from our republic of letters. Freshmen will not emerge from their first year steeped in the lore of Eskimos and Pygmies but ignorant of English composition. Put simply and bluntly, the existing course requirement asserts that we have a common culture and it asserts that it can be defined by a bit of reading in the great works. This has been an affront to a large number of students and faculty, to women and members of minority groups.

The New York Times, 1-19:8

Thomas H. Kean
Governor of New Jersey (R)

5

Good jobs will not matter if our children do not have the skills to fill them. And it starts with education. . . . No more automatic passing of stu-

(THOMAS H. KEAN)

dents from grade to grade. If you can't write or read or count, you don't deserve a high-school diploma.

At Republican National Convention,
New Orleans, Aug. 16/
The New York Times,
8-17:13.

Ronald E. Kutscher
Associate Commissioner,
Bureau of Labor Statistics
of the United States

1

In the year 2000, it's hard to imagine anyone without a high-school diploma being well placed in the job market. We're gradually eliminating prospects for that.

The New York Times,
9-8:9.

Henry Levin
Professor of education, and
director of Center for
Educational Research,
Stanford University

2

[Criticizing the practice of placing slow-learning children in less-demanding classes or adapting classes to their "needs"]: This approach appears to be both rational and compassionate, but it has exactly the opposite consequences. It stigmatizes them with a mark of inferiority and reduces learning expectations both for them and their teachers, and it slows the pace of instruction to a crawl. The result is a school experience that lacks intrinsic vitality, omits crucial learning skills and reinforcement, and moves at a plodding pace. It is also joyless. . . We tell ourselves that these youngsters have to crawl before they can walk, and then we turn them into permanent crawlers.

Interview/
The Washington Post,
1-15:(A)21.

Stephen R. Lewis, Jr.
President, Carleton College

3

Surely, what happens to students while they are at the college is as important as the measure of what they were like when they arrived.

U.S. News & World Report,
10-10:(C)3.

Gary Orfield
Professor of political science,
University of Chicago

4

[On the increasing integration of black, Hispanic and Asian-American students in U.S. school systems]: The black administrators who are inheriting school leadership from whites may have just as much difficulty coping with groups different from themselves as the whites did with blacks.

The New York Times, 6-23:8.

Ronald Reagan
President of the United States

5

Perhaps the greatest difficulty facing our educators today is this: In too many school systems, if you're a teacher, principal or superintendent, and you do something very good for your students, nothing good happens to you. In a word, there are too few rewards. We need to change that. We need to reward excellence in education as we reward excellence in other fields. We need, in other words, to introduce education to some free-market principles, things like incentives and accountability.

At Suitland (Md.) High School,
Jan. 20/
The New York Times, 1-21:11.

Joe Restic
Football coach,
Harvard University

6

Football is just a part of things here [at Harvard], and it's up to me to make it interesting. I have to make sure they enjoy this course

(JOE RESTIC)

as much as any other course. Because I consider this a course—and not just in the game of football. It's a course in character building, in ethics, in building strength as an individual, in learning to handle a variety of experiences. If I can teach them to win gracefully, to lose without bitterness, and to rise above anything that happens, I'll have done my job.

Interview, Harvard University/
The Christian Science Monitor,
11-21:18.

Richard P. Richter
President, Ursinus College

1

[On determining "the best" colleges]: American colleges are not in a baseball league, nor are they racehorses. We are a flock of birds in flight. The one in front is not "winning" even though it is at the head of the V.

U.S. News & World Report,
10-10:(C)3.

David Riesman
Professor emeritus of sociology,
Harvard University

2

I say college and school are a time to learn two life-long musical instruments, two life-long sports, a craft such as plumbing or carpentry, a foreign language, how to give a talk. It's a time for mutuality, generosity, sharing—without ideological trimmings.

The Christian Science Monitor,
9-29:14.

Frank Rose
Former president,
University of Alabama

3

Current statistics on the number of blacks, Hispanics and poor whites attending college reveal we have lost some of our momentum. . . . Too many of our people do not have access to higher education, due to increasing costs. Just as we have made public education available to our elementary and secondary young people, we must find ways of financing higher education. Our country is too wealthy to ignore this need. The additional revenues from college graduates will more than fund such an effort.

At University of Alabama, June 10/
USA Today, 6-9:(A)13.

Arthur M. Schlesinger, Jr.
Historian; Professor of
humanities, City University
of New York

4

[I believe] in the usefulness of composition courses. Writing papers each week is the best discipline for students. One of the defects of contemporary education is that students are no longer asked to write very much. The invention of multiple-choice tests has had a terrible impact. I think it's very important that young people write essays and papers and learn to express themselves in a connected way.

Interview/Writing!, January:12.

Patricia Schroeder
United States Representative,
D-Colorado

5

One quarter of our children do not make it through high school. If we are going to provide for ourselves and our children, Americans must become a people who think for a living. This means attracting first-class teachers, paying them a decent salary, and holding them to high standards. The [foreign] trade competition will be won or lost in our schools.

"Ms.," February:52.

Gilbert Sewall
Educator

6

History books generate a special kind of heat. What they include, how they are slanted, has a lot to do with the next generation's understanding of this country.

The Christian Science Monitor,
2-29:20.

Donna Shalala
Chancellor, University of
Wisconsin, Madison

1

When we call ourselves a research university, we are not pretending that we're only here to teach students. . . The great research universities have been finding solutions to diseases, designing sensitive social policies, and have been on the cutting edge of international research since their existence. We say very clearly that we are here to create new knowledge—to discover the cures for our greatest diseases, to add to our culture, and to find solutions to issues of social policy.

Interview/
USA Today, 11-21:(A)11.

Albert Shanker
President, American
Federation of Teachers

2

[Education] reform . . . is bypassing about 80 per cent of the students in this country. That is, these reforms are very good for kids who are able to sit still, who are able to keep quiet, who are able to remember after they listen to someone else talk for five hours, who are able to pick up a book and learn from it. . . The reform movement is very good for them because now they have to do the things that they should have done and could have done all along. . . But it will not do anything for those students who are not able to sit still and listen for that many hours, and are not able to read that long. It will not do much for those kids who, every time they are asked a question, stand up and are humiliated in front of all their colleagues in class because they never get it right. . . This is not, as some would like to believe, a problem only for the disadvantaged . . . What I'm talking about is not a "special" problem, because the traditional ways of learning don't seem to work for the majority of our kids.

At National Press Club,
Washington, March 31/
The Washington Post,
4-28:(A)22.

Harold Shapiro
President,
Princeton University

3

The simple fact is that we are usually more preoccupied with the discovery of new knowledge and its transmission than with ensuring that we and our students have informed conversations with ourselves and with society on the issues that really matter. We are better at research than at the public discourse required to transmit ideas and values.

Inaugural address, January/
The Wall Street Journal, 1-29:14.

Joel E. Smilow
Chairman and president,
Platex, Inc.

4

[On his donating $1-million to endow the position of head football coach at Yale University]: Clearly, excellence in football is not a core objective of Yale or any other great institution of higher education. However, it is my belief that football is an integral part of the very broad objective of attracting, educating and motivating persons with the potential to become tomorrow's leaders . . . Many individuals who are interested in football would not attend a university that did not afford them an organized opportunity to pursue "their sport."

Sept. 13/
The New York Times, 9-14:28.

Arthur O. Sulzberger
Publisher, "The New York Times";
Chairman,
American Newspaper
Publishers Association

5

Today, up to 60 million Americans—one-third of the adult population—cannot read their local newspaper. [Such people are] cut off from a flow of vital information that is essential to involved and productive lives. This is bad news for our country. As we edge closer to the 21st century,

WHAT THEY SAID IN 1988

(ARTHUR O. SULZBERGER)

life is becoming more complex and will become more difficult for adults who cannot read.

At symposium on literacy,
National Press Club,
Washington, Sept. 8/
The New York Times, 9-9:11.

Charles Sykes
Author; Part-time professor,
University of Wisconsin,
Milwaukee

1

[Professor] tenure is the main reason that a university is so hard to change. In order to frustrate reform, all a tenured professor has to do is say, "I don't want to do it. I don't want to change this. I'm not going to teach more." And there's really nothing you can do about it. And too many professors simply retire after they get tenure. They stop doing either much teaching or much valuable research, and it's one of the reasons why universities have become such vast empires of waste, because most of the resources are going to people who are often producing the very least.

Interview/
USA Today, 11-21:(A)11.

P. Michael Timpane
President, Teachers College,
Columbia University

2

[On the New York City public-school system]: There are no problems here that are different than problems in other school systems. They are just more complicated—and so complicated in fact that they lead to a kind of paralysis in trying to solve them. It is a system with an unsurpassed ability to have nothing happen despite enormous efforts. This has led to very profound cynicism by the people, especially at the lower levels. . . They believe [that] even people who say they are promoting their welfare have got some other agenda. That, I think, is at least somewhat distinctive in the New York City schools. The profound distrust is perhaps, at the bottom, the most difficult thing we are working on.

Los Angeles Times, 5-14:(I)28.

Stephen Joel Trachtenberg
President, University of
Hartford (Conn.);
President-elect, George
Washington University

3

. . . universities are so vulnerable to people who criticize them for not being as authoritative as they used to be. Back in the '50s, for example, those of us attending college still felt the Halls of Ivy ethic all around us. A change in the curriculum might take 20 years to work its way from the proposal stage to what actually got taught in the classroom. Nobody—not even the athletes—seemed in too much of a hurry. Indeed, universities were places where people went in order to slow down and think. Their predominating tone was one of almost religious contemplation. It's a little harder to feel a sense of religious awe when confronted with a university that is trying to respond to demands, needs, wants, signals, shouts and occasional screams from a world so active, so dynamic and so given to rushing forward that it is actually endangering its own continued existence.

At University of Hartford
commencement, May 15/
The Washington Post, 5-17:(A)22.

Carolyn Trice
Associate director of
educational issues, American
Federation of Teachers

4

Unless the experienced teacher has some credential that [school administrators] are desperately looking for, they will hire the young persons right out of college. . . [As a teacher,] it takes you three years to find out what is really going on in the classroom. So the students are being deprived.

The Christian Science Monitor, 7-18:4.

Michael Usdan
President, Institute for
Educational Leadership

5

[On local school boards]: They're part of the warp and woof of the American body politic.

(MICHAEL USDAN)

Even with all the criticism of the schools, no one—no Governor, no state legislature, no blue-ribbon commission—has called for abolishing them. They're like the UN. They've got all kinds of problems, but if you didn't have them, you'd have to invent them.

The New York Times, 11-2:(B)7.

Gary Walz
Professor of education,
University of Michigan

1

[On school guidance counselors]: Relational and developmental roles are the stuff of counseling. Many of the other functions counselors may take on are more administrative. It is critical to view the child over time, not just experiencing a crisis and needing help now. [Guidance should be] a series of enriched experiences that carry through outside the school walls and are seen as very worthwhile. Counseling should give direction and guidance to a child's life. [It should not be] limited to interventions in crises, because crisis counseling isn't necessarily the best counseling. Like in law, hard cases make bad law. It is a special relationship that is not conflictive with the parental role, and certainly is not a substitute for the parental role.

The Christian Science Monitor, 1-22:(B)3.

Richard Warch
President,
Lawrence University

2

Choosing a college is a highly personalized matching process in which student needs and aspirations are aligned with institutional characteristics and cultures.

U.S. News & World Report, 10-10:(C)3.

John P. Whalen
President, ConSern; Former
president, Catholic University
of America

3

Years ago, when I was a boy, it was a rare person who went to college. Then, after World War II and the GI Bill, a college education became the desideratum of the majority. No longer was it just for the elite. Early in our history, this country made an economic accommodation so a person could get shelter, have a home. Later, we developed a second necessity, the monthly payment for a car. Now we have a third necessity, a monthly payment for an education. That shows how we are changing. The first thing, the home, meant stability. The second necessity, the car, gave us mobility. The third thing, education, provides intellectual mobility.

Interview/
Nation's Business, February:38.

Clifton R. Wharton, Jr.
Former chancellor,
State University of
New York

4

The problems of, and for, minorities in higher education are merely symptomatic of much larger and more fundamental challenges to our society at large. Surely, the institutionalization of a permanent "under-class" who have lost all hope or faith in the American dream has become a dominant factor influencing the reality of minorities in higher education.

Before American Council on
Education, Washington, Jan. 19/
The New York Times,
1-20:16.

Merlin Wittrock
Professor of education,
University of California,
Los Angeles

5

Teaching is more than knowing a subject matter and presenting it in clear language. Teaching involves knowing how students think, their preconceptions and misconceptions... It involves learning what motivates students and what genuinely gets their attention and holds it.

Los Angeles Times, 3-16:(I)22.

WHAT THEY SAID IN 1988

Jim Wright
United States Representative,
D-Texas

1

In each year of his Presidency, [Ronald Reagan] has called for major cuts in education. In an age when our children will have to cope with semiconductors, super-colliders and international competition, America will not survive unless they are better educated than we were.

Broadcast address to the nation, Washington,
Jan. 25/Los Angeles Times, 1-26:(I)16.

Edward F. Zigler
Professor of psychology,
Yale University

2

[Criticizing state tests for kindergartners to evaluate their readiness for first grade]: If a child at five is given the message that he or she is a failure [because of the results of such tests], a self-fulfilling prophecy may be perpetuated. Kindergarten should be structured so that no child can fail.

Time, 4-25:86.

The Environment • Energy

Isaac Asimov
Science-fiction writer

1

[Saying a solution to dirty air is trees]: They absorb carbon monoxide and carbon dioxide and give out oxygen. What could be more desirable? And they look good in the bargain. Stop chopping down the rain forests and plant more saplings, and we're on our way.

Interview, New York/
Time, 12-19:82.

Mollie Beattie
Commissioner of Forest,
Parks and Recreation of Vermont

2

The non-traditional approach to forestry asks how you can best imitate the forces of nature while still achieving some of the same [economic] goals. It asks what can be learned by watching— by adjusting the system in relation to these forces.

Interview, Montpelier, Vt./
The Christian Science Monitor,
1-5:21

Lester Brown
President,
Worldwatch Institute

3

Things are happening so fast to the environment. The question is whether our institutions, political processes and values can shift quickly enough ... Societies have to cross a certain threshold of awareness and concern about an issue before there can be an effective political response.

The Christian Science Monitor,
9-14:3.

Gro Harlem Brundtland
Prime Minister of Norway

4

We need a wider definition of national security ... The destruction of the planet's environment is making the world a less stable place, politically, economically and militarily ... Our environmental management practices have focused largely upon after-the-fact repair of damage ... The ability to anticipate and prevent environmental damage will require that the ecological dimensions of policy be considered at the same time as the economic, trade, energy, agricultural and other dimensions.

TV broadcast, "Only One Earth"/
"Ms.," January:74.

George Bush
Vice President
of the United States;
Candidate for the 1988
Republican Presidential
nomination

5

I think we can compatibly have off-shore [oil-drilling] leasing. Right now we're sitting fat, dumb and happy in the United States; [we've] got energy prices down; you have what appears to be a glut of energy. [But] we are becoming more and more dependent on foreign oil, and that is not good national-security policy.

News conference, May 4/
The Washington Post, 6-6:(A)4.

6

I think for too long we've given the playing field away to the Democrats on the environment. I want to make the environment a Republican issue. I'd like to be remembered the same way as Teddy Roosevelt ... the Republican President who first made clear to us that nothing short of defending this country in wartime compares in importance to the great central task of leaving this land a better land for our descendants ... I want to leave a legacy of unspoiled land for our children and our children's children.

Campaign address/
Los Angeles Times, 5-17:(I)16.

(GEORGE BUSH)

1

[On off-shore drilling along the California coast]: Before going forward with new lease sales, we must be assured that the national treasure of the California coastline will not be harmed . . . I was one of the pioneers in the equipment end of off-shore drilling in the Gulf of Mexico, and I know it can be done safely. But there are other important considerations—tourism and marine life and aesthetics—and in some extraordinarily sensitive areas, those considerations may prevail until technology moves forward . . . In the long run, alternative fuels like methanol can reduce the pressure to drill in environmentally sensitive areas, just as they can reduce our dependence on foreign oil. Methanol offers better performance than gasoline, more pep, more pickup, more fun. It is the fuel, incidentally, of the Indy 500 [auto race].

Los Angeles, June 5/
The New York Times, 6-6:10.

George Bush
Vice President
of the United States;
1988 Republican
Presidential nominee

2

[Criticizing Democratic Presidential nominee Governor Michael Dukakis of Massachusetts]: [At the Boston Aquarium] they have an exhibit featuring a "sewage meter" to measure the pollution flowing into what the exhibit calls "the dirtiest harbor in America" [Boston Harbor]. The sewage meter is a measure of the cost of my opponent's neglect of the environment. He delays, and the harbor gets dirtier and dirtier. Half a billion gallons of barely treated sewage a day—into the harbor . . . And the exhibit reveals an appalling fact: The amount of sewage dumped into the harbor in 1986 would cover all of metropolitan Boston up to a depth of 17 feet . . . Boston is the only major city in America to dump it right in its own harbor.

Campaigning, Boston, Sept. 1/
Los Angeles Times,
9-2:(I)15.

3

I believe that we must use clean, safe nuclear power. The more dependent we become on foreign oil, the less our national security is enhanced . . . We're going to have to use more gas, more coal and more safe nuclear power for our energy base.

Presidential debate,
Los Angeles, Oct. 13/
The New York Times, 10-15:13.

4

I do believe that development of our most promising oil and gas reserves is called for, because continued domestic production of oil and gas is vital to the national security of the United States. At the same time, I oppose drilling in those environmental sensitive areas where the risk of [ecological] damage is too great.

Campaigning at
University of California,
San Diego, Oct. 14/
The New York Times, 10-15:8.

George Bush
Vice President,
and President-elect,
of the United States

5

The days a man spends fishing or spends hunting should not be deducted from the time that he's on earth. In other words, if I fish today, that should be added to the amount of time I get to live. That's the way I look at recreation. That's why I'll be a big conservation, environmental President, because I plan to fish and hunt as much as I possibly can.

News conference,
Beeville, Texas, Dec. 29/
Los Angeles Times, 12-30:(I)20.

Prince Charles
Prince of Wales

6

[Criticizing much of modern architecture]: This is very much the age of the computer and the

(PRINCE CHARLES)

word processor. But why on earth do we have to be surrounded by buildings that look like such machines?

Before Royal Institute
of British Architects/
The Wall Street Journal, 7-26:24.

William C. Clark
Ecologist, Kennedy School,
Harvard University

1

If you could tomorrow morning make water clean in the world, you would have done, in one fell swoop, the best thing you could have done for improving human health by improving environmental quality.

At Wingspread Conference,
Racine, Wis., April/
The Christian Science Monitor,
7-25:(B)4.

Paul Josef Crutzen
Director, Max Planck Institute
for Chemistry
(West Germany)

2

[On air pollution]: For a long time, climate researchers and meteorologists thought that [the Earth's atmosphere] was a very robust system. I believe that we must now come to a new way of thinking. Today we are seeing more [dangerous] accelerating effects than stabilizing ones. The ice ages did not make much difference. There were so few people on Earth then. When it got difficult somewhere, groups simply migrated. That won't work any more. When there are 10 billion people on the planet, all of whom want to live as we do, what will happen then? . . . The entire system would be simply impossible to maintain. We cannot wait 50 years before taking steps. They must come soon, and if we in the developed world do not take the initiative in this regard, the developing countries certainly will not follow.

Interview/World Press Review,
September:29.

Frank M. Cushing
Staff Director, Energy
and Natural Resources Committee,
U.S. Senate

3

[Saying public opinion and reasons of practicality may be coming around to support the opening of the now-shut-down Seabrook and Shoreham nuclear-power plants in the Northeast]: Political times change. Constituencies change. Party control in given areas of the country change. People see this as consistent not just from a states' rights standpoint, but from the standpoint of electric-power production and energy policy, too. Here we have two huge plants ready to operate, and we're looking at power outages in the Northeast, and everyone agrees on one thing: It's silly not to operate them.

Interview, Washington, Nov. 21/
The New York Times, 11-21:1.

Charles DiBona
President, American
Petroleum Institute

4

If we continue to see the decline in domestic [oil] production that we're seeing, and if we see the increase in consumption and therefore the increase in imports, then, at some point in the next decade, we will experience tightness in world markets and dependence on OPEC oil that will send prices soaring.

Interview/
USA Today, 11-29:(A)11.

Michael S. Dukakis
Governor of Massachusetts (D);
Candidate for the 1988 Democratic
Presidential nomination

5

If we can't have clean beaches and an attractive coastline and an ocean that we can swim in, then what is life about anyway? There is nothing more important and more precious in the world than the shoreline and the beach and the water and the ocean.

Campaigning,
Linden, N.J., May 29/
Los Angeles Times, 5-30:(I)20.

135

(MICHAEL S. DUKAKIS)

1

[Criticizing the Reagan Administration's policy of withholding funds from international organizations that support the use of abortion as a method of population control]: Given the direct relationship between over-population and environmental degradation, a reversal of the [Reagan Administration's] policy would be both substantively desirable and conducive to restoring our role as a global leader in environmental and population issues.

The Christian Science Monitor,
7-21:10.

Robert Gale
Chairman, advisory committee,
International Bone Marrow
Transplant Registry and
Bone Marrow Transplant Unit,
University of California, Los Angeles

2

[On nuclear power-plant accidents, such as the one in 1986 at Chernobyl in the U.S.S.R. after which he assisted the victims]: Unless we realize that the technologies we are dealing with are of international consequence, that the technologies are very serious, we are headed down a very dangerous and possibly disastrous path. That message is driven home by the Chernobyl accident, where we see that human beings can undermine even the most sophisticated technologies and that an accident anywhere in the world can have global repercussions.

Interview/USA Today, 4-27:(A)9.

Mikhail S. Gorbachev
General Secretary,
Communist Party
of the Soviet Union

3

International economic security is inconceivable unless related not only to disarmament but also to the elimination of the threat to the world's environment. In a number of regions, the state of the environment is simply frightening . . . Let us also think about setting up within the framework of the United Nations a center for emergency environmental assistance. Its function would be promptly to send international groups of experts to areas with badly deteriorating environment. The Soviet Union is also ready to cooperate in establishing an international space laboratory, or manned orbital station, designed exclusively for monitoring the state of the environment.

At United Nations,
New York, Dec. 7/
The New York Times, 12-8:(A)6.

Allan E. Gotlieb
Canadian Ambassador to the
United States

4

[On the problem of acid rain originating in the U.S. and falling on Canada]: The [U.S.] Administration has itself been of not two but several minds on this issue. It is divided between those who want to see action, those who are skeptical that the science justifies the expense, and those who oppose environmental regulation as an act of faith. It is further divided between those who accept that the U.S.A. has a legal obligation to Canada to act, and those who see the whole issue as a Canadian conspiracy to increase electrical exports. This mildly schizophrenic frame of mind has made our work with the Administration a pathway fraught with pitfalls and digressions.

At conference on acid rain,
University of Southern California,
Feb. 12/Los Angeles Times, 2-12:(I)37.

Michael Hooker
Chancellor, University of
Maryland, Baltimore County

5

I'm concerned mostly, I think, about the obscene avariciousness with which we [in Western countries] consume resources. [It is] a reflection of our culture, which tells me that there's something wrong spiritually with us—that, at least in American society, we *consume* material culture, use it up, spend it, waste it.

At Wingspread Conference,
Racine, Wis., April/
The Christian Science Monitor,
7-25:(B)4.

Lady Bird Johnson
Widow of the late President
of the United States
Lyndon B. Johnson

1

My heart has always responded to the environment. When I got to be 70, I thought, I'm going to take time to do what I really yearn to do, and that is work with native plants, wildflowers and trees, and encourage their use in the nation's landscape so they won't just be something of the past but will be passed on to our grandchildren.

Interview, L. B. J. Ranch, Texas/
Good Housekeeping, February:169.

2

I've had a long love affair with the environment. It is my sustenance, my pleasure, my joy. Flowers in a city are like lipstick on a women—it just makes you look better to have a little color.

Time, 5-9:88.

J. Bennett Johnston
United States Senator,
D-Louisiana

3

We have only one planet. If we screw it up, we have no place to go.

USA Today, 8-23:(A)8.

4

[On the "greenhouse effect," a warming of the planet caused by man-made gases released into the atmosphere]: It [the greenhouse effect] is so much more comprehensive, so much more dangerous, so much more revolutionary, so much more life-changing than anything else we have done, that it literally means everything as far as this Congress is concerned and as far as our lifestyles and our very economy is concerned.

Los Angeles Times, 9-1:(I)30.

George M. Keller
Chairman,
Chevron Corporation

5

I'd like to challenge the sincere and dedicated individuals who work for environmental causes to repudiate the more extreme and hostile voices in their movement and to try to work with us to raise the level of dialogue . . . There are some people for whom a love of the works of nature seems to engender a corresponding hatred of the works of man . . . These people need to realize that human technology and the products of our industry are what stand between us and the hostile elements, between us and constant hunger, between us and the ravages of disease and predation . . . I'm not sure what solutions we'll find to deal with all our environmental problems, but I'm sure of this: They will be provided by industry; they will be products of technology. Where else *can* they come from?

Before California Manufacturers
Association/
Nation's Business, June:12.

Frank R. Lautenberg
United States Senator,
D-New Jersey

6

[On recent cases of dumped waste washing ashore at beaches]: The ocean is tired. It's throwing back at us what we're throwing in there.

USA Today, 8-11:(A)10.

Patrick J. Leahy
United States Senator,
D-Vermont

7

[On the global warming trend thought to be caused by increasing man-made carbon-dioxide emissions into the atmosphere]: If we do nothing, many soybean farmers in the Southeast could be out of business. If we do nothing, warming could drive the sugar maple right out of Vermont, which would be a catastrophe for my state . . . Congress can't seem to make up its mind about whether it wants a two-year budget, let alone focus on the effects of global warming which may not occur for several decades. But there is too much at stake to let our normal cynicism—or realism—about Congressional leadership hold sway. It is our job to worry about the long-term future of American agriculture and forestry.

Washington, Dec. 1/
Los Angeles Times, 12-2:(I)41.

Grenville Lucas
Chairman, Survival Services
Commission, International Union
for Conservation of Nature
and Natural Resources

1

There is a growing awareness of governments and people that our wild animals, vegetation and plants are our life-support system, and must be saved. Slowly the trend is changing. My fear is it is not changing fast enough. We are winning the battles—but we are losing the war.

At general assembly of
International Union
for Conservation of Nature
and Natural Resources,
San Jose, Costa Rica/
The Christian Science Monitor,
2-8:13.

George J. Mitchell
United States Senator, D-Maine

2

The quality of the natural environment and the quality of human life are inseparable. Indeed, if the most threatening predictions about the greenhouse effect come true, the very survival of human life may be determined by the quality of the environment. Indiscriminate use of the atmosphere and the oceans as dumps for our wastes has poisoned the atmosphere and fouled the oceans . . . We have found that, just as neglect of pollution controls means dirtier air, emphasis on controls can mean cleaner air. Americans are suffering from a man-made phenomenon that can be controlled. We have developed the technologies of control. We have the resources to apply those technologies. All we lack is the political will to do so.

Before the Senate,
Washington, Oct. 4/
The Washington Post, 10-7:(A)21.

William Penn Mott
Director,
National Park Service

3

[On environmentalist proposals that hotels and concessions be removed from National Parks]: We can't agree with that. We think that it's our responsibility to provide accommodations for various people. Not everybody wants to sleep in a sleeping bag on the ground. Some like tents; some like camper cars; some like a motel kind of accommodation. Our job is to provide a variety of accommodations . . . I think what we need to do is to be sure to design those accommodations so that they do not destroy the very natural and cultural values that we're trying to maintain in the parks. We are not going to overdevelop in this direction, and if accommodations can be provided outside the park, then we would encourage that sort of thing.

Interview/
USA Today, 8-25:(A)7.

Daniel Patrick Moynihan
United States Senator,
D-New York

4

[On the dumping of wastes in the ocean]: The governing classes nowadays want to talk about social justice and projects that provide jobs for lawyers. No one wants to talk about sewers.

USA Today,
8-11:(A)10.

Brian Mulroney
Prime Minister
of Canada

5

Acid rain doesn't discriminate. It's killing lakes and streams in the Eastern United States and in Canada. We have to have a treaty with the United States to reduce this blight. People can't use beaches. Salmon rivers are being polluted. As your neighbor, you're [the U.S.] my friend. I give you the benefit of the doubt. The test of our friendship is that I don't have the right to pollute your front lawn or dump garbage in your back yard. I told [the U.S.] Congress, "We're your best friend. Why are you doing this [sending acid rain] to us?"

Interview,
Ottawa, Aug. 25/
USA Today, 8-26:(A)9.

Dan Quayle
United States Senator,
R-Indiana; 1988 Republican
Vice-Presidential nominee

1

When you bring up the environment, you can't help but think about the environmental policy of the Governor of Massachusetts [Democratic Presidential nominee Michael Dukakis]. He talks about being an environmentalist. Let me tell you about his environmental policy. The Boston Harbor? The Boston Harbor, which is the dirtiest waterway in America. Tons of raw sewage go in there each and every day. What has the Governor of Massachusetts done about that? Virtually nothing. And then he has the audacity to go down to New Jersey and tell the people in New Jersey that he's against ocean dumping. This is the same Governor that applied for a license to dump Massachusetts sewage, waste, off the coast of New Jersey.

At Vice-Presidential debate,
Omaha, Neb., Oct. 5/
The New York Times, 10-7:(A)12.

William D. Ruckelshaus
Former Administrator,
Environmental Protection Agency
of the United States

2

You go into a community and they will vote 80 percent to 20 percent in favor of a tougher Clean Air Act, but if you ask them to devote 20 minutes a year to having their car emissions inspected, they will vote 80 to 20 against it. We are a long way in this country from taking individual responsibility for the environmental problem. Just drive down the highway and watch the guy in front of you throw junk out of his car window. Unless we can get individuals to act differently than they do now, we have a hell of a problem.

The New York Times, 11-30:(A)14.

Marvin Runyon
Chairman, Tennessee
Valley Authority

3

If you were starting from scratch today, you'd find that nuclear power would cost you twice as much as fossil power. [But] the other thing you have to look at is long-term—and this is what I'm trying to find out—how long is fossil fuel going to be available? How much fuel do you have? If you look at other countries, for example Japan, they're building quite a number of nuclear plants. They have no coal to speak of in their country.

Interview/USA Today, 2-2:(A)13.

Robert Rycroft
Director, program in science,
technology and public policy,
George Washington University

4

Our method of doing environmental protection really has depended on a crisis mentality . . . The whole notion of crisis is a short-term orientation that worked in the past to environmentalists' advantage. But I'm not sure it does any more. Sometimes the problems stretch out too long to be able to show real crisis.

The Christian Science Monitor,
9-14:6.

Andrei D. Sakharov
Dissident Soviet physicist

5

The problem of the safety of nuclear energy is a very important question. It became especially acute after the events in Chernobyl [the Soviet nuclear accident in 1986]. The radioactive elements [released into the atmosphere from that accident] surpassed the total radioactivity of all past nuclear disasters. I'm deeply convinced nuclear energy should be developed, but it must be absolutely safe. My proposal is to put nuclear reactors underground.

News conference, Boston, Nov. 7/
USA Today, 11-8:(A)8.

Patricia Schroeder
United States Representative,
D-Colorado

6

We [the U.S.] once led the way in attacking such problems as acid rain, ozone depletion,

(PATRICIA SCHROEDER)

water pollution and toxic wastes. Now our leaders speak and the world laughs. What is their answer to ozone depletion? Hats and sunglasses ... There is an ancient Indian saying: "We do not inherit the earth from ancestors; we borrow it from our children." If we use this ethic as a moral compass, then our rendezvous with reality can also become a rendezvous with opportunity.

"Ms.," February:52.

1

Clean air is an area where the Federal government will wimp out with the slightest bit of pressure.

USA Today, 5-5:(A)6.

Peter Seligmann
President, Conservation
International

2

The President of Bolivia ... is trying to develop an economic program based upon the capacity of the country's resource base. That means a slow-growth economic-development program that will survive over time. Using the resource base as an endowment, it is managed in such a way that resources will be as productive tomorrow as they are today. The philosophy of the Bolivian President and Congress is that, for their own good, that is the way they have to treat their renewable resource base—their forests, their soils, their watersheds and their fisheries. Because otherwise they're going to run out of productive land, and they're going to lose the ability to feed their population ... I see Bolivia as a leader in this ... The only way that the health of our planet will be protected—and that species diversity, rain forests, etc., will be preserved—is if the economies of those nations can be benefited from conservation. And if the people can be fed. You can create parks, and you can educate people about birds and the environment. But if you haven't fed people, you haven't reduced the pressure to clear forests. The only

way conservation can work is if it is seen as just part of the fabric of development—part of the fabric of growth of human society.

Interview, San Francisco/
The Christian Science Monitor,
1-4:4.

Norman Steisel
Former Commissioner of
Sanitation of
New York City

3

People are only aware of garbage when it piles up on the street.

USA Today, 7-11:(A)8.

Russell E. Train
Former Administrator,
Environmental Protection Agency
of the United States

4

No nation in the world has grappled so successfully with [environmental] issues [in the past] as the United States. Without these accomplishments, where would we be today? We would be like Mexico City or Sao Paulo. [But] the problems hitting us now—problems like toxic wastes, acid rain and global warming—are hellishly more complex and difficult, not only technically but politically and economically.

The New York Times, 11-30:(A)14.

Henry A. Waxman
United States Representative,
D-California

5

We have been slow to recognize the danger of acid rain and slower still to respond to it. But the time has now come for the U.S. to listen to its leading scientists and once again play a leadership role in the development of responsible environmental policies.

At conference on acid rain,
University of Southern California,
Feb. 12/Los Angeles Times,
2-13:(I)37.

George M. Woodwell
Director, Woods Hole
Research Center

1

Until now, the environment has been large in proportion to the demands that we've put on it. Now our influences are large.

At Wingspread Conference,
Racine, Wis., April/
The Christian Science Monitor, 7-25:(B)4.

Foreign Affairs

Philip Alston
Professor of international law,
Tufts University

1

[Saying human rights has become an international concept]: This concept of international accountability is a major breakthrough, and a single most important achievement [of the human-rights movement] in global terms. In the '40s, it was assumed that what you did to your own citizens was your own business. That's all changed now. Most states still tend to make a token defense that it's a local matter, but [that defense] never gets anywhere nowadays.

The Christian Science Monitor,
6-8:16.

Daniel arap Moi
President of Kenya

2

U.S. Secretary of State George Shultz is un-American in that he is not arrogant.

Interview/USA Today, 9-16:(A)9.

Georgi A. Arbatov
Director, Soviet Institute of
U.S.A. and Canadian Affairs

3

[On the Soviet Union's new efforts to win the friendship of Western nations]: Even the professional Russia-haters must now admit that things have changed, and they've changed for the better. We are going to do something terrible to you—we are going to deprive you of an enemy.

Time, 5-23:25.

4

What has taken place in the last three years in Soviet-American relations has changed the international agenda. Previously, our goals were more limited ... to reduce tension, to steer events away from confrontation. Now we have the pos-

sibility to move toward demilitarization in Soviet-American relations, to destroy the entire building and infrastructure of the cold war erected in the post-war era ... The first steps have shown that it is possible to destroy the cold war. When there is no enemy, then the whole structure of the cold war starts to destroy itself.

Moscow, May 26/
Los Angeles Times, 5-27:(I)24.

5

[On *perestroika*, reform, in the Soviet Union]: We are acquiring a new image of ourselves. Our views of the U.S. are evolving as well. We are realizing that we cannot achieve security at your [America's] expense. We hope you will feel the same about the Soviet Union. If you are not secure, neither are we. We must find ways of surviving together. I want to emphasize that what we are doing is not for the purpose of impressing others. It is for ourselves. We are doing what we think is necessary in our own interest. We like to believe it is also in your interest and the world interest.

At Dartmouth Conference, U.S.A./
The Christian Science Monitor,
6-6:14.

Michael H. Armacost
Under Secretary for Political
Affairs, Department of State
of the United States

6

[On the Soviet Union's new efforts to win the friendship of Western nations]: We and the Soviets are necessary partners on some issues, like avoiding nuclear war, preventing local crises from becoming wider confrontations and defusing regional conflicts. But we're also geopolitical rivals. That hasn't changed. The Soviets will continue to try to erode the strategic advantages of the U.S. They will do so, however, in a more adroit and sophisticated manner than the

(MICHAEL H. ARMACOST)

old crowd . . . The Soviets are more attentive to the diplomatic methods of solving a problem, as opposed to merely relying on blatant displays of raw muscle. But they're also using diplomacy in pursuit of their traditional goal of hemming us in where necessary, rolling us back where possible.

Time, 5-23:25.

Alfred L. Atherton
Former United States
Ambassador to Egypt

1

Morale [in the U.S. Foreign Service] is worse now than I can remember. The signal has gone out from the [Reagan Administration] that it doesn't see the Foreign Service as a national asset. [Secretary of State George] Shultz has tried to protect the Service, but he is crying in the wilderness.

Interview/
Los Angeles Times, 5-14:(I)1.

Lloyd Bentsen
United States Senator,
D-Texas;
1988 Democratic
Vice-Presidential nominee

2

[Criticizing Republican Presidential nominee Vice President George Bush for not trying to stop the U.S. sale of arms to Iran, which turned out to be an exchange for U.S. hostages held in Lebanon]: You can't trade arms for hostages. When you try to do that, there's no question but what you just encourage more taking of hostages, and that's been the result, by this dumb idea that was cooked up in the White House basement. And I want to tell you that George Bush, attending 17 of those meetings and having no record of what he said—if Lloyd Bentsen was in those meetings, you would certainly hear from him, and no one would be asking where is Lloyd, because I would be saying, "That's a dumb idea, and now let's put an end to it."

At Vice-Presidential debate,
Omaha, Neb., Oct. 5/
The New York Times, 10-7:(A)14.

Stanley Brand
Lawyer; Former General
Counsel to the U.S. House of
Representatives

3

Congress has the power to declare war. Congress has the power to raise armies and navies. Congress has the power to appropriate money for those purposes. And Congress has the power to make all laws that shall be necessary and proper for carrying out those powers. The Executive Branch and Presidents, both Republican and Democratic, have relied on vague, empty phrases, like Commander-in-Chief, to supply what they say are the specific powers to commit American forces overseas. That's Constitutional hogwash.

Interview/USA Today, 3-17:(A)7.

L. Paul Bremer III
Ambassador-at-Large for
Counter-terrorism,
Department of State
of the United States

4

[Saying the U.S. would be critical of any deal that allowed the killer-hijackers of a Kuwaiti airliner to go free after releasing the remaining hostages from the plane in Algeria]: These people, if they go free, will be free to attack another plane . . . We think that one of the hijackers of TWA flight 847 three years ago, [in which a U.S. serviceman was killed] may have been on this plane. In other words, he may have already committed murder twice . . . so it's not a theoretical point about how you deal with terrorism. This is a very practical question of how you deal with criminals.

The Christian Science Monitor,
4-21:5.

Harold Brown
Former Secretary of Defense
of the United States

5

[On the current improved relations between the U.S. and the Soviet Union, which features the forthcoming Moscow summit meeting by U.S.

(HAROLD BROWN)

President Reagan and Soviet leader Mikhail Gorbachev]: The U.S. and the Soviet Union clearly have . . . a considerable stake in maintaining this version of detente. This particular summit . . . is symbolic in the sense of a clearly anti-Soviet President putting his seal of approval on a form of detente . . . and an emphasis on the cooperation part of the cooperation-competition dichotomy that characterizes U.S.-Soviet relations.

The Christian Science Monitor,
5-24:7.

George Bush
Vice President of the United
States, Candidate for the
1988 Republican
Presidential nomination

1

[Criticizing Congress' handling of foreign-policy matters]: You got 535 secretaries of state up there with their own briefcases and their own agenda. The American people see that. All of them running around hauling people in to testify about where you were on the night of the 23rd. The world outside observes and loses faith. Our chaos does not go unnoticed around the world.

Campaign speech,
New Hampshire, Feb. 11/
The Washington Post, 2-12:(A)18.

2

There's an isolationist trend in this country that must not be allowed to happen. Everybody wants everybody else to pay for things and join in, but that's not the real world. The fact is the United States has a disproportionate responsibility. That's the theme I'll be talking about, and I think the public understands it.

U.S. News & World Report, 5-2:23.

3

[On Democratic Presidential candidate Michael Dukakis]: Governor Dukakis draws his foreign-policy views from the latest trend in the Harvard Yard boutique. He says he would rely heavily on multinational organizations such as the UN. Well, the UN does some useful things: It has an active, sometimes effective, economic and social council. But I was our Ambassador to the UN, and I know its limitations.

At Republican Unity Conference,
Denver, June 10/
The New York Times, 6-11:8.

4

[On Soviet leader Mikhail Gorbachev's program of reform in the Soviet Union]: The steel door has opened a crack and the fresh air of freedom is beginning to seep through. Will that door slam shut again . . . or open up to a new age of hope . . . ? We can't know that now . . . We must be bold enough to seize the opportunity to change, but at the same time be prepared for what one pundit called "the protracted conflict."

Before World Affairs Council
of Northern California,
San Francisco, June 29/
The Washington Post, 6-30:(A)14.

5

[On the forthcoming Presidential election in which he will be running against Democratic nominee Michael Dukakis]: A tremendous difference is going to be on the national security of this country, how to deal with the major world problems and who best to sit across the table from [Soviet leader Mikhail] Gorbachev or a wide array of other leaders, who best to lead the alliance, who has enough confidence and experience to chart a course for the future. My case to the American people is, that's me. I'd be better at this than Michael Dukakis.

Interview, Washington/
Time, 7-25:33.

6

The American Century has not drawn to a close. America has set in motion the major changes under way in the world today—the

(GEORGE BUSH)

growth of democracy, the spread of free enterprise, the creation of a world market in goods and
ideas. For the foreseeable future, no other nation,
or group of nations, will step forward to assume
leadership.

Speech, Aug. 2/
The New York Times, 11-2:(A)1.

1

[On the accidental shooting down by a U.S.
Navy warship of an Iranian passenger plane over
the Persian Gulf]: I will never apologize for the
United States of America—I don't care what the
facts are.

Newsweek, 8-15:15.

2

[Criticizing Democratic Presidential nominee
Michael Dukakis on foreign policy]: I do not
think that the United States should [subordi-
nate] its role to multilateral organizations. If we'd
done that in the Persian Gulf, I don't believe
you'd see an Iran-Iraq cease-fire. The United
States has a disproportionate responsibility to
lead. If we'd have listened to [Dukakis] in Angola
and pulled the rug out from under [Angolan rebel
leader Jonas] Savimbi, I don't believe you would
see a potential for Cubans getting out of Angola
. . . And I am certainly convinced that if we listen
to [Dukakis] in Central America, where he is
unwilling to support the contras [rebels fighting
the Sandinista government in Nicaragua] at all,
that we would be a party to locking in a Communist regime right in the heart of those core four
democracies.

Interview, Washington/
Newsweek, 8-22:20.

George Bush
Vice President of the United States;
1988 Republican
Presidential nominee

3

[On Democratic Presidential nominee Michael
Dukakis]: My opponent's view of the world sees

a long, slow decline for our country, an inevitable
fall mandated by impersonal historical forces.
But America is not in decline. America is a rising
nation. He sees America as another pleasant
country on the UN roll call, somewhere between
Albania and Zimbabwe. And I see America as
the leader, a unique nation with a special role in
the world.

Accepting the nomination,
at Republican National Convention,
New Orleans, Aug. 18/
The New York Times, 8-19:8.

4

[On Democratic Presidential nominee Michael
Dukakis]: He does not, I believe, see America as
a leader of the West. It has not, I believe,
occurred to him that if America does not lead the
free countries of the world, the free countries of
the world will not have a leader.

At fund-raising event,
Los Angeles, Sept. 13/
The New York Times, 9-15:15.

5

I've met [Soviet leader Mikhail] Gorbachev.
Met [Soviet Foreign Minister Eduard] Shevardnadze and talked substance with him the other
day. These people are tough. But now [with the
reforms taking place in the Soviet Union] we
have a chance. If we have the experience and the
know-how to handle it. But please do not go back
to the days when the [U.S.] military was as weak
as they could be, when the morale was down and
when we were the laughing-stock around the
world. And now we are back because we have
strengthened the defenses of this country and,
believe me, I don't want to see us return to those
days.

At Presidential debate,
Winston-Salem, N.C., Sept. 25/
The New York Times, 9-26:12.

6

[On Soviet leader Mikhail Gorbachev's programs of *perestroika*—reform—and *glasnost*—

(GEORGE BUSH)

openness—in the Soviet Union]: What I think we ought to do is take a look at *perestroika* and *glasnost,* welcome them, but keep our eyes open, be cautious, because the Soviet change is not fully established yet . . . I'm encouraged by what I hear when I talk to Mr. Gorbachev and [Foreign Minister Eduard] Shevardnadze. But can they pull it off? . . . All I'm suggesting is let's not be naive in dealing with the Soviets and make a lot of unilateral [defense] cuts hoping against hope that they will match our bid.

At Presidential debate,
Winston-Salem, N.C., Sept. 25/
The New York Times, 9-28:12.

1

[It would be] far too simple, even dangerous, to conclude that Soviet foreign policy is driven exclusively by economic weakness. Where we have seen flexibility, it has come because the price of aggression was too high, because we supported the *mujaheddeen* [resistance fighters] in Afghanistan. It has come because intimidation failed, because we deployed the *Pershing* and cruise missiles in Europe in the face of the strong freeze movement. Yes, the Soviets are restrained by their own troubles. But they are also restrained by our strength, our ability to deter aggression, the unity of the democracies. To abandon that, to turn away from that path, is to invite trouble.

At Westminster College,
Fulton, Mo., Oct. 18/
The New York Times, 10-19:(A)10.

2

[Soviet leader Mikhail Gorbachev] is able to reverse course when Soviet policies fail, when the costs become too high. Those costs become too high not only when there is a shortage of food in Moscow but also when we resist aggression and intimidation. The costs become too high when the *mujaheddeen* [Afghan rebels], helped by the United States, fight for freedom in Afghanistan. The costs become too high when

the United States and NATO deploy *Pershing* and cruise missiles in Europe despite Soviet threats. But where those costs have not been clear, the Soviets have not changed. In the Middle East, in the Persian Gulf and in Central America, we see traditional Soviet policies. The opportunity for narrow gains still attracts Moscow.

At University of Michigan, Oct. 19/
The Washington Post, 12-14:(A)25.

3

. . . power remains a very important part of world politics—to protect peace and advance the cause of freedom. A President must have the experience to know when and how to use power, the prudent use of power, and be willing to do so when he has to do that.

At Republican breakfast meeting,
Colorado Springs, Colo., Nov. 6/
The Washington Post, 11-7:(A)17.

4

[On high-level U.S.-Soviet talks]: I've never supported meetings just for the sake of having a meeting. I want some progress to take place, but it doesn't have to be progress on START or on one category or another. We have arms control, we have human rights, we have regional differences. And I can see reasons to talk about any, provided there's reason to believe there will be progress.

News conference, Nov. 9/
The Washington Post, 11-17:(A)21.

5

[On Soviet leader Mikhail Gorbachev's program of reform and openness in the Soviet Union]: We welcome the developments in the Soviet Union, but we should not let our hopes outrun our practical experience. Soviet ideology has proven bankrupt, but Russia remains a formidable military power. [Gorbachev promises more democracy,] but in the final analysis, the Soviet Union will be judged by what it delivers.

Campaigning/
Los Angeles Times, 11-14:(I)14.

George Bush
Vice President, and
President-elect, of
the United States

1

[On the new Administration he is putting together]: We're going to take whatever time is necessary for a thorough review and analysis on our [foreign-] policy objectives, and then come out with our own strategic objectives, and then move this country forward together for a strong America, determined more than ever to work for peace and freedom, to strengthen our alliances, to help those around the world who need our help, to enhance the quest for human rights around the world and to deal realistically with the Soviet Union and other world powers.

News conference,
Washington, Nov. 23/
The New York Times, 11-24:(A)10.

2

Do we have any differences with the Soviets? Absolutely. Are they regional? Yes. Are they on human rights? Yes. Do we have some differences on how we ought to approach the arms-control agenda? Certainly. But am I optimistic about what I see in the Soviet Union? Absolutely. And you just take a look at the human-rights question. There have been some good steps forward there, and I want to see more. I think we come into a great period of opportunity in terms of reduction of regional tensions. But there's an awful lot that the Soviets can do to make me feel I'm right in that.

News conference,
Washington, Dec. 6/
The New York Times, 12-7:(A)9.

3

[On whether the public should have been informed about an anonymous threat against Pan American Airways, which was revealed after a Pan Am passenger plane crashed in Scotland and sabotage was suspected]: I think when you are dealing with intelligence which can be an unsubstantiated threat, can be a crackpot phone call or

it can be a real warning, what you've got to do is evaluate that intelligence. And I think the answer is sometimes, by going public, you give undue attention to what the terrorist wants to call attention to. And so often it's best to handle these matters by aborting the threat. And you've got to evaluate the threat. I found from some experience in the intelligence business that you get enormous numbers of suggestions that there's going to be some kind of terroristic action, and most of them never materialize. So I think you have to look at it on a case-by-case basis. But if you have hard evidence that a specific flight was going to be threatened or that the threat could not be contained, clearly you would want to serve the public good by notifying people.

News conference,
Washington, Dec. 22/
The New York Times,
12-23:(A)10.

Robert C. Byrd
United States Senator,
D-West Virginia

4

There seems to be a great rush today to sign treaties, to enter into treaties, and they seem to be dictated by the calendar all too much, by deadlines that have to be met, by summits that have to be met. I would urge in this summit binge and treaty binge, that we go a little slow, and do the job right, because this Senate is not going to be jerked around and hastened overly in order to meet summits.

Before the Senate,
Washington, March 23/
The New York Times, 3-24:8.

5

[On working out arms-control agreements with the Soviets in the wake of the current summit meeting between U.S. President Reagan and Soviet leader Mikhail Gorbachev]: My suggestion would be that we make haste slowly and not go too fast . . . Summits are fine, good headline media events, but the devil is in the details.

Moscow, June 1/
Los Angeles Times, 6-2:(I)10.

147

Frank C. Carlucci
Secretary of Defense
of the United States

1

[On the recent summit meeting between U.S. President Reagan and Soviet leader Mikhail Gorbachev]: Summitry is no substitute for security. Until we see tangible changes [in Soviet policy] we should not change our defense policies. We are still facing a very substantial military threat . . . [Gorbachev] is not, so to speak, changing the fundamental structure of society; he is just trying to make the [Soviet] system more efficient. If the end result of that is a Soviet Union that is less expansionist in its foreign policy, that stops its human-rights violations or that comes to respect human-rights values, and is more open to a dialogue with the West, then we will all be better off. But if the end result is that the Western alliance relaxes its defense effort and the Soviet Union modernizes its industrial and technological base, and if some time in the 1990s it ends up as a society that can produce enormous quantities of weapons even more effectively than it does today, then we will have made an enormous miscalculation.

Before Japan National Press Club,
Tokyo, June 6/
The Washington Post, 6-7:(A)1.

Fidel Castro
President of Cuba

2

If there's a revolution in a small Caribbean country, the United States screams. But if there is an economic problem that poses bankruptcy for tens of countries in the Third World, and it conflicts with the interest within a small group in the United States, the United States pursues a selfish policy.

Interview/
USA Today, 2-22:(A)7.

3

The American politicians don't have a policy for the Third World. They just improvise it.

Interview/USA Today, 6-2:(A)2.

Robert F. Chandler, Jr.
Founding director,
International Rice
Research Institute

4

. . . we must continue to intensify our struggle to bring a better life to the poverty-stricken people of the Third World. It must be said, however, that the job cannot be done by the richer nations alone. The afflicted countries must come to realize that their survival depends upon their own national efforts. They must fully and wisely utilize not only foreign financial and professional assistance but their own resources, both human and natural . . . I predict that world population will at least double before it becomes stable. If this forecast is true, it will require a herculean effort, with an enormous commitment of financial and human resources, to maintain this planet as an acceptable place in which to live.

Accepting General Foods World
Food Prize, Oct. 4/
The Washington Post, 10-13:(A)18.

Clark M. Clifford
Former Secretary of Defense
of the United States

5

I believe that, on balance, covert activities have harmed this country more than they have helped us. Certainly, efforts to control these activities, to keep them within their intended scope and purpose, have failed.

Before House Intelligence
Committee, Washington/
The Christian Science Monitor,
3-31:13.

Barber B. Conable
President, World Bank

6

I realize that population policy touches upon sensitive cultural and religious values. But the societies in which population is growing so fast must accept that many—perhaps most—of these new lives will be miserable, malnourished and brief . . . Poverty on today's scale prevents a

(BARBER B. CONABLE)

billion people from having even minimally acceptable standards of living. To allow every fifth human being on our planet to suffer such an existence is a moral outrage.

At meeting of World Bank
and International Monetary Fund,
West Berlin, Sept. 27/
The Washington Post, 9-28:(D)1,4.

Milovan Djilas
Author; Former Vice President
of Yugoslavia

1

The crisis of Communism, from Belgrade to Peking, is continuous ... Every Communist country suffers from the inbuilt inadequacies of the system ... Let us be quite clear about one thing: The Soviet leaders' attempt to reform the system is not inspired by some noble realization that the system is unjust or poorly regarded abroad, but by strict necessity. They have come to realize what other Communists in Yugoslavia, Poland, Hungary, Czechoslovakia and China realized much earlier—that Communism doesn't work.

Interview/
The Washington Post, 12-5:(A)23.

Robert J. Dole
United States Senator,
R-Kansas; Candidate for the
1988 Republican
Presidential nomination

2

What alarms me most about [Soviet leader Mikhail] Gorbachev, for all that he brings that is new, [he] also brings something that is very, very old: the convictions of a committed, dedicated, tough-as-nails Communist. He's a Communist still—in his head, in his heart. [Nevertheless, the] emergence of Mr. Gorbachev is a powerful incentive to work even harder for new agreements with the Soviet Union.

At University of Iowa, Jan. 19/
The New York Times, 1-20:12.

3

[Democratic Presidential candidate Michael Dukakis] says that the Monroe Doctrine, which has defined America's security in its own neighborhood for some 200 years, is "obsolete." He says that this country has no choice but to tolerate the existence of Soviet client states wherever subversion might install them. Any other course of action, he tells us, is too dangerous to contemplate. [The Democratic Presidential candidates] have chosen America, and not Communism, as their hemispheric villain. [This] shows how strange and potentially dangerous these times really are ... The salient fact is that each of the dominoes that the attitude of apology helps to topple into the pocket of Communism is also a building block for further Communist power. The mentality, so prevalent among the Democratic candidates, that seeks to limit our options and capabilities in advance is the same mentality that casually accepts the expansion of the Soviet empire into the hemisphere we call our own. It is a mentality which believes that surrender is a prevention of war rather than a provocation.

At Center for Strategic
and International Studies, Washington,
March 23/The New York Times, 3-24:10.

4

[Democratic Presidential candidate Michael Dukakis has made the argument that the U.S.] must not antagonize its enemies or exert itself too strenuously in behalf of its friends. Perverse, but pervasive, this attitude has enveloped the Democratic side of the [Presidential] primary campaign like nerve gas.

At Center for Strategic
and International Studies, Washington,
March 23/Los Angeles Times, 3-24:(I)20.

Michael S. Dukakis
Governor of Massachusetts (D);
Candidate for the
1988 Democratic
Presidential nomination

5

It's one thing to provide—or withhold—support for a government that is restricting or

(MICHAEL S. DUKAKIS)

eliminating the rights of its citizens and the liberties of its citizens. And I think that's appropriate; we should not be supporting nations that don't give their citizens full democratic expression. But there is a difference between that and going in and overthrowing governments whose ideology we don't happen to agree with.

Interview, Brookline, Mass./
U.S. News & World Report, 2-1:25.

1

I think there will continue to be a competition between the United States and the Soviet Union because we happen to have very different ideologies. In [journalist] Tom Brokaw's interview with [Soviet leader Mikhail] Gorbachev, the most striking thing about it was the extent to which Gorbachev bristled when Brokaw started challenging him on human rights. He really got mad, and you could see it. There's a fundamental difference there between our values and perceptions.

Interview/
Los Angeles Times, 5-26:(I)1.

2

Communism and autocracy and dictatorship always have tough consequences for people. That's one of the reasons why I want this country always to be a leader for human rights and democracy. But how we demonstrate that leadership and how we use our power is always the question.

Interview, Washington, July 13/
The Washington Post, 7-14:(A)14.

Michael S. Dukakis
Governor of Massachusetts (D);
1988 Democratic
Presidential nominee

3

[On the Reagan Administration's foreign policy]: Frankly, they're coming a lot closer to where I am, not only on U.S.-Soviet relations,

but with the [Persian] Gulf settlement and southern Africa. Here's an Administration that five years ago was talking about the [Soviet] "evil empire," and now the President is walking arm-and-arm with [Soviet leader Mikhail] Gorbachev in Red Square. I'm very supportive of the President as he moves in this direction.

Interview, Cincinnati, Aug. 9/
Los Angeles Times, 8-10:(I)18.

4

[Criticizing Vice President and Republican Presidential nominee George Bush on foreign policy]: Making tough decisions is a test of leadership. George Bush endorsed the decision to sell arms to Iran, and in doing so he failed that test ... Here's a man who supported the sale of arms to a terrorist nation, one of the worst foreign-policy disasters of this decade; was part of an Administration that was doing business with drug-running Panamanian dictators, funneled aid to the contras [Nicaraguan rebels] through convicted drug dealers, went to the Philippines in the early '80s and commended [then President and dictator Ferdinand] Marcos and his commitment to democracy—and he's talking about judgment?

News conference,
Amherst, Mass., Aug. 30/
The New York Times, 8-31:1.

5

If there's one thing we understand, it is that you cannot make concessions to terrorists—ever—because, if you do, it's an open invitation to other terrorists to take hostages and to blackmail us. And that's the tragedy of the Iran-contra scandal. As a matter of fact [Vice President and Republican Presidential nominee George] Bush was the chairman of a task force on international terrorism which issued a report shortly before that decision was made [that ended in trading U.S. arms to Iran in exchange for the release of American hostages held in Lebanon], and said, and rightly so, that we never, ever, can make concessions to terrorists and hostage-takers. And yet, after sitting through meeting after meeting, he

(MICHAEL S. DUKAKIS)

endorsed that decision, endorsed the sale of arms to the Ayatollah [in Iran] in exchange for hostages—one of the most tragic, one of the most mistaken foreign-policy decisions we've ever made in this country, and I dare say encouraged others to take hostages, as we now know.

At Presidential debate,
Winston-Salem, N.C., Sept. 25/
The New York Times, 9-26:12.

1

I intend to be a President with only one foreign-policy goal: I want to restore respect for American leadership in a changing world. The kind of respect that Franklin Roosevelt earned when he championed the Four Freedoms in crushing Hitler during World War II. The kind of respect that John Kennedy earned when he forced the withdrawal of those Soviet missiles from Cuba and signed the world's first nuclear test-ban agreement.

Sept. 12/
The New York Times, 11-2:(A)1.

2

It's not necessary that everyone love us [the U.S.]. It wouldn't be healthy if everyone feared us. It's not necessary that everyone agree with all our philosophies all of the time. But if we are to lead in this diverse and dangerous world, if our words are to be heard and our warnings are to be heeded, we must be respected.

Campaign speech,
Philadelphia, Sept. 12/
The New York Times, 9-13:10.

3

Some of us [Democrats] do not, and will not, accept the tragedies of the past as a prophecy for the future ... We want to challenge the Soviet leaders, test their intentions and explore the opportunities that may exist to build a safer world. [Soviet leader Mikhail] Gorbachev is a Leninist. He has not abandoned Soviet goals, but

rather seeks to advance those goals through different means ... Mr. Gorbachev presides over a nation that has seen its rate of economic growth fall in every five-year plan since the 1950s ... [He] wants to make this country part of the international economic community. He wants access to Western resources and technology ... What is he prepared to do in return? [The U.S. should] translate Soviet economic weakness into improved Soviet behavior in world affairs [and] hold out the prospect of better economic ties.

Before Chicago Council on
Foreign Relations, Sept. 13/
Los Angeles Times, 10-10:(I)16.

4

[Criticizing Republican Vice-Presidential nominee Dan Quayle]: Three times since 1945, men who served as Vice President have been called to the Presidency. In each case, these men have had to engage in tough bargaining with the Soviet leader ... Dan Quayle is no Jerry Ford. He is no Lyndon Johnson. And he sure ain't Harry Truman. Can we stake our future on the hope that he is a match for [Soviet leader] Mikhail Gorbachev?

Before Chicago Council on
Foreign Relations, Sept. 13/
The Washington Post, 9-14:(A)4.

Rajiv Gandhi
Prime Minister of India

5

We feel the world needs to break down the artificial barriers it has built up: capitalism versus Communism, North versus South. If the world is to progress, then these barriers must be removed. The concept of power blocs must also end. The only way to end power blocs is to be non-aligned.

Interview, New Delhi/
USA Today, 4-29:(A)13.

Robert M. Gates
Deputy Director of
Central Intelligence
of the United States

6

The question I am most frequently asked is whether it is in our interest for [Soviet leader

(ROBERT M. GATES)

Mikhail] Gorbachev to succeed [in his reform program] or fail. The first thing we should acknowledge is that there is little that the United States can do to influence the outcome of the struggle going on inside the Soviet Union. That said, we should ask ourselves if we want the political, social and economic revitalization of the historical and current Soviet system. I think not. What we do seek is a Soviet Union that is pluralistic internally, non-interventionist externally, observes basic human rights, contributes to international stability and tranquility, and a Soviet Union where these changes are more than a temporary edict from the top and are independent of the views, power and durability of a single individual. We can hope for such change, but all of Russian and Soviet history cautions us to be skeptical and cautious. We cannot—and should not—close our eyes to momentous developments in the U.S.S.R., but we should watch, wait and evaluate. As long-time Soviet-watcher William Odom has said, we should applaud *perestroika* [reform] but not finance it. We should not make concessions based on hope and popular enthusiasms here or pleasing personalities and atmospheric or superficial changes there. We should, however, take advantage of opportunities where the terms are favorable to us or where we can bring about desirable changes in Soviet policies . . .

Before American Association
for the Advancement of Science,
Oct. 14/The Washington Post,
11-2:(A)20.

Gennadi I. Gerasimov
Spokesman for the
Foreign Ministry
of the Soviet Union

1

[On whether the Soviet Union, as it did in Afghanistan, would again commit its troops to another country to defend a socialist government]: We will think twice, thrice, before we move in again. I think it's not going to happen. I cannot foresee it.

Los Angeles Times, 5-14:(I)10.

Roy Godson
Professor of government,
Georgetown University

2

There is increasing recognition that the [intelligence] capabilities that we have now will not fully enable us to meet future challenges, threats and opportunities. In the mid-1980s, we had begun to address the apparent weaknesses. But because of [the] Iran-contra [scandal] and the death of [former CIA Director William] Casey, policy-makers were distracted by the leadership shuffle and the investigations. In recent months, the CIA has initiated important reforms. But much remains to be done and many inside the community are good at fending off bureaucratic change.

Los Angeles Times,
12-11:(I)1.

Curt Goering
Deputy director,
Amnesty International

3

Torture done with methods that equal anything the Nazis devised is practiced systematically in more than one-third of the world's nations. It is all systems of government that are at fault: dictatorships as well as democracies, countries with military rule as well as civilian rule, countries with free elections and countries with no elections . . . Today, in countries from South Africa to Vietnam, from Uganda to Israel, thousands upon thousands of political prisoners languish, uncharged and untried, in filthy and overcrowded prison cells, in mountains and in deserts—beaten, humiliated and isolated . . . We frankly don't care whether the government is torturing someone in the name of the revolution, or in the name of fighting the revolution, or in the name of restoring order so that democracy might flourish. All we care about is that the torture stop.

Before Washington chapter of
United Nations Association/
The Washington Post,
12-14:(A)9.

Galia Golan
Professor, Hebrew University
(Israel)

1

The way [Soviet leader Mikhail] Gorbachev is trying to balance interests in the Middle East is part of an over-all strategy that you can find in his policies on Angola, Cambodia, China, the Pacific, the Persian Gulf, South America, Western Europe. All over, really. You don't have to have stars in your eyes to understand that the Soviets these days are after stability, quiet and reduced tensions.

The Washington Post,
11-21:(A)15.

Felipe Gonzalez
Prime Minister of Spain

2

[The U.S.] is not a country that is loved from a general point of view. The Americans want to be loved and that is much more difficult if you are powerful.

Interview, Madrid/
USA Today, 7-15:(A)9.

Mikhail S. Gorbachev
General Secretary,
Communist Party of
the Soviet Union

3

It is time to get rid of delusions that we [Soviets] are insisting on [improving U.S.-Soviet relations] because of weakness—that because the position of the present Soviet leadership is unstable, it is interested in some foreign-policy success—and for this reason is persuading the Americans to agree to cooperation. A real policy cannot be based on such absurdities.

April 22/
Los Angeles Times, 4-23:(I)8.

4

The Soviet Union is working consistently toward settling regional conflicts through political means on the basis of the balanced interests of all sides. The Soviet Union does not foist its approach on anyone and does not pretend to know the ultimate truth. We are for solving pressing problems through the efforts of all nations on the path of dialogue and extensive contacts.

Los Angeles Times, 5-27:(I)24.

5

[Addressing U.S. President Reagan]: I like the notion of realism, and I also like the fact that you, Mr. President, have lately been utterring it more and more often. Normal, and indeed durable, Soviet-American relations, which so powerfully affect the world's political climate, are only conceivable within the framework of realism. Thanks to realism, for all our differences we have succeeded in arriving at a joint conclusion which, though very simple, is of historic importance: A nuclear war cannot be won and must never be fought.

At dinner for President Reagan,
Moscow, May 30/
The Washington Post,
5-31:(A)11.

6

The problems which the developing countries face have turned out to be difficult to the point of tragedy. Glaring backwardness, hunger, poverty and mass diseases continue to beset entire nations, and incredibly high debt has become an excruciating and universal problem. We believe that if the international community, and above all the great powers, are to be of any help, the starting point and the essential thing is to recognize unconditionally the freedom of choice. We are insisting on fairness. We have seriously studied the economic situation in developing nations, and I am convinced that a way out is possible along the lines of a radical restructuring of the entire system of world economic relations, without any discrimination for political reasons.

At dinner in his honor at
U.S. Ambassador's residence,
Moscow, May 31/
The New York Times, 6-1:8.

WHAT THEY SAID IN 1988

(MIKHAIL S. GORBACHEV)

1

[On the just-ended U.S. Soviet summit meeting in Moscow and the generally improved relations between the two countries]: It is not only the peoples of the Soviet Union and the United States that can congratulate themselves, but also their allies and the entire world public, the entire world community. It is a common victory for reason and realism. And it has become possible because today, on all continents, in every nation, in every country, regardless of social choice and of other values which each people chooses for itself, there is a common understanding and awareness that the world had reached the brink and that it had to be stopped . . . and the door had to be opened leading in another direction, toward a nuclear-free and non-violent world, and toward making international relations more healthy.

News conference,
Moscow, June 1/
The Washington Post, 6-2:(A)27.

2

[The Soviet Union] will not accept any advice on how we run our affairs . . . We do not need anyone else's model. We don't need anyone else's values. All the peoples in the world seek ways to a better life, and it is not right not to trust a people, to suspect it of being unable to find this road. Therefore, we reject any lectures addressed to us, and we are not going to teach anyone. The world is not a school where there are teachers and pupils. We all go to school in life and history, and history will show whose values are of a higher standard.

To peace groups, Moscow, June 2/
Los Angeles Times, 6-3:(I)16.

3

[Addressing U.S. President Reagan at the conclusion of their summit meeting]: Mr. President, you and I have been dealing with each other for three years now. From the first exchange of letters to the conclusion of this meeting, we've come a long way. Our dialogue has not been easy but we mustered enough realism and political will

to overcome obstacles and divert the train of U.S.-Soviet relations from a dangerous track to a safer one . . . For my part, I can assure you that we will do everything in our power to go on moving forward. Now, with the vast experience of meetings in Geneva, Reykjavik, Washington and Moscow, and backed up by their achievements, we are in duty bound to display still greater determination and consistency. That is what the Soviet and American peoples, international public opinion and the entire world community are expecting of us.

Moscow, June 2/
The New York Times, 6-3:6.

4

External debt is one of the gravest problems. Let us not forget that in the age of colonialism, the developing world, at the cost of countless losses and sacrifices, financed the prosperity of a large portion of the world community. The time has come to make up for the losses that accompanied its historic and tragic contribution to global material progress . . . Looking at things realistically, one has to admit that the accumulated debt cannot be repaid or recovered on the original terms. The Soviet Union is prepared to institute a lengthy moratorium of up to 100 years on debt servicing by the least-developed countries, and in quite a few cases to write off the debt altogether.

At United Nations,
New York, Dec. 7/
The New York Times, 12-8:(A)6.

5

It is obvious . . . that the use or threat of force no longer can or must be an instrument of foreign policy. This applies above all to nuclear arms, but that is not the only thing that matters. All of us, and primarily the stronger of us, must exercise self-restraint and totally rule out any outward-oriented use of force. That is the first and the most important component of a non-violent world . . .

At United Nations,
New York, Dec. 7/
The New York Times, 12-8:(A)6.

(MIKHAIL S. GORBACHEV)

1

The relations between the Soviet Union and the United States of America have a history of five and a half decades. As the world changed, so did the nature, role and place of those relations in world politics. For too long a time they developed along the lines of confrontation and sometimes animosity—either overt or covert. But in the last few years, the entire world could breath a sigh of relief, thanks to the changes for the better in the substance and the atmosphere of the relationship between Moscow and Washington. No one intends to underestimate the seriousness of our differences and the toughness of outstanding problems. We have, however, already graduated from the primary school of learning to understand each other and seek solutions in both our own and common interests.

At United Nations,
New York, Dec. 7/
The New York Times, 12-8:(A)6.

Albert Gore, Jr.
United States Senator,
D-Tennessee;
Candidate for the 1988
Democratic Presidential
nomination

2

It's important not to learn the wrong lessons from [the U.S. involvement in the Vietnam war in the 1960s and '70s]. One phrase that I remember from Mark Twain is . . . "A cat burned on a stove won't sit on a hot stove again, but it won't sit on a cold one either." And I think it is important to realize that we do have interests in the world that are important enough to defend, to stand up for. And we should not be so burned by the tragedy of Vietnam that we fail to recognize an interest that requires the assertion of force.

Interview, Washington/
U.S. News & World Report,
2-15:17.

3

[Democratic Presidential candidate] Governor Michael Dukakis does not have a single day

of foreign-policy experience. He said it would be perfectly all right with him for the Soviet Union to establish a client state on the mainland of the American continent. Now, that reflects a lack of experience. After seven years of [President] Ronald Reagan, do we want another President who doesn't know beans about foreign policy or what this country ought to be doing in the world?

Campaign speech, Feb. 17/
Los Angeles Times, 2-18:(I)19.

Alexander M. Haig, Jr.
Candidate for the 1988
Republican Presidential
nomination; Former
Secretary of State
of the United States

4

The Soviet Union is continuing to conduct aggression around the world and . . . we have de-linked, so to speak, their international behavior from arms control in a quest for arms control for arms control's sake. [In dealing with the Soviets, we] cannot leave unattended violations of human rights and aggression in the developing world . . . Linkage is an essential vehicle in American foreign policy.

The Christian Science Monitor,
1-8:14.

5

[On Soviet leader Mikhail Gorbachev's program for change in the Soviet Union]: Are we witnessing merely a change in fashion in Moscow or a true change in philosophy? Will Gorbachev practice real Soviet restraint in the use of force, whether in Afghanistan, Cambodia, Angola or in Central America? Will Moscow fulfill at last the human-rights obligations it undertook at Helsinki back in 1975? At this point, the answer must be "we don't know." What we do know and what we do see is a change in fashion. After all, Mrs. Gorbachev wears Gucci shoes. Mr. Gorbachev cut a handsome figure on Connecticut Avenue [in Washington] during the recent summit. And didn't [Nicaraguan leader] Commandante Ortega go to [New York's] Madison

(ALEXANDER M. HAIG, JR.)

Avenue last spring to buy designer sunglasses for himself and his wife? Didn't [Polish leader] General Jaruzelski appear across the table from [U.S. Vice President] George Bush two months ago with a crisply tailored suit? And you know who made the greatest sacrifice of all? [Cuban leader] Fidel Castro; he gave up cigars. But it's important again to remind ourselves that when the cigar smoke clears in Havana, we are still witnessing the smoke of [Soviet] battle in Afghanistan and Angola and right here in our own hemisphere—Central America. Until that smoke clears, I remain highly skeptical of Soviet good intentions.

Campaign speech/
The New York Times,
1-15:8.

1

[On Soviet leader Mikhail Gorbachev's program of *glasnost*, openness, in the Soviet Union]: It's important to remember that *glasnost* is not a product of some procedure on the part of an enlightened Gorbachev to do the West a favor; it's the product of the failures of the Soviet system—and the inevitable demand for reform in the face of these failures. Now, Gorbachev happily seems to be willing to undertake these risks, but for us to buy the line in many Western capitals, including my own, that we should take risks with our own vital interests in order to encourage more *glasnost* and to strengthen Gorbachev, may indeed be a formula that will bring the whole reform movement to a screeching halt.

Interview,
McLean, Va./
U.S. News & World Report,
2-8:12.

Mark O. Hatfield
United States Senator,
R-Oregon

2

This [Reagan] Administration sees the world as black and white, friend or enemy: if they are

not for us they are against us; therefore, we wipe them out.

Interview/
The Washington Post, 10-6:(A)39.

John Healey
Executive director, Amnesty
International U.S.A.

3

Concern for human rights is growing gradually around the world. It is like a wide, shallow river spreading slowly across a dry plain.

U.S. News & World Report,
12-19:31.

Hume A. Horan
United States Ambassador
to Saudi Arabia

4

People often say that Islamic countries and the U.S. don't get along. That's bunk. I think that Americans get along better with foreigners than any other nationality does.

USA Today, 4-1:(A)11.

Gordon J. Humphrey
United States Senator,
R-New Hampshire

5

[On the warming of relations between President Reagan and Soviet leader Mikhail Gorbachev]: I'm afraid the President has fallen under the spell which sooner or later seems to affect all Presidents, which is that [they think] they have a unique talent to tame the Soviet bear. The effect of Presidents falling under that spell . . . has been disastrous.

Interview/USA Today, 6-1:(A)9.

Jesse L. Jackson
Civil-rights leader,
Candidate for the
1988 Democratic
Presidential nomination

6

[On dealing with terrorists who hold American hostages]: We must never do anything to

(JESSE L. JACKSON)

compromise or jeopardize the national interest or national security . . . Having said that, however, we must be willing to talk with anyone to free innocent American hostages . . . Talk does not mean material concessions.

April 25/
The Washington Post, 4-26:(A)4.

1

[Saying he could be of service as Vice President to Democratic Presidential frontrunner Michael Dukakis]: Suppose that my mission [as Vice President] was to facilitate peace in the Middle East and in Africa, Latin America and the rest of the Third World. [Soviet leader Mikhail] Gorbachev could not compete with me in Angola and Mozambique. I [as a black] have credibility among the seven-eighths of the world that comprises the Third World. That seven-eighths say we should have someone with authority and visibility focused on them. The Secretary of State is focused on U.S.-U.S.S.R. relations. Locked out of that preoccupation is the seven-eighths. America is losing more and more ground among that seven-eighths.

Interview/
Los Angeles Times, 6-21:(II)7.

Brian Jenkins
Director, research program
on subnational conflict
and political violence,
Rand Corporation

2

The general feeling in the United States is that raising money for [foreign organizations'] humanitarian purposes is okay; money for lethal weapons is not okay. But you've got to remember money is fungible. A group can move a dollar from its humanitarian budget to its weapons budget to some other budget and it's still a dollar. And if you reduce the burden an organization has to deal with in taking care of its people, you free money for weapons. Dollars are dollars.

Los Angeles Times, 3-3:(I)25.

Michael Josephson
Former professor of law,
Loyola University

3

[On the possibility that President Reagan will pardon those Americans indicted in the U.S. Iran-contra scandal]: A pardon would say that the democratic process is only a valid one sometimes, and that highly committed patriots can set it aside—like Dr. Strangelove. It would send a message that there are times when we will permit high-level government officials to lie to Congress. How could we trust anything afterward?

Time, 4-11:57.

Thomas H. Kean
Governor of New Jersey (R)

4

For me, how a man would deal with foreign policy is a lot more than half the reason I support someone for President. But I know that I'm in the minority. Most people only think about that if there's a crisis in the world, and this time [in this forthcoming Presidential election] we have just the opposite of that.

Interview, Newark, N.J./
The New York Times, 9-16:11.

Geoffrey Kemp
Authority on world security issues,
Carnegie Endowment
for International Peace

5

Neither [Republican Presidential nominee] George Bush nor [Democratic Presidential nominee] Michael Dukakis, nor any foreseeable President, is going to want to be put in the position where he'll have to commit U.S. ground forces [in conflicts overseas]. What the [current] Reagan Administration has shown is that you can use direct and indirect force, covert operations and arms sales to back up U.S. diplomacy. I think we're going to see more operations of this sort [such as the recent U.S. naval escorts of oil shipping in the troubled Persian Gulf].

Los Angeles Times,
11-2:(I)10.

Jack Kemp
United States Representative,
R-New York; Candidate
for the 1988 Republican
Presidential nomination

1

People want better relations with the Soviet Union. Of course, we all do. We want peace on this earth. We want to beat our swords into plowshares, and our spears into prune hooks. We want the lion to lay down with the lamb. But this [the Soviet Union] is a Marxist-Leninist Communist government. It has 120,000 Soviet troops in Afghanistan. They have Bulgarian, East German, PLO, Cuban and Soviet advisers in Nicaragua. Our own hemisphere. They are destablizing Angola, Mozambique, Ethiopia, Cambodia, and they are trying to bring down Mrs. Aquino's very fragile democracy in the Philippines. Ladies and gentlemen, the survival of Western, democratic government and Western civilization depends on having a policy, program and platform that believes the way to peace is not a piece of paper; it's not a person, or just an arms-control process. Peace can only be maintained and strengthened through strength.
Campaign speech/
The New York Times, 1-12:11.

Jeane J. Kirkpatrick
Former United States
Ambassador/Permanent
Representative to the
United Nations

2

[Democratic Presidential nominee] Michael Dukakis is more worried about an American President's misuse of power than about an adversary's use of power against us. The [Iranian leader Ruhollah] Khomeinis, the [Libyan leader Mummar] Qaddafis, [Nicaraguan President Daniel] Ortegas and the proliferation of nuclear weapons make the world too dangerous for America to rely on naive, unrealistic, uninformed strategies to defend our freedom.
At Republican National Convention,
New Orleans, Aug. 16/
The Washington Post, 8-17:(A)23.

3

We need a President who knows the world. We cannot settle for less. Mistakes in economic policy can cost us jobs and profits. But serious mistakes in foreign policy can cost us jobs, profits—and our freedom.
At Republican National Convention,
New Orleans, Aug. 16/
USA Today, 8-17:(A)3.

Henry A. Kissinger
Former Secretary of State
of the United States

4

The Nixon-Kissinger approach to foreign policy wound up getting attacked by both liberals and conservatives because it was too power-oriented for liberals and too relativistic for conservatives. We believed in balance of power but we were hostile to crusades. Eventually, limitation of resources will oblige America to come to that as a nation. Peace requires hegemony or balance of power.
Interview/
Los Angeles Times, 1-24:(V)2.

Lee Kuan Yew
Prime Minister of Singapore

5

This is a plea [to the U.S.]: Don't believe that what has worked in America must work elsewhere. Yes, we are all human beings, but we are different kinds of human beings, different histories, mindsets, ambitions, ideas. The more you try to judge others by your standards, the more you show total disregard for their own circumstances.
Interview, Singapore/
USA Today, 5-13:(A)11.

Stanislav A. Levchenko
U.S. intelligence consultant;
Former Major in the
KGB (Soviet secret police)

6

Americans have a tendency to be naive. During a period of relaxation of tensions and

(STANISLAV A. LEVCHENKO)

betterment of relations with the Soviet Union, a large number of Americans start thinking that Soviet leaders can be trustworthy, that all kinds of exchanges should dramatically transpire between the two countries. And that's where the KGB is fishing very actively.

Interview/USA Today, 10-26:(A)7.

Stephan Lewis
Canadian Ambassador/
Permanent Representative
to the United Nations

1

The UN's peace-keeping budget could be bigger than its regular budget in a year or so, which would give it a sense of relevance and usefulness in the popular perception that it has not enjoyed for decades . . . We could see a new conventional wisdom developing—that the UN is important, after all.

The New York Times, 7-30:5.

Jack Matlock
United States Ambassador
to the Soviet Union

2

[On Soviet leader Mikhail Gorbachev's reform program for the Soviet Union]: If Gorbachev's program of reforms is successful, it will produce a stronger Soviet Union, but it will do so by changing some fundamental ways that the country is ruled and thus make it less threatening to us.

U.S. News & World Report,
7-11:27.

Federico Mayor Zaragosa
Director General, United
Nations Educational,
Scientific and Cultural
Organization (UNESCO)

3

[One] reason why UNESCO is vulnerable [to criticism] is the lack of "visibility" of its activities. What is visible is the controversy and the polemics, not its achievements. We train thousands of people. We have to our credit considerable progress in promoting basic sciences. None of this is really known. It is difficult to manage an organization that produces invisible things.

Interview/
World Press Review, March:44.

George S. McGovern
Senior fellow, Institute for
Policy Studies; Former
United States Senator,
D-South Dakota

4

[Saying the U.S. concerns itself too much with not having good relations with such small Communist countries as Cuba, Angola and Vietnam]: It's stupid. We have a paternalistic view that these little countries ought to behave themselves and do what we want them to do: Why don't they follow a system of free enterprise? Why do they appropriate private corporations? Why don't they behave like little people are supposed to behave and respect a great power like the U.S.A., which wants nothing except to have them do what we tell them to do?

Interview/USA Today, 5-18:(A)11.

Daniel arap Moi
President of Kenya

5

Let me tell you a weakness of [U.S.] democracy. A U.S. President holds office for eight years, but in his eighth year nobody does a thing, and that affects foreign policy. Somebody can do a nasty thing because they know the U.S. can't do a thing about it.

Interview, Nairobi/
USA Today, 4-15:(A)13.

Jonathan Moore
United States Refugee
Coordinator

6

In a period of increased competition for limited resources, our society must find ways to give

159

(JONATHAN MOORE)

greater priority to truly disparate humanitarian-assistance needs abroad. Refugee problems are not peripheral, but integral, to U.S. foreign policy. Affirmative attention to them [serves] our most precious ideals and our most critical political and security interests.

The Christian Science Monitor,
4-21:1.

Richard M. Nixon
Former President
of the United States

1

[Soviet leader Mikhail] Gorbachev is quite aware of how effective charm can be. But while he uses charm, he is not really affected by it. You must not assume that because this man is sophisticated, because he's a man of the world, because he has the right manners, that he is really any different from what he deeply believes than a Nikita Khrushchev, who was none of those things.

Interview/USA Today, 4-5:(A)11.

Manuel Antonio Noriega
Commander of the armed
forces of Panama

2

The United States does not want friendly governments; it wants docile governments. It does not want to *win* friends, but wants to *buy* them.

USA Today, 5-9:(A)8.

Sam Nunn
United States Senator,
D-Georgia

3

It is a dangerous world, with a lot of people who don't have our values or our economic or political philosophies. We like to take care of our own business, but we don't have the luxury of taking a position that is essentially isolationist. If we do that, the world will be [an even] more dangerous place.

U.S. News & World Report,
5-23:15.

Hugh O'Hare
Spokesman, United Nations
Fund for Population
Activities

4

[On the projected rapid population growth in developing countries]: Many people won't have jobs, or any possibility of ever working. The political ramifications of that are ominous, as are the implications for trade. How are the U.S. and others going to trade with whole sections of the world that are impoverished? How does a [poor] country pay its debts when its population is soaring?

The Christian Science Monitor,
7-21:10.

Norman J. Ornstein
Resident scholar, American
Enterprise Institute

5

Clearly, in an ideal world you have the Legislative Branch setting broad guidelines [in foreign policy], leaving a lot of discretion to the Executive Branch to carry them out. Congress is supposed to play an aggressive role in foreign policy, but not in diplomacy. Where individual members of Congress have gotten involved in outrageous acts and screwed up, it's been for intervening in diplomacy ... The vast majority of members now travel, and they are not just going off to London, Paris and Rome. Once they start to travel, they develop contacts among foreign governments and with opposition leaders. They maintain those relationships. And when those people come to Washington, [members of Congress] are much more accessible than State Department figures, ambassadors and diplomats.

Los Angeles Times, 1-27:(I)18,19.

6

[On Congressional distrust of the President in foreign-policy matters]: It's a problem of the post-Vietnam era that is exacerbated by the current President [Reagan] and the current Congress. The fact is that no President can come forward and say: "Trust me. I have more infor-

(NORMAN J. ORNSTEIN)

mation than you have." No Congress will trust a President in foreign policy. They feel they have been lied to by all of them.

Los Angeles Times,
1-27:(I)18.

Vladimir F. Petrovsky
Deputy Foreign Minister
of the Soviet Union

1

[Saying the Soviet Union is changing its policies toward the UN]: We were wrong not to pay for [UN] peace-keeping operations. We are paying up. We were wrong toward international civil servants. Now we accept permanent contracts. We consider the whole UN Charter should be fulfilled, not just parts we like. We were wrong to oppose an active role for the Secretary General. We want a new system for comprehensive security. We need a stable structure for international affairs, and we see the UN as a major way of achieving it.

Interview, July 2/
The New York Times,
7-6:27.

Thomas Pickering
United States Ambassador
to Israel

2

[On U.S. Ambassadorships]: In general, in tough places they [the State Department] have looked for experience. The career diplomat is a known quantity. There is an advantage to being a career diplomat—you have a depth of experience, a knowledge in the field, education on the job. The selection process itself assures a choice of top people—people who have the experience to understand how foreign cultures work, people who are specialists in languages. Would you pick anyone off the street to be a brain surgeon?

Interview/
TWA Ambassador,
April:50.

Colin L. Powell
Assistant to President of the
United States Ronald Reagan
for National Security
Affairs

3

We [in the foreign-policy sector] still have internecine battles. I've never seen a family that does not. But where we have disagreements, disagreements are good. Creative tension in an organization is good. You tend to get the best out of people. What we've tried to do is put in place a process and a system that deals with that tension and with those disagreements in a way that is focused internally. So that when the President makes his decision, everybody feels that they have played in the process, they have presented their view to the President, and now we're going to execute the *President's* foreign policy, not the national-security adviser's foreign policy or the Secretary of State's or the Secretary of Defense's.

Interview/
The Christian Science Monitor,
4-8:32.

4

[On the National Security Council]: We run a moral operation. We run an operation that I feel is accountable to the President and Administration, Congress and American people. Everything we do at the NSC has to be in the name of the American people in the furtherance of their foreign policy as set by the President of the United States . . . We have restored that level of confidence and honesty to the NSC.

Before National Press Club,
Washington, Oct. 27/
The Washington Post, 10-28:(A)3.

5

People keep coming to me and saying, "Why have you lost the initiative to [Soviet leader Mikhail] Gorbachev? Why is he doing all these things [announcing Soviet plans for military reductions and better relations with the West], and you guys are standing around?" I say, when you've got a game-plan that's worked and everybody under-

(COLIN L. POWELL)

stands it, and the Soviets understand it and keep coming to us with human-rights movement, with movement on a solution of regional matters, with signing additional bilateral agreements that are in the best interests of both countries, and when you see progress in arms control without giving away your fundamental positions, it seems to me that's a very good game-plan and I don't know why I would want to jump out of a game-plan peremptorily.

Interview, Washington/
The Christian Science Monitor,
12-15:7.

Muammar el-Qaddafi
Chief of State of Libya

1

Why is [U.S. President] Reagan involved with the contras in Nicaragua, with UNITA in Angola, with Afghanistan? This is the same question. Let's all agree that everyone concern himself only with things in his own borders. [But if Reagan] goes to Chad, then I come to Chad. If he interferes in Palestine, then I will interfere in Ireland. If he comes to Angola, I go to Panama.

Interview, Annaba, Libya, Feb. 7/
The Washington Post, 2-8:(A)16.

2

Terrorism, if it arises, must be terrorism of the masses, and not terrorism of individuals or committees. That is the most dangerous type of terrorism.

To members of Revolutionary
Committee, Tripoli, Libya,
Aug. 29/The Washington Post,
8-31:(A)21.

3

If you want to stop this so-called [international] terrorism, you have to let the Palestinian people return to the West Bank and Gaza, the Zionists must go back to the countries they came from, the British should withdraw from Ireland. It is not terrorism; it is a matter of colonizations.

Interview, Tripoli, Libya, Sept. 5/
The Washington Post, 9-6:(A)23.

Qian Qichen
Foreign Minister of China

4

Americans are fond of talking about democracy and human rights. In our view, democratization is needed in international relations, and the sovereignty of each and every country should be respected in the international community. It is no good for one or two countries to have the final say, nor is it good for a few countries to give the last word.

At United Nations,
New York, June 2/
The New York Times, 6-4:6.

Dan Quayle
United States Senator,
R-Indiana;
1988 Republican
Vice-Presidential nominee

5

[Criticizing Massachusetts Governor and Democratic Presidential nominee Michael Dukakis for vetoing a bill that would have required the Pledge of Allegiance to be recited in his state's schools]: The same mindset that would impede the daily recitation of the Pledge of Allegiance is, in my judgment, the same mindset that could well sterilize public education of its proper role as a transmitter of the values and standards upon which we must rely ... Some may continue to hide behind long-winded legalisms and claim that this great pledge need not be a requirement. But [Republican Presidential nominee] George Bush and I say nothing is bigger than the ideas professed in these words.

Campaign speech,
New York, Sept. 5/
The Washington Post, 9-6:(A)17.

Ronald Reagan
President of the United States

6

We must not delude ourselves into believing that the Soviet threat has yet been fundamentally altered or that our vigilance can be reduced. In the Soviet Union we hear of "new thinking" and basic changes in Soviet policies at home and abroad. We will welcome real changes, but we

(RONALD REAGAN)

have yet to see any slackening of the growth of Soviet military power or abandonment of expansionist aspirations. [We] will continue to judge the Soviets by their actions rather than their words.

Report to Congress on national
security, Jan. 20*/
Los Angeles Times, 1-21:(I)10.

1

[On dealing with foreign policy as President after being a state Governor]: First of all, a Governor's job is an executive job. And you know that you sit at the desk where the buck does stop and, when the decisions have to be made, you have to make them. And even with regard to the principal difference, which would be foreign policy, I recall to you that a former President several times asked me to represent him abroad in meetings with heads of state. I had been in 18 different countries on trips of that kind before I came to this job, so it wasn't a complete, sudden immersion in foreign policy.

Interview, Washington, Feb. 25/
The Washington Post, 2-26:(A)18.

2

[On Oliver North's indictment in the U.S. Iran-contra scandal]: I still think Ollie North is a hero. And, on the other hand, in any talk about what I might do, or pardons and so forth, I think with the case before the courts—that's something I can't discuss now. But . . . I just have to believe that they're going to be found innocent, because I don't think they were guilty of any lawbreaking or any crime.

At seminar sponsored by Center
for the Study of the Presidency,
Washington, March 25/
Los Angeles Times, 3-26:(I)1.

3

[On U.S.-Soviet relations]: We have many differences—deep differences, moral differences.

But we are still fellow human beings. We can still work together to keep the peace. And in working with the Soviet Union, the United States can still remain true to its mission of expanding liberty throughout the world.

Upon leaving for U.S.-Soviet
summit meeting in Moscow,
Washington, May 25/
Los Angeles Times, 5-26:(I)6.

4

[On Soviet leader Mikhail Gorbachev]: The difference that I've found between him and other previous leaders that I have met with is that, yes, we can debate and we disagree, and it is true he's made it apparent that he believes much of the Communist propaganda that he's grown up hearing about our country—the big corporations and whether they dictate . . . to government or not. I try to disabuse him of those beliefs. But there is never a sense of personal animus when the arguments are over.

Interview, Washington/
Los Angeles Times, 5-30:(I)12.

5

[On his just-concluded summit meeting in Moscow with Soviet leader Mikhail Gorbachev]: To those of us familiar with the post-war era, all of this is cause for shaking the head in wonder. Imagine, the President of the United States and the General Secretary of the Soviet Union walking together in Red Square, talking about a growing personal friendship, and meeting, together, average citizens, realizing how much our people have in common. [It was] a special moment in a week of special moments.

Before Royal Institute of
International Affairs,
London, June 3/
Los Angeles Times, 6-4:(I)11.

6

When free peoples cease telling the truth about and to their adversaries, they cease telling the truth to themselves. In matters of state, unless the

(RONALD REAGAN)

truth be spoken, it ceases to exist. It is in this sense that the best indicator of how much we care about freedom is what we say about freedom. It is in this sense that words truly are actions. And there is one added and quite extraordinary benefit to this sort of realism and public candor: This is also the best way to avoid war or conflict.

Before Royal Institute of
International Affairs,
London, June 3/
The Washington Post, 6-4:(A)18.

1

. . . from Afghanistan to the Persian Gulf to southern Africa, we are bringing peace to long-raging conflicts, even as we frustrate aims. In eight years we have not given up one square inch of land to Communism. In fact, we have taken some ground back for freedom. And yet today, relations between the United States and the Soviet Union are the best they've been in decades.

Before American Legion,
Louisville, Ky., Sept. 6/
Los Angeles Times, 9-7:(I)14.

2

Around the world—in Afghanistan, Angola, Cambodia and, yes, Central America, the United States stands today with those who would fight for freedom. We stand with ordinary people who have had the courage to take up arms against the Communist tyranny. This stand is at the core of what some have called the Reagan Doctrine.

At National Defense College,
Oct. 25/
The Washington Post, 10-26:(A)4.

3

Dictators today, from Afghanistan to Nicaragua, do not want to be called czar or commissar. They want to be called Mr. President, and to pretend that they rule in the people's name, even if they don't.

To students in State Dining Room,
Washington, Nov. 14/
The Washington Post, 11-21:(A)2.

4

[On Soviet leader Mikhail Gorbachev's apparent desire for better relations with the U.S. and his more moderate foreign-policy and military policies]: While our hopes are for a new era, let us remember that if that new era is indeed upon us, that there was nothing inevitable about it. It was the result of hard work and of resolve and sacrifice on the part of those [in the West] who love freedom and dare to strive for it.

Before American Enterprise
Institute, Washington, Dec. 7/
Los Angeles Times,
12-8:(I)29.

5

We came to Washington . . . in 1981, both as anti-Communists and as unapologetic defenders of a strong and vibrant America. I am proud to say I am still an anti-Communist. And I continue to be dedicated to the idea that we must trumpet our beliefs and advance our American ideals to all the peoples of the world until the towers of the tyrants crumble to dust.

Before American Enterprise
Institute, Washington, Dec. 7/
The Washington Post, 12-8:(A)36.

Charles S. Robb
United States Senator-elect,
D-Virginia

6

America's foreign policy must always draw a clear moral distinction between those who fight to enlarge the scope of freedom and those who conspire to shrink it.

At Veterans Day ceremony,
Washington, Nov. 11/
The Washington Post, 11-12:(A)14.

William P. Rogers
Former Secretary of State
of the United States

7

[Saying the U.S.-Soviet INF Treaty should not fail because of a few Senators blocking it]: A

(WILLIAM P. ROGERS)

lot of people in the world think we're war-mongers, that we are equally as guilty as the Russians in terms of wanting to dominate the world. [It would be] devastating [if a few U.S. Senators could block this treaty]. I can't think of a more serious setback to American foreign policy and to American interests throughout the world than to have this treaty fail . . .

Before Senate Foreign Relations
Committee, Washington, Jan. 27/
The Washington Post, 1-28:(A)4.

Paul F. Rothstein
Professor of law,
Georgetown University

1

[On the U.S. defendants indicted in the Iran-contra scandal]: I know of no fraud case where so much of the motivation was idealism and not profit-taking. Even if the law may not recognize the defense, the jurors might.

U.S. News & World Report,
3-28:19.

Edward L. Rowny
Special Adviser to President
of the United States
Ronald Reagan
for Arms Control

2

We must not forget that beneath the smiles and the cosmetics of *glasnost* [the new Soviet policy of openness], the Soviet Union remains a dangerous, brutal adversary. We in the West have no choice but to keep our wits about us and patiently, persistently, do what is necessary to preserve our freedom and security.

Before American Association
for the Advancement of Science,
Boston, Feb. 15/
The New York Times, 2-16:3.

Andrei D. Sakharov
Dissident Soviet physicist

3

Should the West fear that as a result of *per-estroika* [reform in the Soviet Union] we will become a new Japan-like economy or military power with expansionist goals? People should fear not the success of *perestroika,* but its failures. Our state will always have enough soldiers, military hardware and scientific-research institutes. We always did have enough. But the failures of *perestroika* would make expansion a political necessity and the country would be extremely dangerous in terms of world balance.

The Washington Post, 11-11:(A)18.

Daniel Schorr
Senior news analyst,
National Public Radio;
Former correspondent, CBS News

4

[On last year's U.S. Iran-contra scandal]: You assume someone got away with something—that it was a success. But it was the Keystone Kops. Nothing succeeded. They [those Americans involved in the scandal] traded arms to Iran for hostages, but the number of hostages stayed basically the same. They sought a moderate Iranian policy; they got a war in the Persian Gulf. They wanted to keep the contras [Nicaraguan rebels] alive; they're about to be axed. I don't know what kind of conspiracy it is when nothing about it worked . . . The President's [Reagan] men did these dumb, stupid, illegal things. They were caught at them and accomplished nothing. They destroyed one of the most popular Presidencies in history and flushed it down the drain. The real result of this report [on the Iran-contra hearings] is the same as the result of the entire Iran-contra affair. Both left the President standing alone, looking like an idiot, anxious for his term to end.

Panel discussion,
New School for Social Research,
New York/Harper's, February:49.

Edward Schuh
Dean, Hubert Humphrey
Institute, University
of Minnesota

5

For a country with our wealth and capacity, our aid level to the Third World is a disgrace.

USA Today, 6-10:(A)12.

Brent Scowcroft
*Former Assistant to the
President of the
United States
(Gerald Ford) for
National Security Affairs*
1

It's hard for us to remain vigilant and cautious . . . in the face of Soviet smiles.

*The Christian Science Monitor,
5-24:7.*

Brent Scowcroft
*Foreign-policy adviser to
1988 Republican
Presidential nominee George
Bush; Former Assistant to the
President of the United States
(Gerald Ford) for National
Security Affairs*
2

We really are in an age of transition from a post-war world where the Soviets were the enemy, where the United States was a superpower and trying to build up both its allies and its former enemies and help the Third World transition to independence. That whole world and all of those things are coming to an end or have ended, and we are now entering a new and different world that will be complex and much less unambiguous than the old one.

*Interview/
Los Angeles Times,
9-4:(I)1.*

3

[On whether the U.S. should economically help the Soviet Union now that current Soviet leader Mikhail Gorbachev has instituted reform and openness in his country]: It is no more of a good idea to subsidize the Soviet economy now than it was three years ago. We should focus on our own interests rather than playing in the internal politics of the Soviet Union.

*Interview/
Los Angeles Times,
11-14:(I)15.*

Natan Sharansky
*Exiled former Soviet
dissident*
4

If I could whisper in the ear of the next President of the United States, I would tell him he must understand the deep, fundamental differences between the Soviet system and Western society—that words are understood differently in Washington and Moscow, whether they be freedom, law, parliament, human rights, prison.

*Interview, Jerusalem/
U.S. News & World Report,
5-23:30.*

Eduard A. Shevardnadze
*Foreign Minister
of the Soviet Union*
5

[On U.S.-Soviet relations and negotiations]: Many difficulties emerged through misunderstandings, and the misunderstandings turn into complex jigsaw puzzles. That seems to be the nature of U.S.-Soviet relations at this stage—that we will continue for a long time to pay the ransom of mutual mistrust.

*News conference, Geneva, May 12/
Los Angeles Times, 5-13:(I)12.*

6

Everything in U.S.-Soviet relations represents a process toward putting our relations on a solid foundation. Look at what's happened in the last 2½ to three years: four summit meetings, 28 meetings at the foreign minister level . . . unprecedented meetings of the ministers of defense. We have not overcome suspicion, but there is more confidence now.

Interview/USA Today, 9-9:(A)13.

Nikolai V. Shishlin
*Spokesman, Central
Committee, Communist
Party of the Soviet Union*
7

I want to be quite frank. I watched the [1988 Presidential-] election campaign in the United

(NIKOLAI V. SHISHLIN)

States very carefully. The statements on foreign policy by both [candidates George] Bush and [Michael] Dukakis showed a lack of imagination. Imagination is necessary in politics. So are courage and daring. And though [U.S.] President Reagan cannot be called a man of progressive convictions, he is a man of imagination and a political figure capable of bold decisions. I would hope [President-elect] Bush will inherit these qualities.

Interview, Moscow/
Newsweek, 11-28:56.

George P. Shultz
Secretary of State
of the United States

1

[On whether he fears there is a growing tendency toward isolationism in the U.S.]: . . . I am trying to fight against any tendency in the United States [to] turn in a protectionist, disengagement direction, and I think it's a threat. I'm a great believer that we are going to be part and parcel of what's going on around the world, that if we are engaged imaginatively and aggressively, we will see things happen that are basically good.

Interview,
Washington, Jan. 15/
The New York Times, 1-16:5.

2

The people who represent the United States abroad serve in the front lines of America's interests. Our diplomats often work in areas which can only be described as combat zones. I am reminded of this every time I enter the State Department and see two plaques on the wall commemorating members of the Foreign Service who died in the line of duty. The older plaque took 187 years to fill up; most of the people listed there lost their lives to accident or disease. The more recent plaque, however, took only 20 years to fill up; and most of the people on it were murdered by terrorists. So don't let anyone tell

you that diplomacy is a tea party or pushing cookies.

Before Anti-Defamation League
of B'nai B'rith, February/
The New York Times, 8-26:19.

3

[On the reform program instituted in the Soviet Union by Soviet leader Mikhail Gorbachev]: We recognize that a potentially important experiment is getting under way in the Soviet Union. It suggests the possibility of a far more satisfactory U.S.-Soviet relationship than we have known in the post-war era, a relationship that could be a constructive element in a changing world. Americans are willing to work with dedication and creativity to fashion such a relationship. It is a goal which is achievable, if the Soviet leadership is willing to join us in making change for the better a permanent reality.

At University of Washington,
Feb. 5/
Los Angeles Times, 2-6:(I)11.

4

We [the U.S.] have to keep fighting the tendency to disengage. We have people talking about protection of our markets [from foreign competition] and people saying we don't like something going on somewhere [in the world] so we should throw up our hands and leave. I say, no, that's not the right way. One hundred and fifty years ago, protected by these two big oceans, we minded our business, and we created a great country. But the big oceans don't do for us what they once did, and we found that out two times in this century, when there was a war in Europe. How much more evidence do you need that if something very important happens somewhere, we're going to be involved? We've got to engage ourselves.

Interview/Esquire, June:152.

5

What you regard, legitimately and necessarily, as sovereign territory in today's world . . . is less

(GEORGE P. SHULTZ)

and less kind of airtight. No sovereign has the ability to completely control its borders . . . Weapons of war can come across those borders in new and different ways. That means the border, and the whole sense of sovereignty of 100 years ago in the political literature, is necessarily different than it is today.

Cairo, June 3/
Los Angeles Times, 6-4:(I)3.

1

While we will never seek to dictate events, decisions or formulas, we will attempt to offer ideas, assistance and understanding in support of the process of change [toward democracy]. And our support will be all the more steadfast when democracies are threatened by hostile external forces. To do less would be to betray our own commitment to democratic values.

Before Korean Newspaper Editors
Association, Seoul, July 18/
Los Angeles Times, 7-18:(I)20.

Gaston J. Sigur
Assistant Secretary for
East Asian and Pacific Affairs,
Department of State
of the United States

2

I disagree with the contention that the United States is stretched hopelessly too thin in its commitments abroad. Our policy role today . . . is not one of "imperial over-stretch," but one of responsible outreach.

Speech, Tokyo/
Los Angeles Times, 5-31:(I)15.

John R. Silber
President, Boston University

3

No university worthy of the name can pretend to be value-neutral in the assessment of the United States and the Soviet Union. A university that promotes the doctrine of moral equiva-

lence between these two nations, presenting them as two equally valid systems of government, or as two equally guilty parties in the political realities of our time, repudiates the conditions for its very existence. The pernicious assertion of the moral equivalence of the United States and the Soviet Union is nothing more than an expression of an ideology that seeks to eliminate the very freedom on which universities depend.

At opening reception of Boston
University's Center for Defense
Journalism, May 8/
The Wall Street Journal, 7-12:26.

Arlen Specter
United States Senator,
R-Pennsylvania

4

If we expect other nations to extradite terrorists to the United States when they have in their custody terrorists whom we want to prosecute, we obviously must lay the legal groundwork. We should move immediately to sign bilateral extradition treaties with the many nations with whom we now have no such agreement. It is astonishing to me that the United States has no extradition treaties with the United Arab Emirates, Bahrain, Qatar, Oman, Yemen, Kuwait, Saudi Arabia, Jordan, Lebanon, Syria, Sudan, Ethiopia and several other countries . . . where terrorists might very well be apprehended. If a nation with custody of a terrorist is beset with external pressures to release him . . . the absence of a formal extradition treaty with the United States may provide a pretext for succumbing to the pressure.

The Washington Post, 5-11:(A)24.

John Steinbrenner
Scholar,
Brookings Institution

5

Not only is the cold war over, but it's been over for much longer than anyone acknowledges. And we've [the West] won it. That's the easy part. The real question now is: What's next? . . . [First,] we must learn how to manage the large standing military forces that still exist on both sides, how to

(JOHN STEINBRENNER)

stand them down in a stable manner to reach new balances at lower levels. [Second,] our own national economy must now find a way to adapt to the new international economic system that our policies have produced. [And third,] we must learn how to accommodate the Chinese and Soviets in the international economic model which they have decided to accept.

Los Angeles Times, 12-10:(I)8.

Monteagle Sterns
Former United States
Ambassador to Greece

1

[Saying the U.S. Foreign Service is not the favorite agency of American Presidents]: All elected officials like to think in terms of opportunities. Presidents want gung-ho, can-do guys . . . [But] the Foreign Service is paid to think in terms of risks.

Interview/
Los Angeles Times, 5-14:(I)14.

Robert S. Strauss
Former chairman,
Democratic National Committee

2

[On President-elect George Bush's naming former Treasury Secretary James Baker to be his Secretary of State]: Jim Baker's probably more qualified than most to be Secretary of State. You can't separate traditional foreign-policy experience from economic foreign-policy experience, which Baker has in abundance. A Secretary of State doesn't have to be the world's greatest expert in every nuance of foreign policy. What he needs to have is a high degree of intelligence; he needs to be a strategic thinker.

Nov. 9/
The New York Times, 11-10:(A)1.

Studs Terkel
Author

3

We [the U.S.] are winners, right? We are the most glorious people who ever lived—nobody

like us, right? Well, in the Vietnam war, we didn't win against little guys in black pajamas. We're the bully on the block, and we're walking down the block with a bloody nose. The world's laughing at us, so we've got to beat somebody. So bam, bam, bam. We kicked the shit out of Grenada. And we cheered because we beat somebody. We're old Muhammed Ali knocking the shit out of Woody Allen. That's what it comes to. We're accustomed to asking not what's right or wrong, but only, "Are we winning?" What lesson have we learned?

Interview/Esquire, June:117.

Margaret Thatcher
Prime Minister
of the United Kingdom

4

[On whether the West should trust the Soviet Union now that Soviet leader Mikhail Gorbachev has instituted a reform program]: Trust and confidence are slow to develop when we have had past histories such as we have and when there have been things like the era of Stalin. They develop because you reach agreements and you see how those agreements are carried out. They develop as you watch and see how a country treats its own people . . . Now we have started this process of building. Yes, of course, each looks at the other to say: "Now, are you going to honor this agreement?" I must say, anything that Mr. Gorbachev has personally promised me he would do, he has done.

Soviet broadcast interview, June 7/
The Washington Post, 6-10:(A)22.

5

[U.S.] President Reagan has rebuilt the strength and confidence of the West—not without a little help—and inspired the democracies to go out and win the battle of ideas. It is vital that Britain and America should always stand together, so the next President of the United States, too, will have the United Kingdom as a staunch ally.

At Conservative Party convention,
Brighton, England, Oct. 14/
Los Angeles Times, 10-15:(I)3.

WHAT THEY SAID IN 1988

1

[On the election of Vice President George Bush as President of the United States]: [The election of Bush] gives Europe enormous confidence and continuity, and I think it gives much of the world the knowledge that the President will already be familiar with their problems. He's been to many of their countries. He knows many of them. Therefore, we'll get perhaps a smoother changeover than we've had for many years.

To reporters, Nov. 9/
Los Angeles Times, 11-10:(I)14.

2

[Addressing President Reagan]: I remember vividly the feeling of sheer joy at your election eight years ago, knowing that we thought so much alike, believed in many of the same things and convinced that together we could get our countries back on their feet, restore their values and create a safer and, yes, a better world . . . Thanks to your courage and your leadership, the fire of individual freedom burns more brightly, not just in America, not just in the West, but right across the world.

At White House dinner,
Washington, Nov. 16/
The Washington Post, 11-17:(A)4.

3

[On East-West relations]: I think the cold war is already at an end. The relationship has moved from a fixed arms-control minimal relationship to a much bigger, wider relationship . . . In the Soviet Union you have much greater freedom of speech . . . coupled with the fact that a far larger number of people have been able to come out. [But] I am very conscious of the fact that these things are administrative decree and not a matter yet of fundamental right. They could be reversed if [Soviet leader Mikhail] Gorbachev does not succeed in climbing through to a rather different kind of political structure.

Interview, Washington/
Newsweek, 1-28:52.

Timothy L. Towell
United States Ambassador-
designate to Paraguay

4

An Ambassadorial post is what all Foreign Service officers aspire to. It's like being head of the bank after starting out as a teller. It's becoming headmaster after being a school teacher . . . The Foreign Service is designed on the principle of upward or out. They won't let you find a nook and let you stay doing that wonderful stuff you love to do for the rest of your life. You keep going onward and upward or bye, bye. If you are going to just sit there quietly, you are going to be gone.

Interview, Washington/
The New York Times, 6-30:10.

Robert Turner
Associate director,
Center for Law
and National Security,
University of Virginia

5

[On the 1973 War Powers Resolution, which limits the power of the President in committing U.S. troops and resources to areas of hostilities]: One of the saddest side-effects of the War Powers Resolution has been the signal Congress has given to the world's aggressors and terrorists. By tying the trigger of the statute to "hostilities," you have gone a good way toward surrendering the initiative to the most radical anti-American forces around the world. Whereas once they knew that killing an American Marine would likely bring down the wrath of God—supported by a few thousand Marines and whatever other force might be necessary to complete the mission—today they know that by killing American soldiers they can possibly start the clock ticking to force a withdrawal of all American soldiers in the area. At minimum, they can start a divisive controversy between Congress and the President—which by itself weakens the United States in the eyes of much of the world. It may well have been unintentional, but it seems to me that Congress has put a "bounty" on the lives of American servicemen around the world. As I

(ROBERT TURNER)

have already mentioned, I think you [Congress] deserve substantial responsibility for the tragic attack which killed 261 fine young Marines in Beirut in October 1983.

Before Senate subcommittee,
Washington, September/
The Wall Street Journal,
11-14:(A)16.

Brian Urquhart
Former Under Secretary General
of the United Nations
for Special Political Affairs

1

[On the founding of the UN]: I don't think you could say that [the late U.S.] President Roosevelt, [the late British Prime Minister] Churchill and [the late Soviet leader] Stalin were starry-eyed idealists. They had been through the fire of war. Did anybody really think, in 1945, that every government would renounce the use of force in its relations with every other government, and agree to settle all disputes with peaceful means, and disarm? This was the aim [of the UN]. The UN Charter was a great beacon set on a hill, the great light toward which we were supposed to be working. We haven't had World War III. I don't see any reason to be downhearted. One should be frustrated, and certainly working in the UN was a great exercise in that. And one should be more determined than ever to keep after the basic objective.

Interview, New York/
Time, 12-5:52.

George S. Vest
Director General,
Foreign Service,
Department of State
of the United States

2

There was a day when going into the Foreign Service meant going to a place where life is more pleasant than it is here. Today, overseas, you face terrorism and harassment.

Interview, Washington/
Los Angeles Times, 5-14:(I)1.

William H. Webster
Director of Central Intelligence
of the United States

3

Despite *glasnost* and *perestroika* [openness and reform in the Soviet Union], we have seen an increase this year in Soviet attempts to recruit U.S. sources [of intelligence information]. We also expect to see greater Soviet efforts to recruit U.S. personnel abroad and a greater effort to penetrate allied governments ... Maybe we're getting better at finding it [Soviet spying] or it's more important to them to know certain things. For instance, on arms control. None of the essential goals of Soviet world domination have changed.

Before American Bar Association,
Toronto, Aug. 9/
The New York Times, 8-10:7.

Fred Wertheimer
President, Common Cause

4

[Criticizing President Reagan's outspoken support for those indicted in the U.S. Iran-contra scandal]: There's no basis, absolutely none, for the President injecting himself into a criminal process that is being brought by the government ... It's really hard to figure out what the President is doing. This leaves the impression that the President has not learned anything about the terrible events that occurred in the Iran-contra scandal.

March 25/
Los Angeles Times, 3-26:(I)20.

John C. Whitehead
Deputy Secretary of State
of the United States

5

Why should the United States and the West support East Bloc economies? Because we are willing to bet that greater economic openness and further integration of Eastern economies into the world market system will help to reduce tensions and advance the prospect of a more secure and

(JOHN C. WHITEHEAD)

more prosperous world for us all. Without greater openness in economic management, [the Communist bloc faces the prospect of] accelerated relative decline. I suspect that such a situation would have uncertain consequences that would most likely be in the interest of neither side.

At Institute for East-West Security
Studies, Potsdam, East Germany,
June 10/Los Angeles Times, 6-11:(I)10.

Charles Z. Wick
Director, United States
Information Agency

1

[On U.S. President Reagan]: Seven years ago, the allies didn't know quite what to make of this guy—an actor, maybe Governor by a fluke, too old to be in the White House. Everyone in the West was worried about the world economy and about the Russians and their SS-20s. A year ago, frankly, he was at a real low point, with his credibility hurt by events at home. Now, by force of character, he has reestablished himself as the leader of the free world, and his values as those that must guide [Western] alliance.

Toronto, June 19/The New York Times, 6-20:7.

Richard S. Williamson
Assistant Secretary for
International Organization Affairs,
Department of State
of the United States

2

[On the Reagan Administration's changing position on the UN, from one of skepticism to one of increasing support]: Our position is that we came in 1981 with the United States in retreat in many ways within the United Nations system, that for a variety of factors there has been progress on a number of fronts, so that while the criticisms in 1981 were valid and there are still problems, the UN has become a more hospitable place for us to help advance our interests and it's come closer to reflecting the original character [of the UN].

The New York Times, 9-26:4.

David Wise
Author; Authority on
U.S. foreign intelligence

3

[On his 1964 book, *The Invisible Government*, dealing with the CIA]: We [the authors] felt very strongly that there were two governments in the United States: one in the civics texts and the other in the real world. We found it both necessary and disturbing. We thought the intelligence agencies were important to our security. But we were troubled about a system based on the consent of the governed when the governed didn't know to what they have consented . . . The invisible government still operates in the shadows. Of course, the public today is much more aware that it exists, but most of the time you can't see what it does. Secrecy is the CIA's cloak, its national security blanket that allows it to hide from the public, even from Congress. Basically, nothing much has changed.

Interview, Washington/
The New York Times, 8-10:10.

Laurie Wiseberg
Director, Human
Rights Internet

4

The human-rights defenders on the front lines [through out the world] are the most at risk. If you kill them off, you close any space for others to operate in. Human-rights groups are not fighting for democracy; they are trying to create the space to let others do that. The moment you kill the defenders you close off the options for political change.

The Christian Science Monitor,
6-8:17.

Manfred Woerner
Secretary General, North
Atlantic Treaty Organization

5

We should seek to engage the Soviet Union in fighting hunger in the Third World, in preserving the global environment and in abiding by the rules of the international trade and payments

(MANFRED WOERNER)

system. Gradually, we may be able to draw the Soviet Union into playing a responsible international role and into working for the vision which animated the founding of the United Nations.

Before Atlantic Council,
Washington, Sept. 13/
The Washington Post, 9-14:(A)18.

Aleksandr N. Yakovlev
Member, Politburo,
Communist Party of the
Soviet Union; Adviser to
Soviet leader
Mikhail Gorbachev

1

From the very first days of my acquaintance with the United States, I have always believed, and believe now, that unless there's a genuine agreement between the U.S. and the Soviet Union, nothing good will come of the world.

Interview, Moscow, Oct. 26/
The New York Times,
10-28:(A)6.

Clayton K. Yeutter
Special Trade Representative
for President of the United States
Ronald Reagan

2

[Foreign] aid programs [for needy countries] will only do so much. They're never an answer. They're a help but not a panacea. The answer is clearly economic growth [in those countries].

USA Today, 6-10:(A)12.

Government

Mark A. Abramson
Executive director, Center for
Excellence in Government

1

The Federal government is like the Pony Express, changing the riders but not the horses. The political appointees are the riders, and they try to beat the hell out of the horses. But the horses know that they have to pace themselves, and that the riders will only be around for a couple of years, while they'll be around for decades.

They New York Times, 7-12:12.

Donnald K. Anderson
Clerk of the United States
House of Representatives

2

Most people who go to the Safeway think the food is grown in the back room. Likewise with the [process of law-making]. People don't give a second thought to the mechanical process by which words, which start as thoughts in the minds of members of Congress, end up on the printed page, headed for the President's desk.

Interview/
The New York Times, 11-2:(A)16.

Bruce Babbitt
Candidate for the 1988
Democratic Presidential
nomination; Former
Governor of Arizona (D)

3

[On whether it is proper for the government to lie to or mislead the American people]: I suppose if it's 24 hours before D-Day at Normandy and a reporter has found his way to a responsible official and asked: "Will there be an invasion on the European mainland in the next 72 hours?" it's perfectly appropriate and acceptable to use any line at all that will protect the truth. [It's] got to be very narrow, and it seems to me it must be directed at the protection of lives in the immediate future. But lying to cover up the consequences of a policy, it seems to me, is just unacceptable.

Interview/
U.S. News & World Report,
1-25:15.

Bruce Babbitt
Former Governor of Arizona (D);
Former candidate for the
1988 Democratic
Presidential nomination

4

It would have been very interesting, during the Democratic [Party debates for this year's Presidential nomination], if one moderator had turned to a candidate and asked, "Do you know the price of a loaf of bread or a dozen eggs?" Because [as a Presidential candidate] you do get removed, you do get cut off. The larger judgments you have to make as President—whether it's on defense, balance of trade, nuclear arms—ultimately have to be illuminated by a cultural and historical perspective.

The Christian Science Monitor,
4-1:17.

James David Barber
Professor of political science,
Graduate School,
Duke University

5

Before [a Presidential] election, all the smart people want to talk about the issues. But afterwards it becomes clear that character is the most important: who the Presidents are and how they operate. There's no such thing as the Presidency. There is simply one President after the other, and each remakes the office in terms of his particular approach.

Los Angeles Times, 11-13:(I)1.

(JAMES DAVID BARBER)

1

The [President] Reagan years are marked by a deterioration of political discourse. What is needed now is a resurrection of a rationality in American politics which was the intent of the Founding Fathers, who were skeptics, not romantics, who were energetic in trying to be realistic, and were not given to the diversion of ideology.

The Christian Science Monitor,
11-17:17.

Mollie Beattie
Commissioner of Forest,
Parks and Recreation of
Vermont

2

Too often we see laws passed that only nibble at the edge of large problems. They create the illusion that someone at the top knows what's going on and will see to it that it all turns out right. We've got hierarchical systems with power vested in the position rather than in ideas, and usually nobody's really in control. Politics is too important to be left to traditional politicians. We need a lot of people who don't look at things in the usual way, and we need them soon.

Interview, Montpelier, Vt./
The Christian Science Monitor,
1-5:21.

William J. Bennett
Secretary of Education
of the United States

3

[On public service]: If you don't like government, then don't govern. I love it. Speak your mind; be truthful and candid. The American people can handle it. I never went anyplace in this country that I did not meet smart people. Talk to the American people because you actually like them and respect them. A lot will respect you, and some will like you.

Time, 9-19:21.

Lloyd Bentsen
United States Senator,
D-Texas;
1988 Democratic
Vice-Presidential nominee

4

[On policy differences with his Presidential running mate, Michael Dukakis]: You have only one President, and he has the ultimate responsibility. He bears the ultimate consequences. So I won't hesitate a minute to come in and make my views known to him very forcefully. I won't win them all. That's obvious. I don't win all of them with my wife.

Interview/
U.S. News & World Report,
7-25:22.

Joseph R. Biden, Jr.
United States Senator,
D-Delaware

5

I think [TV coverage of Senate proceedings has] helped, because when people stand up to be the horses' tails and do that silly stuff, I think it hurts them. I'm not at all sure that you help yourself and your constituents by tying up the business of the Senate for two days and getting seven votes.

Interview/USA Today, 2-1:(A)13.

Bill Bradley
United States Senator,
D-New Jersey

6

[Endorsing Massachusetts Governor Michael Dukakis for the 1988 Democratic Presidential nomination]: It has been said of Michael Dukakis that he is dull, a charge with which I am not unfamiliar. But governance is not an amusement park. It holds lives in the balance.

Jersey City, N.J., March 23/
Los Angeles Times, 3-24:(I)20.

7

A good President knows that public office is one of democracy's marvelous abstractions—

(BILL BRADLEY)

that you exercise power but you must never claim it.

At Democratic National Convention,
Atlanta, July 21/
USA Today, 7-22:(A)3.

Dale Bumpers
United States Senator,
D-Arkansas

1

[On being a Senator]: I don't mind the long hours. I'm sympathetic to the Senators who are younger and have children at home. Mine are out of the nest. You're in Washington where the power is exercised and, at the same time, you get to come home regularly to be with your friends and in your home environment. From a personal standpoint, I think it's the greatest job in the world.

Interview/
USA Today,
2-1:(A)13.

George Bush
Vice President of the United
States; Candidate for the
1988 Republican
Presidential nomination

2

[On qualifications for being President]: I'm not sure that being in Congress all your life is part of the answer; I think it may be part of the problem. We're [he and his competitors] running for President. That's an Executive Branch job. . . How many of them [Congressmen] have built a business? How many of them have met a payroll? How many of them know what it means when you add to the productive base of the country? How many of them know foreign policy, from being there, talking to those leaders, not in a "photo-op" with a group going over there from the Congress?

Speech,
Washington, Jan. 5/
Los Angeles Times,
1-6:(I)1.

3

I made more decisions running the Central Intelligence Agency and intelligence community in a week than I did in four years as a Congressman from Texas. A President's got to consider the national interest. Members of Congress have to consider—by virtue of their job—the special interests. A President leads, and I found as a member of Congress to some degree you follow. And as one humorist put it, it's hard to look up to a leader who keeps his ear to the ground. And there's something to that.

Before Rotary Club,
Nashua, N.H., Feb.1/
The Washington Post, 2-2:(A)7.

4

[There] is the inside-the-[Capital] Beltway favorite sport, and that is, "How's the President screwing up today? What's he doing wrong?" And people love it. People in your profession [the press] love it. The opposition party loves it.

To newspaper editors, Milwaukee/
The Washington Post, 4-11:(A)4.

5

The liberals want government to help people directly; we want government to help people help themselves. They want to empower the government; we want to empower the people.

At Republican fund-raising luncheon,
New York, June 30/
The New York Times, 7-1:8.

6

Absolutely nothing is going to prevent [ethical lapses by government employees and officials]. I don't think you're going to ever legislate the kind of moral standards that I hope this public service deserves. I don't think a code [of ethics] can do that. . . Speak out against it, say it's bad, ferret out the corruption, make people pay the price. White-collar crime is just as bad as some kind of street crime or something of that nature. Say these things. Get a code that sets as high a standard as you can, but not then conclude that every-

(GEORGE BUSH)

thing is so perfect that you're not going to have venality of man. I mean, it just isn't going to work that way.

Interview, Washington, July 5/
The Washington Post, 7-6:(A)4.

1

[Saying the same ethics standards that apply to the Executive Branch should apply to Congress, which is now exempted from many of those standards]: The practice of Congress to legislate rules of conduct for others and not for itself is without justification or excuse. To exempt Congress from any of these rules, as does current conflict-of-interest law, is to establish a double standard that breeds suspicion, breeds cynicism, and in my judgment breeds abuse. No one, no institution, no body of government should be above the law. That is not the American way.

Speech, July 26/
Los Angeles Times, 7-27:(I)1.

2

[On how, as President, he would treat his Vice President]: You want to give him access, so the Vice President can walk down, open the door to the Oval Office, walk in without having been intercepted by staff, and talk frankly to the President. That is exactly the kind of relationship we [President Reagan and he] have. . . But the Vice President can't go out and say "I think the President is wrong". . . . Once I made a decision [as President], he [must] understand I was elected President of the United States and he was elected Vice President.

Interview, Washington, July 26/
The Washington Post, 7-27:(A)4.

George Bush
Vice President of the United
States; 1988 Republican
Presidential nominee

3

There are those who've dropped their standards along the way, as if ethics were too heavy and slowed their rise to the top. There's graft in City Hall and there's greed on Wall Street and there's influence-peddling in Washington, and the small corruptions of everyday ambition. But you see, I believe public service is honorable. And every time I hear that someone has breached the public trust, it breaks my heart.

Accepting the nomination,
at Republican National Convention,
New Orleans, Aug. 18/
The New York Times, 8-19:8.

4

For seven and a half years I've worked with a President [Reagan]—I've seen what crosses that big desk. I've seen the unexpected crisis that arrives in a cable in a young aide's hand. And I've seen the problems that simmer on for decades and suddenly demand resolution. And I've seen the modest decisions made with anguish, and crucial decisions made with dispatch.

Accepting the nomination,
at Republican National Convention,
New Orleans, Aug. 18/
The New York Times, 8-19:8.

5

I think [as President] you have to delegate, because nobody can be expected to know everything about everything. Government is too complex, the problems too enormous. But I think I'd be good in setting a philosophical direction, setting certain objectives, delegating authority and then staying in touch. And I've always done that—in something as complicated as the CIA or for the short period of time I was in business.

Interview/
Los Angeles Times, 9-11(I)20.

6

Those of us in leadership positions in government must be an example of ethical behavior. I am disturbed when those in privileged positions fail to uphold the trust that is placed in them. Public service has been hurt by individuals who

(GEORGE BUSH)

lacked the judgment or character to put the public's business above their own self-interest. We need a revival of traditional ethical standards. Despite our national prosperity, many Americans are troubled over the fact that we have strayed from our fundamental values. But we cannot legislate ethical behavior. We must lead by example.

Interview/
Christianity Today, 9-16:40.

1

I don't think it's a question of whether people like you or not to make you an effective leader. I think it's whether you share the broad dreams of the American people; whether you have confidence in the people's ability to get things done. Or whether you think it all should be turned over, as many of the liberals do, to Washington, D.C. You see, I think it's a question of values, not likability or lovability.

At Presidential debate,
Los Angeles, Oct. 13/
The New York Times, 10-15:10.

George Bush
Vice President, and
President-elect, of the
United States

2

[On his being elected President]: I hate to think of myself as shell-shocked. Nevertheless, that's one way of describing how one feels after the end of the campaign and finding himself elected to be the next President of the United States.

To reporters,
Gulf Stream, Fla., Nov. 14/
The Washington Post, 11-15:(A)14.

3

[On his plans for Vice President-elect Dan Quayle[: Those who are saying the Vice President hasn't even been given specific assignments yet simply missed the point over the last eight years. They just don't understand that the importance of the Vice Presidency has emerged, and one of the reasons it has emerged is that the Vice President is a generalist, has the confidence of the President, and so the mold will be very much like the one that President Reagan cast and forged in 1980, building, incidentally, on the Carter-Mondale operation, which I think elevated the Vice Presidency. And with all apologies to those who traveled with me, close your ears, because I know you don't want to hear it again, but [the late Vice President] Nelson Rockefeller told me one of his great frustrations was when he was assigned specific programs and then, for various political reasons, his legs were cut off by the White House staff. And I'm not going to have that kind of arrangement. And I don't think now-Senator and future Vice President Dan Quayle wants that kind of arrangement.

News conference,
Washington, Dec. 14/
The New York Times, 12-15:(A)10.

Rosalynn Carter
Wife of former President of
the United States
Jimmy Carter

4

[On criticism of her taking a more active role in Presidential affairs, such as sitting in at Cabinet meetings, while her husband was President]: I don't think I would have done anything differently. I cannot imagine anybody in the White House having a chance to go to Cabinet meetings and not going. I had campaigned. I was traveling all of the time and people were asking me questions. I wanted to know what my husband was doing, so I didn't have to ask, "Why did you do this?" every time he got off the elevator. What people don't realize is that the Cabinet meetings are also attended by lesser officials, so there are a lot of people in that room who are not Cabinet level. I just sat back as a spectator. I never knew the details of policy, but I did try to have an overall understanding of what was going on.

Interview/
L. B. J. Ranch, Texas/
Good Housekeeping, February:171.

Michael Checkland
Director general,
British Broadcasting
Corporation

1

It is often said—and I think rightly—that England could learn a thing or two from America on the matter of freedom of information. We will continue to be in the forefront of those demanding free discussion of all matters of public interest where no genuine breach of national security is involved. Democracy thrives on openness and is endangered when the state exerts unjustified pressure on the media.

Before Academy of Television Arts
and Sciences, Los Angeles/
Emmy Magazine, May-June:53.

Tony Coelho
United States Representative,
D-California

2

[Former President Jimmy] Carter and [President] Reagan got elected against the Federal system. They worked against the Federal system while in office and never quite understood it. [President-elect George] Bush is a product of the Federal system and likes it, and the players in this town, regardless of party, see another player come to join them at the table. Instead of cracking the whip, he's creating an ambience of cooperation. It's very shrewd.

Washington/
The New York Times, 12-3:9.

Mario M. Cuomo
Governor of New York (D)

3

I would prefer a system where we [state governments] gave the local goverments less, and gave them the capacity to raise their own revenues so that their people could make judgments as to what you want to pay taxes for and what you want to spend on. The government closest to the people is the best. Let them make more of the decisions.

News conference,
Albany, N.Y., Dec. 27/
The New York Times, 12-28:(A)13.

Thomas A. Daschle
United States Senator,
D-South Dakota

4

[On being a Senator after serving in the House]: It's quite a dramatic transition to make. Once you've developed certain work habits with regard to the legislative process, it requires a significant effort to change your style. The House is a legislative assembly line and the Senate is designed to bring a more analytical view to the process. Using the automobile as an analogy, you could say the House is the gas pedal and the Senate the brake.

Interview/The New York Times, 4-11:26.

Sam Dash
Professor, Georgetown
University Law Center;
Former Chief Counsel,
Senate Watergate Committee

5

[On last year's U.S. Iran-contra scandal]: Today the American public is uncertain where the Constitutional power lies. Does the President have this right? Does Congress? Unlike Watergate, you have a real clash of Constitutional powers between what the President claims are his powers and what the Congress claims are its powers. I would have liked to have heard public testimony by Constitutional experts representing both Congress and the President's points of view. Maybe we would learn that [President] Reagan believes, as [former President] Richard Nixon once said, that he is as absolute a monarch as Louis XIV—only four years at a time—and not subject to the law.

Panel discussion,
New School for Social Research,
New York/Harper's, February:56.

Michael S. Dukakis
Governor of Massachusetts (D);
Candidate for the 1988
Democratic Presidential
nomination

6

[On "kiss-and-tell" books written about Presidents by their disgruntled former aides]: I don't

(MICHAEL S. DUKAKIS)

think any of us demand blind loyalty from the people who work for us. But one aspect of the loyalty I think we have a right to expect is that when you leave, you leave quietly.

May 11/
Los Angeles times,
5-12:(I)18.

1

I think [President Reagan's] is an Administration that is contemptuous of public service and contemptuous of the Congress. They came to office with a view that government and public service were both dirty words. If you come to government with that attitude, then the chances are you are going to pick mediocre people, at best. You are not going to really pay attention to what it means to provide good public services effectively and well. . . I'm not campaigning against Washington. My vocation has been public service. I think it's a very noble calling. That's 180 degrees from where Reagan is and the people around him. I have a rather clear philosophy of public service and what it's all about, and it's an activist view.

Interview/
Los Angeles Times, 5-26:(I)23,24.

Michael S. Dukakis
Governor of Massachusetts (D);
1988 Democratic
Presidential nominee

2

Four years from now, when our citizens walk along Pennsylvania Avenue in Washington, D.C., or when they see a picture of the White House on television, I want them to be proud of their government. I want them to be proud of a government that sets high standards not just for the American people, but high standards for itself. . . . In the Dukakis White House, as in the Dukakis State House, if you accept the privilege of public service, you had better understand the responsibilities of public service. If you violate

that trust, you'll be fired. If you violate the law, you'll be prosecuted.

Accepting the nomination, at
Democratic National Convention,
Atlanta, July 21/
Los Angeles Times, 7-22:(I)6.

3

[On criticism that, as a Governor, he does not have enough experience to be President]: Some of our finest Presidents, some of our strongest international leaders, were Governors: Franklin Roosevelt, Woodrow Wilson, Theodore Roosevelt. It's not the amount of time you spend in Washington, it's not the length of your resume; it's your strength, it's your values, it's the quality of the people you pick, it's your understanding of the forces of change that are sweeping the world and whether or not you're in a position to provide leadership to make those forces of change work for us and not against us. . . So I don't believe that the fact that you've got that long resume, or had that experience, is the real question. The question is values, the question is strength, the question is your willingness to provide the kind of leadership that must be provided.

At Presidential debate,
Winston-Salem, N.C., Sept. 25/
The New York Times, 9-26:12.

Pierre S. du Pont IV
Candidate for the 1988
Republican Presidential
nomination; Former
Governor of Delaware (R);
Former United States
Representative, R-Delaware

4

I won't be a legislator again. Once you've been a leader, going back to sit around a table to take little snippets from here, little snippets from there and craft a compomise—you're not going to get anything done that way. . . They all sweat and they lose sleep and they've got bags under their eyes trying to get that extra quarter of a billion dollars out of some resolution that it turns out doesn't matter because the whole thing's overtaken by events. That's not *doing* anything!

The Washington Post, 2-2:(D)10.

Dennis E. Eckart
United States Representative,
D-Ohio

1

[On the desire of President Reagan to privatize many functions of government]: We're not going to let the President sell the Post Office to Federal Express. But given the budget constraints we're under, given the demands that people make on government services, we ought to look at alternatives and better ways to provide them. The basic Democratic response until now has been "Drop dead," but I think that's a mistake.

The New York Times, 2-15:8.

Stuart E. Eizenstat
Former Assistant to the
President of the United States
(Jimmy Carter) for
Domestic Affairs

2

[Saying new Presidents always sweep the White House clean of any remnants of the former occupant]: Everything in the White House, including the pictures and the Filipino waiters, are somehow considered tainted. . . There are not that many decisions that are totally new, with no writing [already] on the blackboard. [But] a new President removes not only the people who wrote on the blackboard, but also takes away the blackboard.

News conference, Jan. 20/
The New York Times, 1-21:14.

3

[On the transition period after a new President is elected and before he takes office]: There's been a recognition that the transition, in itself, is an important decision-making period. It's not just a period for rest and recreation between an exhausting campaign and a new Administration. During the transition, you're going to appoint several hundred top officials, put together your first budget, and develop two or three key legislative ideas.

Interview/
The New York Times, 9-22:28.

Daniel J. Evans
United States Senator,
R-Washington

4

[On his decision not to seek re-election to the Senate]: I came with perhaps a more romantic idea of what the Senate was all about than I should have. But I looked forward to the debate, the exchange of ideas, the hope that I could influence my colleagues in the Senate by the force of ideas. That has to substitute for seniority, and I think, after all, [that] is the most important thing we're all about in the Senate—the exchange of ideas and importance of ideas. But there is very little debate in the Senate. Debate takes a couple of things. It takes people prepared and understanding of the issues themselves, not their staffs, not just reading the speech, but understanding, and understanding deeply the issues. And secondly, annoyance: the Senators being there and exchanging ideas and entering into debate—but giving a series of set speeches to an almost empty chamber is a pretty pale substitute. The one thing that has frustrated me, or really makes me feel kind of badly about the way the Senate operates is, frankly, the discourtesy on the Senate floor.

Broadcast interview/
"The MacNeil-Lehrer NewsHour,"
PBS-TV, 10-24.

Vic Fazio
United States Representative,
D-California

5

The budget process can be debated and we can theoretically improve it, but it really is more fundamental than that. It really requires people to compromise and to get a little dirty and make enemies of some of their friends, and all that sort of thing. The fundamental structure of our government—a tripartite system—when populated by people who are rigid and antagonistic, unyielding, uncompromising and overly ideological, just doesn't produce results.

Los Angeles Times,
1-26:(I)14.

181

Betty Ford
*Wife of former President of
the United States
Gerald R. Ford*

1

Anyone in public office . . . is always going to be judged on their actions. And that is a part of their moral characteristics. If you run for public office, I think you have to be prepared to know that the press is going to investigate.

*Interview, L. B. J. Ranch, Texas/
Good Housekeeping, February:172.*

Gerald R. Ford
*Former President of the
United States*

2

I strongly believe that when a person in the Cabinet or a comparable position is challenged for alleged misdeeds . . . if his staying in office in any way undercuts or jeopardizes the Presidency . . . he should walk into the Oval Office and offer his resignation.

*Before National Press Club,
Washington, June 6/
The Washington Post,
6-7:(A)8.*

Wyche Fowler
*United States Senator,
D-Georgia*

3

[On being a Senator after serving in the House]: In the House, a specific time-frame is allotted a piece of legislation and you've got to fight to get on the list if you want to talk, much less offer an amendment. Here [in the Senate], we have no such rules. We protect the rights of individuals to offer any amendment at any time, germane or not, and we don't limit a Senator's right to the floor once he has taken it. I think it was either Washington or Hamilton who said, when discussing the different functions of the House and the Senate, that we [the Senate] are the saucer in which legislation is poured to cool.

*Interview/
The New York Times, 4-11:26.*

Anthony M. Frank
*Postmaster General
of the United States*

4

[Criticizing calls for privatization of the Postal Service[: Is privatization simply a code word for union busting? Is privatization an attempt to let private companies selectively skim off the profitable segments of postal business, while leaving the Postal Service to continue serving those groups in areas deemed not profitable? [I am] certainly interested in exploring . . . a genuine effort to promote efficiency, [but I am] not in the business of union busting [or destroying the economic base of the Postal Service].

*Before Cato Institute, April 7/
The Washington Post, 4-8:(A)19.*

5

[Comparing his job as Postmaster General with his previous position as head of First Nationwide Savings[: In this job, everything is 100 times greater. At First Nationwide, we had 2 million customers; here we have 200 million. Before, we had 400 branches; here we have 40,000. We had 8,000 employees [at the bank]; here we have 800,000. . . In private life you want to earn a profit; here your objective is to break even. . . Imagine running a $38-billion business, which would put you in the top 10 of the *Fortune* 500, and not being able to set your own prices [Post Office prices must be cleared through the Postal Rate Commission]. And it's not just stamps and mail rates. We can't even set prices on rental fees for Post Office boxes. And for some reason, while we can sell packing materials at our Post Offices, we can't sell tape. Supposedly that is competitive with the private sector. Hey, I just work here!

*Interview, Washington/
The New York Times, 7-27:12.*

Monroe H. Freedman
*Professor of legal ethics,
Hofstra University*

6

There seems to be a greater number of people who are in government today for selfish reasons.

(MONROE H. FREEDMAN)

Back amid the idealism of the 1960s, many young people sought government service for what they might contribute—not for the sake of enriching themselves.

Los Angeles Times, 2-12:(I)22.

Carlos Fuentes
Mexican author
and diplomat

1

[On Washington]: This has always been a floating city, in a way, a city of passage. You ask: "Where is so-and-so whom I met last spring?" "Oh, she's gone, he's gone, they're gone." Everybody is leaving all the time, everybody is arriving. It is a mutant city . . .

Interview/
The New York Times, 5-30:20.

Jake Garn
United States Senator,
R-Utah

2

[Saying Congress has become less and less effective in getting things done]: I'm to the point where I don't care what is done, as long as we do something. . . Frankly, ladies and gentlemen, I'm getting sick of all of you, just really sick.

To government officials, lobbyists
and reporters at Senate Banking
Committee hearing, Washington/
Los Angeles Times, 1-24:(I)22.

Samuel Gejdenson
United States Representative,
D-Connecticut

3

The hearing process is the lifeblood of the Congress. It is the primary source of information for this legislative body. It is the duty of Congressional committees to protect witnesses that appear before them. Unless our citizens can come before the Congress and speak their minds freely and without fear of retribution, it renders the Congressional-hearings process meaningless.

The Washington Post, 10-3:(A)9.

Richard A. Gephardt
United States Representative,
D-Missouri; Candidate for the
1988 Democratic
Presidential nomination

4

All great political leaders have changed their minds in response to changing circumstances. It's silly to be rigid on things when circumstances change.

Time, 2-22:22.

Paul Gewirtz
Professor of law,
Yale University

5

Our system of government is not made up of three rigidly insulated government bodies. It is a system of overlapping functions.

Newsweek, 7-11:30.

Barry M. Goldwater
Former United States Senator,
R-Arizona

6

One day, we'll have a woman President—not because she's a woman but because she's demonstrably better. But I won't be here.

USA Today, 4-29:(A)2.

Allan E. Gotlieb
Canadian Ambassador
to the United States

7

The exercise of political power in Washington is so extraordinarily complex that the only way one can understand or describe it is through a metaphor. . . Imagine R. F. K. Stadium—only imagine also that the field is magnetic. Each player is an atom or unit and carries an electrical charge. All the particles are moving about,

(ALLAN E. GOTLIEB)

seemingly at random. Some particles have more power than others, but all have some. Some particles attract; others repel. The field is full of players, hundreds of them, thousands of them. Several teams take the field at a time. Several kinds of games are in play at once. Players from one team, without changing uniform, sometimes play for another. There are no referees. The cheerleaders, dressed in power suits and Gucci loafers, send in plays from the sidelines. Political-action committees, dressed as trainers, dispense the steroids of modern politics—money—to the players on all sides. Meanwhile, the crowd's attention is riveted not on the field but on the media. The media sometimes declare what happens on the field, and sometimes they play their own games. Well, who are these particles? The President, the Cabinet, the 4,000 or so political appointments made directly by him, the 350,000 Federal civil servants, the 535 members of Congress, the 18,000 Congressional staffers, the 47,834 lawyers, the employees of the 11,000 associations, the 75 think tanks, the 4,196 political-action committees, the 9,127 lobbyists who registered in the last year, the 18,348 lobbyists who have not registered in the last two years and, last but not least, the 4,326 journalists—a cozy community of, some say, half a million, all shooting off electrical power charges.

At National Press Club luncheon,
Washington, Dec. 20/
The Washington Post, 12-23:(A)18.

William H. Gray III
United States Representative,
D-Pennsylvania

1

When I was elected Chairman [of the House Budget Committee], I told my colleagues a kind of parable about the little boy falling in the well who figures out that the only way out is to tie all the ropes together. That's the way I see my job—if you can't tie the ropes together between the conservatives and moderates and liberals of our Party, then you can't make a policy.

U.S. News & World Report, 2-8:60.

Gary Hart
Candidate for the 1988
Democratic Presidential
nomination; Former
United States Senator,
D-Colorado

2

I'm a political person and, whether each of you likes it or not, so are you, because politics simply means the process by which we govern our lives. And we can pretend—and we often do—that we won't have anything to do with politics, and vice versa, that we won't let it have anything to do with us. But that is simply ignoring reality. Politics and government affect our lives every day and in practically every way.

Campaign speech/
The New York Times, 1-26:13.

Julius W. Hobson, Jr.
Chief Congressional lobbyist
for the District of Columbia

3

We [who reside in Washington] live in a goldfish bowl, surrounded by members of Congress, none of them our own full-fledged representatives, because we've been denied statehood. Any District issue is easy game for any member who wants to tee off on something, or help out a union or an industry or an organization, or who just doesn't like Washington or its people. Congress wants it that way.

The New York Times, 7-19:7.

Jerry R. Hough
Professor of political science,
Duke University

4

The great problem with [government] bureaucracies is that there is no reward for success, only penalties for doing a bad job.

The Washington Post, 6-3:(A)27.

Henry J. Hyde
United States Representative,
R-Illinois

5

The President represents all the people. We [in Congress] have narrow constituencies. We re-

(HENRY J. HYDE)

spond to the loudest of those constituencies and those who have the busiest Xerox machine and the longest letterhead. Our vision of the future does not extend much beyond the next election.

Los Angeles Times, 1-27:(I)18.

Fred C. Ikle
Under Secretary of Defense
of the United States

1

Any Presidency is a combination of the President's views and the nature of his team, and maybe what has changed more than [President Reagan's] views is the team. The President cannot do everything alone. He's the conductor, in a sense, and if the orchestra starts to play a different tune, there's only so far that he can go in conducting the concert.

Interview, Washington, Jan. 18/
The New York Times, 1-20:10.

Michael Josephson
Former professor of law,
Loyola University;
Authority on ethics

2

[On ethics in government]: Being ethical involves more than staying out of trouble. There is an affirmative dimension which focuses on producing good rather than forbidding bad. We cannot require it by law, but we ought to prod and inspire government employees to view their ethical obligations in broad and affirmative terms.

Before Senate subcommittee,
Washington/
The Christian Science Monitor, 11-21:1.

Walter Karp
Author, Historian

3

[On the U.S. Iran-contra scandal hearings' report]: The thing that the report does beautifully is to erect a Chinese Wall between the Presi-

dent and his advisers. The report holds that a President's *ignorance* of what his closest advisers do in pursuit of his avowed policy is to be assumed unless there is—I quote—"direct evidence" of personal participation in a crime. That is an invitation to criminal government in the future.

Panel discussion, New School
for Social Research,
New York/Harper's, February:47.

Thomas H. Kean
Governor of New Hersey (R)

4

Being Governor is the best job in politics right now. It's the one where you can get the most accomplished.

The New York Times,
3-22:8.

5

[Government should be involved in] creating opportunity and removing barriers. Once a child born in the ghetto has the same chance as a child born in the suburbs, then it's up to him. It's not the government's job at all. It's government's job to make sure everybody's in the same place at the starting line.

Interview/
USA Today, 8-15:(A)11.

Jack Kemp
United States Representative,
R-New York

6

[On attempts by the Federal government to take over control of the Teamsters Union because of that union's alleged involvement in criminal activity]: We all believe that breaking the law should and must be prosecuted ... but the United States government is not meant to be in the business of taking things over. It shouldn't take over newspapers. It shouldn't take over schools. It shouldn't take over corporations. And it shouldn't take over [labor] unions.

The New York Times, 7-4:9.

Lewis Lapham
Editor, "Harper's" magazine
1

[On last year's U.S. Iran-contra scandal]: Apparently no one found the confused impulse toward autocracy within [President] Reagan's White House cause for sufficient alarm. Maybe the times have changed since [former President] Richard Nixon was nearly impeached. Is it because the public assumes that politicians will steal and lie, or is it because people think that the world has become such a dangerous place that only scoundrels can guarantee the safety of a democratic republic?

Panel discussion,
New School for Social Research,
New York/Harper's, February:54.

Delbert Latta
United States Representative,
R-Ohio
2

I have been around Congress long enough to know that whenever we get our hands on some more dough, we are going to spend it.

Nation's Business, February:14.

Marvin Leath
United States Representative,
D-Texas
3

I'd like to be able to walk into that [White House] Oval Office and say [to the President], "Sit down, turkey, you've really been screwing up." We tried that with [former President Jimmy] Carter and he would just turn redder and redder, and when it was over he would chew our butts off.

Los Angeles Times, 1-20:(I)16.

Arthur Liman
Counsel to the U.S. Senate
Iran-Contra Committee
4

[Supporting the use of independent counsels and special prosecutors to investigate alleged crimes by Executive Branch officials]: An Administration investigation of Administration officials cannot be credible. And without that credibility, there can be no confidence in government.

Newsweek, 7-11:30.

Robert F. Linowes
Professor of political economics,
University of Illinois; Chairman,
Presidential Commission
on Privatization
5

The government, with its checks and balances, does not lend itself to managing high technology. Government entities have injected themselves well beyond the realm of government into business, to the detriment of both business and government. . . Government should reach out by opening its operations to the creative talents and drive of entrepreneurs.

News conference,
Washington, March 18/
The New York Times, 3-19:8.

Ray Mabus
Governor of Mississippi (D)
6

The abuse of public office for private greed is not recent. It is far older than the corruption that we are now routing out in our own state—but it is also as new as the urgent, seemingly endless crisis of ethics at the highest levels of national power. The issue is not partisan. If we step back from it, we have to ask ourselves: "Why do so many public officials now think they can get away with so much?" I think their conduct merely reflects a more pervasive reality: the loss of respect for the law flows from a lost sense of obligation—an obligation not only to avoid doing wrong, but to meet a higher standard of concern and involvement. The decade of the 1980s has, in too many ways, sanctified selfishness—and invited us to believe that the buck is the only bottom line.

At University of
Mississippi commencement/
The Christian Science Monitor,
7-27:26.

Thomas E. Mann
Director of governmental studies,
Brookings Institution

1

Divided government is the norm rather than the exception in American politics. The fact that the Republicans are a permanent minority party in the House, combined with their success in winning the Presidency, has made comity between the branches difficult.

Los Angeles Times, 1-24:(I)22.

John McCain
United States Senator,
R-Arizona

2

[Comparing the House with the Senate]: In the House, you have members who really have an in-depth knowledge of issues that they've been dealing with for years and years. On the other hand, I would suggest that one of the best things about the Senate is our ability to thoroughly debate an issue, whereas in the House, debate is constrained by the rules. Recently, the House had all of three hours to debate the fiscal 1989 budget.

Interview/The New York Times, 4-11:26.

Eugene J. McCarthy
Former United States Senator,
D-Minnesota

3

[Saying the Vice-Presidency should be abolished]: The Vice-Presidency clutters up the [Presidential election] campaign. . . It's an insult to the electorate. It puts people in line to become either the candidate or the President who shouldn't be there. It wastes good people, takes them out of circulation for eight years and sometimes practically destroys them.

Interview/Time, 11-14:73.

E. Patrick McGuire
Executive director for
corporate relations,
The Conference Board

4

When the Reagan Administration came in and promised to get government off the backs of the people, the people they had in mind were business people, and that was fine—because there were regulatory excesses. [But] they may have gotten them too far off the backs of some people. If you look at the record of the Occupational Safety and Health Administration or the Consumer Product Safety Commission, you wouldn't necessarily be too impressed. . . What has happened is that some of that slack in terms of prosecutorial zeal has been picked up at the state level. It's been happening not only in the regulatory sphere, but also in a lot of other spheres of government activity. When things slow down in Washington, they don't necessarily slow down at all out in the state capitals.

The Washington Post, 8-30:(A)16.

John McLaughlin
Political commentator and
talk-show host

5

[Reflecting on a dinner visit to his house by President Reagan]: Here's the interesting thing: The President becomes one of you, but then it's time for him to go. You usher him downstairs and open the door leading to the garage. All kinds of secret service people are darting in and out. The Presidential limousine is there, backed into the garage, the door open. Nancy Reagan gets in and the President follows. They close the door, and it's like a big bubble. It goes out. You see the flags on the car and the cars in front and behind and the cops on motorcycles, and sirens are going and he goes down the street, and suddenly it dawns on you, after three-and-a-half hours, that he's not yours. He doesn't belong to anybody. He belongs to the people. And it's [an] awesome [realization].

Interview/
Emmy Magazine, May-June:10.

Edwin Meese III
Attorney General
of the United States

6

[On the results of an independent counsel's investigation of him which cleared him of criminal wrongdoing in office]: The filing of the report

(EDWIN MEESE III)

by the independent counsel, in line with his previously stated finding, confirms that, after an exhaustive investigation, he has determined that there is no basis for criminal proceedings with respect to any of the matters that he has examined. I am gratified by this result but not surprised. I knew from the beginning of this investigation that my conduct has been at all times lawful, and that if the truth were told, there would be no grounds for any criminal action. This past year has been enormously difficult for my family and me. . . [But] I have refused to bend to the constant drumbeat of political and media pressure because I have a responsibility to uphold [that] which involves an important principle, not only for myself and this Administration, but for future government officials who are subjected to untrue allegations. As I have said before, to allow myself to be hounded out of office by false accusations or allegations, unjust political attacks and media clamor would undermine the integrity of our system and would abandon the principles of justice [that] I have championed throughout my life.

News conference,
Sacramento, Calif., July 5/
The New York Times,
7-6:12.

Edwin Meese III
Former Attorney General
of the United States

1

Any additional ethics requirements [for government officials] should apply in an evenhanded manner to both the Legislative and the Executive Branch. That certainly is one requirement. And secondly, I think that the objectives should be honest government and the perception of integrity, and the perception as well as the reality of integrity, rather than just a lot of burdensome regulations that don't produce either.

Interview/
USA Today,
12-12:(A)11.

Howard H. Metzenbaum
United States Senator,
D-Ohio

2

[Agreeing with a bill that would, for at least a year after they leave office, prohibit former members of Congress from becoming paid lobbyists who lobby the government for private interests]: For once, Congress is doing the right thing. Day after day, we find former members of Congress are getting unbelievably high fees for influencing their former colleagues. Lobbyists should be paid for *what* they know, not *who* they know.

April 19/
Los Angeles Times, 4-20:(I)1.

Robert H. Michel
United States Representative,
R-Illinois

3

The Congress is becoming unaccountable. The question we have to answer is: Has the machinery of government reached such a state of disrepair that it should be a matter of public concern? My answer—as subjective and prejudiced as it might be—is yes.

Los Angeles Times, 1-24:(I)22.

4

We Republicans have to rid ourselves of the cliches and platitudes of yesteryear and realize that most Americans don't believe government is the enemy. Most Americans believe *bad* government is the enemy.

At "Congress of the Future"
meeting, Houston/
The Christian Science Monitor,
3-30:8.

5

[Saying 34 years of Democratic House rule has, through poor procedural methods instituted by the Democrats, resulted in bad legislative processes]: We see less thoughtful process, sloppier laws, declining productivity and an emphasis on the frivolous as against the substan-

(ROBERT H. MICHEL)

tive. The average citizen's life is made more complicated and more difficult by poorly drafted and often contradictory laws.

Washington, May 24/
The Washington Post, 5-25:(A)3.

Barbara A. Mikulski
United States Senator,
D-Maryland

1

[On Presidents' wives]: When the women are uninvolved [in governmental affairs], they're criticized for being aloof. When they're very much involved . . . they're accused of petticoat politics. So I think a First Lady gets a bum rap no matter what she does.

Interview/USA Today, 6-2:(A)9.

James C. Miller III
Director, Federal Office of
Management and Budget

2

The Postal Service is a monstrosity. It is over-staffed, over-priced and inefficient. Postal patrons are paying more and more and getting less and less in return.

Time, 3-28:50.

Alan B. Morrison
Director, Public Citizen
Litigation Group

3

The separation of powers is one of the remarkable virtues of the Constitution. There are temporary ebbs and flows due to the political climate, but basically each branch has the power to do what it needs to do, and not so much that it can keep the others from doing what they need to do. In this sense, I'm a conservative. I regard the separation of powers as a fundamental part of our system that we shouldn't tinker with. . . The separation of powers is one means of keeping the government accountable. If you can hide the ball, you don't have accountability.

Interview, Washington/
The New York Times, 12-26:(A)10.

Edmund S. Muskie
Former Secretary of State
of the United States

4

The use of political appointees has dipped down into the middle level and the lower level of management in government service to the point that . . . it closes off opportunities for advancement to career people. Opportunity for advancement in government service is as important as it is in the private sector.

News conference, Washington, Oct. 19/
The Washington Post, 10-20:(A)21.

Lyn Nofziger
Former Special Assistant to
President of the United States
Ronald Reagan for
Political Affairs

5

[On his being convicted of violating the Ethics in Government Act due to alleged conflicts of interest]: It's a lousy law. It doesn't apply to Congress. It doesn't apply to the judiciary. It doesn't apply to those below a certain salary level. . . It's like running a stop sign.

Washington, Feb. 11/
The Washington Post, 2-12:(A)1.

Eleanor Holmes Norton
Professor of law,
Georgetown University;
Former Chairman, Federal
Equal Employment
Opportunity Commission

6

One should be careful before one adopts the kind of structural Federalism that says the only way, or the best way, to achieve social change or reform through government is exclusively through state initiatives. We're still groping for the proper balance. . . [But] nobody would want to dilute the creativity now arising in the states. During this [Reagan] Administration, the states have saved the whole idea of government as a force for a kind of humanitarian aid. Without the state initiatives, during this decade we would have had no progress, no innovation in government.

The Washington Post, 8-30:(A)16.

Norman J. Ornstein
Resident scholar, American
Enterprise Institute

1

[Members of Congress] may be frustrated, but they're not leaving. What they get from their friends who have gone out and are practicing law or doing other things, is that the work is pretty boring compared to Congress. So despite the bitching and moaning, it's still a pretty interesting and exciting job.

Los Angeles Times, 1-25:(I)21.

2

I believe there are only two circumstances under which government can act swiftly and sweepingly in changing the status quo. The first is when you have a crisis of sufficient magnitude that the public says to policy-makers, "We're going under for the third time, do whatever is necessary," and the second is when you have a President, Congress, the business community and the academic community declaring, "This is terrible and we've got to act."

Los Angeles Times, 1-26:(I)14.

Bob Packwood
United States Senator,
R-Oregon

3

[Saying U.S. Attorney General Edwin Meese should resign because of allegations of wrongdoing]: [The Reagan Administration] would be better off with his leaving. I think it is unfortunate if the standard is going to be we will all wait until we're indicted. That is the standard for a bank robber and should not be the standard for high public office.

March 30/
Los Angeles Times, 3-31:(I)1.

Leon E. Panetta
United States Representative,
D-California

4

People ask, "Why can't the Congress run the nation?" Well, it wasn't designed to run the nation. We're designed to evaluate proposals, to evaluate bills. A large number of those bills should be generated from the White House. In the last couple of years, there has been almost a vacuum in which the President has not exercised close coordination with Congress or laid out a legislative agenda.

Los Angeles Times, 1-24:(I)22.

Charles Peters
Editor, "The Washington
Monthly"

5

There are many jobs for which orderly minds are very well suited, but President of the United States is not one of them. The United States government does not work in an orderly fashion, and to make it work you have to do a lot of disorderly things.

Interview/
The Washington Post, 6-9:(B)1.

Colin L. Powell
Assistant to President of the
United States Ronald Reagan
for National Security Affairs

6

One of the reasons you have leaks breaking out [in government] and people fighting out issues in public is when they don't think decisions are going to be made inside. But if you have an orderly decision process, and decisions are made, and they're made fairly promptly, you have a better opportunity to have an orderly in-house system rather than a public shouting match.

Interview/
The Christian Science Monitor,
4-8:32.

William Proxmire
United States Senator,
D-Wisconsin

7

Somebody said that the U.S. Senate is a place where somebody stands up to give a speech that nobody listens to, and as soon as he sits down everybody stands up and disagrees with him.

Interview/USA Today, 2-1:(A)13.

David H. Pryor
United States Senator,
D-Arkansas

1

[Questioning the desirability of privatization, contracting out government services to the private sector]: Few, if any, government officials can show money in hand as a consequence of contracting out. . . When they can show that there was actually money saved, we often find that they usually wind up spending the money on some pet project.

Washington, March 30/
The Washington Post, 3-31:(A)21.

2

We [Senators] can take angry constituents, mean-spirited journalists, just about anything you can name; but when [a Senate colleague] asks for a vote and we have to say no, we become discombobulated, totally shattered. We're just not very good at this kind of thing.

The Washington Post, 11-21:(A)4.

Dan Quayle
United States Senator,
R-Indiana; Vice President-elect
of the United States

3

The Vice President submerges himself and implements the policies of the President. That becomes your sole goal and your challenge in the job.

To reporters, Nov. 8/
Los Angeles Times, 11-10:(I)18.

4

[Saying there is more to being Vice President than just attending official ceremonies]: There is ceremony for the funerals, but you can also do a lot of work. You can meet a lot of people. You can have some meetings and you'd be surprised at the kind of information and contact that is made beyond the ceremonial requirements.

Interview, Washington, Nov. 30/
Los Angeles Times, 12-1:(I)18.

Nancy Reagan
Wife of President of the
United States Ronald Reagan

5

A President has advisers to counsel him on foreign affairs, on defense, on the economy, on politics, on any number of matters. But no one among all those experts is there to look after him as an individual with human needs, as a flesh-and-blood person who must deal with the pressures of holding the most powerful position on Earth. . . [Therefore,] no First Lady need make apologies for looking out for her husband's personal welfare. It's an important, legitimate role for a First Lady to look after a President's health and well being. And if that interferes with affairs of state, then so be it.

To spouses of attendees at
World Gas Council Meeting,
Washington, June 9/
Los Angeles Times, 6-10:(I)36.

Ronald Reagan
President of the United States

6

[Supporting privatization of many government operations]: This does not imply the abrogation of government responsibility for these services. Rather, it merely recognizes that what matters the most is the cost and quality of the service provided, not who provides it. In addition, there is an important moral consideration—individual liberty would be enhanced and the debilitating effect of public-sector growth on human freedom would be reduced.

Message to Congress*/
The Washington Post,
1-27:(A)17.

7

[On allegations of wrongdoing by Attorney General Edwin Meese]: I have no evidence of any wrongdoing on his part of the kind that is inferred in the allegations that are being kicked around. I have complete confidence in him. I think that for him to step aside would be what he, himself, once said: that he would then live for the

(RONALD REAGAN)

rest of his life under this cloud, but with nothing that had ever been proven.

News conference,
Washington, May 17/
The New York Times, 5-18:1.

1

Our Constitution is a document in which "we the people" tell the government what its powers are. . . But very carefully, at the same time, the people give the government the power with regard to those things which they think would be destructive to society. . . The government can enforce the laws, but that has all been dictated by the people.

To students at Moscow State
University, May 31/
Los Angeles Times, 6-1:(I)12.

2

Democracy is less a system of government than it is a system to keep government limited, unintrusive, a system of constraints on power to keep politics and government secondary to the important things in life, the true sources of value found only in family and faith.

To students at Moscow State
University, May 31/
USA Today, 6-1:(A)13.

3

As I see it, political leadership in a democracy requires seeing past the abstractions and embracing the vast diversity of humanity, and doing it with humility; listening as best you can, not just to those with high positions, but to the cacophonous voices of ordinary people, and trusting those millions of people, keeping out of their way; not trying to act the all-wise and all-powerful; not letting government act that way. And the word we have for this is *freedom.*

At House of Writers, Moscow,
May 31/Los Angeles Times,
6-1:(I)14.

4

I just have to believe that in any government some of us find ourselves bound in bureaucracy and then sometimes you have to stomp your foot and say unmistakably, I want it done. And then maybe you get through with it. . . I'm afraid I have to confess to you that I think one of the sins of government and one with which we must deal and never have been able to be completely successful with . . . is that the bureaucracy, once created, has one fundamental rule above all others: preserve the bureaucracy.

To reporters, Moscow/
The Washington Post, 6-3:(A)27.

5

[Saying he wants the amendment limiting Presidents to two terms to be eliminated]: When I get out of office, I'm going to travel around . . . and try to convince the people of our country that they should wipe out that amendment to the Constitution, because it was an interference with the democratic rights of the people.

At Moscow University/
Time, 6-13:14.

6

Early in [our Administration's] first term, we set out to reduce Federal regulations that had been imposed on the people, and businesses and on local and state governments. Today, I'm proud to say, we have eliminated so many unnecessary regulations that government-required paper work imposed on citizens, businesses and other levels of government has been reduced by an estimated 600 million man-hours a year.

At Republican National Convention,
New Orleans, Aug. 15/
The Washington Post, 8-16:(A)21.

7

I must say that it is not *my* Presidency, any more than the White House has belonged to me these past eight years. The Presidency of the United States is a trust, a public trust from the great people of this land who every four years

(RONALD REAGAN)

vest their trust in someone who must be humble enough to do their will and firm enough to make sure their will is not thwarted by the twin demons of expediency and fear.

At ground-breaking dedication
of his Presidential library,
Simi Valley, Calif., Nov. 21/
The Washington Post, 11-22:(A)13.

1

[Criticizing what he calls the "iron triangle," consisting of the Congress, the news media and special interests]: When I came into office, I found the Presidency a weakened institution. . . I found a Washington colony that, through the iron triangle, was attempting to rule the nation according to its interests and desires more than the nation's. . . Special-interest groups focus all their resources and members on this line or that in the budget. And members of Congress, particularly liberal members with their dependence on special-interest campaign financing and their fear of bucking any group that is strongly committed to a spending program, take up the banner and join the charge. [I have] the greatest respect for the media and the role they play in our system, [but] it is also clear that too many members of the media approach issues like Federal spending from a superficial perspective. Our positions are reported in caricature; special-interest charges are reported uncritically, and the public's understanding suffers. Shouldn't we expect better of those who act in the name of the public's right to know? In the long run, the situation we have now isn't good for anyone—even the members of the iron triangle. Fundamentally, the American people know what's up, and they don't like it. They may re-elect their Congressmen, but they trust Congress itself less and less. They may watch or read the media, but they stop believing it and they show more and more dislike for special-interest influence. The only question is, when will they say once and for all that they've had enough?

At Constitution Hall,
Washington, Dec. 13/
Los Angeles Times, 12-14:(I)1,31.

Harry M. Reid
United States Senator,
D-Nevada

2

[On being a Senator after serving in the House]: You have to be here to know what it really means. I wasn't prepared for how slowly things move over here in terms of debate. The House whips through bills; if you have the votes, you are going to win. That isn't the case here [in the Senate]. A single Senator can throw a monkey wrench into the process and hold up a bill or an appointment.

Interview/The New York Times, 4-11:26.

Charles S. Robb
Former Governor of Virginia (D);
1988 Democratic nominee
for the U.S. Senate
from Virginia

3

We've got to accept the hard truth that government will never have enough money to solve all our problems. Cutting the [government's budget] deficit means going against the grain . . . the courage to say no to requests that are popular but wrong, and yes to requests that are unpopular but right.

Campaign speech,
Richmond, Va., April 7/
The Washington Post, 4-8:(A)6.

Pat Robertson
Candidate for the
1988 Republican
Presidential nomination;
Former evangelist

4

The crisis we face is a moral crisis, not a government crisis. Unless we address the moral crisis, it won't matter what government does.

U.S. News & World Report,
2-22:15.

Michel Rocard
Prime Minister of France

5

Undoing what others have done and doing what others will later undo—that is exactly the

(MICHEL ROCARD)

kind of politics that the voters do not want any more [from their elected officials].

Before French National Assembly,
Paris, June 29/
The New York Times, 6-30:8.

Robert Rosenzweig
President, Association of
American Universities

1

. . . Congress works best when it has strong and coherent messages from the President. It may not like what it hears, but if it has nothing to rub up against, it tends to flounder . . .

Before Consortium of Social
Science Associations, Dec. 13/
The Washington Post, 12-20:(A)24.

James R. Sasser
United States Senator,
D-Tennessee

2

[On the U.S. Senate]: In my view, it's not the greatest deliberative body in the world any more. It saddens me very much. The most satisfying and enjoyable hours are those in which Senators are on the floor in debate and listening to debate. Now you have filibusters that drone on and on that make meaningful debates few and far between. These debates could be vehicles for great information for the electorate and a tool for constituents.

Interview/USA Today, 2-1:(A)13.

Antonin Scalia
Associate Justice, Supreme Court
of the United States

3

[Saying testing for government-employee drug abuse is not as onerous as requiring financial disclosures by government employees]: We [Supreme Court Justices] think of financial disclosures as an invasion of privacy that is much greater than these tests. If you're asking me to

choose between submitting a urine sample or publishing my entire financial record, you would lose.

Supreme Court hearing, Washington, Nov. 2/
The Washington Post, 11-3:(A)7.

William Donald Schaefer
Governor of Maryland (D)

4

One of the members of the Legislature said we—talking about the Legislature—should not give up our legislative authority to the Governor. Absolutely correct. You should not give up an ounce of the authority you have and give it to me. On the other side, you ought to allow me to do my job. Don't take from me the things that I can do. I'm a different type of Governor. I don't sit and watch the world go by. I'll be bumping heads with you on who does what. But if we have one objective, one objective, and that is to help people, that's the most important thing. I don't want your authority, and I hope you'll let me have mine.

State of the State address,
Annapolis, Jan. 14/
The Washington Post, 1-15:(A)16.

Daniel Schorr
Senior news analyst,
National Public Radio;
Former correspondent,
CBS News

5

You ask too much of televised [Congressional] hearings. Televised hearings have a dynamic all their own. You are dealing with politicians faced with witnesses who are well prepared . . . Politicians want a witness who looks bad on television; then they'll go after him . . . We forget the way in which a witness sits there before an impressive array of power. The camera shows you looking up and the committees are looking down at you, and you're held in judgment. You've got enormous sympathy even before you are five minutes into your testimony.

Panel discussion,
New School for Social Research,
New York/Harper's, February:53.

Patricia Schroeder
United States Representative,
D-Colorado

1

There is no way the leader of the free world [the President of the U.S.] is going to do away with government. Let us restore the concept of public service. We need our best minds working on arms control, the budget, the environment. And where do you work on these problems? In public service.

"Ms.," February:52.

Charles E. Schumer
United States Representative,
D-New York

2

When I was in the state Legislature, you crossed the Speaker, and you were gone. He picked what committees you were on. He picked the committee chairman. Here [in the House], the Speaker has none of those powers. If I want to vote against the Speaker, there is little he could do to me. So it might be a change for the better if we centralized more power in the hands of the Speaker. It would probably be better for the institution.

Interview, Washington/
Los Angeles Times, 1-25:(I)20.

William S. Sessions
Director, Federal Bureau
of Investigation

3

[Saying he will not criticize his boss, Attorney General Edwin Meese, for staying in office despite questions about Meese's ethical conduct]: If it is perceived by parts of society and the American public that the Director of the FBI is not properly, legally and ethically carrying out his responsibility, I always have open the route of resignation for myself. [But] I think there is a great deal of difference between that and the [Meese] circumstances where there is *speculation* about impropriety.

Press briefing, Washington, May 5/
The Christian Science Monitor,
5-6:3.

Philip Stern
Founder, Center for Public
Financing of Elections and
Citizens Against PACs;
Former Deputy Assistant
Secretary of State of the
United States

4

I like to think of Congressional offices as being turnstiles. And who gets in first? One would like to think that the voters get in first, but often it's not. I hear stories all the time from current and former members of Congress of returning from lunch and being handed the telephone-call lists by their secretaries, and on them are the names of 10 constituents whose names they have never heard of and one large [financial] contributor. And whose call gets returned first? The large contributor.

Interview/USA Today, 5-26:(A)15.

Ted Stevens
United States Senator,
R-Alaska

5

[Questioning the desirability of privatization, contracting out government services to the private sector]: Federal employees are the ones paying the costs of contracting out. We have mandated a series of minimum benefits for Federal employees, such as a retirement system, a substantial contribution to health insurance, and annual leave. On two occasions, I have heard of Federal workers, whose jobs have been contracted out, winding up working for the winning contractor without retirement, health insurance or leave time. The savings [to the government] reported are savings from not paying the costs of the benefits we've mandated for Federal workers. I don't see the equivalency here.

Washington, March 30/
The Washington Post, 3-31:(A)21.

John N. Sturdivant
President, American Federation
of Government Employees

6

The government employee after eight years of [President] Ronald Reagan is really shellshocked.

(JOHN N. STURDIVANT)

Unfortunately, you've had an Administration that has tried to rake it out of the hides of the government employees. Not only that, in the area of reduced pay, reduced benefits, you've had attacks on your privacy through drug testing, polygraph screening where people basically have to prove they're innocent... If you had the head of any major corporation talk and treat his employees the way Ronald Reagan has treated Federal employees, then the board of directors would have removed him a long time ago.

Interview, Washington, Sept. 6/
The Washington Post, 9-7:(A)17.

John H. Sununu
Governor of New Hampshire (R);
Chief of Staff-designate to
President-elect George Bush

1

My job will be what George Bush wants my job to be. You know, there are lots of nuances to that that he will determine. Am I to be visible or invisible? I prefer to be invisible for a while. But if he wants me to be visible, that's his choice. The level of detail he wants presented to him, he will determine. The frequency of meetings that he wants to frequent.

Interview, Washington, Nov. 28/
The New York Times, 11-29:(A)13.

Dick Thornburgh
Attorney General
of the United States

2

[The] top leadership [in any organization], from a corner convenience store to a [Federal] Cabinet department, [must transmit to subordinates] clear and explicit signals [about what types of conduct are and are not allowed]. To do otherwise allows informal and potentially subversive "codes of conduct" to be transmitted with a wink and a nod, and encourages an inferior ethical system based on "going along to get along" or on the notion that "everybody's doing it". . . A variety of questions should be addressed: How to avoid any appearance of personal and financial conflict of interest; how to deal with lapses in behavior, whether job-related or not; how should we properly regulate interaction between employees and outside groups; what "perks" are proper and which are out of bounds. . . The goal is to put our ideals and our principles on the record, and to say to the public, "These are our standards and we mean to live up to them. Watch us do it."

To Justice Department employees, Washington, Oct. 7/
The Washington Post, 10-8:(A)3.

Cal Thomas
Political columnist

3

[On revelations that President and Mrs. Reagan utilize astrology in some of their decision-making]: This is the last straw for a lot of religious people who treated Reagan as their political savior. He used to say, "The answer to all life's problems can be found in the Bible." I guess he put God on hold and consulted [astrologist] Jeane Dixon.

Newsweek, 5-16:20.

Strom Thurmond
United States Senator,
R-South Carolina

4

[Urging President Reagan to sign a bill that would restrict former government employees from lobbying the government after leaving office]: The public is deeply concerned about ethics and this bill will inspire greater confidence in our government. It is essential that Congress takes steps to limit the revolving door from government service to the private sector.

Nov. 21/The New York Times, 11-23:(A)12.

Preston Robert Tisch
Postmaster General
of the United States

5

Basically, money is not a big factor in this town [Washington]. It isn't thought about as it is in other cities. What counts is position and power.

Interview, Washington/
The New York Times, 1-11:10.

Paul S. Trible, Jr.
United States Senator,
R-Virginia

1

We [in the Senate] offer amendments, we send out press releases, and we poll our constituents to assess their approval or disapproval. In the process, the Senate has become difficult to lead, consensus is illusory and the whole policy-making process stands on the brink if incoherence.

The Washington Post, 1-4:(A)1.

2

Today you have 535 people in Congress who all want to be an important part of the process, who are unwilling to wait. My sense is that Congressmen and Senators today are better trained and educated than in years past, and they're not willing to yield their responsibilities and prerogatives to others.

Interview, Washington/
Los Angeles Times, 1-25:(I)20.

Chase Untermeyer
Director of Personnel for
President-elect George Bush

3

[On the criteria to be employed by President-elect Bush in making appointments to his Administration]: I would say certainly that people should share the philosophy of the President. It certainly doesn't mean any sort of loyalty test or urine analysis or blood test or any other form of testing of somebody's credentials. It's mostly an effort to make sure that the true troopers, those who helped elect George Bush, who were there, especially in the early days, are not forgotten, as frequently is the case in a new Administration.

News conference/Los Angeles Times, 12-15:(I)21.

Paul A. Volcker
Chairman, National
Commission on the Public
Service; Former Chairman,
Federal Reserve Board

4

Unmistakable evidence is accumulating that government is increasingly unable to attract, retain and motivate the kinds of people it will need to do the essential work of the republic in the years and decades ahead. In recent years there has not just been indifference toward public service, there has been a distinctly anti-Washington theme in much of our political rhetoric.

At American Enterprise Institute,
Washington/
The Christian Science Monitor, 11-17:17.

Fred Wertheimer
President, Common Cause

5

[Common Cause] believes that full-time public officials should be adequately and fully compensated by the public to whom they are responsible and should not receive private fees, such as honoraria, from individuals or groups who may have matters pending before the government. Today, most members of Congress supplement their taxpayer-funded income with private income provided by narrow special interests whose affairs are regulated by Congress.

Before Federal Commission on
Executive, Legislative and Judicial
Salaries, Washington/
The Washington Post, 11-12:(A)3.

6

[Criticizing President Reagan's pocket veto of a bill that would place stricter controls on lobbying by former government officials]: Now, as he departs office, President Reagan leaves not only the legacy of an Administration that was wracked by ethics scandals but, with his veto, he also leaves the door wide open to further abuses and sleaze in government.

Nov. 23/
The Washington Post, 11-24:(A)35.

Jim Wright
United States Representative,
D-Texas

7

Members of Congress are not immune from prosecution if they violate laws. The Justice

(JIM WRIGHT)

Department is not prohibited from investigating and prosecuting a member if he or she should violate the law. There has been greater emphasis than ever before upon seeking any evidence of any wrongdoing on the part of anybody high in the government.

Interview/USA Today, 1-7:(A)9.

1

I've seen the growth in honoraria [for members of Congress] by trade associations, and the appearance of it has been made to look evil, so let's get rid of it. The day is coming. I'm ready right now. I don't know whether members are. It would be a very healthy thing for Congress.

To reporters, Washington, Aug. 1/
The Washington Post, 8-2:(A)5.

Ron Ziegler
Former Press Secretary
to the
President of the United States
(Richard Nixon)

2

[On Presidential news conferences]: It is up to the President of the United States as to how he chooses to communicate and exert his leadership. Therefore, I think any recommendation of a strict formulation [as to how many news conferences should be held] made by any outside entity is not appropriate. [But] the more Presidential press conferences that are held, the better for the Presidency and the better for the American people in terms of formulating their opinions.

The Washington Post,
10-17:(A)13.

Melvin Belli
Lawyer

1

I am imbued with the spirit of this great profession. It means we teach a lesson, and we do one hell of a lot of good. We lawyers are the ones who pull the Constitution out of its glass case and make it operate for "we the people." We are the ones who give you life, liberty and the pursuit of happiness—as much as the good Lord will give you in this world.

Interview/USA Today, 9-1:(A)9.

Robert H. Bork
Former Judge,
United States Court
of Appeals for the
District of Columbia

2

[Saying those in the law have become more timid in what they say because of the difficult time he had at last year's Senate Judiciary Committee hearings on his nomination to the U.S. Supreme Court, which was turned down by the Senate]: I know of several instances now in which . . . lawyers have submitted articles to magazines, and withdrawn them explicitly on grounds of what happened to me. I think this has been very bad for the intellectual life of the law . . . [It has now become] "express only noble sentiments, and arrive at only non-controversial results."

Broadcast interview,
"Good Morning America," ABC-TV/
The Wall Street Journal, 2-26:14.

Steven Brill
Editor and publisher,
"American Lawyer" magazine

3

[On the high growth in income of the nation's large law firms]: For most of the law's heavy hitters, business has been so good that law is fast becoming not just a source of wealth for the few, but one of the country's largest sources of high income.

USA Today, 7-6:(B)2.

Arnold I. Burns
Former Deputy Attorney
General of the United States

4

[Criticizing the Justice Department under Attorney General Edwin Meese, in which he, Burns, served until recently resigning]: You get a flavor of what life was like in the Department of Justice. It was a world of Alice in Wonderland— a world of illusion and allusion; a world in which up was down and down was up, in was out and out was in, happy was sad and sad was happy.

Before Senate Judiciary Committee,
Washington, July 26/
The New York Times, 7-27:8.

George Bush
Vice President of the United States;
Candidate for the
1988 Republican
Presidential nomination

5

[On calls for U.S. Attorney General Edwin Meese to resign because of allegations of wrongdoing]: It seems to me that the Justice Department has to be above reproach and it's an agency that has special responsibilities. So let's wait and see what the facts are. But it troubles me, no question about it.

March 30/
The New York Times, 3-31:9.

6

I am strongly committed to the concept of providing legal services to indigent persons. The Legal Services Corporation plays an important role in organizations and legal clinics that furnish

(GEORGE BUSH)

these services. However, even under the best of circumstances, the Federal government is unable to cover the costs for all the legal services required by indigent persons. Thus, I strongly commend efforts by the American Bar Association, and bars of all states, to promote and provide *pro bono* legal services to those who cannot afford to pay.

Interview/
The New York Times, 9-23:22.

1

[On his Supreme Court nominations if he becomes President]: I don't have any litmus test, but what I would do is appoint people to the Federal bench that would not legislate from the bench, who will interpret the Constitution. I do not want to see us go to again—and I'm using [the] word advisedly—a liberal majority that is going to legislate from the bench.

At Presidential debate,
Los Angeles, Oct. 13/
USA Today, 10-14:(A)6.

Robert C. Byrd
United States Senator,
D-West Virginia

2

[Saying U.S. Attorney General Edwin Meese should resign because of allegations of wrongdoing]: He ought to get out. [He is the] crown jewel of the sleaze factor in this [Reagan] Administration. The country cannot have confidence in the Justice Department when the top law-enforcement official is spending his time defending himself on his own problems . . . We're talking about the country's top law-enforcement officer. It's just cloud after cloud after cloud, building in layers over his head to the point where all confidence in this agency is being seriously eroded. The President ought to ask somebody, if he doesn't want to ask him himself, to ask Mr. Meese to step aside, step down.

March 30/
The New York Times, 3-31:9.

Rosalynn Carter
Wife of former President
of the United States
Jimmy Carter

3

The [U.S.] Supreme Court has such an impact on the lives of people, and I think it should more closely represent the people of the United States. In a choice between a well-qualified woman or a well-qualified minority and a well-qualified man, I think that the woman or minority should be put on the Court.

Interview, L. B. J. Ranch, Texas/
Good Housekeeping, February:172.

Frank M. Coffin
Judge, United States Court of
Appeals for the First Circuit

4

Precedent is certainly real, and we learn to live with it. But if precedent clearly governed, a case would never get as far as the Court of Appeals: The parties would settle.

Interview/
The New York Times, 1-29:12.

Michael S. Dukakis
Governor of Massachusetts (D);
Candidate for the 1988 Democratic
Presidential nomination

5

The rule of law is the most conservative principle in the history of mankind. I know, because we got it from the ancient Greeks. And we've got a bunch of self-styled conservatives in the [Reagan] White House who wouldn't understand the rule of law if it hit them in the face.

Campaign speech/
The New York Times, 1-4:9.

Michael S. Dukakis
Governor of Massachusetts (D);
1988 Democratic
Presidential nominee

6

While a Dukakis Administration will encourage private attorney-involvement programs, it is

(MICHAEL S. DUKAKIS)

clear that *pro bono* work alone cannot meet the legal needs of the poor. The budget of the Legal Services Corporation has been savaged . . . and I will do all I can—within the constraints of a massive Federal budget deficit—to strengthen our commitment to this vital program.

Interview/
The New York Times, 9-23:22.

1

I don't have political litmus tests for the judges that I appoint. I don't know what their party registration is—I don't care. I don't ask them where they stand on particular issues. I'm looking for independence, integrity, intelligence, judicial temperament, a clear understanding of the Constitution, balance, good sense.

Interview/USA Today, 11-1:(A)6.

Frank H. Easterbrook
Judge, United States Court of
Appeals for the Seventh Circuit

2

Given that litigation is so expensive, why are parties willing to take their cases up? It's because precedent doesn't govern. Precedent covers the major premise. But the mind-set of the judge governs the minor premise.

Interview/
The New York Times, 1-29:12.

Mikhail S. Gorbachev
General Secretary,
Communist Party of
the Soviet Union

3

The activities of the courts are of immense importance. The future of many people, the protection of their rights and the inevitability of a penalty for offenses against the law depend on the accuracy of the scale of justice. Bearing all this in mind, it is extremely important to restore Lenin's vision of the role to be played by the courts of law within the system of our democracy. We should

abide strictly by the principle that judges are to be independent and guided only by the law.

At Soviet Communist Party
conference, Moscow, June 28/
The New York Times, 6-29:8.

Henry J. Hyde
United States Representative,
R-Illinois

4

[Saying President Reagan should issue pardons to Oliver North and John Poindexter who have been indicted for involvement in the U.S. Iran-contra scandal]: How do you achieve justice by forcing two retired military officers to defend themselves without funds against a prosecution team that has 26 lawyers and has spent $8-million? If that's a level playing field, I'm Carmen Miranda.

The New York Times, 11-23:(A)12.

James M. Ideman
Judge, United States District Court
for the Central District
of California

5

[Criticizing the idea of independent commissions establishing sentencing guidelines for judges to use]: It seems the term "sentencing guidelines" is a misnomer. It seems these are not guidelines, but hard and fast rules. It's as cold and implacable and immutable as a computer. You push a button and out comes the sentence.

At hearing on sentencing guidelines,
Pasadena, Calif., April 18/
Los Angeles Times, 4-19:(I)3.

Arthur J. Kropp
President, People for
the American Way

6

[On Attorney General Edwin Meese, who has announced his resignation]: Ed Meese leaves a record of shame. He spent his time at the Justice Department dodging scandals and gutting civil-rights enforcement. Meese will be remembered

WHAT THEY SAID IN 1988

(ARTHUR J. KROPP)

not only for his endless ethical problems, but for his on-going vendetta against basic Constitutional principles.

July 5/
The Washington Post, 7-6:(A)6.

William M. Kunstler
Lawyer

1

[I began representing] the poor, the persecuted, the radicals and the militant, the black people, the pacifists and the political pariahs. Every time I have a different case, I want to be the color or race. I want to be Indians. Sikhs I want to be. Blacks I want to be. I'd like to experience it all. I'd like to speak all the languages.

Interview, Bronx, N.Y./
The New York Times, 7-28:12.

Sol M. Linowitz
Lawyer; Former American diplomat

2

We've created the impression that it's in the large law firms that the real "there" is there, that it's where things happen, where you develop the leadership of the bar and get your own sense of personal fulfillment. I don't believe that's true. But a lawyer who may want to devote himself or herself to human problems finds that he or she will be paid far less to do that. The quid pro quo at large firms is dazzling. We attract them, we lure them, we bribe them, and in the process we don't tell them that they're going to be giving up a decent way of life.

Interview, Washington/
The New York Times, 4-22:23.

Edwin Meese III
Attorney General of the United States

3

[Refuting charges by two of his ex-aides that the Justice Department has been in disarray because of legal controversies surrounding him]:

One of the most certifiably false bits of conventional wisdom in Washington is that the Justice Department has somehow been in disarray, an agency dead in the water because of political controversies aimed at me. The foolishness of this conventional wisdom is apparent to all who have read beyond the headlines ... During this period, the Department has moved to take the Teamsters union out of the hands of organized crime, launched the largest defense-procurement fraud case in the history of the Department [and] convicted and won a sentence of life without parole for one of the most powerful and notorious drug traffickers [in Colombia].

Before International Platform
Association, Washington, Aug. 3/
The New York Times, 8-4:11.

George J. Mitchell
United States Senator, D-Maine

4

[Saying U.S. Attorney General Edwin Meese should resign because of allegations of wrongdoing]: The reality is that in terms of legal and judicial ethics, the appearance of impropriety is an important factor, and it can't be dismissed lightly. The reality is the Attorney General has displayed an almost spectacular casualness in his personal affairs in his giving the appearance of aiding others who have in turn provided financial assistance to him, directly or indirectly.

Broadcast interview/
"Face the Nation," CBS-TV, 4-3.

Robert M. Morgenthau
District Attorney of Manhattan (New York City)

5

Too many lawyers in our litigious society seem willing to press spurious claims on behalf of any client who can meet their skyrocketing fees. There is far too little early case-assessment, with the result that too many practitioners, quite literally, are just going through the motions. The reputation of the bar, and with it respect for the law, can only suffer by their actions.

Accepting the Fordham-Stein Prize
for contributions to the bar, Oct. 27/
The New York Times, 11-4:(B)12.

Louis Nizer
Lawyer

1

Trials are not won by eloquence. Law requires hard work and thorough preparation. You must establish the facts.

Interview/USA Today, 6-8:(A)2.

David O'Brien
*Legal scholar, University
of Virginia*

2

[On the Reagan Administration judicial appointments]: This is the first time an Administration has looked on judgeships not just as symbols but as the instruments of Presidential power—which goes well beyond the attempts of F. D. R. or even [Richard] Nixon to pack the courts. As of 1982, Reagan knew he could not get his social agenda through Congress, so the only way was to concentrate on the courts.

*The Christian Science Monitor,
11-18:18.*

William H. Rehnquist
*Chief Justice of the
United States*

3

For years there has been discussion and apparent agreement on the need for a tribunal that would resolve disputes among the Federal circuits. The Supreme Court does not and cannot consider every conflict among the circuits that reaches its docket for review each year. A national court of appeals or inter-circuit tribunal would provide a forum for an earlier determination of those issues and promote greater uniformity of interpretation in Federal law.

Annual report on the Supreme Court/
The New York Times, 1-6:10.*

4

Those of you who preside over courts in states which have the death penalty may be as familiar as are the members of our Court with the sort of chaotic conditions that often develop within a day or two before an execution is scheduled. The practical result of this is that judges of both state and Federal courts are called upon to make important Constitutional decisions, often without as much time as would be ideal for making them.

*At National Conference of Chief
Justices, Williamsburg, Va., Jan. 27/
The Washington Post, 1-28:(A)20.*

5

[Criticizing the confirmation process for Federal judicial nominees, such as Robert Bork, who was turned down by the Senate last year]: [A judge should not be] measured by his capacity to come up with instant answers to impromptu questions [at a confirmation hearing, but by his ability to make decisions based on] real-life facts [and long study of the law. That] is something which cannot possibly be duplicated in a committee hearing room; and since it cannot be duplicated, no nominee who is both prudent and honest can give categorical answers to detailed questions of Constitutional law . . . I think I speak for a great number of my fellow citizens of the United States when I say there is a general feeling of dissatisfaction with the process attending Judge Bork's nomination—a feeling which is shared by many of those who were happy to see him denied confirmation. [The Bork hearings consisted of] exhaustingly detailed examination of the nominee on his views of Constitutional law, and in particular on his view of the extent to which our Constitution recognized a right of privacy. The nadir of the public debate was reached when newspapers publicized a list of home movies which the judge had checked out in the months preceeding his confirmation hearing to look at on his home movie viewer.

*At Bicentennial Australian Legal
Convention, Canberra, Aug. 29/
The New York Times, 8-30:7.*

Elliot L. Richardson
*Former Attorney General
of the United States*

6

[Saying Attorney General Edwin Meese should resign because of accusations against him

(ELLIOT L. RICHARDSON)

of ethical and legal wrongdoing]: Some things can be taught through experience. Others should be known. One of them is sensitivity to the feelings and interests of others. This sensitivity is markedly lacking in our present Attorney General. He seems not to grasp the fact that his responsibility is to establish and observe standards transcending the minimum requirements of the law. We hear a lot about "role models" nowadays. For you who are about to assume the practice of law, he is an anti-role model.

At Pace University School of Law commencement, White Plains, N.Y., June 12/The New York Times, 6-13:12.

Antonin Scalia
Associate Justice,
Supreme Court of the United States

1

[On conferences among the Supreme Court Justices to discuss cases]: To call our discussion of a case a conference is really something of a misnomer. It's much more a statement of the views of each of the nine Justices, after which the totals are added and the case is assigned. I don't like that. Maybe it's just because I'm new. Maybe it's because I'm an ex-academic. Maybe it's because I'm right.

At George Washington University's National School of Law Center, Feb. 16/ The New York Times, 2-22:20.

William S. Sessions
Director, Federal Bureau of
Investigation

2

[On accusations of unethical or illegal conduct by Attorney General Edwin Mees]: ... a lawyer's responsibility to adhere to the highest ethical standards is very important. I think it's even more important when you're dealing with a person who is in fact the Attorney General of the United States, and I think Mr. Meese would strongly agree with that. [As to the question of] the effect that there might be on lawfulness of

American citizens, that in some ways the accusations against the Attorney General might weaken the fabric of law enforcement, I think it's a very, very important item. To me, I think there's a general feeling in the United States that all of us can . . . choose those laws which we would obey or disobey.

News conference, Washington, May 5/ The Washington Post, 5-6:(A)17.

3

We are a country of law. We govern ourselves by law. We choose to do that. Therefore, the rule of law is extremely important to us and part of the fabric and strength of American society.

News conference, Washington, May 5/Los Angeles Times, 5-6:(I)6.

Ralph Steinhardt
Authority on international law,
George Washington University

4

[On the U.S. Justice Department's decision to prosecute deposed Philippines President Ferdinand Marcos and his wife on racketeering charges involving embezzlement of money from the Philippines and investing it in the U.S.]: Obviously, what we have here is a mixed bag [of acts committed both inside and outside the U.S.], and the Justice Department has evidently decided that the pattern of corruption doesn't break down on national boundary lines; but in order to get a full sense of the true corrupt practices they have to go back and look at actions taken abroad . . . If you look at what's going on in securities, antitrust, tax cases, increasingly the United States is taking an aggressive view of its jurisdiction, so long as there is an intent to have an effect in the United States and so long as there is an effect here.

The Washington Post, 10-26:(A)4.

Dick Thornburgh
Attorney General of the United States

5

It's no secret I feel there should be a very limited role for independent counsels [used in

(DICK THORNBURGH)

investigations of government officials]. My sense is that the public-integrity section [of the Justice Department's Criminal Division], and the U.S. attorneys, of late have done a very good job with prosecuting such cases.

Interview,
Washington, Aug. 23/
Los Angeles Times, 8-24:(I)19.

1

Subordinates [in the Justice Department] cannot be left to speculate as to the values of the organization. Top leadership must give forth clear and explicit signals, lest any confusion or uncertainty exist over what is and is not permissible conduct. To do otherwise allows informal and potentially subversive "codes of conduct" to be transmitted with a wink and a nod, and encourages an inferior ethical system based on "going along to get along" or on the notion that "everybody's doing it."

At Department of Justice,
Washington, Oct. 7/
The New York Times, 10-8:7.

Bill Wagner
Lawyer; President,
American Trial Lawyers
Association

2

Many people have a warped view of the legal system that's based on some of the current television series and courtroom dramatizations. When people learn more about how the legal system operates, they have a better appreciation of their rights, privileges and responsibilities. They also have a greater interest in protecting their freedom and the legal structure.

The Christian Science Monitor,
11-17:19.

Franklin Williams
Chairman, New York State
Judicial Commission on
Minorities

3

When a black person walks into a court and sees a white judge, white prosecutors, white clerks, white stenographers, do you think they're going to believe they're going to get justice?

Time, 8-8:17.

Politics

Roone Arledge
President, ABC News

1

[On the national political conventions held every four years to nominate Presidential and Vice-Presidential candidates]: The conventions as currently structured are anachronistic and they are part of what is turning people off in this country to political [news] coverage. Clearly, the time has come for political parties to look at whether they want to have a four-day anachronistic meeting where no business is transacted, or very little.

The Washington Post, 7-22:(A)1.

2

[On the recent Presidential-election campaign]: It's been an awful campaign. The people at home are unhappy, with good reason. Everything is staged by Hollywood producers; no one discusses anything; the [TV] commercials were among the nastiest in memory. But the tone was set by the candidates, not by the evening news [broadcasts].

USA Today, 11-11:(A)5.

Lee Atwater
*Manager of Vice President
George Bush's 1988
Republican campaign
for the Presidency*

3

The key [for a Presidential candidate] is not to over-dress—no candidate wants to appear foppish—or to under-dress. That's why you see a lot of blue suits, a lot of blue shirts, a lot of red ties. I've never worked with a candidate who wasn't aware of his appearance, but I've also never worked with one who wanted to be known as the best-dressed man in town.

*U.S. News & World Report,
5-30:12.*

4

One of the reasons that the Republican Party is where it is is because the big growth group in the Party has been among baby-boomers. If there are two things that I would say about the Republican Party today that are vastly different than the Republican Party in 1978, they are: A) It's much younger; B) It's much more Southern. Baby-boomers are not liberal on social issues. They are libertarian, meaning tolerant. That whole notion of tolerance is very, very important. We Republicans need to establish that we are a tolerant party. [President] Ronald Reagan did a good job on that in 1984; he is a tolerant man. So is George Bush . . . If we got to the point where the so-called far right of the Party was perceived as being dominant and on social issues being intolerant, then it would cause a big problem with baby-boomers. But, frankly, social issues are not top-burner issues for these voters.

Los Angeles Times, 9-4:(I)14.

5

[Saying Democratic Presidential nominee Michael Dukakis made a mistake politically by acknowledging that he is a liberal after months of denying it]: [The Dukakis team has] shown an uncanny knack for being able to step on any kind of movement they ever get in this race. When the history books are written, just as it's universally accepted that the big mistake of '84 was [Walter] Mondale's pledge to raise taxes, I think this ranks right up there with that. [Dukakis] spent the last several months denying the fact that he was a liberal, and then he comes out eight days before the election and says he is. I think he loses on two fronts—ideologically, and as a flip-flopper.

The Washington Post, 11-1:(A)12.

Lee Atwater
*Chairman-designate, Republican National
Committee; Former manager,
Vice President George Bush's
1988 campaign for the Presidency*

6

I am convinced, after going out this year, [that] we've [the Republican Party] got an opportunity

(LEE ATWATER)

in the black community like we've never had before. There is a kind of 45-and-under black that I find in every state who is prone to listen to our message and is tired of being considered of being in the hip pocket of the Democratic Party, and who is not tied to the current black leadership out in these states.

> *At Republican Governors Conference,*
> *Point Clear, Alabama, Nov. 21/*
> *The Washington Post, 11-22:(A)2.*

Gerald F. Austin
Manager of civil-rights leader
Jesse Jackson's 1988
Democratic campaign for
the Presidency

1

If [Jackson] doesn't win another delegate or another vote, he's already won . . . Certainly when the campaign is over, we will determine who the candidate will be, ratifying the candidate, defining our priorities . . . We're satisfied with what we've been able to accomplish . . . It's not just delegates and votes. That's just not the only thing it is. Jesse Jackson is needed for the rest of the campaign to get people involved. If he gets them involved in the primary, they're going to stay involved in the general election. This is all about Democrats winning the White House, and he's a vital cog in that wheel to turn it, even if he didn't win New York and Pennsylvania [in the primaries].

> *April 27/*
> *Los Angeles Times, 4-28:(I)16.*

Bruce Babbitt
Candidate for the 1988
Democratic Presidential
nomination; Former
Governor of Arizona (D)

2

[On his decision to pull out of the Presidential race]: Was it unfair or amazing that I didn't succeed? No. You've got to be around for a while. You almost never can ride in out of the outback

and take the town the first time. Most serious contenders have to try at least twice . . . Politics, at its best, is a transcendent process. What's important is the debate about our future. If you don't speak up about what you believe to voters, then it's just a giant cattle show where you're saying, "I'm shinier than the next guy."

> *Washington, Feb.17/*
> *The New York Times, 2-18:10.*

Bruce Babbitt
Former candidate for the
1988 Democratic
Presidential nomination;
Former Governor of Arizona (D)

3

[On why the Democratic Party keeps losing the Presidency]: What we need is a vigorous, wide-spread debate about why it is that the voters slam the White House door in our faces every four years . . . You run for Senate or Governor on specific issues to specific constituencies. A Presidential race is about two issues, peace and prosperity, otherwise known as economics and foreign affairs. That's the core of our problem. We have not laid out a convincing message on those two issues.

> *The New York Times, 11-11:(A)10.*

Dan Balz
National editor,
"The Washington Post"

4

Polls are clearly so much a part of the political landscape that it is often hard not to pay attention to them, even though we recognize that sometimes they are flawed and out of date.

> *The New York Times, 3-31:11.*

William Barnard
Political historian,
University of Alabama

5

[On black civil-rights leader Jesse Jackson, who is running for the 1988 Democratic Presidential nomination]: Whites are taking him more

(WILLIAM BARNARD)

seriously than four years ago. And they're proud to listen to him; it proves they're not bigots. They walk away and say, "Boy, can that man talk!" But when it comes to the lick-log, as they say in the Alabama Legislature, they'll walk into that voting booth and, generally, vote for somebody else.

Los Angeles Times, 2-13:(I)27.

Robert Beckel
Former manager of
Walter F. Mondale's
1984 Democratic campaign
for the Presidency

1

If you win early [in the Presidential primaries], money comes. If you don't, you're out. The lack of money is the single biggest eliminator in Presidential politics.

Los Angeles Times, 2-5:(I)14.

2

People say that issues don't matter in a [political] campaign, and it's a self-fulfilling prophecy. Issues don't matter if you don't raise them. It's wrong that people don't care about issues. If you present them with a controversy, they do care. They'll listen to it. But if you don't give it to them, if you give them balloons and happy talk and bullshit every night, there's no controversy there. The only controversy the press found during the entire [1976 Presidential] campaign was [Democratic Vice Presidential candidate] Geraldine Ferraro; it was the only significant, major, sustained issue in that campaign. Except, for a very brief period of time, [President] Reagan's age.

Esquire, May:82.

William J. Bennett
Secretary of Education
of the United States

3

[Criticizing Massachusetts Governor and Democratic Presidential nominee Michael

Dukakis for vetoing a bill that would have required the Pledge of Allegiance to be recited in his state's schools]: I lived in that Brookline-Cambridge [Mass.] world for eight years and these are people who don't like things like the Pledge. They have disdain for the simple and basic patriotism of most Americans. They think they're smarter than everybody else and they don't like these kinds of rituals . . . I think the crowd with which Mike Dukakis runs . . . do think they are smarter . . . They don't like what most Americans think and believe.

Broadcast interview/
"Meet the Press," NBC-TV, 9-4.

Lloyd Bentsen
United States Senator,
D-Texas;
Candidate for the 1988
Democratic Vice-Presidential
nomination

4

[On the Democratic Party's campaign for the forthcoming Presidential election]: This truly is a politics of inclusion. There are those who would like to take the approach of perhaps a St. Ignatius view of politics, that what you want is purity of ideology. And if you find that and work toward that to the ultimate, finally you have a party of one, and you sure don't win any elections. But what you have seen here is a politics of inclusion, of bringing people together, and people who share a common view on things that are important to this country of ours . . .

Atlanta, July 18/
The New Yorks Times, 7-19:9.

Lloyd Bentsen
United States Senator,
D-Texas; 1988
Democratic Vice-Presidential
nominee

5

We Democrats don't march in lockstep behind some narrow, rigid ideology of indifference. We are not gray grains of oatmeal in a bland porridge of privilege. Our way, the Democratic way, is to

(LLOYD BENTSEN)

tackle the tough problems. Our way is to search out the honest answers and stand by our principles. Of course, we have differences of opinion. But on the basic issues of justice and opportunity, we stand united.

> *Accepting the nomination, at*
> *Democratic National Convention,*
> *Atlanta, July 21/*
> *Los Angeles Times, 7-22:(I)7.*

1

[Criticizing the Reagan Administration's nearly eight years in office]: My friends, America has just passed through the ultimate epoch of illusion: an eight-year coma in which slogans were confused with solutions, and rhetoric passed for reality; a time when America tried to borrow its way to prosperity, and became the largest debtor nation in the history of mankind; when the Reagan-Bush Administration gave lip service to progress, while fighting a frantic, losing battle to turn back the clock on civil rights and equal opportunity; a time of tough talk on foreign policy amid strange tales of double-dealing Swiss bank accounts and a botched campaign against a drug-running tinhorn dictator [in Panama] . . . At long last, the epoch of illusion is drawing to a close. America is ready for the honest, proven, hands-on, real-world leadership of [Democratic Presidential nominee] Michael Dukakis, backed by the power of a united, committed Democratic Party.

> *Accepting the nomination,*
> *at Democratic National Convention,*
> *Atlanta, July21/*
> *The Washington Post,*
> *7-22:(A)31.*

2

[On the controversy about Republican Vice-Presidential nominee Dan Quayle having avoided Vietnam war service by joining the National Guard]: Recently, [Republican Presidential nominee] George Bush stood before the VFW and told you how he saw the qualifications for the

Vice Presidency . . . I'm also running for Vice President . . . I went down and volunteered as a private in the Army [during World War II]. I flew 34 combat missions. I volunteered for two weeks of front-line duty with the infantry airborne, and I have the usual things they pin on your chest in combat when they run out of aspirin.

> *Before Veterans of Foreign Wars,*
> *Chicago, Aug. 25/*
> *Los Angeles Times, 8-26:(I)14.*

3

[Criticizing Republican Vice-Presidential nominee Dan Quayle for being too young and inexperienced to be Vice President]: He'd have to have some on-the-job training. Sometimes you don't have time for that. I wouldn't say he wouldn't grow into the job, but I would hope not too much important happened while the transition was taking place . . . What I see here is a man that was chosen to satisfy the hard right, who is much more in tune with the philosophy of [conservative Senators] Jesse Helms and Gordon Humphrey than he is with [Republican Presidential nominee] George Bush . . . No one has ever questioned *my* qualifications insofar as [becoming] Vice President of the United States. Like Harry Truman, I'm ready. Ready to help lead America to a new era of greatness. I'm ready to help [Democratic Presidential nominee Michael Dukakis] create jobs and opportunity for all Americans. I'm ready to help him make America a strong and reliable guardian of freedom in this world. And, if any tragedy should ever strike the President of the United States, I think I'm ready to lead America. If a Presidential candidate [Bush] does not choose a running mate with those kinds of qualifications, he does not respect the importance and dignity of the office of Vice President.

> *Campaigning,*
> *Independence, Mo., Sept. 28/*
> *Los Angeles Times, 9-29:(I)19.*

4

[On Republican Vice-Presidential nominee Senator Dan Quayle's saying he has as much

(LLOYD BENTSEN)

experience in Congress to run for Vice President as the late John Kennedy had when he became President]: Senator [Quayle], I served with Jack Kennedy. I knew Jack Kennedy. Jack Kennedy was a friend of mine. Senator, you're no Jack Kennedy.

At Vice-Presidential debate,
Omaha, Neb., Oct. 5/
The New York Times, 10-7:(A)14.

1

[Critizing Republican Vice-Presidential nominee Senator Dan Quayle after their recent public debate]: I listened to Dan Quayle try to put the mantle of [the late President] John F. Kennedy on [himself]. Incredible. When I think of Jack Kennedy, I think of a war hero, a man who was a Pulitzer Prize winner, a man who helped bring about an atmospheric nuclear test ban, who stood up to [then Soviet leader Nikita] Khrushchev. What an incredible misfit [is Quayle] . . . When I think of some of the heavyweights in the Republican Party, I think of [Senators] Bob Dole, Alan Simpson and Dick Lugar. Then I think of the shock in the United States Senate when Dan Quayle was chosen [for Vice-Presidential nominee].

Before Dallas Democratic Forum,
Oct. 7/
The Washington Post, 10-8:(A)12.

2

[Criticizing Republican Presidential nominee George Bush's campaign tactics against the Democratic ticket of Presidential nominee Michael Dukakis and himself]: [The Bush campaign] is one of the most outrageous displays of negative campaigning ever seen in our nation's history . . . They've said things about [Dukakis] that we wouldn't say in Texas about a rattlesnake on the lawn at a church picnic. They don't seem to mind if what they say is untrue . . . if it sounds good, say it. If it sells, package it. If it looks good, nominate it [referring to Republican Vice-Presidential nominee Dan Quayle] . . . We've been a

little too flabbergasted sometimes to make a proper response. I don't think we ever imagined that George Bush . . . would be so willing to debase the precious currency of our democracy by conducting a campaign that resembles a demagogic race for county sheriff.

At University of California,
Los Angeles, Oct. 18/
The Washington Post, 10-19:(A)7.

Earl Black
Political scientist,
University of South Carolina

3

[Saying black civil-rights leader Jesse Jackson's strong influence in the Democratic Party will help the Republicans in this Presidential-election year]: When a lot of white Democrats begin to associate the Democratic Party with Jesse Jackson, it's going to be devastating. The Republican Party doesn't have to do anything except exist.

The Washington Post, 3-3:(A)17.

David Brinkley
Commentator, ABC News

4

[On election-year Presidential debates]: [To call them] "true debates" is a distortion of the English language. We [in the media] don't have any control over them. It's essentially a boring press conference.

Interview/USA Today, 12-6:(A)4.

William E. Brock
Former Secretary of Labor
of the United States

5

We have created our own monster [in politics]. Three P's: Platforms, Primaries and PACs. The combination of all this reform [lets] the ideological activists of both parties dominate the nomination . . . I really do worry about what we've done to politics and the parties—the [diminished] incentive for participation . . . It's theatre now, not politics.

Interview, New Orleans/Newsweek, 8-29:5.

Hugh Brogan
*U.S. historian, University
of Essex (England)*
1

[On U.S. Vice President George Bush's victory in the recent Presidential election]: [The victory reflects] the dearth of real political talent in the Republican Party. He seems to be seriously under-qualified for the job and really owes [his victory] to the patronage of [outgoing] President Reagan.

Nov. 9/
The Christian Science Monitor,
11-10:10.

Willie Brown
*Speaker of the California
Assembly (D)*
2

[On why Democratic Presidential nominee Michael Dukakis is behind in the polls for the forthcoming election]: My guy didn't understand that to win in this country these days you've got to campaign down to a 13-year-old's level of mental development. It's Dukakis' fault. You can't blame the staff or the advisers. It starts with the head guy. He has to read the situation and decide what tactics to follow. By this late stage, people have given up on Dukakis. When you manage to go from a 17-point lead to an 11-point deficit in a matter of eight short weeks, they're not inclined to buy a lottery ticket from you, never mind electing you President.

Interview, San Francisco/
The New York Times, 10-31:(A)13.

Patrick Buchanan
Political columnist
3

[On the current Democratic National Convention at which Michael Dukakis was nominated for President and Lloyd Bentsen for Vice President instead of civil-rights leader Jesse Jackson]: This has been Jesse Jackson's convention. Jackson's constituency may have loved it, but all it did was to deliver bales of votes to [likely Republican Presidential nominee George] Bush.

So far, Dukakis is the man who wasn't there. Moreover, Dukakis has another problem: After [Senator] Teddy Kennedy and Jesse Jackson, Dukakis and Lloyd Bentsen are pure vanilla. When they get up and speak, they simply are not glowing. There are not two men in America who are less powerful and articulate than Dukakis and Bentsen. As [former] President [Richard] Nixon says, people still want poetry in their politics. But Michael Dukakis is a word processor, a Zorba the clerk.

Interview/USA Today, 7-21:(A)9.

Horace Busby
Political analyst
4

[Republican President-elect George] Bush will use the White House to show blacks that blacks are welcome. It will not be a difficult thing for Republicans to turn this around, because it has become apparent this year to most black voters that there is not a prayer for the blacks to win the Presidential nomination in the Democratic Party. [1988 black Presidential candidate] Jesse Jackson was not rejected by Republicans, but by Democrats.

The Christian Science Monitor,
11-23:3.

George Bush
*Vice President of the United States;
Candidate for the
1988 Republican
Presidential nomination*
5

The entire record of this [Reagan-Bush] Administration will be an issue in the [forthcoming Presidential election] when I am the [Republican Presidential] nominee. That means the people will evaluate how we have dealt with the economy, with the creation of jobs and with our educational system. It means our record of dealing with the Soviets, with our allies and the developing nations will be evaluated. We have an outstanding record of accomplishment, and we have some areas in which we have not succeeded. When the entire record is examined, the scales

(GEORGE BUSH)

tip strongly in our favor. I believe my experience gives me the best opportunity to build on what we have done well and gives me the insight to avoid mistakes. It is this experience that translates into Presidential leadership that the voters will look for in the primaries and in the general election. I am proud to be judged by this standard.

Interview/
The Washington Post, 1-14:(A)7.

1

I have a tendency to avoid going on with great eloquent statements of belief . . . These days, I think of Lincoln: "Here I stand, warts and all" . . . There are others who are better orators . . . I don't always articulate well, but I always feel and I care . . .

Campaign speech, February/
U.S. News & World Report,
2-22:19.

2

The challenges we [Republicans] face will never be met unless we do it together, hand in hand, as brothers and sisters, as blacks and whites, Northerners and Southerners, east and west, the wealthy and the wanting—we must meet the challenges as a big party with a big open door.

Madison, Wis., March 30/
Los Angeles Times, 3-31:(I)19.

3

[On criticism that his political style is uninspired]: What's wrong with being a boring kind of a guy? Is that what you mean and are too polite to say it? My wife doesn't think that. I don't know about Mrs. Dukakis, what she thinks, Mrs. Jesse Jackson [wives of the two Democratic frontrunners]. People aren't looking for a lot of pizzazz out there. They're looking for someone who's stable. Someone who's had some experience, a lot of conviction, a record of achievement, values they can identify with, hopefully the

stability and strength to lead this country. So I think to kind of suddenly get my hair colored and dance up and down in a miniskirt or do something, show I've got a lot of jazz out there, drop a bunch of one-liners—we're talking about running for President of the United States. It's a serious business. And a lot of complexity is involved in it. I've got a record . . . let that stand out there rather than some of these labels that people try to attach to people. I kind of think I'm a scintillating kind of fellow. We'll let the American people decide that.

To reporters,
Cincinnati, April 26/
The Washington Post, 4-27:(A)1.

4

The most important of all [election] campaign reforms has already been achieved—financial disclosure of receipts and expenditures. I have long supported full disclosure laws and believe it must be kept strong to prevent ethical misconduct. I agree that special interests have too much power, especially over the Congress. But special interests do not decide national elections—the people do.

USA Today, 5-3:(A)11.

5

The things I have run in my life have been clean. Nobody has ever . . . leveled any charge against me in terms of conflict of interest or sleaze or anything of that nature. I heard these charges [by Democratic Presidential candidates Michael Dukakis and Jesse Jackson] trying to link me in to [Panamanian leader and suspected drug trafficker Manuel] Noriega in some way . . . What is their evidence? . . . If Dukakis has some allegations and wants to confront me with the charge . . . do it directly to my eye.

To his supporters/
The Christian Science Monitor,
6-29:4.

6

[On his running for the Presidency]: It's an uphill fight, an uphill fight, for our Republican

(GEORGE BUSH)

·team this year, and I'm talking team, from top to bottom. After eight years of one party in the White House, no matter how successful, some good people yearn for change—hoping that "change" will mean "improvement." It's our job to let them know that this time, in this case, change and improvement come from the Republican Party and from experience.

At Republican Party
fund-raising luncheon,
New York, June 30/
Los Angeles Times, 7-1:(I)9.

1

[Criticizing Democratic Presidential nominee Michael Dukakis for running away from the issues in his campaign for President]: I have made five specific speeches on five specific proposals, relating from energy to the environment to ethics, and talking specifics, and they're still in the mold on the other side of saying "ideology doesn't matter, just competence," and avoiding the issues ... It's not negative to ask that he [Dukakis] be specific on the issues. He's trying to run away from a record in Massachusetts [where Dukakis is Governor] on the very, very far liberal fringe of the political spectrum, and I have to pin him down. And I have to say what he's really for. He's unwilling to do that because he thinks he can pre-empt the middle [moderate voters].

To reporters, Pittsburgh, Aug. 9/
Los Angeles Times, 8-10:(I)16.

2

[On the forthcoming Presidential election]: We must remind [the voters] that peace and economic growth are not blanketing our land by accident. They've not fallen out of the sky. But rather, they've grown from carefully cultivated seeds planted by the men and women in this room [the members of the Reagan Administration]. And now the task is to plant where no flowers have bloomed before, to grow to heights previously unimagined.

To members of the Reagan Administration,
Washington, Aug. 12/Los Angeles Times, 8-13:(I)18.

3

[On his running for the Presidency against Democrat Michael Dukakis]: I've been underestimated over and over again, by political observers and political opponents, and here I am. A lot of people have fallen by the wayside. So no, he [Dukakis] is not driven more. I will outwork him, outhustle him, outrun him and outknowledge him. He has his strengths, but one of them isn't wanting to be President more than I do.

Interview, Washington/
Time, 8-22:21.

4

[On the criticism by Democratic Presidential nominee Massachusetts Governor Michael Dukakis of U.S. Attorney General Edwin Meese, who was accused by some of illegal or unethical conduct]: All I've heard out of the opposition is assailing Ed Meese. Ed Meese was not indicted. But Mr. [Gerard] Indelicato in Massachusetts was indicted. So please tell me what the difference is, Governor [Dukakis]. One was a high-ranking state education official, indicted, convicted and on his way to prison. And here is a man [Dukakis] standing there with all the *chutzpah* in the world, pointing the finger at somebody else. And, I might say, to get one last political shot in here—the analogy [used by Dukakis describing the Reagan Administration] of a fish rotting from the head down was very offensive to a lot of people in this country. And you're looking at one of them.

Interview, Washington/
Time, 8-22:21.

George Bush
Vice President of the United
States; 1988 Republican
Presidential nominee

5

[On the forthcoming Presidential election in which he is running against Michael Dukakis]: Some say [as did Dukakis] this isn't an election about ideology, that it's an election about competence. Well, it's nice of them to want to play on our field. But this election isn't only about com-

(GEORGE BUSH)

petence, for competence is a narrow ideal. Competence makes the trains run on time but doesn't know where they're going. Competence is the creed of the technocrat who makes sure the gears mesh but doesn't for a second understand the magic of the machine. The truth is, this election is about the beliefs we share, the values that we honor and the principles that we hold dear.

Accepting the nomination, at
Republican National Convention,
New Orleans, Aug. 18/
The New York Times, 8-19:8.

1

I may not be the most eloquent, but I learned early on that eloquence won't draw oil from the ground. And I may sometimes be a little awkward, but there's nothing self-conscious in my love of country. And I'm a quiet man, but I hear the quiet people others don't—the ones who raise the family, pay the taxes, meet the mortgage. And I hear them and I am moved, and their concerns are mine.

Accepting the nomination, at
Republican National Convention,
New Orleans, Aug. 18/
The New York Times, 8-19:8.

2

[On criticism that his Vice-Presidential choice, Dan Quayle, avoided Vietnam war service by joining the National Guard]: You've seen the controversy about my running mate, Senator Quayle. Let me give you my views. Because I served in active combat, because I saw my countrymen, some of them killed, as many of you did, I think I can speak from a sound perspective. First, I salute the Vietnam veterans here today, those who fought in the rice paddies. Thank God, America has finally come around to doing what it should have done from the very beginning, saluting you, too . . . But let me say this: Many others served, too. Some were in the reserves and were not sent overseas, some served in the National Guard and were not sent over-

seas, but they served. And my running mate was one of them. Now, 20 years later, he's a seasoned United States Senator, a leader in defense matters, a strong supporter of American veterans. Dan Quayle served in the National Guard, signing up in a unit that had vacancies at the time. And now he is under shrill, partisan attack. So let his attackers cast the first stone, let them cast it. He served honorably . . . He did not go to Canada, he did not burn his draft card, and he damn sure didn't burn the American flag. And I am proud to have him at my side.

Before Veterans of Foreign Wars,
Chicago, Aug. 22/
The New York Times, 8-23:10.

3

[Criticizing Democratic Presidential nominee Governor Michael Dukakis of Massachusetts for vetoing a bill to require the Pledge of Allegiance in public schools]: I believe that our schoolchildren should have the right to say the Pledge of Allegiance to the flag of the United States. I don't know what his problem is with the Pledge of Allegiance. I can't help but feel that his fervent opposition to the Pledge is symbolic of an entire attitude best summed up in four little letters: ACLU. He says—here's an exact quote— he says, "I am a card-carrying member of the ACLU." Well, I am not and I never will be.

Campaigning,
San Antonio, Texas, Aug. 25/
The Washington Post, 8-26:(A)6.

4

[Defending his choice of Senator Dan Quayle who, because of his youth, is being criticized as being too inexperienced to run for Vice President]: I have placed my confidence in a whole younger generation. And people forget [Richard] Nixon was elected at 39—I mean on the ticket— [John] Kennedy at 42, Teddy Roosevelt president before he was 40. And this man [Quayle] has had plenty of experience. He was a leader in the Job Training Partnership Act, he's an expert on defense, and when I mention him now to young people in the rallies we have, the place

(GEORGE BUSH)

goes wild. And he will be a tremendous asset to me.

Broadcast interview/
"USA Today: The Television
Program," 9-12.

1

[Saying Democratic Presidential nominee Michael Dukakis' patriotism has not been questioned by him]: Not by me, it hasn't. Never. I have never challenged his patriotism. But if you're referring to the issue of the Pledge of Allegiance, don't I have a right to say I would have signed a bill he vetoed [that would have required the Pledge to be recited in schools in Governor Dukakis' state of Massachusetts]? He's not willing to talk about it. And there's nothing to do with patriotism. It's a lot to do with judgment.

Broadcast interview/
"USA Today: The Television
Program," 9-12.

2

Anybody that gets into this political arena and has to face you guys [of the press] every day deserves a word of praise, because it's gotten a little ugly out there. It's gotten a little nasty. It's not much fun sometimes . . . I salute those who participate in the political process. [The late House Speaker] Sam Rayburn had a great expression on this. He said, you know, here are all these intellectuals out there griping and complaining and saying there's negative coverage. Rayburn says, "Yeah, and that guy never ran for sheriff, either." [Democratic Presidential nominee] Michael Dukakis has run for sheriff and so has George Bush.

At Presidential debate,
Los Angeles, Oct. 13/
The New York Times, 10-15:11.

3

[On Democratic Presidential nominee Michael Dukakis]: I would hate to be my opponent, the

man who doesn't like the big L word [liberal]; I would hate to be him, going around the United States telling everybody how bad things are. Things are not bad in the United States, and I want to keep this expansion going until every American benefits by this expansion, the longest in American history . . . I'm not the one who said: "I am a progressive liberal Democrat." That was the liberal Governor of Massachusetts [Dukakis]. And I'm not the one who said: "I am a card-carrying member of the ACLU." That was the liberal Governor of Massachusetts that said it. What's happening for us, I think, [is] the American people understand that I share their values and share the direction they want to see this country go in.

Campaign speech, Illinois/
The New York Times, 10-24:(A)10.

4

[On the current Presidential race]: Today, when you strip away all that rhetoric, all the words, all the analysis, the question . . . the American people are going to decide this election on is the same: Are you better off today than you were eight years ago? When all the evidence is in, when you go past all the sound bites and the horse race and the tank rides, the answer is a clear "Yes." Now, they contend that the American people are rallying to our [Republican] cause because we make better television commercials. But they've missed the whole point, no question about it. [President] Ronald Reagan is a warm and friendly man . . . But the American people have chosen us to lead because of our principles, not personalities. And they're going to vote on November 8 for the best ideas, not the best images.

Before Chamber of Commerce,
Waterbury, Conn., Oct. 24/
The Washington Post, 10-25:(A)6.

5

I feel that the old party distinctions and loyalties are beginning to change in the United States. A lot of mainstream Americans feel that the national Democratic Party, 1988, just simply

(GEORGE BUSH)

doesn't represent them any more. It's like what the most famous of all former Democrats, [Republican President] Ronald Reagan, said: They didn't leave the Democratic Party, the Democratic Party left them. It drifted farther and farther off to the left. You might say that the Democratic Party today suffers from a split personality. With the rank and file made up of the best of America, the silent majority . . . a source of strength for this great nation. But the leadership, much of it, is the remnant of the '60s, the New Left, those campus radicals grown old, the peace marchers and the nuclear-freeze advocates. That's not where the heartbeat of most of the neighborhood Democrats is.

Speech, California, Oct. 28/
The Washington Post,
10-29:(A)17.

1

[On those who say they're scared of Republican Vice-Presidential nominee Dan Quayle because of his youth and the possibility he would become President if Bush is incapacitated]: It doesn't scare me as much as having [Democratic Presidential nominee Michael] Dukakis as President. It doesn't scare me at all, because . . . when steel is put in the fire it's tempered, toughened. My running mate has been subjected to the darnedest fire I've ever seen in politics . . . If I'm elected, he'll be included and he'll be a strong and good Vice President. And besides that, I think there's something very exciting about putting some confidence in a person in his 30s or 40s. You don't all have to be long in the tooth like we are to serve.

Broadcast interview/
"Today" show, NBC-TV, 11-3.

2

[On Democratic Presidential nominee Michael Dukakis]: I am getting sick and tired of my opponent's complaining about the rough-and-tumble of this campaign—something he does every time just before an election. He seems to forget those

personal attacks, night after night, on *me,* on my character, at that idiotic Democratic Convention [earlier in the year]. Those 20 negative commercials that he produced and ran until he found out the American people weren't buying any of that. And all the last minute attacks his squad are heaping on us. The American people are fair—they see through this last-minute smokescreen, and so now all that's left [for Dukakis] is this daily whining about a "negative campaign" [by Bush]. Let me give the Governor [Dukakis] a little advice. If he can't stand the heat, he ought to get out of the kitchen. Every time he gets into a little bind, he attacks the other guy. But this election is about big things . . . So don't listen to the crying of the far left.

At rally, Los Angeles, Nov. 6/
The Washington Post,
11-7:(A)1.

George Bush
Vice President, and
President-elect, of the
United States

3

Some people don't understand the [Presidential-election] campaign. They think that when you run against someone in a campaign, that that injures friendships. And, as I saw the other day [in discussions] with the Democrats, that's not true. It's wonderful the way the American political system works.

Washington, Dec. 2/
Los Angeles Times, 12-3:(I)18.

Jimmy Carter
Former President of
the United States

4

I think [1988 Democratic Presidential nominee Michael] Dukakis has learned a lot in the campaign against [former Democratic Presidential candidate] Jesse [Jackson]. He's learned that he has to be attentive to a broad constituency, to be broad in his seeking of advice and accommodating to a heterogeneous constituency. When Dukakis and his top advisers accept the black

(JIMMY CARTER)

and Hispanic leadership as in integral part of their process of getting elected and governing, it's not a yielding on principle, it's not a defeat for them, but it's a great victory for them, because it gives them a strength, politically and otherwise, that they couldn't have any other way.

U.S. News & World Report, 8-1:14.

1

[Defending Democratic Presidential nominee . Michael Dukakis whom Republicans are criticizing for not signing a bill as Massachusetts Governor that would have required the Pledge of Allegiance to be recited in his state's schools]: I have a great respect for the flag, [but] if the government . . . passed a law saying that I had to pledge allegiance to the flag, I don't think I would do it. I have always felt that I lived in a country . . . where if I wanted to worship God as a Baptist I could do so. If I were an atheist, I could be one. If I wanted to be a Catholic but was born a Jew, there's no condemnation . . . from a government authority.

At Emory University, Sept. 14/
Los Angeles Times, 9-16:(I)17.

John Chancellor
Commentator, NBC News

2

After seven years of [President] Ronald Reagan, we get [as candidates for the Presidency in 1988, Vice President George] Bush and [Massachusetts Governor Michael] Dukakis, the least charismatic candidates in the field. It looks as though we'll have a grilled-cheese sandwich running against a chocolate milkshake this fall.

Before American Newspaper
Publishers Association,
Honolulu/USA Today, 4-28:(B)2.

3

The [national political] conventions don't belong to the television networks [that cover them].

The conventions belong to the American people . . . and if occasionally [they] turn out to be boring, [changing them is not] up to television executives.

USA Today, 8-8:(D)2.

John Chubb
Senior fellow,
Brookings Institution

4

[Saying that Jesse Jackson has not earned the Vice Presidential position on the 1988 Democratic ticket, even though he came in second to Michael Dukakis in the primary voting]: There isn't much historical precedent for saying the person who comes in second earns anything. It's an argument they [the Jackson campaign] are concocting for this year's circumstances. I don't think he's earned it.

The Christian Science Monitor, 6-10:3.

Tony Coelho
United States Representative,
D-California

5

[On the prospective 1988 Democratic and Republican Presidential nominees, Massachusetts Governor Michael Dukakis and Vice President George Bush]: This is not a contest between liberal and conservative, left and right. It's a contest between vastly different profiles of leadership—between a man of action [Dukakis] and a man of absence [Bush], between a man of noble purpose and a man with a noble pedigree, between a miracle from Massachusetts with a real Texas accent and a fellow who wears cowboy boots over argyle socks. We [Democrats] can't help but win.

At Democratic National Convention, Atlanta,
July 19/Los Angeles Times, 7-20:(I)5.

John B. Connally, Jr.
Former Governor of
Texas (D); Former
candidate for the Republican
Presidential nomination

6

[On the current Presidential campaign between Democrat Michael Dukakis and Republi-

(JOHN B. CONNALLY, JR.)

can George Bush]: Dukakis is not well liked in this state [Texas]. People are a little afraid of him. He's an unknown quantity. Texas is put off by his stand on the death penalty, gun control, that sort of thing. But the really big thing is that the Bush people did a job on him in the five weeks after the conventions. They defined the agenda for the rest of the campaign, and he let them do it. Never seen anything like it in my life, and I still don't understand what the devil the Dukakis people thought they were doing all that time.

Interview/
The New York Times, 10-17:(A)13.

Ann Crigler
Assistant professor of
political science,
University of Southern
California

1

[On the current Presidential-election campaign]: My work suggests that most people can only conceptualize politics in simple, personal terms. They can't manage abstract ideas. In-depth interviews suggest that no matter how much people may complain about negative [campaign] commercials, they remember them and believe them, especially if the other side fails, as the Democrats have this time, to counter with slogan-like thoughts of their own . . . [Republican Presidential nominee George] Bush is succeeding because he is playing on something very basic—he's playing on people's fears. Look at his commercials: "Vote for *us,*" they say, "and vote for hard-working, warm, life-enhancing people. Vote for *them* and vote for muggers, for drug addicts, for brutes who kill unborn children." Not subtle, but strong.

The New York Times, 10-29:8.

Walter Cronkite
Former anchorman,
CBS News

2

I know liberalism isn't dead in this country . . . It simply has, temporarily we hope, lost

its voice. About the Democratic [Party's] loss of this [1988 Presidential] election . . . it was not just a campaign strategy built on a defensive philosophy. It was not just an opposition that conducted one of the most sophisticated and cynical campaigns ever . . . It was the fault of too many who found their voices stilled by subtle ideological intimidation. We know that unilateral [U.S.] action in Grenada and Tripoli [Libya] was wrong. We know that "Star Wars" [the proposed U.S. space defense system] means uncontrollable escalation of the arms race. We know that the real threat to democracy is the half a nation in poverty . . . We know that no one should tell a woman she has to bear an unwanted child. We know that religious beliefs cannot define patriotism . . . Gawd Amighty, we've got to shout these truths in which we believe from the housetops. Like that scene in the movie *Network,* we've got to throw open our windows and shout these truths to the streets and the heavens. And I bet we'll find more windows are thrown open to join the chorus than we'd ever dreamed possible.

Before People for the American Way/
Newsweek, 12-5:8.

Mario M. Cuomo
Governor of New York (D)

3

[Supporting Massachusetts Governor Michael Dukakis in his race for the Presidency against Vice President George Bush]: There are two people in the race, and they're both good Americans, both people who have served their country and served it admirably well. They're both people to whom we should feel gratitude and for whom we should feel respect. But only one of these good Americans [Dukakis] has ever run a complicated government, been able to balance a budget, reduce taxes, put people to work, supply housing, provide health insurance, deal with the elderly. Only one of these two good Americans has ever proven that he can do it. One of these two good Americans says: "I offer the status quo." The other good American says: "I'm not satisfied yet . . ." There are two good Americans, and the choice between them is clear.

The Washington Post, 10-17:(A)11.

(MARIO M. CUOMO)

1

[Criticizing what he says was the "negative" tone of the recent Presidential campaign]: If there's anything about this election that strikes me, that I find debilitating, it's the harshness, the crassness, the negativism. [The theme was] you do what you have to do to win. On the way there, you gouge out eyes, you lie, you cheat. I find that disconcerting.

News conference,
New York, Nov. 9/
The New York Times, 11-10:(A)23.

2

[On civil-rights leader Jesse Jackson, who ran for the Democratic Presidential nomination this year]: We have to start treating Jesse like everyone else. No more condescension. No more double standards. Give him the dignity he demands—and all the scrutiny we demand of others. Only then can white Democrats legitimately compete for black voters in the primaries and still have their heavy participation in the general election, without which we lose. Only then are you credible when you say, "We white office-holders are the ones who can actually deliver what Jesse talks about."

Time, 12-12:29.

John Deardourff
Political analyst

3

[The Presidential primary] campaigns have degenerated into either endless airport visits— the "Tarmac Campaign," where you just fly into one little airport after another, hoping that the television cameras from the local station will be there. Or you can stay in some fixed location where you can communicate via satellite, and local stations can conduct their own interviews with you by long distance. You see very few people. You don't deliver major speeches on the issues. You're not really talking to the voters; you're talking to them over the electronic airwaves.

Interview/USA Today, 3-8:(A)11.

Walter Dellinger
Professor of law,
Duke University

4

[On Republican Presidential nominee George Bush's criticism of Democratic Presidential nominee Governor Michael Dukakis' veto of a bill mandating the Pledge of Allegiance in Massachusetts public schools]: It has generally been considered out of bounds in Presidential politics to label one's opponents unpatriotic or un-American. If the Vice President [Bush] gets away with this cheap trick, we are going to see patriotic issues like this become a staple of American politics.

Los Angeles Times, 9-3:(I)22.

George Deukmejian
Governor of California (R)

5

[Democratic Presidential candidate Michael Dukakis is a] Walter Mondale when it comes to taxes . . . a Tip O'Neill when it comes to spending . . . a Teddy Kennedy when it comes to the issues of crime, and . . . a George McGovern when it comes to defense issues.

Broadcast interview/
The Christian Science Monitor,
6-9:1.

6

[On why he wouldn't accept the Vice-Presidential nomination under 1988 Republican Presidential nominee George Bush]: [It would be] a very, very high honor, [but] I'm also fully aware that it would bring about a total change in your entire life and that of your family . . . I wouldn't be eager to have to take on the kinds of responsibilities that go along with the office—the constant travel, the expectations the public has and the Party has for a person who holds that position, in addition to the countless major tasks that would be assigned, I think, to whoever the Vice President is under George Bush. Because with George Bush's experience in that office, I think he would be relying on his Vice President to be carrying on a lot of major responsibilities . . . I

(GEORGE DEUKMEJIAN)

think it would involve a tremendous amount of work. And I have to say, I'm not eager to jump at having to take on those additional burdens.

Interview,
Sacramento, Calif., July 14/
Los Angeles Times 7-15:(I)32.

Robert J. Dole
United States Senator,
R-Kansas;
Candidate for the 1988
Republican Presidential
nomination

1

A year ago people said there was no alternative [to Vice President George Bush as the Republican Party's 1988 Presidential nominee], and now people realize there is one and his name is Bob Dole. He understands the issues. He comes from a background where people can say he's one of us. He attended public schools. He's one of us. He's had some hard knocks in his lifetime. Nobody gave him anything. He's one of us, and I think that makes a difference.

Campaign rally,
New Hampshire, Jan. 5/
The New York Times, 1-7:9.

2

[On those who say the Republican Party does not care enough about the poor or blacks]: I think we do care, but I believe there is a perception [that we don't]. Otherwise, why would so many people be in the other party—because the Democrats promise more spending? Not necessarily. I happen to believe that one way to change that is to reach out—give somebody reason to join the Republican Party. There are good reasons for a lot of Americans—hard-working, real people.

Interview/
U.S. News & World Report, 1-11:29.

3

I think the President [Reagan] came in as sort of an outsider—after another outsider, Jimmy Carter—and he was not convinced you couldn't do all these things people said you couldn't do, so he did them. He lowered taxes. He dealt with inflation. He put people back to work. And he's done a good job. I think he has brought back respect to America around the world.

Interview/
U.S. News & World Report,
1-11:29.

4

[On the race for the 1988 Republican Presidential nomination]: I can beat [Vice President George Bush, who is also running], but I can't beat [President] Ronald Reagan [who is nearing the end of his two terms]. Bush has been standing next to him for seven years, while I've been doing all the work [as Senate Republican leader] and he's been piling up credits. It's a phenomenon I don't understand.

March 10/USA Today, 3-11:(A)1.

5

The Republican Party, like our nation, must have an open door to all Americans. We need to reach out, sincerely reach out, to new legions of Hispanic voters, blacks, Asian Americans and other ethnic groups eager to show that they can play a dynamic role in the American political process.

To his campaign staff,
Washington, March 28/
The Washington Post, 3-29:(A)4.

Robert J. Dole
United States Senator,
R-Kansas; Former
candidate for the
1988 Republican
Presidential nomination

6

We [Republicans] must cast off the restrictions of privilege and class. We must offer help to those who need it. We must support and defend civil rights . . . Our [Republican] leaders should not be timid about discussing issues that affect

(ROBERT J. DOLE)

the homeless and the hungry. We must speak out on issues like drugs, day care, the environment, education, long-term health care, medicaid and Medicare, to mention just a few.

The Christian Science Monitor,
3-30:4.

1

[Criticizing newspaper coverage of the Presidential primary campaign, citing a letter he received from *The New York Times*]: [The letter informed] me that *The Times* had assembled a "team of reporters" who would be preparing a series of "in-depth profiles" on Presidential candidates. In fact, it was a letter that heralded the kind of coverage Presidential candidates could expect in the coming months on the campaign trail: issueless and negative. The *Times* letter made no reference to issues, nor did it request any such information. Instead, I was asked to provide my driver's license, my marriage license, my high-school and college transcripts, my military records, my medical records, a list of my friends and a waiver of my privacy rights.

Before the Senate,
Washington, April 26/
The New York Times, 4-27:12.

William Donahue
Former fellow,
Heritage Foundation

2

[On Republican Presidential nominee George Bush's criticizing Democratic nominee Michael Dukakis for being a member of the ACLU]: The ACLU has, at least in the last 20 years, become an extremist organization . . . Now it's coming home to roost. [It] is the legal arm of the liberal left. The ACLU is a partisan organization and it follows the logic of the liberal left community.

The Washington Post,
10-3:(A)8.

Frank Donatelli
Political Director for
President of the United
States Ronald Reagan

3

[President] Reagan is as revolutionary a figure in the Republican Party as F.D.R. was in the Democratic Party. The Party needs successful role models. The Democrats routinely recite F.D.R., Kennedy, Truman. I think future Republicans will talk about the Reagan years.

USA Today, 8-15:(A)1.

Michael S. Dukakis
Governor of Massachusetts (D);
Candidate for the 1988
Democratic Presidential
nomination

4

I'm not a great fan of the momentum theory of politics. I'm a great fan of the marathon theory of politics—step by step, mile by mile, working hard, state by state.

News conference,
New York, April 5/
Los Angeles Times, 4-6:(I)10.

5

I hope you're as proud as I am of the fact that in 1988, in the United States of America, the two leading candidates for the Democratic [Presidential] nominee is the son of Greek immigrants from Massachusetts [himself] and a black man who grew up poor in South Carolina [Jesse Jackson].

At Democratic Party dinner,
Philadelphia, April 19/
The New York Times, 4-20:15.

6

Federal elections have become fund-raising and spending marathons that are largely dominated by political action committees. As a candidate for President, I will not accept PAC money . . . I also believe there should be absolute limits on expenditures in Congressional elections, just as there are in Presidential elections.

USA Today, 5-3:(A)11.

(MICHAEL S. DUKAKIS)

1

[On the forthcoming Presidential election campaign]: [Americans] aren't interested in slashing attacks. They want to judge our positive ideas for change. Every day of this race, the strength of our character—our integrity and independence—will be scrutinized. [This race will be a] golden opportunity [for Democrats]. And what quicksand for our [Republican] opponents if they waste this opportunity on mudslinging and name-calling. Because the American people are not interested in what [Republican candidate Vice President George] Bush thinks of me or what I think of him. They want to know which one of us has the strength and the ability and the values to lead our country.

Speech upon winning California
Democratic primary,
Los Angeles, June 7/
Los Angeles Times, 6-8:(I)10.

2

[On civil-rights leader Jesse Jackson, who is also running for this year's Democratic Presidential nomination, which appears will be won by Dukakis]: I want Jesse Jackson to play a major role in this campaign. I want his supporters, who are out there by the millions, to be deeply involved in this campaign. They're going to be an essential part of the coalition we build coming out of this convention to win a Democratic victory in November . . .

Atlanta, July 18/
The New York Times, 7-19:9.

Michael S. Dukakis
Governor of Massachusetts (D);
1988 Democratic
Presidential nominee

3

[On the forthcoming Presidential election]: We're [Democrats] going to win because we are the Party that believes in the American dream. A dream so powerful that no distance of ground, no expanse of ocean, no barrier of language, no distinction of race or creed or color can weaken

its hold on the human heart . . . And, my friends, if anyone tells you that the American dream belongs to the privileged few and not to all of us, you tell them that the Reagan era is over. You tell [them] that the Reagan era is over and that a new era is about to begin.

Accepting the nomination, at
Democratic National Convention,
Atlanta, July 21/
Los Angeles Times, 7-22:(I)6.

4

[On the forthcoming Presidential election]: This election is not about ideology. It's about competence. It's not about overthrowing governments in Central America; it's about creating jobs in middle America. That's what this election is all about. It's not about insider trading on Wall Street; it's about creating opportunity on Main Street. And it's not about meaningless labels. It's about American values. Old-fashioned values like accountability and responsibility and respect for the truth. And just as we Democrats believe that there are no limits to what each citizen can do, so we believe that there are no limits to what America can do.

Accepting the nomination, at
Democratic National Convention,
Atlanta, July 21/
The New York Times, 7-22:8.

5

[Vice President and Republican Presidential nominee] George Bush has some of the highest negatives ever recorded in the history of American politics, and I think one of the reasons for it is people have seen his campaign as an essentially negative campaign. I think the way I'm going to win the Presidency is not by responding every day to what some speech writer has put in front of Mr. Bush. It's going to be by defining myself, my Party, my values, this country, its future, and the kind of society I think all Americans want.

Boston, Aug. 8/
Los Angeles Times, 8-9:(I)13.

(MICHAEL S. DUKAKIS)

1

[On his vetoing a bill to require the Pledge of Allegiance in Massachusetts public schools, a veto which has been criticized by Republican Presidential nominee George Bush]: I encourage children to say the Pledge of Allegiance. I say the Pledge of Allegiance. That's not the issue, and the Republicans know it . . . If a serious candidate for the Presidency seriously suggests that he would sign a bill even though the Supreme Court of the United States told him it was un-Constitutional, then how can he be qualified to be President of the United States? What does it mean to take the oath of office?

News conference, Aug. 23/
The New York Times, 8-24:10.

2

[In the 1930s, the Republicans] put together the most vicious campaign of propaganda, lobbying and intimidation ever seen [to attack Speaker of the House Sam Rayburn and Presidential nominee Franklin Roosevelt]. Sam Rayburn didn't back off. He snorted: "Hell, I'm a conservative, but even a conservative can smell garbage in his front yard." Sam Rayburn knew that when you fight for the real people the other side will attack your patriotism. He saw that when he passed the Wall Street reform bills. He saw it again in the 1950s, when the Republicans cheered as Joseph R. McCarthy slandered good Democrats and called them Communists and Soviet sympathizers. Those Republicans haven't changed a bit. Just as they did to Franklin Roosevelt and Sam Rayburn, now they're attacking my patriotism. And just as they did in the 1930s and 1950s, the American people can smell the garbage.

At East Texas State University,
Sept. 9/
Los Angeles Times, 9-10:(I)20.

3

[Criticizing Republican Presidential nominee George Bush's choice of Dan Quayle as his Vice-Presidential running mate]: This was the first Presidential decision that we as nominees were called upon to make, and that's why people are so concerned . . . Mr. Bush picked Dan Quayle, and before he did he said, "Watch my choice for Vice President; it will tell all." And it sure did.

At Presidential debate,
Los Angeles, Oct. 13/
USA Today, 10-14:(A)6.

4

I've been in public life for a quarter of a century, and I've been there when the tough decisions are made. I know there are times when the three most important words a Governor, a Vice President or a President must say are: "This is wrong." Does anyone doubt what I would have said if I was in the room when [the Reagan Administration] made those decisions to sell arms to the Ayatollah [in Iran], to put [Panamanian leader and accused drug-trafficker Manuel] Noriega on the payroll, to veto civil rights and women's rights, or to choose people like [current Republican Vice-Presidential nominee] Dan Quayle and [former Attorney General] Ed Meese and [former Interior Secretary] James Watt and [Senate-rejected Supreme Court nominee] Robert Bork? I would have said three simple words: This is wrong. These aren't issues of right and left; these are issues of right and wrong.

Campaign speech, Boston, Oct. 16/
The New York Times, 10-17:(A)12.

5

The business of polls [during Presidential election campaigns] is really having a terrible effect . . . It's terrible. Now we've got a new set of numbers that has absolutely no relationship to anything we have or other people have, so you spend two or three days responding to questions about it.

Ohio, Oct. 17/
The Washington Post, 10-18:(A)1.

6

I'm a liberal in the tradition of Franklin Roosevelt and Harry Truman and John Kennedy.

(MICHAEL S. DUKAKIS)

But I'm also somebody who balances budgets, something [Republican Presidential nominee George] Bush has never done. I mean, I'm fiscally a lot more conservative than George Bush . . . Like most Americans, I'm liberal in some ways, and I guess I'm conservative in others. I was always taught that the first thing a conservative did was pay his bills.

Interview/USA Today, 11-1:(A)6.

1

I think all of us have combinations of liberal and conservative about us. I'm not a liberal.

Broadcast interview/
Time, 11-7:22.

2

I don't know if the American people are particularly happy about this [Presidential] campaign. There have been a lot of smears, fears and issues raised which don't have much to do with the Presidency of the United States. People have been watching furlough ads [Republican ads criticizing Massachusetts' prison furlough program] playing politics with human tragedy. This is not a campaign about furloughs and flag factories [where Republican nominee George Bush had a photo session]. This is a campaign about the future of America.

Broadcast address to the nation,
Nov. 7/
The New York Times, 11-8:(A)11.

3

[On Republican Presidential nominee George Bush]: First he tried to steal our heroes—Franklin Roosevelt, Harry Truman, John Kennedy. Then he tried to steal our issues—jobs, education, the environment, health care. Now he's trying to steal our cause—the cause of average Americans and working people and working families all across the country. Before you know it, he'll try to steal the Democratic donkey.

Campaigning, Nov. 7/
The Washington Post, 11-8:(A)1.

4

[On his losing the 1988 Presidential election to George Bush]: Look, there's no question that the negative campaigning [by Bush] hurt us. I had hoped that it would be possible to run a good, strong, positive campaign without having to take a lot of time responding to those attacks. I think one of the lessons of this campaign is you have to respond, you have to respond quickly.

News conference, Boston, Nov. 9/
The New York Times, 11-10:(A)15.

5

[On his losing the just-held Presidential election to Republican George Bush]: I don't see a mandate [for Bush]. Not when the [Congress] has increased its Democratic membership. The American people . . . have expressed a desire to have some continuity in the Presidency [but] I don't think you can look at those results on the Congressional side and not say they're also expressing some very strong progressive feelings about what this country has to do.

News conference, Boston, Nov. 9/
The Washington Post,
11-10:(A)37.

6

[On this year's Presidential election, which he lost to George Bush]: I really enjoyed the primary [election]. I talked to real people [in the primaries], about real problems, and you are learning. But when I got to the general [election], I asked myself, "Where is the world? Where are the people?" You are spending half your life on the plane. The average sound bite got down to, I think, eight seconds.

Interview, Boston/
The Washington Post, 12-27:(A)2.

Carter Eskew
Democratic Party media
consultant

7

The belief for as long as there has been paid media [ads] was that you never used negative ads

(CARTER ESKEW)

in a Presidential campaign, because it looked un-Presidential. Well, the last bastion of conventional wisdom has been shattered this year because candidates have already gone negative, and you can be sure others will follow. The new reality is that negative ads work especially well in this environment.

U.S. News & World Report,
2-29:12.

Frank J. Fahrenkopf, Jr.
Chairman, Republican
National Committee

1

Support [for the Republican Party] is much stronger among men voters ... not only for the Vice President [George Bush, who is running for the Presidency] but for the Party itself. We are particularly vulnerable, if I can use that word, among young women between the ages of 18 and 35 who work outside the home and, particularly within that subgroup, those young women who are single parents. [The reason is] a perception that the Republican Party has not been responsive to their needs.

The Washington Post,
5-11:(A)8.

2

[On charges that the national political conventions have become boring for TV viewers]: Some of the network people indicated to me that professional wrestling actually did better on some of the alternative channels than the Democratic and Republican conventions [this year] ... There has been criticism by many in the media that these events have become nothing more than staged activities in which nominees give canned speeches. By the same token, there are many in the parties and many academicians who believe that the conventions are ... a healthy catalyst for political activity.

News conference,
Washington, Dec. 7/
Los Angeles Times, 12-8:(I)9.

Thomas S. Foley
United States Representative,
D-Washington

3

To run for President, you have to have an enormous passion. You have to want it with a compelling urgency. You have to be prepared to sacrifice all kinds of things—financial security, your privacy, family well-being—on the altar of that desire, and even then the odds will be profoundly against you ... I think the way we choose Presidents has terrible flaws. I know of any number of people who I think would make good Presidents, even great Presidents, who are deterred from running by the torture candidates are obliged to put themselves through.

Interview, Spokane, Wash./
The New York Times, 11-4:(A)12.

Gerald R. Ford
Former President
of the United States

4

[On the long Presidential primary- and general election season in the U.S.]: I wish we were as smart as our British friends and could have an election in five weeks and it's over. The candidates would come out of it better mentally and physically.

Before political scientists,
University of California, Davis/
Los Angeles Times,
6-9:(I)20.

Donald L. Fowler
Chief executive officer, 1988
Democratic National
Convention

5

We [Democrats] need to show the nation that we are a party that can handle the real problems of real people in the 1990s. Americans are not really riled up about anything. They have a reasonable sense that their world is okay today, but a brooding apprehension about the future. We need to demonstrate that we are capable of leading them into that future.

The Washington Post, 6-18:(A)1.

225

Michael Gartner
President, NBC News

1

[Defending TV's practice of announcing winners in Presidential elections before all the results are tallied, by using exit polls and analysis of partial results]: Our duty is to tell the viewer what's happened. And when the polls have closed, and we're sitting here knowing who's won, it's incumbent on us to say.

USA Today, 11-8:(A)10.

Richard A. Gephardt
United States Representative,
D-Missouri; Candidate for the
1988 Democratic
Presidential nomination

2

We [Democrats] cannot prevail as a Yuppie Party, or simply by bashing the Republicans on issues where the voters may share our positions but not our passion, or by offering the technocratic argument that we can administer the status quo with a little more efficiency, or a little more compassion.

Campaign speech,
Waco, Texas, Feb. 24/
The Washington Post,
2-25:(A)10.

Newt Gingrich
United States Representative,
R-Georgia

3

[On Speaker of the House Jim Wright]: This is a situation where the man who is third in line to the Presidency is the least ethical person to serve as Speaker in the 20th century. That is terrifying in its implications for the future of the House of Representatives and, therefore, since we have oversight over the CIA, and the IRS, and the FBI, it is frightening in its implications for the country.

The Christian Science Monitor,
5-31:6.

Ira Glasser
Executive director,
American Civil
Liberties Union

4

[On Republican Presidential nominee George Bush's criticizing Democratic nominee Michael Dukakis for being a member of the ACLU]: We have absolutely no desire to get into the middle of a political campaign. We're not going to get into the business of attacking Bush or defending Dukakis. [But] we are worried that the way in which a lot of people have jumped on the anti-ACLU bandwagon for their own purposes has the effect of eroding understanding of what the Bill of Rights is all about . . . Being a member of the ACLU should be seen as an act of patriotism, not the reverse.

The Washington Post, 10-3:(A)8.

Barry M. Goldwater
Former United States Senator,
R-Arizona

5

If the press is going to make strict adherence to morality the guiding light for engaging in politics, then we're going to run out of candidates real fast, including women.

USA Today, 4-29:(A)2.

Albert Gore, Jr.
United States Senator,
D-Tennessee;
Candidate for the 1988
Democratic Presidential
nomination

6

My definition of the Democratic Party is a party that has as big a heart as it has ever had and the same soul it has always had—but also has an understanding of how the world has changed and how important it is for us to match our policies to the circumstances in which we find ourselves.

Interview, Washington/
U.S. News & World Report,
2-15:17.

(ALBERT GORE, JR.)

1

[Democratic Presidential candidate Michael Dukakis] has been a good Governor of Massachusetts, and I think he should stay as Governor. His program for the country is so vague and fuzzy as to have no substance. That's true in domestic policy and it is especially true in foreign policy. Anybody who talks to him about foreign policy and defense policy comes away with a question mark about his experience.

Interview, March 9/
Los Angeles Times, 3-10:(I)21.

2

[Criticizing Massachusetts Governor and Presidential candidate Michael Dukakis for not challenging Presidential candidate Jesse Jackson's views]: He's [Dukakis] scared to death he'll be misinterpreted [as being anti-black, since Jackson is black]. He's very uneasy with the whole subject. It's just ludicrous. He is absurdly timid when it comes to uttering the slightest sound that might somehow be interpreted as containing an unfavorable view of one of Jesse Jackson's positions . . . If the country is going to mature to the point where we are color-blind and see candidates in terms of their ability and leadership, then we must be prepared to engage in the rough-and-tumble of politics. It's just ludicrous to me to take any other position.

To reporters/
The New York Times, 4-4:10.

Phil Gramm
United States Senator,
R-Texas

3

[On Democratic Presidential nominee Michael Dukakis]: Is there anybody who doubts that a President Dukakis would raise our taxes . . . spend our workers into poverty . . . cut defense and wimp America and endanger peace . . . expand the power of government and its control over our lives? No, we don't doubt it, and that's why there is not going to be a President Dukakis.

At Republican National
Convention, New Orleans/
Los Angeles Times, 8-19:(I)4.

George W. Grayson
Virginia State Legislator (D);
Professor of government,
College of William and Mary

4

[On Democratic Presidential candidate Jesse Jackson]: It would be a minor miracle if Jackson got even one-third of the vote in the general election [if he was nominated by the Party]. It would be another [George] McGovern, [Walter] Mondale reverse landslide. It would cost the Party seats from the White House to the courthouse . . . It's a tremendous dilemma. Jackson certainly has paid his dues to the Democratic Party, and black voters [Jackson is black] have been the most loyal component of the Democratic electoral results. Yet because of Jackson's free-lancing in foreign policy, combined with his glibness on issues, it's doubtful whether he can expand on what is already a narrow base.

The Christian Science Monitor,
3-31:6.

Fred I. Greenstein
Political scientist,
Princeton University

5

In a way, the historical memory of the [Jimmy] Carter Presidency is just the reverse of what the historical memory of the [Franklin] Roosevelt period did for Democrats in earlier periods. In the '40s and '50s, and even into the '60s, Democrats could say, look back and think what F.D.R. did for us—he brought us a return to prosperity from a terrible crisis and brought us international strength. What did the Democrats do last time [during the Carter years]? The voters are likely to think of high inflation, gas lines and a hostage crisis [in Iran].

The New York Times, 9-21:10.

Lawrence Grossman
President, NBC News

6

I happen to think . . . that when people are judging an election, personality and character—leadership—is undoubtedly the most critical

227

(LAWRENCE GROSSMAN)

factor. And in any event, that is the aspect of it that television is particularly suited to bring.

Esquire, May:82.

Alexander M. Haig, Jr.
Candidate for the 1988 Republican Presidential nomination; Former Secretary of State of the United States

1

[On Vice President and Republican Presidential candidate George Bush]: The role of the Vice President is very difficult, but Bush chose to be Vice President. And having made that decision he's got to pay the price. As far as I'm concerned, he will. And that price is paucity of accomplishment. He's enjoyed an unusual delegation of authority from the President [Reagan], and he's shown very little. He's been running for '88 instead of running to accomplish the missions he was assigned by the President. He was responsible for curbing drugs, dealing with terrorism, crisis management and reduction of regulation and the size of bureaucracy. And he's been totally lackluster. And I don't believe a lackluster leadership is adequate for this country.

Interview, Manchester, N.H./
The New York Times, 1-11:9.

2

[On his quest for the Presidential nomination]: I came in to see this through. I'm prepared to. But when you get down to it, it's the resources available to the candidate. You can get all the good-will in the world but, if you don't have the resources, it's not doable. Frankly, it's more of a business than I thought it was.

Interview, Manchester, N.H./
The New York Times, 1-11:9.

David A. Harris
Washington representative, American Jewish Committee

3

Jews defy political trends in this country by defining themselves along a moderate-to-liberal spectrum and not a moderate-to-conservative spectrum, as a majority of voters do. Jews are a curious phenomenon—they are the only group that in most elections votes against their class interests [by voting Democratic]. As the Jewish community becomes better educated, and moves to the middle class and upper middle class, one would argue that they ought to be moving more toward the Republican Party, and yet they are not in such numbers.

The Washington Post,
10-17:(A)10.

Gary Hart
Candidate for the 1988 Democratic Presidential nomination; Former United States Senator, D-Colorado

4

The theme of this [his campaign for President] will be the national interests, [not] special interests. Part of the education process [of the campaign] is that the voters need to understand that they owe the country something. They at least owe it their votes. My themes are going to be responsibility and citizenship. And if they don't vote for it, then I'll go back to Kittredge [Colorado] and live happily ever after.

Interview, Exeter, N.H., Jan. 6/
Los Angeles Times, 1-7:(I)20.

5

[On his re-entering the Presidential race after withdrawing from it last year after a sex scandal]: My religion tells me all of us are sinners. The issue of character of leadership has been with us for 200 years. We have not expected perfection from our leaders and I don't think we should now. In the past, people who have not led perfect lives have been some of our finest leaders.

At debate among Democratic
Presidential candidates,
Des Moines, Iowa, Jan. 15/
The New York Times, 1-16:9.

(GARY HART)

1

I think one of the reasons why it's kind of fashionable these days to run politics down is because people have the sense that the politicians are not giving them the straight facts on public issues that affect their lives. And further, people have a sense that there is so much emphasis placed these days on polls and media and raising money and political endorsements, what I call the tactical or "inside baseball" aspects of politics, that we've lost sight of what all this is about . . . There are some bad politicians, and there are too many of them. Either they don't understand the problem, or they don't know the answers. Or if they know that some kind of bold or innovative action is going to be required and that will be unpopular, they don't want to say anything that might upset somebody. But the people—that is to say all of us—are to blame, also, because we always seem to want simple answers.

Campaign speech/
The New York Times, 1-26:13.

2

[On the controversy about his alleged marital infidelity]: Why are my personal life and campaign finances front-page, eight-column, banner-headline news and lead stories for nightly news when the real [campaign] issues—hunger, homelessness and illiteracy—are routinely buried by those same organizations? While the media criticizes [President] Ronald Reagan and [Vice President and Presidential candidate] George Bush for not answering questions about their conduct or national policies, why do few show any interest in examining *my* policies, instead preferring to focus on personal and private issues that are of importance only to me and my family? And why are my personal life, my contributor list, my campaign finances endlessly scrutinized, and not those of other candidates? I wonder and have wondered for a long time. And I don't know the answer. My guess is it's mostly a combination of the fact that I'm independent and don't always play by the rules. I've always been a reformer and I don't make any deals or arrangements with powerful interests, and I won't take their money.

At University of Northern Iowa,
Jan. 28/
The New York Times, 1-29:10.

Gary Hart
Former United States Senator,
D-Colorado; Former
candidate for the 1988
Democratic Presidential
nomination

3

The system for selecting our national leaders . . . reduces the press of this nation to hunters and the Presidential candidates to being hunted.

USA Today, 4-27:(A)4.

Peter Hart
Democratic Party political
analyst

4

[Presidential] candidates tend to be monochromatic. They all have the same consultants, and all the consultants are reading the same things; and once they've all read the same things, they're all advising the same things, so everybody ends up in the same blue suit with a light-blue shirt, and the red power tie. Does it work against them? Sure. It's like any uniform—you become "it" instead of who you are.

U.S. News & World Report,
5-30:12.

5

[On Democratic Presidential nominee Michael Dukakis trailing in polls for the forthcoming election]: The Democrats had a wealth of things to go after, and they didn't take one path and just make it stick. You can't bring [a message] out there for a day, ask the question and disappear. The Republicans knew exactly what arguments they were going to make. They told you in June, they made them in July, sharpened them in August and kept them going in September. What it really comes down to is [Republican Presidential nominee]

(PETER HART)

George Bush has done a better job of making Mike Dukakis unfavorable [and] unlikable.

To reporters, Washington, Oct. 31/
The Christian Science Monitor,
11-1:3.

Orrin G. Hatch
United States Senator,
R-Utah

1

[Democrats] are the party of homosexuals. They are the party of abortions. They are the party that has fought school prayer every step of the way. They are the party that has basically, I think, denigrated a lot of the values that have made this country the greatest country in the world.

St. George, Utah, Aug. 31/
Los Angeles Times, 9-4:(I)36.

Stephen Hess
Scholar,
Brookings Institution

2

[Political] caucuses measure interest and intensity [in an election campaign]. You have to work hard to get people out on a February night for anything.

USA Today, 2-5:(A)12.

3

The Republicans have been in office for eight years and, in our system, that is a strength for the Democrats. The country tends to get bored with one party in office. We have a history of throwing the rascals out, even if they are doing a good job.

The Christian Science Monitor,
4-21:1.

Benjamin L. Hooks
Executive director,
National Association for the
Advancement of Colored People

4

Too many civil-rights leaders . . . gave their lives seeking the right to vote. We blacks have an obligation to vote [in the forthcoming Presidential election] whether we dislike the Republican candidate because we don't like his Party or whether we dislike the Democratic candidate because we don't like his treatment of Reverend Jesse Jackson . . . I would like to see every state pass a law allowing immediate, on-the-spot registration of any qualified voter. Getting people to register and vote—not only blacks, but all Americans—to the ballot box is our goal.

At NAACP convention,
Washington/
The Christian Science Monitor,
7-18:8.

Jesse L. Jackson
Civil-rights leader;
Candidate for the 1988
Democratic Presidential
nomination

5

I want to be your President. It's time for a change . . . all this talk about Jesse Jackson can't win—whoever gets the most votes can win. If I get your vote, I can win. If I can win, any American can become President. If I cannot win, most Americans cannot become President. If I can win, it means never again will race, sex or religion stand between you and the White House. If I cannot win, most of you can never win. Together we can win.

Campaign speech/
The New York Times, 1-19:12.

6

[On his current front-runner status for the Democratic Presidential nomination and speculation about whether he, a black, could win it]: The voters are obviously in front of the press on this question. That's why the voters are voting according to what they feel and see. I'm using old math: the most votes, the most delegates equals the nomination. I'm not familiar with any other way of counting.

To reporters en route
to campaigning in New York,
March 28/Los Angeles Times, 3-29:(I)13.

(JESSE L. JACKSON)

1

It is a threat to the very idea of democracy if only candidates capable of raising millions of dollars can run for office successfully. It should not be possible for a candidate to "buy" an election, by heavily outspending an opponent, or for a special-interest PAC to "buy" a Congressman by contributing thousands of dollars to his/her campaign.

USA Today, 5-3:(A)11.

2

[On his running for the Democratic Presidential nomination]: I am a survivor. I am competing with [the other Democratic Presidential candidate Michael] Dukakis and [the Republican Presidential candidate Vice President George] Bush. That's Harvard and Yale. They have the prestige. They have the power. They have the power structure. They have the press. They have the pundits. They have the party. They have the cultural expectation. And yet I must not surrender the will to lead.

At North Carolina A&T State
University commencement, May 8/
The New York Times, 5-9:10.

3

What do I want in the Atlanta [Democratic Party Convention] platform? What kind of agenda am I putting forth? What is the Jesse Jackson bill of priorities? One is the right to a useful and remunerative job. Two is the right to earn enough to provide adequate food, clothing and recreation. Three is the right of farmers to raise and sell their product to give their family a decent living. What do I want in Atlanta? The right of every family to a decent home. The right to adequate medical care. The right to adequate protection for the economic fears of old age and sickness. The right of everybody to a good education. All these rights spell security. These radical recommendations, this Jackson agenda, is a direct quotation from [Franklin] Roosevelt 44 years ago. I seek to return our Party to its roots, to

its basic beginnings, its basic obligation to invest in people, to reinvest in America.

News conference,
Trenton, N.J., May 31/
The New York Times, 6-1:13.

4

[Saying he is available for the Vice-Presidential nomination if Michael Dukakis wins the Democratic Presidential race]: If the issue is that he wants someone from the South, I'm from the South. If [he needs] someone who has had the impact on Southern politics, I've done that. If it's someone who can mobilize a mass of Democrats, I've done that. If it's someone who is not limited to regional appeal but has national appeal, I've won primaries from Vermont to Puerto Rico, from Mississippi to Michigan, from Texas to Alaska.

News conference, Los Angeles,
June 8/
The Washington Post, 6-9:(A)21.

5

[Saying he should be considered for the Vice Presidential spot if Michael Dukakis wins the Democratic Presidential nomination]: Any combination of criteria used historically [to select running mates], I match those criteria . . . No one else at this point that's active in politics has shown the breadth of support I have shown at the voting polls. No one else has shown the ability to impact upon the country's tone and the Party's priorities as I have shown. So the other persons considered are by comparison speculative. They may have state credentials. [But] they've not shown themselves to have national and vote-pulling power in every region in the country.

News conference,
Carlsbad, Calif., June 10/
The New York Times, 6-11:8.

6

[On those who criticize him for seeming to be overtly running for the Vice Presidency on the ticket with Democratic Presidential frontrunner

(JESSE L. JACKSON)

Michael Dukakis]: Those of us who are behind have always had to be more animated for our quest for justice. Voters never got the impression that [Walter] Mondale was overtly campaigning [to be Jimmy Carter's running mate in the 1976 election], but he didn't have to be overt; he had important sponsors. When Mondale [was the Democratic Presidential nominee in 1984 and] broke new ground by naming a woman as his running mate, Geraldine Ferraro didn't have to campaign for the nomination. She had big-name sponsors like [then-Speaker of the House Thomas P. O'Neill, Jr.]. I don't have that. I'm the stepchild, and my peculiar circumstances breed what might appear to be peculiar behavior. But as long as the outcome is ultimately fair, legal and just, that's all right.

Interview/
Los Angeles Times, 6-21:(II)7.

Jesse L. Jackson
Civil-rights leader;
Former candidate for the
1988 Democratic
Presidential nomination

1

[On whether he is angry that he was not chosen by Democratic Presidential nominee Michael Dukakis to be his Vice-Presidential running mate]: No. I'm too controlled. I'm too clear. I'm too mature to be angry. I'm focused on what we must do to keep hope alive. Anger reflects a crisis and emotions and, therefore, irrational behavior. I simply have been in this struggle long enough to be able to keep my eyes on the prize and keep doing what I've done throughout this campaign: maintain a moral tone, lift the campaign, keep my focus on where we ought to be . . . I've honored the process throughout. I've honored the rules throughout.

News conference, July 12/
USA Today, 7-13:(A)11.

2

[On 1988 Democratic Presidential nominee Michael Dukakis]: Tonight I salute Governor

Michael Dukakis. I have watched a good mind fast at work, with steel nerves, guiding his campaign out of the crowded field without appeal to the worst in us. I have watched his perspective grow as his environment has expanded. I have seen his toughness and tenacity close up, know his commitment to public service. [His ancestors came to America on immigrant ships, while mine] came to America on slave ships. But whatever the original ships, we are in the same boat tonight.

At Democratic National
Convention, Atlanta, July 19/
The Washington Post, 7-20:(A)1.

3

[On his recent quest for the 1988 Democratic Presidential nomination, which he lost to Michael Dukakis]: My mission has been to transform the mind of America. It's not just politics, small p, as in delegates and votes. But politics, big P, as in transforming our minds and changing our self-concept.

At convention of black lawyers,
Washington/The New York Times,
8-13:9.

4

[Criticizing 1988 Republican Vice-Presidential nominee Senator Dan Quayle]: He has not earned the nomination, he has inherited it [a reference to his wealthy family]. [Leadership results from] a combination of struggle and suffering, sacrifice and pain. All these are foreign to him.

Interview, Aug. 22/
Los Angeles Times, 8-23:(I)11.

5

[Criticizing the campaign style of Republican Presidential nominee George Bush]: One day I'm called a Chicago hustler, then my proximity to the Democratic ticket is called a three-headed monster, then the Bush campaign presses rumors about [Democratic Presidential nominee Michael] Dukakis seeing a psychiatrist, and then

232

(JESSE L. JACKSON)

Bush challenges Dukakis' patriotism. The pattern of behavior is not just conservative; it's reactionary and mean-spirited.

Interview,
Washington, Sept. 11/
Los Angeles Times,
9-12:(I)1.

1

It was liberals who got women the vote, who got black people the vote, who gave us rural electrification and better health care . . . [Unless liberalism is defended against current attacks such as those by Republican Presidential nominee George Bush], we are about to have a generation of children who've grown up thinking that to be liberal is to be dirty, inadequate, subversive.

Before Hollywood Women's
Political Committee,
Beverly Hills, Calif., Oct. 16/
Los Angeles Times, 10-18:(I)17.

2

If the white Democrats don't come to their senses, then we're [blacks] going to have to reconsider our religious loyalty to the [Democratic] Party. [Republican President-elect George] Bush took me seriously the other day [in a meeting between the two of them], after [current Republican President] Reagan had the unwelcome mat out for eight years. If [Bush] acts as well as he talks, then we'll have to re-examine our historical alliances.

Time, 12-12:29.

Kathleen Hall Jamieson
Professor of communications,
University of Texas

3

[On the current Presidential-election campaign between Democrat Michael Dukakis and Republican George Bush]: This is the first year that I can remember in Presidential history in which we've seen nationally aired ads—ads aired in major regional markets—that are actively distorting the other person's record, not just prompting false inferences, but stating as true something that's false. The Bush campaign is far guiltier [of distortion] than the Dukakis campaign . . . Over-all, in terms of fairness and accuracy, Bush is running the dirtiest campaign that I've seen since 1964.

Broadcast interview/
"Meet the Press," NBC-TV,
10-23.

Sonia Jarvis
Director, National Coalition
for Black Voter Participation

4

[On the current Presidential-election campaign]: Both candidates [Republican George Bush and Democrat Michael Dukakis] are so busy beating each other over the head going after the "Reagan Democrats," so where does that leave the black voter? During the campaign of the 30-second sound bites, how many pictures have you seen of Michael Dukakis in black neighborhoods? You can count them on one hand. I know, because I have.

Los Angeles Times, 10-20:(I)28.

Thomas H. Kean
Governor of New Jersey (R)

5

We [Republicans] have to reach out to people who are black, people who are members of unions, the Hispanic community and so many others, to voters who listen to [Bruce] Springsteen as well as [Frank] Sinatra, who eat burgers as well as brie and who wash those burgers down with Schlitz [beer], not just Chardonnay.

At rally, Princeton, N.J./
The Washington Post, 3-22:(A)8.

6

At the [recent Democratic National Convention], they were terribly worried because they thought somebody was going to say something that would lose them a few votes, so they really

(THOMAS H. KEAN)

said nothing. We're [the Republicans] not that kind of a party. Some people are going to disagree with some of the things we're going to say at [the forthcoming Republican National Convention]. But they're going to know what we believe.

Interview/USA Today, 8-15:(A)11.

1

A [political] party, year after year, cannot serve up the same issues and the same rhetoric. If we try to run on the issues that won for us in 1980, then we will lose in 1988 . . . There is a static element to conservatism within the [Republican] Party that is disturbing. If you want to conserve, you've got to create.

The Washington Post, 8-15:(A)17.

2

[When running for Governor,] you have to make yourself physically available to people who don't usually see a Governor . . . I've been to various black organizations, black community centers, black churches that Governors, Senators, usually don't get invited to, or if they are invited, they don't accept.

The Christian Science Monitor, 8-16:28.

Karlyn Keene
Editor, "Public Opinion" magazine

3

[On the politics of the "baby boom" generation, born between 1946 and the mid-1950s]: Right now, they're in their peak child-bearing age. They've got marriages, they've got mortgages and they've got kids. And those tend to be stabilizing or conservatizing influences. They still are fairly liberal to moderate on life-style, but there's a conservatism on other matters. As Winston Churchill said, if you're not a socialist at 20 you have no heart, and if you're not a conservative by the time you're 40 you have no head.

Los Angeles Times, 8-18:(I)9.

Jack Kemp
United States Representative, R-New York; Candidate for the 1988 Republican Presidential nomination

4

When I was growing up . . . the conservative movement was essentially against things. You always knew what conservatives were against. With all due respect, we were against the Commies, we were against government, we were against spending, we were against deficits, we were against this and that, and there is nothing intellectually wrong with being against things. The Ten Commandments are against a lot of things. You need to know what you're against. But, ladies and gentlemen, you can't beat the liberals just [by] being against something. It is essential that we show people that we can be *for* them and *for* certain core principles and ideas.

Campaign speech/ The New York Times, 1-12:11.

Jack Kemp
United States Representative, R-New York; Former candidate for the 1988 Republican Presidential nomination

5

[Saying the Republican Party should go after minority voters]: Republicans many times can't get the words "equality of opportunity" out of their mouths. Their lips do not form that way.

Newsweek, 7-18:17.

6

Playing pro football gave me a good sense of perspective when I entered the political arena. I had already been booed, cheered, cut, sold, traded and hung in effigy.

Los Angeles Times, 11-10:(III)2.

Edward M. Kennedy
United States Senator,
D-Massachusetts

1

Not being a [Presidential] candidate has given me both time to spend as a legislator and . . . additional credibility as to motives. When you're a candidate and you talk about an issue, you probably get higher visibility, but you get questioning about your motivation. And when you're not [a candidate], you probably get not as high a visibility, but a greater willingness to consider the substance of the matters.

Los Angeles Times, 7-3:(I)5.

Joseph P. Kennedy III
United States Representative,
D-Massachusetts

2

It is so hard to run for public office. It is hard for me, and I am a Kennedy. You can imagine how difficult it is for someone who doesn't happen to have my money and my background and my name, and you tell them to run.

USA Today, 7-20:(A)9.

Bob Kerrey
Former Governor
of Nebraska (D);
Winner of Congressional
Medal of Honor for service
in the Vietnam war

3

[On the controversy regarding Republican Vice-Presidential nominee Dan Quayle's avoiding service in the Vietnam war by joining the National Guard]: I had a lot of friends who joined the National Guard, got married, had babies, became teachers to stay out of the draft. It's not a major event if his family [used influence to keep him out of the regular Army]. We were all avoiding the draft. Only a handful . . . were saying, "You know what I want to do next year, Bob? I want to go to Vietnam."

USA Today, 8-19:(A)2.

Paul G. Kirk, Jr.
Chairman, Democratic
National Committee

4

As a vibrant, competitive institution, the Democratic Party . . . is stronger today than it has been in modern political history. Over the past four years, we paid off our debt, we developed fully computerized voting lists, conducted in-depth polling and targeting, deployed a trained, professional party election force, increased our direct-mail capability and closed ranks with our election officials. [As a result, despite the Republicans winning the Presidency in the last three elections,] there is no Republican majority of Governors. There is no Republican House. There is no Republican Senate. There is no Republican realignment. And there is no Republican mandate.

At Democratic Party conference,
Phoenix, Nov. 18/
The Washington Post,
11-19:(A)2.

Henry A. Kissinger
Former Secretary of State of the
United States

5

. . . I am of the moderate wing of the Republican Party, which barely exists any more. Logically, one would have to say that unless there's a recession, the Republican candidate [for President in the 1988 election] will have a better chance than the Democratic candidate. On the other hand, there are some similarities with the situation in 1960 when another popular President [Dwight Eisenhower], getting on in years, was leaving office and the public was looking for a new face; that produced John Kennedy. I really think it's a very close election. The personalities of the leading candidates are not so remarkable when you consider the basic differences. Right now they're spending all their time fighting each other within each party.

Interview/
Los Angeles Times,
3-13:(V)6.

235

Andrew Kohut
President,
Gallup Organization

1

[The] Iran-contra [scandal] remains the pivotal event in the Reagan Administration that will determine whether [Vice President George] Bush gets elected [President in November]. People do want to forget Iran-contra, but it undermined a fragile confidence in government and the Administration . . . Reagan has not recovered and Bush continues to deal with the legacy of Iran-contra, [Panamanian leader] Noriega, etc. It's all indicative of one thing to people—things aren't right in Washington.

The Christian Science Monitor,
7-27:3.

Ted Koppel
Broadcast journalist,
ABC-TV

2

[Saying TV debates between Presidential nominees are too limited in format]: If we'd like to hear what's really going on in the candidates' minds, or what thoughts they really have for the economy, or defense, or the environment, then wouldn't it be wonderful if we could just let them talk, exchange views, criticize one another at length? And do it not in terms of clever one-liners that have been written by somebody else, but do it in the context of allowing the public to see what these men are really made of, what they stand for, what they think, what they believe.

Interview/
USA Today, 10-11:(A)11.

Irving Kristol
Political analyst

3

[On the forthcoming 1988 Presidential election]: I don't think Americans want a strong leader right now. That's why I think that [Vice President] George Bush will be President.

U.S. News & World Report,
2-8:63.

H. Martin Lancaster
United States Representative,
D-North Carolina

4

I think the whole fallacy of our [Presidential] nominating process is that the people who turn out to caucuses and primaries should have the final word on the nominee, when in some states only 10 or 15 per cent involve themselves in that process. In my opinion, you end up with a very skewed process . . . You do not end up with the nomination of a candidate who can win.

The Washington Post, 5-17:(A)8.

Bert Lance
Political adviser to
civil-rights leader
Jesse Jackson

5

In my judgment, Jackson's made the transition from civil-rights leader to political leader . . . That was very evident when he stepped off that bus in Atlanta [to attend the Democratic convention at which Michael Dukakis won the Party's Presidential nomination]. What Jackson is doing is not going to end. It's not going to end when we leave Atlanta. It's not going to end [after the election] in November. It's not going to end for him in January when we're successful in electing Dukakis. That's not going to end as long as Jackson is able to . . . stir people.

Interview/Newsweek, 8-1:4.

Frank R. Lautenberg
United States Senator,
D-New Jersey

6

[On complaints about "negative" political campaigning]: It's unfortunate. I hate it. But negative campaigns are the mode of the day. They're winning all over. People like them, the same way that they like wrestling and violence in the movies.

Interview/
The New York Times, 11-4:(A)13.

Mickey Leland
United States Representative,
D-Texas

1

[Civil-rights leader] Jesse [Jackson] could win [the 1988 Democratic Presidential nomination] if he was playing on a level field. He could win if people would view him for what he's worth . . . Many people treat him as a throwaway, and he is not a throwaway, because he's right on the issues. He's the most articulate candidate in the race.

Ebony, March:161.

Eddie Mahe
Republican Party political
analyst

2

The incumbent [in an election] is the product the voters are now using. If they're perfectly happy with that product, they're not going to switch. So before a challenger can get his message across, before he can even get people to pay attention to him, he has to explain why they should be dissatisfied with what they have. That means negative ads. That means bringing it down to the level where people feel they are being hurt, their safety is jeopardized, their pocketbook, something.

The New York Times, 11-4:(A)13.

Jarol Manheim
Director of political
communications, George Washington
University

3

[On election-year broadcast debates between Presidential candidates]: [Through the debates,] people learn what kind of people they are voting for. They learn about the character of the individuals, they learn about personality quirks . . . about who can deal with pressure . . . about who can think on their feet . . . about who is a nice person and who is not . . . It's not that the debates are earth-shattering events in themselves, but that they might come along at a time when anything could make just enough difference to matter.

The Christian Science Monitor,
9-9:5.

Greg Markus
Political scientist,
University of Michigan

4

[On the forthcoming Presidential election]: Political campaigns are determined not principally by campaign events, but by larger, slower-moving events: partisan strength, strength of the economy, over-all satisfaction with foreign affairs. In those terms, any Republican Presidential nominee would have had to work awfully hard to lose this election.

The Washington Post,
10-28:(A)10.

John McCain
United States Senator,
R-Arizona

5

After eight years as Vice President and a year of campaigning for the Presidency, George Bush has no real public image. Everything about him and his views is fuzzed up. We've reached the point where it's less important whether what he says and does is left, right or center; the really important thing is that he and the electorate know who he is.

Interview, Washington, Aug. 3/
The New York Times, 8-4:1.

6

The American people are very happy with what they have today. [But there is also] a great uneasiness out there, a great uncertainty as to what's going to happen in the next year or so. If we're [Republicans] going to run, as I think we are, on the peace and prosperity theme, we've got to . . . present a vision of the future that will calm those fears.

Interview, New Orleans/
The Washington Post, 8-15:(C)10.

Paul N. McCloskey, Jr.
Former United States Representative,
R-California

7

The difficulty with the Iowa [political] caucus system is that so few Iowans choose to partici-

237

(PAUL N. McCLOSKEY, JR.)

pate. Zeal and organizational skill alone can win for an otherwise unqualified candidate. Iowa demonstrates one of America's best-kept secrets—that political power goes not to the majority but to those minorities who care most.

Interview/
USA Today, 2-5:(A)12.

Robert McElvaine
Professor of history,
Millsaps College

1

[President] Reagan's legacy is the ability to create illusion and get everybody to buy it.

Newsweek, 11-21:29.

George S. McGovern
Former United States Senator,
D-South Dakota;
1972 Democratic
Presidential nominee

2

I believe that a majority of the American people now accept the views I advocated in 1972. To repudiate the McGovern Democrats in 1988 is to repudiate what is now the mainstream of the Democratic Party.

Speech/
The Washington Post,
6-22:(A)6.

Barbara A. Mikulski
United States Senator,
D-Maryland

3

We know about the enormous cost of running for the Senate—where you spend more time raising the funds. Congress should not be coin-operated. I think that the sting's going to come out of these kinds of races fairly soon and that we're going to try to change that process.

Interview/
"Ms.," September:59

Walter F. Mondale
Former Vice President of
the United States;
1984 Democratic
Presidential nominee

4

[Criticizing the 1988 Presidential-election campaign tactics of nominees George Bush and Michael Dukakis]: There is no substance. The candidates are hidden. You don't get to ask questions. The negatives have taken over . . . Politicians are permitted to throw mud from privileged sanctuaries, and the negatives are driving substance off the playing field. They can mount an attack and then not take questions about that attack. First Bush, then Dukakis. You couldn't get a hold of any of them for questioning and for context.

Interview/
The Washington Post, 11-21:(A)8.

Daniel Patrick Moynihan
United States Senator,
D-New York

5

[On the long nomination and campaign process in U.S. national elections]: The endless, debilitating ordeal denies dignity to the defeated and diminishes the stature of the victorious.

USA Today, 4-4:(A)8.

Brian Mulroney
Prime Minister of Canada

6

[On U.S. President Reagan]: Here is a guy who has just come back from the Soviet Union. He is as vigorous as you are ever going to see anyone even close to that age. He's leading the most powerful economy in the world and he's the most popular President in the recent history of the United States. Believe me, you're not talking to a lame duck [when you talk to Reagan]. You're talking to a vigorous, very dynamic guy who is in charge of his business and knows exactly what he wants to do.

Interview/
The New York Times, 6-20:7.

Nancy M. Neuman
President, League of
Women Voters

1

[On the Presidential primary-election process]:
I think it has put somewhat of a barrier between
the voter and the candidates, in that it's hard for
the voters to find out who these people are. We
are really getting packaged and managed candidates.

The Christian Science Monitor, 7-20:14.

2

[On debates her organization arranges between Presidential and Vice-Presidential candi-
dates]: The public needs a time to see the candidates when they're in a forum they cannot control. Our debates are the only events left that are
not packaged.

USA Today, 9-7:(A)10.

3

[On why her organization dropped its support
for the second 1988 Presidential debate between
the nominees, George Bush and Michael
Dukakis]: Throughout these negotiations, I
asked that the campaigns open the door to the
League. I was certain that the voters' interest
would be better served if there were a third party
in the room keeping campaign manipulations in
check. The campaigns said no, keeping the
voters' interest out of their discussion. Between
themselves, the campaigns had determined what
the television cameras could take pictures of . . .
how they would select those who would pose
questions to their candidates . . . that the press
would be relegated to the last two rows of the
hall . . . that they would pack the hall with their
supporters. The campaigns' agreement was a
closed-door masterpiece.

News conference, Oct. 3/
The Washington Post, 10-4:(A)15.

Richard M. Nixon
Former President of
the United States

4

[On the Watergate scandal of 1972]: In 1972,
we went to China. We went to Russia. We ended
the Vietnam war effectively by the end of the
year. Those were the big things. And here was
this small thing [Watergate], and we fouled it up
beyond belief. It was a great mistake. It was
wrong, as I've pointed out again and again. It was
a small thing, the break-in [at the Watergate
Democratic Party offices], and break-ins have
occurred previously in other campaigns as well.
At that point, we should have done something
about it. We should have exposed it, found out
who did it, rather than attempting to contain it, to
cover it up. It was the cover-up that was wrong,
and that was a very big thing; there's no question
about it at all.

Broadcast interview/
"Meet the Press," NBC-TV, 4-10.

5

[On a meeting he just had with Vice President-
elect Dan Quayle, who has been criticized for not
being of Vice-Presidential caliber]: This is the
first time I had a chance to have a talk with
Senator Quayle . . . I was very surprised. He is a
very different man from the intellectual midget
who has been portrayed among the media. This is
a man who has strong views. He's highly intelligent. He's highly dedicated. I think he's going to
be an excellent Vice-President.

News conference,
Washington, Nov. 21/
Los Angeles Times, 11-22:(I)2.

Peggy Noonan
Speechwriter for
Vice President, and
President-elect, of
the United States
George Bush

6

A political speech is a soliloquy, a moment of
prepared self-revelation that has no equal. I
never sit down to work on something important—
Bush's acceptance speech [for the Presidential
nomination], for example—without, quite literally, thinking: "To be or not to be."

Interview/"Ms.," December:84.

Gary Nordlinger
Democratic Party political
analyst

1

I happen to like our [Presidential] primary [election] system. It really weeds out the good candidates from the bad candidates. You have ample opportunities to make mistakes. It shows your ability to manage money, your ability to manage people and . . . get a message across, [to] sell yourself. I have a lot of respect for the American electorate, and I think that given enough time and exposure they can pretty well sense out . . . who is going to be a good office-holder and who is a fraud.

The Christian Science Monitor,
7-20:14.

Sam Nunn
United States Senator,
D-Georgia

2

[On why he declined to be considered for the Vice-Presidential slot on the ticket with 1988 Democratic Presidential nominee Michael Dukakis]: I told him that I enjoy very much what I do now. I also told him, which is something I've done a lot of thinking about, that I cherish my independence, and that's a big consideration. I'm able to say what I think is the appropriate response on national security and foreign policy, independent of who's President of the United States, and that's something from this position I can continue to do.

Washington, June 29/
The New York Times, 6-30:14

Kirk O'Donnell
Director, Center
for National Policy

3

Politics has become a marketing game of ideas where those who catch the attention of the right patron—like a Congressman, Senator, Cabinet official or even an op-ed-page editor—can prevail.

U.S. News & World Report, 2-8:58.

Norman J. Ornstein
Resident scholar, American
Enterprise Institute

4

[On George Bush's selection of Senator Dan Quayle as his Vice-Presidential running mate in the forthcoming Presidential election]: I didn't think Quayle was a serious possibility and I don't think he should have been a serious possibility. If you take any of the criteria—winning electoral votes, a signal of change, depth of experience and responsibility—he doesn't stack up. I wouldn't call him one of the 25 worst Senators, but he's certainly not in the top 25.

Aug. 16/
Los Angeles Times, 8-17:(I)5.

Gary Owen
Speaker of the Michigan
House of Representatives

5

Unfortunately, the Democratic caucus is not a good indicator of a [candidate's] popular appeal, because you are dealing [in the caucuses] with a very liberal, traditional party-type person who will go to the polls. That doesn't give a fair representation of the electability of the candidates in November.

The Christian Science Monitor, 3-25:3.

Maynard Parker
Editor, "Newsweek"
magazine

6

[In elections,] people care about issues last. When I walk into a bar or a party, people don't ask me about [candidate Gary] Hart versus [candidate Walter] Mondale on a certain issue. They ask who's ahead, what's he really like as a person, what kind of executive ability does he have.

Esquire, May:82

Dennis Patrick
Chairman, Federal
Communications Commission

7

[Saying the FCC should not regulate political-campaign TV advertising, which some people

(DENNIS PATRICK)

say has degenerated into negative mud-sling-ing]: How are we to distinguish between "un-fair" negative ads and truthful, but equally uncomplimentary, ads? Do we really want gov-ernment making these judgments?... The mes-sages [in the ads] are over-simplified, it is said. But these critics fail to appreciate that not everyone wants or needs to make a career out of the process of choosing a candidate. Because the message is simple or presented in an enter-taining way does not make it either unimportant or counter-productive. If it is misleading, it can be countered by opposing candidates, other voters, or other media.

Before American Council of
Young Political Leaders,
Washington, Nov. 9/
Daily Variety, 11-10:1,22.

Donald M. Payne
United States Representative-elect,
D-New Jersey

1

[On his winning election to Congress, after twice before having failed]: Sometimes a politi-cal leader is marching a little in front or a little behind the people. But once in a while the marcher and the drumbeat are in exactly the same cadence, and then, finally, good things happen.

Newark, N.J., Nov. 9/
The New York Times, 11-10:(A)23.

Kevin P. Phillips
Republican Party political
analyst

2

[Saying recent scandals and policies under-mine the view that the Reagan Administration has restored its credibility]: The Iran-contra affair, the decline of U.S. influence, astrology—all these prove the view to be pretty ephemeral. There were analyses in '84 that Reagan would be ranked in the second tier of U.S. Presidents. The question now is whether he's going to be in a respectable third tier.

The Christian Science Monitor, 5-10:1.

William Proxmire
United States Senator,
D-Wisconsin

3

When George Bush and Michael Dukakis are nominated [for President at their parties' conven-tions this summer], the country will have the best choice for President our country has had in this Senator's long memory... [Vice President] Bush would be the first genuine war hero who has been a candidate for President since General [Dwight] Eisenhower. Courage and patriotism should count in a President. Bush showed both as a fighter pilot in World War II. Imagine having a President who thoroughly understands the Cen-tral Intelligence Agency as only one who has run the Agency can understand it. How fortunate to have a President who has a genuine and substan-tial background in foreign policy... Michael Dukakis offers a superlative record of public ser-vice. He has what, I believe, is a rare qualifica-tion. He has been elected Governor of Massa-chusetts. Then he was defeated. After four years, he came back. He was re-elected as Governor. What I like about that record is that Dukakis knows what it means to lose. He has shown that rare and precious quality—the ability to learn from his mistakes. Unlike the reaction most of us have to defeat, Dukakis actually built on it. After his first defeat for re-election, Mike Dukakis spent four constructive years, teaching, studying, running a highly successful public-information television program... Unfortunately, the re-maining months of the 1988 campaign are likely to be marred by negative criticism of their oppo-nent by both of these good men. Criticism makes news... But the American people should not be deceived. George Bush and Michael Dukakis are two superlative candidates for President. The country will be served well by either.

Before the Senate, Washington,
July 6/
The Washington Post, 7-8:(A)22.

4

This Senator would give very strong odds that, sometime in 1989 or 1990, recession and prob-ably depression will hit. The next President and

241

(WILLIAM PROXMIRE)

his party at that time will be in a political dilemma from which there will be no escape. [If the prospective Democratic nominee Michael Dukakis wins, Democrats might be kissing] the Presidency goodbye for 40 years. Let us face it. You will not get one in 100 to admit it, but the best thing that could happen to the Democrats might be to lose the [forthcoming] Presidential election.

Interview/
The Washington Post, 7-14:(A)14.

Paul Pryde
Political analyst

1

The distinction between the liberals of today and the liberals of yesterday is that today's liberals are no longer innovators. They are the defenders of the orthodoxies. The innovators of today are likely to be the people we call neoconservatives . . . There are two groups of conservatives: those who don't want to do anything, and those who want to do things differently. That second group includes people like myself; it includes Republicans like Jack Kemp, Democrats like Doug Wilder and Chuck Robb, who say that some of the things we have tried haven't worked very well and that we need to try something different. It even includes [liberal Democrat] Jesse Jackson, who for years has been preaching an essentially conservative message of personal responsibility and economic participation. In Jesse's case, however, he sings conservative words to liberal music. Most conservatives don't have the musical ear of a Jesse Jackson.

Interview/
The Washington Post,
10-26:(A)23.

Dan Quayle
United States Senator,
R-Indiana; 1988 Republican
Vice-Presidential nominee

2

I would've been quite happy spending my life in Huntington [Indiana] in the newspaper business, watching my kids grow, seeing a community with plenty of opportunity to go around. But I looked around me in the mid-'70s and saw threats to the future of my family and to the values that could once be taken for granted in our country. Beyond my town there were communities torn by crime and drugs and there were neighborhoods where the very word "opportunity"—it didn't exist because there were no jobs. I decided to try to change these things to make opportunity replace despair and to make the future just as good as the past for the family of many Huntingtons of our great land. That was 1976, when I was first elected to the House of Representatives. But both houses of Congress and the White House were in the hands of liberal Democrats. It was a lot tougher than I ever imagined to turn my determination into reality.

Accepting the nomination, at
Republican National Convention,
New Orleans, Aug. 18/
The New York Times, 8-19:11.

3

[On criticism that he joined the National Guard to avoid combat duty during the Vietnam war]: . . . I wanted to continue my legal education as soon as possible. And as far as continuing a legal education at that time, I was willing to go forward with active duty, which was about six months, and to get into law school. And also to serve your country. And I decided to serve the country in the Indiana National Guard. I might add that I was doing that for six years. No one knew how long that Vietnam war was going to go on. and if the Vietnam war would have dragged on to '74 or '75, I was still in the Guard and I could have been called. And if my unit had been called to Vietnam, I would have been proud to go.

News conference,
Huntington, Ind., Aug. 19/
The New York Times, 8-20:8.

4

[On criticism that he joined the National Guard to avoid combat duty during the Vietnam war]: I'm not looking for any medals, [but] I served loyally. The National Guard has had

(DAN QUAYLE)

a long and distinguished history as part of America's national defense. Three hundred thousand National Guardsmen fought in World War II, 15 won the Medal of Honor, and nobody called them "weekend warriors." When I entered the Guard, I was not seeking special treatment. I wasn't looking for favors. No rules were broken. And, in the words of virtually every single person involved two decades ago, no efforts were made unfairly to influence the process . . . I served loyally and I served to the best of my ability. Nearly 20 years ago I had no reason to be ashamed of my service. And you know what? I'm sure as hell not ashamed of it now!

Before past and present
National Guard members,
St. Louis, Aug.24/
Los Angeles Times, 8-25:(I)19.

1

[On criticism that he had a mediocre school record]: Winston Churchill was not a great student, [but] he was a great leader. F.D.R. failed the bar examination a number of times, [but] he turned out to be a great President. I am not going to focus on what I've done in the past. The American people will judge me on what I say and what I have done in the last 12 years in the Congress of the United States.

News conference,
Moore, Okla., Sept. 15/
The Washington Post, 9-16:(A)16.

2

[On whether he is qualified to be Vice President]: I stand before you tonight as the most investigated person ever to seek public office. Thousands of journalists have asked every professor I've had, all my teachers, and they know, and I have never professed to be anything but an average student. I have never said that I was anything more than that. But it's not whether you're an average student, it's what are you going to do with your life. And what am I going to do with my life?—I have committed it to public service since

I was 29 years of age. Elected to the House of Representatives. Elected to the United States Senate when I was 33.

At Vice-Presidential debate,
Omaha, Neb., Oct. 5/
The New York Times, 10-7:(A)15.

3

Senator [Lloyd] Bentsen [the Democratic Vice-Presidential nominee] is the Number 1 PAC raiser. As a matter of fact, he used to have a $10,000 breakfast club. A $10,000 breakfast club! It only cost high-paid lobbyists, special interests in Washington, to come down and have breakfast with the Chairman of the Senate Finance Committee, the one that oversees all the tax loopholes in the Tax Code, $10,000. I'm sure they weren't paying to have corn flakes. But I'll tell you the kind of campaign reform I'm supporting. I think it's time that we get rid of PAC money. Support our legislation where we totally eliminate contributions by special interests and political-action committees, and let's have the individual contribute and the political parties contribute. That's the kind of campaign reform that Republicans are for.

At Vice-Presidential debate,
Omaha, Neb., Oct. 5/
The New York Times, 10-7:(A)13.

4

The question goes to whether I am qualified to be Vice President, and in the case of a tragedy whether I'm qualified to be President. Qualifications for the office of Vice President or President are not age alone . . . I will be prepared not only because of my service in the Congress but because of my ability to communicate and to lead. It is not just age, it's accomplishments, it's experience. I have far more experience than many others that sought the office of Vice President of this country. I have as much experience in the Congress as Jack Kennedy did when he sought the Presidency.

At Vice-Presidential debate,
Omaha, Neb., Oct. 5/
The New York Times, 10-7:(A)12,14.

243

(DAN QUAYLE)

1

[On Democratic Presidential nominee Michael Dukakis]: You and I know, as we listen to the man from Massachusetts, how he preaches to us and how he sort of looks down upon America. He looks down upon America because of his conceited liberal ideology ... They think they're better than we are.

Campaigning, Kankakee, Ill./
The Washington Post,
11-14:(A)19.

Dan Quayle
United States Senator,
R-Indiana;
Vice President-elect
of the United States

2

[On his upcoming role as Vice President]: I've worked with a number of conservatives in the past; a lot of good friends are conservatives. But I'm not the point man for the conservatives in this [forthcoming] Administration ... You won't see me being the so-called spear-carrier for all the so-called conservative issues. There's not a penny's worth of difference in philosophy [between himself and President-elect George Bush].

Interview, Washington, Nov. 30/
Los Angeles Times, 12-1:(I)18.

Ronald Reagan
President of the United States

3

[On his Administration, which is in its final months]: We've got a lot of work left before this old cowboy climbs up on his horse and rides into the sunset. When the credits roll up on the screen for the hit show "GOP Administration—1981 to 1989 and Beyond," the last credit will read, "Don't miss the exciting sequel: GOP House of Representatives in the '90s."

March 22/USA Today, 3-23:(A)1.

4

[Saying people are cautious in criticizing Democratic Presidential candidate Jesse Jackson on the issues, because Jackson is black]: More attention is being paid to the difference in color than is being paid to what he is actually saying. A great many of us would find ourselves in great disagreement with the policies that he is proposing, and would perhaps be more vocal about them if it wasn't for concern that that be misinterpreted into some kind of a racial attack.

Before American Society
of Newspaper Editors,
Washington, April 13/
USA Today, 4-14:(A)4.

5

Just think of the year 1979 [the last year a Democrat was President]. In that one year, Iran, Nicaragua and Grenada were all lost. Iran fell to the Ayatollah [Khomeini]. Nicaragua and Grenada were taken by Communists. In that one year, our Embassy in Iran was seized, not once, but twice. Our Ambassador to Afghanistan was assassinated by gunmen, and that country invaded by Soviet troops. Add to that the economic decay at home. That was 1979. Don't we have a right to ask the American people tonight: If the Democrats return to the White House, what happens in 1989?

At Republican Congressional
fund-raising dinner,
Washington, May 11/
The Washington Post, 5-12:(A)6.

6

[Criticizing likely Democratic Presidential nominee Massachusetts Governor Michael Dukakis]: The American people understand what liberalism means and don't like it, so our opponents plan to go to the voters incognito, and they're putting on political trench coats and sunglasses ... [But] what do you call a Governor who raises taxes $115-million and declares a victory? Out-and-out liberal ... Our opponents' candidate has fought for weekend furloughs for dangerous convicts, including drug dealers. Our candidate [Vice President George Bush] has led the fight against drug smugglers. Their candidate favors abortion on demand; our candidate is

(RONALD REAGAN)

pro-life . . . Their candidate has opposed requiring the Pledge of Allegiance and allowing prayer in schools. Our candidate, well, he and I both find it hard to believe that anyone could take these positions.

At Grassroots Conservative
Conference, Washington, July 5/
Los Angeles Times, 7-6:(I)5.

1

Like so many of us [Republicans] . . . I started out in the other party [the Democratic Party]. But 40 years ago, I cast my last vote as a Democrat. It was a party in which F.D.R. promised the return of power to the states. It was a party where Harry Truman committed a strong and resolute America to preserving freedom. F.D.R. had run on a platform of eliminating useless boards and commissions and returning autonomy to local governments and to the states. That party changed, and it will never be the same. They left *me*. I didn't leave *them*. So it was our Republican Party that gave me a political home. When I signed up for duty, I didn't have to check my principles at the door. And I soon found that the desire for victory did not overcome our devotion to ideals.

At Republican National
Convention, New Orleans,
Aug.15/The Washington Post,
8-16:(A)21.

2

[Endorsing Vice President George Bush for the 1988 Republican Presidential nomination]: It will take someone who has seen this office from the inside, who senses the danger points, will be cool under fire and knows the range of answers when the tough questions come. That's the George Bush I've seen up close, when the staff and Cabinet members have closed the door and when the two of us are alone. Someone who's not afraid to speak his mind and who can cut to the core of an issue. Someone who never runs away from a fight, never backs away from his beliefs and never makes excuses.

At Republican National
Convention, New Orleans,
Aug. 15/The Washington Post,
8-16:(A)21.

3

[On the campaign of Democratic Presidential nominee Michael Dukakis]: Up until Sunday, the opposition objected to being called liberal. Not because it was false, but because it was true. Now they've come clean; they admit it. They're liberals . . . Their views can only be described by the dreaded L-word: liberal, liberal, liberal.

At rally, Reno, Nev., Nov. 1/
Los Angeles Times, 11-2:(I)15.

4

[On the current Democratic Party control of the Senate]: I wish we [Republicans] could have regained control of this body. But I believe that it won't be too long before the Republicans win control of the Congress, the same way we keep winning the White House. Sooner or later, the other party is going to have to take the hint and put themselves out of their misery.

At dinner for Republican Senators,
Washington, Nov. 29/
The New York Times, 11-30:(A)12.

Donald T. Regan
Former Chief of Staff to
President of the United States
Ronald Reagan

5

[Saying he knew President Reagan would be furious at his new book which says the President and the First Lady consult an astrologer when making important decisions]: That [Reagan's anger] was not my concern. My concern was to get my story out truthfully and wholly, which I submit I have done. I have not attacked his wife. Certainly to paint an accurate picture is not to attack. Did anyone think of my wife's feelings when I was being stabbed in the back by all this

WHAT THEY SAID IN 1988

innuendo [when he was fired]? No one thought of my feelings. Why am I supposed to be the one who agrees to play victim and doesn't retaliate? ... I submit that I didn't set the time for my leaving this Administration, or the conditions under which I left this Administration. Accordingly, I then thought I was free to write about this Administration. I know of no rule that says you wait until the President is absolutely finished, and he writes, his wife writes and then you take your turn.

Interview, Alexandria, Va., May 9/
Los Angeles Times, 5-10:(I)1.

Ann Richards
State Treasurer of Texas

1

[Vice President and Republican Presidential candidate] George Bush and [President] Ronald Reagan have one serious problem in common—bad memory. Reagan can't remember selling arms to the [Iranian] Ayatollah, and neither can Bush. But Bush has got it worse. He can't recall a thing he said when he ran against Reagan eight years ago. All that talk about voodoo economics has just sort of faded into the fog. It's like [the late House Speaker] Sam Rayburn said: "If you can tell the truth the first time, you don't have to remember what you said."

At Texas Democratic
State Convention/
Los Angeles Times, 7-18:(I)4.

Charles S. Robb
Chairman, Democratic
Leadership Council;
Former Governor of
Virginia (D)

2

I talk to all of the candidates [for President in the 1988 elections], on both sides of the aisle, and they'll come back from [campaigning in] Iowa and they'll say, "You can't believe the kind of demands—non-negotiable demands—that I was presented with by X, Y or Z group. I say to them,

if you yield to the kind of pressure that you are receiving, all I can do is suggest the same thing is going to happen to you that happened to [former Vice President Walter] Fritz Mondale—a very decent, honorable, capable man. But the public perception of him [as the 1984 Democratic Presidential nominee] was ... that he was beholden [to special interests]. He lost his individual identity. It is my view that the American people [are] inherently distrustful of the accumulation of too much power in any single individual or interest group in [the election] process.

Interview/
The Christian Science Monitor,
1-19:6.

Cokie Roberts
Political correspondent,
National Public Radio

3

The South has become the swing area in Presidential campaigns. The popular wisdom is that for the Democrats to win the Presidency, they have to win the South. That's what they keep trying to figure out a way to do.

Interview/USA Today, 3-8:(A)11.

Pat Robertson
Candidate for the
1988 Republican
Presidential nomination;
Former evangelist

4

I'm very, very proud of the fact that I'm a strong believer in God and in the Bible. I don't ever want to play that down. But I am running for Chief Executive of the United States, not chief pastor.

Greer, S.C./Newsweek, 2-29:18.

Michael J. Robinson
Associate professor
of government,
Georgetown University

5

[On a movement to draft former President Jimmy Carter to run for the 1988 Democratic

(MICHAEL J. ROBINSON)

Presidential nomination]: If Carter were to announce, he might quickly emerge as a challenge to Gary Hart [who re-entered the race after withdrawing because of a sex scandal] as phantom front-runner. But Gary hart is more likely to emerge as winner, because when push comes to shove, the public still prefers a scoundrel to a fool.

USA Today, 1-8:(A)4.

Ed Rollins
Republican Party political
analyst

1

[On Vice President and 1988 Republican Presidential nominee George Bush]: If George Bush gets in a slashing knockdown campaign [for the Presidency], particularly with the problems that he has with the gender gap today—women voters like negative campaigns even less than men voters do—I think it will turn some people off . . . If he does go out and define a strong persona, that may be sufficient to turn some of [his negatives] around. If he doesn't, and the little characters that [cartoonists] Herblock and Gary Trudeau and others have made of him [leave] the impression that he is a silly man . . . then it is going to be very, very hard . . . to get this race back on track.

Interview, New Orleans/
Newsweek, 8-29:5.

Warren B. Rudman
United States Senator,
R-New Hampshire

2

Do I think that [Senate minority leader] Bob Dole and [President-elect] George Bush will ever have the warm personal relationship that Howard Baker had with Ronald Reagan? No. Bob Dole is not a person that has a lot of warm personal relationships. They will not ever become great and fast friends, but they'll become solid political allies.

The New York Times, 11-28:(A)10.

Larry J. Sabato
Professor of government,
University of Virginia

3

[On charges of dirty campaigning in the current Presidential race]: Presidential elections in the 1800s were far more personal and vicious than this one. And 1988 is not particularly negative compared to 1964 [the Johnson-Goldwater race] . . . The root cause of all this disaffection is the candidates' focusing on nitpicking issues, rather than root issues like the budget deficit. Why aren't the candidates discussing the root issues? Because voters are not in a mood to hear what needs to be done. You cannot blame a candidate for not talking about solutions to issues that will result in his defeat.

Interview/
The Christian Science Monitor,
10-12:6.

4

[On Democratic Presidential nominee Michael Dukakis, who is trailing in the polls]: Dukakis is just all over television now. [In 1968, Democrat Hubert] Humphrey was desperate for TV time. He also made the rounds and grabbed for every free minute of TV time. It helped Humphrey close the gap. But two conditions were present then that aren't present now. Then, many Americans still had a relatively strong Democratic Party identification; and secondly, Humphrey was selling a product that many people still wanted to buy, New Deal liberalism. That's the difference. Now the Party is much weaker and New Deal liberalism is passé . . . The problem is you have to have something to sell that people want to buy. And [Dukakis'] fundamental problem seems to be that people don't want to buy what Dukakis is selling.

The New York Times, 10-28:(A)11.

Paul S. Sarbanes
United States Senator,
D-Maryland

5

I don't think that politics ought to be a sort of highly emotional-charged context at all times,

(PAUL S. SARBANES)

although on occasions it's important to have emotion. But the democratic system depends in part on a reasoned discourse, a rational exchange. The most successful user of emotion in politics in the 20th century was probably Hitler, and look what he did. That's not to reject the need for emotion in politics, but it's to point out some of the dangers of it.

The Washington Post, 2-22:(A)6.

Jonas Savimbi
*Leader, National Union
for the Total
Independence of Angola*

1

The art of politics is not to believe what your friends tell you, but to understand what they cannot tell you.

*Interview/
The Wall Street Journal,
12-12:(A)10.*

Richard Scammon
Public-opinion analyst

2

[On the current Presidential campaigns]: This is the game of the 50 million. You've got to get 50 million people to vote for you, come November. You cannot get 50 million Americans to vote for you on a concrete, specific, 28-[point] program. You are necessitously in the ambivalent middle, simply because that's where the people are.

*The Christian Science Monitor,
8-25:3.*

William Donald Schaefer
Governor of Maryland (D)

3

I am a Democrat and I support the Democratic Party, but ... because of the absolute importance of selecting the right person for President, I don't think [voters] should be bound to vote just because they happen to be Democrats or Republicans. Now, that I don't guess is the answer a

total party loyalist would give, but I feel very strongly about it.

The Washington Post, 7-20:(A)22.

Helmut Schmidt
*Publisher, "Die Zeit" (West
Germany); Former
Chancellor of
West Germany*

4

With its [Presidential] political campaign, America could become mired in impossible promises in 1988. What bothers me most is the prospect that the new President will have talked so much about what he is going to do, and the additional welfare he will provide, that he will find it very difficult, first, to understand how much nonsense he has been talking; second, to take the decisions to change course; and third, to convince his followers.

*Interview, Bonn/
U.S. News & World Report,
1-11:39.*

John Sears
*Manager of Ronald Reagan's
1976 Presidential
campaign*

5

[On Presidential-election campaigns]: Once the process starts, you don't get many questions about what your stands on the issues are because the interest of the press becomes much more pronounced on the question of who is winning and who is losing, and which part of the press can indicate that first. That, particularly, is the influence of television.

Esquire, May:82.

Paul Simon
*United States Senator,
D-Illinois;
Candidate for the 1988
Democratic Presidential
nomination*

6

This [Presidential] election is not about fancy television commercials, not even about election

(PAUL SIMON)

speeches. In this election we ought to be looking for three factors—consistency, judgment and trust. Consistency is not just what we say today about where we stand. But where we have been through the years.

Campaign speech,
Goose Lake, Iowa, March 31/
The Washington Post, 2-2:(A)7.

Alan K. Simpson
United States Senator,
R-Wyoming

1

[On 1988 Republican Presidential nominee George Bush]: The folks at this [Republican National] Convention have come here saying, "Oh boy, this time we can take [Democratic Presidential nominee Michael] Dukakis apart" or "The issues are on our side. The economy is on our side. Peace is breaking out all over." Very few are saying, "We believe in our candidate. We want George Bush in the White House."

Interview, New Orleans/
Newsweek, 8-29:5.

Stuart Spencer
Republican political-campaign
adviser

2

[On the forthcoming Presidential election]: Republicans have been in power eight years. Things are relatively good in the country. We're at peace. The economy is going well. People should be happy. But we've also been in power for eight years. The American people have this thing about change. They like to keep everybody honest. So I'm a firm believer that [even] with things as good as they are today—particularly overseas—it's not helping [Republican Presidential nominee George] Bush. If there is a real threat overseas and George Bush was perceived as the person with the most experience, compared to a Governor of Massachusetts [his opponent Michael Dukakis], then it would play to his

advantage . . . This election is going to get down to who makes the last mistake.

Interview/
The Washington Post, 9-13:(C)4.

Robert S. Strauss
Former chairman,
Democratic National
Committee

3

[On Republican Vice President George Bush's chances of winning the Presidency in 1988]: George doesn't have any enemies. I'm his friend. But that doesn't mean he should be President. I've got a lot of friends in the scientific community, but I've never been nominated to be a rocket scientist . . . George has had a hard time, because when he gets excited his voice rises a little and gets squeaky. The Republicans are having a dickens of a time trying to figure out what to do with George Bush to make him look Presidential . . . It has nothing to do with character or personality. It's just that George is George, and he will always be George.

To reporters, May 5/
The New York Times, 5-6:9.

4

[On the forthcoming Presidential election]: This is not going to be a campaign of great macro issues. My judgment is that people are not interested in hearing these candidates talk—unhappily—about nuclear war. Their eyes glaze over when you talk about the [Federal budget] deficit . . . This is going to be a campaign where people are thinking of "what affects my life," and that goes to drugs, the ability to walk the streets at night, potholes . . . education of their children.

The Washington Post, 7-18:(A)1.

5

[On recent Republican Presidential-election victories]: The Republicans seem to have had the ability since 1980 to press a button and bring out the old pros who are good, who know what they are doing. The Democrats press the button and we reinvent the wheel.

The Christian Science Monitor, 9-21:5.

Studs Terkel
Author
1

[Saying he would do away with TV campaign ads for political candidates]: The very idea that the guy who has dough to spend [on TV ads] can beat the guy who hasn't the dough makes a mockery of what our country is about. All the cosmetics have to go... all the mascara of politics, the pomade and the powder. Let's see the face.

Interview, Chicago/
TV Guide, 6-11:3.

Margaret Thatcher
Prime Minister of
the United Kingdom
2

[On politics]: You really have to think out what you believe and why you believe it. Some think politics is only public relations. That is just the packaging. You first have to get the content right.

Interview, London/
USA Today, 9-2:(A)1.

James R. Thompson
Governor of Illinois (R)
3

[On criticism that 1988 Republican Presidential nominee George Bush is too elite]: Nobody [but Bush] in this campaign has been dogged by *Burke's Peerage.* Now, what's he supposed to do? I suppose if you want to be fair, go back and find a horse thief in his background somewhere and then everything will be equal again ... He should leave [his image] alone. Walking around talking about eating pork rinds is not leaving it alone.

Interview, New Orleans/
Newsweek, 8-29:5.

Mario Vargas Llosa
Peruvian author
4

[Politics] brings out the worst in people. Power awakens the worst appetites. You take a position inspired by ideals and suddenly you see the interests that are really at stake. You also soon discover that loyalty is not an unlimited human quality.

Interview, Lima, Peru/
The New York Times, 8-29:4.

C. William Verity, Jr.
Secretary of Commerce of
the United States
5

I am an activist. I believe strongly in this President [Reagan], what he's been trying to do. I think he's done a marvelous job in setting the nation on a course of confidence in itself, creating a new entrepreneurial spirit ... This Administration, whether they felt that way all along—and I think they probably did—there isn't any question in my mind now that this Administration stands for business, industry, labor, education, all working together, to tackle the truly difficult problems.

Interview/
The New York Times, 1-20:10.

Kathy M. Vick
Member, Democratic
National Committee
6

[On the string of Democratic Party Presidential-election losses]: The key question is why is it we can elect people to every office in the land except for President. Is our nominating process flawed? Are we delivering the wrong message? Or are we not delivering the right message well?

The New York Times, 11-11:(A)10.

Richard Viguerie
Political analyst
7

[On civil-rights leader Jesse Jackson's bid this year for the Democratic Presidential nomination]: This year, Jesse Jackson has dominated the media and intimidated the Party. They are afraid to tell him to shut up and sit down. If he were white, with those pro-Soviet foreign policy,

(RICHARD VIGUERIE)

pro-homosexual and pro-socialist economic views, he wouldn't get the time of day. Jackson is bordering on being a disaster for the Democrats. He is great theatre but bad politics. For every vote he inspires, he will turn off 10.

Interview/USA Today, 7-21:(A)9.

Carl Wagner
Democratic Party political
analyst

1

[On Gary Hart's decision to re-enter the race for the 1988 Democratic Presidential nomination after having withdrawn last year because of a sex scandal]: Can a man with negatives of huge proportions turn them around? Can a guy who is completely rejected by the establishment of his party win? Can a guy who everybody in the other party would love to run against win the nomination? Yes, he can. His name is Ronald Reagan, and he did it in 1980, even though he had negatives in January that were pretty close to what Hart has now. He won because he had an agenda people could buy.

The Washington Post, 1-12:(A)5.

Vin Weber
United States Representative,
R-Minnesota

2

The dislike [by Republicans] of [former House Speaker "Tip"] O'Neill was ideological. He was really the symbol of Northeastern liberalism. The dislike of [current] Speaker [Jim] Wright is different. Republicans think he is basically and fundamentally unfair; that he does not have the respect for the institution like Tip; that deep down he is a mean-spirited person, ruthless in the truest sense of the word.

The New York Times, 3-16:28.

Fred Wertheimer
President, Common Cause

3

[Criticizing the donations of "soft money" in Presidential campaigns, money given by backers

to state parties which legally skirts direct-donation limitations but which benefits the candidates anyway]: Soft money allows a Presidential campaign to raise campaign contributions that the Presidential campaign finance law was enacted to ban. It opens the door for "fat cats" and special-interest givers to provide large sums of money to help a Presidential candidate, and thereby creates the opportunity for these givers to buy influence with the President of the United States.

News conference, Aug. 4/
Los Angeles Times, 8-5:(I)14.

4

The PAC-rigged system for financing Congressional elections is creating a challenger-proof House of Representatives. When House incumbents can't lose, regardless of performance, and House challengers can't win, regardless of talent, then we don't have real elections and we don't have representative government.

Newsweek, 11-14:22.

John White
Former chairman,
Democratic National Committee

5

[On Presidential candidate Jesse Jackson]: [His is] not a radical message. It's not a left-wing message. It's the same message that Harry Truman had. The same message that John Kennedy had. The same message that Lyndon Johnson had. And the same message that Jimmy Carter had—like human rights and civil rights and economic progress for have-nots of this country. And that's not radical. That's not liberal. That's the main core of the Democratic Party.

To reporters/
The Christian Science Monitor, 3-31:6.

Charles Whitehead
Chairman, Democratic Party
of Florida

6

I would be less than honest with you if I didn't tell you there is absolutely an awful lot of apprehension out there among an awful lot of Democrats about the [possible] nomination of [civil-rights leader] Jesse Jackson [as the 1988 Democratic Presidential nominee]. Sure there is. They're afraid of nominating someone that they consider unelectable.

Washington, March 30/
The New York Times, 3-31:11.

William Winpisinger
President, International Association
of Machinists
and Aerospace Workers

1

[Placing in nomination civil-rights leader Jesse Jackson for the 1988 Democratic Presidential spot]: . . . I stand before you tonight to place in nomination the name of that one person in this vast nation of ours who has roused the moral conscience of the populace and our Party, a man who has shown us the way to thaw the ice of indifference, smug self-satisfaction and meanness that too long has masked the heartbeat of America. A man who has ignited the fires of passion, the fires of justice in our souls as no other contemporary has. A man who has dared to sound our call to greatness. He has brought us together here in the phoenix of Atlanta, amidst the smouldering ruins of two decades of defeat, challenging the Democratic Party to reclaim its heritage and rainbow identity. He has brought us together on the common ground of conscience, passion, equality, justice, economics, political and social justice for all. He is the personification of feeling and reason united.

At Democratic National Convention,
Atlanta, July 20/
The New York Times, 7-21:10.

Jim Wright
United States Representative,
D-Texas

2

[On the election of Republican George Bush as the next President]: This is the first time in 80 years—since 1908—that the American people have elected a President of one party while enlarging the majority for the other party [the Democrats] in both House and Senate and in Governors' offices throughout the country. And so, if there is any clear mandate, perhaps the American people are telling both parties—both President and Congress—to work together to achieve those things that so desperately need to be done for our whole country . . . So, for today, let's lay aside those things that have divided us and think instead upon those bigger things that unite us. In these areas in which we already agree, let's come together quickly and get the job done! In those areas where we may disagree, let us start by opening the doors of our minds to the search for common ground.

Broadcast address to the nation,
Nov. 12/The Wall Street Journal,
11-30:(A)16.

Daniel Yankelovich
Public-opinion analyst

3

[On Jesse Jackson's run for the Presidency in 1988]: . . . a lot of people will engage in an elaborate rationalization, and disguise their true feelings by saying that they would gladly vote for a qualified black but not for Jackson, despite the credible mainstream campaign he's waged this year. And this tendency is, I think, especially true among the two groups the Democrats must capture to regain the White House—independent voters and blue-collar white Southern Democrats.

U.S. News & World Report, 5-9:14.

Andrew Young
Mayor of Atlanta

4

Unfortunately, to win an election you have to go after the sheep that are lost, in Biblical terms. How do you do that without alienating those who stayed in the Party? That's the [Democrats'] current problem [in the forthcoming Presidential election].

Interview, Atlanta/
Los Angeles Times, 7-19:(V)2.

Social Welfare

Henry Aaron
Economist, Brookings
Institution

1

The baby-boom generation is not going to impose burdens on future workers through Social Security, because today's workers are paying a fair price for the benefits they will receive. Consequently, no basis exists for cutting Social Security benefits on the grounds that they will be excessively burdensome in the future.

Before National Academy of
Social Insurance, Dec. 15/
The Washington Post, 12-26:(A)25.

Abel Aganbegyan
Director, economic section,
Soviet Academy of Sciences;
Chief economic advisor to
Soviet leader Mikhail Gorbachev

2

Under the current Soviet reforms, our social guarantees will be preserved, but a welfare mentality will be discouraged. The welfare mentality does not make people work harder or produce goods of better quality. Rather, it impedes the growth of society's wealth.

Interview/
World Press Review, January:17.

Douglas Besharov
Analyst, American
Enterprise Institute

3

If you believe that work and responsibility is good and positive, you have to give [President] Ronald Reagan credit for some of the change in attitudes and behavior. He'll be criticized for the fact that benefits have not increased. But even Congressional Democrats are not talking about increasing benefits, and that's a part of his legacy—the turnaround from cash maintenance to what someday will be educational work programs.

The Christian Science Monitor, 11-15:16.

Barry Bosworth
Economist, Brookings
Institution

4

Social Security has always been a pay-as-you-go system, but now we need to think of it more like a pension, in which we prudently invest money now, so we won't have to raise taxes so much on workers in the future. Putting the trust fund off-budget would foster that approach.

Los Angeles Times, 5-22:(I)28.

George Bush
Vice President of the United States;
Candidate for the
1988 Republican
Presidential nomination

5

There are those who need help; there are those who have been hurt. And as far as I'm concerned, we will never be a truly prosperous nation until all within it prosper... When wealth becomes an end in itself, our economic triumph becomes hollow... Prosperity with a purpose means helping your brothers and sisters—whoever they are, wherever they are, whatever their needs.

Los Angeles Times, 1-3:(I)1.

6

The suggestion that you have to be born poor to understand poor people is absolutely offensive to me in terms of our way of life in this country.

Interview, Washington/
The Christian Science Monitor,
1-7:5.

7

[Advocating a tax-credit plan for child care and opposing a large Federal child-care program proposed by the Democrats]: I am abso-

(GEORGE BUSH)

lutely convinced the problem is so big and so diverse that the Federal government alone cannot have a bricks-and-mortar child-care program that's going to be effective. You have to have choice, parental choice, family choice, and you have to have diversity.

Campaigning, Virginia, July 29/
Los Angeles Times, 7-30:(I)18.

George Bush
Vice President of the United States;
1988 Republican Presidential nominee

1

Think of the children you know. They're not the hollow-eyed children of the ghetto. They live in warm, well-lit homes and they have clothes to wear and more good food than they choose to eat. Some, perhaps many, have $40 jeans and $50 sneakers. We've showered our children with material things and still we have a sense of unease. Do they know they're fortunate? Do they know it wasn't always like this for America—or for mankind in general? Do they have a sense of thanks? Of citizenship? Do they realize that perhaps they ought to be thinking of giving something back? Or are they cut off from their affluence, removed from the cares and concerns of others?

Before Comstock Club,
Sacramento, Calif., Oct. 4/
The Washington Post, 10-5:(A)16.

John Cogan
Former Associate Director, Federal
Office of Management and Budget

2

[On the increasing Social Security fund reserves and the possibility that Congress may dip into them for an additional source of revenues]: There is tremendous confusion over this issue, which is *the* budget dilemma of the 1990s. There are good reasons why we should be accumulating Social Security reserves, but I'm skeptical that Congress will ever be able to resist the tremendous political pressure to spend the surplus.

Los Angeles Times, 5-22:(I)1.

Mario M. Cuomo
Governor of New York (D)

3

A staggering number of our children are under-educated, under-fed... Unless we act, many more of today's youth, the work-force of the 21st century, will not be able to do the work. If compassion were not enough to encourage our attention to the plight of our children, self-interest should be.

State of the State address,
Albany, N.Y., Jan. 6/
The Washington Post, 1-7:(A)21.

Robert J. Dole
United States Senator,
R-Kansas;
Candidate for the 1988
Republican Presidential nomination

4

I believe I'm a good conservative Republican. I understand the need for government restraint. But I also understand we have an obligation to some people who are down and out or who are left out. Maybe they get food stamps... Maybe they're cold. Maybe they're hungry. But in America, we're going to provide for people who can't do it themselves.

Los Angeles Times, 1-23:(I)25.

Michael S. Dukakis
Governor of Massachusetts (D);
Candidate for the
1988 Democratic
Presidential nomination

5

As President, I will not accept an America where some people do well, while others are left behind. As President, I will not settle for a country where some regions and communities are full of opportunity for our workers and farmers, while others are shrugged off as inevitable casualties of change. As President, I will not buy into the belief that Americans who have been left behind deserve their hardship; that they do not want to lift themselves out of poverty and become self-sufficient citizens. We know better. As Presi-

(MICHAEL S. DUKAKIS)

dent, I want to be a force for positive change. I don't want to go to the Oval Office to put my feet up. I want to roll my sleeves up and go to work.

Campaign speech/
The New York Times, 1-4:9

1

[On pending child-care legislation]: Just one word from the President [Reagan], I think, would get this bill passed and done before the [forthcoming Presidential] election, and get it off the table as a partisan issue and get going. He keeps telling us stories about California, and we're trying to explain to him that the vast majority of people on welfare these days are single mothers with young children, and it's a combination of real training for real jobs, combined with day care, that makes a difference.

To reporters, Washington, Feb. 22/
The Washington Post, 2-23:(A)3.

Michael S. Dukakis
Governor of Massachusetts (D);
1988 Democratic Presidential nominee

2

What are our values? Isn't it providing housing for families of low and moderate income? Isn't it making possible for young families, first-time home buyers, to own their own home someday, something that's part of the American dream? I think so. You know, back after World War II, when we had hundreds of thousands of GIs who came back from the war, we didn't sit around; we went out and built housing. The government was very much involved; so was the housing industry; so was the banking industry; so were housing advocates; so were non-profit agencies; so were Governors and Mayors and people all over this country who believed deeply in home ownership and affordable housing. Now, that's the kind of leadership that I want to provide as President of the United States. This isn't a question of a little charity for the homeless; this is a question of organizing the housing community.

At Presidential debate,
Winston-Salem, N.C., Sept. 25/
The New York Times, 9-26:11

Robert Greenstein
Director,
Center on Budget
and Policy Priorities

3

Many of the states with large holes in their safety nets [for the poor] are outside the South, traditionally the area with the weakest programs; and some are states that rank in the top half of states in per capita income levels, such as Colorado, Florida, Nevada, Ohio, Hawaii, Illinois, Missouri, New Hampshire and Virginia. These findings indicate that serious weaknesses in the safety net are widespread.

May 18/
The Washington Post,
5-19:(A)22.

4

The [economic] data show that the recovery is increasingly leaving the poor behind. While unemployment rates returned to the levels of 1978, poverty levels are far higher than the 11.4 per cent figure for that year, and 8 million more Americans are poor. One of every three blacks and one of every two young black children now are poor, according to the Census Bureau report. And the typical poor family fell further below the poverty line in 1987 than in any year since 1960. The gap between rich and poor families is now at its widest level in 40 years.

Aug. 31/
The Washington Post,
9-1:(A)6.

William Handel
Director, Center for Surrogate
Parenting, Beverly Hills, Calif.

5

Surrogate parenting is going to continue, it is going to grow, because Number 1, it works, Number 2, it is a necessary alternative for people who otherwise cannot obtain a child, and Number 3, no one loses. The surrogate mothers walk out fulfilled and satisfied, as, of course, do the parents who now have a child. Keep in mind that there have only been six women in the history of surrogacy that have changed their minds and

(WILLIAM HANDEL)

tried to take the baby back, out of almost a thousand babies.

Interview/USA Today, 2-8:(A)15.

Dorcas R. Hardy
Commissioner, Social Security Administration of the United States

1

[Criticizing legal limitations on outside earnings by Social Security recipients]: Many older Americans who want to continue working—who want to continue being active, productive members of our society—are being penalized by their government for no good reason other than the fact that, in addition to working, they happen to be over 65 and eligible for Social Security. I believe the earnings penalty is antiquated and that it should be eliminated.

Before House Social Security Subcommittee, Washington, Sept. 29/ Los Angeles Times, 9-30:(I)4.

Martin Hoffman
Chairman, department of psychology, New York University

2

[On street beggars in New York]: With beggars, my observation is that the vast majority of New Yorkers have become habituated to them, have made them just another part of the scenery, so they no longer look at them or give them money. But even if you are habituated, it has some psychological cost. I don't think people feel nothing. A tiny little low-scale war is going on inside. Sometimes it comes out as anger.

The New York Times, 7-29:12.

Jesse L. Jackson
Civil-rights leader; Candidate for the 1988 Democratic Presidential nomination

3

When the family farm is auctioned, the lights go out. When the plant gate closes on the workers, the lights go out. When you cannot get into the hospital because you don't have insurance, and almost 40 million people do not, the lights go out. And when the lights go out, you can't use color for a crutch, because everybody looks amazingly similar in the dark, when the lights go out. For many people, the lights have been turned out. And the only way to get those lights back on is for people to come together, and together move toward economic justice. Move toward raising minimum wage; move toward comparable worth for women; move toward day-care centers for children; move toward rebuilding and building affordable housing. The people must make that kind of demand for economic justice.

Interview/ The Christian Science Monitor, 3-3:13.

4

Where is the incentive [for welfare recipients] to work when nearly one-half of the new jobs created since 1979 pay less than $7,400 per year? An economy which dashes opportunity is a root cause of babies making babies and children losing hope and choosing dope.

The Christian Science Monitor, 4-15:3.

5

. . . most poor people are not on welfare. They work every day. They take the early bus. They work every day. They care for other people's babies and they can't watch their own. They cook other people's food and carry leftovers home. They work every day. They are janitors running the buffing machines. They are nurses and orderlies wiping the bodies of the sick. A loaf of bread is no cheaper for them than it is for the doctor. They work every day. They put on uniforms and are considered less than a person: "Hey, you, maid." They work every day. They change beds in the hotels. Sweep our streets. Clean the schools for our children. They're called lazy, but they work every day. They work in the hospitals. They mop the floors. They clean

(JESSE L. JACKSON)

out the commodes, the bed pans. They work every day. No job is beneath them. And yet, when they get sick, they cannot afford to lie in the bed they've made up every day.

Campaign speech/
The Washington Post, 4-18:(A)10.

1

You see me on TV running for President and you say, "He does not care. He does not understand my situation". . . I do understand. Born in a three-room house. Parents did not have health insurance. I understand. Bathroom on the back porch. Slop jar by the bed. I understand. Had to hang clothes on nail. I understand. Wallpaper used for windbreaker, not decoration. I understand. Had to stand by an open stove to get heat. I really do understand. Could not eat turkey at 3 o'clock on Thanksgiving Day because Mama was preparing someone else's turkey at 3. . . I really do understand.

At North Carolina A&T State
University commencement, May 8/
The New York Times, 5-9:10.

John E. Jacob
President, National
Urban League

2

[On the Reagan Administration]: We've had a disastrous eight-year experiment with government withdrawal from solutions to the problems of black people, poor people and the cities. That experiment failed. It helped deepen the problems, not solve them. Government has a role to play today, just as it did when it created a white middle-class with the GI Bill, FHA and VA lending programs, and a host of other steps that largely ended white poverty. Today, it has to act again, with full-employment programs that reach the underclass, with welfare reform that encourages work, with education aid that gives the disadvantaged access to the mainstream, and with programs that stimulate the urban economy.

News conference, May 5/
The Washington Post, 5-6:(A)9.

Jack Kemp
United States Representative,
R-New York

3

The Democrats measure compassion by how many people receive government assistance. We [Republicans] measure compassion by how few *need* it.

At Republican National Convention,
New Orleans, Aug. 15/
USA Today, 8-16:(A)3.

4

[On his forthcoming role as HUD Secretary]: I want to wage war on poverty. I don't want to wage war on Congress. I don't want to wage war on programs that can work. And I don't believe we're going to balance the [Federal] budget by cutting housing.

News conference,
Washington, Dec. 19/
Los Angeles Times, 12-20:(I)20.

Edward I. Koch
Mayor of New York

5

If we were required to do away with rent control, I honestly believe that there would be people thrown out on the street—not people who are in abject poverty, but middle-class people who could not afford to pay the rent. It's not rent control that prevents new construction of housing; it is the high cost of housing construction, which has nothing to do with rent control.

New York, Jan. 7/
The New York Times, 1-8:9.

6

[Criticizing a court ruling striking down an anti-loitering law that would have affected homeless people]: These homeless people, you can tell who they are. They're sitting on the floor, occasionally defecating, urinating, talking to themselves—many, not all, but many—or panhandling. We thought it would be reasonable for the authorities to say, "You can't stay here unless

(EDWARD I. KOCH)

you're here for transportation [if they are in a train station]." Reasonable, rational people would come to that conclusion, right? Not the Court of Appeals. The Court of Appeals said: "No. How do you know they're not there shopping?"

Before American Institute of Architects,
New York, May 18/
The New York Times, 5-19:15.

1

In most cases, in my judgment, the money you give in the street to beggars goes for booze and drugs. The best thing you can do is to give the money to a church or the Salvation Army or a legitimate agency that will then use the money for a good purpose. If you want a job, a job is available. A lot of people don't want a job. They just want to sponge off society. . . We're easy marks.

To reporters, New York, Aug. 10/
The Washington Post, 8-11:(A)3.

Richard D. Lamm
Former Governor
of Colorado (D)

2

Poverty in America wears a diaper much more often than it wears a hearing aid. Money desperately needed by poor kids is going to rich elderly. . . The myth is that people get their money back from Social Security. Not true. You get somebody else's money back. This is an intergenerational transfer. The elderly are 12 per cent of America, and they get 56 per cent of Federal entitlements. A compassionate and equitable society does not spend such a disproportionate amount on the elderly while it's abandoning a bunch of kids.

Interview/USA Today, 10-20:(A)7.

Patrick J. Leahy
United States Senator,
D-Vermont

3

I have seen poverty in the Third World that was worse than any I have seen in the United States. But the sense of hopelessness that I encountered in the South Bronx [New York] was as deep as any that I have encountered in South America. Thirteen million children in the richest, most powerful nation in the world live in poverty. Forty per cent of the poor in America are children. . . We have a moral obligation to find solutions. . . The moral issue is very, very clear. We must find solutions.

The Washington Post, 4-18:(A)13.

4

[Applauding the Senate's approval of a $1.5-billion expansion of Federal nutrition programs]: It's a great thing. The Senate, at least, has faced up to what I regard as a moral responsibility. There are no votes in it for anybody. One-fourth of the children in this country are poor—and they don't vote. And 40 per cent of the money in this bill goes to children. . . Since coming here 14 years ago, I've seen hunger as more of a moral issue than a political issue.

Washington, July 26/
The Washington Post, 7-27:(A)21.

Irene Levine
Associate director, program
for the homeless mentally ill,
National Institute of
Mental Health

5

At Federal, state and local levels, mental-health and housing authorities vociferously argue that someone else should have the major responsibility for providing services to the homeless mentally ill.

U.S. News & World Report,
2-29:35.

Beryl Levinger
Deputy executive director,
CARE

6

I would never tell a fellow citizen, "Don't support people in your own community in order to support the Third World." I think most people

(BERYL LEVINGER)

can do both. We're living increasingly in an interdependent world. We have to be concerned about fellow Americans; but if our concern stops there, we're not creating a secure future for fellow Americans, either. The kind of person who can make this leap of faith and go beyond his or her own perspective and immediate environment is a very special and perhaps unusual person; but I think increasingly we're going to have to have more and more of our citizenry fall into that basket.

Interview/
USA Today, 12-19:(A)11.

Jay F. Morris
Deputy Administrator,
Agency for International
Development of the
United States

1

Hunger, even famine, is still just a natural-disaster away for many [of the world's] people. Hunger experts have a word for this; they say that much of the world is still not "food secure." "Food secure" means having enough to eat even if there is a natural disaster... "Food secure" also means more than having enough food to keep from starving. It means having enough of the right kinds of foods to ensure healthy bodies and healthy minds. The United States is food secure. We just had our worst drought in decades—but grocery stores remained stocked. On the other hand, much of Africa is food insecure. More than 100 million Africans—one in four—don't get enough food to fuel an active working life.

At Presidential End Hunger
Awards, Oct. 13/
The Washington Post, 10-19:(A)22.

Daniel Patrick Moynihan
United States Senator,
D-New York

2

[Saying there should be more information made available to the public regarding their

Social Security record and benefits]: We receive monthly statements from our banks and credit-card companies, yet every month, in every pay-check, we see money withheld for Social Security, but we hear nary a word from the Social Security Administration.

The Washington Post, 8-17:(A)17.

William Mulch
Director, Harbor Light
Salvation Army, Los Angeles

3

I think lumping the homeless all together as one is a disservice. The Salvation Army for years has been addressing the problem of what makes them homeless. It's just recently become a sexy issue that sells newspapers... Food is not a problem, but housing is. You can eat several times a day within an eight-block area, but there are six to eight people in a family living in one room, whole families living in cars and garages, afraid to say anything because many are illegal aliens. These are the real homeless.

USA Today, 2-5:(A)13.

Leon E. Panetta
United States Representative,
D-California

4

It is a sad day commencing in America when there is a need to introduce an Emergency Hunger Relief Act. In a land blessed with the greatest agricultural production and wealth, it is a disgrace that we face a hunger emergency in this country... [The Reagan Administration's] vision is a country in which hunger does not exist. At most, it is anecdotal, if not measured by statistics collected by a Washington bureaucracy. There is no "hunger problem" because after eight years in office, the Administration has not identified an acceptable methodology to measure hunger.

Before the House,
Washington March 2/
The Washington Post,
4-18:(A)13.

(LEON E. PANETTA)

1

[On the demands of the elderly for government aid for medical costs in the future]: There will be a tremendous competition for resources, and not a hell of a lot of room. There are a lot of priorities [besides the elderly], from deficit reduction to more spending for children's programs and education and roads and bridges. If the money is just consumed on the elderly side, there will be strong resentments by other competing interests.

Los Angeles Times, 6-11:(I)16.

H. Ross Perot
Industrialist

2

If I could have one wish for our country, it would be a strong family unit in every home. That's the most efficient unit of government that's ever been created—good parents. Sadly enough, it's going the other direction in our country. Really sadly, we've got so many single-parent families, so many disadvantaged children from single-parent families.

Interview/USA Today, 6-29:(A)9.

Peter Peterson
Investment banker

3

The most egregious concept in the entire [Federal government] entitlement package, to me, is the idea that people like Peter Peterson, to take a specific example, should be getting three to five times what I've put into Social Security, plus interest, plus my company contribution, plus interest, and that I should be receiving a lot of it tax-free. The argument that is used to support this system is that you need to bribe the well-off so that they will support the poor. Translated, what that's saying is everybody better get on the wagon getting subsidies from the Federal government. But the awkward question that leaves is if everybody is on the wagon, then who pulls it? So I think the single most egregious thing is the idea that in a time of profound fiscal stress in this country, we've got billions and billions of dollars going to well-off people under the guise of universal entitlements.

*Interview, New York/
Time, 10-31:66.*

Samuel R. Pierce, Jr.
*Secretary of Housing and
Urban Development of
the United States*

4

[Saying he bases his budgetary decisions on three principles]: First, individual rights and responsibilities belong to the poor as much as anyone else. Second, the poor need not always remain poor, nor should we assume they will. Third, the poor often are capable of making their own decisions and improving their condition in life.

*Before Senate Appropriations
subcommittee, Washington, April 18/
The Washington Post, 4-19:(A)17.*

Dan Quayle
*United States Senator,
R-Indiana;
1988 Republican
Vice-Presidential nominee*

5

... the family has always been the very heart of civilization. We know the importance of the family to a child growing up. We know the help a family can be to a kid out of school, out of hope, out of luck. And we know the importance of family where one generation helps take care of another, young and old.

*Accepting the nomination, at
Republican National Convention,
New Orleans, Aug. 18/
The New York Times, 8-19:11.*

6

[On child care]: There is a difference in the way Republicans and Democrats approach this issue. We are more inclined to put taxpayer money in the parents' hands, and let them make the determination on what they think the child needs rather than creating this bureaucracy and

(DAN QUAYLE)

the Federal control. Conservatives haven't figured out what they want in child care and how we are going to provide that care. If the question is who is going to spend more for child care, the Democrats will win.

Interview/Time, 8-29:25.

1

... the biggest thing we [Republicans] have done for poverty in America is the Tax Simplification Act of 1986. Six million working poor families got off payroll. Six million people are off the taxpaying payroll because of that tax reform, and they're keeping the tax money there. To help the poor, we'll have a commitment to the programs, and those programs will go on. And we are spending more in poverty programs today than we were in 1981—that is a fact. The poverty program that we are going to concentrate on is creating jobs and opportunities so that everyone will have the opportunities that they want.

At Vice-Presidential debate,
Omaha, Neb., Oct. 5/
The New York Times, 10-7:(A)12.

2

In 1983 Republicans and Democrats dropped their political swords and in a bipartisan effort saved the Social Security System. Republicans and Democrats banded together because we know that this program is not a Republican program. It's not a Democrat program. It's a program for older Americans. And that program is actually sound to the turn of this century.

At Vice-Presidential debate,
Omaha, Neb., Oct. 5/
The New York Times, 10-7:(A)12.

Ronald Reagan
President of the United States

3

[Welfare programs have become] a crippling poverty trap. . . They keep the poor poor. Now, much of the push for child care is designed to rec-

tify the ills of earlier programs, and many of these efforts are timely and good. But in this area, more than any other, government should tread carefully.

Before National Governors' Association,
Washington, Feb. 22/
The Washington Post, 2-23:(A)3.

4

There are always going to be [homeless] people who live in the streets by choice [instead of staying in shelters]. They make it their own choice for staying out there. There are shelters in virtually every city, and shelters here [in Washington], and those people still prefer out there on the grates or the lawn to going into one of those shelters.

Broadcast interview, Washington/
Interview with David Brinkley,
ABC-TV, 12-22.

Lisbeth Schorr
Lecturer,
Harvard University

5

There are people who believe that when resources or money are allocated to programs for the aged, then kids lose out, and when resources are allocated to kids, then old people lose out. I think that it's a total misunderstanding of social policy in this country. I think the issue is whether people, regardless of age, are going to get the services they need, and whether programs, government and non-government, are going to work for them.

Interview/USA Today, 10-20:(A)7.

Patricia Schroeder
United States Representative,
D-Colorado

6

More than a quarter of American children live in poverty—an unbelievable disgrace. Dollar for dollar, money spent on children and families programs are the most cost-effective use of government funds. Solving poverty is cheap; I only

(PATRICIA SCHROEDER)

wanted $10-million for a domestic-abuse shelter program. We can't even get [an airplane's] tail section for that.

"Ms.," February: 52

1

The American family has changed, but policies have not kept pace. The family is the primary social and economic unit in America. It's the basic building block of our society. Yet, there are so many myths surrounding the family—myths that fuel talk and inhibit action. The American family is no longer a Norman Rockwell painting. We have become a nation of two-income families, of single-parent families—a nation of families under stress... We are all pro-family. But what are we prepared to do about it? There is a family gap in America—the gap between what American politicians say about families and what they do for families.

At University of Pennsylvania commencement/
The Christian Science Monitor, 7-27:26.

Deborah Steelman
Domestic policy director of
Vice-President George Bush's
1988 Republican campaign
for the Presidency

2

Women feel this responsibility for their families. For dinner being on the table at 6 o'clock. For everyone having a good time at a party. They feel guilty when they leave their babies to go to work. They feel guilty if they quit their jobs. And they feel this terrific guilt if they see things going wrong. This is why the homeless is such an important issue; I think women feel more guilty than men when they walk past a homeless person. I know I feel guilty as hell. I feel like I should be taking care of them in my basement. And I want a man [as President] who is going to recognize that things like homelessness are wrong, and is going to help me be responsible.

The Wall Street Journal,
10-13:(A)16.

Ben Wattenberg
Senior fellow, American
Enterprise Institute

3

Social Security, probably the greatest social-engineering program in U.S. history, interposes the government between the middle-aged adult and his or her parents in the following way: Instead of middle-aged adults giving money to elderly parents or grandparents, and resenting it, and the grandparents resenting getting it, the middle-aged adults, by law, have some money deducted from their paychecks which they think is going for their own retirement, which, of course, is not saved for their retirement but more or less sent to their fathers or mothers in a Social Security check.

Interview/USA Today, 10-20:(A)7.

J. J. Wuerthner, Jr.
Executive director, Americans
for Generational Equity

4

We have a contract between the generations, and it roughly is, "Hey, parents, you take care of me as a youngster. When you retire, I will continue to pay into your Social Security fund on the basis that I'm going to have a contract with my own children—your grandchildren." And that's what generational equity is all about.

USA Today, 10-20:(A)7.

Transportation

Joseph Allen
Executive vice president,
Space Industries, Inc.;
Former American astronaut

1

[On why we should have laboratories in space]: The philosophical reason is that it is a new environment. In the history of people on the earth, when transportation systems have been invented to take people to new environments, two things have happened. One is that humankind's vision of itself has been enlarged. In addition, every time we've invented a new transportation method to take us to a new environment, lots of commerce has followed that has to do with that environment. You can think of barges down rivers, canals that cross land masses, clipper ships across oceans, railroads across continents and airplanes through the atmosphere.

Interview/
USA Today, 1-19:(A)13.

Lana Batts
Vice president,
American Trucking
Association

2

Historically, people have only looked at the benefits of deregulation [of the transportation industry]. There is now a recognition that those benefits may have come at a cost. In the railroad industry, there is a monetary cost to captive shippers. In the airline and trucking industry, they have come at a cost to safety... Safety is the biggest issue that we are looking at. It establishes credibility on a lot of issues. If you are not a safe industry, no one wants to talk to you about tax issues, productivity issues or labor-shortage issues. No one wants to go to work for an unsafe industry.

Interview/
The New York Times,
9-13:30

Jim Burnett
Member, National
Transportation Safety Board
of the United States

3

[On FAA concerns about pilot performance relating to airliner accidents]: When you're talking about pilot performance in the cockpit, those are hard issues to tackle with a regulation. A whole lot depends on the attitudes on the part of an airline. Their leadership, their responsibility. It becomes relatively difficult to do real enforcement. [But] in the deregulated environment, someone has to play referee. I don't know who can do it better than the government.

The Washington Post, 12-21:(A)3.

James H. Burnley
Secretary of Transportation
of the United States

4

Because the FAA is charged with promoting and protecting the [airline] industry's commercial interests, it is sometimes reluctant to take safety and enforcement actions that impose significant costs and burdens on that industry. [At times,] it has been necessary to use the bureaucratic equivalent of a cattle prod to get the FAA to take needed safety actions.

Before Senate Aviation Subcommittee,
Washington, March 23/
The Washington Post, 3-24:(A)23.

5

Mass transit is useful at the margin in some cases, but what you see in most communities is that people like you and me refuse to give up what we recognize now to be a sacred right, which is to get in our automobile and go where we please. By ourselves. Often. But there are things going on in the research-and-development field right now that hold out a lot of promise... General Motors is putting up 25 automobiles, and we are going to

(JAMES H. BURNLEY)

experiment around Los Angeles with computer software in these cars. That technology would tell if the highway's backed up, and give alternative routes. And we're building something called a "smart highway." It would monitor the highway and control the access ramps, know the backups that have occurred, and get help there quickly; and that immediately could be transmitted to drivers. That's the kind of area in which we ought to spend a lot more time.

Interview/
USA Today, 8-11:(A)11.

Paul Dempsey
Professor of transportation law,
University of Denver
1

[Since deregulation of the airline industry,] flying has become a miserable experience. The planes are filthy, delayed, canceled and overbooked, our luggage disappears and the food is processed cardboard.

USA Today, 10-5:(A)13.

Albert Gore, Jr.
United States Senator,
D-Tennessee;
Candidate for the
1988 Democratic
Presidential nomination
2

. . . there are public benefits to an efficient mass-transit system that are larger than the amount of money which can ever be recovered through the fare box. If one attempts to increase operating revenue by raising fares, one risks getting into a vicious cycle. . . As fares go up, ridership frequently goes down. I think we have a national interest, therefore, in having public subsidies of efficient mass-transit systems so as to keep ridership high and increasing.

Interview/
The New York Times, 4-11:12.

Lee A. Iacocca
Chairman,
Chrysler Corporation
3

Looking 20 years out at what we [automobile manufacturers] will be making, there will be lots of changes, but we will still have a car that is much the same as we see it today. It will have four wheels—perhaps the spare tire will be gone—it will be made essentially of steel, though 20 per cent to 25 per cent of it could be plastic. Despite all those years of research in turbines, electric power and so forth, it will be powered by an internal-combustion engine. It is tough to knock that engine out, even after two fuel crises. With the electronic controls, we've gotten rid of the rough spots. It will stay around for another century.

Interview/Fortune, 8-29:43.

4

The American car buyer honestly feels we [U.S. auto manufacturers] don't have his best interest at heart . . . and he's telling us that loud and clear . . . he's buying imports. . . The car buyer wants a car that will take him back and forth to work—not back and forth to the shop. You don't buy a new car to have problems.

USA Today, 9-7:(A)5.

M. L. Johnson
Chief engineer for structures,
Boeing Company
5

[On the factor of aging on the safety of commercial aircraft]: In theory, there's no reason why a plane can't last forever. As long as you do the proper maintenance, it could fly forever. However, at some time, the airline could decide that the cost was higher than they could justify [and they could retire the plane].

Interview/The New York Times, 5-9:11.

Daniel Patrick Moynihan
United States Senator,
D-New York
6

[Calling on the U.S. to develop a high-speed magnetically elevated train]: The problem is that

(DANIEL PATRICK MOYNIHAN)

nobody in this town [Washington] thinks we do things like this any more. For all the talk about competitiveness, we are now in a mindset that says we can't afford to be first; we don't have the money, we don't have the means... The Japanese are roaring ahead. They have put almost a billion dollars into maglev [the elevated train] already. Consider: They are on the threshold of being able to commercialize a technology that will dominate transportation in the 21st century, just as air transport has dominated the 20th century... Economically, the history of the world is the history of transportation. The 20th century was inaugurated at Kitty Hawk, and it was ours.

The New York Times, 4-5:10.

John Riley
Administrator, Federal
Railroad Administration

1

Under the rule that's in effect today, even when an employee [of a railroad] fails a reasonable-cause drug test, we [in the Federal government] cannot do anything to him because we don't have jurisdiction over the employee. We can require the company to test, but we cannot require it to respond. The big improvement that will come from the passage of the railroad-safety bill is that this agency, for the first time, will have the authority to suspend the operating privilege of an employee who brings drugs into the workplace. And you don't have to look any farther than the accident statistics of the last year to know we need that authority.

Interview/USA Today, 6-7:(A)11.

Harriet Stanley
Finance specialist, High
Speed Rail Association

2

[Applauding Congress' passage of legislation permitting the sale of tax-free bonds to help finance high-speed rail systems in the U.S.]: [This is] the single, most critical factor to determine if high-speed rail can be built anywhere in the nation. I've worked on or been exposed to every high-speed rail system proposed in this country, and the expense for each one is not land or construction, but financing.

The Christian Science Monitor,
12-21:3.

Dean D. Thornton
President, Boeing Commercial
Airplane Company

3

[On Boeing's success in the commercial-airliner business]: We're being burned by our own success. We've got too much on our plate. We've got too many inexperienced workers—green peas, we call them—and not enough of the old-timers who know how to do things. We're working too much overtime. We're stretched right now.

Los Angeles Times, 11-27:(IV)5.

Stephen Wolf
Chairman, United Airlines

4

[On the possibility of United losing its position as the biggest air carrier in the U.S. because of rapid expansion of other airlines]: I'm not too concerned about that. I think our employees would not care to have that happen. It is a consideration. But it's not the driver. The driver is to become qualitatively best. If an airline truly does a superior job and has a superior maintenance program—so there's not a safety issue—why can't you sell your seat for 25 cents more, or $1.80 or $10? I think our focus should be on the quality side. If we're successful quality-wise, earnings will come and we'll take those earnings to plow them back into the airline to grow it.

Interview/
USA Today, 7-28:(B)2.

265

Urban Affairs

Piero Antinori
Director, House of Antinori,
winemakers (Italy)

1

In the cities [today], the rhythm of life is faster and people no longer take the time for an extended meal at noon, with a bottle of wine at the table and a siesta afterward. Now they eat a snack in the middle of the day. You do not open a bottle of wine with a sandwich. You drink a soda.

World Press Review, March:52.

Victor Ashe
Mayor of Knoxville, Tenn.

2

What bothers me most [about being Mayor] is when I ask that something be done and I discover later that it wasn't.

USA Today, 1-20:(A)3.

Alan Beals
Director, National League
of Cities

3

Our national leaders could learn some good habits and important lessons from city hall to take the place of the various gimmicks being used in Washington to duck Federal budget responsibility. Home-town America is holding the bag for a lot of dubious, deplorable and sometimes destructive Federal policies.

The Washington Post,
7-16:(A)13.

J. Thomas Cochran
Director, United States
Conference of Mayors

4

A Mayor is the most scrutinized person on the globe, even in small towns.

USA Today, 1-20:(A)3.

Terry Goddard
Mayor of Phoenix; President,
National League of Cities

5

Cities can do much for themselves, but even Phoenix, with . . . a growing economy, a supportive business community and progressive citizen backing, needs help, especially from Federal and state governments . . . We want . . . to inform the new Administration [of President-elect George Bush] that cities are in crisis. We want Capitol Hill to be aware of our needs before it sets a national policy . . . Look at housing. Contracts that set subsidies for newly constructed affordable housing built in the '60s and '70s are expiring. The Feds have cut back new housing during the '80s. We are looking at more homelessness today.

Boston/
The Christian Science Monitor,
12-13:3.

James W. Hughes
Professor of urban planning,
Rutgers University

6

[Saying casino gambling in Atlantic City, N.J., has not brought improvements to the city as a whole, as was promised]: It was promised as a unique tool of urban revitalization, but those promises were naive. Outside the tinsel on the boardwalk, Atlantic City looks like the South Bronx.

USA Today, 8-4:(A)10.

R. Paul Lasley
Associate professor of sociology,
Iowa State University

7

[On dying rural towns]: They've survived so far by using up their capital. And now many of these communities are struggling to make it. And some won't. They won't just shut off the lights.

(R. PAUL LASLEY)

But they'll become pockets of poor, elderly people. The farm crisis has focused attention on this fundamental restructuring of rural communities. But, in fact, it's been an onward march of a trend toward urbanization that's been going since the 1920s.

The New York Times, 8-4:1.

Sal Panto, Jr.
Mayor of Easton, Pa.

1

The U.S. is an urban nation. We're only as strong as our cities, where 75 per cent of all Americans live.

Washington/
The New York Times, 1-22:24.

Carrie Saxon Perry
Mayor of Hartford, Conn.

2

I cannot in earnest and candor stand before you and parlay the image that everyone's fortunes in Hartford have skyrocketed . . . When I cite growth and development, I am alluding to downtown development and regional growth. When we turn to the central, the inner city, we see people and human services that are in stark contrast to the boomlet less than a mile away.

At forum sponsored by New York University
Urban Research Center,
New York/
The Christian Science Monitor,
5-17:4.

John Rousakis
Mayor of Savannah, Ga.

3

[The Reagan Administration's] interest in local government is at the zero level. We have to fight for every bit of interest. While there may have been too many dollars and programs in the past, the problems are still there: poverty, homelessness, hunger, crime, disease and drugs.

Washington/
The New York Times, 1-22:24.

Stuart Spencer
Republican political-campaign
adviser

4

[Republican Vice-Presidential nominee] Dan Quayle doesn't know about cities. He doesn't know who lives there—ghettos, traffic, race, crime, housing—all that stuff. But we'll teach him. My team is working on it.

Newsweek, 10-31:15.

PART TWO

International Affairs

Africa

Anatoly L. Adamishin
*Deputy Foreign Minister of
the Soviet Union*

1

[If SWAPO takes over in Namibia,] I don't think they're going to build socialism in this part of the world. And there are few people in the Soviet Union who would advise them to build a socialist society in this particular situation in Africa. Everybody has to deal with realities. And one of the realities of Namibia is that it has very strong economic ties with South Africa.

*Brazzaville, Congo, Dec. 13/
Los Angeles Times, 12-14:(I)20.*

Ibrahim B. Babangida
President of Nigeria

2

[Saying he wants Nigeria to have two-party democracy by 1992]: I don't like the idea of one party—it doesn't sound democratic. As long as we are going to practice democracy, someone has to have a choice. The two-party system provides that choice . . . In the 1990s, the military in our country will be strictly confined to the roles assigned to it by a constitution. We are trying to educate the military to make them know that they are subordinate to constituted authorities.

*Interview, Lagos/
The New York Times, 10-22:3.*

Hastings Kamuzu Banda
President of Malawi

3

Any politician who interprets democracy in Africa in terms of the British [system], does not know what he is doing. Britain is tolerant today because government has been established for centuries . . . There was a time in Britain when they did worse things than we are going to do now.

The Washington Post, 9-12:(A)16.

Chadli Bendjedid
President of Algeria

4

We are 23 million Algerians, and 6 million of us are in schools and universities. Forty per cent of our national budget goes to education. That is what occupies us very much . . . We seek to sensitize the Algerian people to building a developed society open to the world, where quality, not quantity, counts. [But] we cannot just make decisions that go against the spiritual values of our people.

*Interview, Algiers/
The Washington Post, 2-6:(A)2.*

Adriaan Botha
*Executive director,
American Chamber of
Commerce in South Africa*

5

[New U.S. economic sanctions to protest South Africa's apartheid system] would devastate this economy and still not change the minds of the powers that be. [Once South Africa's economy is ruined,] the possibility of a phoenix arising from the ashes, as some pro-sanctions people expect, is absolutely nil.

Los Angeles Times, 7-25:(I)7.

Pieter W. Botha
President of South Africa

6

[On South Africa]: This beautiful country, with its wealth of diversity, deserves less negative propaganda and actions [about its apartheid system]. South Africa deserves more patriotism. [We should] remain calm, restore balance and recognize each other's rights. If we wish to live together peacefully . . . the time has come to reflect on what unites us instead of emphasizing what divides us.

*Before South African Parliament,
Cape Town, April 21/
Los Angeles Times, 4-22:(I)7.*

WHAT THEY SAID IN 1988

(PIETER W. BOTHA)

1

There are politicians in the U.S. who apparently want to use [the issue of South Africa's apartheid system] for their internal political fights in the U.S., and I object to that. In South Africa, we don't use the U.S. as an electioneering cry.

Interview/USA Today, 6-2:(A)2.

2

[Saying his government is extending the state-of-emergency regulations imposed to deal with anti-apartheid violence]: It is, indeed, the aspiration of the government that conditions will change to such an extent that the declared state of emergency can be lifted. In the meantime, the government has an overriding responsibility to protect the lives and possessions of all our citizens and to ensure that their daily lives can continue without fear, intimidation and terror. By declaring a state of emergency, these processes and community life can be protected and stability will be ensured.

Cape Town, June 9/
The Washington Post, 6-10:(A)27.

3

[Criticizing U.S. Congressmen who voted for tough new economic sanctions against South Africa to protest that country's apartheid system, sanctions which he says could jeopardize plans for a peaceful settlement of the Namibia problem]: The recklessness of members of Congress who do not care in the least whether their actions adversely affect the search for a peaceful solution to the problems of southern Africa as a whole is astounding.

Aug. 12/
Los Angeles Times, 8-13:(I)5.

4

[On anti-apartheid leader Nelson Mandela, who has spent a quarter of a century in prison]: Personally, I don't think that at his age and condition it would be wise for him to choose to go back

to prison [from the hospital where it is said he is being treated for tuberculosis]. And I hope he will make it possible for me to act in a humane way [by releasing him from imprisonment if he agrees to certain conditions] so that we can have peace in South Africa... The ANC must get one message: Lay down your arms, come back like decent people, and let's talk about a Constitutional future for South Africa. I am not prepared to create chaos in the name of so-called human rights. I hate no Colored man, I hate no Indian and I hate no black; but I have my own life-style and I want to see it continue.

At Natal Province congress of
National Party, Durban,
South Africa, Aug. 18/
The New York Times, 8-19:6.

5

[On the current talks regarding his country's withdrawal from Namibia]: The day the territory becomes independent as a result of a free choice by its people, and the Cubans have withdrawn from Angola, then South Africa will be able to say: The struggle was not in vain; we contributed to the peace and stability of the whole of southern Africa.

Before South African Parliament,
Cape Town, Aug. 24/
The New York Times, 8-25:4.

6

[Encouraging blacks to take part in forthcoming nation-wide municipal elections]: To boycott is easy, but it leads nowhere. To co-operate is sometimes difficult, but we remember those who build and not those who destroy.

At opening of job-training center,
Cape Town, South Africa, Aug. 26/
The Washington Post, 8-27:(A)17.

Joaquim A. Chissano
President of Mozambique

7

[Criticizing the rebels who are fighting his government]: [They are] a horde of criminals

(JOAQUIM A. CHISSANO)

created by the South African regime. [South African authorities hope] to keep the Mozambican people in a permanent state of weakness and terror, blocking the success of any independent development project and keeping the country indefinitely as a client state of South Africa.

At international conference on Mozambique sponsored by the United Nations, Maputo, Mozambique, April 26/ The New York Times, 4-27:6.

Alan Cranston
United States Senator,
D-California

1

[Criticizing the U.S. Reagan Adminstration for being soft on apartheid in South Africa]: I think the White House has been wimpy on the moral issue of apartheid. We can flex our superpower muscles against tiny Grenada, or against the oddball leadership of Libya. But when there's a tough nut to crack, involving the real strategic interests of the United States, as they are in South Africa, the Reagan Administration quivers and quakes.

At Senate Foreign Relations Committee hearing, Washington, June 22/The Washington Post, 6-23:(A)8.

Dennis DeConcini
United States Senator,
D-Arizona

2

The [U.S.] State Department, while pressing for the removal of all foreign forces [in the civil war in Angola], is not insisting that UNITA be included in the negotiating process. There can be no peace in Angola without national reconciliation, and there can be no national reconciliation without UNITA.

The New York Times, 5-20:4.

Yonas Deressa
President, Ethiopian Refugees
Education and Relief Foundation

3

[Ethiopian leader Mengistu Haile Mariam] has destroyed the traditional farming economy with Communist controls on prices, by confiscating all land, and by making the state the sole buyer and seller of food. Since 1979, the agricultural output has fallen in Ethiopia by 15 per cent. Before the Communists, my country not only fed itself, it even exported food. Now, even in good years, seven or eight million people are on the verge of starvation. Ethiopia has become an economic basket case. Life has become so horrible that over three million people have fled, most of them trudging for up to a month through the wilderness, risking death from thirst or starvation.

At U.S. forum sponsored by Heritage Foundation, July/ The Wall Street Journal, 9-16:16.

Michael S. Dukakis
Governor of Massachusetts (D);
Candidate for the 1988
Democratic U.S.
Presidential nomination

4

I think our [U.S.] support of [Angolan rebel leader Jonas] Savimbi and UNITA is absolutely bizarre. We've got a situation where we're supporting this group, whose principal patron is South Africa, which attacks American oil companies that are defended by the Cuban army. If we're serious about building the kind of relationship with the front-line African states that I think we must, if we're serious about getting tough with South Africa, this policy has got to end . . . Being aligned with South Africa in Angola—that's not what the United States is all about. Believe me, if I'm President, we are going to change it. Our policy down there has been disgraceful, as it has been in so many other places.

Interview/ Los Angeles Times, 5-26:(I)22,23.

WHAT THEY SAID IN 1988

Fred du Plessis
Chairman, Sanlam Corporation
(South Africa)

1

Unless we have an economic upswing [in South Africa], an economic revival to make it possible to look at political reforms [such as reform of the apartheid system], it won't be possible to solve either our economic or our political problems. The only way to have a more equitable distribution of wealth is to create more wealth so you can give without taking from others. Trying to improve a person's material position through political freedom is putting the cart before the horse.

Los Angeles Times, 2-15:(I)12.

Kent Durr
Minister of the Budget of
South Africa;
Chairman, Foreign Trade
Relations Committee

2

[On possible new U.S. economic sanctions to protest South Africa's apartheid system]: We've studied the effects down to every man, woman and child. We're ready for it, and we'll survive. Certainly we're not going to be blackmailed into doing things we know to be wrong. We're not going to allow a Marxist government in South Africa in the name of "liberty." We're simply not going to do it. Forget it.

Los Angeles Times, 7-25:(I)7.

Ray Ekpu
Editor-in-chief,
"Newswatch" (Nigeria)

3

Africa is a study in paradox, a continent of contrasts. It has the largest reserves of untapped natural resources in the world; it occupies one-fifth of the Earth's land surface; [and] it has enormous human resources—more than 500 million. If properly husbanded, these resources would have led to the creation of a continent on which poverty would belong to the realm of fiction. Problems could have been ameliorated, if not solved, by Africa's leaders if many of them

had not become the problem rather than the solution. Many of the immediate post-independence leaders must have misunderstood their brief: They took their participation in the extirpation of colonialism as a mandate, [and] their reward was the headship of their countries for as long as they wished. In the last few years, a few of them have eased themselves out of office.

Accepting "World Press Review"
International Editor-of-the-Year
award, New York/
World Press Review,
July:34.

Deon Geldenhuys
Political scientist,
Rand Afrikaans
University
(South Africa)

4

[On the South African government's crackdown on anti-apartheid violence in its own country and threats from neighboring black nations]: The South African government increasingly is acting like a regional desperado. They know how the West will respond after each incursion or crackdown, but they don't care. Security is more important than world opinion.

The Christian Science Monitor,
3-8:9.

Ahmed Houderi
Member, People's Committee
for Foreign Liaison Bureau
of Libya

5

[Calling for improved relations between Libya and the U.S.]: After so many years of hostility, it's not our choice to make the United States our enemy. It was their choice. There's room to sit down and talk, starting with economic issues . . . As they say, business makes friends.

Interview/
Los Angeles Times,
11-30:(I)25.

Jesse L. Jackson
American civil-rights leader;
Candidate for the 1988
Democratic U.S.
Presidential nomination

1

When the [1988 U.S. Democratic Party] convention is called in Atlanta, I want South Africa called by its proper definition. It is a terrorist state.

The Washington Post, 6-6:(A)4.

John Paul II
Pope

2

[On poverty in Africa]: The consciences of many are rightly perturbed and there exists a growing public opinion that more must be done. [But] the countries of Africa themselves must be in charge of their own development and historic destiny. Outside aid is urgently needed, but it will only be helpful in the long run if the essential force of growth and development is truly African.

To diplomatic corps, Harare,
Zimbabwe, Sept. 11/
The New York Times, 9-12:2.

Aneerood Jugnauth
Prime Minister of Mauritius

3

Since [taking office in] 1983, I had to follow a tough line, inculcate discipline at all levels, especially among the working class. I had to insure industrial and social stability. Of course, [that has been] coupled with political stability, which brought in the confidence required on the part of investors to come here. I must say, I have had lots of problems since I started, but I think I have a strength in that I am sincere in what I am doing. I believe that our country has a great future. I have always believed that we are destined to play an important role in this region, especially economically, and I have always had the will to pull on. Unlike many other politicians, I don't mind even if I have to take unpopular measures in the interest of the country to do it.

Interview, Port Louis, Mauritius/
Los Angeles Times, 12-11:(I)8.

John Kane-Berman
Director, South African
Institute for Race Relations

4

[On apartheid in South Africa]: Faced with the unworkability of its discriminatory policies, government is retreating gradually and reluctantly, but nevertheless steadily, from ideology into pragmatism. Whereas ideologies are impervious to the influence of others, pragmatists are not.

The Washington Post, 5-25:(A)26.

Richard G. Lugar
United States Senator,
R-Indiana

5

The lack of formal discussions in South Africa of how white and black civil rights could be obtained and then preserved in a unique, democratic and constitutional plan has tended to perpetuate the worst fears of racial polarization and dominance. American political and economic action to encourage thoughtful internal dialogue in South Africa is based on faith that there is still time for reasonable conversations, negotiations and then the drafting of a constitution with adequate and enforceable safeguards. These conversations must take place and must involve those who are truly representative of all elements in South Africa.

Before Washington International
Trade Association, July 28/
The Washington Post, 8-2:(A)20.

David MacDonald
Canadian Ambassador
to Ethiopia

6

[On Ethiopia's civil war]: For three years, famine was a very clear concern and priority of the [Ethiopian] government. But that has gone by the boards. No one should doubt the Ethiopian people's commitment to keeping this country together. To give up [the province of] Eritrea [to rebel forces], the front door of the country, is not something that is easily contemplated.

Los Angeles Times, 5-30:(I)9.

275

WHAT THEY SAID IN 1988

Mengistu Haile Mariam
President of Ethiopia

1

[On his country's controversial policy of re-settling peasants, which used to be forced, but is now voluntary]: Supposing it was not voluntary? Is it proper to watch someone die, perching on hills and sitting on parched land? Is it right to watch him die? Are we leading people or destroying people? What is the purpose of a government or a party unless it provides guidance?

Interview, Addis Ababa, Nov. 26/
The New York Times, 11-28:(A)6.

Thabo Mbeki
Director of information,
banned African National
Congress (South Africa)

2

To know us [the ANC] is not necessarily to love us, but most people find that we are not so terrible, certainly not the villains and murderers that the [South African] regime has described . . . For whites, this sometimes is such a revelation that they go back and question everything they believed about us, about apartheid, about the struggle against it . . . Often they come to the conclusion that what we want for South Africa—a country for all the people who live in it, a democratic and just political and economic system—is what they want and that, consequently, they belong with us. And when they come, we welcome them.

Interview, Lusaka, Zambia/
Los Angeles Times, 5-10:(I)8.

Daniel arap Moi
President of Kenya

3

We want Kenyans to be understood in our business and our government. We want you [the U.S.] to know we value friendship, and it must be supported in every way. If countries like the United States can assist Kenyans in a big way, we'll appreciate it. We want Kenyans to prosper, to have population growth reduced and, above all, security should be on the priority list. Every

country in Africa is shaken by forces that don't bode well for them. Kenya is the only [African] country that is truly friends with the U.S.

Interview, Nairobi/
USA Today, 4-15:(A)13.

Sam Nujoma
Leader, South-West Africa
People's Organization

4

[On the tentative agreement whereby South Africa will withdraw from its rule of Namibia]: After 23 years of war, I believe it is essential to have national reconciliation. Peace is much needed by everyone, and the South-West Africa People's Organization must initiate a process to eliminate racial hatred in our country . . . I believe that the South African government is genuine—that this time they will be honest people.

Interview,
Kabwe, Zambia, Aug. 18/
The New York Times, 8-19:6.

Julius K. Nyerere
Former President
of Tanzania

5

What I see now [in Africa] is the strengthening of nationalism. We are engrossed in building nation-states. The whole purpose of building the OAU was [a united] Africa. I doubt if the new generation of African leaders has this perception. We are so preoccupied with our national problems that the continental problems are in danger of being forgotten.

World Press Review, August:51.

Lawrence Oyelakin
Nigerian Ambassador to
the Congo

6

[On South Africa's recent initiatives aimed at improving its relations with black African countries]: We look at it as two halves of a cake. The Angolan talks and the Brazzaville agreement [on

(LAWRENCE OYELAKIN)

Namibia] are good for Africa. But until South Africa starts talking to its own people [by addressing its apartheid problem], I don't think many people in Africa will want to talk to South Africa.

Los Angeles Times, 12-27:(I)9.

Muammar el-Qaddafi
Chief of State of Libya

1

[On U.S. attempts to isolate him in the region]: When we are speaking in this logic, that means we are speaking about illogic ... It is unjust, unfair and a type of tyranny that the United States tries to meddle in affairs between Tunis and Algiers and Tripoli. If America wants to appoint itself as an international policeman, it will have to pay the price.

Interview/Newsweek, 2-22:33.

Ronald Reagan
President of the United States

2

The Ethiopian regime recently ordered all foreign famine relief workers to leave the [drought-] afflicted northern region. That leads us to the horrible conclusion that starvation and scorched earth are being considered as weapons to defeat the rebellion [against the government] ... [There is a] tremendous human catastrophe in the making. Is the world to know another holocaust? Is it to see another political famine? [The Soviet Union, as] the principal arms supplier and primary backer [of the Ethiopian government] can stop this disaster before it happens. I appeal to them to persuade the Ethiopian regime, as only they can, to change its decision and to allow the famine relief efforts to continue.

Before World Affairs Council
of Western Massachusetts,
Springfield, April 21/
The New York Times,
4-22:4.

Charles E. Redman
Spokesman for the
Department of State of the
United States

3

[Criticizing the Ethiopian government for interfering with civilian relief operations in its war with Ethiopian rebels]: Over 2 million people are facing starvation. We deplore the decisions made by the government in Addis Ababa to neglect or sacrifice millions of its citizens in pursuit of military objectives. Assurances that the decision was made for the security of those involved, that the expulsion [of foreign relief workers] is "temporary," and that indigenous organizations can take up the slack ring hollow against the sheer magnitude of the disaster. The world cannot stand idly by and allow innocent people to die. To avert this tragedy, the government's callous decision must be reconsidered ... Relief workers are willing to take the risk so that millions of Ethiopians might live ... It is incumbent upon both government and rebels to honor the sanctity of lives and to permit relief operations to go forward unimpeded.

April 13/
The Washington Post, 4-14:(A)29.

George P. Shultz
Secretary of State of the
United States

4

[Arguing against increased U.S. economic sanctions against South Africa to protest that country's apartheid system]: We're against apartheid. We're for a different kind of political process that gives everybody a crack at governing themselves ... But it's important [for the U.S.] to be there and be part of the process ... So, as far as bills that would cause us to end all trade, to end all investment, to end all contact between the United States and South Africa, we're opposed to that. It doesn't make sense.

Press briefing,
Washington, June 15/
The Washington Post,
6-16:(A)5.

WHAT THEY SAID IN 1988

Oliver Tambo
*President, banned African
National Congress
(South Africa)*

1

[On his organization's fight against South Africa's apartheid system]: The enemy's campaign of intense repression has tested the strength of our commitment to liberation, our determination and ability to fight on and the firmness of our adherence to the principle of the seizure of power by the people through struggle. We have come through that test as tempered steel . . . We have survived this determined offensive because we have sunk roots deep in the struggle for the overthrow of the apartheid regime. We have suffered reverses, but the enemy has failed in its objective—and that is a great victory for us.

*News conference,
Lusaka, Zambia,
Jan. 8/
Los Angeles Times,
1-9:(I)11.*

Desmond M. Tutu
*Anglican Archbishop of
Cape Town
(South Africa)*

2

It is sad that South Africa is noted for its vicious violations of human rights [its apartheid system]. But it is also very sad to note that there is less freedom in some independent African countries than there was in the much-maligned colonial period.

*At All-Africa Conference of Churches,
Nairobi, Kenya/
The Wall Street Journal,
1-7:18.*

3

[Saying the West should break off diplomatic relations with South Africa because of that country's apartheid system and state-of-emergency regulations]: We want to tell the South African

government that they do not deserve to be part of decent society. They have behaved in an abominable fashion and until they show that they can participate in decent society, they should be treated as pariahs.

*News conference,
Nairobi, Kenya,
March 2/
The Washington Post,
3-5:(D)10.*

4

[On those who say foreign economic sanctions against South Africa to protest that country's apartheid system do not work]: . . . who is saying they are not effective? Why do you get lobbies from South Africa asking that sanctions not be applied? In any case, these people are saying, let's judge how effective sanctions are after less than a year. That's a very short period of time. We should say that if sanctions don't work, then what is going to work, because constructive engagement—stressing diplomatic dialogue rather than economic sanctions—has not worked. What does, in fact, persuade the South African government to change [it's pro-apartheid stance]? . . . In my heart, I don't want sanctions. I don't want anything that would harm a country that I love very passionately. But the onus is really on those who say they don't want sanctions to provide us with an alternative that will work. And they have not yet come up with anything that we could say is a viable alternative.

*Interview/
USA Today, 5-11:(A)11.*

5

I've just been to Namibia and seen the suffering that is caused by apartheid. It is caused to a large extent by Chester Crocker, U.S. Assistant Secretary for African Affairs, who is linking the independence of Namibia to an extraneous thing—the Cuban presence in Angola. I hope that he will have significant success to be able to tell his children what were the consequences of

(DESMOND M. TUTU)

his policy of "constructive engagement." The same people who support the contras [anti-government rebels in Nicaragua] are supporting UNITA, the rebels in southern Africa, and are helping to destabilize the southern region. And they are doing it with U.S. tax dollars in conjunction with South Africa. This is one story many Americans still don't know about or understand. If they did, they wouldn't tolerate it.

Interview/
USA Today, 5-11:(A)11.

1

I think [U.S.] President Reagan, [British Prime Minister Margaret] Thatcher, [West German] Chancellor [Helmut] Kohl and the Japanese government have made a moral decision [when they decided to continue doing business with the government of apartheid South Africa]. They have decided that South African blacks are expendable, that profits matter more than the lives of black children . . . These people are perhaps not racist . . . but, for the victims, that is only of irrelevant, academic interest. For apartheid's victims, capitalism and free enterprise as we have experienced them have been the most effective partners in our oppression. They are the best recruiters for Communism.

Before National Press Club,
Washington, May 11/
The Washington Post, 5-12:(A)4.

Stoffel van der Merwe
Deputy Minister of Information
and Constitutional Planning
of South Africa

2

It has become imperative to restructure the whole [South African] economy. It is useless to proceed, or even to try to proceed, with reform [of the apartheid system] on a Constitutional, political or social level if the economy is not in good shape, and this economy hasn't been in good shape for years . . . Reform costs money, and some reform measures have come to very little

. . . because there was not a sufficient economic basis for them. A major economic restructuring is absolutely necessary if we are to proceed with reform.

Los Angeles Times, 2-15:(I)12.

3

We [in the ruling National Party] want to get some more definition into the [apartheid] reform process. Whites need to know that there is life after compromise. The troubles of the National Party have stemmed from a lack of clarity or lack of a blueprint for reform, plus a lack of visible progress, which has created uncertainty . . . When people become uncertain, they are vulnerable to the siren song of the right wing.

Interview, Johannesburg/
The Washington Post, 4-22:(A)14.

David Welsh
Teacher of political studies,
University of Cape Town
(South Africa)

4

[On the possibility of South Africa's Conservative Party gaining strength in forthcoming elections against the National Party, and thus forcing a retreat from liberalizing the apartheid system]: The barbarians are at the gate. While it's unlikely the conservatives will take over, they could capture enough seats to have considerable power over a government already reduced to quivering Jello by their advance.

The Christian Science Monitor,
10-26:9.

Elie Wiesel
Historian; Professor of
humanities, Boston
University; Winner, 1986
Nobel Peace Prize

5

[On his opposition to South Africa's apartheid system]: What did I really learn from my life? When it comes to mass humiliation, a compromise is already playing the other side's game.

WHAT THEY SAID IN 1988

(ELIE WIESEL)

And what is apartheid but collective humiliation; furthermore, it is legal humiliation. In South Africa, humiliation is the law of the land. Therefore, we cannot make any compromises.

March 22/The New York Times, 3-23:9.

Howard Wolpe
United States Representative,
D-Michigan

1

[Calling for increased U.S. economic sanctions against South Africa to protest that country's apartheid system]: It is not that sanctions will in and of themselves bring down apartheid—they will not and we ought to have no illusions on that score. But they will increase significantly the costs the white minority regime must bear for its repressions and its inhumanity; and those external costs will reinforce the internal pressures that have been building within South Africa for many years.

Before the House,
Washington/
The New York Times,
6-6:4

The Americas

Elliott Abrams
Assistant Secretary for
Inter-American Affairs,
Department of State of
the United States

1

[Supporting continued U.S. aid to the contras, rebels fighting the Sandinista government of Nicaragua]: We have the Sandinistas in a corner. The only possible escape route [for them] is through [the U.S.] Congress [cutting off aid to the contras]. It'll be the Democratic leadership in the [U.S.] House that is rescuing [Nicaraguan President Daniel] Ortega [if contra aid is cut off]. It's really crazy. It's just unbelievable.

Broadcast interview/
"This Week With David Brinkley,"
ABC-TV, 1-24.

2

[On U.S. support for the contras, rebels fighting the Sandinista government of Nicaragua]: The [U.S. Reagan] Administration should have taken this question to the American people very soon after the inauguration [of President Reagan], should have stated that this was a major national-security problem, should have launched a large campaign to use the President's popularity to get the people behind open and significant actions to counter the Communist threat that was coming from Nicaragua.

Interview/
The New York Times, 4-4:4.

3

The [former U.S.] Carter Administration did the easy thing about Panama, which was to hand over a piece of paper that said, "This is the Panama Canal Treaty, and it gives Panama title to the Canal." You could argue that by its warm dealings with dictator [the late Omar] Torrijos, and sweeping under the rug certain of his activities, you can argue that it set back democracy in Panama. But I'm not making that argument. [When U.S. President Reagan assumed office,] we were left with this guy [Panamanian leader and alleged drug trafficker Manuel] Noriega, to whom we're supposed to give the Panama Canal. It's an impossible situation . . . Anyone who is dedicated to keeping those treaties should recognize that it is critical to get rid of Noriega . . . A few more years of Noriega, and [the Canal treaties] will be endangered.

The New York Times, 10-28:(A)12.

Raul Alfonsin
President of Argentina

4

We have serious economic difficulties caused by the foreign debt and the fall of international prices. The U.S.A., with generosity, launched the Marshall Plan after World War II to help European democracies. Something similar now is happening in Latin America, where there is also a democratic revival taking place within the context of an extremely difficult economic situation. But instead of receiving the support of a Marshall Plan, in the last five years Latin America has transferred wealth to the developed world.

Interview, Buenos Aires/USA Today, 3-11:(A)11.

5

[On the economic crisis in Latin America]: This reality is what prompts us to promote a new hemispheric dialogue. We are ready to foster a new phase in the relations of our region with the United States . . . one that understands that an independent Latin America, democratic and prosperous, is the guarantee of stability in the hemisphere. A dynamic and hopeful region, without the weight of a crushing debt and distorted subsidies, is a pre-condition for international commercial growth and for every domestic economy, including the American economy.

At Latin American summit meeting,
Punta del Este, Uruguay, Oct. 27/
Los Angeles Times, 10-28:(I)15.

Luis Alberto Arias
*Former Director, National
Bank of Panama*

1

[Criticizing the U.S. policy of economic embargo against Panama as a way to get Panamanian strongman Manuel Noriega to leave the country]: The U.S. hasn't been able to get Noriega out, but it has managed to destroy the country. If the U.S. has achieved anything, it has spawned a real anti-American sentiment in the opposition [to Noriega]. Their businesses are either destroyed or left with no possibility to develop.

The Christian Science Monitor,
5-24:13.

Oscar Arias
President of Costa Rica

2

[On the reaction of Nicaraguan President Daniel Ortega following the U.S. Congress' vote to cut aid to the contras, rebels fighting Ortega's Sandinista government]: Ortega said the war would continue, and nothing to stimulate the dialogue. He is wrong if he thinks [the vote in Congress] was a triumph for him. It was a triumph for the peace plan. Those who voted [against aid] expect him to choose now. The Sandinistas have to choose between a military and a democratic fight. They like to choose the military; that's what they do best. For a Marxist regime, democratization is their Achilles heel. We must move rapidly now to a cease-fire. Nicaraguans are dying.

Interview, San Jose, Costa Rica/
The New York Times, 2-9:31.

3

Our ancestors decided 120 years ago to introduce compulsory and free education; that's why we have an illiteracy rate of 6½ per cent. We have many, many universities, about 75,000 university students. Per capita-wise, I think we have more university students than any other Latin American country. We built a welfare state more than 40 years ago. Today, we have a national-

security system which covers the whole population. The poorest Costa Rican can get the best, the most sophisticated surgery in one of our hospitals, and not have to pay a penny. Life expectancy here is 75 years, the same as the U.S. Nevertheless, we have an income per capita that is one-tenth of the U.S. . . . I am determined to make Costa Rica the most developed country in Latin America. For that, we need to introduce some important economic changes, some structural changes. Here the extent of debt plays an important role. We cannot grow as fast as we want if we have to pay our external debt as it was arranged or scheduled. So we are in the process of rescheduling our debt. We don't want any fresh money from private banks but want better conditions to pay.

Interview, San Jose, Costa Rica/
USA Today, 2-26:(A)7.

4

Being certain that the Nicaraguan Army invaded Honduras [to attack bases of anti-Sandinista Nicaraguan contra rebels], my government condemns it categorically and with firmness. I deplore that this happens shortly before the [Sandinista-contra peace] meeting begins, and it appears to me lamentable because Costa Rica feels that the manner of resolving problems is through direct dialogue and not through war. We are putting in danger the much or the little that we have achieved in the Central American peace process, and the eyes of the world are placed on the isthmus to find out what we are capable of.

News conference,
San Jose, Costa Rica, March 17/
The Washington Post, 3-18:(A)1.

5

[Criticizing the Sandinista government of Nicaragua]: I told [U.S. Secretary of State George] Shultz that the Sandinistas today are bad guys, and you [the U.S.] are good guys, that they have unmasked themselves, that they are proving to the world that they were not honest when they committed themselves to democratize. On the contrary, they have sent to jail people

(OSCAR ARIAS)

who have disagreed with them. This is not justifiable. It shows they fear democracy and freedom more than they fear war.

To reporters,
San Jose, Costa Rica, Aug. 4/
Los Angeles Times, 8-5:(I)6.

1

[On the recent crackdown on the opposition by the Sandinista government of Nicaragua]: They are proving to the world that there is no political will in Managua, that they were not really honest when they committed themselves to democratize and advance toward a pluralistic society . . . [But] more military pressure [against them by the U.S.-backed contra rebels] is going to allow the Sandinistas to find an excuse for more repression . . . [They will] use it to take more backward steps than they've already made, to eliminate all kinds of pluralism, and make the Nicaraguan government a much more authoritarian, tyrannical and dictatorial regime. For the first time, Washington [instead of Nicaragua] is not isolated. But as soon as aid to the contras is approved again [by the U.S.], once more they won't get the support of the Western Hemisphere.

Interview,
San Jose, Costa Rica, Aug. 4/
The Christian Science Monitor,
8-8:28.

2

[Arguing against U.S. military aid to the contras, rebels fighting the Sandinista government of Nicaragua]: My position is to support humanitarian aid and not to support military aid. I disagree with military aid even if it is conditional. To continue providing military aid to the contras does not help the peace process.

To reporters,
Quito, Ecuador, Aug. 11/
The Washington Post, 8-12:(A)20.

3

Thanks to the [Central American] peace I have worked for, Costa Rica can become the first Latin American country free of slums. Our neighbors buy tanks and cannons and warplanes, and they get poorer by the day. But our country is growing.

Speech upon granting loans for
workers to build homes,
San Jose, Costa Rica/
Los Angeles Times, 12-27:(I)1.

Prosper Avril
President of Haiti

4

[On his new Administration, which took power in a recent coup]: We dream of a Haiti where freedom flourishes, where human rights are guaranteed, a country where dialogue is the order of the day.

Los Angeles Times, 9-27:(I)6.

5

My vision is to enter history as one who has saved the country from anarchy and dictatorship and who has asked for the establishment of an irreversible democracy . . . Some believe six months would be ideal [for a free election to be held], others nine months and others 2½ years. In any case, the timing will be decided by consensus. The date depends on the return to stability. I don't see how we can achieve that stability without American aid. It is an urgent matter. The longer it takes to come, the longer it will take to achieve stability . . . What we fear most, and what justifies our immediate request for assistance, is the deadly infiltration of extremist elements who would like to appropriate the legitimate demands of the people to create more anarchy.

To reporters,
Port-au-Prince, Haiti, Sept. 29/
Los Angeles Times, 9-30:(I)8.

M. Delal Baer
Specialist on Mexico,
Center for Strategic and
International Studies, Washington

6

Democracy [in Mexico] is a risk; it does not automatically produce what the U.S. wants. But

WHAT THEY SAID IN 1988

(M. DELAL BAER)

the risks of a closed system are even greater.

The Christian Science Monitor,
7-15:3.

Max Baucus
United States Senator,
D-Montana

1

[On the possibility that Canada won't ratify its recent free-trade agreement with U.S.]: Canada wanted this agreement in the first place, and they wanted it more than we did. If Canada now turns around and rejects it, and if they come forward with a proposal in another area like acid rain, it would be a bit more difficult. Americans may think: "Here they come again. We listened to their entreaties on trade; they backed down and said no. How can we be sure they'll follow through?"

The New York Times,
11-18:(A)6.

Marc Bazin
Former candidate for
President of Haiti;
Former economist,
International Bank for
Reconstruction and Development
(World Bank)

2

[Saying the recent Presidential elections in Haiti were a fraud]: We don't accept the elections. We don't believe they are valid and we believe that everything that comes out of them is invalid ... The way they have gone about announcing the results is confirmation that the elections were a sham, a charade. They came with the results like a robbery, visiting barefoot in the night, with everyone sleeping and the robber hoping that the next morning everybody would accept the crime as a dream.

Jan. 24/
The New York Times,
1-25:7.

Lloyd Bentsen
United States Senator,
D-Texas; 1988
Democratic U.S. Vice-
Presidential nominee

3

[Although supporting U.S. aid to the contras, rebels fighting the Sandinista government of Nicaragua,] my big difference with [the Reagan] Administration is they look at the contra aid program as the only way to resolve that problem. They concentrate on that. And I really think we have to give peace a chance. And that's why I've been a strong supporter of the Arias plan—a plan that won the Nobel Prize for President Arias, the President of Costa Rica. I believe that you have to work with the leaders of those other Central American countries to try to bring about the democratization of Nicaragua by negotiation, by pressure, by counseling, by diplomatic pressure—that we ought to be trying that first. But in concentrating so much just on the contras, this Administration has not paid enough attention to the rest of Central America.

At Vice-Presidential debate,
Omaha, Neb., Oct. 5/
The New York Times, 10-7:(A)13.

Enrique Bermudez
Commanding general of the
contras, rebels fighting the
Sandinista government of
Nicaragua

4

[On the U.S. Congress' vote to cut aid to his contras]: It isn't what we wanted, of course. [But] this is like losing a battle. We have not lost the war. We are in a struggle for democracy in Nicaragua, and we haven't achieved this goal yet. The causes that made us take up this struggle have not disappeared yet. We have taken a decision to continue the struggle.

Interview, Feb. 4/
The Washington Post, 2-5:(A)18.

5

[On the truce and negotiations between the contras and Sandinistas]: We will comply with

(ENRIQUE BERMUDEZ)

the truce. We will do our part. But we won't dismantle—we'll keep our forces cohesive under our control . . . What the Sandinistas want is a totalitarian regime . . . They are doing it [the cease-fire] to win time and achieve a better international image. [At the same time,] we are testing the Sandinistas. They . . . will have the last word if this peace-negotiating process is going to succeed. The only thing we are going to do is stop fighting and wait [to see] if they comply . . . [As to whether the negotiations will bring more war,] I'd bet on war. But I'd be glad to lose [the bet].

Interview, Miami/
Los Angeles Times, 3-31:(I)11.

1

We are an armed movement. Political opposition and civic opposition will never get the democracy we want in Nicaragua. The only way to get it is through armed struggle . . . [If we could] reach an agreement by negotiation, we'd be delighted to do that. We have proposed to give up our weapons if you [the Sandinistas] agree on this: freedom of expression, stop the persecution of the church, separation of the Army and Party, a judicial system independent of the government. All the democratic principles that exist in democratic countries. There is nothing extraordinary here, nothing the Sandinistas can't accomplish . . . But that decision remains with the Sandinistas . . . There is no climate to negotiate at this time.

Interview, Washington/
The Christian Science Monitor,
8-3:3.

Christopher S. Bond
United States Senator,
R-Missouri

2

The recent elections in El Salvador once again have proved a strong desire of the people of that country to live in a democratic government. The U.S. observer mission, of which I was a member, concluded that the elections were conducted in a fair and proper manner . . . The government of El Salvador can only hope to keep the support of its citizens if they are treated fairly and humanely. It is a difficult task, fighting against a well-financed group of Communist guerrillas, to make the government sound, stable and secure. The FMLN [rebels], which is backed by regimes in the Soviet Union, Cuba and Nicaragua, has made it very difficult for the still-fragile democracy in El Salvador to survive.

Before the Senate,
Washington, March 31/
The Washington Post, 4-5:(A)20.

Tomas Borge
Minister of the Interior
of Nicaragua

3

[On Nicaragua's freeing of 100 prisoners as part of a cease-fire agreement between the Sandinista government and the contra rebels fighting it]: For many, this [prisoner release] is a dramatic and painful decision. There has never been a negotiation that did not imply mutual concessions. We have sought new and audacious formulas. We talked for long hours, and we have made difficult, necessary and just decisions. If freeing 100 or 1,000 prisoners helps to save just a single drop of blood for one of the people's fighters, or for any other Nicaraguan, then freeing 100 or 1,000 prisoners is welcome.

The New York Times, 3-28:4.

4

[On his Sandinista government's negotiations with the contra rebels]: . . . we cannot expect anything with the contras and the ultra-rightists. They are playing the same games: sit down at the negotiating table, make unacceptable proposals, leave, and then, with all the communications media at their disposal, say that we are intransigent, war-like, stubborn narco-atheists. We are not and will not be willing to surrender our principles, the basis of our existence as a revolution.

Speech, Bluefields, Nicaragua/
The New York Times,
8-15:2

Aquilino E. Boyd
Panamanian representative at
the Organization of American States;
Former Panamanian Ambassador
to the United States

1

The most important thing the United States can do for democracy in Panama is to normalize relations with us as soon as possible. We want to open avenues of communication and cooperation with the United States in the next four weeks, to clear the atmosphere before [U.S. President-elect George] Bush takes the oath of office. If you [the U.S.] found a way to make deals with [Soviet leader Mikhail] Gorbachev and [PLO leader Yasir] Arafat, why not with [Panamanian leader Manuel] Noriega?

Dec. 21/
The New York Times, 12-22:(A)3.

John Edward Broadbent
Leader, New Democratic
Party of Canada

2

I am convinced that social democratic parties have done best where they have also proven to be effective in insuring that the economy is doing well—areas that people do not normally associate as being a top priority of a social democratic government.

Interview/
World Press Review, January:44.

3

[Criticizing the new U.S.-Canadian free-trade agreement]: There are on this North American continent of ours two strongly competing images of the good life—the American way [unrestrained capitalism, and the Canadian way, which places] a sense of community [ahead of profit]. If this deal is consummated, the odds are very great that it will be at once witness and participant to the triumph of one image over another.

The New York Times,
10-3:(A)8.

George Bush
Vice President of the United
States; Candidate for the
1988 Republican
U.S. Presidential nomination

4

Currently, we're in an effort to protect civilian rule in Panama against [Panamanian leader Manuel] Noriega, an indicted drug trafficker. And so far, he's stood up to this considerable economic pressure that we've applied, and I can tell you one reason why. Several reliable sources indicate that he's receiving millions of dollars in support from Libya. We support democracy in Panama, as we do throughout Latin America. And I'm convinced that if we handle it correctly, Noriega will go, democracy will prevail, and we can do it without exacerbating tensions of the past.

Before American Society of Newspaper
Editors, Washington, April 15/
The New York Times, 4-16:10.

5

[On U.S. relations with Cuba]: There have been no accommodations made with [Cuban President Fidel] Castro's corrupt, Communist government, and there will be no accommodations made with that government as long as Ronald Reagan is in the White House—and . . . if I'm elected [President], I can guarantee you [there won't be]. There will be no diplomatic or economic agreements that prolong the tyranny of Communists and the suffering of the Cuban people. And freedom there is not a bargaining chip of any kind at all.

Before Cuban American National
Foundation, Washington, June 13/
The Washington Post, 6-14:(A)4.

George Bush
Vice President of the United
States; 1988 Republican
Presidential nominee

6

[On charges that, as part of the Reagan Administration, he was involved in dealing with

(GEORGE BUSH)

Panamanian leader Manuel Noriega, who is suspected of drug-trafficking]: Seven [U.S.] Administrations were dealing with Mr. Noriega. It was the Reagan-Bush Administration that brought this man to justice [he was indicted in a U.S. court] . . . there was no evidence that Mr. Noriega was involved in drugs, no hard evidence, until we indicted him. And so I think it's about time we get this Noriega matter in perspective. Panama is a friendly country. I went down and talked to the President of Panama about cleaning up the money-laundering. Mr. Noriega was there, but there was no evidence [against him] at that time.

At Presidential debate,
Winston-Salem, N.C., Sept. 25/
The New York Times, 9-26:10.

George Bush
Vice President, and
President-elect,
of the United States

1

[On how high a priority he will give, now that he will be President, to aiding the contras, rebels fighting the Sandinista government of Nicaragua]: It will have a high priority because freedom and democracy in this hemisphere have a high priority, and I know these leaders in this hemisphere. I can't say I know [Nicaraguan President] Daniel Ortega that well, but I met him a time or two. And I will press to keep the pressure on the Sandinistas to keep their commitment to the Organization of American States, the commitment being one to democracy and freedom.

News conference, Houston, Nov. 9/
USA Today, 11-10:(A)13.

Adolfo Calero
President, national directorate,
Nicaraguan Democratic Force

2

[Criticizing the recent U.S. Congressional vote to cut aid to the contras, rebels fighting the Sandinista government of Nicaragua]: It is sad

that the Soviet Union can be a more consistent ally [of the Sandinistas], and that the United States is an inconsistent ally [of the contras], not as it should be. The cutoff of aid to the Nicaraguan resistance is affecting us more every day, because without resources it is very difficult to maintain a war against an [adversary] that has full Soviet support.

Contra radio broadcast, March 10/
The New York Times, 3-12:3.

Cuauhtemoc Cardenas
Democratic Front candidate
for President of Mexico

3

We need to view the [Mexican foreign] debt as being made up of two principal components. Part of the debt was contracted when everyone was certain that Mexico would be able to pay it back. But another portion was contracted when lenders and borrowers alike already knew that the Mexican economy did not have the capacity to repay it. Thus the [foreign] banks share responsibility for these loans, just as if they had been made to insolvent individuals or corporations; there is no real reason why nations should be treated differently . . . I think therefore that we would be justified in limiting payment of the debt to a percentage of export earnings, non-petroleum export earnings, or gross domestic product. The option of suspending payments on the debt, for all its potential problems, is something that should be looked at seriously . . . I think we have to engage in a tough renegotiation of the debt, with an exclusive eye to Mexico's interest and not to external considerations. We should state clearly from the outset the maximum we are able to pay, and begin negotiating from there. If it takes a suspension of debt servicing to get the banks to negotiate with us on those terms, then we must suspend debt servicing.

Interview/The Washington Post, 7-14:(A)18.

Jimmy Carter
Former President of the
United States

4

Last year I spoke quite optimistically about developments in the Americas and about the region's hope for a successful transition to democracy. Recent events there give cause for concern, however. This is true, especially, of the perpetuation of dictatorship in Haiti, a new wave of killings in El Salvador and Guatemala, the crackdown on political opponents in Nicaragua and Panama, the apparent political and economic disintegration of Peru and, in general, the growing fear in a number of these countries that military coups are again a real possibility. These conditions, the drug problem and the tremendous strain that the mounting foreign debt is placing on many countries in this hemisphere call for an imaginative U.S.-Latin America policy, designed to bring economic recovery to the region. Without such progress, freedom and democracy may be doomed.

At 1989 Carter-Menil human-rights ceremony, Dec. 10/ The Washington Post, 12-27:(A)14.

Fidel Castro
President of Cuba

1

When the revolution was victorious here, the people were armed. The people have weapons here. If the people wanted to remove the revolution, they wouldn't have to wait for the CIA to send the weapons. They could do that in three days because they have the weapons. The people have the power. They are the force from which the revolution emanates. How long would other governments last if they gave the power to the people?

Interview/ USA Today, 2-22:(A)7.

2

There is not even a semblance of a Soviet missile in Cuba. Not one. I repeat, not one. It's insane to think about . . . But the idea that Cuba might be a military threat to the United States, that is Walt Disney fantasy . . . With your [the U.S.'] sophisticated satellite spying, you know when a cat is walking on the roof of a house in Cuba. If an elephant goes into the White House, we don't find out.

Interview/USA Today, 2-22:(A)7.

3

We must state right here, once and for all, that we don't need more than one [political] party [in Cuba] . . . in the same way that Lenin didn't need more than one party to make the [Soviet] October Revolution.

Speech to his supporters, July 26/ The Washington Post, 7-28:(A)23.

Vinicio Cerezo
President of Guatemala

4

[Saying he carries a pistol to defend himself]: There are still people here who think violence is a means to resolve political differences. If I need to be defended, I want to participate. Independence and autonomy depend on your capacity to do things yourself—in every sense.

Los Angeles Times, 2-19:(I)1.

5

[On the Sandinista government of Nicaragua]: Political reality puts the Sandinistas against the wall. Either they take a different path, which implies a reduction of their power over the medium term, or they will soon have to impose a dictatorship. The economic situation will produce movements—not necessarily political—but social movements, aimed against them. They need to make some choices.

Interview/ The New York Times, 12-13:(A)6.

Alfredo Cesar
Leader, Nicaraguan Resistance, contra group fighting the Sandinista government of Nicaragua

6

Our objective is to achieve democracy in Nicaragua. Some people thought the only way to do that was to overthrow the Sandinistas. But I

(ALFREDO CESAR)

never thought that ... We [contras] saw that there was no political will in the United States to keep supporting the war, but neither was there a desire to abandon us. It was clear that the political will was somewhere in the middle. So we decided to test the Sandinistas' intention [by agreeing to hold peace talks with them] and see if they were willing to make concessions for democracy.

The New York Times, 4-4:4.

1

The government is avoiding commitments. We explain what our position is, and they say, "We understand; that's fine." But when we try to put it clearly in an agreement, they avoid that. We are not getting from the discussions what the resistance [the contras] needs for an agreement.

Managua, June 8/
The New York Times, 6-9:3.

2

[On recent contra-Sandinista negotiations to end the war]: The round [of negotiations] failed because we were not able to get a firm commitment from the Sandinistas to get the democratic reforms which Nicaragua needs to end the war. The resistance [contras] is acting in good faith, has been acting in good faith all through these negotiations. The Sandinistas have not done the same thing.

Washington, June 14/
Los Angeles Times, 6-15:(I)9.

Manuel J. Clouthier
Conservative National Action Party
candidate for President
of Mexico

3

[American growers] asked me why we Mexicans thought we had a right to sell tomatoes in the United States, anyway. I said, "I'll tell you why. Because I get up every morning and shave with a Gillette razor, I open a General Electric refriger-

ator for breakfast, I get in my Ford car to go to the office and dictate on my Remington [voice recorder] ... That's why I have a right to sell tomatoes to the United States."

Interview,
Monterrey, Mexico/
Los Angeles Times, 6-14:(I)6.

Leslie Cockburn
Producer, CBS News;
Producer, "Frontline," PBS-TV

4

[On U.S. Lt. Col. Oliver North's involvement in last year's Iran-contra scandal]: The documents show that North was running this war openly within the [U.S. Reagan] Administration—as if he were mowing his lawn. He was blatantly telling [Nicaraguan contra rebel leaders] Adolfo Calero and Enrique Bermudez what to do and where to go. He was getting intelligence information from the Pentagon and regularly informing such senior people as then Chairman of the Joint Chiefs of Staff General John Vessey. People at the FBI were on call when North needed them and ever willing to show him their reports on his operation. The documents reveal that this scandal was much broader than the [Iran-contra hearing] report indicates.

Panel discussion,
New School for Social Research,
New York/
Harper's, February:47.

Tony Coelho
United States Representative,
D-California

5

[Criticizing U.S. President Reagan's decision to send more arms to the contras, rebels fighting the Sandinista government of Nicaragua]: Basically, it proves that the White House does not want peace in Central America. They want a military victory at all costs. They don't care about anything else.

Jan. 19/The New York Times,
1-20:6.

289

Arturo Cruz
*Former high official in both
the Nicaraguan Sandinista
government and the anti-
Sandinista contra rebels*

1

The most repugnant aspect of their [the Sandinistas'] perversion of the revolution is their belief that they are a vanguard that can use state power for Party purposes. They make concessions, but they never recognize rights . . . [But] the Sandinistas were working in the catacombs while we in the traditional opposition were out of touch with the rising expectations of the masses. The Sandinistas have broken barriers in Nicaragua that had to be broken, and that is irreversible . . . I've made powerful enemies, starting with the [U.S.] CIA and the Sandinistas. It's because I wouldn't keep my mouth shut in either place. I didn't want to be someone's clown or a pet monkey that rides a bicycle in circles. If you're in the center, you are always in opposition. The people at the extremes hold power.

*Interview, Miami, Jan. 6/
The New York Times, 1-8:3.*

Roberto D'Aubuisson
*Leader, Republican National
Alliance Party (ARENA) of
El Salvador*

2

[Saying the U.S. does not do enough to help the Salvadoran government in its fight against the rebel insurgency]: The United States must learn to respect us. They have imposed this low-intensity conflict on us. They give us the money, and we give the bodies.

*Campaigning for the Presidency
of El Salvador/
U.S. News & World Report,
3-21:43.*

Miguel de la Madrid
President of Mexico

3

[Calling for a negotiated end to the war in Nicaragua and for non-intervention by the U.S.

in Latin American political affairs]: War will continue to generate regrettable events. Not only death, but poverty, absence of hope, and great resentment of the United States—not only among Nicaraguans, but also among other Latin Americans who say: "We cannot accept the United States as the supreme judge of our political system, to say who is good and who is bad and, if it says that someone is bad, to try to remove that government."

*Interview, Mexico City, Feb. 2/
The New York Times, 2-5:5.*

Eric Arturo Delvalle
Former President of Panama

4

[On his being ousted as President by Panama's Legislature, which is effectively under the control of armed-forces General Manuel Noriega]: I don't have a seat of government, or military support, but I do have 2 million Panamanians who are tired . . . of living under a regime that one man has governed capriciously.

*Feb. 26/
Los Angeles Times, 2-28:(I)1.*

Christopher J. Dodd
*United States Senator,
D-Connecticut*

5

[On the renewed effort by some in the U.S. Senate to send more American aid to the Nicaraguan contra rebels after Nicaragua's Sandinista government launched an attack on contra bases in Honduras]: Obviously, the [U.S. Reagan] Administration and those who favor aid have the upper hand now. The Sandinistas are stupid. They've once again snatched defeat from the jaws of victory. [But] this issue is one that's been decided by a margin of six votes among 535 members of the House and Senate [and can change quickly with the news from Central America]. Tell me what the headline is tonight, and I'll tell you what the vote will be tomorrow.

*March 18/
Los Angeles Times, 3-19:(I)13.*

Robert J. Dole
United States Senator,
R-Kansas; Candidate for the
1988 Republican U.S.
Presidential nomination

1

[Criticizing U.S. Democratic Presidential candidates for not standing up against the Sandinista government of Nicaragua]: Every Democratic candidate has had an opportunity to stand up and be counted on an issue that is as symbolic for our time as [Adolf] Hitler's brazen aggression was for an earlier generation. The call to defend the freedom of Nicaragua, which should be easy for them to answer, instead produces endless foot shuffling and sophistry . . . What will the Democrats say [when Sandinista-like or inspired revolutions or take-overs occur in adjacent countries]? [Will they say,] well, we have learned to live with Communist Nicaragua, just as we once learned to live with Communist Cuba, [and] it follows that we could learn to live with a Communist Costa Rica, Panama or even a Communist Mexico? The fact that they [U.S. Democrats] have chosen America—and not Communism—as their hemispheric villain shows how strange and potentially dangerous these times really are.

At Center for Strategic and
International Studies,
Washington, March 23/
Los Angeles Times, 3-24:(I)20.

Charles F. Doran
Director, Center of Canadian
Studies, Johns Hopkins
University

2

[Saying if Canada fails to ratify its recent free-trade agreement with the U.S., industries may seek protectionist measures from the government]: Any aggrieved party, any interest group that feels it's been treated badly in this arrangement, will come to Congress and ask for protectionist measures, to make sure that a free-trade agreement like this never happens to them again.

The New York Times,
11-18:(A)6.

Jose Napoleon Duarte
President of El Salvador

3

[On his suffering from a serious stomach disease]: You all know me. I have been a man of crisis, a man of battle, a man who fights. I have fought against all the vicissitudes, against dictatorships for so many years in search of democracy, against the country's biggest crisis, against an earthquake, three droughts. And now God gives me this other test. I am going to fight and, God willing, I'll come out all right.

To reporters, San Salvador, May 31/
The New York Times, 6-1:9.

Michael S. Dukakis
Governor of Massachusetts (D);
Candidate for the 1988
Democratic U.S.
Presidential nomination

4

[Criticizing U.S. support for the contras, rebels fighting the Sandinista government of Nicaragua]: [Under U.S. President Reagan, the U.S. has] run guns, mined harbors, consorted with torturers and thugs, counseled political assassination, lied to Congress, sold arms to the Ayatollah [of Iran to finance contra aid], squandered hundreds of millions of dollars and repeatedly broken the laws of our land in an effort to overthrow the Sandinista government.

Campaign speech,
Muscatine, Iowa, Jan. 29/
Los Angeles Times, 1-30:(I)24.

5

[Criticizing U.S. aid for the contras, rebels fighting the Sandinista government of Nicaragua]: [In Nicaraguan hospitals,] you almost always see a child or two or three, without an arm, without a leg, without vision, a child who has been hurt in a contra raid, a child who has been playing around with a Sandinista mine, a victim of this war. And when spokesmen for the [U.S. Reagan] Administration talk about keeping up the pressure on the Sandinistas, we have to know what pressure really means: kids with their

(MICHAEL S. DUKAKIS)

arms blown off, pregnant women assassinated and raped, villages and farms destroyed. That's the human face of "pressure"...And that's why I say: Not one dollar of contra aid. Not one. Not one!

Campaigning in Iowa, Jan. 30/
The Washington Post, 2-1:(A)10.

1

[On U.S. President Reagan's statements that the Nicaraguan contra rebels are a 20th-century equivalent of America's Founding Fathers]: Anybody who knows anything about the history of Nicaragua, of Central America, couldn't possibly make that statement. I think the [Costa Rican President Oscar] Arias peace plan [for Nicaragua] is the best opportunity we've had in a long, long time. I think we ought to seize it. I wish the [Reagan] Administration would stop attempting to undercut it or weaken it or sabotage it. The Administration just has what amounts now to an ideological obsession with overthrowing [the Nicaraguan Sandinista] government.

Interview, Brookline, Mass./
U.S. News & World Report, 2-1:25.

2

There is no room in this hemisphere for military bases from which the Soviet Union might project military force against ourselves, our allies or friends. And if Nicaragua, or any other government in Central or South America, seeks to overthrow or subvert its neighbors, we have the right and the responsiblity to stop them.

Campaign speech,
Manchester, N.H., Feb. 14/
The Washington Post, 2-15:(A)11.

3

[On the possibility of a Soviet satellite state in Central America]: There are two fundamental issues here. One is the presence of a foreign military power in the hemisphere that threatens our security. That's problem Number 1. And we can't tolerate that. The second is efforts by any nation in this hemisphere to subvert its neighbor. We can't tolerate that, and it's prohibited in any event by the [OAS] Charter. That applies to us and it applies to any other nation in the hemisphere. Now, if you have a Soviet satellite—at least, as that phrase is commonly defined—then you'll have both a foreign military presence, which threatens our security, and an ideology which systematically attempts to subvert neighbors. We can't tolerate either one.

Interveiw/
Los Angeles Times, 5-26:(I)22.

4

Every time [the U.S.] intervened [in Latin America], we did so in the name of democracy. And almost without exception, the legacy of our intervention has been tyranny. We put ourselves above the law. We tried to go it alone. We tried to impose our views, instead of helping to build a democratic tradition.

Time, 7-18:23.

Michael S. Dukakis
Governor of Massachusetts (D);
1988 Democratic U.S.
Presidential nominee

5

Last year alone, we spent almost twice as much trying to overthrow the government of Nicaragua as we did in the war against drugs in all of Latin America. That's absurd. And for years, while [Panamanian leader Manuel] Noriega was doing business with drugs in Panama, we were doing business with General Noriega. That, my friends, is criminal. How can we ask our neighbors in Latin America to crack down on drugs when we have an Administration that's in bed with one of the biggest thugs on the continent?

Campaign speech, Cleveland, Aug. 25/
Los Angeles Times, 8-26:(I)15.

6

The drug cancer is eating away the foundation of fragile democracies throughout this hemis-

(MICHAEL S. DUKAKIS)

phere. It's corrupting governments, destroying economies, ravaging communities, spawning terror and crippling lives. It's the single greatest cause of violence in the Americas today.

Campaign speech, Cleveland, Aug. 25/
The New York Times, 8-26:1.

Roderick Esquivel
Former Vice President
of Panama

1

[On Manuel Noriega's rule over Panama which resulted in Esquivel's ouster as Vice President]: If peaceful means and the economic measures are not sufficient to achieve democracy [in Panama], then I am the first to say that democracy must be obtained by fighting for it.

USA Today, 3-10:(A)8.

Marlin Fitzwater
Assistant to President of
the United States Ronald Reagan
for Press Relations

2

[Criticizing Panamanian leader Manuel Noriega's offer to step down as head of government if his opponents would agree to negotiations with him]: [The offer] was nothing more than a transparent ploy to legitimize [the Presidency of Manuel Solis, installed by Noriega's supporters after ousting the previous President]. Such a step would leave General Noriega in actual control of the Panamanian Defense Forces. This proposal is like getting the fox out of the henhouse, then giving him quarters next door.

Washington, March 22/
The New York Times, 3-23:4.

Carlos Fuentes
Mexican author and
diplomat

3

Between 1932 and 1952, [the U.S. and Latin America] had 20 years of excellent relations

based on respect for the internal dynamics of each Latin American country, whatever the ideological makeup. I think the way to respond to a perceived Soviet menace or challenge in that part of the world is still [the late U.S. President Franklin] Roosevelt way. The really big issues that are going to decide the destiny of the continent are debt, drugs, migration. We haven't even started to consider these things seriously and the future of the continent will depend upon them. They will make the [current rocky] Central American situation look like a tea party in years to come.

Interview/
The New York Times, 5-30:20.

Alan Garcia
President of Peru

4

Peru needs much deeper changes than the system allows. The Peru of today is the result of 160 years of economic and political centralization. Only a restructuring over 10 or 20 years would allow real change. But, as always, the urgent prevents us from dealing with the important.

Interview, Lima, Oct. 23/
The Washington Post, 10-26:(A)20.

5

I am sure that the American people know that a disunited Latin America is not a good neighbor and that an impoverished Latin America is not a good market. Now, a few days before the [U.S. Presidential] election . . . is the moment to make this proposal: Whoever wins, he must take up the proposal of Latin America to work together on the great problems of the future.

At Latin American summit meeting,
Punta del Este, Uruguay, Oct. 27/
Los Angeles Times, 10-28:(I)15.

Bob Graham
United States Senator,
D-Florida

6

One week from today the United Nations Human Rights Commission will adjourn its

(BOB GRAHAM)

annual meeting in Geneva. The United States delegation ... has offered a resolution for an international investigation of human-rights abuses in Cuba ... The same resolution to investigate allegations of abuses in Cuba was defeated by one vote in Geneva last year. That vote was a disgrace. Human rights can never be held pawn to politics. Such callous disregard for the people of Cuba was loudly defended as condemnation of the United States for its own imperfections. We say that we all live in glass houses, but in [Cuban President Fidel] Castro's house the drapes are always drawn. This year we have the chance to fling wide those drapes and bring all of Cuba's dark secrets to light.

Before the Senate,
Washington, March 4/
The Washington Post, 3-8:(A)18.

Ramiro Gurdian
Leader, Democratic Coordinator,
coalition in opposition to Sandinista
government of Nicaragua

1

The leader of the Nicaraguan opposition is called hunger. People are hungry now, and when people don't see any solution, economic discontent becomes political discontent.

Interview, Managua/
The New York Times, 7-29:5.

Lee H. Hamilton
United States Representative,
D-Indiana

2

[On U.S. support for the contras, rebels fighting the Sandinista government of Nicaragua]: We should insist that President [Daniel] Ortega of Nicaragua keep his promises. But we must also be realistic. Democracy cannot blossom overnight. We cannot require standards other democracies in the region do not meet. In the near term, the Sandinistas will remain whether we vote for or against contra aid. If our objective is to moderate Sandinista behavior, then the

[Arias] peace plan holds promise. If our objective is to overthrow them, then this peace plan doesn't make sense ... During six months of the Central American peace plan, more positive changes in Nicaragua have been achieved than during six years of contra war. Those with the most at stake here are not Americans, but the ordinary people of Central America who will have to fight and die if the war continues.

Radio broadcast, Jan. 23/
The Washington Post, 1-27:(A)18.

3

[Criticizing U.S. President Reagan's request for more aid to the contras, rebels fighting the Sandinista government of Nicaragua]: The President's request ignores the most important problems in Latin America. Fragile democracies in the hemisphere worry about debt, poverty and their future. We are devoting limited resources and time to Nicaragua, which has less than 1 percent of Latin America's population or economy. Our policy-makers must focus on the key regional problems that affect us—immigration, drugs, debt and economic growth. Our neglect of these problems erodes our influence in Latin America.

Broadcast address to the nation,
Washington, Feb. 2/
USA Today, 2-3:(A)9.

Tom Harkin
United States Senator,
D-Iowa

4

[On the U.S.-backed contras, rebels fighting the Sandinista government of Nicaragua]: It was the contras, not the Sandinistas, who were responsible for the collapse of the latest round of peace talks ... If the Sandinistas begin to open up the political process, the United States Embassy begins to promote insurrection, distortion and chaos. On the other hand, if the Sandinistas close down the political space, then the [U.S.] Administration will use that to promote military aid to the contras.

The New York Times, 7-15:4.

294

Gary Hart
Candidate for the 1988
Democratic Presidential
nomination; Former
United States Senator,
D-Colorado

1

[Criticizing U.S. aid to the contras, rebels fighting the Sandinista government of Nicaragua]: The war against Nicaragua is wrong and we ought to stop it. It is beneath this country's dignity. It's a political and military failure and, worst of all, it violates our own democratic ideals. The problem is, in Central America and elsewhere, we are simply letting the vast tidal waves of change in the world confuse us and baffle us and make us look weak and foolish.

Campaign speech/
The New York Times, 1-26:13.

Ernest F. Hollings
United States Senator,
D-South Carolina

2

[On U.S. funding of the contras, rebels fighting the Sandinista government of Nicaragua]: How ironic that several months ago we heard a remarkable outcry here that $100-million was too much to give the contras. One hundred million? Nine years ago, we gave $117-million to the Sandinistas. The Soviets now have given the Sandinistas $4.7-billion. The Sandinistas have run up a foreign debt of another $9-billion. So they have had plenty of money to consolidate their iron grip and build the largest army in Central American history. They have had plenty of money to build their political prisons. At the same time, they have done away with free newspapers' independent radio, and every other freedom. Yet now they dare to play on the inexhaustible gullibility of Americans by enticing us with empty gestures of so-called democratization [so that the U.S. will stop funding the contras]. Indeed, they have received expert advice on how to manipulate the Congress. We have witnessed the disgraceful cynicism of a gentleman speaking on the House floor who had recently gone to Central America to advise [Nicaraguan President Daniel] Ortega on what to do. We have U.S. Congressmen coaching the team down there, saying, "If you give a little bit of that, we can make a case on the [House] floor and keep the contras from getting aid." Who is kidding whom? There is no education in the second kick of a mule. We trusted Ortega once and were betrayed.

Before the Senate, Washington/
The Wall Street Journal, 2-8:26.

Richard N. Holwill
Deputy Assistant Secretary of
State of the United States

3

[Saying the U.S. should not yet impose new economic sanctions against Haiti]: [The new government of Haitian President Leslie F. Manigat] has shown a determination to move Haiti in a democratic direction. We should not expect perfection before we offer assistance.

Before House Foreign Affairs
subcommittee, Washington, March 23/
Los Angeles Times, 3-24:(I)2.

Jesse L. Jackson
American civil-rights leader;
Candidate for the 1988
Democratic U.S.
Presidential nomination

4

The CIA has been involved in the drugs-for-arms operations [with the Nicaraguan contra rebels] and with the Honduran generals. Some of it came out of the hearings about the [U.S.] Iran-contra [scandal last year]. Our dealings with the contras is a sleazy operation. We are heavily implicated in that situation . . . I'm convinced that our CIA is deeply involved in the sleazy and corrupt behavior in Central America and Latin America, and that we should have a full and complete investigation . . . [The] reality is our CIA has been involved in that whole drug operation. It is beneath the dignity of our government. It should never be allowed to happen again.

At Washburn University,
March 18/
Los Angeles Times, 3-19:(I)22.

(JESSE L. JACKSON)

1

[Criticizing U.S. economic sanctions against Panama to try to force Panamanian leader Manuel Noriega from office]: If, in a day or two, the full-court press of setting the forest on fire to smoke Noriega out had worked, it would have been a more temporary pain [for the Panamanian people]. But now as the days go on, Noriega is insulated with his wealth and his military. [Because of the sanctions,] the common people cannot get food, cannot get medicine, some cannot get water. We stand the danger . . . of stirring up anti-American hysteria, the kind of nationalism that will limit our impact in the region.

Speech, Milwaukee, Wis., April 4/
Los Angeles Times, 4-5:(I)16.

2

[Saying the U.S. should help Mexico and the rest of Latin America financially]: It's better to have prosperous neighbors instead of impoverished neighbors. So long as there is poverty on one side of the border, there will be emigration to the other side. Let's build up Latin America, with 400 million neighbors, allies and customers. We should be exporting grain and tractors and medicine and computers and infrastructure. If they're buying and we're selling, and they're selling and we're buying, we both live together as brothers and sisters and not apart as fools.

Campaign speech,
San Diego, May 17/
Los Angeles Times, 5-18:(I)15.

John Paul II
Pope

3

I cannot silence the sadness which invades my heart as a pastor to see that the noble Peruvian people continue suffering the scourge of violence . . . I have perceived once again the clamor for peace which comes from the throats of so many Peruvians of good will. The long and cruel years of fighting between brothers, which has caused so many wounds among the people and the society, must not prevent the achievement of a just and lasting peace.

Speech, Lima, Peru, May 16/
Los Angeles Times, 5-17:(I)11.

Henry A. Kissinger
Former Secretary of State of
the United States

4

Nobody knows any more what we [the U.S.] are trying to accomplish in Central America. The [U.S. Reagan] Administration made a mistake to begin with by putting forward a request for aid [for the contra rebels in Nicaragua] that was so small it could not convince the American public that the security of the United States was involved. Secondly, they defined the peace process in terms of criteria that permit no objective assessments. If we had said that the Cubans must leave Nicaragua and that the Nicaraguan Army should be reduced to historic Central American dimensions, that would have been concrete criteria the public could understand. But when you say that you want democracy in a country [Nicaragua] which has never known democracy in its whole history, then you create a criterion with no clear-cut objective definitions.

Interview/Los Angeles Times, 3-13:(V)6.

Luis Larrain
Deputy Director, Office of
Planning of Chilean
President Augusto Pinochet

5

[Saying the economy of Chile is improving]: This process of growth, sooner or later, reaches all the people. Yes, the rich are getting richer, but the poor are also getting richer.

Interview/Los Angeles Times, 9-12:(I)8.

Sol M. Linowitz
Lawyer;
Former United States delegate
to the Organization of
American States

6

[Saying Latin American nations are uneasy about current U.S. economic sanctions against

(SOL M. LINOWITZ)

Panama to try to force out Panamanian leader Manuel Noriega]: What troubles them is that in their eyes this is economic intervention. And when they look upon what is going on in Panama, they see this as a precedent that could be used in their country if in the judgment of the United States it becomes necessary.

The New York Times, 4-6:6.

Anthony P. Maingot
Editor, "Hemisphere" magazine;
Professor of sociology, Florida
International University

1

Given the history of racism, when the non-white populations of the world were supposed to be incapable of self-government, the Caribbean people have undoubtedly proven their capacity to govern themselves. All the [island] chain—these are well-governed societies with high regard for human rights and a good standard of living . . . The critical measure by which to judge any society or government is its infant mortality rate, the life expectancy of its citizens, the state's education system, and whether or not the jails are full of political enemies. For the most part, the Caribbean has nothing to be ashamed of.

Ebony, October:127.

Leslie F. Manigat
Candidate for President
of Haiti

2

[On criticism of unfairness in the just-held national Presidential elections which show him as the leader]: Our little country has no chance. Instead of understanding our little country, a campaign of disinformation has begun . . . Irregularities are natural in Haiti, because this is the first time Haitians have been called upon to participate in the democratic process. You are going to ask a weak, fragile, nascent democracy, an infant democracy, to do what big democracies do? That's not fair to us.

News conference, Jan. 18/
Los Angeles Times, 1-19:(I)5.

Leslie F. Manigat
President of Haiti

3

The people [of Haiti] can't take any more. They are tired of being hungry, of being sick, of being badly housed, of being without shoes and clothing, of being illiterate, of being unemployed, of being beaten, of being despised, of being badly off—in a word, of not being full-fledged citizens of this country.

Inaugural address,
Port-au-Prince, Haiti, Feb. 7/
Los Angeles Times, 2-8:(I)6.

Bosco Matamoros
Spokesman for the contras,
rebels fighting the Sandinista
government of Nicaragua

4

We [contras] have faith in [U.S.] President Reagan's commitment to our cause, but there is a grim reality. The Sandinistas are hunting our forces like rabbits on the ground, and [the U.S.] Congress has not provided us with the material to defend ourselves. You have given the Sandinistas a license to wipe us out, as long as they do it discreetly.

Los Angeles Times, 10-15:(I)4.

George S. McGovern
Senior fellow, Center for
Policy Research; Former
United States Senator,
D-South Dakota

5

[Criticizing the hostile U.S. policy toward the Sandinista government of Nicaragua]: You would think, listening to the rhetoric coming out of the [U.S. Reagan] Administration about Nicaragua, that they had 750 million people, all armed with nuclear weapons, ready to take over North America. We should remind ourselves we're dealing with 3 million impoverished people in a country that can't feed itself. It's no threat to anybody except maybe to itself.

Interview/
USA Today, 5-18:(A)11.

297

WHAT THEY SAID IN 1988

Richard L. Millett
*Professor of history, and
authority on Latin American
affairs, Southern Illinois University,
Edwardsville*

1

[On the U.S. desire to oust Panamanian strongman Manuel Noriega, who has been indicted in the U.S. on drug-smuggling charges]: You don't want to get too far out and convert this into a Noriega-U.S. fight. Other Latin American governments are moving on this—Costa Rica, Guatemala, Argentina, Bolivia. It's not a finished issue. Noriega will go this year and, though an [U.S.] embargo could speed the process, it would damage the [Panamanian] economy . . . and why damage the whole country to get rid of Noriega?

*The Christian Science Monitor,
3-2:28.*

Jaime Morales Carazo
*Negotiator for the contras,
rebels fighting the Sandinista
government of Nicaragua*

2

We [in the contra movement] all have the same goal of a democratic Nicaragua, but some of us think we have to negotiate with a pistol on the table and others think we have to treat the Sandinistas with courtesy. But before we can deal with the enemy, we have to overcome the rivalries and jealousies within our own house.

Los Angeles Times, 4-28:(I)1.

Ambler Moss
*Dean, School of International
Studies, University of Miami;
Former United States Ambassador
to Panama*

3

[Criticizing U.S. economic sanctions against Panama to try to force Panamanian leader Manuel Noriega from the country after being indicted in the U.S. for drug trafficking]: The wrong methods have been used. I think the drug-trafficking indictment helped lock him in Panama

because it would have been impossible for him to leave with that hanging over his head. Second, to try to run him out of Panama by taking economic measures was an ill-chosen method . . . One thing that I don't think has seriously been attempted throughout all this is serious negotiations with him—which only now in the last few days seem to be beginning.

Interview/USA Today, 4-25:(A)9.

Brian Mulroney
Prime Minister of Canada

4

On a good day, you can't get 50 per cent of the people of Canada to agree on anything. That's just the way it is. I won the largest majority in the history of Canada in 1984, and I got 50 per cent of the vote, which meant at the moment of my highest popularity 50 per cent of the people voted against me. That has to tell you a lot about the [Canadian] psyche.

*Interview, Ottawa, April 22/
The Washington Post, 4-26:(A)23.*

5

[On the new U.S.-Canada Free Trade Agreement]: You have the two largest trading powers in the world. This is an exchange of $200-billion a year. It sets precedents in terms of investments, dispute settlements. We've just done the biggest deal in history. Already, the U.S. does more business with this province [Ontario] than it does with Japan. The U.S. does more business with Canada [as a whole] than it does with West Germany. Canada is indispensable to the economic well-being of the United States, and vice versa.

*Interview, Ottawa, Aug. 25/
USA Today, 8-26:(A)9.*

6

[On the forthcoming national election in Canada, in which the recent free-trade agreement with the United States has become an important issue in his re-election campaign]: Remember, this election is for four years. Not just the 30 seconds it takes to tear up a treaty.

(BRIAN MULRONEY)

Governing is not a single destructive blow. It is a continuing series of positive acts, of making complex and difficult decisions, of building Canada step by step.

Campaigning/
The New York Times, 11-17:(A)4.

1

Americans might reflect on the fact that there is in Canada, as in other industrialized countries, a well of anti-Americanism. It happens that it's not enough to elect a dog-catcher, but this doesn't stop people from trying to whip it up.

News conference, Baie Comeau,
Canada, Nov. 22/
The New York Times, 11-23:(A)6.

Richard M. Nixon
Former President of the
United States

2

[Supporting U.S. backing of the contras, rebels fighting the Sandinista government of Nicaragua]: We hear [from critics of U.S. policy], "No more Vietnams." But people fail to realize that by supporting the contras, we are avoiding another Vietnam, because the contras—the anti-Communist freedom fighters—are doing the fighting that Americans might have to do in the event that the Nicaraguan Communist government solidifies its position, and if the increased Russian arms become a threat to its neighbors and to the Panama Canal.

Interview/USA Today, 4-5:(A)11.

Manuel Antonio Noriega
Commander of the armed
forces of Panama

3

[On U.S. attempts to drive him from office because of his alleged involvement in drug trafficking]: The aggression against us has a name and a purpose. Its name is the [U.S.] military bases, and its purpose is the continuity of a foreign [U.S.] army above the national army on our own territory. The [U.S.] State Department, and others, say the solution is Noriega out or dead. But they are wrong. They are wrong because this is a struggle for national liberation.

Speech, Santiago, Panama, Feb. 8/
The New York Times, 2-10:8.

4

[On U.S. charges that he is involved in international drug trafficking]: The accusations are a low political blow. For 18 years I have been cooperating in the battle against drugs . . . When nobody else was working to combat drugs, Panama was.

Broadcast interview/
"60 Minutes," CBS-TV, 2-28.

Sam Nunn
United States Senator,
D-Georgia

5

So erosive is the loss of the [U.S. Reagan] Administration's credibility [on Central America that] . . . you reach the stage where people just don't believe things. It goes way back to the mining of the harbors [of Nicaragua by the U.S.]. From that point on, there's been one case after another that's undermined the Administration's credibility on Central America.

Los Angeles Times, 3-19:(I)14.

Miguel Obando y Bravo
Roman Catholic Archbishop
of Managua, Nicaragua

6

[On the war between the Sandinista government of Nicaragua and the contra rebels]: The principal obstacle to peace is that there are two incompatible concepts of democracy. The contras favor the Western style, while the government says it will not accept a democracy like those in Argentina, Venezuela or Costa Rica.

To reporters/
The New York Times, 8-26:4.

Daniel Ortega
President of Nicaragua

1

[Criticizing U.S. support for the contras, rebels fighting his Sandinista government]: [The contra war] has left more than 25,000 of my countrymen dead, and the number grows everyday. Isn't it time to say: Enough!? To be sure, Nicaragua and the United States have their present differences. But I am convinced that none of them is irreconcilable. It is not only possible for our two countries to co-exist, it is possible to be friends, even partners. This is my government's and my own personal profound desire.

Letter to U.S. President Reagan,
Jan. 25/
Los Angeles Times, 1-26:(I)24.

2

[On the U.S. Congress' vote not to fund new aid for the contras, rebels fighting his Sandinista government]: We won't let down our guard. As long as the war goes on, all Nicaraguans must remain massively, permanently mobilized to defend our revolution by every means . . . and to complete the total defeat of the mercenary forces [the contras]. The war will only come to an end when the United States accepts a cease-fire in Nicaragua and renounces its policy of force and the possibility of using its military might to invade Nicaragua.

Broadcast address to the nation,
Managua, Feb. 4/
The Washington Post, 2-5:(A)1.

3

[On U.S. Democratic Presidential nominee Michael Dukakis]: We can trust Dukakis' administrative ability, and the administrative ability of a future Democratic Administration to change U.S. policy [which is now anti-Sandinista in Nicaragua]. I think that with Dukakis we could have better conditions to work for a new dialog. [Former U.S. President Jimmy] Carter did not enter into a dirty war against Nicaragua; he always wanted to resolve problems through diplomatic means. It was when [current U.S.

President] Ronald Reagan came to office that the dirty war began.

Interview, Managua, July/
Forbes, 8-22:40.

4

Our socialism is a socialism that gives all economic sectors the opportunity to produce and contribute. It protects all . . . who have a true desire to produce, to be efficient and to share their wealth with everyone else. This is the only thing we ask and demand.

Speech at rally marking 9th
anniversary of the Sandinista
government's rise to power,
Juigalpa, Nicaragua, July 19/
Los Angeles Times, 7-20:(I)18.

5

[On the U.S. policy opposing his Sandinista government]: In January 1989, when [U.S.] President Reagan ends his term, the Sandinista revolution will remain firm. The Sandinista revolution will be here, and President Reagan will be gone with his history of terror, leaving a sad example for the peoples of the world.

Speech at rally marking 9th
anniversary of the Sandinista
government's rise to power,
Juigalpa, Nicaragua, July 19/
The New York Times, 7-20:3.

6

[On U.S. policy against his Sandinista government]: The responsibility for the future of peace in Central America doesn't depend on Nicaragua. It depends on the Yankee government . . . Yankee pressure doesn't make the Sandinistas more flexible. It makes the Sandinistas harder.

To workers at electric plant,
Managua/The Washington Post,
8-5:(A)26.

Humberto Ortega
Minister of Defense
of Nicaragua

7

[On the breakdown of peace talks between the Sandinista government of Nicaragua and contra

(HUMBERTO ORTEGA)

rebels who are fighting against it]: It wasn't peace that died today. Peace is going to be closer, because if it cannot be obtained at the negotiating table, it will come faster on the battlefield. By wanting to kill peace, [the contras] are committing suicide. Their days are numbered.

Managua, June 9/Los Angeles Times, 6-10:(I)17.

Eden Pastora
Exiled former leader of
guerrillas fighting the
Sandinista government of Nicaragua

1

[Criticizing both Nicaragua's Sandinista government and the contra rebels fighting it]: Nicaragua needs a third way, a revolutionary program that addresses the needs of the immense poor majority but also respects press freedom and human rights. Our country needs to be truly anti-imperialist, free from both Washington and Moscow ... In the early days after the [Sandinista] revolution, I advocated following the line of the 15-year-old girl. Everyone wants her and she flirts with everyone, but she never commits herself. Unfortunately, my idea was ignored, and Nicaragua climbed into bed with one suitor [the Soviet Union] right away. The other great error of the Sandinistas has been their arrogance, their belief that only they know what is best for Nicaragua. They insist that whoever opposes them is betraying the nation. It doesn't matter to them that they have destroyed small business, frightened away foreign investment and upset the lives of the peasantry ... A contra government would be worse than what we have now because it would be guided by hatred and revenge rather than a desire for social justice.

Interview,
San Jose, Costa Rica, July 5/
The New York Times, 7-7:4.

Claiborne Pell
United States Senator,
D-Rhode Island

2

[On his recent talk with Cuban President Fidel Castro]: The Cubans expressed sincere interest in my suggestion that [U.S.-Cuban] relations can be improved by each country taking small steps to demonstrate good will and upon which other, progressively more difficult but mutually beneficial steps, can be taken. We've tried invasion, assassination and a full embargo, and our relations are just as sterile today as they were in 1960. It is an appropriate time to attempt to move toward more rational and normalized relations with Cuba.

News conference,
Washington, Nov. 30/
Los Angeles Times, 12-1:(I)5.

Augusto Pinochet
President of Chile

3

[On his losing a referendum which would have extended his rule to 1997]: I will hand over my post to the person that citizens elect freely, secretly and in an informed fashion on December 14, 1989.

Oct. 21/
Los Angeles Times, 10-22:(I)4.

Dan Quayle
United States Senator,
R-Indiana; 1988 Republican
U.S. Vice-Presidential
nominee

4

[Supporting U.S. backing of the contras, rebels fighting the Sandinista government of Nicaragua]: If [Sandinista leader Daniel] Ortega got complete control of the country ... and they would invade Costa Rica, we would have some military decisions to make and they wouldn't be pleasant. And that's why I am convinced that we should do the right thing and help the people who want to help themselves [the contras], and we won't ever have to be confronted with that choice.

Interview, Sept. 4/
The Washington Post, 9-6:(A)16.

5

[Referring to U.S. Democratic Presidential nominee Michael Dukakis]: There's no doubt in

(DAN QUAYLE)

a Dukakis Administration that the aid would be cut off to the democratic resistance in Nicaragua [the contra rebels], and that is unfortunate. It is beyond me why it's okay for the Soviet Union to put in billions of dollars to prop up the [ruling] Communist Sandinistas, but somehow it's wrong for the United States to give a few dollars to the democratic resistance.

At Vice-Presidential debate, Omaha, Neb.,
Oct. 5/USA Today, 10-6:(A)11.

Eric Ramirez
Leader, Social Christian Party
of Nicaragua

1

[On Nicaragua's Sandinista government]: Everything here is "Sandinista." Sandinista Army, Sandinista government, Sandinista television. How can there be a democracy when one party controls all this?

The Christian Science Monitor,
5-27:11.

Ronald Reagan
President of the United States

2

[On his support for the contras, rebels fighting the Sandinista government of Nicaragua]: It's clear that it's the freedom fighters [contras] that have brought the Sandinistas to the negotiating table and have wrung from them the limited reforms they've made. Without the freedom fighters, the hope of democracy in Nicaragua would be lost. The consolidation of totalitarian power would be complete, and the Soviets would have succeeded in establishing another Cuba, this time on the American mainland.

White House speech,
Washington, Jan. 20/
The New York Times, 1-21:6.

3

[On the possibility of the U.S. Congress' cutting aid to the contras, rebels fighting the

Sandinista government of Nicaragua]: If Congress cuts off aid to the freedom fighters next week, there is little chance that the Sandinistas will bargain seriously. [The late U.S.] President Teddy Roosevelt once said diplomacy is utterly useless where there is no force behind it. I didn't come to Washington to preside over the Communization of Central America.

Speech, Washington, Jan. 27/
The New York Times, 1-28:4.

4

With Cuban and Soviet-bloc aid, Nicaragua is being transformed into a beachhead for aggression against the United States. It is the first step in a strategy to dominate the entire region of Central America and threaten Mexico and the Panama Canal. That's why the cause of freedom in Central America is united with our national security. That is why the safety of democracy to our south so directly affects the safety of our own nation.

Broadcast address to the nation,
Washington, Feb. 2/
The New York Times, 2-3:6.

5

[On 1983's U.S.-led invasion of Grenada to throw out its Communist government]: [I] can't help but be proud that there is an island now down in the Caribbean where there aren't any signs "Yankee go home" but where somebody sent me a postcard the other day . . . a photograph of a wall . . . painted with all kinds of graffiti . . . about "God love the U.S.A." . . . That was Grenada, of course.

Interview, Washington, Feb. 25/
The Washington Post, 2-26:(A)18.

6

There cannot and must not be any normalization of relations with Cuba, [so long as Cuba] remains an inhuman Communist dungeon, exports terrorism and revolution, [props up] brutal Communist dictatorships [and] is used as the personal instrument of [Cuban President] Fidel

(RONALD REAGAN)

Castro's violent anti-Americanism. [There is] an unbridgeable gulf between the governments of the United States and Cuba . . . the gulf between freedom and tyranny . . . Freedom for Cuba, liberty for her people, is a non-negotiable demand.

> *At Republican fund-raising luncheon,*
> *Miami, June 29/*
> *Los Angeles Times, 6-30:(I)20.*

1

Let me offer here a simple, straightforward message: No more Vietnams; no more Nicaraguas; no more Bay of Pigs. Never again . . . I stand with the Nicaraguan resistance [to the Sandinista government]. We will not rest until we have won for them the full support they need—and until they have won for themselves the genuine democracy and freedom for which they have so bravely struggled.

> *At Republican fund-raising luncheon,*
> *Miami, June 29/*
> *The New York Times, 6-30:4.*

Charles E. Redman
Spokesman for the
Department of State of
the United States

2

[On Panamanian leader Manuel Noriega]: We see Noriega's continued presence in Panama as untenable. He appears to be placing his own interests above those of Panama . . . The situation is deteriorating. It has been—it continues to be. Noriega continues to lose control. Inevitably, he's going to have to leave. So we would hope at this stage that Noriega could obviate the need for further deterioration and further [anti-Noriega] chaos [in Panama] and just simply undertake a prompt departure that would save himself an amount of trouble. It would save the Panamanian people and the Panamanian Defense Forces [which Noriega also heads] as an institution.

> *Washington, March 21/*
> *Los Angeles Times, 3-22:(I)11.*

Riordan Roett
Director of Latin American
studies, School of Advanced
International Studies,
Johns Hopkins University

3

There has been a deliberate effort [in Latin America] to isolate the Chilean regime. The Chileans have not been included in any of the major collective efforts of the early 1980s . . . The carrot that the United States and the Latin American countries can hold out [if Chile becomes a democracy] is that Chile can take its place again at the conference table with other Latin American nations.

> *Los Angeles Times, 10-8:(I)8.*

Pelayo Ruenes
Deputy Foreign Minister
of Cuba

4

[Criticizing U.S. policy of not allowing Americans to visit Cuba]: Why is Cuba singled out? Americans are free to visit the Soviet Union. They go to the People's Republic of China . . . Yet you are not even allowed to visit here as an individual. Are we, a nation of 10 million, so dangerous?

> *The Christian Science Monitor,*
> *9-7:11.*

Jeffrey Sachs
Economist,
Harvard University

5

[Saying high inflation imperils democratic governments in Latin America]: It is becoming virtually impossible to govern in Argentina, Peru and Brazil. There is a tremendous risk of destabilization . . . The military eventually intervenes in these kinds of circumstances, if and when leftist or populist governments take power or are about to take power . . . As long as the United States continues to demand full repayment [of loans made to hard-pressed Latin American countries], which is a completely idiotic policy, we're going to have all the good guys in government going under in this region.

> *Los Angeles Times, 8-18:(IV)1,6.*

Carlos Salinas de Gortari
*Economist; Institutional
Revolutionary Party nominee
for President of Mexico*

1

I am convinced that drug production or transportation is a threat to our national security. I am convinced that we must use all the power of the Mexican state to fight drug production and transportation, not only because it hurts some people in the United States, but mainly because of all the harm it can do to the Mexican political and social system. [The drug trade] corrupts some Mexican authorities, it uses the most modern armaments, it has lots of money. [But] I would say that sometimes [Mexican] drug problems have been presented more politically in the United States than in relation to facts. I hope we do not have this in the future.

*Interview,
Queretaro, Mexico, Jan. 15/
The New York Times, 1-18:6.*

2

I have [committed myself to] clean elections. I have said that I don't want to break a record in numbers, but a record in credibility. I think that you should understand that a political system that has allowed more than 60 years of peaceful transfer of power is something that you cannot put aside easily. I have made a [commitment] to modernize it but not to [make it] disappear.

Newsweek, 6-27:38.

Carlos Salinas de Gortari
President-elect of Mexico

3

[On the priorities of his Administration]: First, to participate in the enormous transformation that is going on in the world. There's a realignment of financial, commercial, economic and political relationships. Second, to recognize, then promote, advances in our democratic life. Third, a war on poverty in Mexico. The fourth is a new development strategy that calls for recovering growth.

Interview/Time, 7-18:31.

Carlos Salinas de Gortari
President of Mexico

4

[Calling for a renegotiation of Mexico's foreign debt]: The priority will no longer be to pay [creditors], but to return to growth. This is not demagoguery or an admonition. It is a reasoned argument that derives from the needs of my people and the enormous effort we have made. I will avoid confrontation. But I declare emphatically and with conviction that the interests of Mexicans are above the interests of creditors.

*Inaugural address,
Mexico City, Dec. 1/
The New York Times, 12-2:(A)7.*

5

[On his statements that Mexico's foreign debt must be renegotiated]: I never said we won't pay. I just said that, in order to pay, first we must grow. As someone said, a dead client will never pay. And second, let me tell you: Banks, when they made bad loans, do write-offs to private clients. So it surprises me that they cannot do it when they make wrong decisions, with the wrong ones we made also, and solve the problem in similar ways.

*Interview/
The Wall Street Journal,
12-5:(A)14.*

Jose Sarney
President of Brazil

6

Latin America must lift itself out of stagnation and under-development. Because we are confronted with nuts as hard to crack as the "North American common market" [Canada and the U.S.], the West European Common Market, and tomorrow possibly a Sino-Japanese common market, we must work toward our own economic integration.

*Interview/
World Press Review, March:39.*

7

We have always had very good relations with the United States. We were allies in the two

(JOSE SARNEY)

world wars. [But] I would be insincere if I said that our relations are going through a favorable period. We are the two great brothers in the continents of the North and South. But the U.S. is concerned more about internal policies than with external ones and political issues. Our trade relations are in a way contaminating our relationship, and we should avoid this.

Interview, Brasilia, Brazil/
USA Today, 3-4:(A)9.

James R. Sasser
United States Senator,
D-Tennessee

1

[On U.S. support for the contras, rebels fighting the Sandinista government of Nicaragua]: I still do not believe that military aid to the contras is the best policy for the United States. I frankly do not believe that the contras can ever hope to win a military victory in Nicaragua. But if the Sandinistas continue to reaffirm that they are anti-democratic, if they continue to be repressive, if they continue to adhere to the Marxist-Leninist doctrine, they will give us no alternative but to consider re-funding the contras, and with military aid.

July 14/
The New York Times, 7-15:4.

George P. Shultz
Secretary of State of the
United States

2

[On Haiti's difficult road toward democracy after the overthrow of dictator Jean-Claude Duvalier]: Obviously, there are various humanitarian needs in Haiti which we want to continue to work with. There is a line between doing something about these governmental actions [the recent shootings by government troops at polling places] and doing things that, in a sense, punish the people of Haiti. We're not trying to punish the people of Haiti. They are having a tough enough time as it is. But we are trying to affect the processes that the government of Haiti goes through, in an effort to move them in a democratic direction.

News conference,
Washington, Jan. 7/
The New York Times, 1-8:4.

3

The United States will not tolerate the subversion or destabilization of the democratic governments of Central America. Such an act, direct or indirect, is a threat to the security interests of the United States of America. It will be resisted by all appropriate means, including military cooperation, in the collective self-defense of the democracies.

News conference,
San Jose, Costa Rica, July 1/
Los Angeles Times, 7-2:(I))4.

4

[Criticizing the OAS for its negative attitude toward U.S. support of the contras, rebels fighting the Sandinista government of Nicaragua]: I must be frank. This organization has not always been out front on issues concerning democracy. Too often it has been one step behind when it has needed to be one step ahead. As we challenge others to adopt democracy, we need to hold them to their promises and commitments. I need not remind members of this organization that commitments to a "pluralistic" political system were made by Nicaragua to this body as long ago as 1979. Those earliest commitments have not yet been fulfilled.

Before Organization of American
States, San Salvador, El Salvador,
Nov. 14/The Washington Post,
11-15:(A)22.

5

The time has come for a new [U.S.-Latin American] diplomacy, a diplomacy based on democratic solidarity and on the aggressive advocacy of democracy by democratic states. The dictators and the totalitarians must be told

(GEORGE P. SHULTZ)

that they are not free to subjugate their peoples ... If new democracies are threatened, we must rally to support them ... No would-be coup plotters looking to overthrow a democratic government—whether they be of the left or right, civilian or military—should count on our indifference.

Before Organization of American States, San Salvador, El Salvador, Nov. 14/ Los Angeles Times, 11-15:(I)6.

Manuel Solis Palma
President of Panama

1

[On U.S. accusations that Panamanian leader Manuel Noriega is involved in drug trafficking]: What the United States government has done is to introduce into world public opinion an image of Panama and its leaders which is nothing more than a product of its own invention, a fiction manufactured by its agents.

At United Nations, New York, Sept. 27/ The Washington Post, 9-28:(A)25.

Alfredo Stroessner
President of Paraguay

2

In today's Paraguay, we live without social and political crises, without tumult, without street unrest, without political prisoners, without hate that makes blood flow between brothers and without mothers in mourning because of political fanaticism. Here we don't suffer the scourge of terrorism, hunger or drugs. In Paraguay, we live in a democracy, with regular and clean elections ...

Welcoming Pope John Paul II, Asuncion, Paraguay, May 16/ Los Angeles Times, 5-18:(I)9.

Victor Hugo Tinoco
Vice Foreign Minister of Nicaragua

3

[For Nicaragua's ruling Sandinistas, democratization means] guarantees for free and fair elections so that every party has an opportunity to impose their political program on the country if they win. There is already democracy here, revolutionary democracy.

To reporters, Managua/ The Christian Science Monitor, 5-27:11.

4

In the United States, a political party is like a business or a profession. Here [in Nicaragua] it is a life option, almost like priesthood.

Los Angeles Times, 10-17:(I)10.

John N. Turner
Leader, Liberal Party of Canada

5

[Criticizing a free-trade bill negotiated between the U.S. and Canada]: We are here to debate a bill which will finish Canada as we know it and replace it with a Canada that will become nothing more than a colony of the United States. It is a dream come true for Americans. At long last, they have found a government in Ottawa dumb enough, stupid enough, patsies so craven in the face of American demands that they just caved in to every request made of them.

Before House of Commons, Ottawa, June/ The New York Times, 8-29:22.

6

[Addressing and criticizing Canadian Prime Minister Brian Mulroney for his recent signing of a free-trade agreement with the U.S.]: We built a country east and west and north. We built it on an infrastructure that deliberately resisted the continental pressure of the United States. For 120 years we've done it. With one signature of a pen, you've reversed that, thrown us into the north-south influence of the United States and will reduce us, I am sure, to a colony of the United States, because when the economic levers go, the political independence is sure to follow.

Broadcast debate with Mulroney, Oct. 25/ The Washington Post, 10-27:(A)45.

Gabriel Valdez
Former president,
Christian Democratic Party
of Chile; Former Foreign
Minister of Chile

1

[On the recent large demonstrations in Chile against President Augusto Pinochet in anticipation of the forthcoming Presidential plebiscite]: This is the first time in 15 years that we have been allowed to express ourselves without being beaten with sticks or arrested . . . There is now a nation-wide pressure for freedom. The young people, especially, are much less ideological, less sectoral now than in the past. In Chile, people have suffered greatly, and they don't want another failure of democracy.

Santigo, Chile, Sept. 4/
Los Angeles Times, 9-5:(I)12.

Joaquin Villalobos
Leader, People's Revolutionary
Army (El Salvador)

2

[On his rebels who are fighting the government of El Salvador]: From a geo-political perspective, we are not interested in aligning ourselves with either superpower bloc. We do not want to base anyone's missiles in our country, nor do we want to participate in an arms race. What we do want is an economic model which we feel could even promote better economic relations with the U.S. Now, does our model imply radical social changes? Yes, it does. Are socialist ideals part of this model? Most certainly. They have to be. The U.S. must understand that we cannot copy their model. You [the U.S.] developed a capitalist society by exploiting and oppressing our continent. But who do we have to exploit? Where are we going to get slaves? From whose mines are we going to sack the gold and silver? There are none. We have to build our country with our own sweat and labor. We only ask that we be allowed to do so in peace.

Interview, Perquin, El Salvador/
The Christian Science Monitor,
3-21:8.

William G. Walker
United States Ambassador to
El Salvador

3

[On U.S. policy in El Salvador]: Neither my political nor my moral conscience bothers me one whit about pursuing what this Administration is doing—helping the [political] center and consolidating democracy at the expense of the extremes on both sides.

Interview/Los Angeles Times, 9-27:(I)8.

Jaime Wheelock
Minister of Agrarian Reform
of Nicaragua

4

[Addressing Nicaraguan sugar workers]: The revolution rewards, but it also punishes. If anyone raises a strikebanner here, we will cut off his hands.

At ceremony opening the sugar
harvest, November/
The Washington Post, 12-16:(A)39.

Fred W. Woerner
General, United States Army;
Commander, U.S. Southern
Command

5

[The military] is, has been and forever will be a major player [in Latin America, and] I say it's important [for the U.S.] to have relationships with them. That military overwhelmingly has stepped out of the role of determinant of the political process and has stepped into a very new role for it—that of guarantor. So we see, hemispherically, an overwhelming trend in the last decade from military rule to democratically elected civilian rule.

To military writers,
Washington, Feb. 5/
The Washington Post, 2-6:(A)4.

Jim Wright
United States Representative,
D-Texas

6

[On U.S. backing of the contras, rebels fighting the Sandinista government of Nicaragua]:

(JIM WRIGHT)

Congress is prepared to continue humanitarian [non-military] aid, but I don't discern a desire on the part of Congress to rekindle hostilities. We tried that for six years, and it did us no good. We ought to give peace every chance we can.

July 12/Los Angeles Times,
7-13:(I)8.

1

We have received clear testimony from CIA people that they have deliberately done things to provoke an overreaction on the part of the [Sandinista] government of Nicaragua [against which the U.S.-backed contra rebels are fighting]. I do not believe it is the proper role of our government to try to provoke riots . . . or deliberately to try to antagonize government officials into foolish overreactions.

To reporters, Sept. 20/Los Angeles Times, 9-21:(I)2.

Rufus Yerxa
Staff Director,
Ways and Means Committee,
U.S. House of Representatives

2

[On the possibility that Canada may scrap the new U.S.-Canadian free-trade treaty if a new Canadian government is elected]: The Canadians cannot expect things to remain calm and passive if this agreement goes down in flames. It's going to have repercussions for the trading relationship. We won't be looking for ways to penalize Canada, but we will be a lot less inclined to find ways of accommodating them in certain problems that we have.

The New York Times, 11-9:(C)1.

Asia and the Pacific

Corazon C. Aquino
President of the Philippines

1

[On the Communist insurgency in her country]: The insurgency war cannot be fought by programs and speeches, nor by commissions and committees. It must be fought, and it will be won, only by you and the men you will lead. The solution is simple to formulate: Military action . . . It is your small victories in the field that will add up to a final victory in the war, even as our economic initiatives and social reforms should absolish its roots forever.

At Philippine Military Academy
graduation, Baguio/
Los Angeles Times, 3-20:(I)12.

2

[On the Communist insurgency in her country]: The presence of the insurgence, of course, has a great deal to do with the economic situation in our country. Where people do not have employment and where people suffer certain injustices, this is perhaps some of the reason why they turn against the government. It is the goal of the Administration to seek a better life for the Filipino people.

Interview/
USA Today, 5-31:(A)11.

3

[After coming to power in 1986,] I was offered the support of the [ousted President Ferdinand] Marcos parliament, if I would keep it alive. If I accepted its modest terms, there would be stability immediately. I refused the offer. I refused injustice to our people to whom the parliament had lied. I abolished parliament. I became, to put it bluntly, the legislator under the Freedom Constitution. It was essential that no one be able to obstruct me, for I meant to give our people democracy swiftly and to weaken their enemies

permanently. With God's help and the people's continuing support, I succeeded in doing both.

Speech,
Nov. 21/
The Washington Post,
12-2:(A)26.

4

[On the U.S. military bases in the Philippines]: Our deadline for advising the U.S. government as to whether they have to leave is September 1990, or one year before the termination of the present military-base agreement. I still have time . . . Both countries should do what each feels is in its best interest. It's not up to me to tell the Americans: "Please stay." Guam and Palau have been mentioned as alternatives. My goodness, if that's what you believe is in your interest, then we would respect it. Anyway, we have no choice in the matter.

Interview/
Newsweek, 12-5:38.

5

The inhumanity of people obsessed by power or possessed by dogma, whether in the uniform of the regular army or in the casual wear of the insurgency, will be with us for some time yet. But for as long as Filipinos have a democracy, human-rights violations will never become the pattern and policy of government in this country. Sadly, I cannot speak for all Filipinos. I cannot speak for those who refuse to adopt peaceful means to express their rejection of democracy. If there is a pattern of human-rights violations, if there is a conscious policy of terrorism in this country, you will find it among them.

Speech on 40th anniversary of
Universal Declaration of Human Rights,
Dec. 10/The Washington Post,
12-22:(A)24.

Richard L. Armitage
Assistant Secretary for
International Security Affairs,
Department of Defense of
the United States

1

[Saying that Japan is paying a large share of the costs for U.S. military bases and personnel stationed there]: Our major bases and more than 100 other military facilities in Japan are provided to us totally rent-free, and our nuclear-powered and nuclear-capable forces visit Japan frequently without restriction. In 1988, the government of Japan will spend over $2.5-billion on behalf of 55,000 U.S. service personnel on duty there, or more than $45,000 per person.

Before Senate Subcommittee on
Military Construction, Washington/
Los Angeles Times, 5-31:(I)15.

Chester G. Atkins
United States Representative,
D-Massachusetts

2

[On his recent visit to Vietnam as leader of a delegation of U.S. Congressmen]: It would appear that there is a major campaign under way to sell the "new Vietnam." There is no way at this point to tell whether they are just launching a p.r. effort, or representing genuine change. It was very clear in our conversations with leaders in Vietnam that they failed with the old product. They are pariahs in the international community for their occupation of Cambodia, and are presiding over an internal economic disaster . . . [In meeting with Vietnam's Foreign Minister Nguyen Co Thach who engaged in conciliatory diplomacy,] I haven't seen a performance like that since Arthur Fiedler conducted the Boston Pops.

News conference,
Bangkok, Thailand, Jan. 17/
The New York Times, 1-18:3.

Joaquin Bernas
President, Ateneo University
(Philippines)

3

[On Philippine President Corazon Aquino]: There are those who ask whether her sacred regard for human rights as manifested during the [1985 Presidential election] campaign is still with her. There is a growing perception that she is becoming a captive of the military mind. As far as social justice is concerned, she has not shown herself as pursuing this goal with vigor.

The Washington Post, 2-26:(A)25.

Benazir Bhutto
Pakistani opposition political
leader

4

[Criticizing Pakistani President Mohammed Zia ul-Haq's proclamation that candidates in the forthcoming national elections will not be able to campaign on the basis of party affiliation]: How can you say it is a democratic election when I cannot campaign as party leader outside of my own small constituency? And without a party flag or symbol on the ballot [which is banned by Zia's ruling], in a country where there is 27 per cent literacy and no one can read the names of candidates, how can it be a reflection of the will of the people?

Interview/
Los Angeles Times, 7-22:(I)15.

Benazir Bhutto
Prime Minister of Pakistan

5

We will eradicate . . . poverty, we will provide shelter to the shelterless, jobs to the unemployed, education to the illiterate. If on the one hand you have heaps of wealth and on the other, poverty, that we will not tolerate.

Broadcast address to the nation,
Dec. 2/
The Washington Post, 12-3:(A)1.

6

[On the opposition in Pakistan to her new Administration]: The first thing we have done is to try to build confidence. We have tried to build up confidence by saying whoever is there, we are prepared to deal with them. We are a reality, you are a reality. So rather than try to do away with

(BENAZIR BHUTTO)

each other, let's come to terms with each other [and] discuss the issues.

Interview, Islamabad/
The Washington Post, 12-7:(A)31.

Erich Bloch
Director, National Science
Foundation

1

[On the Asian industrial and scientific challenge to the United States]: The [Soviet] *Sputnik* [space satellite] thing [in the 1950s] was, first of all, a highly visible item. You could look up into the sky and see it. You could hear it bleep. Secondly, it affected in a clear way the military security of the U.S. What we have today isn't highly visible. Yes, the Japanese are selling more cars, and the Koreans are selling more semiconductors. But the man in the street doesn't see that. Or when he sees it, it's to his benefit, because he can buy a Hyundai [car] cheaper than he can buy a [U.S.] Ford. So you don't get a feeling that there's a catastrophe here at all. Also, I don't think our industries realized what was happening until very late in the game. Finally, the Japanese aren't the Russians; that puts the security issue in a different light.

Interview/The Wall Street Journal, 11-14:(R)32.

Bill Bradley
United States Senator,
D-New Jersey

2

No country is more important to our [the U.S.'s] economic future than Japan. You want Japan to assume more foreign-policy responsibility in the world, but in partnership with the U.S. The key is to get them to assume more responsibility without getting them to re-arm.

Time, 7-4:28.

Choi Seh Hyung
Executive director, Korea
Foreign Trade Association

3

[On South Korea's new democratic government, elected after years of dictatorial rule]: In a

democracy, everyone can urge that the government should do this or not do that. Government must accommodate all those kinds of demands. Before, the government economic policy was made by a few people and they would suddenly announce it one day.

The Christian Science Monitor,
3-1:8.

Manning Clark
Australian historian

4

[Most Australians are] unable and unwilling to see where they are going, or what they want to be. If anyone asks us, we lapse into the great Australian silence.

U.S. News & World Report, 2-1:34.

Ray Cline
Professor of international
relations, Georgetown
University; Chairman, United
States Global Strategy Council

5

[On the recent death of Pakistani President Mohammed Zia ul-Haq, who was killed in a plane crash which may have been caused by sabotage]: Zia and his influence on the whole region and on the future of Afghanistan were very important. It's hard not to suspect that somebody on the Soviet-Afghan side was interested in wiping him out . . . Zia was viewed by many people in the Soviet Union as an enemy, a person who frustrated the Soviet Union and who threatened to destroy the Soviet-sponsored government in Afghanistan . . . I would say that the Communist Najibullah government in Afghanistan is the group you would point the finger to most directly because it would have an enormous interest in getting rid of President Zia.

Interview/USA Today, 8-18:(A)9.

Diego Cordovez
Under Secretary General of
the United Nations

6

[On the Soviet decision to withdraw its troops from Afghanistan]: One thing annoys me tremen-

(DIEGO CORDOVEZ)

dously. I have been told for six years—a million times—that the key to the whole thing is the withdrawal of the Soviet troops. Those people who are saying now how difficult it is [without a provisional government] are the same ones who were telling me for years to get the Soviets out and things would work out in Afghanistan. There is an increasing recognition that [the current Soviet-backed ruling party] cannot be ignored because it has existed since 1965. It consists of 40,000-80,000 people in a well-organized party. I told them I'm not going to get involved in your business—you decide whatever you want. But I think it's very wise, what the European community has said, that the future government of Afghanistan should be one whose independence cannot be challenged.

Interview/
U.S. News & World Report,
5-30:29.

Gerald L. Curtis
Director, East Asian Institute,
Columbia University
1

[On Japan's increasing expenditures for foreign aid]: From the U.S. point of view, the more the Japanese spend, the more Japan's influence is going to increase . . . If we see the Japanese increasing aid substantially in Latin America—in our own back yard—and it results in more Japanese exports to the region, instead of American exports, I think there are going to be problems. [Japan's growing role] isn't the end of the story. It's the beginning.

Los Angeles Times, 7-23:(I)12.

Dalai Lama
Exiled leader of Tibet
2

[Calling for China to give Tibet more self-determination if not independence]: I will continue to counsel for non-violence, but unless China forsakes the brutal methods it employs, Tibetans cannot be responsible for a further

deterioration in the situation [of recent unrest]. The Chinese leadership needs to realize that colonial rule over occupied territories is today anachronistic. A genuine union or association can only come about voluntarily, when there is satisfactory benefit to all the parties concerned.

June 15*/Los Angeles Times, 6-16:(I)12.

John Gunther Dean
United States Ambassador
to India
3

[On relations between the U.S. and India]: Our basic national interests are not only compatible but even supportive of one another. That which unites us is far stronger than that which divides us.

USA Today, 4-29:(A)13.

Le Dang Doanh
Vietnamese government
economic adviser
4

For a long time, the leaders [of Vietnam] held ultra-conservative theories of trying to maintain two economies. But now they admit to pure economic reality. Creating a capitalist sector is the highest priority of Vietnam. It's the only way to create jobs . . . Socialism still remains. But we must be extremely creative in interpreting Marx. He lived in a different time. It would be extremely treasonous to treat Marxism as a bible. Vietnam's situation is different than the Europe that he knew.

The Christian Science Monitor, 12-22:7.

Marlin Fitzwater
Assistant to President of the
United States Ronald Reagan
for Press Relations
5

[On the withdrawal of Soviet troops from Afghanistan and its effects on the Soviet-backed Afghan government]: As the Soviets leave, we remain confident that a broad-based government, chosen by the Afghan people, and not imposed from outside, will replace the Kabul regime.

May 16/USA Today, 5-17:(A)4.

Rajiv Gandhi
Prime Minister of India

1

When you look at a country like India with 800 million people, and look at the percentage below the poverty line, which is about 37 per cent, one sees a country which is very poor. But if you translate the percentage into numbers, then we have over 100 million people who are part of the middle class.

Interview, New Delhi/
USA Today, 4-29:(A)13.

2

It was in quest of our treasures, of our fabled material wealth, of our silks and our spices, of our textiles and our technologies, that the West sought out Asia. The voyages of discovery that began with Marco Polo and Vasco da Gama ended, however, in the inequity of imperialism. In different ways, each of us [in Asia] succumbed to the depredations of the European powers. Then, each of us, in our separate ways, rose once again to freedom and independence.

At banquet,
Peking, China, Dec. 19/
Los Angeles Times, 12-20:(I)5.

Mikhail S. Gorbachev
General Secretary,
Communist Party
of the Soviet Union

3

. . . the governments of the Soviet Union and the Republic of Afghanistan have agreed to set a specific date for beginning the withdrawal of Soviet troops—May 15, 1988—and to complete their withdrawal within 10 months.

Moscow, Feb. 8*/
Los Angeles Times, 2-9:(I)11.

4

The Soviet Union is for the broad participation of the United States in the affairs of the Asian and Pacific region, worthy of its position and its political and economic potentialities. But it should be equal, without great-power manners and the tricks of power politics.

Speech, Krasnoyarsk, U.S.S.R.,
Sept. 16/Los Angeles Times,
9-17:(I)12.

5

Aware of the Asian and Pacific countries' concern, the Soviet Union will not increase the amount of any nuclear weapons in the region—it has already been practicing this for some time—and is calling on the United States and other nuclear powers not to deploy them additionally in the region. [Also,] if the United States agrees to the elimination of [its] military bases in the Philippines, the Soviet Union will be ready . . . to give up the fleet's material and technical supply station in Cam Ranh Bay [Vietnam].

Speech, Krasnoyarsk, U.S.S.R.,
Sept. 16/Los Angeles Times,
9-18:(I)1.

Alexander M. Haig, Jr.
Candidate for the 1988
Republican U.S.
Presidential nomination;
Former Secretary of State
of the United States

6

[On the U.S. pull-out from the Vietnam war of the 1960s and '70s]: I have frequently said it wasn't the work of the dissidents [in the U.S.]—and, above all, it wasn't the work of the American press, as some have suggested—that caused us to come out of Vietnam in a very unsatisfactory way. That was the product of bad policy. In one respect, you have to give these [dissidents] credit for recognizing it was bad policy, and I included in there the American press. The difference I would have with them was that their judgment was flawed in determining why it was bad policy. I think it was bad policy because if we decided to shed one drop of American blood, it should have been under a formula in which we had intended to take all of the actions necessary to win—and win decisively and promptly.

Interview, McLean, Va./
U.S. News & World Report,
2-8:12.

Han Xu
Chinese Ambassador to the
United States

1

In 1987, 300,000 American tourists came to China. Quite a number of Chinese also came over to the United States. Trade has increased eight times since 1978. In 1978, there was not a single Chinese student in the U.S.A. Now, there are 32,000 Chinese scholars. We have no fear, otherwise why would we send so many? We are convinced this is good for both countries. We believe this is a bridge of friendship, from generation to generation.

Interview/
USA Today, 12-20:(A)11.

Robert Hawke
Prime Minister of Australia

2

We [in Australia] have got the capacity to be of assistance to a number of countries in the region. One of the most exciting is China, and we have a better relationship with China than probably any other country. I mention China because of the changes that are taking place there. But it is an indication of the commitment we have to making sure that Australia is not isolationist.

Interview, Canberra/
USA Today, 5-6:(A)13.

Ronald Hays
Admiral, and
Commander-in-Chief/Pacific
Command, United States Navy

3

There's a threat [in the Pacific] from the Soviet Union. The Soviets are making a play in the Pacific. They've built up their military forces, despite what [Soviet leader] Mikhail Gorbachev has promised by way of a new era of peace and cooperation. The political activity has picked up as well. So combine that with the Communist insurgency [in the Philippines], and you have to be concerned.

Interview/
USA Today, 3-23:(A)11.

4

There is an urgent need for [the U.S.] to provide economic assistance, security assistance, to [the Philippines]. The Republic of the Philippines, of course, is faced with a lot of problems now. But it's my view that despite the apprehension that you read about so often as to the future of the Republic of the Philippines, they're going to make it. Democracy is going to survive in the Philippines. They're on the right road.

Interview/
USA Today, 3-23:(A)11.

Hyun Hong Choo
Adviser to, and Director of
Office of Legislation of,
South Korean President
Roh Tae Woo

5

[On South Korean President Roh Tae Woo]: Sometimes it will be viewed by outside observers that he is too conservative, too cautious. But that kind of cautiousness is important for us now. We've seen too much of leaders . . . taking personal command, making dramatic announcements out of the blue sky. I don't think we'll see that kind of thing again in Korean politics.

The Washington Post,
6-29:(A)20.

Kuniko Inoguchi
Associate professor of political
science, Sophia University,
Tokyo

6

Japanese don't care about elections in France or Britain, but we know a lot about American politics. I think people in Tokyo probably have a greater interest in the primaries than your typical American citizen . . . People are watching the debates, and saying, "Why don't we have them in Japan?" The rule has always been that silence is golden. But we'll soon see a new generation of LDP leaders who are more open and clear and eloquent.

Los Angeles Times, 3-18:(I)15.

Ji Shaoxiang
Foreign affairs director,
Xinhua News Agency (China);
Representative of China in
Hong Kong during that colony's
impending transition to
Chinese rule

1

[On how Hong Kong will change after Chinese rule takes effect in 1997]: Foreign affairs will be handled by the Chinese government; defense will be handled by [China's] People's Liberation Army. [But] people will keep their existing lifestyles, local law will remain the same, the central government will not levy any taxes here, and most civil servants will stay. The one big question is the Executive Council of Hong Kong. Will that change? We don't know.

Interview, Hong Kong/
USA Today, 5-13:(A)11.

Kim Dae Jung
Leader, New Korea
Democratic Party of
South Korea

2

To be an opposition leader like myself, you have to be a little bit dumb; you cannot be clever. You have to be persistent . . . like a bulldog, [and] you cannot be afraid of going to prison.

World Press Review, May:54.

Kim Young Seok
Professor of communications,
Yonsei University
(South Korea)

3

[On televised government hearings into abuses committed during the recent Administration of former South Korean President Chun Doo Hwan]: People are overwhelmed. It is the first time in Korea that the past is being exposed. The core system is changing. Things that were secret are being opened. I think in the future, because of this kind of hearing, those in power cannot act as before. It is a gigantic step toward democracy.

The New York Times, 11-22:(A)3.

Henry A. Kissinger
Former Secretary of State
of the United States

4

. . . India is becoming the predominant military country in its region and has shown no hesitation to use its power to achieve its national interests. I think India's long-range interest in the Indian Ocean is very similar to the U.S. interest. That is to say, they will not want the Soviet Union—or any other major power—to dominate the Indian Ocean, and they will not want a great power to be dominating the Persian Gulf [either].

Interview/
Los Angeles Times, 1-24:(V)2.

Conrad Lam
Member, Legislative
Council of Hong Kong

5

[On the 1997 reversion of Hong Kong to Chinese rule]: If we can make the system of "one country, two systems" work in Hong Kong, we will have 50 years to show the people of China that there is a system superior to the system they have. So we are here not only helping the modernization of China, but also giving the Chinese people a broader perspective, so that one day the political situation and the atmosphere of China would be more approaching the Western style.

Interview/
Los Angeles Times, 2-10:(I)6.

Muhammad Javad Larijani
Deputy Foreign Minister
of Iran

6

[On the effects of the pull-out of Soviet troops from Afghanistan on the Soviet-backed Afghan government which has been fighting *mujahideen* rebels]: It is very difficult to imagine any of the [Najibullah Afghan government] group which is now in power [remaining] in the country . . . They are the symbol of people who invited foreign troops into the country, so they don't have

(MUHAMMAD JAVAD LARIJANI)

any internal dependency, and are thought of as the cause of this huge trouble for the nation of Afghanistan. We look to the *mujahideen* as the true representatives of the people. We will support them all the way . . . If we will be of any help [in the formation of an interim government], definitely we don't have any hesitations. Our position is well known: The *mujahideen* should be the major part of any interim or permanent government [in Afghanistan].

Interview, United Nations, New York/
The Christian Science Monitor, 4-12:11

Lee Kuan Yew
Prime Minister of Singapore

1

We [Singapore] were almost a hopeless case in the '60s. This was a dirty, filthy place going down the drain. But I said we will "clean and green" Singapore. It worked because we have a hardworking people. Very few sit under a coconut tree playing tiddlywinks.

Interview, Singapore/
USA Today, 5-13:(A)11.

2

It's the software in the younger generation which will determine whether Singapore continues to thrive, to prosper, to be a dynamo as it used to be, as it has been; or whether it will plateau like so many Western societies, like Europe or Britain, where they've just lost steam. They don't see the point of striving and achieving any more. They're just comfortable and they're happy.

To university students/
The New York Times, 11-5:4.

Lee Teng-hui
President of Taiwan

3

There are two very important aspects to the [Chinese] mainland regime's current policy toward Taiwan. One is that they have never

repudiated the possibility of reunifying China by military force. These words seem very forceful. Indeed, they seem to be saying, "I'm more powerful, and I'll strike you if you are not obedient." This attitude itself causes a problem. The other is that they are promulgating the "one-country-two-systems" idea, and treating us as a local government.

News conference, Taipei, Feb. 22/
Los Angeles Times, 2-23:(I)5.

4

From the past 40 years of economic, political and other development on Taiwan, we learn that the truly most appropriate political ideology is not socialism, and it is not Communism, but rather a free and democratic society . . . The faster we progress, the faster and more thoroughly we carry out our political reforms, the more the mainland [Chinese] will be unable to take any other direction . . . A free and democratic system is what the [mainland] Chinese people have been pursuing since the beginning of history.

News conference, Taipei, Feb. 22/
The Christian Science Monitor,
2-23:7.

David Li
Chairman, Bank of East Asia
(Hong Kong)

5

We are drawn to the United States as a magnet because it is still the most dynamic, most open society in the world. The Japanese reputation is still tainted by the past and by their reluctance to make trade with Asia the two-way street it should be.

Los Angeles Times, 9-17:(I)9.

Li Peng
Acting Premier of China

6

The situation in the past five years shows that . . . we sometimes have to make a detour. On the one hand, we should adhere to our original

(LI PENG)

goals, maintain our direction in construction and reform, keep up our morale and be more confident. On the other hand, we should be prepared for possible difficulties on the road ahead [and] take into account what the state, the enterprises and the masses can tolerate . . . Although reform will ultimately bring immense benefits to the people, certain specific measures of reform may not bring them immediate benefits and may even work temporarily against the interests of some people. We must face up to this problem . . . We should help the masses to gain a clear idea of the content, significance and necessity of the measures we take.

Before National People's Congress,
Peking, March 25/
Los Angeles Times, 3-26:(I)4.

1

[On changes in the Chinese economic structure]: [It will be difficult to] move from a society in which people are merely assured of adequate food and clothing to one in which they lead a fairly comfortable life. Nevertheless, that is what we have to do. [But it will take] hard work and even great sacrifice . . . If we are to make China strong and prosperous and our people well off, we shall have to go through a long period of hard struggle during which living standards can improve only step by step.

Before National People's Congress,
Peking, March 25/
The Washington Post, 3-26:(A)17.

James Lilley
United States Ambassador to
South Korea

2

I am particularly disturbed that some people [in South Korea] seem to be linking anti-Americanism with the problem of reunification [of North and South Korea]. We realize it is a very emotional question for Koreans. The U.S. has always supported peaceful efforts to reunify . . . [As for U.S. influence in establishing a South

Korean government after World War II,] I think the U.S. made the right decision, and I think any Korean who seriously considers what it would be like to be living under [North Korean leader] Kim II Sung probably agrees.

Interview/The Washington Post,
6-28:(A)1,12.

Nguyen Van Linh
General Secretary,
Communist Party of Vietnam

3

[Saying his country wants improved relations with the U.S. following the Vietnam war of the 1960s and '70s]: Vietnam wants to forget the past, let bygones be bygones. We also want to push back that bitter past. We don't want to remember it. We just want to look ahead so we can have good relations.

To journalists, January/
The Washington Post, 2-11:(A)54.

4

[Saying private enterprise is encouraged in the south of Vietnam, which used to operate that way before being taken over by the Communist North]: We are just one country, but there are two different states of economic development, and the ways of thinking and the way of doing business are different as a consequence. Under the regime of centralized bureaucratic subsidization, it was the people in this Ho Chi Minh City [in the South] who were striving to break all the restrictions that were checking their production.

News conference,
Ho Chi Minh City, Vietnam,
Jan. 21/The New York Times,
1-22:2.

Fang Lizhi
Former vice president,
University of Science and
Technology (China);
Former member, Communist
Party of China

5

The most important [thing] is for China to have a multi-party system. One can't expect everyone

317

(FANG LIZHI)

in Chinese society to hold the same views as the Communist Party demands. "One heart and one mind for the whole nation"—that's impossible! Only with different parties can we achieve balance and compromise ... I believe that a democratic environment is actually more stable. Forced stability isn't real stability. Consider the case of a natural phenomenon: the typhoon. People feel that typhoons are very destabilizing. But if there weren't a typhoon, the weather would be even worse. Every once in a while you need a typhoon to adjust things.

Interview/
The Christian Science Monitor,
11-18:36.

Alexei D. Lizichev
General, Soviet armed forces;
Member, Soviet Communist
Party Central Committee

1

[On the Soviet military involvement in Afghanistan]: In any conflict, there are casualties, and we have suffered serious losses. Yet Soviet soldiers are leaving Afghanistan now and returning home with a sense of having fulfilled their internationalist duty to help the Afghan people [fight against Afghan rebels]. They have gone through a heavy test in Afghanistan, but they have shown courage.

News conference,
Moscow, May 25/
Los Angeles Times, 5-26:(I)1.

Winston Lord
United States Ambassador
to China

2

[In 10 years, the U.S. and China have] gone from almost no trade at all to over $13-billion in 1988. Neither country had any investments in the other. Now the U.S. has over $3-billion committed in over 400 joint ventures. At the same time, the Chinese are beginning to invest in some significant amounts in the United States. We've

gone from no scientific cooperation to over 30 protocols covering a wide range of subjects: outer space to earthquake prediction. Our militaries cooperate. Countless cultural and educational business delegations cross the Pacific every week ... Our shared interest in making sure that no country dominates Asia or the world is our strongest link. I think our most difficult challenge is that two nations with greatly different histories, cultures, values, social and economic systems produce some cultural and political frictions and misunderstanding.

Interview/
USA Today, 12-20:(A)11.

Ma Ying-chiu
Deputy secretary general,
ruling Nationalist Party
of Taiwan

3

[Saying the recent death of Taiwan President Chiang Ching-kuo will not inhibit reform in the country]: First of all, it is part of our ideals to have a constitutional democracy. Secondly, the society here has become so affluent, and the people so educated, they certainly want to make their voices heard in the political process. Any political party must reflect social realities. So we believe the time has come to move to a more advanced stage of constitutional democracy.

Los Angeles Times, 2-8:(I)4.

Raul Manglapus
Foreign Secretary of the
Philippines

4

[On the U.S. Clark and Subic Bay military bases in the Philippines]: The powerful shadow of America remains cast over our land. The Americans solved their problem by crawling away from the British shadow, thus speeding their growth. [But] the long, fixed shadow of Subic and Clark stretches over the land and mind of the Filipino.

Speech, March 29/
Los Angeles Times, 4-4:(I)8.

(RAUL MANGLAPUS)

1

[Saying the U.S. should be prepared to pay much more to keep its two military bases in the Philippines when the lease agreement is up in 1991]: If the United States cannot afford it, I don't think they should be here. It's up to the United States. If they can afford it, they can stay. If they cannot, they should go.

To reporters, Manila/
The Washington Post, 5-17:(A)16.

Mike Mansfield
United States Ambassador
to Japan

2

A shift is occurring away from Europe to the Pacific Asia area. I think the [U.S.] trade figures tell the story. In 1975, our two-way trade with these states, including Japan, amounted to about $42-billion. Last year, it was somewhere around $220-billion. So you can begin to get an idea of what's occurring in this part of the world. I think without question in my mind that the next century will be the century of the Pacific.

Interview, Tokyo/
USA Today, 5-27:(A)15.

3

The Japanese have carried responsibility extremely well ... Japan has proved to be a staunch and reliable ally and friend to the U.S. When others lacked support for some of our policies, the Japanese were always there at our side.

Interview, Tokyo, Nov. 14/
The Christian Science Monitor,
11-15:8.

Ferdinand E. Marcos
Exiled former President
of the Philippines

4

[On what has happened to the Philippines since he was ousted and replaced by Corazon Aquino as President]: I left the country solid and now it's bankrupt. I left the country with $28-

billion in the treasury. No one can account for it now. The Communists have increased. At the very most, there were 15,000 when I was there. We had obtained the surrender of many Communists. Now the Communists are in the city and are free to roam ... The soldiers of the armed forces are not skilled in the use of power. They are not indoctrinated. They are not skilled. When I left them, we had organized 68,000 with training of at least six months ... [President Aquino] has the support of the American government and that's an important thing. I said it didn't appear that she would sit easy in her stolen Presidency. There would be attempts to unseat her, and they could succeed. I've always told our people there that violence begets violence.

Interview, Hawaii/
USA Today, 5-31:(A)11.

Jamsheed K. A. Marker
Pakistani Ambassador to
the United States

5

[Saying the U.S. should continue to supply weapons to rebels fighting the Soviet-backed government of Afghanistan even though the Soviets are removing their troops from the country]: The only thing that will make the Soviets get out of Afghanistan is resistance, and the prospect of continuing resistance, as long as they remain there. The Soviet Union is trying to find ways to shore up a doomed regime. We don't want them to get, through delays and negotiations, what they failed to get through sheer brute military power.

Interview,
Washington, Nov. 4/
The New York Times, 11-5:4.

John David Morley
Author; Authority on Japan

6

Japan has never had a foreign policy. It has had wars, it has colonized parts of Asia. But apart from that, its experience in dealing with other nations is still very primitive.

Time, 7-4:29.

319

Richard M. Nixon
*Former President of
the United States*

1

China is awake and inevitably will be an economic and military superpower. The question is, what will it do with that power? If the Chinese had the same aggressive foreign policy as the Russians, we would be out of our minds to be cooperating and trading with them. But, at the present time, the Chinese have recognized that their first priority is progress at home . . . They could be very dangerous in the world. That is why the move we made toward China in 1972 was so important, because if China had moved forward and became an economic and military superpower, and was still an enemy of the United States, as it was before 1972, it would be a far more dangerous world than it is today. So it's critical that we—the Europeans, Japanese, the free world—continue to give the Chinese a stake in peaceful relations with us through our economic cooperation.

Interview/USA Today, 4-5:(A)11.

2

[On democracy in the Philippines which was established with the advent of current President Corazon Aquino's Administration]: Thomas Hobbes, a British philosopher, once said that democracy is nothing more than an aristocracy of orators. That is the essence of the problem in the Philippines. The Filipinos are great orators, but they have not been very good at government. Mrs. Aquino is honest; at the beginning she brought a new spirit to the Philippines. But the more things change, the more they stay the same.

Interview/USA Today, 4-5:(A)11.

3

I would say the major mistake I made as President was one—this will surprise you—was not doing early in 1969 what I did on May 3 of 1972 and on December 15 of 1972, and that was to bomb and mine North Vietnam [during the Vietnam war]. I wanted to do it. I talked to [then Secretary of State] Henry Kissinger about it, but

we were stuck with the bombing halt that we had inherited from the Johnson Administration, with Paris peace talks. I knew that, just like the [current] cease-fire talks down here in Nicaragua, I didn't trust them at all. And they proved to be, of course, phony. But if we had done that [the early bombing] then, I think we would have ended the war in Vietnam in 1969 rather than in 1973. That was my biggest mistake as President.

*Broadcast interview/
"Meet the Press," NBC-TV,
4-10.*

Robert A. Peck
*Deputy Assistant Secretary of
State of the United States*

4

[On the announced Soviet pull-out of its troops from Afghanistan]: Our estimate is that the [Soviet-supported Afghan] government could splinter and fall of its own weight even before the final Soviet pull-out . . . Once the Soviet protectors are gone, the regime will be unable to project power into the countryside, and its early demise will be inevitable . . . Almost all effective fighting [against the U.S.-backed Afghan rebels] has involved the use of Soviet ground forces together with Afghans, as well as Soviet air and artillery support. This will be gone once the Soviets start to pull out.

*Before House Asia Subcommittee,
Washington, Feb. 25/
Los Angeles Times, 2-26:(I)5.*

Qian Qichen
Foreign Minister of China

5

Following the decision of the Soviet Union to pull its troops out of Afghanistan, the international community has voiced an even stronger demand for Vietnamese troop withdrawal from Kampuchea [Cambodia] and to an end to the war of aggression. Regrettably, however, what the Vietnamese authorities have been doing runs counter to the desire and the demand of the international community.

*At United Nations,
New York, Sept. 28/
Los Angeles Times, 9-29:(I)13.*

Burhanuddin Rabbani
*Leader, rebels fighting the
Soviet-backed government
of Afghanistan*

1

[Saying his rebels are keeping up their fight even though the Soviets are in the process of withdrawing their troops from Afghanistan]: We do not trust the Russians. The Russians have not stopped the war themselves. So how can we stop our military operations? Decreasing our military operations might encourage the Russians to remain longer in Afghanistan. As long as the Russians are there, we feel a necessity to keep pressure on their military bases.

*Washington, Nov. 9/
The New York Times, 11-10:(A)3.*

Ronald Reagan
President of the United States

2

In the very near future we anticipate the signing in Geneva of an agreement that will result in the total withdrawal of Soviet forces from Afghanistan. If that accord is complied with, and the Soviets withdraw irrevocably from that long-suffering country, this will be a great victory for [Afghanistan's] heroic people—whom we shall continue to support.

*Speech, Las Vegas, Nev./
The Washington Post, 4-11:(A)21.*

3

[On the Soviet Union's announced plans to pull their troops out of Afghanistan]: The Soviets have rarely before—and not at all in more than three decades—left a country, once occupied. They have often promised to leave, but rarely in their history, and then only under pressure from the West, have they actually done it . . . Have the Soviets really given up these ambitions [to dominate Afghanistan and the region]? We don't know. We can't know, until the drama has fully played.

*Before World Affairs Council
of Western Massachusetts,
Springfield, April 21/
The New York Times, 4-22:6.*

4

[On the possibility of Americans still remaining in Vietnam 13 years after the end of the war]: If there are living Americans being held against their will, we must bring them home. Should there be anyone remaining voluntarily, their family deserves to know. And every American who has perished deserves to rest on United States soil. And until our questions are fully answered, we will assume that some of our countrymen are alive.

*Before National League of
POW-MIA Families,
Washington, July 29/
Los Angeles Times, 7-30:(I)1.*

Edwin O. Reischauer
*Former United States
Ambassador to Japan*

5

There will continue to be a tremendous mutual dependence between the U.S. and Japan. If they [the Japanese] turned uncooperative, it would be a disaster for us, but it would also be a disaster for them.

Time, 7-4:31.

Thomas W. Robinson
*Authority on Chinese
military affairs, American
Enterprise Institute*

6

[For China,] the Americans have not been a threat for a while, and the Russians are no longer a serious threat. For the [Chinese People's Liberation Army], the question is, who are your enemies now? The answer is the Vietnamese, and possibly the Indians or Taiwan, and in the long run, Japan.

Los Angeles Times, 8-25:(I)1.

Roh Tae Woo
President of South Korea

7

The day when freedoms and human rights could be slighted [in South Korea] in the name of

(ROH TAE WOO)

economic growth and national security has ended. The day when repressive force and torture in secret chambers were tolerated is over . . . I do not want to be a President who pushes his fellow countrymen around. But I will not be one who is pushed around by mobs either . . . We will have an era of mature democracy when human rights are inviolable and freedom with responsibility prevails, so that both economic development and national security are assured . . . The people want an honest and ethical government. I intend to give them one. All leaders, including myself, will be honest and truthful . . . My Administration will resolutely reject any form of privilege, irregularities and corruption.

Inaugural address, Seoul, Feb. 25/
Los Angeles Times, 2-25:(I)1,25.

1

Gone are the days [in South Korea] when, on the strength of its numerical superiority, the ruling party could get away with arbitrarily running the legislature and forcing anything through it. In this new era, the people do not want any more of the wasteful and debilitating past politics characterized by antagonism and schism . . . Under the new situation, no political party can run the show alone, and nobody can reject politics of partnership and cooperation.

Before South Korean National
Assembly, Seoul, May 30/
The Washington Post, 5-31:(A)15.

2

The danger from North Korea has not diminished. It continues to exist. Since the armistice, we have lived under that threat. As long as North Korea maintains its policy of reunification by force and Communism, we will have to be prepared. We have been able to build up our defense and are now spending 6 per cent of GNP on defense. Although North Korean [relations] are cooling with China, the Soviet Union is coming in very strong. Altogether, the Soviet military power is stronger in this region than over-all U.S. military power here.

Interview, Seoul/USA Today, 6-3:(A)13.

3

[South] Korea was devastated in the 1950s during the war. The U.S. came to our aid. We are allies forged in war. We built our nation from the ashes of war. We've achieved spectacular economic results and we are approaching a more mature democratic republic. We are one country you can be proud of contributing your efforts to.

Interview, Seoul/
USA Today, 6-3:(A)13.

4

The basic policy in the past was to try to change the North Korean position by isolating them further. We have changed this. We think that by encouraging them to be more open, we can have peace in this part of the world . . . We will approach the North Koreans on more friendly terms, and we would like our friends to help us draw them out into the international community.

Interview, Seoul, July 1/
The Washington Post, 7-2:(A)1,18.

5

I believe we have now come to a historical moment when we should be able to find a breakthrough toward a lasting peace and unification on the Korean Peninsula, which is still fraught with the danger of war amidst persisting tension and confrontation . . . I believe that if the entire 60 million Korean people pool their wisdom and strength, the South and the North will be integrated into a single social, cultural and economic community before this century is out.

July 7/
Los Angeles Times, 7-7:(I)1,19.

6

I will keep my promise to build a new democratic nation. I will not abuse any government power to advance the interests of the governing party. I will even more greatly respect pluralism and freedom in all segments of society. I will take the lead in reforming any [undemocratic] laws and institutions. I will take the initiative in

(ROH TAE WOO)

implanting democratic principles on all spheres of national life.

Before National Assembly,
Seoul, Oct. 4/
Los Angeles Times, 10-4:(I)8.

1

. . . I do have a feeling that our hopes and expectations [for better relations between North and South Korea] will somehow be met in the future. As more and more socialist countries begin to understand us [South Koreans] better and develop cooperative relations with us, that is bound to have some influence on North Korea. Changing external circumstances will be helpful in our efforts for reunification. I believe that process has now begun.

Interview, Seoul, Oct. 31/
Los Angeles Times, 11-1:(I)14.

2

[On anti-Americanism in South Korea]: The Number 1 element is propaganda from North Korea . . . Some of the left-leaning elements inside [South Korea] tend to side with the North . . . The other element in this anti-American feeling is that some of the youth, either from their sense of national self-esteem or from ignorance of the exact relationship between our two countries . . . believe that we are dependent and subjugated to American interests economically and politically, which is very wrong.

Interview/Newsweek, 10-31:38.

Rene Saguisag
Philippine Senator

3

I want the [U.S. military] bases out [of the Philippines] by the end of 1991 . . . At some point, we have to just stand on our own two feet. We have to grow out of our innocence.

Los Angeles Times, 7-13:(I)5.

Leticia Ramos Shahani
Philippine Senator

4

[On the two U.S. military bases in the Philippines]: I think it's obvious that, sooner or later, the bases will have to go, but the real question is how and when. We have to cut the umbilical cord at a certain point or we will always be a neo-colony . . . But it's like you've been addicted to drugs, and a sudden withdrawal could cause more trauma. If you do it all right away, you might even die.

At discussion session/
Los Angeles Times, 4-4:(I)8.

Shao Yu-ming
Director, Government
Information Office of Taiwan

5

We will only accept reunification [with mainland China] if Communism is removed [from there]. When and how China's reunification is going to take place depends on how fast and how genuine is the disappearance of Communism from the soil of China. We feel that time is on our side. The longer we compete, the better position we'll be in, because the gap between the two sides across the Taiwan Strait is being widened every day . . . It took us [Chinese] 90 years to get rid of the Mongols of the Yuan Dynasty. It took us 268 years to get rid of the Manchus. The Chinese Communists have had 40 years so far. I don't think they will last very long—not [as] long as the Mongols or the Manchus.

Los Angeles Times, 1-23:(I)9.

Eduard A. Shevardnadze
Foreign Minister of the
Soviet Union

6

[On Soviet military involvement in Afghanistan against Afghan rebels fighting the government]: We would like 1988 to be the last year of the presence of Soviet troops in [Afghanistan] . . . Having discussed this question with [Afghan] President Najibullah, we have arrived at the conclusion that the necessary conditions

323

can be ensured shortly. In other words, we believe the conditions for a political settlement of external aspects of the Afghan problem will be ensured ... We shall leave Afghanistan with a clear conscience and an awareness of duty fulfilled when outside interference is stopped. We have complete understanding with the Afghan leadership to this effect.

Interview/
Los Angeles Times, 1-7:(I)6.

Nikolai V. Shishlin
Spokesman, Central Committee,
Communist Party
of the Soviet Union

1

I think it's quite clear that the first desire of the Soviet Union is to withdraw our troops from Afghanistan, and really we are interested to see Afghanistan as a neutral, non-aligned and friendly country to my country.

U.S. broadcast interview/
"This Week With David Brinkley,"
ABC-TV, 12-11.

George P. Shultz
Secretary of State of
the United States

2

[On the war in Afghanistan between U.S.-backed rebels and the Soviet-backed government]: We will do our part to see an Afghanistan which rules itself, where the refugees can return, an Afghanistan that is ... neutral. And, of course, the objective of our support for the resistance has been to bring about those conditions and, as those conditions emerge, obviously we wouldn't have to continue that support ... Make no mistake. We're going to support the resistance in the attainment of their objective. And it's very important to emphasize that, even as the objective may seem close at hand. As far as our side is concerned, we look for Soviet agreement to a firm schedule for withdrawal [of Soviet troops]. We think that schedule must be front-end loaded, so that once it starts, there's a certain inevitability to it, there's no turning back.

News conference,
Washington, Jan. 7/
Los Angeles Times, 1-8:(I)5.

3

[Saying the Philippines may want unacceptable financial terms to allow the U.S. to keep its military bases there]: There are those in the Philippines who think that they have a great asset there and they should rent it out to us for a staggering amount of money. And we have told them that we just don't accept the concept at all, and if that's their view, we'll have to find some other place to have our ships and planes and so on, because we only want to be at a place where we have an ally that wants us there.

Before Senate Foreign Operations
Subcommittee, Washington,
June 16/The New York Times,
6-17:7.

4

[On the 1986 overthrow of Philippines dictator Ferdinand Marcos and the establishment of democracy in the Philippines]: The United States rejoiced—there is no other word for it—when the Philippine people joined together two years ago in one of the most dramatic political transformations of this era.

Manila, July 11/
Los Angeles Times, 7-12:(I)5.

5

[China] is seeking elimination of the remaining obstacles in the way of Sino-Soviet relations, a prospect that can be welcomed to the extent that it strengthens an environment of security and stability for all the countries of Asia as they try to focus their energies on national economic construction.

At banquet in his honor,
Peking, July 14/
Los Angeles Times, 7-15:(I)13.

(GEORGE P. SHULTZ)

1

[American troops] will remain in Korea as long as the people and governments of both the United States and the Republic of [South] Korea deem them necessary to ensure peace. North Korea should have no doubt that even as we will support the efforts of our ally in the south to promote dialogue and national reconciliation, we will also stand firm in the face of violence and efforts to intimidate.

Before Korean Newspaper Editors
Association, Seoul, July 18/
Los Angeles Times, 7-18:(I)20.

2

[On U.S. pressure on South Korea to open its markets to American products]: An awful lot of people have said to me that you shouldn't keep pressing for those market-opening measures, because it's causing Koreans to be anti-American. And I have to say, well, if that causes you to be anti-American, help yourself.

Seoul, July 18/
The Christian Science Monitor,
7-20:9.

3

In the next century, America's engagement with Asia must intensify because—and not despite the fact—that there is an ever-growing number of capable countries coming onto the world scene. Our engagement [with Asia] must be more active than ever, because the socialist powers are seeking to become more actively involved in the region as well.

At University of Hawaii, July 21/
Los Angeles Times, 7-22:(I)23.

4

Since the Second World War, the United States has been the indispensable stabilizing influence in [Asia and the Pacific] ... Longtime adversaries have become allies, friends and trading partners. Once-poor nations have become prosperous. Nations once divided from

each other are working together pragmatically to realize shared interests and concerns. And authoritarian political orders of the past have given way to the give-and-take of democratic politics.

At University of Hawaii, July 21/
The Washington Post, 7-22:(A)18.

Josef Silverstein
Professor of political science,
Rutgers University

5

[On the current unrest in Burma]: This is one of the few examples of a pure popular revolution that we are seeing anywhere in the world. There are no leaders [of the revolution], there is no organization and there is no international movement outside the country pushing the people one way or the other. What surprised me is that the Burmese government has held on for so long, that this upheaval did not come at an earlier point.

The New York Times, 9-10:1.

M. R. Srinivasan
Chairman, Atomic Energy
Commission of India

6

The intent of India has been from the very beginning to concentrate on a comprehensive program of nuclear technology exclusively for our energy needs. India's political leadership over the last 40 years has been remarkably responsible in this matter. It has not launched a weapons program in spite of the fact the technology basis of the Indian energy program is quite comprehensive.

Interview, Bombay/
The New York Times, 5-7:1.

Ted Stevens
United States Senator,
R-Alaska

7

[Saying Japan should pay more toward maintaining U.S. military bases and personnel stationed there]: We've got to make them realize

(TED STEVENS)

that they are not paying their fair share. Why should my children and my grandchildren pay the costs of keeping our troops there for their national defense?

Los Angeles Times, 5-31:(I)15.

R. R. Subramanian
Senior analyst, Institute for Defense Studies and Analyses (India)

1

With a large coastline, India is concerned over naval threats, particularly from China, which has the world's third-largest, though obsolescent, navy. The possibility of the Chinese Navy linking up with Pakistan in a war must be weighing heavily in the minds of our policy-makers.

The Christian Science Monitor, 1-22:1.

Noboru Takeshita
Prime Minister of Japan

2

We have undertaken to make Japan a nation which contributes more to the world. We are embarking on this course of our own will and initiative, and not merely responding to the requests of others ... Our ability to communicate with each other sometimes lags behind the extraordinary speed with which our two countries [Japan and the U.S.] are interacting. When communication lags, there can be misunderstandings and even prejudices. [But] to those people ... who view our relationship as confrontational and to those ... who worry about the future course of Japan-U.S. relations, I have only this to say: Japan is fully aware that the prosperity of the United States constitutes the very foundation of our own prosperity.

At National Press Club, Washington, Jan. 14/ Los Angeles Times, 1-15:(I)11.

Nguyen Co Thach
Foreign Minister of Vietnam

3

[On the U.S.-Vietnam war of the 1960s and '70s]: The people of the U.S. ended the war against us. The politicians started it.

Interview/USA Today, 6-2:(A)2.

4

In Cambodia, we have withdrawn half our forces. We will withdraw totally by 1990. But why is the United States so concerned about the Vietnamese presence in Cambodia, and they do not concern themselves with China, which has supported the Pol Pot regime's genocide? I think because we are small and China is big.

Interview/USA Today, 6-10:(A)13.

5

We [in Vietnam] have neglected the law of supply and demand, the law of value. Charity is not working. Without some capitalism there can be no socialism. We must learn from [the U.S.].

Interview/USA Today, 6-10:(A)13.

Nathaniel Thayer
Director of Japanese studies, School of Advanced International Studies, Johns Hopkins University

6

Regardless of the trade dispute, we are in the midst of building a single, Japanese-American economy. We don't have one economy yet, but we have two economies that are already so close that they have a profound, unexpected and unwelcome effect on each other ... The two governments do not resolve trade problems. They talk about resolving trade problems until the trade problems resolve themselves.

Los Angeles Times, 5-19:(I)1.

S. C. Tsiang
President, Chung Hua Institution for Economic Research (Taiwan)

7

People here [in Taiwan] have enjoyed [trade] protection from [American] imports for a long

(S. C. TSIANG)

time and, if it is removed, they will take the matter to the streets. The United States is starting to be seen as a [economic] bully rather than a friend.

Los Angeles Times, 9-17:(I)9.

Sosuke Uno
Foreign Minister of Japan

1

Japan . . . intends not only to expand its contributions in the economic field but also to embark on new forms of contribution in the political and diplomatic fields, with a view to finding solutions to regional conflicts, and relaxing tensions . . . [But] although it has the second-largest economic capability in the free world, Japan refuses to become a military power and maintains an exclusively defensive posture.

At meeting of Association of
Southeast Asian Nations,
Bangkok, Thailand, July 8/
Los Angeles Times, 7-9:11.

Rudy Von Bernuth
Director of programs,
CARE (international relief
organization)

2

[On Bangladesh]: The country is one of the poorest in the world. It has a very large population, currently estimated to be over 110 million, in an area of only 55,000 square miles, which is comparable, say, to New Jersey in size. It has very few natural resources. It has very little industrial capacity, and it has not coped well with its independence.

Interview/USA Today, 9-8:(A)9.

Wu Xueqian
Foreign Minister of China

3

There are a lot of countries in the world that sell weapons, but newspaper commentaries are always picking on China . . . Why is it that some people always harass China with this so-called

issue? Our attitude on the question of arms sales is a serious and responsible one; it is not a question of China selling arms to all countries in the world.

News conference, Peking, April 6/
The Christian Science Monitor,
4-8:11.

Tadashi Yamamoto
President, Japan Center for
International Exchange

4

The majority of Japanese would like to see [U.S. President-elect George] Bush take a much more serious look at the twin deficits [U.S. deficits in its Federal budget and in trade]. And I think we're bracing ourselves for what will be the inevitable consequence of neglect on that issue: more pressure [on Japan] about the trade deficit and defense burden-sharing. That's why we are terribly concerned about Mr. Bush's determination not to raise [U.S.] taxes.

The New York Times, 11-25:(C)4.

Zhao Ziyang
Chairman, Communist Party
of China

5

[On the death of Taiwanese leader Chiang Ching-kuo]: Mr. Chiang Ching-kuo had upheld a one-China policy, opposed the independence of Taiwan and had stood for the reunification of the country. He had said that he would not let history down and had made certain efforts to help relieve tension over the relations between people on both sides of the Taiwan Strait . . . We hope the new [Taiwan ruling party] Kuomintang leadership will size up the situation in line with the fundamental interest of the Chinese nation and the common aspirations of the people, and work to promote the promising momentum beginning to appear in the relationship between the two sides of the Taiwan Strait, and make a positive contribution to ending the division of the country and realizing peaceful reunification as soon as possible . . . The people of Taiwan have a glorious patriotic tradition, long for reunification and

(ZHAO ZIYANG)

oppose division. Together with compatriots residing in Hong Kong, Macao and overseas, they have in recent years made efforts for peaceful reunification and for peace talks between the Communist Party and Kuomintang.

Jan. 14/
The New York Times, 1-15:5.

1

[On relations between China and Taiwan]: The situation in the Taiwan Strait has been improving, although the Taiwan authorities still stick with their three "no" policies: no communication, no negotiations, no direct contact with the People's government [mainland China]. Nevertheless, the Taiwan authorities have relaxed their control over visits of the people of Taiwan to the mainland. In fact, relations across the Taiwan Strait have relaxed quite a bit . . . I see the situation moving toward relaxation, and the return of Taiwan and the reunification of the country are more and more possible. Our hopes of this are higher and higher every day. If you ask me when will the mainland and Taiwan be reunited, I can't answer that. But I think the situation is improving steadily.

Interview, Peking/
USA Today, 5-9:(A)9.

2

Although the United States regards China as a non-aligned, friendly country, actually, in terms of technology transfer, China is still discriminated against. So the term "non-aligned, friendly country" does not match what the United States is actually doing or trying to do. Some members of [the U.S.] Congress often say things which irritate the Chinese people, and some of their statements are, as a matter of fact, actions interfering in China's international affairs.

Interview, Peking/
USA Today, 5-9:(A)9.

Mohammed Zia ul-Haq
President of Pakistan

3

[On Pakistan's support for the *mujahideen*, rebels fighting the Soviet-backed government of Afghanistan]: If Pakistan continues to support the *mujahideen*, then the fallout will be in the form of some arm-twisting and some border bombings and some other things [by the government of Afghanistan]. Pakistan is prepared to pay such a price until the Afghans have won their objective of changing the regime in Kabul. Pakistan will face the music.

Time, 4-25:51.

4

[Saying candidates in the forthcoming national elections in Pakistan will not be allowed to campaign on the basis of party affiliation]: As your [the U.S.'] George Washington once said, America would do better without political parties. And you are living in a vast country where democracy has been developed over years—centuries. We always labor to look to the U.S. as a democratic model, but they only have two parties there. Here we have a ton of them, and our parties rely more on rhetoric and sloganeering than on the candidate's personal character and his politics.

News conference, July 21/
Los Angeles Times,
7-22:(I)15.

5

I really have been a reluctant ruler. Really. You can say that. A reluctant ruler. But I am not a person to just give up in disgust and walk away. I am determined to stay here until I solve all of the many problems that continue to face our country. Only then will I disappear and start playing as much golf as I wish I were playing right now.

Interview,
Islamabad, Pakistan/
Los Angeles Times, 8-1:(I)8.

Europe

Leonid I. Abalkin
Director, Soviet Economics Institute

1

One cannot deny that positive shifts have occurred in the [Soviet] economy . . . But there have been no radical breakthroughs in the economy, and it still remains in a state of stagnation . . . The state of the consumer market has worsened. Of particular concern is the situation with scientific and technological progress, where the gap from world levels is increasing and assuming ominous proportions. One of the main causes is that, in drafting the 12th five-year economic plan, we opted for both quantitative growth and qualitative transformation. From an academic point of view, these two tasks are incompatible. Whatever doubts there were about this were confirmed by the midway results of the current five-year plan. We faced a choice of quantity or quality. Having considered our traditions and experience, it is clear what choice we made.

At Soviet Communist Party
conference, Moscow/
The New York Times, 7-1:4.

Robert Adley
Member of British Parliament

2

[Criticizing New York Mayor Edward Koch for saying the British are an occupying Army in Northern Ireland]: What Mayor Koch and his creepy-crawly colleagues in New York should realize is that most of the Protestants have been in Northern Ireland longer than they have been in America. If there are to be any occupying forces withdrawn, it is the whites who should get out of the United States and hand the country back to the Red Indians.

The New York Times,
8-1:9.

Yuri F. Afanasyev
Soviet historian

3

[On the World War II pact between the Soviets and Germany which resulted in the Baltic states, including Estonia, being incorporated into the U.S.S.R.]: The signing of the pact resulted in the occupation of Estonia. We are speaking now of historical injustices, and we have no right to be silent about this . . . In no other country has history been falsified to the extent that it has been in the Soviet Union.

At rally protesting the pact,
Tallinn, Estonia, Aug. 23/
Los Angeles Times, 8-24:(I)5.

Abel Aganbegyan
Director, economic section,
Soviet Academy of Sciences;
Chief economic adviser to
Soviet leader
Mikhail S. Gorbachev

4

We are not deterred by the failure of earlier attempts to change the Soviet economy. The Kosygin-era reforms embraced only industrial and agricultural enterprises without involving other sectors. Bureaucratic management methods were unchanged; ministers' jobs were unchanged. Economic reforms in industry and agriculture, moreover, were not reinforced by social reforms. Today, things are different. *Perestroika* [reform] involves all spheres of the economy and of society. Now the principal motivating force is democratization. That is why we are so very optimistic. We are sure we will succeed because we have no other choice. People are sick of living in the old way. As [Soviet leader] Mikhail Gorbachev has said, "We have nowhere to retreat."

Interview/
World Press Review,
January:18.

329

Georgi A. Arbatov
Director, Soviet Institute of
U.S.A. and Canadian Affairs

1

[On Soviet leader Mikhail Gorbachev's policy of *glasnost,* openness]: We've been questioning all the things that are basic in our society. I personally have been surprised at the extent of Gorbachev's impact on Soviet society. We are acquiring a new image of ourselves. We are able to look squarely at our inadequacies, having become the victims of our own excesses and formulations. We are able to talk freely about the sufferings and injustices we have had to endure.

At Dartmouth Conference, U.S.A./
The Christian Science Monitor,
6-6:14.

Alexander Askoldov
Soviet motion-picture
director

2

I often have the feeling that what is happening in my country is being distorted in the Western press. The idea that art and spirituality in Russia have been smothered by the bureaucracy alone is a particular danger one might fall into. Alone, bureaucracy would be incapable of doing such a thing. The cooperation of strike-breakers and immoral people among the intelligentsia was required as well. That's where the essential tragic contradiction of our internal situation lies.

Interview, California/
The Wall Street Journal, 5-24:32.

Wladyslaw Backa
President, Polish National
Bank; Member, Politburo,
Communist Party of Poland

3

Those who create, those who work, those who provide, should win, while those who are lazy should lose. Unfortunately, our social system has a hard time adjusting to the creation of fortunes.

The Christian Science Monitor,
1-6:7.

4

A considerable number of Poles are frustrated, not so much by low earnings but rather by the unceasing necessity to overcome difficulties they come across in everyday life. This applies equally to villages and towns. A Pole hunts for basic medicines, he carries his own single-use injector when going to a clinic, wastes 45 minutes at a bus stop, to no avail asks the dustman to come for litter, spends weeks asking housing-administration people to repair the roof. In this way, the citizen's everyday life becomes not only difficult but also extremely humiliating. The disappointment stems not only from the present economic situation; there is also a spreading conviction that Poland will remain bogged in the economic crisis for many years—a conviction that the present economic policy is unable to cope with the existing obstacles, that the situation will deteriorate rather than improve. This happens six years after the beginning of the economic reform. We cannot overlook this.

Before Polish Communist Party
Central Committee, Warsaw/
Los Angeles Times, 8-30:(I)8.

Naili B. Bikkenin
Editor, "Kommunist," Soviet
Communist Party journal

5

[Agreeing with Soviet leader Mikhail Gorbachev's reform program for the country]: Our intention is to create a human face for socialism, and that means making over socialism to serve the human being ... We are going back to Lenin's methods. Lenin wanted Communists to lead not by strength of power but by strength of talent, strength of knowledge, strength of experience and strength of vision, and to exercise that leadership through its members in the government and other bodies ... Our main aim is ending the alienation of the Soviet people from power. That alienation began in the 1930s [under Stalin], but it continues to today. We have had formal organs of people's power, but they have not had real power. The Supreme Soviet functions as a rubber stamp.

Press briefing, Moscow, June 27/
Los Angeles Times, 6-28:(I)1,12.

Pyotr S. Bogdanov
Chief of Police of Moscow

1

[Saying the Soviet government is showing more tolerance now for dissident demonstrators]: It is our responsibility to make sure it does not interfere with the order of the city, not to have an uncontrollable situation. But in general, if somebody says he wants to demonstrate for clean air, or if they want to demonstrate to leave for another country, that's their right. We won't interfere. If before we used one set of measures, now we are using more democratic methods with respect to the public expression of views. It is no longer our policy to detain these people.

Interview/The New York Times, 6-8:6.

Mihai Botez
*Romanian mathematician
and political dissident*

2

[Romania is] extremely unsophisticated, the simplest and most Stalinist in nature. [Romanian leader Nicolae] Ceausescu is really a leader of the 1930s, which means he has no doubts—he is a true believer. He was certain from the beginning that Communism is good and capitalism is bad; that central planning is good and markets are bad; that any private ownership or the introduction of even a semblance of market mechanisms would be heretical, that central planning and the vanguard of the [Communist] Party can solve all the problems of humankind. In this view, people are bad because they waste their energy on marginal activities and are not sufficiently committed to the Master Plan—thus, they need a firm hand ... Romania in this situation is extremely isolated, because there is only pressure from below, and no pressure for reform at the top. This lack of reformist will at the top has created an extremely tense atmosphere in Romanian society.

Interview/The Wall Street Journal, 7-29:12.

Willy Brandt
*Former Chancellor of
West Germany*

3

[West Germany's] history and our geography constrain us [militarily]. It is not easy; it is like squaring the circle. We are expected to have an army weak enough not to worry our allies to the West, but strong enough to defeat the Soviet Union. For us, the problem is to be less powerful than the Russians, but to be sufficiently powerful so they are not tempted to attack Europe.

*Before Nobel Prize winners, Paris/
World Press Review, June:50.*

Edgar M. Bronfman
*President,
World Jewish Congress*

4

It has always been the view of the World Jewish Congress ... that Soviet Jews should also first be accorded full cultural and religious rights within the U.S.S.R., enabling them to live as full-fledged Soviet citizens. I have argued to Soviet officials that their nation will derive palpable benefit from such reform. Those Jews who stay, given status to live dignified lives while holding to their heritage, will be there to contribute their knowledge and skills and talents to their nation's progress. Tentative steps have been introduced in the last year that would give them accessibility to religious material and limited availability of such related items as kosher food ... I believe, however, that until these tentative steps become accepted policy and general practice, the foundation for creating trust and an environment in which trade can flourish between the United States and the Soviet Union will be absent.

*Before House Foreign Affairs
subcommittee, Washington,
April 20/The Washington Post,
4-21:(A)22.*

Zbigniew Brzezinski
*Professor of government,
Columbia University;
Former Assistant to the
President of the United States
(Jimmy Carter) for National
Security Affairs*

5

[Saying that in the light of *perestroika*, reform in the Soviet Union, the West should prod

331

(ZBIGNIEW BRZEZINSKI)

Eastern European countries to moderate their regimes as well]: If we don't do anything, revolution could break out [in Eastern Europe]. If there is a revolution, there will be suppression. If suppression fails, there will be Soviet intervention. If there is Soviet intervention, that's the end of *perestroika*.

Newsweek, 5-9:26.

Vladimir Bukovsky
Exiled Soviet dissident

1

Let's not make a mistake. It's not [Soviet leader Mikhail] Gorbachev and his team who are introducing democracy in our country; they have their own agenda. Their agenda is to get socialism working. But the people have their own agenda. What Gorbachev wants is irrevelant, because he wouldn't get democracy if he asked the Politburo for it, anyway. But the people used this opening [reform in the Soviet Union] to promote their own agenda. And, suddenly, Gorbachev has much more than he bargained for. He has people coming up to him with demands for religious freedoms, for human rights, with social and environmental agendas. The Soviet country is becoming slowly uncontrollable. There is a chance the Soviet authorities will not be able to control the process they started, and that is a most fascinating thing. The country is in a struggle. It is a struggle between the people and the system.

At conference hosted by
Philanthropic Rountable, June/
The Wall Street Journal, 11-25:6.

Fyodor M. Burlatsky
Soviet political scientist
and adviser to Soviet leader
Mikhail Gorbachev

2

[On Soviet leader Mikhail Gorbachev's policies of *glasnost*, openness, and *perestroika*, reform, in the nation]: An immense struggle is unfolding within Soviet society. It is taking place on the basis of socialism, but the notions we have had of socialism are changing... All is in flux ... and the future is at stake.

Los Angeles Times, 5-29:(I)20.

George Bush
Vice President of the United
States; Candidate for the
1988 Republican U.S.
Presidential nomination

3

My trip to Poland [in 1987] drove home to me the disproportionate responsibility of the United States. I know enough about the churning in Eastern Europe today to think that maybe there is a chance—not a 50-50 but a longer-shot chance—of having more freedom for the people there if we handle our policy of differentiation correctly and build on it. I want to offer the hope of freedom to countries around the world because that's the basis of our very being in this country, our own freedoms.

Interview, Washington/
Time, 8-22:20.

George Bush
Vice President of the United
States; 1988 Republican
Presidential nominee

4

The Iron Curtain still stretches from Stettin to Trieste. But it's a rusting curtain. Shafts of light from the Western side, from our side, the free and prosperous side, are piercing the gloom of failure and despair on the other side. The truth is being sought as never before. And the peoples of Eastern Europe, the peoples of the Soviet Union itself, are demanding more freedom, demanding their place in the sun ... [The Soviets] do face a serious situation. You see, the people they rule want to know why they lack bread and why they lack freedom, and why life expectancy has decreased, and why public services and consumer goods are so poor and in such short supply. So 70 years after the Russian Revolution, Marxism is losing its luster.

At Westminster College,
Fulton, Mo., Oct. 18/
The New York Times, 10-19:(A)10.

Richard Carlson
Director, Voice of America

1

[On the Voice of America's service now that Soviet radio has opened up somewhat due to the new *glasnost* policy]: Our most important job is supplying what [orchestra] maestro [Mstislav] Rostropovich once described as "daily bread for people," and that is what we are doing, intellectually feeding hungry people . . . Our role is changing in that part of the world and we consider ourselves more competitive now. However, we think we have a real influence on the information that is given out by the Soviets. They have come a long way, but they have come from zero and the Soviet press is still basically a cheerleader for the government there.

The New York Times, 10-7:(A)16.

Lord Carrington
Secretary General, North
Atlantic Treaty Organization

2

In terms of public perception in our own countries, if you argue that one of the reasons why you must maintain nuclear weapons in Europe is the conventional imbalance between the Warsaw Pact and NATO, then you are not credible if you don't make a genuine effort to do something about the imbalance [in conventional weapons that favors the Warsaw Pact]. Therefore, we really have got to tackle the conventional-stability problem, seriously and energetically. It is not very easy . . . But it's got to be done.

Interview, Brussels/
Los Angeles Times, 3-1:(I)7.

3

It's much easier to hold the [NATO] alliance together when they're frightened than when they're not.

USA Today, 3-2:(A)10.

4

There was general agreement [among the members of NATO] on the need to keep up the level of our defense expenditures in spite of the fact that there is a very welcome reduction in tensions [between the U.S. and the Soviet Union] . . . Whatever else may have changed in the Soviet Union [under *glasnost,* openness, and *perestroika,* reform], the [Soviet] military machine is still, so far, operating at exactly the same level as it was in the days before *perestroika* and *glasnost.*

Madrid, June 10/
The New York Times, 6-11:6.

Victor Chebrikov
Director, KGB (Soviet
secret police)

5

[On anti-government ethnic protests in [some] areas of the Soviet Union]: It is an open secret that secret services of imperialist powers and foreign anti-Soviet centers actively join extremist nationalist actions [in the Soviet Union]. One should not underestimate the danger of this method of subversive action against this country . . . You know that anti-social actions of nationalistic nature took place in a number of regions of the country. Attempts were even made to put forward demands on the revision of the existing state-national and administrative-national borders.

Speech, Cheboksary, Soviet Union,
April 13/Los Angeles Times,
4-14:(A)28.

Jacques Chirac
Premier of France

6

[Criticizing the Berlin Wall]: Destruction of the wall that separates Berlin in an inhuman way must constitute an essential step in [European] confidence. We do not want a Europe with barbed wire sticking out. We do not want a walled-up Europe.

At luncheon for visiting East
German leader Erich Honecker,
Paris, Jan. 8/
The Washington Post, 1-9:(A)16.

Jacques Chirac
Premier of France;
Candidate for President
of France

1

I want to make our country the most dynamic power in Europe by the end of the century. Some will say this is a mad idea, but history goes against those who lack ambition.

Campaign speech, Jan. 24/
Los Angeles Times, 1-25:(I)16.

Ciriaco De Mita
Prime Minister of Italy

2

The solidarity between Italy and the United States has been constant since the Second World War. One factor is the presence of a very large Italian community in the United States. Also, after Fascism, we learned a lesson. It was that our own development could only take place together with the free and democratic countries of the world, and so this also lies behind our solidarity with the United States.

Interview, Rome/
USA Today, 7-29:(A)11.

Milovan Djilas
Author; Former Vice
President of Yugoslavia

3

The Soviet Union is a military empire and, in history, military empires change very slowly. But my view is that the Soviet Union is in a deep crisis, to the extent that it is becoming rotten.

Interview/
The Washington Post, 1-20:(A)22.

4

[On Soviet leader Mikhail Gorbachev's program of reform in the Soviet Union]: Gorbachev has so far tackled only the foothills of the mountain range he has to climb. There has been much sermonizing, criticism, encouragement and some limited legislation—none of which has yet begun to bite. His difficulties will begin in three or four years when decentralization, privatization and self-management will confront him with the painful fact that none of these reforms can be made really effective without revamping the political profile of Soviet society. This is the experience we have had in Yugoslavia and that is what the Hungarian Communists, too, are now discovering to their dismay. Up will go the demands for political pluralism. This is going to cause trouble, because while members of the *apparat* may well be forced, lured or cajoled into supporting reforms for a more productive economy, they cannot be lured or cajoled into underwriting the dissolution of the Party and the destruction of their own jobs and security.

Interview/
The New York Times, 12-3:15.

Alexander Dubcek
Former First Secretary,
Communist Party of
Czechoslovakia

5

[On the 1968 Soviet invasion of Czechoslovakia, which ousted him and stopped his plans for liberalization of the Czech Communist system]: Twenty years ago, we defined as "socialism with a human face" our movement for the rebirth of socialism. We wanted to express in the most precise and significant manner the relation between human values and the aspirations of socialism. We tried programmatically to unite socialism with democracy. I must reaffirm here my clear conviction: Without the external intervention in the affairs of our Party and of Czech society [by the Soviets], our attempt would have been crowned with success. The necessary conditions were there in our society. It was, in this sense, more mature than any other.

Accepting honorary degree from
University of Bologna (Italy),
Nov. 13/The New York Times,
11-14:(A)6.

Alain Duhamel
French political analyst

6

The ideological evolution in France over the past several years has effectively been the victory

(ALAIN DUHAMEL)

of Protestant ideology [over mainstream French Catholicism]—more tolerance, more modernity, more individual responsibility, more spirit of competition, more opening to the outside world. The French governing class has become Protestant without knowing it.

The New York Times, 6-11:4.

Michael S. Dukakis
Governor of Massachusetts (D);
Candidate for the 1988
Democratic U.S.
Presidential nomination

1

Even conventional [non-nuclear] warfare in Europe—given the number of nuclear power plants there—would itself be an absolute disaster for Europe and for the world. If [the Soviet nuclear-plant accident at] Chernobyl was as dramatic an experience as it was for all of us, think of what would happen if conventional warfare broke out in Europe and, as almost certainly would happen, the energy sources and power plants of the combatants were the first targets. You'd have a nuclear holocaust with conventional warfare.

Interview/
Los Angeles Times, 5-26:(I)22.

Michael S. Dukakis
Governor of Massachusetts (D);
1988 Democratic
Presidential nominee

2

[On the unrest in Poland involving the Solidarity trade union]: It is time for the Polish government to follow the call of the true leader of the Polish people, [Solidarity leader] Lech Walesa, and, finally, legalize Solidarity. Poland cannot solve its economic problems and expect expanded economic assistance, unless the government is prepared to respect basic human rights and enter into a dialogue with the church and the workers.

Aug. 22/*
The New York Times, 8-23:9.

3

[Criticizing the Soviet Union's policies in Eastern Europe]: Free trade unions do not endanger security [for the Soviets]; political parties do not endanger security; and the right to worship God can be a threat to no civilized power. [Soviet leader Mikhail] Gorbachev must understand that in Eastern Europe it is the status quo that creates instability.

Before Chicago Council on
Foreign Relations, Sept. 13/
Los Angeles Times, 9-14:(I)27.

4

[On Soviet leader Mikhail Gorbachev]: Where his predecessors were ponderous in diplomacy, Mr. Gorbachev is nimble. Where they were predictable, he has a facility for surprise. Where they were orthodox, he has used the pulpit of our open Western press to place before the world an image of a Soviet Union on the verge of far-reaching change at home and in world affairs.

Before Chicago Council on
Foreign Relations, Sept. 13/
The New York Times, 9-14:16.

5

I don't see how you can look at the Soviet Union and not conclude that some very significant things are taking place. We don't know at this point how much, how far. We don't even know whether [Soviet leader Mikhail] Gorbachev himself can survive politically. But we do know that the Soviets are in very deep trouble domestically, that their economy is stagnating. I think that's the principal reason why we appear to have a Soviet Union that's much more willing to sit down and negotiate seriously about arms control.

Interview/
Reader's Digest, October:66.

Oskar Fischer
Foreign Minister of
East Germany

6

It is not helpful to anybody to lament over the partition or the division of Europe, and to call for

(OSKAR FISCHER)

ending it. The socialist countries accept realities as they exist, and expect others to do likewise.

At meeting of Institute for
East-West Security Studies,
Potsdam, East Germany, June 9/
Los Angeles Times, 6-10:(I)14.

John R. Galvin
General, United States Army;
Supreme Allied Commander/
Europe

1

[Saying he is wary of Soviet leader Mikhail Gorbachev's policy of *perestroika*, reform, in the Soviet Union]: When I read *Perestroika* [Gorbachev's book], I find nothing that says they've changed their external policies or their ideology. They still want nuclear weapons, America and NATO out of Europe. That's what they've wanted since the 1950s . . . You have times when Americans and Europeans think there's an enormous [Soviet] threat. Then a little thing will happen, and because we all so much desire peace and quiet and prosperity and happiness, we have the urge to will it into effect. But the geopolitical aims and goals of the Soviet Union haven't changed, and the military power that back them up has not changed.

Interview, Mons, Belgium/
The New York Times, 4-28:7.

Hans-Dietrich Genscher
Foreign Minister of
West Germany

2

The time has come when we must press forward with a decisive process of European unification so that we can develop the power of 320 million consumers. Therefore, I am of the opinion that we need clear progress in currency and financial policies: a monetary union and a European central bank. We have in the European Community really great reserves of growth for the world economy. All that we're doing now to keep the economy going, or to stimulate it, is

relatively little . . . in comparison with the effect the EC internal market could have.

Interview, Bonn/
The Christian Science Monitor,
4-1:10.

3

[On improved Soviet-West German relations]: Progress in bilateral relations will not only be to the benefit of further improvement of cooperation all over Europe, but also to the benefit of East-West relations. The far-reaching projects to restructure and modernize the Soviet economy offer many opportunities for [West Germany] as the most important Soviet trade partner.

Oct. 21/
Los Angeles Times, 10-22:(I)6.

Felipe Gonzalez
Prime Minister of Spain

4

Spain has managed to accomplish a peaceful revolution [after the Franco dictatorship which ended in 1975]—a democratic revolution—which hasn't been normal during our history. This democratic transformation, done peacefully without any vengeance or civil confrontation, has been accompanied by a spectacular opening of our borders. Spain is the fifth country in importance in the European market. All this has taken place in just one decade. This is a country which is beginning to flourish economically. It was traditionally considered a poor country. Now it's considered the country with the greatest potential for growth and development in Europe. I need to make that image known.

Interview, Madrid/
USA Today, 7-15:(A)9.

Mikhail S. Gorbachev
General Secretary,
Communist Party
of the Soviet Union

5

[On his program of reform in the Soviet Union]: The task is indeed a daunting one. We

(MIKHAIL S. GORBACHEV)

are just leaving the period of stagnation . . . We perhaps have not realized completely how widespread various negative phenomena—parasitic attitudes, leveling of pay, report padding, parochialism, illegal actions—became in the years of stagnation. Deplorably, a widely current attitude is that one can work ten times less, a hundred times less than others, can do nothing at all, and at the same time enjoy all the benefits in the same degree as people do whose work makes a large contribution to the country's development.

To editors and publishers, Moscow, Jan. 8/Los Angeles Times, 1-13:(I)8.

1

It is necessary to remove the rust of bureaucratism from the values and ideas of socialism. We are striving in the present conditions to revive the Leninist look of the new system, to rid it of accumulations and deformations, of everything that shackled society and prevented it from realizing the potential for socialism in full measure . . . We have lost and keep losing a lot because of our failure to unshackle grass-roots initiative, endeavor and independence completely. This is the biggest, the hardest, but also the most important task of *perestroika* [reform]. And it will not be an exaggeration to say that everything today hinges on its fulfillment.

Before Soviet Communist Party Central Committee, Moscow, Feb. 18/The New York Times, 2-19:1.

2

[On his program of reform in the Soviet Union]: We want our decisions, at least our principal decisions, to be prepared with the involvement of the whole society. We want them to be prepared democratically. This, we believe, is the main guarantee against mistakes. So that is why we are so persistent in developing the process of democratization and openness and public debate, *glasnost,* in our society. We shall not retreat from that . . . And that means an end to stagna-

tion, an end to apathy. This is a turbulent time, a turbulent sea in which it is not easy to sail the ship, but we have a compass and we have a crew to guide that ship. And the ship itself is strong.

Interview/Newsweek, 5-30:25.

3

In the whole complex of measures that are covered by the term radical economic reform [in the Soviet Union], prices and price formation occupy a significant place. . . prices should be consistent with actual economic processes, with real costs and with the real contribution of the workers. That would create a healthier financial system . . . Along the way we will be able to better satisfy the demands of the people and improve the means of production of goods and services, and we are planning to encourage higher quality of both goods and services.

Interview/Newsweek, 5-30:26.

4

Everyone who wants to do business with us will find it useful to know how Soviet people see themselves. We see ourselves even more convinced that our socialist choice was correct, and we cannot conceive of our country developing without socialism, based on any other fundamental values. Our program is more democracy, more *glasnost* [openness], more social justice with full prosperity and high moral standards. Our goal is maximum freedom for man, for the individual and for society.

At dinner for visiting U.S. President Reagan, Moscow, May 30/The New York Times, 5-31:8.

5

I would like to dwell particularly on the political freedoms that enable a person to express his opinion on any matter. The implementation of these freedoms is a real guarantee that any problem of public interest will be discussed from every angle, and all the pros and cons will be weighed; and that this will help to find optimal

(MIKHAIL S. GORBACHEV)

solutions with due consideration for all the diverse opinions and actual possibilities. In short, comrades, what we are talking about is a new role of public opinion in the country. And there is no need to fear the novel, unconventional character of some opinions; there is no need to over-react and lapse into extremes at every turn of the debates.

At Soviet Communist Party
conference, Moscow, June 28/
The New York Times, 6-29:8.

1

The Soviet people want a clear perspective . . . full-blooded and unconditional democracy. *Glasnost* [openness] in all things, big and small. Respect for hard work, and talk, and faithful service for the cause and the good of society. We need no social utopias.

At Soviet Communist Party
conference, Moscow, June 28/
Time, 7-11:24.

2

We see in the future a Europe whose East and West no longer bristle with weapons trained on each other but, on the contrary, draw unprecedented benefits from exchanges of goods and values, enterprise and knowledge, people and ideas.

Before Polish Sejm (Parliament),
Warsaw, July 11/
The Washington Post, 7-12:(A)17.

3

[On Polish Prime Minister Wojciech Jaruzelski]: I will tell it directly to you Poles: You were lucky that at this stage of history there has appeared a man of high moral standards and tremendous intellectual abilities who loves this land and is a great internationalist. I consider comrade Jaruzelski my great friend.

To shipyard workers,
Szczecin, Poland, July 13/
The Washington Post, 7-14:(A)26.

4

[On his program of *perestroika,* reform in the Soviet Union]: We are moving slowly so far, and we are losing time, and this means that we are losing . . . It was not easy to elaborate a concept of *perestroika,* but this was still easier than to embody it in specific actions . . . Some people have panicked when they have come face to face with the difficulties and realities of this revolutionary process. And really, comrades, the inertia that has gathered in our society over decades is tremendous. To bring the country out of this state, we need colossal efforts. Many problems have their roots and their history. A lot still has to be done to rock the old trees, to pull them up and to plant a new forest and gather its fruits.

Speech, Sept. 23/
Los Angeles Times, 9-26:(I)1,8.

5

The forthcoming months will be the most active in all the years of *perestroika* [his reform program] in terms of switching to new forms of economic management. Our intention is to lead the entire economy along this road, starting with agriculture . . . By having torn people away from the land and from the means of production [over the past half century], we have turned them from the masters of their land into hirelings . . . If a man wants to own land and create his own farm, we will not oppose it.

At agricultural conference, Oct. 12/
Los Angeles Times, 10-14:(I)14,15.

6

[Criticizing recent proclamations of semi-independence by the local government of Estonia]: The amendments adopted by the Supreme Soviet of the [Estonian] Republic say that Estonia's land, its mineral resources, the atmospheric air, inland and territorial waters, the shelf, forests and other natural resources are its exclusive property. According to the amendments, transport and communication facilities, state banks, trade, communal and other enterprises organized by the state, the available housing of the cities, as well as other facilities

(MIKHAIL S. GORBACHEV)

needed for the fulfillment of tasks by the Republic of Estonia, also belong to it. This is a principled deviation from the existing Constitution . . . There is only one aim, comrades. We are one family, we have a common home, and we have accomplished much, thanks to concerted effort. Some people omit that now, or even try to idealize the bourgeois period in the development of the Baltic republics or the past of other regions. But we know how backward Lithuania was, or when the greatest number of people left Estonia because life there was impossible. Our future is not in weakening ties among the republics, but in strengthening them, in broadening cooperation.

Before Presidium of Supreme
Soviet, Moscow, Nov. 26/
The New York Times, 11-28:(A)4.

1

Today I can report to you that the Soviet Union has taken a decision to reduce its armed forces. Within the next two years their numerical strength will be reduced by 500,000 men. The numbers of conventional armaments will also be substantially reduced. This will be done unilaterally, without relation to the talks on the mandate of the Vienna meeting. By agreement with our Warsaw Treaty allies, we have decided to withdraw by 1991 six tank divisions from East Germany, Czechoslovakia and Hungary, and to disband them. Assault landing troops and several other formations and units, including assault crossing units with their weapons and combat equipment, will also be withdrawn from the groups of Soviet forces stationed in those countries. Soviet forces stationed in those countries will be reduced by 50,000 men and their armaments by 5,000 tanks. All Soviet divisions remaining, for the time being, in the territory of our allies are being reorganized. Their structure will be different from what it is now; after a major cutback of their tanks, it will become clearly defensive. At the same time, we shall reduce the numerical strength of the armed forces and the numbers of armaments stationed in the European part of the Soviet Union. In total, Soviet armed

forces in this part of our country and in the territories of our European allies will be reduced by 10,000 tanks, 8,500 artillery systems and 800 combat aircraft.

At United Nations,
New York, Dec. 7/
The New York Times, 12-8:(A)6.

2

The problem of exit from and entry to our country, including the question of leaving it for family reunification, is being dealt with in a humane spirit. As you know, one of the reasons for refusal to leave is a person's knowledge of secrets. Strictly warranted time limitations on the secrecy rule will now be applied. Every person seeking employment at certain agencies or enterprises will be informed of this rule. In case of disputes, there is a right of appeal under the law. This removes from the agenda the problem of the so-called "refuseniks."

At United Nations,
New York, Dec. 7/
The New York Times, 12-8:(A)6.

Boris I. Gostev
Minister of Finance of the
Soviet Union

3

[On the disclosure of large, long-standing Soviet budget deficits]: This is not a problem that has cropped up all of a sudden. It is a result of an unbalanced economy, of excessive subsidies, of huge losses caused by extensive management methods, parasitic attitudes and passive financial policy.

Before Supreme Soviet,
Moscow, Oct. 27/
The New York Times, 10-28:(A)7.

Gerald Greenwald
Member, board of directors,
Chrysler Corporation

4

Europe's ambitious plan to create a truly free internal market by 1992 offers great opportuni-

(GERALD GREENWALD)

ties for U.S. business. [But] the American business community must exercise vigilance to ensure that companies from outside the European Community are not denied parity of access to that market.

The Washington Post, 10-6:(F)4.

Karoly Grosz
General Secretary,
Communist Party of Hungary

1

Anyone can express an opinion in [Hungary], and anyone can demonstrate. But our Constitution stipulates the government's duty to keep order. We are not ready for a multi-party system. It is impossible to turn back the wheel of history.

Interview, Budapest/
Newsweek, 7-18:38.

Carl Hagen
Member of Norwegian
Parliament; Leader, Progress
Party of Norway

2

Why is it, when everyone wants to be rich, that it can be wrong for someone to succeed? If someone makes it in Silicon Valley [in the U.S.] or in American business, he's considered a good man and you look up to him. In Norway, it's the other way around—you get a negative reaction. When a society gets into that way of thinking, it takes a hell of a long time and a lot of effort to change it. I'm trying to change it.

Interview, Oslo/
Los Angeles Times, 12-14:(I)16.

Lord Hailsham
Former Lord Chancellor of
the United Kingdom

3

[On British Prime Minister Margaret Thatcher]: You've got to put her in the same category as Bloody Mary, Elizabeth I, Queen Anne or Queen Victoria. Her handling of men is not altogether dissimilar [to that of Elizabeth I]. If you'd been a courtier of Elizabeth I, you would never know whether you were going to get the treatment of an admired male friend or a poke in the eye with an umbrella.

BBC-TV documentary/
The New York Times, 1-5:7.

Armand Hammer
Chairman, Occidental Petroleum
Corporation (United States)

4

[On what his close ties to the Soviet Union have shown him about Soviet leader Mikhail Gorbachev's reform policies]: Change is everywhere. I never dreamed I would see people criticizing high officials. The Politburo is actually encouraging them to write letters. People are not so much afraid. They used to be afraid to hear a knock on the door, that the KGB would be there . . . Of all the [Soviet] leaders I have met, [Gorbachev] stands out with Lenin. He has done a remarkable job in three years, and we must give him time to continue. I think he is sincere in not wanting to export Communism. He just wants to help his country.

Interview, Moscow/
USA Today, 5-31:(A)5.

Arthur A. Hartman
Former United States
Ambassador to the
Soviet Union

5

[On the economic reforms currently taking place in the Soviet Union]: When you begin something like this—trying to produce more quality products—you cut back on the quantity of things that you did before. So that means your general production goes down. When you raise prices, people are immediately unhappy, because they don't have the money right away to pay for these things. They feel themselves to be worse off. When you're trying to make progress like that, the first effects are very bad—bad for people.

Interview/USA Today, 12-6:(A)11.

(ARTHUR A. HARTMAN)

1

[Despite friendlier Soviet relations with the West,] Europe is still divided. The Soviets are not going to allow a reunification of Germany, for example. The Soviets say they will not allow pluralistic societies in East Europe. That means those countries are going to continue to feel unhappy about the regime that's been imposed on them.

Interview/USA Today, 12-6:(A)11.

Charles J. Haughey
Prime Minister of Ireland

2

The challenge that we face over Northern Ireland is to create a solution that will restore political cohesion through the exercise of self-determination by the Irish people . . . There are no instant formulae that can be summoned to our assistance. Violence must first cease, as it can have no place in the building of the Ireland of the future that we desire. There will have to be a deliberate and careful assembling of the elements of a solution.

At Harvard University, April 22/
The Washington Post, 5-5:(A)22.

Francois Heisbourg
Director, International
Institute for Strategic
Studies, London

3

If you eliminated nuclear weapons today, then the Soviets would have an [military] edge [in Europe]. You can quibble about the extent of that edge, but it's there.

Los Angeles Times, 1-31:(I)15.

John Hume
Member of British
Parliament from
Northern Ireland

4

[On the religious/political strife in Northern Ireland]: The territory of Ireland is already

united. It's the people who are divided. And you can't unify people through violence. An "eye for an eye" leaves everyone blind.

USA Today, 9-2:(A)15.

Gordon J. Humphrey
United States Senator,
R-New Hampshire

5

[Arguing against the U.S.-Soviet INF treaty in Europe]: The Soviets give up missiles which they don't need, because they have so many others not covered by the treaty which they can use in place of those which are being destroyed. The U.S. gives up missiles which are essential to the defense of Europe . . . The effect is likely to be the denuclearization of Europe—precisely what the Soviet Union is seeking. The problem is the conventional-force imbalance in Europe. The Soviet Union will become dominant in Western Europe, just like the United States is now.

Interview/USA Today, 6-1:(A)9.

Jesse L. Jackson
American civil-rights leader;
Candidate for the 1988
Democratic U.S.
Presidential nomination

6

Our [the U.S.'] World War II allies and enemies are now our economic competitors, yet we still spend over $150-billion a year to defend Europe against threats that even the military considers remote. As [former U.S. Secretary of State] Henry Kissinger has recommended, Western Europe should be responsible for its own conventional defense.

The Christian Science Monitor,
4-1:6.

Milos Jakes
First Secretary, Communist Party
of Czechoslovakia

7

[We are] expanding the rights and responsibilities of state enterprises and making them accoun-

341

(MILOS JAKES)

table, self-financing and self-managing. Workers will be electing their management from among competing candidates and will help development strategies and the distribution of profits. They will have the right to recall managers found to be unsuited to their tasks. Workers will think of themselves as real co-owners and co-managers of their enterprises; thus, they will be interested in results. Some workers will have to be trained or relocated. They will have to adapt, and nobody likes to do that. People want to be comfortable. It is not exactly pleasant when you've been sitting somewhere in a chair for 20 years and you are supposed to go somewhere else and start new. Reform will affect the laggards, those who do not like to work, the parasites.

Interview, Prague/
Time, 4-18:42.

1

Extending democracy in no way means making room for the legalization of political opposition which, as all experience so far has shown, cannot but be anti-socialist.

Newsweek, 4-25:38.

Wojciech Jaruzelski
President of Poland; Chairman,
Communist Party of Poland

2

Democratic transformations [in Poland] have reached very deep and they will go deeper. Relations with the Catholic Church in Poland have undergone normalization, and the Church is a very meaningful power in this country. This process of democratization of public life is no short-term flash in the pan. It's something that's here to stay. We are not masochists, and we are not a bunch of fools. We have become quite convinced that democratization in an over-simplified manner inevitably leads to catastrophe. The road that we have selected is the correct one.

Interview, Warsaw/
USA Today, 8-1:(A)13.

3

Historically, the Poles have understood that they should be close to the Soviet Union due to the guarantees that such an alliance gives us. The situation today is that this understanding remains the same. But now, the Polish heart is beginning to beat in both East and West directions and is large enough to accommodate both. The thing is that we should be real friends [with the West]—not in words, but in deeds and reality.

Interview, Warsaw/
USA Today, 8-1:(A)13.

John Paul II
Pope

4

[On Poland, his native country]: The problem of sovereignty, that is, independence, of our country [must] be rooted most profoundly in another problem, the problem of the sovereignty of society and of the people of Poland today. One can speak of sovereignty, of independence of a nation, only when, in the context of this nation, there is a people sovereign and independent who can, by rule and fact, decide their common life.

Homily, May 3/
The New York Times, 5-4:10.

Ilya Kabakov
Soviet artist

5

We [in the arts in the Soviet Union] find ourselves living in a post-utopian world. We're no longer involved in describing the fearful, megalomaniac visions of Russia in the 1920s, but we send in reports on the conditions in which we live today, which are just as sad, hopeless and horrible, though perhaps a little more friendly.

Interview/Newsweek, 5-23:67.

Janos Kadar
First Secretary, Communist
Party of Hungary

6

No qualitative changes have taken place in our economy, restructuring is sluggish and the inter-

(JANOS KADAR)

nal and external financial balance has deteriorated. As a consequence, conditions are lacking for a perceptible rise in the living standard, and even for safeguarding it in all aspects.

At Hungarian Communist Party
Congress, Budapest, May 20/
The New York Times, 5-21:4.

Tom King
British Secretary of State for
Northern Ireland

1

[On his position in strife-torn Northern Ireland]: When you first take on the job, I think there are moments when you would be mad if you didn't have concern in certain situations... People are dying for nothing. That is awful. You can look at other causes where you understand people dying. All they're doing now is dying for the mythology of the IRA, the mythology of old Irish causes. But the reality of the scene has long passed them [the IRA] by.

Interview, London/
The New York Times, 4-4:7.

Neil Kinnock
Leader, Labor Party
of Britain

2

Those [in the Labor Party] who are afraid of developing the alternatives that will gain the support of the British people, those who say they don't want victory at such a price, had better ask themselves this: If they won't pay any price for winning, what price are they prepared to pay for losing?

At Labor Party convention,
Blackpool, England, Oct. 4/
The Washington Post, 10-7:(A)28.

Henry A. Kissinger
Former Secretary of State of
the United States

3

[Expressing reservations about the U.S.-Soviet INF treaty in Europe, but saying the U.S. should

ratify it]: Failure to ratify the treaty, or insistence on amendments requiring re-negotiation, would not cure its defects. It would, on the contrary, vastly magnify all difficulties. [Senate rejection at this point would] generate a crisis in the Atlantic Alliance which would in the end almost certainly lead to the unilateral withdrawal of U.S. missiles from Europe and undermine the cohesion of the Alliance ... The Soviet strategy of dividing the Atlantic Alliance would be greatly enhanced.

Before Senate Foreign Relations
Committee, Washington, Feb. 23/
The Washington Post, 2-24:(A)6.

4

[On the U.S.-Soviet INF arms-control treaty for Europe]: I agree with the flexible-response doctrine, but I think that the INF agreement has made flexible response more difficult, because it means that you cannot retaliate *from* Europe against an attack *on* Europe to the same degree that you could before. It leaves only tactical weapons in Germany and strategic weapons in the United States. It leaves a small number of airplanes that can perform a strategic mission but that could shorten the conventional period because, in order to avoid using up its airplanes in the conventional phase, NATO would have to go earlier to the nuclear phase.

Interview/
Los Angeles Times, 3-13:(V)2.

Helmut Kohl
Chancellor of West Germany

5

[On the U.S.-Soviet INF arms-control treaty for Europe]: [The treaty] has for the first time in history opened the way toward genuine disarmament. The INF agreement is in the interest of the United States of America and in the interest of the Atlantic Alliance, and not least in the interest of our own country.

To reporters,
Washington, Feb. 19/
The Washington Post, 2-20:(A)16.

(HELMUT KOHL)

1

[After World War II,] the Americans came to our aid. The Marshall Plan was initiated. The money connected with the Marshall Plan was not that important, although it was a large sum. What was important was that someone extended a hand to us and said "come on." For many, that was a very personal experience. You know that I am the one in Europe who was attacked the most from within the Soviet Union for his pro-American position. But why do I do this? Because it's correct. When we were starving, the Americans helped us . . . Our American friends should know that they have friends here [in West Germany]. They should not mistake demonstrations against the U.S. for the opinion of the Germans in general. The Germans don't say: "Americans go home."

Interview, Bonn/
USA Today, 8-5:(A)15.

2

[On the Nazi era in Germany]: We Germans will neither forget, nor dismiss from our minds, nor play down the darkest chapter in our history. The unspeakable suffering inflicted in the name of the Germans and by German hands in those years, primarily on the Jews, is ever-present in our memory. We know that the Holocaust is without parallel in the history of mankind, its cold-blooded, inhuman planning and its deadly effectiveness.

The Washington Post, 11-8:(A)18.

Stanislav Kondrashov
Journalist, "Izvestia"
(Soviet Union)

3

We have a new feature in our newspaper. It consists of letters from readers who begin by saying that they are certain we wouldn't dare publish their views. Most of these letters complain about everyday life. The writers say that our political elections are a sham. Or they complain about the drabness of life, or about the shabby quality of the merchandise in the shops,

or the cramped conditions of their housing, or about the way the bureaucrats abound everywhere and complicate and frustrate their lives. And you know what? They are right.

At Dartmouth Conference, U.S.A./
The Christian Science Monitor,
6-6:14.

Brian Lenihan
Deputy Prime Minister
of Ireland

4

[On the prospects for reunification of Ireland with Northern Ireland]: I believe reunification is possible, but I have no timetable. Our policy is to move toward a reunification of minds, which will lead to political reunification.

Interview/USA Today, 8-19:(A)13.

Jean-Marie Le Pen
National Front Party
candidate for President
of France

5

[Referring to French President Francois Mitterrand, whom he calls "Tonton"]: Seated on the French throne, Tonton is nonetheless always sitting on his derriere. He is the Tonton of decline, he is the Tonton of three million unemployed, six million new poor, six million immigrants, of the collapse of our demography, the Tonton of decadence!

Campaigning for the Presidency/
The New York Times, 3-29:6.

Roy Medvedev
Soviet historian

6

Westerners who understand democracy and its institutions come here and they somehow think the Soviet Union can just adopt democracy, assume a different tradition. But most people here are so used to life as it has been that their main concern is that things don't get worse than they already are.

The Washington Post, 4-29:(A)23.

(ROY MEDVEDEV)

1

The Stalinist mood [in the Soviet Union] is still strong. Conservative moods dominate among the greater part of the [Communist] Party leadership. But as the Russian saying goes, "A word is not a sparrow. Once it flies, you can't catch it."

The New York Times, 5-20:4.

2

The Stalinist mentality still exists [in the Soviet Union]. You can see it in the blind obedience of the people, the absence of civic freedoms, the priority given to the state over the individual ... The authorities have [lately] opened the door. Now journalists, publicists, ordinary citizens are trying to push through the door and make the opening as wide as possible. Of course, it is always possible that the authorities can close the door that they have opened. We are still at a transitional stage.

The Washington Post, 12-27:(A)12.

Francois Mitterrand
President of France

3

[Criticizing the Berlin Wall]: That which we expect in all European countries is constant progress concerning free movement, multiplication of contacts, free debate of ideas. What a paradox it would be if, at a time when ... exchanges of material goods and merchandise grow, anachronistic barriers to circulation of people and ideas were not also dismantled.

At banquet for visiting East
German leader Erich Honecker,
Paris, Jan. 7/
The Washington Post, 1-9:(A)16.

4

[On France and West Germany setting up a joint defense council]: What two other nations, torn by three wars, have done more, have done better, than France and West Germany in forging a community of joint destiny? ... There is no French-German axis [in setting up the council].

The aim of French-German cooperation is to advance Europe.

At signing of the defense-council
agreement, Paris, Jan. 22/
Los Angeles Times, 1-23:(I)12.

5

[On whether he believes the Soviet Union is no longer a military threat to Western Europe because of Soviet leader Mikhail Gorbachev's policies of reform]: I'm not inside Mr. Gorbachev's head. My job, like that of other Western leaders, is to create the conditions for peace and security, not to deliver psychological observations on the state of mind or hidden thoughts of the Soviets. That said, I don't believe they are warmongers. Let's not ignore the fact that at the head of the Soviet Union we now have a worldly man who considers disarmament a fundamental element for his foreign policy. Disarmament is, after all, necessary to improve the buying power of the Soviets. I think it would be a miscalculation to refuse economic help to the Soviet Union on the pretext that the Soviet economic situation would improve. One gains nothing by the worst.

Interview/
U.S. News & World Report, 3-7:43.

6

The problem facing the U.S. in regard to Europe is a major political problem, but simple. Either Americans consider that Europe is still an indispensable element of their own security, that Europe represents a factor necessary to the equilibrium of the world and its historical values, or they no longer think so. Either the U.S. considers that it has a global role or it no longer wants that role. The choice is America's. I continue to believe in their solidarity.

Interview/
U.S. News & World Report, 3-7:44.

7

[On his decision to run for re-election as President]: There is a risk that France could fall back into the quarrels and the divisions that have so

(FRANCOIS MITTERRAND)

often undermined it. I want France to be united. It will not, if it is taken over by intolerant views, by parties that want everything, by clans, by gangs.

Broadcast interview,
Paris, March 22/
The New York Times, 3-23:3.

1

[On his being re-elected for a second term]: I will continue to exercise a mission whose grandeur and burden I have been able to experience for seven years but which, renewed, obliges me even more to do what I can to rally all the French who would assent to it. Liberty, equality and respect for others, the refusal of exclusions, which one can also call fraternity, have not ceased to keep alive the hope of men.

To his supporters,
Chateau-Chinen, France, May 8/
The New York Times, 5-9:1.

2

Through increasingly close cooperation in the Atlantic Alliance, certain European countries have undertaken to build the core of a common European defense system. Other countries find that the current situation [of strong U.S. involvement] suits them better, even if all of them recognize that Europe, once it has found the way toward political union, must ensure its own defense. In maintaining its armed forces in Europe, the U.S. is keeping its commitment to NATO and protecting its global interests. The progress of European cooperation in defense will not erase the reasons for the U.S. presence in Europe.

Interview/Time, 5-16:50.

3

No nation in Europe, however ancient and glorious, can control in isolation its development. The surest way of preserving our national heritages, as well as our ways of thinking and doing things, is to pool our resources, our currencies, our knowledge and our industries, much as we have done for our agriculture.

Interview/Time, 5-16:50.

Allen Moore
Under Secretary of
Commerce of the
United States

4

[On Europe's plans for an internal free market by 1992]: If the EC program falls prey to protectionist forces, the United States' largest foreign market will be at risk . . . We need to make sure that Europe does not use the single internal market as a powerful "private preserve" that will give Europeans advantages in competing for our markets. We have made this position clear to the European Community, and we will continue to do so.

The Washington Post, 10-6:(F)4.

Phyllis Oakley
Spokeswoman for the
Department of State
of the United States

5

Free labor unions can help the Polish economic reform effort, not hinder it. Indeed, it is hard to see how economic reform can succeed without the participation of free trade unions. Economic reform is a truly national undertaking. It must include all the people.

Washington, Aug. 23/
Los Angeles Times, 8-24:(I)11.

Andreas Papandreou
Prime Minister of Greece

6

It is evident that progress in Greek-Turkish relations is directly affected by the solution of the Cyprus problem, and the solution of that problem is directly linked to the withdrawal of Turkish troops from the island.

At dinner for visiting Turkish
Prime Minister Turgut Ozal,
Athens, June 13/
Los Angeles Times, 6-14:(I)10.

Cecil Parkinson
Secretary of Energy of the
United Kingdom

1

[The] coal [industry in Britain] will be privatized. By the next Parliament [in 1991 or 1992], we shall be ready for this, the ultimate privatization . . . Just think: Miners will be shareholders with a stake in their own industry. From the days when the miners' leaders thought they owned the government—to the day when every miner owns part of his own mine.

At British Conservative Party
convention, Brighton, England,
Oct. 12/Los Angeles Times,
10-13:(I)5.

Imre Pozsgay
Member, Politburo,
Communist Party of Hungary

2

The [Hungarian Communist] Party's power must be controlled. We must open up for dialogue and give an outlet for citizen's emotions . . . We should have taken these steps 20 years ago, but unfortunately we couldn't because there was no [Soviet leader Mikhail] Gorbachev. For the first time, Hungary can go ahead and reform, because the most important socialist states are reforming . . . The conservatives say that we must not move too fast in order to maintain stability. I say our greatest enemy is the unchanged situation.

Interview/
The Christian Science Monitor,
5-24:11.

Charles H. Price II
United States Ambassador to
the United Kingdom

3

[British Prime Minister Margaret] Thatcher is an Atlanticist, but she is also a very practical person. As a consequence, she can see the collective advantage associated with the stronger integration [of Western Europe] and freer, more unrestricted markets in the European Community which can compete with the U.S.

The Christian Science Monitor,
11-15:7.

Dan Quayle
United States Senator,
R-Indiana; 1988 Republican
U.S. Vice-Presidential nominee

4

[On Soviet leader Mikhail Gorbachev]: As far as Gorbachev is concerned, he's new . . . he has a different approach to things, and his mannerisms and style are unfortunately pleasing to the West . . . [I say] unfortunately, because I don't think from an ideological point of view he's any different from [the late Soviet leader Leonid] Brezhnev, or anybody else. In fact . . . he and his wife both are very rigid ideologues and have very deep convictions. I mean, *perestroika* [Gorbachev's policy of reform in the Soviet Union] is nothing more than refined Stalinism: kick their people out and bring your people in. That's his reorganizing. It's not changing the system.

Interview, Sept. 4/
The Washington Post, 9-6:(A)16.

Mieczyslaw Rakowski
Member, Politburo,
Communist Party of Poland

5

Now we must have a different economic approach [in Poland]. We must accept differing political orientations within the system and find new structures for them. We must accept the role of the church. We know now that the [Communist] Party is not alone and will not be alone in the future. If the market leads the economy, the Party cannot dictate how it should work. We have to take this problem of the role of the Party seriously, even if we have no answer . . . Maybe my generation is not ready; maybe we are prisoners of the past. This is a task for the next generation. The Party is not prepared for such change. In the past it used simple instruments, all connected with dictatorship.

Interview, Warsaw/
The New York Times, 1-5:25.

Mieczyslaw Rakowski
Prime Minister of Poland

6

To be consistent in rebuilding our economy means, in effect, that enterprises will go under,

(MIECZYSLAW RAKOWSKI)

that thousands of people will face the necessity of changing their workplace or even of a temporary job hunt. Will we get public approval for that, for men seeking jobs and not jobs seeking men?

Before Polish Parliament,
Warsaw, Oct. 13/
The Washington Post, 10-14:(A)28.

Ronald Reagan
President of the United States

1

While we note recent Soviet policy statements regarding "reconstruction" and economic reform, the Soviet economic system remains at this point fundamentally incompatible with participation in free-world institutions. Policy statements must be translated into positive actions before such participation can be considered.

Report to Congress on national
security, Jan. 20*/
Los Angeles Times, 1-21:(I)10.

2

[On Soviet leader Mikhail Gorbachev's program of reform in the Soviet Union]: We cannot afford to forget that we are dealing with a political system, a political culture and a political history going back many decades, even centuries. Swings between *glasnost* [openness] and the Gulag are not new or even peculiar to the Soviet regime. In history, they recurred again and again as the throne passed from czar to czar and even within the reign of a single czar. We cannot afford to mortgage our security to the assessed motives of particular individuals or to the novel approaches of a new leadership, even if we wish them well.

Satellite broadcast address to
Europe, Washington, Feb. 23/
The Washington Post, 2-24:(A)4.

3

[Addressing Europeans]: If you are not at peace, we [the U.S.] cannot be at peace. An attack on you is an attack on us . . . Simply put: An attack on Munich is the same as an attack on Chicago . . . Our goal is not a nuclear-free, or a tank-free, or an army-free Europe. A war-free Europe is what we have today. A war-free Europe is what we want to preserve.

Satellite broadcast address to
Europe, Washington, Feb. 23/
The Washington Post, 2-24:(A)4.

4

NATO has kept the peace in Europe, and kept American security, for 40 years. A free and democratic Europe is essential to a free and democratic America.

Before American Legion,
Washington, Feb. 29/
USA Today, 3-1:(A)4.

5

The purpose of this [NATO] summit is not self-congratulations. Our responsibility is to the future. Our first priority is to maintain a strong and healthy partnership between North America and Europe, for this is the foundation on which the cause of freedom so crucially depends.

Speech before leaving for Brussels,
Washington, March 1/
The New York Times,
3-2:8.

6

[Praising the Soviets for alleged human-rights improvements in that country]: Over the past three years, some 300 political and religious prisoners have been released from labor camps. More recently, the incarceration of dissidents in mental hospitals and prisons has slowed and, in some cases, stopped completely. And while the press remains tightly controlled by the [Communist] Party and state, we've seen the publication of stories on topics that used to be forbidden—topics like crime, drug addiction, corruption, even police brutality . . . We applaud the changes that have taken place and encourage the Soviets to go farther. We recognize that changes

(RONALD REAGAN)

occur slowly, but that is better than no change at all.

Before National Strategy Forum,
Chicago, May 4/
Los Angeles Times, 5-5:(I)14.

1

[Criticizing the Soviet Union for not adhering to various aspects of the Helsinki human-rights accords]: Thirteen years after the Final Act [of the accords] was signed, it's difficult to understand why cases of divided families and blocked marriages should remain on the East-West agenda, or why Soviet citizens who wish to exercise their right to emigrate should be subject to artificial quotas and arbitrary rulings. And what are we to think of the continued suppression of those who wish to practice their religious beliefs? Over 300 men and women whom the world sees as political prisoners have been released. There remains no reason why the Soviet Union cannot release all people still in jail for expression of political or religious belief, or for organizing to monitor the Helsinki Act. The Soviets talk about a common European home, and define it largely in terms of geography. But what is it that cements the structure of clear purpose, that all our nations pledge themselves to build by their signature of the Final Act? What is it but the belief in the inalienable rights and dignity of every single human being? What is it but a commitment to true pluralist democracy? What is it but a dedication to the universally understood democratic concept of liberty that evolved from the genius of European civilization? This body of values, this is what marks, or should mark, the common European home.

Speech,
Helsinki, Finland, May 27/
The Washington Post, 5-28:(A)20.

2

[Addressing Soviet dissidents during his visit to Moscow]: I came here to give you strength, but it is you who have strengthened me. While we

press for human lives through diplomatic channels, you press with your very lives, day in and day out, year after year, risking your homes, your jobs and your all.

Moscow, May 30/
Los Angeles Times, 5-31:(I)1.

Charles E. Redman
Spokesman for the
Department of State
of the United States

3

[On Spain's insistence that the U.S. remove 72 of its fighter planes from Spain within three years]: It is a fact that we disagree with the Spaniards on the withdrawal of the 401st Tactical Fighter Wing. But the Spaniards insisted on the withdrawal, and we are complying with their sovereign decision. [The move] points toward a new defense agreement that will have important positive elements for the United States and Spain, and for allied defense and security . . . On balance, it could be said that the agreement in principle is good for all concerned with that one substantial exception [the removal of the planes].

Washington, Jan. 15/
Los Angeles Times, 1-16:(I)1.

4

The current [labor] strikes in Poland demonstrate more clearly than ever that successful economic reform and recovery require genuine dialogue between the government and society. In our view, such dialogue must allow for the expression of working people's concerns and rights.

May 4/
The Washington Post, 5-5:(A)33.

Rozanne L. Ridgway
Assistant Secretary for
European and Canadian
Affairs, Department of State
of the United States

5

The Warsaw Pact countries have a substantial superiority in conventional forces on the

(ROZANNE L. RIDGWAY)

ground in Europe, comprised largely of massive forward deployment of Soviet armed forces organized and equipped for rapid, large-scale offensive operations . . . While we have heard a great deal of language about the change in doctrine as it is being taught in Soviet military academies, we have seen nothing on the ground, we see nothing in the production of these kinds of equipment, that would indicate a change in the Soviet posture.

Briefing, Nov. 25/
The Washington Post,
11-26:(A)17.

Michel Rocard
Prime Minister of France

1

[French President] Francois Mitterrand's re-election forcefully signaled that a more efficient and more just France now depends on political reconciliation. My priorities are not going to be those of one half of France against the other half.

Before French National Assembly,
Paris/The Christian Science Monitor,
7-15:10.

Bernard W. Rogers
General, United States Army (ret.);
Former Supreme Allied
Commander/Europe

2

[Criticizing the proposed U.S.-Soviet INF Treaty]: I'm concerned because this treaty, I believe, puts Western Europe on the slippery slope of denuclearization, which is something the Soviets want, because it would make Europe safe for conventional war . . . It is not in the best interests of our Western European allies, short term or long term, and in the long term will not be in the best interest of the United States.

Before National Press Club,
Washington, Jan. 29/
Los Angeles Times, 1-30:(I)8.

Dusan Rovensky
Spokesman for foreign affairs
of Czechoslovakia

3

[On whether his country will adopt *perestroika*, the reform being carried out in the Soviet Union]: We see in this some valuable concepts—an increase in democracy, an increase in efficiency and reorganization of management. We are doing these things in special conditions. We consider these concepts important, and we want to put them into effect under conditions we have here. I say that because some people say we in Czechoslovakia refuse *perestroika*, but that is not true. Czechoslovakia is sympathetic to *perestroika*, but we must respect the conditions we live in.

Interview/
Los Angeles Times, 1-23:(I)35.

Edward L. Rowny
Special Adviser to President
of the United States Ronald Reagan
for Arms Control

4

It's in our [U.S.] interests to stay [militarily] in Europe, and while we believe that Europeans should do more and there should be a burden sharing, it would be irresponsible for us to say, "Well, if you don't, we'll pull out." That doesn't do them any good, and it doesn't do us any good to pull that sort of bravado or bluff tactics.

Interview/USA Today, 5-25:(A)11.

Andrei D. Sakharov
Dissident Soviet physicist

5

Up until now, the [human-rights] situation [in the Soviet Union] was very difficult, but it was a clear one. It was clear that there were problems with human rights, and it was clear that there were problems with peace [such as the Soviet intervention in Afghanistan]. That put a very heavy pressure for [human-rights activists]. Now I would say that the situation has become more

(ANDREI D. SAKHAROV)

complex. It has become more complex because it has become better.

At dinner for visiting human-rights
activists, Moscow, January/
The Washington Post, 2-8:(A)14.

1

[On Soviet leader Mikhail Gorbachev's policy of *perestroika,* reform in the Soviet Union]: An expression of trust in *perestroika* at this time would encourage it and also improve the human-rights situation. We should even give an advance measure of confidence in [its observance of] human rights. I believe that, as time goes on, there will be even further improvements ... Mikhail Gorbachev is an outstanding statesman, and one of the chief architects of *perestroika.* From the bottom of my heart, I wish success for the cause with which his name is associated.

News conference, Moscow, June 3/
Los Angeles Times, 6-4:(I)1,16.

2

[On Soviet leader Mikhail Gorbachev's program of reform in the Soviet Union]: The fact that I find myself in this hall today reflects a change in this country, not a change in me ... Considerable changes have taken place. The changes are not exhaustive and they do not ensure full implementation of human rights. But it is necessary to view the situation overall. [Gorbachev and his policies of reform] are deserving of trust, and to a certain extent we should give an advance measure of confidence in the human-rights area.

News conference, Moscow, June 3/
The Washington Post, 6-4:(A)1,20.

3

[Criticizing Soviet leader Mikhail Gorbachev's assuming the Presidency of the country, as well as being Communist Party chief]: A head of state with such power in a country that does not have a multi-party system is just insanity. This is practically boundless power. Today it is Gorbachev,

but tomorrow it could be somebody else. There are no guarantees that some Stalinist will not succeed him. Once more, everything boils down to one person, and this is extremely dangerous for *perestroika* [reform] as a whole and for Gorbachev personally. This is an extremely important question, on which the fate of our country depends.

At conference of Soviet and
American scholars, Moscow, Nov. 1/
The Washington Post, 11-2:(A)1.

4

The great danger to the world as a whole would be the failure of *perestroika* [reform in the Soviet Union]. [It] would mean the simultaneous failure of internal reform that would necessitate external expansion of the military-industrial complex.

News conference, Boston, Nov. 7/
The Christian Science Monitor,
11-8:3.

Richard Schifter
Assistant Secretary for
Human Rights, Department
of State of the United States

5

[Saying the number of political prisoners in the Soviet Union has declined recently]: Objectively speaking, freedom is still severely limited, but at least people are not being punished quite the way they used to be ... There's no question that the kinds of offenses for which, as recently as a few years ago, you would have been sent to Siberia for really long stretches, now are punished usually by being roughed up by the police, detained for a few hours, and being sent home. This is different ... [but] there is no change in terms of the ultimate result.

Washington, May 13/
Los Angeles Times, 5-14:(I)5.

James R. Schlesinger
Former Secretary of Defense
of the United States

6

[On the INF treaty reducing U.S. and Soviet nuclear arms in Europe]: It is a form of parochial-

WHAT THEY SAID IN 1988

ism in Europe to suggest that the Soviets have basically been deterred by a relative handful of warheads in Europe, none of which were deployed before 1983. It is the over-all strength of America's strategic forces that has been the principal element in Europe's nuclear deterrent in the past and will remain so in the future. If the Soviet Union is not deterred by the 12,000 warheads in America's strategic forces that can reach Soviet soil, then the Soviet Union will not be deterred by the 12,400 warheads that could reach Soviet soil when we throw in a handful of weapons presently based in Europe that will be withdrawn under this treaty.

At Senate INF treaty hearings,
Washington/
The Washington Post, 2-5:(A)22.

Natan Sharansky
Exiled Former
Soviet dissident

1

[On *glasnost,* the current policy of openness in the Soviet Union]: For all its *glasnost,* the Soviet Union remains a closed society, a totalitarian regime trying to destroy an individual's rights to his own views on politics, religion, ethics, nationalism.

Interview,
Jerusalem/
U.S. News & World Report,
5-23:31.

Eduard A. Shevardnadze
Foreign Minister of the
Soviet Union

2

Those who take care of the security of the state must realize that a true threat to our country will arise when we find ourselves economically insolvent and will not be able to get the feel of world-wide economic progress and join the mainstream of scientific and technological progress.

Speech/
The Washington Post, 12-29:(A)16.

Nikolai Shmelyev
Soviet economist

3

We have to introduce into all spheres of [Soviet] social life the understanding that all that is economically ineffective is immoral, and all that is effective is moral.

Interview/
The Washington Post, 2-8:(A)14.

Hedrick Smith
Pulitzer Prize-winning reporter,
"The New York Times"

4

[The Soviet] system just became totally rigid. There was no sufficient avenue for people with different ideas, good ideas—and I'm not talking about anti-Communists—I mean within their own framework, making the economy work better, modernizing their technology, dealing with some of their nationality problems; they were congealed. For all the stalemates we have had and all the frustrations that divide our government [in the U.S.], we simply don't have problems on a comparable level. On the other hand, when the Soviets set their minds to something like a military buildup—and they have decided on that in 1962 and gotten their leadership behind it—by God, they have pursued that with a continuity over 10 or 15 years that overcomes a lot of this business of being congealed. They can decide to build a railroad across Siberia if they think that's what they need and build enormous dams, and they don't go through the repeated votes on appropriations that we go through ad infinitum and ad nauseum. Basically, the real problem is, they don't innovate.

Interview/
Los Angeles Times, 4-4:(V)6.

Andrzej Stelmachowski
President, Catholic
Intellectual Club, Warsaw, Poland

5

[On whether negotiations could lead to the relegalization of Solidarity, the now-banned militant Polish trade union]: It is possible. The government wants guarantees that a renewed Solidarity will be constructive and not ruin the

(ANDRZEJ STELMACHOWSKI)

present system. The government remembers Solidarity from 1980 and 1981 and fears that a renewed Solidarity will destroy it. But it realizes that it cannot guard a monopoly on power. The opposition also remembers the past. In 1980, it was without experience and acted according to its emotions. It wanted everything. It was impatient. Now it has learned to choose its goals. It is like a poker game. At first, you cannot be sure what kind of solution can be reached. But the ideas are clear... A new trade union must concentrate on trade-union matters, and let political goals be realized within political clubs.

Interview, Warsaw/
The Christian Science Monitor,
9-13:9.

Margaret Thatcher
Prime Minister of the
United Kingdom
1

[On her becoming Britain's longest-serving 20th-century Prime Minister]: When I first walked through that door [of the Prime Minister's residence in 1979], we were known as suffering from the "British disease." Now we're known for the British cure and people come to us, a newly confident country, to see how we've done it.

London, Jan. 3/
Los Angeles Times, 1-4:(I)6.

2

The defense of Western Europe is, first of all, NATO, and for this defense to remain effective, it is vital that American forces remain in Europe. This does not exclude numerous bilateral relations [among NATO countries], but, and I insist on this point, within NATO.

Interview/
The Washington Post, 1-30:(A)16.

3

The nicer the Russians get, the more dangerous they are.

USA Today, 3-2:(A)10.

4

[Saying some men resent a woman Prime Minister]: Yes, it is rather patronizing. The best compliment they [men] can give a woman is that she thinks like a man. I say she does not; she thinks like a woman. The House [of Commons] is still very much male-dominated, and there is something about them, a sort of "little woman" thing. It would be all right... if I had followed Florence Nightingale. A Prime Minister has a task of leadership. If the trumpet gives an uncertain sound, who shall prepare himself to the battle? All right, so I give a certain sound.

Interview/
Los Angeles Times, 5-9:(I)2.

5

I think some people are being very superficial when they say, [since] there is a United States of America, why don't we have a United States of Europe? It is not possible to have a United States of Europe... I was really very much with [the late French President Charles] de Gaulle that this is a Europe of separate countries working together.

Broadcast interview/
The Christian Science Monitor,
7-29:8.

6

[On the apparent movement toward more freedom in Communist countries]: They've realized that the might of the Soviet Union as a superpower is dependent only on its military might. Not upon the standard of living, or social services, or housing or technology. I was the first to meet with [Soviet leader Mikhail] Gorbachev and say, "He's a man I could do business with." I was the first to publicly encourage reforms [in the Soviet Union]. We are fortunate there is a person [like Gorbachev] with such vision and courage there.

Interview, London/
USA Today, 9-2:(A)15.

7

[Addressing Polish leader Wojciech Jaruzelski]: You will only achieve higher growth [for

353

(MARGARET THATCHER)

Poland], only release enterprise, only spur people to greater effort, only obtain their full-hearted commitment to reform, when people have the dignity and enjoyment of personal and political liberty, when they have the freedom of expression, freedom of association and the right to form free and independent trade unions.

At banquet in her honor,
Warsaw, Nov. 3/
Los Angeles Times, 11-4:(I)7.

1

[On U.S. Vice President George Bush's victory in the recent Presidential election]: The main advantage [of the Bush victory] is [that] the same positive policies of the last eight years, which are very similar to our own, will continue into the future. I think that gives Europe enormous confidence in continuity.

To reporters,
London, Nov. 9/
The Christian Science Monitor,
11-10:9.

Carlisle A. H. Trost
Admiral and Chief of
Operations, United States Navy

2

I think there has been too narrow a focus in our [U.S.] overseas [military] policy with the emphasis on Europe. Having said that, how can you criticize a NATO alliance that's deterred war going on 45 years?

The Christian Science Monitor,
12-27:28.

Jerzy Urban
Spokesman for the
government of Poland

3

[Criticizing the current Gdansk shipyard-workers' strike, which involves the banned Solidarity trade union]: The government will not talk to illegal structures, Solidarity. We might

talk to individuals who were in Solidarity, but not to Solidarity as a union. The strikes which are now going on, and which they are still trying to organize, do not pose a threat to the socialist government; it has firm domestic and external support. But they threaten economic reform.

News conference, Warsaw, May 3/
The New York Times, 5-4:10.

4

[On recent changes in the Polish economic system favoring more private enterprise]: We are no longer afraid of radical reforms. The Poland you will see several years from now will have a different economy than it has had until now.

Warsaw, Dec. 23/
The Washington Post, 12-24:(A)1.

George Vassiliou
President of Cyprus

5

The Cyprus state we want to build must be free, united and demilitarized, without settlers or refugees, with a functional democratic federal system. A smoothly functional system of government. A viable solution will be in the interests of Turkish Cypriots also, because only such a system can safeguard the human and democratic rights of all the citizens of Cyprus, so that Greek and Turkish Cypriots may develop sincere cooperation which will consolidate our peaceful coexistence.

The New York Times, 8-1:6.

Mikhail P. Vyshinsky
Deputy Minister of Justice of
the Soviet Union

6

[On reform in the Soviet Union]: What we are aiming for is the creation of a society where democracy, law and human freedom can flourish. Up until now, we have needed relatively few laws because [Communist] Party policies and Party decisions covered almost everything. As we strive to become a nation of laws, however, we find we have nowhere near enough laws to sup-

(MIKHAIL P. VYSHINSKY)

port the reforms we have undertaken. So we are making an all-out effort to write and enact new legislation almost across the board, and it will be pushed through as a top government priority.

News conference,
Moscow, June 26/
Los Angeles Times, 6-27:(I)6.

Kurt Waldheim
President of Austria

1

One must say openly time and again that in 1938 the criminal policy of the National Socialist [Nazi] regime led us [Austrians] into an abyss, a policy many discerned when it was already too late . . . Tens of thousands of our fellow citizens, whose families had helped shape Austria's politics, culture and economy for generations, became in those tragic years victims of racial hatred. Let us beware of such a frame of mind; let us beware of hostility to foreigners and intolerance. Let us give the members of our minorities the certainty that they can feel as equal fellow citizens and have a sheltered home in Austria.

New Year's address to the nation,
Vienna, Jan. 1/
The Washington Post, 1-2:(A)27.

2

[Saying that he knew of atrocities carried out by his German army group during World War II but kept silent about them]: Practically every soldier in the Balkans knew that reprisal actions were carried out [by the Nazis]. The fact that, as a staff officer, I was, here and there, better informed could be true, but I did not volunteer for the job. I pay the deepest respect to all those who offered resistance, but I ask for understanding for the hundreds of thousands who did not, but were still not personally guilty. We certainly didn't do any more than try to survive the war. Yes, I admit I wanted to survive.

Interview/
Los Angeles Times, 2-13:(I)1.

3

[On persistent criticism that he was involved in Nazi atrocities during World War II]: I want to take a stand in all clarity. You, my dear Austrians, have elected me Federal President with a convincing majority in a secret and direct election for six years. Thus it is no longer a matter of the man Kurt Waldheim. In view of the slanders, I have often asked myself in the last two years whether I should carry on. It is a fundamental principle of our democracy that an election result cannot be subsequently corrected. A head of state must not retreat in the face of slanders, hateful demonstrations and wholesale condemnations.

Broadcast address to the nation,
Vienna, Feb. 15/
Los Angeles Times, 2-16:(I)5.

Lech Walesa
Former chairman,
now-banned Solidarity
(independent Polish trade
union); Winner, 1983 Nobel
Peace Prize

4

[On the current shipyard workers' strike in Gdansk]: The shipyard [workers are] fighting to put the country on the road to reform. If we don't achieve a real reform this time, then we will have a bloody revolution. [The Polish government] made us the beggars of Europe, the beggars of the world. How ashamed I am that they are begging the world for credit while only throwing us a few pennies.

To striking workers,
Gdansk, Poland, May 3/
Los Angeles Times, 5-4:(I)1.

5

[On whether Poland should be a capitalist or a socialist society]: Labels are not important. It doesn't matter who bakes the bread—whether it be a capitalist or socialist loaf—only that plenty of good bread is produced at prices the worker can afford.

Interview/
The Christian Science Monitor, 3-10:9.

355

(LECH WALESA)

1

[On the current labor strikes in Poland]: When things are so hard in Poland, strikes are bad. But how [else] do you talk with people who are bad managers, who suppress initiative and are destroying the country? . . . If the Communists don't come to their senses, then I am determined to put the whole country on its feet. If I have to, I'll go out there and scream my head off.

Interview/Newsweek, 5-9:27.

2

[On whether Communist domination of Poland will end]: We must look at this with Polish eyes. We say that the world has tested pluralism and it works. But to implement pluralism does not necessarily mean transplanting what exists in the West. It is like bananas and oranges. They will not grow in our climate, however much we might like to have them.

Interview, Gdansk, Poland/
Time, 10-3:37.

Robert D. Waller
British Conservative Party
political analyst

3

[On British Prime Minister Margaret Thatcher]: Our democracy is not the best for resisting authoritarian politicians. We seem rather to like these strong popular leaders. Among the people as a whole, as long as she can deliver bread and circuses, as long as the prosperity is there, she can go on and it will be hard to stop her.

Interview, London, Jan. 4/
The New York Times, 1-5:7.

John C. Whitehead
Deputy Secretary of State of
the United States

4

The new atmosphere of reform and restructuring [in the Soviet Union initiated by Soviet leader Mikhail Gorbachev] has come to Eastern Europe as well as the Soviet Union . . . The

leaders of the East European countries regard the new attitudes in the Soviet Union as giving them the freedom to change their societies in their own way.

Interview/
The Washington Post, 5-11:(A)31.

Manfred Woerner
Secretary General, North
Atlantic Treaty Organization

5

It is our task, and it can be accomplished, to explain to our populations that the success of our policies and the change in the Soviet Union and Eastern Europe [toward better relations with the West are] largely due to the political cohesion and the initiatives of the [NATO] alliance. To maintain a credible defense posture is one of the conditions to make further success possible.

News conference, Brussels, Dec. 9/
Los Angeles Times, 12-10:(I)5.

Aleksandr N. Yakovlev
Member, Politburo,
Communist Party of the
Soviet Union; Adviser
to Soviet leader
Mikhail Gorbachev

6

[On Soviet leader Mikhail Gorbachev's reform program in the Soviet Union]: There are certain periods in history when the course of events depends very much on a particular personality. You have to be realistic about this. But you can look at it another way. Do you think the changes in the Soviet Union wouldn't happen if someone else were in this post? I think it would happen, but later. I think that Gorbachev's personality just speeded up events, thanks to his personal qualities, his political acumen, his education and his surprising ability to understand the rhythm and demands of the time. The times have persistently demanded changes, knocked at the door, and he, earlier than others, understood that the door should be open.

Interview, Moscow, Oct. 26/
The New York Times, 10-28:(A)6.

(ALEKSANDR N. YAKOVLEV)

1

[On the reforms in the Soviet Union instituted by Soviet leader Mikhail Gorbachev]: A most important theoretical and political question is being posed today: Are the effects of *perestroika* [reform] really socialist? Democracy, openness, cooperative ventures, self-financing, the socialist market, self-management, the sovereignty of the people, the pluralism of opinions—all this is penetrating our life deeply. It disturbs our life and sometimes deprives certain people of sleep and rest. It gives rise to passions, to sharp emotions and to new, quite real contradictions . . . Democracy, *glasnost* [openness] and the pluralism of opinions still frighten us, as if each of us is absolutely sure of himself and always thinks in comfortable cliches. The excesses of democracy frighten us. We speak about spiritual revival and moral purification, but we are still suspicious of the clashes of passions that are going on between young people, the intelligentsia, the working class and the peasantry.

At Soviet Communist Party
regional conference,
Perm, U.S.S.R., Dec. 17/
Los Angeles Times, 12-18:(I)5.

Boris Yeltsin
Former Moscow Chief,
Communist Party
of the Soviet Union

2

The top echelons [of the Soviet Communist Party], without exception, should be limited to two terms of office, and should be eligible for a second term only if there are tangible results in the first. We should introduce a clear age limit of 65 for all officials, including those in the Politburo . . . The Party exists for the people and the people should know everything it does. Unfortunately, this is not the case. There should be detailed reports from the Politburo and Secretariat on all matters except state secrets.

At Soviet Communist Party
conference, Moscow, July 1/
The Washington Post, 7-2:(A)19.

Tatyana Zaslavskaya
Director,
Center for the Study
of Public Opinion
(Soviet Union)

3

Under the old administrative-bureaucratic system [in the U.S.S.R.], nobody cared what the people thought. As we build a democratic system, our leaders are finding that they must keep a finger on the popular pulse . . . Take ecology, for example. For many years, Soviet people considered pollution as a fact of life. If they lived next to a chemical plant that was poisoning them, they regarded this as their fate. Since we've begun discussing these problems openly, however, they take a very different attitude. Environmental awareness has grown enormously here.

Interview/
The Washington Post,
10-20:(A)38.

Vitaly Zhurkin
Director,
Institute of Western
Europe, Soviet Academy
of Sciences

4

[On Soviet leader Mikhail Gorbachev's policy of democratization in the Soviet Union]: After a thousand years under czarism and dictatorship, we know it will not be easy, and we know it will not happen overnight. We also know that the changes will be resisted up and down the line by all those who have a stake in perpetuating the old system. Do not make the mistake of thinking that Gorbachev can bring about democracy by simply issuing some decrees. It will take time and it will be difficult, but Gorbachev's aim is nothing less than a complete redesign and restructure of our society.

At Dartmouth Conference,
University of Texas, Austin/
The Christian Science Monitor,
6-6:14.

The Middle East

Yasir Abed Rabbo
*Head of Palestine Liberation
Organization delegation at
talks with the United States
on the Arab-Israeli conflict*

1

We're here [at the U.S.-PLO talks] to achieve the goals and aims of the uprising [by Palestinians in the West Bank and Gaza]. It will end with the establishment of a Palestinian state, with Jerusalem as its capital.

*Carthage, Tunisia, Dec. 16/
The New York Times, 12-17:5.*

Youssef Abou Samra
*Psychologist, Bir Zeit University
(Israeli-occupied
West Bank)*

2

The *intifada* [the current anti-Israeli violence by Palestinians in the West Bank and Gaza] has been a catharsis. We [Palestinians] were a divided, frustrated and disintegrating community. Drug addiction was spreading, and we had no sense of self-worth. The Israelis were the active stimulus, and we were the passive response. Now it's reversed. We are the stimulus and the Israelis are the response.

The Washington Post, 12-9:(A)36.

Morris B. Abram
*Chairman, Conference of
Presidents of Major
American Jewish Organizations*

3

[On charges that Israel uses excessive force in countering anti-Israeli violence by Palestinians in the West Bank and Gaza]: With regard to the issue of beatings in the occupied territories, I can state today that Israel does not have a policy of indiscriminate beatings. Such a policy would be wrong and inconsistent with Israel's historic policy and practice ... The [anti-Israeli] violence is real; the weapons that are being used by the Palestinians are Molotov cocktails, rocks, crowbars and knives. The targets are often small, isolated groups of Israeli soldiers who are the victims of hit-and-run attacks intended to maim and kill. We understand that, in any democratic society, that to preserve democratic institutions, order is required, and order, sometimes in the face of extreme violent protests and violent actions ... requires force.

*News conference,
New York, Jan. 27/
Los Angeles Times, 1-28:(I)7.*

4

[On the PLO's recent statements indicating its acceptance of Israel as a nation]: [The PLO must] repeal the Palestine national covenant, which calls for the destruction of Israel. As long as that convenant serves as the basic political document of the PLO, there can be no progress toward peace. No matter how many commas [PLO leader Yasir] Arafat inserts or semicolons he removes, his statement is merely words. Peace requires deeds. And the first deed is to repeal the covenant.

*Interview,
New York, Dec. 14/
Los Angeles Times, 12-15:(I)7.*

Bassam Abu Sharif
*Adviser to Palestine
Liberation Organization
chairman Yasir Arafat*

5

[Saying the PLO will declare the Israeli-occupied West Bank and Gaza Strip independent and will form a Palestinian government in exile for those areas]: I know it does not mean sovereignty. Sovereignty will come after putting an end to occupation. We have no other choice

(BASSAM ABU SHARIF)

but to proceed unilaterally. We will go ahead in fulfilling the requirements for the declaration of independence. We have the land, although it is occupied. We have the people, part of which is under occupation. We will be forming our government. And the fourth element will be world recognition.

Interview, Baghdad, Iraq, Aug. 26/
The New York Times, 8-27:4.

Brock Adams
United States Senator,
D-Washington

1

[On the current U.S. military presence in the Persian Gulf to protect shipping during the Iran-Iraq war]: I am concerned that we have no strategy in the Gulf. We have some objectives, most of which I share, but no plan to achieve them. We go from day to day. We are allowing Iran to set the agenda. That is not a strategy. That is a prescription for disaster. What we have in the Persian Gulf is an open-ended commitment. We do not know how to tell if we have won; we do not know how to tell if we have lost. All we know is that we are there and will be there for a long time.

The New York Times, 7-5:7.

Yehuda Amital
Leader, Meimad Party
of Israel

2

The great tragedy of Israel is that the image of religion is also the image of extremism. In the Jewish value system, security and peace have to take precedence over land. We have to give up land, even if it hurts.

Interview/
The New York Times, 10-18:(A)6.

Yasir Arafat
Chairman, Palestine
Liberation Organization

3

The Palestinian people whom I represent are committed to peace based on justice. The people of Palestine do not fight for the sake of fighting. Like other people in the world, we yearn for peace, freedom, democracy and national independence. Palestinian people have played throughout history, and aspire to play in the future, a role achieving peace and progress for themselves and the rest of humanity.

Before members of European
Parliament, Strasbourg, France,
Sept. 13/The New York Times,
9-14:3.

4

[On Western charges that he is a terrorist]: George Washington was called a terrorist by the British. De Gaulle was called a terrorist by the Nazis. What can they say about the PLO, except to repeat this slogan? We are freedom fighters, and we are proud of it. According to international law and the United Nations Charter, I have the right to resist Israeli occupation. I don't want to harm anybody. But look how [the Israelis] are treating my people. These savage, barbarian, fascist practices against our children, our women! . . . What are we [Palestinians] looking for? We want a place for our bodies to be buried in and a place where our new generations, our children, can live as freely as other human beings. We want an end to daily massacres, sometimes in Beirut, sometimes inside the [Israeli-occupied Arab] territories, sometimes in Nablus, in Gaza. Forty years of continuous massacres! Continuous genocide! You know that. The world knows it. It is enough.

Interview/Time, 11-7:48.

5

[On the PLO's plan for Arab-Israeli peace]: First: That a serious effort be made to convene, under the supervision of the Secretary General of the United Nations, the preparatory committee of the international conference for peace in the Middle East . . . Second: In view of our belief in international legitimacy and the vital role of the United Nations, that actions be undertaken to place our [Israeli-] occupied Palestinian land under temporary United Nations supervision, and that international forces be deployed there to protect our people and, at the same time, to supervise the withdrawal of the Israeli forces from our country. Third: The PLO will seek a comprehensive settlement among the parties concerned in the Arab-Israeli conflict, including the state of Palestine, Israel and other neighbors, within the framework of the international conference for peace in the Middle East on the basis of [UN] Resolutions 242 and 338, and so as to guarantee equality and the balance of interests, especially our people's rights in freedom, national independence and respect the right to exist in peace and security for all . . . I ask the leaders of Israel to come here under the sponsorship of the United Nations, so that, together, we can forge that peace . . . And here, I would address myself specifically to the Israeli people in all their parties and forces, and especially to the advocates of democracy and peace among them. I say to them: Come, let us make peace. Cast away fear and intimidation. Leave behind the specter of the wars that have raged continuously for the past 40 years.

At the United Nations, Geneva, Dec. 13/The New York Times, 12-14:(A)10.

1

[On the PLO's recent statements indicating acceptance of Israel as a nation and the establishment of an independent Palestinian state]: . . . we have made our position crystal clear. Any more talk [by critics of the PLO] such as "The Palestinians should give more"—you remember this slogan?—or "It is not enough" or "The Palestinians are engaging in propaganda games and public-relations exercises," will be damaging and counter-productive . . . I declare before you and I ask you to kindly quote me on that: We want peace. We want peace. We are committed to peace. We are committed to peace. We want to live in our Palestinian state, and let live.

News conference, Geneva, Dec. 14/ The New York Times, 12-15:(A)7.

2

Our decision was and has been to continue the *intifada* [the anti-Israeli violence in the West Bank and Gaza] until the occupier is pushed from our territories, and until our people get a chance to enjoy their sovereignty under PLO leadership on their national soil. The whole world has taken our side. . . Israel continues to remain isolated and to defy the will of the international community.

Speech, Belgrade, Yugoslavia, Dec. 20/Los Angeles Times, 12-21:(I)14.

3

[On speculation that the crash of a Pan American Airways passenger plane in Scotland was the result of a Middle Eastern-terrorist bomb]: This is an inhuman, criminal action which we condemn. It is against our peace mission. It is not against a state; it is directed against humanity as a whole. Another proof that we should all fight against terrorism.

News conference, Rome, Dec. 23/ Los Angeles Times, 12-24:(I)3.

Abdul Karim Musawi Ardebili
Chief Justice, Supreme Court of Iran

4

[On the cease-fire in the Iran-Iraq war]: Brothers and sisters, beware lest you begin to think that with the breakup of the war we will have leisure time to enjoy ourselves. It would be a catastrophe for the revolution and the state. It is a disaster to assume that the end of the war means welfare and consumption, and that foreign companies will arrive to bring with them things we will enjoy. This would mean an end to the revolution, not the war.

The Christian Science Monitor, 8-19:6.

Moshe Arens
Foreign Minister of Israel

5

[Criticizing the U.S decision to talk with the PLO]: We express great sorrow that our allies,

(MOSHE ARENS)

the United States, who once stood shoulder to shoulder with us against international terror, have forgotten . . . that the PLO is the premier terror organization. Any sort of recognition only encourages them and extremism.

Interview, Jerusalem, Dec. 23/
Los Angeles Times, 12-24:(I)11.

Michael H. Armacost
Under Secretary for
Political Affairs,
Department of State
of the United States

1

[Saying that, as part of its new negotiations with the PLO, the U.S. will monitor Middle East terrorism to determine PLO culpability]: If attacks occur and if it appears [to be] the responsibility of elements that are close to the PLO, we would expect [PLO leader Yasir Arafat] to disassociate from them, certainly to expel any elements that are involved in this from the PLO. We're not talking simply about condemning. We're talking about disassociation and expulsion.

Broadcast interview/
"Face the Nation," CBS-TV,
12-18.

Hafez al-Assad
President of Syria

2

War will continue [between the Arabs and Israel], sometimes with rifles, other times with rocks, sometimes through demonstrations and other times in the form of an open military confrontation. [But] we will not close the doors in the face of others who may choose other options to reach a settlement. We will deal with it with an open mind.

At 25th anniversary celebration of
his Baath Party's ascent to power,
Damascus, March 8/
The Washington Post,
3-9:(A)18.

Shlomo Avineri
Professor, Hebrew University
(Israel)

3

If you ask me, the worst damage that Arab enmity has inflicted on us over the years is this: It has kept Israel so preoccupied with struggling for its very existence that we have never had time to decide on its essence.

The Washington Post, 4-18:(A)19.

George W. Ball
Former Deputy Secretary of State
of the United States

4

[On U.S.-Israeli relations]: In the first place, part of the mythology is that their strategic interests and ours coincide. They diverge to a very considerable degree. Secondly, all you have to do is look at their [Israel's] behavior toward minorities [the Palestinians living in the occupied territories], and you get a very clear idea that if it's a democracy, then South Africa's [apartheid system] is a democracy. Now, having a special relationship [between the U.S. and Israel], well, that's simply a figure of speech.

Interview/USA Today, 1-5:(A)9.

Bandar Bin Sultan Bin Abdulaziz
Saudi Arabian Ambassador
to the United States

5

The world is getting smaller. When the U.S. sneezes, we catch cold. When Saudi Arabia sneezes, the U.S. catches cold.

USA Today, 4-1:(A)11.

Abolhassan Bani-Sadr
Exiled former President
of Iran

6

[On the current government in Iran]: Today we have become the purveyors of scandals in the world. From now on anyone who says Iran, says corruption, terrorism, fanaticism.

Interview, Versailles, France/
The New York Times, 4-5:4.

Johanan Bein
*Acting Israeli Ambassador to
the United Nations*

1

[Criticizing the UN's decision to move a General Assembly meeting to Geneva to permit PLO leader Yasir Arafat to speak, after Arafat was denied a visa by the U.S. to speak at the UN in New York]: This assembly is asked to pack its bags and go to another continent for the dubious pleasure of lending an ear to the person who conceived, instigated and organized some of the world's cruelest atrocities against the innocent citizens of many nations.

*At United Nations, New York,
Dec. 2/Los Angeles Times,
12-3:(I)9.*

Meron Benvenisti
Israeli demographer

2

[On the current anti-Israeli violence by Arabs in the West Bank and Gaza]: [U.S. Secretary of State George] Shultz is working on the premise that the conflict is an international, interstate conflict. But that view has been overtaken by events. It is now an intercommunal conflict between Jews and Arabs, Israelites and Palestinians in the Holy Land. It has become a cultural, primordial, almost tribal conflict. It is a clash over psychological space, not physical space or land.

*Interview/
The New York Times, 6-4:3.*

Alexander Bessmertnykh
*First Deputy Foreign Minister
of the Soviet Union*

3

[Recognizing the Palestine National Council's recent proclamation of an independent Palestinian state]: Faithful to the fundamental principle of freedom of choice, the Soviet Union recognizes the proclamation of the Palestinian state ... The Palestinian leadership has displayed a great deal of responsibility and realism. They have provided for the creation of their state, but at the same time have stressed the importance of a Middle East settlement [of their conflict with Israel]. A situation is shaping where all the sides directly involved in the conflict recognize that the path to peace ... lies through talks on the basis of [UN] Security Council Resolutions 242 and 338, and that a Jewish and Arab state have equal rights to exist in Palestine.

*News briefing, Moscow, Nov. 18/
Los Angeles Times, 11-20:(I)1,15.*

Hyman Bookbinder
*Washington representative,
American Jewish Committee*

4

One of the most quoted descriptions of what Israel aspires to be, and what it has to a large extent fulfilled, is to be "a light unto the nations." But people have also got to understand that Israel is a state, and [as such] it must do certain things, like putting down rebellions [as in the current Arab violence in the occupied territories], like collecting garbage, like taxing people.

*The Christian Science Monitor,
3-4:17.*

L. Paul Bremer III
*Ambassador-at-Large,
Counter-terrorism Office,
Department of State of
the United States*

5

[On foreign criticism of the U.S. decision to deny PLO leader Yasir Arafat a visa so he could address the UN]: One of the striking things about the reaction to the decision is that nobody in the Arab world or among the Europeans or at the UN denied that Arafat is responsible for terrorism. It is true as a general proposition that terrorism in the Middle East has declined in 1988. But that doesn't detract from the basis of [the no-visa] decision, that elements loyal to the PLO were involved in terrorism, some of which affected Americans. You're getting into an argument over how much terrorism is acceptable, and that's not a proposal we can entertain.

Los Angeles Times, 12-3:(I)8.

Zbigniew Brzezinski
Professor of government,
Columbia University;
Former Assistant to the
President of the United States
(Jimmy Carter) for National
Security Affairs

1

I see no reason [for Israel] not to talk to the PLO. The French talked to the Algerians, the U.S. talked to the North Vietnamese, and at this moment the [Nicaraguan] contras are talking to the Sandinistas. Israeli insistence on not talking with the PLO is in effect a dodge to prevent any negotiations at all.

Time, 4-11:33.

George Bush
Vice President of the United States;
Candidate for the
1988 Republican U.S.
Presidential nomination

2

[On his role in the scandal involving the covert sending of U.S. arms to Iran, which resulted in the release of U.S. hostages in Lebanon]: Do I support arms for hostages? No, I don't . . . Did I care about the hostages? Yeah. Did I think it right to reach out to moderates in Iran? Yeah. Was I smart enough to see in the very beginning that this was arms for hostages? No. Did the President [Reagan] see it? No.

Campaigning in Manchester, N.H.,
Jan. 6/Los Angeles Times, 1-7:(I)21.

3

[On criticism that he was involved in the deal between the U.S. and Iran that resulted in American arms being traded for the release of U.S. hostages held in Lebanon]: The President and the Vice President, when Americans are held hostage, probably care more about that than others . . . So maybe I'll put a little more emphasis on getting Americans freed from tyranny, from being held by terrorists; and maybe we reached out a little bit more in retrospect than we should have. But I have no regrets about erring on the

side of human life . . . And I think the American people identify with that; I think they feel that this matter has been thoroughly examined . . . I don't think anyone has ever accused me of anything dishonest. Nothing culpable in that sense, at all. And if one wants to fault one's judgment in retrospect, fine. I've said I'll take my share of the responsibility for that. [But] give me half the credit for all the good things we've done.

News conference,
Des Moines, Iowa, Jan. 7/
The Washington Post, 1-8:(A)6.

4

Even to say that a Palestinian state would be okay if the parties themselves accept it is [ridiculous]. It's a concept that won't work. The parties *won't* accept it, and if you're running for President [of the U.S.], you have to know that when you begin. Hypothesizing about something that can't happen makes no sense.

U.S. News & World Report, 5-2:23.

5

[On the U.S. military presence in the Persian Gulf]: We will always have a mission in the Gulf. We always have had, will always continue to have, as far as I'm concerned. We have to have the presence, sometimes sporadic, sometimes quasi-permanent as we are now. We have to keep the Straits [of Hormuz] open. We have to show the flag there. We have enormous interest in terms of our energy base . . . So the concept that we someday can pull our presence out, I just don't agree with that.

Interview, Washington, July 5/
The Washington Post, 7-6:(A)4.

6

[On the accidental downing of an Iran passenger plane by a U.S. warship on patrol in the Persian Gulf]: The United States has never willfully acted to endanger innocent civilians, nor will it ever. Contrast this, if you will, to the willful detention in inhuman conditions of Americans, and others, held hostage against their will [in the

363

(GEORGE BUSH)

Middle East by groups sympathetic to Iran]. One course is civilized—and the other barbaric.

At United Nations,
New York, July 14/
Los Angeles Times, 7-15:(I)1.

George Bush
Vice President of the United
States; 1988 Republican
U.S. Presidential nominee

1

I have made it very clear that I am opposed to an independent Palestinian state for a very simple reason. Such a state would be a threat to the security of Israel and of Jordan, which is crucial to any lasting settlement of the [Arab-Israeli] conflict. And, I would add, it would also be contrary to America's interests. Anyone who has trouble making up his mind on this issue, or who proposes to leave it open, just doesn't understand the dangers to Israel and the United States, just doesn't understand the very real threats that continue to exist. My Administration would not support the creation of any Palestinian entity that would jeopardize the security of our strategic ally, Israel.

Before B'nai B'rith,
Baltimore, Sept. 7/
The Washington Post, 9-8:(A)14.

Frank C. Carlucci
Secretary of Defense of the
United States

2

[On the U.S. military presence in the Persian Gulf to protect neutral shipping against attacks stemming from the Iran-Iraq war]: We are not policemen of the Gulf, nor do we wish to be. [But] we cannot stand by and watch innocent people be killed or maimed by malicious, lawless actions when we have the means to assist and perhaps prevent them.

April 29/
The Washington Post,
4-30:(A)1.

3

[On the accidental downing of an Iranian passenger plane by a U.S. warship on patrol in the Persian Gulf]: The principal responsibility of a commanding officer [of a warship], . . . under the rules of engagement, is to protect his ship. I believe that, given the operating environment, Captain [Will C.] Rogers [of the U.S. ship] acted reasonably and did what his nation expected of him in the defense of his ship and crew.

News conference, Washington, Aug. 19/
Los Angeles Times, 8-20:(I)1.

4

The real casualty, if the [U.S.] Congress ultimately deals the United States out of a military partnership in the Arab world [by blocking U.S. arms sales to Arab nations], will be the peace process itself—a result equally damaging to Israel as well as moderate Arab states . . . I see foreign soldiers and advisers on Jordanian and Saudi installations, providing training and maintenance assistance, where American servicemen have served until now. I see tens of billions of dollars worth of jobs going abroad instead of sustaining our key defense industries and bolstering the U.S. economy.

Before American-Arab Affairs Council,
Huntington, W.V.,
Oct. 21/Los Angeles Times, 10-22:(I)18.

Jimmy Carter
Former President of the
United States

5

. . . the unnecessarily harsh Israeli response to the Palestinian uprising in the West Bank and Gaza [continues]. More than 300 civilians have been killed, and Israeli authorities have stated that several thousand are held in detention without trial. Not only does this play into the hands of the most obstructionist of the Arabs who want no peace with Israel, but it perpetuates more than two decades of military domination of an increasingly restive people [the Palestinians]. Both Jews and Arabs continue to suffer.

At 1989 Carter-Menil
human-rights ceremony, Dec. 10/
The Washington Post, 12-27:(A)14.

Joe Clark
Minister of External Affairs
of Canada

1

[Criticizing Israel's methods in putting down anti-Israeli violence in the West Bank and Gaza]: The use of live ammunition to restore civilian order, the withholding of food supplies to control and collectively penalize civilian populations, the use of tear gas to intimidate families in their homes, of beating to maim so as to neutralize youngsters and pre-empt further demonstrations, have all been witnessed.

Before Canada-Israel Committee,
Ottawa/The Christian Science
Monitor, 3-30:10.

Tony Coelho
United States Representative,
D-California

2

[Criticizing U.S. military presence in the Persian Gulf—which is intended to protect oil shipping from attacks stemming from the Iran-Iraq war—especially after the accidental downing of an Iranian civilian airliner by a U.S. Navy cruiser]: Every time you get into an embarrassing situation like this, it makes it much harder to consider getting out of the Gulf. It would look like you are trying to walk away . . . We're basically at the beck and call of anybody who wants to move their goods. There are countries in Europe and the Pacific Basin who are direct beneficiaries of our presence in the Gulf who take no responsibility.

July 6/The New York Times, 7-7:6.

3

[Advocating caution before the U.S. makes compensation payments to Iran for the accidental downing of an Iranian passenger plane by a U.S. warship on patrol in the Persian Gulf]: We're dealing with a country that hates the U.S.; whose leaders, every day, are talking about how to go after us; that has repeatedly killed innocent American citizens and held Americans hostage. I say, slow down, let's make sure, before we do anything.

The New York Times, 7-18:12.

Alan Cranston
United States Senator,
D-California

4

[Criticizing U.S. Reagan Administration arms sales to Arab countries]: I am disappointed that the Reagan-Bush Administration, which has sold over $25-billion worth of sophisticated arms over eight years to the nations of the Persian Gulf, would now complain about Congressional restraint [in such sales]. Congress has had a modest deterrent effect on a number of irresponsible sales. I wish we had been able to block more sales, including the 1981 Saudi [surveillance plane] deal and the arms-to-[Iran] scheme.

Oct. 21/
Los Angeles Times, 10-22:(I)18.

William J. Crowe, Jr.
Admiral,
United States Navy;
Chairman, Joint Chiefs
of Staff

5

[On the recent accidental downing of an Iranian civilian airliner over the Persian Gulf by a U.S. Navy cruiser]: If a country [Iran] is going to wage combat operations in a certain area and then send a commercial airline in the area during that, of course it's an accident waiting to happen.

Press briefing/Newsweek, 7-18:22.

Robert J. Dole
United States Senator,
R-Kansas

6

No nation has endured greater tragedy in this century than Lebanon. Wracked by communal hatred, beset by aggression and intervention, struggle against war and terrorism—a once prosperous and progressive nation is fighting for its very existence . . . We shall never have true peace in the Middle East until Lebanon is again at peace. We shall never get a firm handle on the scourge of international terrorism until Lebanon is at peace. And because the stakes are so high, Lebanon must remain a high priority of Ameri-

(ROBERT J. DOLE)

can foreign policy. The fundamental goal of our policy should be the preservation of the unity of the nation of Lebanon. If Lebanon disintegrates, it will be a major blow to any hopes of establishing peace and stability in the Middle East . . . The political leaders of every major faction in Lebanon better wake up before it is too late. Unless they begin to place a higher priority on the preservation of the nation than on their narrow parochial interests, Lebanon will not survive.

Before the Senate,
Washington, Sept. 28/
The Washington Post, 10-5:(A)24.

Michael S. Dukakis
Governor of Massachusetts (D);
Candidate for the 1988
Democratic U.S.
Presidential nomination

1

[On the current anti-Israeli violence by Palestinians in the West Bank and Gaza]: It is critically important that the world understand who is responsible for the turmoil and the violence. It is not the generation of young Palestinians who have grown up in uncertainty, and who have been taught by their elders to hate. It is not a government in Jerusalem that struggles to maintain order while seeking an opportunity to negotiate with responsible Arab leaders about the future of the [occupied] territories. It is, regrettably, Arab leaders themselves who have time and again rejected the chance to sit down with Israel and negotiate peace.

Before Conference of Presidents of
Major American Jewish Organizations,
New York, April 11/
The New York Times, 4-12:13.

2

I don't think you negotiate with the PLO as long as they engage in active terrorism and are committed to the destruction of Israel. And I haven't seen anything in the course of the past weeks or months or years which seems to have changed that basic view. And every time [PLO leader Yasir] Arafat is pressed, he gets very ambiguous. I don't see what's so difficult about the PLO or other Arab nations standing up and doing what [the late Egyptian President] Anwar Sadat did, which is basically to say: "Yes, we agree that the people of Israel have a right to exist within secure borders with dignity and freedom, and we'll negotiate on that basis." I mean, what's so difficult about that?

Interview/
Los Angeles Times, 5-26:(I)22.

3

If Israel wants its capital in Jerusalem, then, as far as I'm concerned, its capital is in Jerusalem [even though the U.S. has resisted moving its Embassy from Tel Aviv]. I think it's a basic principle of doing business with other nations. They say their capital is in "X", then that's where we go.

Interview/
Los Angeles Times, 6-11:(I)18.

4

[A Dukakis Administration] will not sell weapons that would threaten the security of Israel to any nation. And we will work to persuade our NATO allies to join us in that policy. The Republicans have sold AWACS to Saudi Arabia, *Mavericks* [missiles] to Kuwait, *Stingers* [missiles] to Bahrain and billions of additional dollars worth of sophisticated arms to Arab countries that refuse to make peace with Israel. [U.S. Republican Presidential nominee] George Bush has supported those sales, and [Republican Vice-Presidential nominee] Dan Quayle voted for them. [Democratic Vice-Presidential nominee] Lloyd Bentsen and I are going to say "no" to Arab shopping lists that endanger the security of Israel.

Before B'nai B'rith, Baltimore,
Sept. 7/The New York Times,
9-8:12.

5

There can never be a role in [Arab-Israeli] negotiations for the PLO unless it renounces

(MICHAEL S. DUKAKIS)

terrorism in word and deed, unless it accepts UN Resolutions 242 and 338 and unless it clearly and explicitly renounces its own covenant, which states that peace can only come at the price of Israel's right to exist. A Dukakis Administration will never recognize a unilateral declaration of a Palestinian state or government in exile.

Before B'nai B'rith,
Baltimore, Sept. 7/
The New York Times, 9-8:12.

Michael S. Dukakis
Governor of Massachusetts (D);
1988 Democratic
Presidential nominee

1

[Criticizing U.S. Republican Presidential nominee Vice President George Bush for not trying to stop U.S. arms being sent to Iran in exchange for U.S. hostages held in the Middle East]: I think the question in this particular case was why the Vice President stood silently by, doing very little to try to stop it. One of the reasons I picked my [Vice Presidential] running mate was because Lloyd Bentsen would walk into the Oval Office and say, "Mr. President, this is outrageous. It has got to stop." And that just didn't happen [with Bush]. So I think the question is, why didn't he and other responsible members of the Administration realize that when you grant concessions to terrorist nations and hostage-takers, the consequences are devastating? You encourage terrorism by doing so. And that's why you never, ever, make concessions to terrorists or terrorist nations.

Interview/
Reader's Digest, October: 67.

Abba Eban
Member of Israeli Knesset
(Parliament); Former
Foreign Minister of Israel

2

[On current anti-Israeli violence by Palestinians in the West Bank and Gaza]: We are the predominant military power. That doesn't mean to say that we should use words of arrogance and contempt, and that I'm going to tell you that our neighbors are either flies or grasshoppers [as did Israeli Prime Minister Yitzhak Shamir recently in describing the Palestinians involved in the uprisings]. Once you start comparing your adversaries to insects, you are rehearsing the rhetoric of extermination. You are dehumanizing that which is—despite the depth of our conflict—an intra-human tragedy and an objective conflict between rival claims. And the fact that such words come from such high places indicates how deeply [Israel's] values have been affected by this unresolved issue.

Newport Beach, Calif., April 10/
Los Angeles Times, 4-11:(I)14.

Warren W. Eisenberg
Director, International
Council of B'nai B'rith

3

[On the PLO's recent statements indicating acceptance of Israel as a nation]: The PLO has to show through deed that it has finally come to terms with Israel's existence and intends to pursue the path of peace and eschew violence. [PLO leader Yasir Arafat's] history of artful zigs and zags on the issues of peace, together with his organization's blood-drenched record of disdain for human life and peaceful accommodation with Israel, leave us exceedingly skeptical.

Los Angeles Times. 12-16:(I)15.

King Fahd
King of Saudi Arabia

4

[On his country's decision to seek armaments from countries other than the U.S., which had been almost its exclusive supplier in the past]: The Kingdom of Saudi Arabia is not tied to anyone and does not take part in any pact that forces upon it any sort of obligations. If we find what we need among friendly nations and if they give us what we ask, they do so for money. We are not getting anything for free. So if things become complicated with a certain country, we will find

(KING FAHD)

other countries, regardless of whether they are Eastern or Western.

To Saudi armed forces leaders,
July 26/The New York Times,
7-28:6.

Munir Fasheh
Sociologist, Bir Zeit University
(Israeli-occupied
West Bank)

1

[On the Israeli occupation of the West Bank and Gaza]: British, Turks, Christians, Hebrews—all kinds of colonizers have come and gone. The Arab is here to stay. I am not saying that the *intifada* [violence by Palestinians against Israelis in the territories] will succeed in the short run. But it has made fundamental changes in the mind. It freed the imagination from the idea that Israel is here forever.

Los Angeles Times, 12-5:(I)17.

Marlin Fitzwater
Assistant to President of the
United States Ronald Reagan
for Press Relations

2

[On whether the U.S. will negotiate with Iran regarding the release of Americans held hostage in the Middle East]: Our position remains the same: that we are always available to talk, any time, any place, about the safety or release of our hostages. But we will not negotiate for them. We won't negotiate, we won't pay ransom, we won't talk *quid-pro-quos,* we won't give or take. The answer to the release of the hostages is to release them . . . They took them off the streets; they can put them back on the streets.

Los Angeles Times, 7-26:(I)6.

Elias Freij
Mayor of Bethlehem, Israeli-
occupied West Bank

3

[On the current anti-Israeli violence by Palestinians in the West Bank and Gaza]: I am the

Mayor of Bethlehem and I am a Christian, but first and foremost I am a Palestinian Arab. What do the Israelis really expect from us? To bow our heads and say Lord bless the occupation? . . . What is the Israeli option for peace? Is it more threats, more repression, more detention orders, more jails, more suppression? Why can't they comprehend and acknowledge that the *intifada* [uprising] is a protest against continuing Israeli occupation, not against Israel or against the Jewish people?

Interview, Bethlehem/
The Washington Post, 12-24:(A)12.

Reuven Gal
Former chief psychiatrist, Israeli Army

4

[On the Israeli armed forces' use of force against protesting Palestinians in the West Bank and Gaza]: The need to employ violence against a civilian population over time produces two kinds of psychological reactions [in soldiers]. On the one hand, it produces symptoms of insensibility and the inability to distinguish between violence justified by the circumstances and violence for the sake of violence. On the other hand, it leads to confusion, inner conflict, lack of motivation and depression.

Los Angeles Times, 2-20:(I)9.

Amin Gemayel
President of Lebanon

5

[On the lack of elections in Lebanon]: I leave the Presidency today worried and filled with anxiety. Today should have been a festival in which we rejoice over the election of a new President that would take the helm and the oath of office, as I and my predecessors did. But the people of war were stronger than peace.

Farewell address, Sept. 22/
Los Angeles Times, 9-23:(I)1.

Gennadi I. Gerasimov
Spokesman for the Foreign Ministry
of the Soviet Union

6

[On the accidental shooting down of an Iranian passenger plane by an American warship on

(GENNADI I. GERASIMOV)

patrol in the Persian Gulf]: The unprecedented buildup of American warships and planes in the area has made and keeps making for an explosive situation there. [The] tragedy has borne out once again that the U.S. Naval fleet must leave the Persian Gulf without delay. The Soviet Union consistently supports seeking political solutions in conflict situations and [has] regularly warned that the path of military action could not bring about a normalization of atmosphere [in the Gulf].

Press briefing, Moscow, July 4/
The Washington Post, 7-5:(A)15.

Mikhail S. Gorbachev
General Secretary,
Communist Party of
the Soviet Union

1

The Palestinians are a people with a difficult fate. But they receive broad international support, and this is the guarantee for resolving the main question for the Palestinians—self-determination. In the same way, recognition of the state of Israel, consideration of its security interests—the solution of this question is a necessary element for the establishment of peace and good-neighborliness in the region, based on principles of international law.

Moscow, April 9/
The Washington Post, 4-11:(A)1.

2

We cannot decide for the Arabs how the Palestinians participate in the international conference [proposed to settle the Arab-Israeli conflict]. Let them decide for themselves; let the Arabs decide. What we should do, the Americans and the Soviet Union, we should respect their decision. It's a vast Arab world out there, and we must recognize Israel's right to security. We must recognize the right of the Palestinian people to self-determination. In what form? Let the Palestinians, with their friends the Arabs, decide on that.

News conference, Moscow, June 1/
The New York Times, 6-2:8.

3

[Criticizing the U.S. refusal to grant a visa to PLO leader Yasir Arafat that would allow him to speak before the UN]: In the context of the problem of settling regional conflicts, I have to express my opinion on the serious incident that has recently affected the work of this session. The chairman of an organization which has observer status at the United Nations was not allowed by U.S. authorities to come to New York to address the General Assembly. I am referring to Yasir Arafat. What is more, this happened at a time when the Palestine Liberation Organization has made a constructive step which facilitates the search for a solution to the Middle East problem, with the involvement of the United Nations Security Council . . . We voice our deep regret over the incident and our solidarity with the Palestine Liberation Organization.

At United Nations,
New York, Dec. 7/
The New York Times, 12-8:(A)6.

Mohammad Hallaj
Director, Palestine Research
and Education Center,
Washington

4

[On the high education level of Palestinians]: When an agrarian society loses its land [such as the Palestinians did, to Israel], it loses not only property, but livelihood. For that reason, education became an obsession. Over the past 20 years particularly, there has been an unparalleled upsurge because it was necessary for survival. A mobile or insecure population can't rely on fixed economic activity, like industry. It has to have mobile "capital" that it can carry in its head.

The Christian Science Monitor,
1-22:12.

Yehoshafat Harkabi
Professor of international
relations, Hebrew University
(Israel); Former chief of
Israeli military intelligence

5

[On the current anti-Israeli violence by Palestinians in the West Bank and Gaza]: Our choice

(YEHOSHAFAT HARKABI)

is not between good and bad. That is easy. Our choice is between bad and worse. Israel cannot defend itself if half its population is the enemy. The Arabs understand that if there is no settlement, then there will be hell, for them and for us . . . We must re-open the national debate, must think with our heads and not our hearts. We need a Zionism of quality, not of acreage.

Interview, Jerusalem/
Time, 4-4:50.

1

[Israel] will always be a small country, even if we annex the entire West Bank. We can survive with insecure borders, but we cannot survive as a Jewish state with half our own population out to destroy us. All of our choices are bad ones, so we must choose the least bad.

The Washington Post, 4-18:(A)19.

David Hartman
Director,
Shalom Hartman Institute
for Jewish Study (Israel)

2

[On current Palestinian violence in the West Bank and Gaza against Israeli occupation and the forceful Israeli reaction to put it down]: Most of us feel ashamed about what's happening in the territories. Our actions there threaten Jews everywhere. Israel is the Jewish people's synagogue. Jews all over the world have chosen Israel for their identity, and if Israel doesn't exist as a *mensch* [human], then the Jewish culture will disappear. Therefore, we must risk compromise in order to save the Jews *as Jews,* not just as 3 million people here in Israel. In our souls we must know that we have reached out, that we have tried, that we have been reasonable. At the very least, we need to feel that way, in order to be able to fight.

U.S. News & World Report, 4-4:36.

3

Forty years [of Israeli nationhood] should bring the beginning of some sort of wisdom. Our

adolescence is over. We've had some great teen-age fantasies like the Six-Day War, and we've had some knocks like Lebanon. The conflict now is between traumatized politics and the politics of vision. People are ready for leadership, but the country is still ghettoized, and the politics are very small-minded. It's very difficult for anyone to express a truly national vision.

The Washington Post, 4-18:(A)19.

Geoffrey Howe
Foreign Secretary of the
United Kingdom

4

[On the Arab-Israeli conflict]: Time is not on [the Israelis' side]. We admire very much the courage with which the people of Israel have established their own country after all the long historic sufferings of those people. But they, too, must recognize that they cannot build their future on the insecurity and hostility of the Palestinians.

Los Angeles Times, 12-16:(I)16.

Hussein I
King of Jordan

5

The U.S. seems to be more and more under the influence of extremist elements, short-sighted elements, in Israeli society; and by that I mean their influence is, of course, tremendous over decision-makers, policy-makers in the U.S. Look at the United Nations Security Council, where the U.S. recently joined the other members denouncing Israeli deportations of Palestinians, then immediately issued a statement to the effect that this would be the last resolution against Israel. Well, how do you know what Israel will do next? . . . It seems to me that the decision-makers [in The U.S.] are under the influence of the extremists in Israel, people who cannot see beyond tomorrow, or the day after tomorrow, let alone years from now.

Interview, Amman, Jan. 27/
The Washington Post, 1-29:(A)17.

6

[Criticizing Israel and the U.S. for opposing an international peace conference for the Middle

(HUSSEIN I)

East which would include the U.S., Soviet Union and the PLO]: The United States continues to oppose it until it secures the approval of [Israeli Prime Minister Yitzhak Shamir]. Israel must bear the responsibility for the faltering peace process, and those who are in a position to influence the Israeli position, yet fail to do so, must share the blame. We are still hopeful that the United States will assume responsibilities as a superpower and reconsider its position . . . The truth is that the time factor has made the problem far more intense [because of current anti-Israeli violence in the West Bank and Gaza]. Time has bred a generation of Palestinians who see Israel as nothing more than a ruthless occupier.

To West German foreign-policy
group, Bonn, Feb. 9/
The Washington Post, 2-10:(A)32.

1

If no action is taken to resolve the Palestinian problem [in the West Bank and Gaza], by the turn of the century, the Arab population in Palestine will be almost equal to the Jewish population. But the Arab population will be full of bitterness as a result of unjust treatment and denial of their rights. This is a recipe for disaster . . . I have a feeling that the trend in Israel now is toward greater extremism, because they fear that Israeli Palestinians and Palestinians in the occupied territories are getting together. I hope this will change to a clearer vision of what is at stake and what needs to be done. Without jeopardizing their rights, we could be on the verge of giving them the kind of life and the kind of peace that they have never imagined.

Interview/Time, 5-2:38.

2

The United States has no Middle East policy other than support for Israel. The United States approach to the problem of the Arab-Israeli conflict is, unfortunately, based on a policy of crisis management. The United States takes no political steps or initiatives until there has been a recent eruption in the region taking on the aspects of war.

At Arab League meeting,
Algiers, June 8/
The New York Times, 6-9:7.

3

[Saying his country is giving up its claim to the Israeli-occupied West Bank]: Jordan is not Palestine . . . The independent Palestinian state will be established on the occupied Palestinian land after its liberation, God willing. There the Palestinian identity will be embodied, and there the Palestinian struggle shall come to fruition as confirmed by the glorious uprising of the Palestinian people under occupation. We assure you that these measures do not mean the abandonment of our national duty, either toward the Arab-Israeli conflict or toward the Palestinian cause. These steps were taken only in response to the wish of the Palestine Liberation Organization . . . and the prevailing Arab conviction that such measures would contribute to the struggle of the Palestinian people.

Broadcast address, Amman, July 31/
The New York Times, 8-1:4.

4

[On the PLO's recent agreement to the creation of a Palestinian state and the acceptance of UN Resolutions 242 and 338 as a way to settle the conflict with Israel]: I believe the PLO has gone as far as it was asked to go and has contributed its share for progress toward a just and comprehensive peace. I believe that if there is any intransigence—and there is indeed—it is in the Israeli position that hasn't changed and, up to now, the United States' position.

Broadcast interview/
"Face the Nation," CBS-TV, 11-20.

Faisal Husseini
Palestinian nationalist;
Director, Arab Studies Center,
Jerusalem

5

We always like to look at the beautiful face, with an international [peace] conference, self-

(FAISAL HUSSEINI)

determination, a Palestinian state. But the other side of the coin is the ugly one—recognition of Israel, negotiations with it, a two-state solution.

Interview, Jerusalem/
Los Angeles Times, 7-23:(I)10.

Henry J. Hyde
United States Representative,
R-Illinois

1

Unofficial, informal talks with the PLO must be held; because no matter how long we wait for other leadership to rise up in the West Bank and Gaza, it never rises, and it always comes back to the PLO.

Interview/
The Washington Post, 3-9:(A)25.

Jesse L. Jackson
American civil-rights leader;
Candidate for the 1988
Democratic U.S.
Presidential nomination

2

[On what he would do as President about the Arab-Israeli impasse]: I would first face the fact that Israel and the Palestinians are now locked into a death grip, bound by mutual fear, distrust, hatred, and that we must do for both of them what neither can do for the other—mutual security in exchange for mutual recognition. They cannot offer the other that because they are too insecure and too threatened . . . Occupation [by Israel of Arab lands] is untenable for Israel. It leaves Israel with false security, and the Palestinians with no security. America is standing by unable to protect its interest or its allies' interests. Occupation is divisive politically, is too costly economically, is too bloody militarily, and it's too draining emotionally. And that's where our coming in with Camp David-type leadership, with Israelis on one side and Palestinians on the other, must begin to break the jam.

Interview/
The Christian Science Monitor, 3-3:13.

3

The fact of the matter is we must talk with the PLO sooner or later . . . As a matter of principle, I support the [formation of a] Palestinian state. As a matter of fact, the PLO is by far the most representative organization of the Palestinian people. And . . . we must bring Israel security by convincing its adversary to cease being its adversary.

Interview/
The New York Times, 4-16:8.

4

In the case of the PLO, we [the U.S.] have opted not to talk. Since we can't talk, we can't act, and if we can't act, we can't influence. When all is said and done, if you can't talk with your enemy, you can't stop your enemy from being your enemy . . . We have given up the right to talk, we have given up the right to act, thus we have given up the right to change things.

Political debate,
New York, April 16/
Los Angeles Times, 4-17:(I)21.

5

[Criticizing Israeli occupation of Arab land]: . . . the occupation is too great a burden to bear. Economically, it's too expensive; we [the U.S.] are basically footing the bill. Economically, Israel cannot grow. Israel cannot expand to its true world potential; it cannot expand toward Africa; it cannot expand toward the Arab countries; it is rejected by most nations of the world. It cannot grow under this arrangement. Emotionally, it is terribly draining to the people who live there. Militarily, it's too bloody. We must do the harder thing than just choose sides. We must use our strength to bring sides together. That requires courage.

Interview/
Los Angeles Times, 5-27:(I)30.

6

[On the shooting down of an Iranian civilian airliner over the Persian Gulf by a U.S. Navy

(JESSE L. JACKSON)

cruiser]: The issue is not the efficiency of the head of the ship, of the Admiral, of the crew. The issue is not their honor. Even they regret the tragic accident. The crew did not make the policy to go into the Gulf [where the U.S. Navy is protecting oil tankers against attacks stemming from the Iran-Iraq war. The issue is] how shall we respond diplomatically and with a sense of humanity to a technological error resulting in the loss of 290 lives [aboard the plane]. Sixty-six children. That must be the focus of our diplomacy, our humanity, our compassion. Let us seize this moment to talk it out and not shoot it out.

News conference,
New York, July 6/
The New York Times, 7-7:10.

Adnan Khair Allah
Minister of Defense of Iraq

1

[On charges that his government is using poison gas against Iraq's Kurdish population]: The policy is to not use and to not encourage others to use [chemical weapons]. We believe in this policy. But I want to tell you that if this is the rule, then each rule has an exception.

News conference,
Baghdad, Sept. 15/
The New York Times, 9-16:4.

Salah Khalaf
Deputy chief, Fatah faction of
Palestine Liberation
Organization

2

[On the Palestine National Council's adoption of a peace platform calling for an independent Palestinian state and negotiated resolution of the conflict with Israel]: We have tried here to demonstrate our serious intent to achieve a peaceful settlement. But if we don't make good on this intention, if we fail, then the next PNC will see the rise of the extremists and the fall of the moderates. If there is no peaceful solution, then next time the fanatics will take the floor.

Algiers, Algeria/
Los Angeles Times, 11-19:(I)16.

3

[Saying that, despite the PLO's renunciation of the use of terrorism, the U.S. should not expect PLO attacks against Israeli military targets to cease]: [U.S. President] Reagan may stop his government's dialogue with the PLO now if he thinks he will be able to stop our attacks against Israeli military targets. [PLO leader Yasir] Arafat's denunciation of terrorism in Geneva did not include military attacks against Israel. Our struggle will continue until we raise the Palestinian flag over Jerusalem.

News conference,
Abu Dhabi, Dec. 18/
Los Angeles Times, 12-19:(I)7.

Ali Khameini
President of Iran

4

[On the Iran-Iraq war]: The main issue in our view is to prevent aggression in the region by defining who the aggressor is, and punishing him. We know if it's determined who the aggressor is, it's very important for the future of Iran and Iraq, and there won't be any further aggression in the future. This is why we are so persistent in determining that Iraq started the war.

Interview, Teheran/
The Christian Science Monitor,
3-11:12.

5

Today, the system of the Islamic Republic of Iran, for all the ineffective efforts of the enemies, has turned into an important power in the whole of the region. The nation of Iran is counted as an armed and established military force in the region.

At prayer gathering,
Teheran, Aug. 12/
The Washington Post, 8-13:(A)18.

373

Ruhollah Khomeini
Spiritual leader of Iran

1

The best prayer for the likes of the American President [Reagan] and his servants, such as [Iraqi President] Saddam [Hussein] is that God should give them death. Every day that passes for the likes of them, their hell becomes worse.

Broadcast address to the nation, Teheran, May 17/ Los Angeles Times, 5-18:(I)7.

2

The courageous Iranian people should vote for candidates [in the forthcoming national elections] . . . who have tasted the bitterness of poverty, and defend in their words and deeds the Islam of the bare-footed of the earth, the Islam of the downtrodden. They should shun those who uphold the Islam of capitalism, the oppressors, the free-from-pain well-to-do, the hypocrites, the comfort seekers, the opportunists, and in one word—[those who practice] pro-American Islam.

Speech/ The Christian Science Monitor, 5-26:9.

3

[Saying he agrees to a cease-fire with Iraq to end their eight-year war]: Taking this decision was more deadly than taking poison. I submitted myself to God's will and drank this drink for his satisfaction.

Statement read on Teheran radio, July 20/The New York Times, 7-21:1.

Henry A. Kissinger
Former Secretary of State of the United States

4

[On U.S. Secretary of State George Shultz's planned attempt to negotiate a settlement to end the anti-Israeli violence in Israeli-occupied Arab territories]: Secretary Shultz has a different deck of cards than I had. When I was out there [in the

1970s], the Israelis had the Egyptian Third Army surrounded in the Sinai and were pressing at the gates of Damascus. In addition, you now have a pair of extremely tough guys in [Prime Minister] Shamir and [Foreign Minister] Peres . . . Shultz doesn't know it, but it's in the nature of things that the Israelis won't settle until everyone's reached exhaustion, just to make sure they get a good deal. If Shultz doesn't watch his step, he'll have the worst of all worlds. The Israelis will blame him for betrayal, and the Arabs will dismiss him as Israel's lawyer . . . You've got to find some solution which balances the Arab need for self-esteem with Israeli security. I'm not sure it exists.

Interview, Washington/Time, 3-7:40.

Noel Koch
Former Principal Deputy Assistant Secretary for International Security Affairs, Department of Defense of the United States

5

I want to address the term "terrorist organization." Apologists for the activities of [many of the PLO groups] are at pains to make terrorist activity into a noble endeavor that simply has to be viewed with the right squint. [PLO leader Yasir] Arafat, a master squinter, demonstrated the proper form in an interview he gave to *Time* magazine earlier this month, rejecting the term "terrorist." "George Washington was called a terrorist by the British," he declared, adding, "We are freedom fighters, and we are proud of it." We see here the peculiar depravity of people who can make no distinction between confronting the regularly constituted military forces of a powerful nation—as George Washington did—and throwing burning gasoline on a young mother and her three infant children, as happened within the past month in Israel. George Washington never did that. Or attacking a nursery school in Ma'alot [Israel] in 1974 and killing 22 children, three older people, and wounding 66. George Washington never did that, either . . . [Or] the hijacking of an Air France commercial

(NOEL KOCH)

liner to Entebbe in 1976 and a Lufthansa commercial liner to Mogadishu in 1977 . . . Or the murder of a cripple in a wheelchair in a botched hijacking master-minded by the Palestine Liberation Front's Abu al-Abbas, one of Mr. Arafat's underlings in the PLO . . . It is important that we know what we mean when we discuss terrorism, and that we not be seduced into the intellectual sloth that says, "One man's terrorist is another man's freedom fighter."

Before U.S. Special Trade
Representative, Nov. 17/
The Washington Post, 12-9:(A)26.

Teddy Kollek
Mayor of Jerusalem

1

. . . it is impossible to accept any change in Jerusalem's status as one united city, under Israeli sovereignty and as captial of the state of Israel. Any attempt or suggestion to change this situation means . . . returning to the difficult days of a divided and neglected city, cleft by high walls and barbed wire. Only under Israeli rule has the city known conservation of its historical heritage, freedom of worship and free access for all to the holy places of all faiths, and guaranteed rights for all the religions and nationalities in the city.

Interview, Jerusalem/
Los Angeles Times, 12-18:(V)5.

Bernard Lewis
Professor emeritus of Near East studies,
Princeton University

2

When Iranians went to the [UN] Security Council and other international bodies with what they thought was a cast-iron case to obtain a denunciation of the United States [for the downing of an Iranian passenger plane by a U.S. warship on patrol in the Persian Gulf], and found they couldn't, that brought home to them, in a dramatic way, how utterly isolated and friendless they were in the world.

The New York Times, 7-22:4.

Samuel W. Lewis
Former United States Ambassador
to Israel

3

[On criticism by U.S. Jews of the harsh methods used by Israel to put down anti-Israeli violence by Palestinians in the West Bank and Gaza]: American Jews criticize, understandably, excesses; and there have been excesses. The defensive reaction from most Israelis is, "What would you suggest? If you want to tell us what to do, come over here and join us; don't sit on Park Avenue and give us advice" . . . It's a very complicated play that goes on, and it's colored by the special nature of the Jewish people and by the fact that Israel is not a nation-state like any other. Israel is connected to a people who are scattered around the world and concentrated heavily in the United States—people who are very passionately concerned about the future of that state. Israelis don't want to lose the support of American Jewry; at the same time, they cannot accept the proposition that American Jews who don't share their risks can tell them how to deal with those dangers.

Interview/
The Washington Post, 5-12:(A)20.

Robert Lifton
President, American
Jewish Congress

4

[The Israelis] have to face the problem that if they enfranchise [the Arab population in the occupied territories], Israel would no longer be a Jewish state. And if they refused to enfranchise that population, they would have a population which is a second-class citizenry in a state that was not democratic.

Interview, New York/
The Christian Science Monitor, 4-1:7.

Clovis Maksoud
Chief Arab League
representative at
the United Nations

5

[Criticizing the U.S. refusal to allow PLO chairman Yasir Arafat to enter the U.S. that

(CLOVIS MAKSOUD)

would allow him to speak at the United Nations, on grounds that he is a terrorist]: The Palestine National Council has [recently] taken very important and substantive decisions [regarding Arab-Israeli relations] that need to be communicated to the world body at the highest level. And it is not for the U.S. to decide who speaks for the Palestinians on a particular issue. If this [refusal of entry] is allowed to become a precedent, it will be a very dangerous one.

News conference,
United Nations, New York,
Nov. 28/
The New York Times, 11-29:(A)3.

Theodore R. Mann
President, American
Jewish Congress

1

[On current anti-Israeli violence by Palestinians in the West Bank and Gaza]: Israel cannot continue indefinitely to keep control over territories with so many Arabs without jeopardizing the Jewish state. Either they get rid of the Arabs—which most Jews here [in the U.S.] and Israel regard as abhorrent—or they get rid of the territory, which sooner or later is absolutely essential for Israel to do. However, it will only be able to do so if there are adequate security arrangements. It is up to the Arabs to make these arrangements, and it is up to Israel to make that compromise.

Newsweek, 1-25:30.

2

[On Israel's policy of beatings in response to anti-Israeli unrest in the occupied territories of the West Bank and Gaza]: The current policy of force and beatings as it has been implemented on the ground is regarded by us as inhumane and simply unacceptable. Moreover, on another level, its costs in terms of the loss of support for Israel is far, far too great.

News conference,
Jerusalem, Jan. 25/
The New York Times, 1-26:4.

Francois Mitterrand
President of France

3

[Approving the U.S. decision to talk with the PLO after that organization's recent statements indicating its acceptance of Israel as a nation]: I regard the most recent decision of the United States as a real step forward. [I praise] the courageous stand by the leader of the PLO, Yasir Arafat, to renounce terrorism and recognize Israel. The PLO has thus acquired the representativeness which some denied but France acknowledged.

Casablanca, Morocco, Dec. 15/
The New York Times, 12-16:(A)7.

Mohammad Ibn Fahd
Prince, and Governor
of the Eastern Province,
of Saudi Arabia

4

People criticized us [Saudis] for spending so much in the 1970s, but look at what happened. If we didn't do it then, we couldn't have done it today, given the current oil prices. We feel we can't spend too much on defense or the welfare of our people. We've done in 15 years what it has taken others 50 or 100 years or more to do ... We have probably better relations with the U.S.A. than any other Arab country does. Americans should know that we are not backward and are spending our money wisely to improve health care, education, housing.

Interview, Riyadh, Saudi Arabia/
USA Today, 4-1:(A)11.

Hosni Mubarak
President of Egypt

5

Why should the Israelis fear an international conference [between Arab and Israeli leaders to help solve Middle East and Palestinian problems]? It is not going to bite them ... Direct talks, for sure, are going to start. The problem of the Golan [Heights] will then be between the Israelis and the Syrians; and the problem of Jerusalem, the West Bank and Gaza will be between the

(HOSNI MUBARAK)

Israelis and the Jordanians, having some Palestinians in their delegation . . . The initiative now lies with Israel . . . I'm telling them to put us in a corner. You, [Israeli Prime Minister Yitzhak] Shamir, put the Arabs in a corner. Say you agree to an international conference . . . All the other problems will be solved after that, for everybody will be eager for the peace process to go forward. It will give hope to all the parties, [especially] to those people who are suffering in the West Bank and Gaza. It will relax the whole situation, and the other problems will be resolved more smoothly.

Interview, Cairo, Jan. 21/
Los Angeles Times, 1-22:(I)26.

1

[Calling on Israeli Prime Minister Yitzhak Shamir to make Israel part of an international conference to work out Arab-Israeli problems]: The international conference has been accepted by countries all over the world now: Europe, the United States, the Soviet Union, the Eastern Bloc. Everybody except Shamir. But believe me, if we could reach a comprehensive settlement in the international conference, this would be in the interest of not only the Europeans and the Americans but also for the Israelis. They will live in peace. Peace is very precious. There has to be some kind of sacrifice to achieve peace.

Interview, Heliopolis, Egypt/
USA Today, 3-7:(A)9.

Richard W. Murphy
Assistant Secretary
for Near Eastern and
South Asian Affairs,
Department of State of the
United States

2

The opportunities [for peace] in the Middle East don't last. They come and they go, and they're normally missed.

To Congressional committee,
Washington/Time, 3-28:35.

Hanna Nasser
President, Bir Zeit University,
Israeli-occupied West Bank

3

[On the PLO's declaration of an independent Palestinian state]: In itself, declaring independence may not bring us [Palestinians] any closer to living in Ramallah or Jerusalem. On the other hand, if we don't do this, if we don't say Palestine is a country under occupation, then who lays claim to this land, now that Jordan has pulled out? This may not lead us to actual independence, but it's the first step in that direction.

Nov. 14/
Los Angeles Times, 11-15:(I)10.

Robert Neumann
Director, Middle East studies,
Center for Strategic and
International Studies

4

Over Israel hangs a demographic time bomb. Since 1984, more Arab babies have been born than Jewish babies, speaking of the whole territory. Any Jewish child born today would have to expect when it goes to high school [that] half of its classmates will be Arabs. If Israel is to be a Jewish state and a democratic state, as its founder wanted it, the situation [of anti-Israeli Palestinians in the West Bank and Gaza] cannot last.

Interview/USA Today, 1-5:(A)9.

Richard M. Nixon
Former President of the
United States

5

I sympathize with the Israelis. I have always been a defender, and I still am. In their own interests, however, they should now make a settlement with their neighbors. Israeli has won five wars, and they'll win the next one—but in the long run they will lose, because there are so many more Arabs. Israel should make a settlement while they basically still are superior . . . They should insist upon a settlement that provides for defensible borders, one which does not divide the

RICHARD M. NIXON)

city of Jerusalem. One which all the states in the area—and the Palestine Liberation Organization, which in not a state—must recognize. If these conditions are met, Israel should then make a settlement. And then there should be self-government for the Palestinians.

Interview/USA Today, 4-5:(A)11.

Sari Nusseibeh
Professor of Islamic philosophy,
Bir Zeit University,
Israeli-occupied West Bank

1

You Israelis keep mentioning the word *terror* [by Palestinians against Israel]. But let's be fair. Terror is practiced by two sides. And right now, the predominant terror is practiced by Israel against Palestinians. It's *our* villages where people are being harassed, tortured, killed. Do Palestinians practice what you call "terror" as part of their natural behavior, or is it a reaction to dispossession, to the denial of national dignity, to 40 years of diaspora and refugee life? I believe that if we address the cause, if we satisfy our national aspirations in the context of a sovereign state in the West Bank and Gaza, then the chances for violence will greatly diminish. People's national energies will then be directed not against Israel but toward constructing the future Palestinian state.

Discussion, Jerusalem/
U.S. News & World Report, 4-4:45.

Reza Pahlavi II
Son of the late Shah of Iran

2

[Comparing Iran under his late father with the Iran of today under the Ayatollah Khomeini]: As far as talking about human-rights violations and actual brutality, [consider those such as accused airliner hijacker and killer Mohammed Ali Hamadi]. Well, there were hundreds of Hamadis in the jails [of Iran] in the past. They [Khomeini's followers] let them loose. They take hostages, they blow up embassies, they commit acts of

terrorism here and there. That's precisely why they belonged in those jails. Anybody unhappy about the fact that those kind of people were put in jails [during the Shah's reign] should be picketing the Hamadi trial right now in Germany. Of course, I'm not saying that the justice system in [the Shah's] Iran was perfect. There was corruption, I can't deny that. Yes, there were a lot of mistakes made, be it in terms of violence, be it in terms of corruption, be it in terms of opulence, whatever. We were not perfect. But to say that all of these were an instrument of our state policy would be ridiculous ... In the past 10 years, the Islamic Republic [of Iran] has not managed to come up with even 10 names of people who might have disappeared under the system. One has to put things into perspective.

Interview, Los Angeles/
Los Angeles Times, 10-3:(V)2.

Claiborne Pell
United States Senator,
D-Rhode Island

3

[On the reported use of poison gas by Iraq against Kurdish rebels]: A crime of unthinkable proportions is emerging. For the second time in this century, a brutal dictatorship is using deadly gas to exterminate a distinct ethnic minority. There can be no doubt but that the Iraqi regime of Saddam Hussein intends this campaign to be a final solution to the Kurdish problem.

Before the Senate,
Washington, Sept. 8/
Los Angeles Times, 9-9:(I)9.

Shimon Peres
Foreign Minister, and former
Prime Minister, of Israel

4

[On whether the current Palestinian unrest in the Israeli-occupied West Bank and Gaza will increase]: I don't think it will happen, because the residents of the territories also have their own limitations. Whoever disobeys will make his own life miserable ... Whoever suggests making con-

(SHIMON PERES)

ditions more difficult will just be kicking the ball into his own net.

Israeli Army radio broadcast,
Jan. 5/Los Angeles Times,
1-6:(I)10.

1

I am convinced that it is the task of my generation, and myself, to hand over to the younger people [an Israeli] state free of two great dangers. One is that, demographically, we shall lose our majority and it will stop being a Jewish state. The other, that we shall lose a chance for peace [with the Arabs], and then be in a state of belligerency for many years to come.

Interview/
The New York Times, 1-28:23.

2

[Saying Jewish settlements in the Israeli-occupied Arab territories contribute to the current Palestinian unrest in those areas]: Let each of us ask himself: Do the settlements, this dandy enterprise, provide security [for Israel]? Have they strengthened our position in the [Arab-Israeli] negotiations? Let each of us ask himself: If we did not have to keep so many troops in Gaza, could we not bring about quiet in the place that is most essential to us today—Jerusalem?

Before Israeli Labor Party central
committee, Feb. 11/
The Washington Post, 2-13:(A)24.

3

For wars, we don't need the Americans; for peace, we do. We've never asked American soldiers to participate in our wars, but we've always asked American diplomats to participate in our peace meetings [with the Arabs]—and I don't see a replacement.

Interview, Jerusalem/
U.S. News & World Report,
3-21:38.

4

We don't want to dominate the Arabs, because the Arabs don't want to be dominated . . . And believe me, it is so difficult to govern the Jewish people, why should we try and govern somebody else, anyway?

At Jewish Theological Seminary
commencement, New York/
Time, 6-13:74.

5

[On the election campaign between himself and Yitzhak Shamir for Prime Minister of Israel]: Every evening I hear on TV from the Likud [Shamir's party] that we're [Peres' party] selling the country, that we're returning to 1967 borders [before Israel gained control of the West Bank and Gaza]. What kind of talk is this? How does the Likud dare all the time to spread such slander and such deceptions among the people . . . Did [Israeli founder David] Ben-Gurion sell the state when he decided to establish a Jewish state on part of the Land of Israel? This is what you have to say? This is how you talk to the people? I'm not saying that there will be peace tomorrow [with the Arabs if he is elected], or peace immediately. I am also not willing to pay any price for peace. I'm just saying, if you give me a chance we can begin negotiations. The whole picture in the Middle East will change. We will not only talk war and make war and have an arms race. We could devote ourselves to the basic things of our life—economy, education, health, preparing jobs for the younger generation. There is a big chance.

Debate with Shamir, Oct. 23/
Los Angeles Times, 10-24:(I)7.

6

[Saying Israel should be more accommodating to Palestinian demands for more freedom in the West Bank and Gaza]: What will we answer when the Americans and Soviets press for [Arab-Israeli] peace? Where will we get money to build industry when we have to spend endlessly on defense? What will become of a Jewish state when 40 per cent of its population is Arab?

Election-campaign address,
Negev Desert, Israel/
U.S. News & World Report, 10-31:38.

Daniel Pipes
Director, Foreign Policy
Research Institute
(United States)

1

All this interest in the 1948 period [of Israeli history] is due to the fact that the Arab-Israeli conflict has gone back to where it was. It was primarily then between the Israelis and the Palestinians. Then, after that, all the other states got involved. Now, it's reverted to where it was before.

The New York Times, 7-28:4.

Muammar el-Qaddafi
Chief of State of Libya

2

We must not beat around the bush. The one and only enemy of the Arabs is the United States. We must all recognize this, and anyone who refuses to do so, or who collaborates with America, can go to hell.

At Arab League meeting,
Algiers, June 8/
Los Angeles Times, 6-9:(I)6.

Yitzhak Rabin
Minister of Defense, and
former Prime Minister,
of Israel

3

[On anti-Israeli violence by Palestinians in the West Bank and Gaza]: We can use our force to maintain tranquility, but not to achieve a political solution to the conflict. By no means do I pretend that by force we can solve it politically. Politically it can be solved only by negotiations. We have to make it clear to the Arab world, to the Palestinians and to the international community, that [while] we cannot solve it by military means only, they cannot solve it by violence or terror or wars ... The people who started it did not wait for any outside help. Maybe they cling to the PLO as a symbol, but I hope that once the dust will settle down they will be strong enough to be the masters of their own fate and they'll realize

that through violence they'll achieve nothing, and they will be ready to negotiate.

Interview, Tel Aviv, Jan. 18/
The Washington Post, 1-19:(A)12.

4

[On Israel's use of beatings to quell Palestinian unrest in Israeli-occupied Gaza and the West Bank]: The first priority is to use force, might, beatings ... We've gone in with force, beating without playing games—but without using arms. From this no one has died yet, and we also have fewer injured. I prefer a [news] photo of curfew over shooting, burning tires and petrol bombs.

The New York Times, 1-22:6.

Hashemi Rafsanjani
Speaker of the Iranian
Parliament

5

One of the wrong things we did in the revolutionary atmosphere [in Iran] was to constantly make [foreign] enemies. We pushed those who could be neutral into hostility and did not do anything to attract those who could become friends. It is part of the new plan that in foreign policy we should behave in a way not to needlessly leave ground to the enemy.

July 2/The New York Times, 7-4:4.

6

[On the accidental downing of an Iranian passenger plane by a U.S. warship on patrol in the Persian Gulf]: I have a report that the U.S. people believe the commander of the ship did the right thing [in shooting down the plane]. If it is true, I am sorry for the Americans. It proves that they have forgotten they are human beings. If the Nicaraguans were to shoot down your [U.S.] aircraft [flying over their territory], would this be reasonable? If the Filipinos were sick and tired of your [military] bases and were to shoot down an aircraft, would that be acceptable? If the Panamanians had taken such action, would that be acceptable?

At prayer service, Teheran,
July 8/The Washington Post,
7-9:(A)18.

(HASHEMI RAFSANJANI)

1

[On the announced cease-fire in the Iran-Iraq war]: Islamic Iran is proud before God for performing its holy duty of protecting justice, and the Iraqi Baathists should answer God and the people as to why they kindled the fire of war and what they gained from it.

Iranian radio broadcast, Aug.9/
The New York Times, 8-10:6.

2

We still have a lot of unanswered questions with regard to [Iranian] society. We still have not been able to clarify for people economic problems as befits Islam. We have differences of opinion among ourselves over these issues [and] we have not come forward with clear principles in our foreign policy . . . [or in] religious matters that vastly differ today from earlier eras of Islam.

To clergymen, Qom, Iran, October/
The Washington Post, 10-27:(A)54.

Ronald Reagan
President of the United States

3

[Americans] have no better friends then the people of Israel. The fact is, a strong Israel depends on a strong America. An America that will lose faith in a strong defense is an America that will lose faith in a nation at arms, like Israel.

Accepting Simon Wiesenthal
Center Humanitarian Award,
Los Angeles, Oct. 30/
The New York Times,
10-31:(A)14.

4

[On PLO leader Yasir Arafat's recent meetings in Sweden to further recent proclamations about his organization's readiness for peace with Israel]: We thought in the last few days that there was a statement that came out of that meeting in Sweden that appeared to be clean-cut and not with the things around the edge that then diffused what seemed to be a pledge. But we had to wait until his press conference and what he said. And I have to say that, again, he has left openings for himself where he can deny that he meant this or meant that that sounded so clean-cut. It's up to him. We are willing to meet with him and walk with him and I'm sure the Israelis would be, when once and for all it is clear-cut that he is ready to recognize Israel's right to be a nation, that he is ready to negotiate on behalf of the Palestinian people for a homeland for them, and so forth.

News conference,
Washington, Dec. 8/
The New York Times, 12-9:(A)8.

5

The Palestine Liberation Organization today issued a statement in which it accepted United Nations Security Council Resolutions 242 and 338, recognized Israel's right to exist and renounced terrorism. These have long been our conditions for a substantive dialogue. They have been met. Therefore, I have authorized the State Department to enter into a substantive dialogue with PLO representatives. The Palestine Liberation Organization must live up to its statements. In particular, it must demonstrate that its renunciation of terrorism is pervasive and permanent. The initiation of a dialogue between the United States and the PLO representatives is an important step in the peace process, the more so because it represents the serious evolution of Palestinian thinking toward realistic and pragmatic positions on the key issues. But the objective of the United States remains, as always, a comprehensive peace in the Middle East. In that light, we view this development as one more step toward the beginning of direct negotiations between the parties, which alone can lead to such a peace. The United States' special commitment to Israel's security and well-being remains unshakable. Indeed, a major reason for our entry into this dialogue is to help Israel achieve the recognition and security it deserves.

Dec. 14/USA Today,
12-15:(A)9.

Charles E. Redman
Spokesman for the
Department of State of the
United States

1

[Criticizing Israel's use of beatings to quell unrest in Israeli-occupied Gaza and the West Bank]: We are disturbed by the adoption of a policy by the government of Israel that calls for beatings as a means to restore or maintain order. [Israel can maintain order] through the use of humane measures which do not result in civilian casualties.

Jan. 21/
The New York Times, 1-22:6.

2

[On the recent proclamation of an independent Palestinian state by the Palestine National Council and its acceptance of UN Resolutions 242 and 338 as a way of negotiating an end to its conflict with Israel]: There are signs that there are Palestinians who are trying to move the PLO in a constructive way. That's encouraging, and it should continue. But measured against the requirements of the negotiating process, more movement on key issues will be required. And measured against the positions the PLO must adopt in order for the United States to engage in dialogue with it, the results of the PNC session fall short of meeting those requirements ... [The PNC's stand on Resolutions 242 and 338] is ambiguous both in its placement in the text and its meaning. Possibly implied, or indirect, reference to Israel's right to exist is not sufficient. Recognition must be clear and unambiguous.

Nov. 16/
The Washington Post,
11-17:(A)27.

Zaid Rifai
Prime Minister of Jordan

3

[On recent comments on the Arab-Israeli conflict by Jordan's King Hussein]: His Majesty had in mind the Israeli Likud [Party's] declared position regarding the peace process. They claim that all the land of Palestine is the Land of Israel; they claim that there is no such thing as Palestinian occupied territory; they claim that the Palestinians living in the West Bank and Gaza Strip are foreigners living on Israeli soil, and yet they say, "We want to negotiate a peaceful settlement." This is the recipe for disaster that His Majesty had in mind. The platform of the Likud excludes any possibility of a peaceful settlement, and they will be condemning the area to many more years of violence, terrorism, extremism, maybe eventually even war ... I don't know what the final Israeli position will be, but we do know that without the participation of the PLO at an international peace conference, you are not going to have a meaningful peace process; and the sooner the United States and Israel accept this, the better it is for the chances of peace.

Interview, Amman, Nov. 1/
The Washington Post, 11-2:(A)34.

4

[On the apparent close victory by the hard-line Likud Party in the recent Israeli election]: The unfortunate result of this is that there won't be any movement toward peace [with the Palestinians who have been engaged in anti-Israeli violence in the West Bank and Gaza]. The status quo will continue and eventually deteriorate. This is a recipe for disaster, because we've reached the point where either we move toward peace or things will deteriorate into more violence, extremism and terrorism. The situation cannot continue as it is ... It's not Likud itself we're against, but what it stands for. When they declare they have no intention of accepting the basic tenet of peace, and no intention of attending an international [peace] conference ... then what kind of bridges can you build with such a party?

Interview, Amman, Nov.2/
Los Angeles Times, 11-3:(I)9.

Elyakim Rubinstein
Cabinet Secretary for Israeli
Prime Minister Yitzhak Shamir

5

[Criticizing the U.S. decision to talk with the PLO]: It is upsetting to us. Is there someone in

(ELYAKIM RUBINSTEIN)

the United States prepared to buy a used car from [PLO leader Yasir] Arafat, let alone begin negotiations with him? Two weeks ago, they didn't let him in [to the U.S. to speak before the UN], referring to the voice of the blood of [terrorism victim Leon] Klinghoffer crying from the Mediterranean Sea.

Dec. 15/
The Washington Post,
12-16:(A)45.

Alexander M. Schindler
President, Union of
American Hebrew
Congregations

1

[On why he has criticized the Israeli policy of beatings used to quell anti-Israeli violence in the occupied West Bank and Gaza]: The first [reason] involved the moral factor. It is jarring to the Jewish spirit to hear about a policy of indiscriminate beatings of Arabs. The second reason was, if you will, tactical. This kind of policy is self-defeating. It will not restore order. It can only increase the cycle of violence. The third reason . . . was political. The responsibility for the Palestinians' plight certainly is not primarily Israel's. They are victims of the Arab governments and of the leaders of the PLO, who consistently have chosen terrorism and military confrontation over accommodation and political settlement. These latest events must not be allowed to obscure that point. And finally, if this Israeli policy is not stopped, it is bound to erode support for Israel among its American friends.

Interview, Jan. 24/
Los Angeles Times, 1-25:(I)16.

Yitzhak Shamir
Prime Minister of Israel

2

[On U.S. criticism of tough Israeli handling of anti-Israeli violence by Palestinians in the West Bank and Gaza]: It is impossible to dictate to someone from afar how to defend oneself against

anarchy, riots, attacks on the state, its citizens, its peace and security. It seems to me that the American public needs to understand the problems of a democratic state defending itself against anti-democratic elements that want to destroy it.

To U.S. and Israeli businessmen,
Jan. 1/
Los Angeles Times, 1-4:(I)6.

3

[On foreign criticism of Israel's forceful crackdown on anti-Israeli violence by Palestinians in the West Bank and Gaza]: Nations that didn't open their mouths when we [Jews] were brought to slaughter [by the Nazis] are now going crazy at the sight of rioters getting their punishment. It is difficult to understand the injustice and the lack of proportion in these responses [to the Israeli crackdown]. It's nothing but the fact that they [the critics] like to see us beaten and knocked down, and hate to see us defending our country with strength, forcefully, and remaining alive.

Feb. 29/
The New York Times, 3-1:5.

4

The United States is Israel's greatest and most loyal friend. But we do not have to accept even from our best friend things likely to endanger our state. A blow from a friend hurts no less, perhaps hurts more, than a blow from an enemy.

Before National Religious Party,
Jerusalem, March 6/
The New York Times, 3-7:6.

5

[On why he has not agreed to an international conference to work out Arab-Israeli problems, as Egyptian President Hosni Mubarak has urged him to do]: First of all, I cannot accept his position that he is not ready to meet me without knowing that I support an international conference. It's a pre-condition. This is a very important subject: peace in our area. Why not meet and discuss it? He says, no, he wants to know, before,

WHAT THEY SAID IN 1988

(YITZHAK SHAMIR)

that I support an international conference. I am ready to order direct negotiations on all the subjects, resolve all the subjects, without any limitations; but I don't see the need for an international conference.

Interview, Jerusalem/
USA Today, 3-7:(A)9.

1

We don't like very much the involvement of the United Nations in the peace-making process. They don't have a record of achievement in this regard. In the United Nations, we have always an automatic majority against us—for the most simple subjects. For instance, Israel will bring a proposal to the United Nations that today is Thursday, and we will have an automatic majority against us. It's always the same.

Interview, Jerusalem/
USA Today, 3-7:(A)9.

2

[Criticizing those who advocate that Israel give up occupied Arab territory as a way of securing Arab-Israeli peace]: Now we are told that the only thing needed to achieve a true and lasting peace is for us to declare our readiness to give up territories in Judea, Samaria and Gaza. I am astonished at some people's short memory. Did we have peace when we did *not* have these territories? Don't they remember that the two most dangerous attempts to destroy us—in 1948 and in 1967—were made when we did not control any of these territories? Do they want us to go back to a situation which would inevitably invite another such attempt?

Before United Jewish Appeal,
Washington, March 14/
The Washington Post, 3-15:(A)1.

3

[On the current anti-Israeli violence by Palestinians living in the West Bank and Gaza]: We will not surrender to violence. We cannot. Nor

will we ever get tired. We could put an end to it in a few days, but our Army is under strict orders not to shoot except in cases of personal danger. We don't want to kill people, because we know it is our destiny to live together with these people on the same land. You know, in Jordan or in Egypt, such demonstrations wouldn't last for a week. You'd immediately have large numbers of people killed, and it would be finished. In Syria, they massacred 20,000 when there were demonstrations in the town of Hamra. We don't want to be Goliaths, but we also don't want to be Davids.

Interview, Jerusalem/
U.S. News & World Report,
3-21:39.

4

We have to strengthen our economy by going more in the direction of privatization. There has been a tradition of Israeli governments in the past to be inclined more toward socialistic methods. Now it's clear for the great majority of people that the only way to improve our economy is the way of privatization, of giving priority to the business sector.

Interview/USA Today, 3-25:(A)13.

5

[On the current anti-Israeli violence by Palestinians in the West Bank and Gaza]: If the Arabs of Israel do not come to their senses, the reality will be harder and laden with impending disaster. A test of strength between us and them is like a test of strength between an elephant and a fly.

Interview/
The Washington Post, 3-29:(A)13.

6

[The Palestinians] say they want the West Bank and Gaza [for a Palestinian state], but what they really mean is Tel Aviv, Haifa and all of Israel . . . We want peace, but we will never allow a PLO state.

Election-campaign rally,
Hadera, Israel, Oct. 22/
U.S. News & World Report, 10-31:38.

(YITZHAK SHAMIR)

1

[Arguing against an international conference to foster Arab-Israeli peace]: An international conference as a beginning [of negotiations] is the beginning of defeat, of Israeli surrender . . . because . . . all the Arabs that are for it know that such a conference will decide upon an Israeli withdrawal to 1967 borders, at least, and on the establishment of a Palestinian state. Therefore, this is not a chance for peace, but the contrary.

Debate with his election opponent,
Shimon Peres, Oct. 23/
Los Angeles Times, 10-24:(I)7.

2

I hope that for the sake of promoting the chances of peace and advancing the struggle against terror and violence, the United States will never establish any contact with the PLO. We shall not negotiate with the PLO under any conditions, nor recognize it. From our point of view, the PLO is no partner for any peace process. It is a terrorist organization aimed at undermining our national existence and bringing about the destruction of the state of Israel.

News conference,
Jerusalem, Dec. 13/
Los Angeles Times, 12-14:(I)1.

3

[Criticizing the recent U.S. decision to talk with the PLO]: We always said the United States and Israel are allies; there is an alliance between us, and it can happen that there are serious disagreements between allies. This week, something happened that puts that principle to a serious test. The United States decided to enter negotiations with Israel's most extreme enemy [the PLO]. It is no wonder that this caused shock, and no wonder that we are all thinking and weighing what happened, why did it happen and what should be done . . . There is an atmosphere in the world, even a fashion—and fashions can be crazy sometimes—of sympathy for this terrorist body [the PLO]. The United States was swept up by this wave.

Dec. 17/
Los Angeles Times, 12-18:(I)1.

4

The battle today is against the very establishment of a Palestinian state [in the West Bank and Gaza]. It is time to present a united front against all factors endangering our position. What we are talking about is an international effort to push us within a year or two back to 1967 borders [that existed before the Six Day War gave Israel control of those territories].

To Likud Party,
Jerusalem, Dec. 20/
Los Angeles Times,
12-21:(I)1.

5

[Addressing Palestinians in the West Bank and Gaza who have been rioting against Israeli occupation]: Those who called on you to go out to the streets and to seize violent means won't achieve anything for you except for declarations and empty banners. There is one way to achieve this purpose. It is through direct negotiations with Jordan, with Palestinian Arab representatives who are not connected to terror groups, the PLO or its ilk. There's no room or reason for a second Arab [Palestinian] state within the land of Israel, and it won't arise. The way to solve the problem of the Arabs and the state of Israel is found in the Camp David agreements. We're obliged to fulfill them and convinced that they're the framework for a just and fair solution.

At ceremony marking the
beginning of his new four-year term
of office, Jerusalem, Dec. 22/
The New York Times,
12-23:(A)8.

Farouk Shareh
Foreign Minister of Syria

6

Any Lebanese national who believes that the Syrian presence in Lebanon is a foreign presence, harms Lebanon in the first place, and does not want to see a unified, sovereign and independent Lebanon.

September/
Los Angeles Times, 10-12:(I)6.

WHAT THEY SAID IN 1988

Ariel Sharon
*Former Minister of Defense
of Israel*

1

[Saying that, if he becomes the next Israeli Minister of Defense, he will be tough on anti-Israeli violence by Palestinians in the occupied territories]: [I feel] a moral duty to take over a matter I believe is in my ability to handle today in the best way and better than anyone else. My philosophy is, if it's a terrorist, kill him . . . It's incredible, this terrible weakness [Israel is now showing against the Palestinian violence]. Here we are allowing this terror for a whole year in Jerusalem. Stones thrown, petrol bombs. Can you imagine for one minute that in [the U.S.] capital, Washington, if cars and buses were attacked with petrol bombs and stones? It would be taken care of in one day, and everybody would understand.

*Interview/
The New York Times, 11-9:(A)8.*

Rashad Shawa
*Former Mayor of Israeli-
occupied Gaza*

2

[Anti-Israeli] riots [in Gaza] will resume. Maybe it will be next week, maybe next month, maybe in three months. And they will become more and more violent. Because most people here, and especially the youth, are desperate. They feel that they have nothing to lose.

Los Angeles Times, 1-3:(I)8.

George P. Shultz
*Secretary of State of the
United States*

3

[On Israeli criticism of a U.S. vote in the UN opposing Israel's deportation of some Palestinians involved in anti-Israeli violence in the West Bank and Gaza]: Of course, we are upset with the violence in the West Bank and Gaza. [But] I think it's important for everyone to understand that the United States regards its friendship and the strength of its relationship with Israel as key and unshakable. No one should misinterpret a vote as meaning anything else. In fact, I suppose the ability to differ occasionally with a friend shows the depth of that friendship . . . Israel is a democratic country seeking stability and peace and the ability to pursue its destiny. And we support those objectives. And we work closely with Israel . . . Occasionally we disagree, but through all of that, this relationship, as I said, is unshakable—that's what that means.

*News conference, Jan. 7/
The Washington Post, 1-8:(A)14.*

4

[On his forthcoming trip to the Middle East to try to help end the violent anti-Israeli turmoil in Israeli-occupied Arab territories]: It's going to be tough. I don't think many people give me much chance, and that's the drift of their questions everywhere: intense skepticism. [But] I believe that if there are chances, even if the chances are small, it's worthwhile trying. You can't be too afraid of failing. Suppose I go and don't succeed? What am I saving myself for? So we'll try, and people want to have the U.S. come, and maybe we'll get somewhere.

*News conference,
Brussels, Feb. 23/
The Washington Post, 2-24:(A)20.*

5

[On the anti-Israeli violence by Palestinians in the West Bank and Gaza]: As I have read the intelligence, there are various opinions about the unrest, and I think its fundamental origins are essentially indigenous. But there has also been interaction with outside forces, and that's developed over a period of time. But there is an underlying problem consisting of a large number of people in an occupied area who don't have the basic rights of governance. And so we seek, among other things, consistent with Israel's security, to look at things that will help Palestinians gain legitimate rights.

*To reporters enroute to Israel,
Feb. 25/
The New York Times, 2-26:5.*

(GEORGE P. SHULTZ)

1

Israel needs to focus on the fact that there is a very large, clearly ticking demographic time bomb—many, many [Arabs] who are disenfranchised and who are there [in the West Bank and Gaza]. And in some manner or another, that problem must be dealt with; it cannot be ignored. Moves toward peace that will grapple with that problem successfully are very important . . . There is no doubt that we live now in the world of the missile. And missiles that go further and further and are more and more accurate are becoming more and more common. Security [for Israel], of course, will always have to reflect defensible borders and arrangements of that kind. But when somebody who's a long way away from you can inflict very, very damaging blows, then your concept of defense has to be different, and I think, fundamentally, that concept has to be one of seeking peace in the neighborhood.

Before House Foreign Operations
Subcommittee,
Washington, March 10/
The New York Times, 3-11:1.

2

The fate of Zionism and Palestinian nationalism are interdependent, although many on both sides refuse to recognize this. Arabs and Israelis are not engaged in a winner-take-all competition. A fair settlement is possible even though people have difficulty conceiving how to achieve it.

Cairo, June 3/
Los Angeles Times, 6-4:(I)3.

3

[On why the U.S. has resisted moving its Embassy from Tel Aviv to Jerusalem, which Israel considers its capital]: Our view is that Jerusalem must remain a unified city . . . but that its status remains subject to negotiations. I have no doubt that the capital of Israel will stay there, will be a unified city, and so on. But in the meantime, if you want to proceed with negotiations [with the Arabs], you don't wind up, in effect, declaring an outcome that hasn't been agreed to yet.

Broadcast interview, Madrid/
"Today," NBC-TV, 6-10.

4

[On the U.S. military intervention in the Persian Gulf to protect shipping there during the current Iran-Iraq war]: The increase in our [naval] presence took place in response to problems. If the problems go away, the ship presence will go down. [But] we'll be there as long as it takes to serve the peaceful and proper mission that we undertook.

To reporters, Tokyo, July 19/
The Christian Science Monitor,
7-20:9.

5

[Expressing concern that advanced weaponry is being introduced into the Middle East]: As we can see in the [Persian] Gulf war [between Iran and Iraq], less-developed countries fighting age-old battles on religious, ethnic or political grounds have ready access to such highly destructive armaments. And it is ironic that just as the major powers are making progress in getting their arms competition under some control, the developing world is increasingly burdened by this flow of advanced weaponry.

Speech, China, July/
Los Angeles Times, 7-31:(I)1.

6

[Jordan's King Hussein] has to be a partner [in future peace talks with Israel, because] Jordan has the longest border with Israel of any Arab state. [So] if there is going to be peace between Israel and its neighbors, then Jordan is involved . . . The PLO, if it wants to be a partner in the peace process, has to change its ways . . . We need to keep the pressure on the PLO to recognize that Israel is there, Israel is going to stay there. It's a fact of life. And they might as well accept that fact.

Broadcast interview/
"Face the Nation," CBS-TV, 7-31.

(GEORGE P. SHULTZ)

1

[Arab-Israeli] peace cannot be achieved through creation of an independent Palestinian state or through permanent Israeli control or annexation of the West Bank and Gaza . . . The status of the West Bank and Gaza cannot be determined by unilateral acts of both sides, but only through a process of negotiations. A declaration of independent Palestinian statehood or government-in-exile would be such a unilateral act . . . The United States cannot accept "self-determination" when it is a code word for an independent Palestinian state. [However,] Israel must find a way to respond to expressions of Palestinian grievances. It cannot claim there is no one to talk to while suppressing political expression and arresting or deporting those who speak out—even those who speak in moderate terms.

At conference sponsored by
Washington Institute for Near East
Policy, Queenstown, Md., Sept. 16/
The Washington Post, 9-17:(A)19.

2

[Saying his decision not to grant PLO leader Yasir Arafat a U.S. visa that would allow him to speak at the UN was based on the PLO's involvement in terrorism]: If the thing I am remembered for most of all is a strong and great resolve to resist and combat terrorism, I won't feel that's a blot on my record. I'll feel that is a proud accomplishment . . . In the case of Mr. Arafat, he's the [PLO's] chairman; he must know about the [terrorist] activities of these people, and his organization must give them sustenance and support. So he condones it; he is an accessory. And therefore we connect him with these acts. I feel that the [world-wide] negative reaction to the [no-visa] decision that I made on behalf of the United States only highlights the fact that people tend to forget too quickly the horrors and difficulties and threat of terrorism. It's something we must keep very high on our agenda or civilization will go down the drain.

Interview, Nov. 30/
The Washington Post, 12-1:(A)59.

3

[On his decision not to grant a U.S. visa to PLO leader Yasir Arafat that would allow him to speak at the UN]: We carefully preserved our right to exclude people who we think threaten the security interests of the United States. There is a law in the United States that finds the PLO to be a terrorist organization and denies visas to members of the PLO. Do we have the right to exclude anybody that the UN invites? The answer to that is, clearly, yes, we do. And then, second, within the scope of that reservation, given our law, was it proper to exclude Arafat on the grounds of terrorism and terrorism's relationship to our security? And I think the answer to that is yes.

Broadcast interview/
"This Week With David Brinkley,"
ABC-TV, 12-4.

4

[The U.S. has had] for a long time certain set things that we have said must be said by the PLO, positions they need to adopt if we are to have substantive dialogue with them. And they're well known. It is the acceptance of UN Resolutions 242 and 338 as a basis for negotiations of Mideast peace. Number 2, recognition of Israel's right to exist. And Number 3, their denunciation of terrorism and all its forms, and they pledge not to engage in it. Those are the things that we have insisted on. And it is our view that they need to be said directly, not inferentially, not conditioned . . . If they meet these conditions, then we're prepared for a substantive dialogue [with the PLO]. We've said that. We'll continue to say that. That's our position.

News conference,
New York, Dec. 7/
The New York Times, 12-8:(A)12.

5

The Palestine Liberation Organization today issued a statement in which it accepted UN Security Council Resolutions 242 and 338, recognized Israel's right to exist in peace and security, and renounced terrorism. As a result, the United States is prepared for a substantive

(GEORGE P. SHULTZ)

dialogue with PLO representatives . . . Nothing here may be taken to imply an acceptance or recognition by the United States of an independent Palestinian state. The position of the U.S. is that the status of the West Bank and Gaza cannot be determined by unilateral acts of either side, but only through a process of negotiations. The United States does not recognize the declaration of an independent Palestinian state. It is also important to emphasize that the United States commitment to the security of Israel remains unflinching . . . I'm only saying that for the period since 1975, the U.S. has had a position in effect that if the PLO meets these conditions we will have a substantive dialogue, and since they have met the conditions, we are carrying through on our policy. And that's the sum and substance of it.

News conference,
Washington, Dec. 14/
The New York Times, 12-15:(A)6.

David Sidorsky
Professor of philosophy,
Columbia University

1

The Israeli model is that there is one Jewish nation scattered around the world and the Jews of Israel are the vanguard. Elsewhere is the periphery, the rear guard. The frontline does the fighting and the periphery pays the bills, provides the support. And this is something the American Jewish community can't accept.

At American Jewish Congress
conference/The Washington Post,
12-12:(A)19.

Henry Siegman
Executive director,
American Jewish Congress

2

[On the current anti-Israeli violence by Palestinians in the West Bank and Gaza]: We have urged Israel to find a political way of ending its control over a million and a half resentful Arabs.

We believe Israel ought to do that as a favor to itself. Because the current situation, for demographic reasons alone, will cause Israel endless grief.

Interview/USA Today, 1-5:(A)9.

Lawrence J. Smith
United States Representative,
D-Florida

3

[Criticizing U.S. arms sales to various Middle Eastern countries]: I am absolutely frustrated and amazed at this [U.S. Reagan] Administration's desire to arm the entire Middle East to the teeth. It's another example of how our government uses arms sales as a substitute for diplomacy.

Interview/
The New York Times,
5-13:5.

Arlen Specter
United States Senator,
R-Pennsylvania

4

[On his meeting in January with Syrian President Hafez al-Assad]: I'd met with [Syrian Foreign Minister Farouk] Sharah before, and there was fire in his eyes. That was in 1984, and he clearly wanted Israel at the bottom of the Mediterranean, and me along with her. This time, though, it was all very cordial, and Assad expressed his readiness to talk, for three reasons: His economy is in terrible shape; he doesn't want [Egyptian President Hosni] Mubarak to become the dominant Arab leader in the region as [the late Egyptian President Anwar] Sadat was before him, and the Soviets are being even tougher on Assad than we knew from the press accounts of [Soviet leader Mikhail] Gorbachev's rebuff of him in Moscow last April. I'm still skeptical, but maybe something positive will come if the Israelis can get their act together.

U.S. News & World Report,
3-14:14.

Howard Squadron
Honorary president,
American Jewish Congress

1

A strong Israel was supposed to be the answer to anti-Semitism in the world. Instead, there are times when it has become the cause.

At American Jewish Congress
conference/The Washington Post,
12-12:(A)19.

I. F. Stone
American journalist and
political analyst

2

You cannot in the 20th century deny the Palestinian Arabs the right to self-determination. That's unjust. You can't have peace [between the Palestinians and Israel] without a modicum of justice. If there is a moral ground for a Jewish state in what was Palestine, there's an equal moral ground for an Arab state in Palestine if the Palestinian Arabs want it. I think the Jewish soul is at stake. [For Israel] to hold the Arabs [in Israeli-occupied Arab territories] in a kind of bondage, to deny them their rights, to push down their living standards and then to use them as cheap labor in the Jewish cities, that's terrible, that's poison, and it undermines the moral foundations of the Jewish state and of everything that the Jews of the Diaspora depend on.

Interview, Washington/
The Washington Post, 3-10:(C)2.

John H. Sununu
Governor of New Hampshire (R);
Chief of Staff-designate to
President-elect of the United
States George Bush

3

[On his 1986 refusal to sign a document condemning the UN's 1975 resolution equating Zionism with racism]: I have no problem in stating rather clearly that the key to tranquility and peace in the Middle East—one of the keys—is the assurance of the integrity and protection of

the state of Israel—Zionism that promotes that I have no problem with.

Concord, N.H., Nov. 16/
The Washington Post, 11-17:(A)22.

Avraham Tamir
Director General, Foreign
Ministry of Israel

4

Everyone knows that the PLO is, for the Palestinians, for the Palestinian people, their national organization. There is no replacement for them. So the question is not how to replace the PLO, but how to change it. Until now, they did not want to reach the right solutions which might enable them to participate in the peace process, because they don't want to split . . . Some people think that maybe we can wait and wait and wait till there will be a change in the Arab world, and they will crawl on their knees and be ready to accept a peace on the basis of our conditions. But as long as there is no peace process, the Palestinian uprising will continue.

Washington, Aug. 31/
The New York Times, 9-2:2.

Robert G. Torricelli
United States Representative,
D-New Jersey

5

[On polls that show Americans oppose U.S. compensation payments to Iran for the accidental downing of an Iranian passenger plane by a U.S. warship on patrol in the Persian Gulf]: The [U.S. Reagan] Administration clearly underestimated the depth of American antipathy toward Iran. Iran represents a challenge to most of the things that Americans think are special about our country; they question our values, our morals, what we represent in the world.

The New York Times, 7-18:12.

Vernon A. Walters
United States Ambassador/
Permanent Representative
to the United Nations

6

Israel must face up to the need for withdrawal from occupied territories and to the need to

(VERNON A. WALTERS)

accommodate legitimate Palestinian political rights. We must tell the parties [Israel and the Palestinians] that their dispute is resolvable. We must tell them that we are tired of this conflict and tired of their unwillingness to make fair compromises. We must tell them the time has come to agree that a negotiated settlement is required.

At United Nations, Geneva, Dec. 14/
Los Angeles Times, 12-15:(I)9.

Ezer Weizman
General, Israeli armed forces;
Former Minister of Defense
of Israel

1

We live in a particularly small area where a defense equation begins with political agreements. We would have much more land—the Sinai—if we didn't have a peace treaty with Egypt, but would we be more secure? Of course not. So the notion of trading land for peace *can* make us more secure if the peace that's made is the right one—and if we don't relax our strength. I'm like everyone else here—from dove to hawk. I know we're not loved. I know we continue to exist because of our power. And that's why the second political reason for us to compromise is so important. I need my F-16s [U.S.-built fighter planes] in reserve. To have that kind of backup and the economic assistance we need as well, and also to have a decent chance of denying our enemies a comparable military capability, I must retain the good-will of America, and others. So we must take into account the views of our friends. And their views—which happen in this instance to coincide with my own—demand that we compromise.

U.S. News & World Report, 4-4:35.

Paul Wilkinson
Specialist in terrorism,
department of international
affairs, University of Aberdeen
(Scotland)

2

[On Iranian involvement in international terrorism]: They have a lot of wild men. These are the people we really need to worry about, people who single-handedly hijack an aircraft with little hope of success. But they've been indoctrinated that to die in a *jihad* [holy war] means they will go to paradise. That's not something fanciful, as many Westerners believe. These people really believe it, and this attitude has to be understood more in the West if we're to be able to combat this kind of fanaticism. This poses a big threat to secular states that don't seem to understand the nature of the beast they're up against in what I believe is going to be a very difficult period. We should have taken effective steps to curb this long before now. Iran is not Libya. The Iranians have an intensity of revolutionary fervor that leaves the Libyans at the starting block. And, unlike Libya, Iran is a regional power that's playing for high stakes.

Los Angeles Times, 4-3:(I)5.

Zvi Yaacovson
Spokesman, Shas Party
of Israel

3

[On the Israeli-occupied territories of the West Bank and Gaza, where there has been anti-Israeli violence by Palestinians]: In Judaism, there is only one way, the Halacha [sacred Jewish law], which says sanctity of life before all else, before the territories. If it can prevent the death of one Jew to return the territories, they will be returned. But not if it will cause the death of two others.

The New York Times, 11-8:(A)6.

James Zogby
Executive director, Arab-American Institute,
Washington

4

In the last 20 years, the majority of the world community has come to understand this Palestinian need [for their own state]. In the United Nations, the overwhelming majority of nations have to come to recognize that. It's only the United States government that has taken the side of Israel and has refused to accept the need to implement Palestinian rights in order to have a comprehensive peace in the Middle East.

Interview/USA Today, 1-5:(A)9.

WHAT THEY SAID IN 1988

Elmo R. Zumwalt, Jr.
Admiral (ret.), and former
Chief of Operations, United States
Navy

1

[On the accidental shooting down of an Iranian passenger plane by a U.S. warship on patrol in the Persian Gulf during the Iran-Iraq war]: The Persian Gulf is probably the worst place in the world for naval power to have to be used in a neither-war-nor-peace environment. If we were at war and could shoot anything that wasn't ours, it would be a piece of cake for this kind of technology. If we were at peace, obviously there would be no problem. But when you're put in there in a police role, with both commercial activity and war activity going on, you are at the maximum level of complexity for a human.

Interview/USA Today,
8-9:(A)11.

War and Peace

John Araka
Nigerian journalist

1

If we want to achieve peace in a nuclear age, the emphasis really should be on communication... As more and more nations acquire nuclear technology without necessarily improving their economic system, such countries can turn out to be very dangerous in the future—because, out of frustration, out of annoyance, they can press the button.

At Wingspread Conference,
Racine, Wis., April/
The Christian Science Monitor,
7-25:(B)9.

Oscar Arias
President of Costa Rica

2

Peace is a never-ending process, the work of many decisions by many people in many countries. It is an attitude, a way of life, a way of solving problems and resolving conflicts. It cannot be forced on the smallest nation or be enforced by the largest. It cannot ignore our differences or overlook our common interests. It requires us to work and live together.

At Harvard University
commencement/The Christian
Science Monitor, 7-27:26.

William J. Crowe, Jr.
Admiral, United States Navy;
Chairman, Joint Chiefs
of Staff

3

The intriguing thing about war is how many mistakes are made. My conclusion, from military history, is that successful generals are wrong 95 per cent of the time. For unsuccessful generals, it's 99 per cent. In the fog of war, there's so much uncertainty ... The canvas [of battle] has greatly expanded. It involves the whole globe, including the sea depths and a large chunk of space. Weaponry has expanded the scale of destructiveness. But the uncertainty of war has not disappeared, and the tendency for things to go wrong has increased. Battles are still fought by people, and their state of mind will still influence the outcome more than weapons.

Interview/Time, 12-26:74.

Miguel de la Madrid
President of Mexico

4

[I] believe that there is already a logical, a real need to avoid the grave economic waste represented by the arms race. It is not just the danger of the disappearance of life, a fact which of itself supports disarmament, but also the argument of the world economy and the argument of peace. We cannot continue to advance in a world in which economic differences are so large. The industrialized countries cannot live in security in such a world.

Interview, Mexico City, Feb. 2/
The New York Times, 2-5:5.

Edward Luttwak
Authority on war and
military affairs, Center for
Strategic and International
Studies, Georgetown University

5

What everybody agrees on is that war has become absurd on the human plane. To think about war is therefore to be deliberately engaged in talking about the absurd. For myself, I know only one thing. That is, precisely when everybody agrees that war is absurd, that is when people do not make the sacrifices necessary to avoid it, either by strong armament or by being willing to make political concessions. It is precisely then that war becomes feasible.

Interview/
American Heritage, July-Aug.:78.

Robert S. McNamara
Former Secretary of Defense
of the United States

1

No well-informed, coolly rational political or military leader is likely to use nuclear weapons. But leaders, in moments of severe crisis, are likely to be neither well informed nor coolly rational.

USA Today, 2-2:(A)12.

2

[Non-aligned nations should be saying to the U.S. and Soviet governments,] "If you ever carry out your NATO and Warsaw Pact strategy, you're going to destroy yourselves. Up until recently, we thought if you were stupid enough to pursue [such] a strategy, that was your problem. [But now] we are learning that through climatic conditions you will destroy *us*. We will not tolerate that. We wish you to present to us a verifiable agreement that—starting next year or certainly in the 21st century—you will no longer put our nations at risk. It's immoral. It's illegal. We won't tolerate it."

At Wingspread Conference,
Racine, Wis., April/
The Christian Science Monitor,
7-25:(B)9.

Benjamin Netanyahu
Former Israeli Ambassador
to the United Nations

3

[Discussing the effect of TV news coverage on modern warfare]: Most modern wars of democracies are fought not only on the ground, but also in the living rooms of the Western democracies, starting with the United States.

USA Today, 4-1:(A)10.

Miguel Obando y Bravo
Roman Catholic Archbishop
of Managua, Nicaragua

4

Peace means not only the absence of war and end to battles, but also fraternity and well-being.

At Mass, Managua, March 27/
The New York Times, 3-28:4

Javier Perez de Cuellar
Secretary General of the
United Nations

5

[On the UN's peace-keeping troops]: Never before in history have military forces been employed internationally not to wage war, not to establish domination and not to serve the interests of any power or group of powers, but rather to prevent conflict between peoples . . . Collective responsibility for peace can be evolved in a truly representative international system.

Accepting Nobel Peace Prize,
Oslo, Dec. 10/
The Christian Science Monitor,
12-12:6.

Ronald Reagan
President of the
United States

6

True peace means not only preventing a big war but ending smaller ones as well.

Broadcast address to Soviet
people, Jan. 1/
The Washington Post, 1-2:(A)1.

Margaret Thatcher
Prime Minister of the
United Kingdom

7

If there were an absence of arms, you would have cause to be alarmed. The presence of arms . . . is reassuring, because it means we are prepared to defend what we believe in. It was [Romanian President Nicolae] Ceaucescu who said to me years ago, "Don't you think it is very alarming if you are talking to a person and you notice he has a gun in his luggage?" I said: "No. I don't find it alarming at all, because if I talk to certain people, I would want a gun in *my* luggage as well. Then neither would go off."

Interview/
U.S. News & World Report,
12-19:19.

William H. Webster
Director of Central
Intelligence of the
United States

1

[On alleged use of chemical weapons in the recent Iran-Iraq war]: During World War II, even during the most desperate battles, both sides refrained from using chemical weapons, weapons that Winston Churchill referred to as "that hellish poison." The Iran-Iraq war ended that restraint and set a dangerous precedent for future wars. These weapons are thought to offer a cheap and readily obtainable means of redressing the military balance against more powerful foes.

Before World Affairs Council,
Washington, Oct. 25/
The New York Times, 10-27:(A)6.

Aleksandr N. Yakovlev
Member, Politburo,
Communist Party of
the Soviet Union; Adviser to
Soviet leader Mikhail
Gorbachev

2

. . . in my opinion, people are tired of confrontation. The policy of force is out of fashion these days. Arms will soon become as common a word as ecology. People will struggle against arms as against environmental pollution. This is the way it is. And not only nuclear arms. Nuclear arms are direct environmental pollution. Only police weapons must remain on the earth as long as crimes exist.

Interview, Moscow, Oct. 26/
The New York Times, 10-28:(A)6.

PART THREE

General

The Arts

Alvin Ailey
Choreographer

1

[On the annual U.S. government-sponsored Kennedy Center Honors]: I'm very glad that the arts are still being celebrated yearly by these higher-ups who seem to care on one level but, on the other hand, don't seem to care so much when it comes to [Federal arts-] budget slashing. We've all had to suffer with that part of the arts. So I hope that the new Administration will be more sensitive to the needs of the country's artists.

Interview, New York/
The Christian Science Monitor,
12-5:22.

Pedro Almodovar
Spanish motion-picture
director

2

Censorship is always very irrational. It forces you as an artist to say things between the lines, because you never know what disturbs the censor or whether they understand the implications of it. After a while, you become so oblique that it becomes a style in itself.

Interview, Los Angeles/
Los Angeles Times, 12-20:(VI)8.

Stephanie Barron
Curator, Los Angeles County
Museum of Art

3

It is unfair to expect the public in all cases to understand why a thing is hanging in a museum. Making art accessible and interesting to the public is the responsibility of the curator. We have to provide a context and an explanation.

Interview/Los Angeles Times,
12-25:(Calendar)5.

Robert L. Burns
Dean, College of Arts and
Sciences, Washburn University

4

In an urban university, the arts are especially important—not only to the quality of cultural life in the entire community we serve, but to its economic life as well. Too often, the arts are seen merely as "extras." We are blessed here with people who don't see it that way.

Interview, Topeka, Kan./
Horizon, Jan.-Feb.:49.

Sarah Caldwell
Artistic director,
Opera Company of Boston

5

[Applauding increased U.S.-Soviet cultural exchanges]: It's tremendously exciting and tremendously important for us to be speaking with each other. We're so ignorant of the Soviets and they're so ignorant of us, there is just a frightful lack of knowledge on both sides. This extends not only to music but to life-styles and what we believe. We are just beginning to try to understand one another.

The New York Times,
2-17:17.

Francis Ford Coppola
Motion-picture director

6

. . . creative people should never give up. They can't give up. The society needs them . . . Creative people are seen as dangerous. And expensive. The question now is, "How cheap can you get them?" and it's asked by executives whose salaries are astronomical.

Interview,
Rutherford, Calif./
Los Angeles Times,
8-7:(Calendar)4.

399

Dennis Russell Davies
Music director of Bonn, West
Germany; Former music
director, Stuttgart Opera

1

You may have a problem initially with funding [for the arts] until people see that it works, but those are hardly reasons not to make art. Those are obscene reasons for not doing something. People who run major arts organizations are supposed to have a passionate commitment to the art. That's what I find scandalous—the careful, fearful approach to doing something. I make music that I'm passionately involved in doing and eager to play, whether it's *Tristan Und Isolde* or Phillip Glass's *Aknahten*. Artist, conductor, performer, singer—you're supposed to be putting yourself on the line. And if you find yourself in a position of authority and responsibility, then you have the authority and responsibility to do something about these ideas you're supposed to be committed to.

Interview/
The Wall Street Journal,
1-12:26.

Margaret DeMott
Director of programs,
Durham (N.C.) Arts Council

2

[On public—outdoor—art]: One of the important things about public art is that you don't go around imitating other places. You can learn a lot by looking at what other people do and what procedures they use, but it's a fatal error to say, "There's a Calder in downtown Minneapolis; we'll do something just like that," because public art has got to respond to the community. So it is important to say, "What is special about the Southeast? As a region, what elements do we have that are different from what's happening elsewhere across the country?" Public art is not a closed-in definition. It is a wide-open definition, and it's not prescriptive. We're still figuring it out and we should always be figuring it out.

Interview/
Horizon, September:59.

Helen Frankenthaler
Artist

3

The nature of my work is such that I must often be alone—in body, mind and spirit. The making of it is, literally, physically, with my hands and head. No one can fill in lines for me. No one can decide on colors. The preparation for this requires a certain amount of anxiety, boredom, research—by which I mean that I need to look around, whether at a contemporary piece, a painting by an Old Master, or landscapes. I follow my own rhythms. It's very important to me to be in a cocoon of sorts before I fly into the studio and make something. I might be in a pencil-sharpening mood, or in a mood to listen to Vivaldi or Sinatra, or look at reproductions of paintings, or cook, or walk. Whatever it is, it's *my* mood, and I'm on my own . . . You can't fake art. Real art doesn't lie. You know it when you see it or feel it or hear it. And that's the relief and the beauty and the pain of truth. And it's being yourself.

Interview/Lear's, Nov.-Dec.:32,34.

Jack Golodner
Director, department for
professional employees,
American Federation of
Labor-Congress of Industrial
Organizations

4

Anybody who is in the creative arts today feels threatened by the ease with which their work can be copied or exploited without their knowledge or compensation. Musicians, actors, artists, filmmakers, photographers—they all say the same thing: "A lot of people are making money from my labor."

The New York Times, 3-3:20.

Daniel Hechter
Fashion designer

5

When I started in the 1960s, I felt that fashion should be for everyone, not just for the privileged. *Haute couture* is concerned with maybe 1,000 or

(DANIEL HECHTER)

1,500 people worldwide ... Fashion speaks an international language, just as sports have an international language. But there is something in Paris that does not exist anywhere else. One can find inspiration in many places, but it is in Paris where inspiration is realized.

World Press Review, March:52.

Frank Hodsoll
*Chairman, National
Endowment for the Arts of
the United States*

1

Like other school subjects, the arts must be taught sequentially and to all students, not just the especially talented. Do we teach math only to those students who are good at it? ... While 15 per cent of the elementary-school day is devoted to the arts, it is likely taught by general classroom teachers who lack relevant training in the arts. [And] although 17 per cent of the junior high/middle school day is occupied by the arts, it is likely focused on creation and performance, with no attempt to impart historical or aesthetic context. It is almost entirely confined to visual art and music, with very little dance or drama and no attention to the design or media arts ... As we move in the weeks, months, years and even decades ahead, toward making the arts as basic in our schools as the three Rs ... we will be counting on the voices of the American people to join us in one loud chorus for arts education.

*News conference,
Washington, May 3/
Los Angeles Times, 5-4:(VI)1,8.*

2

[Criticizing the state of arts education in the U.S.]: We think that cultural literacy is at stake. We have found that the arts are in triple jeopardy: They are not viewed as serious; knowledge itself is not viewed as a prime educational objective, and those who determine school curricula do not agree on what arts education is.

*May 3/The Washington Post,
5-4:(A)3.*

Wolf Kahn
Painter

3

[As a painter,] I never tried to find a way of my own; I never *tried* to be original. I was never afraid to be influenced by, and to steal from, anybody whose work I was fond of. I still do. A lot of times I see somebody who's younger than I and I steal from him or her, because I think there's something worth appropriating. That's how a culture is formed, by people stealing from each other. No disgrace in it. The disgrace, I think, lies in this frantic search for originality, which is apt to bring forth abominations.

*Interview, Brattleboro, Vt./
The Christian Science Monitor,
12-12:30.*

4

Van Gogh saw colors, undoubtedly, that no one else saw. It didn't take the rest of the world very long to catch up to him, however. Now, everybody sees colors the way he did. He saw the landscape sort of rippling across in ribbons, and it didn't take very long for everyone to be aware that the landscape was composed of rippling ribbons. I think the artist focuses things for people.

*Interview, Brattleboro, Vt./
The Christian Science Monitor,
12-12:30.*

Elia Kazan
Motion-picture director

5

In the end, the best art, even in a form that's collaborative, requires one guy with an insistent vision. It may be the director, or it can be the writer or producer. But if a work doesn't follow one person's vision, it'll be wishy-washy mush. There'll be a softness in its core. Some guy has got to stand up and say, "This is the way this is going to be," and make it like that.

*Interview/
U.S. News & World Report,
6-6:55.*

Andrew Kramer
Architectural photographer

1

We are profoundly influenced by our physical environment. Well-designed architecture moves us beyond the immediate experience of the environment itself to other dimensions of response. Like any good work of art, good architecture has an intangible quality of abstraction which takes us to higher and deeper levels of awareness—both conscious and unconscious.

Interview/Horizon, July-Aug.:22.

Hilton Kramer
Editor, "New Criterion"
magazine

2

[On increased U.S.-Soviet cultural exchanges]: I don't approve of it. It reminds us of what short political memories American artists and cultural bureaucrats have. They can so easily put aside the history of suffering that artists and ordinary citizens have endured and continue to endure in the Soviet Union. I think it's deplorable that just out of pure self-interest these exchanges are so hotly pursued.

The New York Times, 2-17:17.

Jack Lang
Minister of Culture and
Communication of France

3

In my little life I have encountered many controversies . . . I like this atmosphere of controversy. The worst thing is when art creates only indifference. When you have struggles, it is perhaps a sign that art is living.

Interview, Paris/
The New York Times, 7-26:16.

George Lucas
Motion-picture director

4

Art is the retelling of certain themes in a new light, making them accessible to the public of the moment.

Interview, Nicasio, Calif./
The New York Times, 6-9:17.

Robert MacNeil
Co-anchor, "MacNeil-Lehrer
NewsHour," PBS-TV

5

It matters that [a Presidential candidate] at least have encountered some of the monuments of our spiritual culture. Has he taken the time to develop his own soul? Has he had a liberal-arts education—either from his schooling or through his own encounters with some of the great works of the culture? It's a hard question [for a candidate] to say "No" to—to say, "No, it doesn't matter" . . . Maybe it's part of the American machismo that big men who want to be tough don't want to admit they go to the ballet. They'd much rather say they went to the Super Bowl.

The Christian Science Monitor,
4-1:16,17.

Samuel C. Miller
Director, Newark (N.J.)
Museum

6

The Newark Museum was founded in 1909 by John Cotton Dana, a social activist. Dana thought a museum should be a teaching institution and a mini-Smithsonian which would embrace all aspects of culture. We are still very much guided by that philosophy. What makes this museum really special is our belief that art should be relevant, lead to questioning and thus promote learning, as Dana said. You see that in the fact that this museum started collecting African art back in the teens of this century. We had the first show of black art in 1931.

Interview, Newark/
The New York Times, 12-13:(B)2.

Bruce Nauman
Artist

7

There is a tendency [in art] to clutter things up, to try to make sure people know something is art, when all that's necessary is to present it, to leave it alone. I think the hardest thing to do is to present an idea in the most straightforward way. What I tend to do is see something, then re-make

(BRUCE NAUMAN)

it and re-make it and re-make it and try every possible way of re-making it. If I'm persistent enough, I get back to where I started. I think it was Jasper Johns who said, "Sometimes it's necessary to state the obvious."

Interview/
Art in America, September:142.

Yuri Norstein
Soviet animated-film maker

1

What is art except the ideal to which we're aspiring, which we cannot achieve in real life? When this happens, when art tends to express the ideals and the path toward this ideal, then it has real authenticity and meaning.

Interview, Washington/
The Washington Post, 4-30:(C)13.

Randy Ray
Director, Kentucky
Derby Museum

2

Fine art is a medium that transcends language. This museum has as its mission promoting and educating the public on thoroughbred racing and the thoroughbred industry. Art is a wonderful way to express that mission. We use art as a tool.

Interview/Horizon, May:24.

Ronald Reagan
President of the United States

3

In the last few years, freedom for the arts has been expanded in the Soviet Union. Some poems, books, music and works in other fields that were once banned, have been made available to the public, and some of those artists who produced them have been recognized. We in the United States applaud the new thaw in the arts. We hope to see it go further. We want this not just for your sake, but for our own. We believe that the greater the freedoms in other countries, the more secure both our own freedoms and peace. And we believe that when the arts in any country are free to blossom, the lives of all people are richer.

At House of Writers,
Moscow, May 31/
Los Angeles Times, 6-1:(I)14.

Robert Redford
Actor

4

[On whether he could have "made it" as an artist]: You have to define what you mean by "make it." Do I think I could have become world renowned? I have no idea. Could I have made it in the sense that I could have made a living and been happy with what I was doing and who I was? Yes. But look at what art means: In many cases an artist has to wait a hundred years before somebody decides that he had talent. What do you do in the meantime? Cut off your ear? If I didn't think I could've made it as an artist, I wouldn't be so uneasy about being an actor.

Interview/Esquire, March:120.

Ned Rorem
Composer

5

An artist retains that which only children have—except that an artist is an improvement on a child. A child might have a vast imagination, but he has little sense of form. And art is nothing if not imagination snared.

Interview/Opera News, October:70.

Arthur M. Schlesinger, Jr.
Historian;
Professor of humanities,
City University of New York

6

We've [the U.S.] had nearly a quarter of a century of experience with public [government] support of the arts. I think an unnoticed revolution has taken place in these years, in which the endowments have become solidly established as national policy. The reason this has been so is that it represents a national consensus.

Interview, New York/
The New York Times, 4-14:22.

Vincent Scully
Architectural historian,
Yale University

1

In 1963, [author Norman] Mailer described modern architecture as "creating the empty landscapes of psychosis." It's an exact, precise description, one of the best things said about architecture in the 20th century. What I like about Mailer is that he always tries to have a dialogue, he always tries to liberate from stereotypical thinking, And that's what we need—that's fundamental.

Interview/
Publishers Weekly, 9-30:48.

Martin Segal
Founder, International
Festival of the Arts,
New York; Former director,
Lincoln Center for the
Performing Arts, New York

2

You hear so much about the problems of the world. And here we are right in the middle of a period where some of the most creative and beautiful works have been done by people from different countries and enjoyed by different countries. I believe the arts and cultural exchange is a great force for peace and understanding, because people don't come to concert halls with machine guns, or with spears and animosity. They come to share each other's creativity. That's the way the world should function, in my opinion.

Interview, New York/
The Christian Science Monitor,
6-9:22.

Peter Sellars
Stage director

3

Our audiences have been so mistreated. They have been desensitized. They have been fed a sanitized concept of culture. Everything, we are told, has to be the smoothest, the silkiest, the creamiest ... I value art that is hard to look at. Events can shift in time and dimension. Deep emotional colors are crucial. I don't want people to just come and sit and clap. I want to return genuine friction to the cultural arena.

Interview, Chicago/
Los Angeles Times,
10-23:(Calendar)64.

Alan Shestack
Director, Museum of Fine Arts,
Boston

4

Museums have become part of the entertainment industry, and to some extent are in competition with movies, television, professional sports, theatre and music for a share of leisure-time attention and leisure-time dollars. And this is where the strain comes. We are still trying to collect the best art, provide art research, and stay at the cutting-edge of conservation.

Interview, Boston/
The Christian Science Monitor,
1-11:20.

Hugh Sidey
Washington correspondent,
"Time" magazine

5

If you look at the current crop [of candidates for the 1988 Presidential election], you see that the profile of their lives is just grubbing for power. A President needs some sense of why people respond in certain ways: their joys, hopes, sorrows. I think [a knowledge of] art defines that for us in very basic ways.

The Christian Science Monitor,
4-1:16.

Roger L. Stevens
Chairman, Kennedy Center
for the Performing Arts,
Washington

6

[On his heading the Kennedy Center]: A quarter of the time I have big hits; a quarter of the time artistic successes; a quarter of the time the critics were crazy; and a quarter of the time I was crazy. It figures out pretty well that way.

The Washington Post, 1-15:(B)3.

Giuseppe Taddei
Opera singer

1

Don't be in a hurry to succeed. An artist needs the experience of maturity. In life, many sufferings and sacrifices happen on the way. If you get your satisfaction too soon, they will vanish too soon. The first disillusion after the first success is the most painful.

Interview, New York/
Opera News, 2-13:11.

John Wilmerding
Deputy director, National
Gallery of Art, Washington

2

If there is anything that I think is important, it's that the work of art and the ideas about the work have to be brought together. You have to be able to appreciate an object on its own, as a thing of beauty, but also as possessing and carrying ideas.

Interview, Feb. 21/
The New York Times, 2-22:9.

Journalism

Bruce Babbitt
Former Governor of Arizona (D);
Former candidate for the
1988 Democratic
Presidential Nomination

1

[For those] who worry that the press is a giant conspiracy that controls politics: You have nothing to fear. The press has little or no influence.

USA Today, 4-27:(A)4.

Conrad M. Black
Canadian press executive

2

The power of the press has been a hackneyed theme for many decades, but it has been given a new twist by the abdication of many publishers, and even many editors, from their former operating pre-eminence in favor of the individual journalists. There has been a general decline in the editorial role of the media proprietor and executive. With the rise of the newspaper chain, and the heavy emphasis on commercial aspects of the newspaper business, the publisher has often become a local purser and paymaster, answerable to his absentee owner on economic matters.

Speech, April 20/
The Wall Street Journal, 7-19:22

Daniel Brenner
Director, communications
law program, University of
California, Los Angeles;
Former senior legal advisor
to former Federal
Communications Commission Chairman
Mark Fowler

3

ABC News Nightline is an example of market forces at work. It is on the air because it is economically successful. [Similarly,] some day it may be written that the most important thing in

the history of broadcast news was Cable News Network. It, too, was market-driven, and obviously the public benefited from this.

Emmy Magazine, Jan.-Feb.:41.

David Brinkley
Commentator, ABC News

4

The Washington press corps [today] is quite different from what it was then [in the 1930s and '40s]—because the world is different. Until sometime in the 1930s, the newspapers had a monopoly. Radio was new and unimportant. The newsmagazine was just being invented. Television, of course, did not exist. So the newspapers owned journalism, and there were relatively few of us in the press corps. When I covered the White House in the '40s, there would be only about 20 or 25 of us standing in a semicircle around [President] Roosevelt's desk, holding our pads and pencils and asking questions. We went to him. He didn't go into the East Room; he didn't go anywhere. It was rather informal. Now a newspaper, to be self-respecting, feels it must have a Washington bureau—so do a lot of television and radio stations. Today there's a press corps of about 3,000.

Interview/
U.S. News & World Report,
4-25:(57).

Rosalynn Carter
Wife of former President
of the United States
Jimmy Carter

5

I think there has to be a very careful balance between what the press reports about somebody and what shouldn't be reported, because certain things tell a good bit about character. But then, where do you stop? The press needs to impose some voluntary standards. In the Gary Hart situation [in which the press exposed an alleged

(ROSALYNN CARTER)

extramarital affair of that Presidential candidate], there was as much written about how the press handled that as there was about the incident.

Interview, L. B. J. Ranch, Texas/
Good Housekeeping, February:172.

Edward Cony
Associate editor, "The Wall Street Journal"

1

I think investigative reporting is important, but there are some editors who don't agree. The Associated Press Managing Editors association asked journalists about the importance of investigative reporting, and 2 per cent to 3 per cent said they didn't think it was important. My feeling is that maybe those people should leave the occupation and go somewhere else.

Interview/USA Today, 4-13:(A)9.

Alistair Cooke
Journalist, Commentator

2

I think I've lasted because I found out that what people really wanted to know was anything that you notice in life, and especially things that touch everybody, touch a bishop and a farmer. That's become the thing I love more than television, more than print—to write for talking. Ideally, you would like to talk like the first chapter of Genesis, or John Bunyan or Defoe— the language that anyone can understand. It's not easy, because you're disciplining your imagination every step of the way.

Interview, San Francisco/
The New York Times, 11-19:12.

Christine Craft
Broadcast journalist

3

There are a number of people who do [TV] news who are both attractive and bright. But there are an awful lot of people who are beautiful and stupid who are getting anchor credibility, who don't know what it is they're talking about.

Interview/USA Today, 2-9:(A)11.

Mario M. Cuomo
Governor of New York (D)

4

[On persistent news stories that he wants the 1988 Democratic Presidential nomination, even though he has consistently denied it]: I wish somebody sometime would write a piece that says, "Let's face it, he was telling the truth." Nobody has . . . You've [the news media] done everything but call me a liar. You said that I was cute. You said that I misplayed the game. You said that I was really waiting for another scenario . . . It really comes down to my credibility or yours. What you're really saying is, "I want to tell you privately that I was wrong, but I won't say it publicly because that would cost me credibility." Well, the net result of that is it costs *me* credibility because you spent all those months saying I was conning people. All through my career I have made promises and lived up to them. I told you in '84 [that he wasn't running], I told you in '86, I told you in '87. And you guys then do columns that say, "What did he really intend? Did he have a Mafia background? Did he have skeletons in his closet? Did his son get involved? Did he think he couldn't win?" Why don't you just write the truth? . . . What you're really saying is, "He's supposed to run. He doesn't have the right to say, 'I'm not going to be a candidate.' We have a political expectation of him . . . We're going to assume that he has some undisclosed motivation." Who *are* you people to suggest that? I think that it is the height of arrogance, and I think you people do it over and over, and so far none of you has admitted it.

Interview, New York/
The Washington Post, 6-29:(D)6.

Robert J. Dole
United States Senator,
R-Kansas; Former
candidate for the 1988
Republican Presidential
nomination

5

Look in the newsrooms. Let's face it—they tend to be liberal. In my judgment, reporters try to be objective. But try as they do, they just can't

(ROBERT J. DOLE)

help but see the world through liberal-colored glasses.

Before the Senate,
Washington, April 26/
The New York Times, 4-27:12.

Jerry Falwell
Evangelist

1

[Criticizing a Supreme Court ruling upholding the right of Larry Flynt's *Hustler* magazine to parody public figures such as Falwell]: I fully appreciate the deep concerns the Court has shown for the sacredness of the First Amendment. However, I respectfully disagree with their ruling. Just as no person can scream "Fire!" in a crowded theatre when there is no fire, and find cover under the First Amendment, likewise, no sleaze merchant like Larry Flynt should be able to use the First Amendment as an excuse for maliciously and dishonestly attacking public figures as he has so often done. I believe the Supreme Court has given the green light to Larry Flynt and his ilk to print what they wish about any public figure at any time with no fear of reprisal.

Feb. 24/
The New York Times,
2-25:14.

Katherine Fanning
Editor, "The Christian Science Monitor"

2

More than half of all American newspapers— 55 per cent—still have no minorities on their staff. This is deplorable. And it is a weakness which must be corrected if we are to serve this country as we should.

At American Society of Newspaper
Editors convention, Washington/
The Christian Science Monitor,
4-15:5.

Gerald R. Ford
Former President of the United States

3

[On Presidential news conferences]: The fact is, anybody bright and experienced enough to be President can always dominate a news conference. After all, it is his house, and the media are his invited guests.

The Washington Post,
10-17:(A)13.

Mikhail S. Gorbachev
General Secretary, Communist Party of the Soviet Union

4

The Soviet press is not a private shop. Let us recall again Lenin's promise that literature is part of the common cause of the Party. This is a fundamental provision and we continue to be guided by it.

To Soviet editors/
The New York Times, 1-13:5.

Marvin Kalb
Director, Barone Center on the Press, Politics and Public Policy, Harvard University

5

. . . we need to have frequent, routine, undramatic news conferences by the President. Whether it's every week, two weeks, is not so important. We want the President to get in the habit of holding them on a routine basis, so they don't become huge events of state. So it's not the number, it's that they should be routine . . . The press, in our system, is the surrogate for the American people in posing questions directly to the President. When you break the bond and don't see the press for a long time, it is almost in my mind as if you were breaking a bond of trust between the President and the people.

The Washington Post,
10-17:(A)13.

Yevgeny Lanfang
Deputy editor, "Moscow News" (Soviet Union)

1

[On how Soviet leader Mikhail Gorbachev's policy of openness has affected the press]: *Glasnost* [openness] has given us all a headache. The headache comes from not being used to any of this, from having to think and read in completely different ways. Our heads hurt.

The Washington Post, 4-20:(A)23.

Edwin Meese III
Attorney General of the United States

2

Why does the media take out after me the way they do? I don't understand that totally, although I can make some speculation as to why it is. I think that there are some news people who are resentful because I refused to leak [confidential material to the press] for 7½ years; and, as some of the books that are now coming out reveal, if you play the game and feed the people unauthorized information, you get better press.

Interview,
McLean, Va./
The Washington Post, 6-2:(C)1.

Kay Mills
Editorial writer, "Los Angeles Times"

3

[On whether women journalists cover stories differently than men]: They have broadened the definition of news. Men have tended to see stories as politics, diplomacy, crime. Women write those stories, too, and, after all, people don't cover fires any differently. But I think they also see other things that men might not hear about, so they have broadened the kinds of questions the politicians are asked. They have written more about children, health issues, how people live.

Interview/
USA Today, 2-9:(A)11.

Bill Moyers
Broadcast journalist

4

A journalist is a professional beachcomber on the shores of other peoples' wisdom.

At University of Texas at Austin
commencement/Time, 6-13:74.

Roger Mudd
News correspondent,
Public Broadcasting Service

5

Having penetrated the ballot box with an exit-poll system breathtaking in its simplicity and startling in its accuracy, the [broadcast] networks now find themselves unable to make full use of that system because of a public-relations problem with the public and the politicians. Having helped remove the drama from the nominating conventions, having helped them turn into scripted, predictable, bland gatherings, the networks now talk about reducing their coverage of them because they are bland and predictable. Having encouraged political parties to add more and more primaries because they would bring politics out into the open, they now want to roll back on their coverage of the primaries, because they might produce muddled results. Having literally taken over daily campaign coverage, and having caused candidates to rearrange their entire style of campaigning to fit television's peculiar requirements, the networks now regard such steady coverage as a luxury, not worth the money for the news it produces, and are no longer sending a full complement of correspondent, producer and camera crew with each candidate. The net effect on politics, it seems to me, has been to water it down. It's not that television has not performed an enormous good by opening up politics to the American voter and viewer by educating the viewer on the intricacies of the system, and by bringing what we call "the process" into their homes. It is that we're not sure that what we're seeing and who we're seeing are the real thing.

At Public Television Annual
Meeting, Arlington, Va., April 11/
The Washington Post,
4-26:(A)18.

Ike Pappas
Former correspondent,
CBS News

1

[On his being fired by CBS News as part of a general cutback in news personnel at the network]: I didn't feel like, "Gee, after all this time, look what they've done to me." Because as far as I'm concerned . . . I gave to them and they gave to me. They gave me a hell of a job a long time ago, and I did well with it. Nevertheless, they supported my career, gave me 23 years of a life that would be the envy of any reporter in the world. I went and saw things that I never would have seen and done otherwise. I was a part of the history of the '60s and '70s and a good part of the '80s. I witnessed the world first-hand. I never thought that any of that was coming to me. I thought CBS put a lot of faith in me over the years. And as I looked at it over the long term, I looked at the people who ran CBS news at the time I was laid off as not my people—and that CBS News had fallen into alien hands.

Interview/
Los Angeles Times, 2-13:(VI)12.

Uri Porath
Director General, Israeli
Broadcasting Authority

2

What I see in American television [news] is not journalism—it's fabrication. When you don't film the provocation, and only film the response to provocation, that's a half-truth and that's worse than a lie.

The New York Times, 3-3:6.

Jody Powell
Former Press Secretary to the
President of the United States
(Jimmy Carter)

3

No President is going to sign a blood oath to [have a specific number of news conferences]. And the big problem for journalists is that the public doesn't seem to care very much whether the President has a press conference. There's no doubt it is in the public interest, but journalists have not figured out any way to give a practical weight to their concern. In fact, what happens too often is that a President weighing the pluses and minuses quickly realizes that the press will reward you if you're inaccessible and punish you if you're accessible.

The Washington Post, 10-17:(A)13.

Dan Quayle
United States Senator,
R-Indiana; 1988 Republican
Vice-Presidential nominee

4

I have a strong affection for members of the press. I was one of them one time. I'm not going to second-guess the media. The media can review itself. They know their biases and instincts.

Interview/USA Today, 8-29:(A)4.

Dan Rather
Anchorman, CBS News

5

Everything in my experience is [that], in the end, editing a good newspaper or editing a good newscast has to be in the hands of real people putting it together for real people. The higher you go, the more difficult it is to make that happen. And with something as large as a network operation, if you aren't careful, it becomes a journalistic fudge factory in which nobody's responsible, nobody's to blame, and nobody cares.

Interview, Jan. 11/
The Washington Post, 1-12:(B)4.

6

[On news interviews]: Trying to ask honest questions and trying to be persistent about answers is part of a reporter's job and, however it might be seen at a given time, the intention of even persistent questions in a spirited interview is to do an honest, honorable job. The fact that more attention is sometimes given to the heat than the light is regrettable, but it goes with the territory.

TV broadcast/
"Evening News," CBS-TV, 1-26.

(DAN RATHER)

1

[Saying TV networks should not cut back covering the national political conventions because of decreasing audiences at home and the dullness of the conventions themselves]: The selection of the President of the United States is a good story, as good as it gets. Conventions are a chain of history going back to 1832. I don't want us to do anything that would contribute to breaking that chain. Not everything in life should be made for television. There are things more important.

The Washington Post, 7-22:(A)29.

2

Not everything about democracy is exciting. Some things are simply important. That is reason enough to cover them.

USA Today, 8-19:(A)12.

James Risser
Director, Knight
Journalism Fellowships,
Stanford University;
Pulitzer Prize-winning
journalist

3

One funny effect [of winning the Pulitzer Prize]—you get a lot of phone calls to give speeches on topics that you don't know anything about, domestic and foreign. You also become an instant expert on journalism. There's a mystique and awe about a Pulitzer. People think that you are important. I think it's important that journalists not let the award go to their heads. The award is wonderful and I was proud to get it, but sometimes you are treated with more respect than you deserve.

Interview/USA Today, 3-31:(A)9.

Jack Rosenthal
Editorial-page editor,
"The New York Times"

4

[On newspapers making endorsements during political election campaigns]: In our case, endorsing has nothing to do with king-making, but with responsibility. When a paper sets out to comment on government and politics, it assumes a larger responsibility also. We shouldn't hide from the reader when the time comes to draw the line and add it all up.

USA Today, 11-11:(A)13.

John Sears
Manager of Ronald Reagan's
1976 Presidential campaign

5

[On the press's coverage of elections]: Television is still essentially an entertainment medium, not a journalistic medium. Ratings mean so much, even in the news department, that it's inevitable that the horse race [in the election] is going to be the more entertaining story [than the issues]. So they rush to cover that, and that puts a lot of pressure on the newspapers.

Esquire, May:82.

Tom Selleck
Actor

6

[Criticizing some media coverage of celebrities, such as himself]: I'm not anti-press—its freedom is essential—but it scares me that this pervasive news-as-entertainment will violate everyone's privacy. Then you could have a backlash against an institution that's vital to a democracy . . . I do not want approval of what's written. Form any opinion of me you wish—just don't make things up. Media's largely a bunch of very bright people who've been more than fair to me. But the tabloid element that hides behind the First Amendment, wraps itself in the flag, screams "Press Freedom!" and then abuses the responsibility—we're now seeing that line stepped across all the time.

Interview/
Cosmopolitan, December:169.

I. F. Stone
Journalist

7

It takes me several hours to read *The [Washington] Post* and *The [New York] Times* and I

WHAT THEY SAID IN 1988

read them with pleasure, because that for me is like reading history unfolding. I read history like the daily paper. I read the daily paper like history.

Interview, Washington/
The Washington Post, 3-10:(C)2.

1

You can't be a cynic and a good reporter. You have to believe, not in cliches, but essentially that people are sufficiently reasonable that they can be moved by argument, reason and compassion.

Mother Jones, June:37.

Margaret Thatcher
Prime Minister of the
United Kingdom

2

The press has an enormous role to play. It consists, of course, of criticism, but also of upholding the great institutions, traditions, heritage. If you had all the press in the West debunking and undermining [the West], and all the press in the Communist world saying only to the outside world what a marvelous system Communism is—which it isn't—how is the Third World to judge?

Interview, London/
USA Today, 9-2:(A)15.

Helen Thomas
White House correspondent,
United Press International

3

[On the American press's experiences dealing with Soviet officials during the current U.S.-Soviet summit meeting in Moscow]: Everything is *nyet*. They're still rooted in the old Soviet traditions. I don't think they know what to make of us—a rambunctious, thundering herd who question everything, every rule that doesn't make sense.

Moscow/
USA Today, 6-1:(A)2.

Richard E. Wiley
Former Commissioner,
Federal Communications Commission

4

[Criticizing the FCC's decision to rescind the broadcast Fairness Doctrine]: The battle ain't over yet. If the Fairness Doctrine is ultimately declared un-Constitutional in the courts, what then happens to other program-content regulations of the FCC, including the equal-time [provision for political candidates]? What then happens to the basic premise upon which all broadcast licenses are premised—that broadcasters are public trustees?

Emmy Magazine, Jan.-Feb.:42.

Jean Gaddy Wilson
Director of women and media
research, School of Journalism,
University of Missouri

5

No matter what size newspaper, television station or radio station, even when a majority of the employees are female, management for women never tops 25 per cent. The media have been male-dominated organizations. Because of that, there have not been expectations that women would enter management. And women have not been in positions where they could move into management . . . Since 1977, women have outnumbered men in journalism schools. If education is the key to management positions, then women are there, ready for management. In journalism, they've been there a decade.

Interview/USA Today, 2-9:(A)11.

Tom Wolfe
Author, Journalist

6

There are no special techniques to reporting, no tricks. It's so much easier than anyone would think. I mean, anyone could have done what I did if they wanted to. If you hang around the courthouse, people will wonder who you are, and as soon as they wonder, you introduce yourself. As soon as you introduce yourself, you have a chance to make a friend. And once you make a friend, that friend can introduce you to someone else.

Interview/Cosmopolitan, April:190.

Literature

Isabel Allende
*Exiled Chilean author
and journalist*

1

[Comparing journalism with writing novels]: You can reach more people in journalism—including the printed press and television—but only on a momentary basis. Books achieve a different goal, a very emotional goal. For example, in Europe, people have forgotten about Chile. But in Germany a million copies of my first novel were sold. That means a million people have been reminded about Chile. Novels defy the process of time.

*Interview/
The New York Times,
2-4:16.*

2

Storytelling is a way of preserving the memory of the past and keeping alive legends, myths, superstitions and history that are not in the textbooks—the real stories of people and countries. I have tried desperately to do that in all my novels.

*Interview/
U.S. News & World Report,
11-21:67.*

3

Writing is like a catharsis; it's a way of getting inside the past, inside your own memories. And when you write about other people, you write about yourself. Why do you choose those characters? Those anecdotes? It's because they're meaningful to you. While writing . . . books I learned a lot about myself, and the world became more tolerable. Living with myself was more tolerable, too.

*Interview/
Mother Jones, December:44.*

Isaac Asimov
Science-fiction writer

4

[On book publishing]: An incredible number of my editors went to other houses. I always publish with the house that signed my books up, but the editors who move on always get me to write something for their new publisher. They're like bees carrying me like pollen from house to house.

The New York Times, 2-2:23.

5

I had planned to make my living as a teacher and scientist. I wrote for pleasure and didn't care whether I published or not; or, if published, whether I sold or not. When I received a check for a royalty from a single book that was equal to 3½ times my annual teaching salary, I rather got the idea that I had made it as a writer. If you don't enjoy writing, there are other ways of making a living. If you are easily discouraged, there are other ways of making a living. If you don't want to spend your life working in more or less isolation, there are other ways of making a living.

*Interview/
Writer's Digest, December:30.*

Margaret Atwood
Canadian author

6

[On what is good fiction]: Well, it does not depend on genre. A well-written thriller can be better fiction than a badly written novel. Also, the element of surprise is important. If a book does not hold the attention of the reader, no matter how worthy its contents may be on Page 250, then it is of no use. If we can anticipate everything about a book at the beginning, we are not interested in finishing it.

*Interview/
World Press Review,
June:60.*

413

Saul Bellow
Author

1

I don't care too much for scholarly research [by others about his books]. It makes me feel too self-important . . . I can very rarely read things that are written about my work. They make me uneasy. They sometimes intriguingly misunderstand what I have written.

Interview, Chicago/
The New York Times, 5-5:20.

2

[On the state of fiction in today's magazines]: I had already suspected for a long time that they are not interested in fiction very much any more. Most of the serious magazines feel it is necessary to have one story per issue, and the minimalists are much in favor because they don't take up too much space. That way you can have all that room for advertisements. But if it were something about politics or sex, no amount of space would be excessive.

Interview, Chicago, Sept. 21/
The New York Times, 9-22:20.

William Boyd
Author

3

I almost know how a book's going to end before I start. In some cases, I have the good last paragraph before I start on page one. Iris Murdoch writes that way. She says the real pleasure is in the invention, a process that takes place without putting pen to paper. That can take a year: to invent the characters, find jobs for them, flesh it all out. But it means that I then write the book faster than somebody who is inventing as he goes along.

Interview/
Publishers Weekly, 4-29:57

Anthony Burgess
Author

4

I am a hard worker by temperament. E. M. Forster wrote six novels, and that was enough.

Virginia Woolf? Not much more. Me, I have to write an average of 1,000, sometimes 2,000, words a day. That's hard work. Every morning, I begin by drinking a big cup of tea with six or seven teabags, and I compose the expositionary part of a fugue to get the brain stirred up. Only then do I sit down to work. I write fast. So what? No one would criticize a craftsman for being too fast on the job.

Interview/
World Press Review,
September:59.

5

Literature will always be superior to music, because it is not just a structure. It has a semantic force that gives it meaning.

Interview/
World Press Review,
September:59.

6

[Author Vladimir] Nabokov and I like each other's work, but it's dangerous to get in too close touch with people like that. There's always the danger that one's admiration of the writing will be qualified by one's lack of admiration for the person.

Interview, New York/
TWA Ambassador, October:47.

Richard Burgin
Assistant professor of English,
Drexel University

7

[On the literary magazine *Ploughshares'* agreement with the National Writers Union for the first labor contract with a literary journal]: As a writer, I suffer when I submit a story and I wait a year and a half while nothing happens. Of all writers, literary writers are the most powerless. It's good to see their rights recognized. This contract is a victory for writers and, therefore, ultimately for society.

The Christian Science Monitor,
10-17:21.

414

Tom Clancy
Author

1

[As a writer,] write the kind of book that you like to read, and would pay money for. Your first audience, and your first critic, is yourself . . . if you're honest.

Interview/
Writer's Digest, December:30.

Clive Cussler
Author

2

[Saying aspiring writers should copy successful authors]: You don't steal their concept, or their story. What you steal is their style of writing . . . It's like football. When the team comes back at the beginning of the year, the coach doesn't care if you're a big star or not. You start right in with the blocking and tackling . . . going back to basics. That's structure. Very simple stuff. For example: Are you going to write first person? Third person? How are you going to divide it up? Are you going to have a prologue? An epilogue? How are you going to switch chapters back and forth? How will you start the next chapter? And how does it all tie in? Take Hemingway: He did a great job of plotting. Fitzgerald, on the other hand, is a prime example of what I call the literary writers. Beautiful words and phrases, but no plot. But then, I consider myself an entertainer. I write for the reader. I tell a story.

Interview/
Writer's Digest, April:34.

Robertson Davies
Canadian author

3

There's no central theme in the Canadian novel because there is no unifying Canadian problem. Government can influence themes. You can see it in the 19th-century Russian writers who had to suffer under oppressive regimes. Canada doesn't have an oppressive government. It's hard for people in the [United] States to recognize this, but Canada is a socialist monarchy, like Sweden, Denmark and Norway. We have a leg in both camps—a limited welfare state and also a monarchy that causes a kind of clinging to the past. Canadian writers are different from the Americans, who have an optimism in their writing that we don't have.

Interview, New York/
The New York Times, 12-29:(B)2.

Don DeLillo
Author

4

Eventually, a novel begins to reveal its themes to me, but I might be working on it for a year and a half before I have the faintest idea what it eventually is going to be about, what will sail above the heads of the characters, so to speak . . . That's how I operate as a writer.

Interview/
Publishers Weekly, 8-19:55.

Rita Dove
Poet; Winner,
1987 Pulitzer Prize in poetry

5

No poet can expect the acclaim of a rock star, a Michael Jackson. Black poets discover there's a dearth of calls for their works in most magazines. Poets know they will not be rich.

Interview, Boston/
The Christian Science Monitor,
2-5:(B)4.

Lawrence Durrell
Author

6

Everybody [today] is writing bad novels. We are drowning in dime-a-dozen stuff. Absolutely unreadable books bring in millions of dollars and then vanish overnight. [Norman] Mailer is an excellent writer, but he is so money-hungry that there is nothing he would not do—even rewrite the Book of Exodus—badly. It is true that other writers have done it before; Dickens wrote serials for newspapers. But Dickens did not become a millionaire. He lived comfortably and bought a house, but that was all.

Interview/
World Press Review. October:41

Thomas B. Flanagan
Author; Professor of English,
State University of New York,
Stony Brook

1

I bumped into a poet friend of mine and I told him that it was funny but for the first 25 years that I was teaching, I didn't write any fiction. And he said that during that time I was probably thinking about the story, working it out, writing the novel without knowing it . . . When I teach, I'm a professor, not a creative writer. The gears simply get changed. I go into my study upstairs and work on the novel. Different parts of the brain are involved in the two processes. Sometimes when I'm writing fiction I think, my God, this is the easiest job I've ever done—why didn't I get started on it earlier?

Interview/
The New York Times, 1-18:15

Carlos Fuentes
Mexican author
and diplomat

2

I believe in books that do not go to a ready-made public. I'm looking for readers I would like to *make*. To *win* them, to *create* readers rather than to give something that readers are expecting. That would bore me to death.

Interview, Fairfax, Va./
The Washington Post, 5-5:(C)2.

3

My business is writing. Bureaucracy, you see, is the antithesis of writing. Bureaucracy is dispersion and jumping from one subject to another. Writing is concentration. It is deciding what adjective to use during a whole morning.

Interview/
The New York Times, 5-30:20.

A. Bartlett Giamatti
President, National (baseball)
League; Former president,
Yale University

4

The act of creating a work of literature had an ethical purpose for Dante, Spenser, Milton and Shakespeare. It isn't necessary to accept Dante's doctrinal religious framework, but there is a moral perspective to his writing. I've always found it immensely satisfying that literature has an ethical impulse.

Interview, New York/
The New York Times, 12-28:(B)3.

Nikki Giovanni
Poet

5

Unfortunately for whatever "success" means to a living poet—and that is certainly specious—there is no secret. You simply work your tail off—as it were—trying to find your audience. The Puritans may have had their faults, but they were right about one thing: Nothing beats sticking to the job until you know it's the best you can do. Conversely, nothing beats quitting when you know it's never going to work . . . As the commercial says, "There are three *nevers* in poetry: Never write something just because it sounds good. Never refuse to write something because you are afraid of public reaction. And never, never let them see you sweat."

Interview/
Writer's Digest, December:31.

Graham Greene
Author

6

[On writing]: People you know can serve as models for secondary characters because you can explore their eccentricities. But you cannot use people you know as protagonists, because no matter how well you know them, if you try to put them in a book you discover that you do not know them well enough to draw a well-rounded main character . . . [Those fictional heroes come] from the depths of my unconscious.

World Press Review, March:53.

Jeff Greenfield
Syndicated columnist

1

[When writing,] respect your reader. The niftiest turn of phrase, the most elegant flight of rhetorical fancy, isn't worth beans next to a clear thought clearly expressed.

Interview/
Writer's Digest, December:29.

Alex Haley
Author

2

The way to succeed [as a writer] is never quit. That's it. But really be humble about it. The best way to approach writing is as you would approach painting, or something like that. It needs to be done almost like on the Elizabethan apprenticeship level. You start out lowly and humble and you carefully try to learn an accretion of little things that help you get there.

Interview/
Writer's Digest, December:25.

3

There's a saying that a writer who has just finished the manuscript of a big book is kind of like a lady who just had a baby. It's something you've been full of—and all of a sudden it's gone and you don't know what to do with yourself.

Interview, Knoxville, Tenn./
The Washington Post, 12-26:(D)2.

Donald Hall
Poet

4

Historically, if you look at the lives of poets, you learn that, though poetry can be very satisfying and pleasurable, it requires hard work. The chance for writing something good *quickly* is very small. Learning how to play a guitar requires hard work; learning how to do anything requires hard work. But the joy is in the work. The great pleasure is in the act of writing itself: sitting at the desk, working it through, trying to make it better, seeing something grow, not even

thinking about it, losing consciousness of time, of hunger, of hot and cold, of oneself, in the total immersion in the work. As the sculptor loves the material, as the wood-carver loves the grain of the wood, so the poet loves manipulating language.

Interview/
Writing!,
February:20.

5

There's inspiration [in writing poetry], and when that inspiration batters at the door, it will come through anything. There are times when I am inspired. These days, it may be one week every two years. Then, everything that I look at—a dandelion, a shooting star, traffic in the city—will seem laden with significance, and I have the ability to read through the external circumstances and see something living and meaningful at the center of it. These are the times when poems begin.

Interview/
Writing!, February:21.

Anthony Hecht
Poet

6

["Success" is a] bothersome word, in particular as it applies to poetry. A novelist can be a best-seller and even sell his books to films and TV; and a six-figure income, team of agents and several homes will testify to some variety of "success." But for a poet, "success" can rarely be very much more than winning the ungrudging respect of the *best* of his fellow poets. Discovering just who the best are will take much study and thought.

Interview/
Writer's Digest, December:31.

John Jakes
Author

7

Without practice, a dedication to write and keep writing, the writer's inherent talent never develops or matures—unless he or she happens

417

(JOHN JAKES)

to be born a genius, which the great majority of professional writers are not. Continue to slug away at the Three Ps for writers: Practice—the only way to improve your writing skills; it's just like golf. Persistence—the only way to overcome periods when you write badly, the whimsicalities of the market, personnel changes at publishing houses, et. al. Professionalism—without the ability to judge your work critically, slash it and fix it, you're not a writer.

Interview/
Writer's Digest, December:32.

Vladimir V. Karpov
Head, Soviet Writers' Union

1

There is one genre that has sprung up [in Soviet literature] that is raising a lot of fuss but not producing much—this is the genre of criticism. Unfortunately, along with the serious analytical stories has arisen a cacophonous chorus that sounds like a quarrel in the kitchen of a communal apartment. We must confess that not only critics but also the representatives of all other genres participate in it. The motivating forces behind it are the mob passions, old insults and, I would say, prejudices born in our Soviet times. Many critical stories are written with the aim to "eliminate." Their authors think that such a style creates for them a reputation as an active restructurer. There is logic in this: The louder the cry, the heavier the obscenities, the more attention it enjoys—people will say, "Look how original and brave the author is." Today, reading these angry, ungrounded and yellow stories, I see the old style of denouncing and a desire to compromise or "destroy" a person. In such stories, analysis and the arguments are practically absent; all their efforts are aimed at gaining a label of some kind. It is possible to understand the bearer of these faults—this is the way he was brought up, this is what he is like inside. However, we cannot understand the editors who agree to publish them.

At Soviet Communist Party
conference, Moscow/
The New York Times, 7-1:4

Paula T. Kaufman
University librarian,
Columbia University

2

[Criticizing an FBI program to monitor the use of American libraries by Soviet spies looking for information]: It seems to me that our society faces a far greater threat from the loss of our basic rights of privacy and access to public information than from the use of unclassified material by foreign nationals in our libraries. Any threat to our national security which results from the exercise of these rights is the necessary price we must pay to remain a free and open democratic society.

Before House Civil and
Constitutional Rights Subcommittee,
Washington, June 20/
The New York Times, 6-21:11.

Jonathan Kellerman
Author

3

Character and motivation are very important to me, but I never see myself abandoning plot and story. It's not the glamorous part of writing—we all like to play with words, come up with the brilliant phrase—but plot still frames the structure. It's the necessary carpentry before you put in the decoration. And it's why I write crime novels.

Interview/
Publishers Weekly, 2-19:63.

William Kennedy
Author

4

A sense of place is very important for a novelist, and most great novelists have that. There's Steinbeck's California, Bellow's Chicago, Hemingway's Spain and Paris, Camus's Algeria and Tolstoy's and Dostoyevsky's Russia; the list goes on and on. Albany, New York—my hometown—is the locus of everything I write. Maybe that's because I had a great feeling for the work of William Faulkner and the way he used Yoknapatawpha County [Miss.], and the way J. D. Salinger interlocked his stories about the

(WILLIAM KENNEDY)

Glass family. I found that this created more energy than novels that were not connected. So almost from the very beginning of my career, I thought about doing something similar.

Interview/
U.S. News & World Report,
6-20:66.

Ken Kesey
Author

1

Writing is a lonely business, done pretty much on mountaintops. If you get stuck on the mountaintop, you'll die of loneliness.

People, 6-27:63.

Laurence J. Kirshbaum
President, Warner Books

2

The first axiom of publishing is that there is always a shortage of the books that sell and an over-abundance of the books that don't.

The New York Times, 1-18:14.

Vyacheslav Kuprianov
Soviet poet

3

[On internationally known Soviet poets who have gained fame by visiting other countries, especially the U.S.]: . . . their prominence in people's minds far exceeds their significance as poets. People know them as people better than they know what they actually write . . . I call them made-in-America poets, because very often they got their reputations because, if they were popular in the United States, how could we fail to recognize them ourselves?

At forum sponsored by Esalen
Institute, Los Angeles/
Los Angeles Times, 1-25:(V)1.

Lewis Lapham
Editor, "Harper's" magazine

4

[Readers of *Harper's*] are responsive, intelligent readers, to begin with—people who care about words and have an appreciation of good writing and can separate the wheat from the chaff. However, they are non-ideological—not interested in slogans. I sense that readers of *Harper's* share our editorial philosophy, which is a novelistic approach to journalism, much resembling Stendhal's dictum that a novel is a mirror walking down the road. The writer's function is to describe and tell a story, not shove an idea down people's throats. Our readers expect to think for themselves.

Interview, New York/
Publishers Weekly, 2-5:75.

Jean-Claude Lattes
President, book division,
Hachette (France)

5

[On the problems of today's book business]: There are too many titles being produced, while the space to display them is not expanding, and so the extra books have no place to go. The smaller points-of-sale are the first to feel the strain; in fact, the larger stores and the chains are doing better, on average. And then there are reasons external to the book business: In the past 10 years there has been a change in how people spend on leisure activities, in a context in which income is not growing. Vacation time has increased, there are more channels on TV, we have video cassettes, compact disks, home computers and even a new interest in sports.

Interview, Paris/
Publishers Weekly, 9-9:102.

Wendy Lesser
Editor, "Threepenny Review"

6

[Expressing concern about a possible trend toward union contracts for writers who write for literary magazines]: We're not Hollywood moguls making millions of dollars and under-paying our screenwriters. The world of little magazines is the world of people who, for good or bad, have left the world of business. I'd be horrified if our world began to resemble the world of commercial publishing.

The Christian Science Monitor,
10-17:21.

R. W. B. Lewis
Professor,
Yale University; Pulitzer
Prize-winning biographer

1

The articulation of literary values can always be difficult, but it's a little like what Justice Potter Stewart said about pornography: "I can't define it, but I know it when I see it." We know Faulkner is great and Jacqueline Susann is trivial.

The New York Times, 1-6:12.

Spark M. Matsunaga
United States Senator,
D-Hawaii

2

[On the post of Poet Laureate of the United States]: Poets have had political patrons in the past, as the title "Poet Laureate" suggests. There are those wo believe that such a designation has no roots or place in American egalitarian tradition, but I would beg to differ. The United States Poet Laureate is not servant of a crown. He or she serves we, the people, and enjoys governmental recognition, because democratic government exists to insure the pursuit of happiness on the part of the governed.

Washington, March 7/
The New York Times, 3-8:21.

Charles McCarry
Author

3

As I see it, it is the function of the writer not to be an interesting person, but to write. Fifteen minutes of fame is not worth a lifetime of writing for the wrong reasons. If you keep on going on the *Today* [TV] show, there is a danger of creating expectations in your audience and yourself that you can only fulfill at the expense of your original intentions as a writer.

Interview, Washington/
Publishers Weekly, 7-22:39.

Iris Murdoch
Author

4

My problem is not being great. I'm in the second league, not among the gods like Jane Austen, Henry James and Tolstoy. My characters are not as memorable as theirs. I'd like to think people enjoy reading my books and consider me a good storyteller—like Dostoyevsky or Proust—at my own modest level.

Interview/People, 3-14:126.

Howard Nemerov
Poet Laureate of the
United States

5

I've never read a political poem that's accomplished anything. Poetry makes things happen, but rarely what the poet wants.

News conference,
Washington, Oct. 3/
The Washington Post, 10-4:(D)4.

Peggy Noonan
Speechwriter for Vice
President, and President-elect,
of the United States George Bush

6

A great speech is literature. Speechwriting is a tributary off the river of American prose, but it *is* American prose. I wish literature students would go into speechwriting. Or poets. Now, that's an idea. Except . . . wait. They'd just write speeches for the other side. There aren't any politically conservative poets.

Interview/
"Ms.", December:85.

Marsha Norman
Pulitzer Prize-winning
playwright

7

To me, concentration is the key to writing. Focus is so important that you have to be able to work for 48 hours straight if that's necessary, have nothing standing in your way. There should be no excuses like, "Well, my writing would be better if I didn't have to work full-time." People who hedge their bets, who write in their spare time, may never know the answer to the question, "Could I be a writer, with a capital W?"

Interview/
Writer's Digest, September:34.

Rosamunde Pilcher
Author

1

There's a big market there—light reading for intelligent ladies. Intelligent ladies want something to go to sleep on. They don't want a lot of drivel; they don't want to read a semi-political novel; they don't want to read about somebody being tortured to death. I took one of those on holiday and suddenly threw it down. Someone asked me why I did that, and I said, "I haven't come to Spain to sit in the sun to read about people being tortured—not my idea of holiday reading."

Interview/
Publishers Weekly, 1-29:412.

Reynolds Price
Author

2

American literature is full of wonderful writers—Fitzgerald, Wolfe, Hemingway—who were never really able to make their apparatus function in a reliable way. Virtually all were fairly wild romantics who saw themselves as puppets really, at the whim of their talent. It's sad to see how many great novelists have done their best work before they were 40 and were pretty much dead or dying volcanoes before they were 50. It's a problem European artists generally seem not to have had. The pattern in European fiction is that of fairly sober, bourgeois citizens who get up every morning, do their day's writing and have dinner with the wife and children.

Interview/
U.S. News & World Report,
6-13:62.

Anne Rice
Author

3

The important thing to remember is that writing is an artistic realm—even if you're writing the most commercial fiction or non-fiction. That means there's no justice. It doesn't matter how hard you work; it doesn't matter who you know. What ultimately matters is what you put

on that page—and whether somebody wants it at the moment. That's why people who want to go into this profession have to, a) believe in themselves, b) work like demons, and c) ignore the [publisher] rejections. When you mail out a manuscript, you are not turning in a paper for a grade. You can mail out a perfectly wonderful and publishable novel, and have it rejected 10 times. And the reason it's rejected is because you hit 10 different [publishing] people who for various reasons don't want to work with this idea . . . The main thing to remember is that you can't take seriously anything these people say, because they're *not* writers. Just because somebody has a sign that says "Editor," and has paid vacation and medical insurance and works for a publishing company, doesn't necessarily mean that person knows very much or is very smart or is worth listening to. So don't take it seriously if they brush off your manuscript with a couple of lines.

Interview/
Writer's Digest, November:44.

Augusto Roa Bastos
Exiled Paraguayan author

4

The day of the independent writer—especially the Latin American fiction writer—is over. As long as the multinational publishing houses hold all the cards, he cannot compete. I myself am published by multinationals. I am still a freelancer, but with a very clear idea about the world I come from. This is part of the nightmare of the average writer, who now finds himself in a system that is completely closed but that continues to give lip service to independence.

Interview/
World Press Review, May:60.

Tom Robbins
Author

5

One of the hardest things for a writer to deal with is the loneliness caused by that life-style. And yet it's absolutely necessary. If you spend too much time with other people, you find that

(TOM ROBBINS)

you're having only secondhand ideas, for one thing. You also shouldn't talk about your work. I've watched people fall into that pothole. They talk all their juice away. A lot of talented writers just talk their books away, their stories away. They go to bars and talk about writing to the point where they talk all the sizzle out of them. Their work is either flat or never gets finished at all because it's already done; they did what they had to do with it in talking, rather than putting it on a page.

Interview/
Writer's Digest, March:36.

Don Robertson
Author

1

At one time, the publishing world was full of Maxwell Perkins-types. Then it became hamburger merchants—selling books by the pound. It used to be they'd take a writer in the hope that every third book would make money. Now they want every book to make money ...

Interview/
The New York Times, 1-23:13.

Philip Roth
Author

2

I don't want a contract or money until I'm done [writing a book]. *All* done. I want to be able to abandon a project at any point. I don't want the pressure to finish something because I have a check.

Interview/
Publishers Weekly, 8-26:69.

Thomas Savage
Author

3

I have never written a book that I didn't know the last line before I started. I wouldn't think of using an outline because that ties you down. But if you write to the last line, you know where you're going from the very beginning.

Interview, Boston/
Publishers Weekly, 7-15:46.

Arthur M. Schlesinger, Jr.
Historian; Professor of
humanities, City University
of New York

4

I can write all day. I rarely get tired. I think it's easier for historians, because they don't have to invent anything. They don't have to imagine anything. You have the facts to stimulate you. Your job is to arrange and interpret them. Find a logical order; tell a story.

Interview/Writing!, January:14.

Stirling Silliphant
Screenwriter

5

I developed the most critically important element we writers must all have, and that is discipline. If I had to, I could sit down right now and go to work while you'll still asking me questions. That comes from doing it. From doing the work. Over and over and over again. I know it's very arrogant of me to say this, but I have no patience with the concept of writer's block. I can understand that some writers are emotionally tortured—they may have deep personal problems. But as a creative person, you have an obligation to take charge of yourself and of your work, regardless of the pain involved. That's where the joy lurks—out there beyond easy reach. You have to go out and grab it.

Interview/
American Film, March:14.

Elizabeth Spencer
Author

6

My idea of a story is that it's something that should go on living in your mind. I judge books and novels and stories like that, that there's something I can feel I'm living in, and after I finish that I can meditate on its various angles. I try to aim for that effect, because it's what I like to read. I have this optimism that the good things do have a tendency to last.

Interview/
Publishers Weekly, 9-9:112.

Danielle Steel
Author

1

When it's 1:30 or 2 in the morning and I feel like reading something, I don't want to read Thomas Mann. I want to read Jackie Collins. Some long esoteric treatise may be good for your mind, but it's awful hard to read. And, after you pass the age of 12, you have enough pressure and stress that you just want something you can flow with.

Interview, San Francisco/
Los Angeles Times, 1-6:(V)4.

Gay Talese
Author

2

Modesty is a most becoming quality for so-called "successful" writers to adopt. Too often, writers take their success too seriously, let their egos influence their future work, and end up producing writing that is self-centered and shallow.

Interview/
Writer's Digest, December:29.

John Updike
Author

3

I think of myself as a man who's had plenty to do with women in many capacities, beginning with my mother, and two daughters, and two wives, and a lot of female editors. Women have been colleagues of mine as well as domestic companions, and I never thought of myself as anything in my role of novelist but fair and sympathetic. But what comes up when you venture before college audiences is that there aren't enough women in my books who have jobs; they're not career-minded; they merely are wives, sex objects and purely domestic creatures. And my only defense would be that it's in the domesticity, the family, the sexual relations, that women interest me. I don't write about too many male businessmen, and I'm not apt to write about too many female businessmen.

Interview, New York/
The New York Times, 3-2:20.

Mario Vargas Llosa
Peruvian author

4

Prosperity and stability are very damaging for literature. But when the old institutions and the established order enter a process of decomposition, that pushes writers to create with great impetus, originality and audacity. Sometimes they give testimony to what is dying; sometimes they help along the process of transformation and change; sometimes they just give artificial security to people who feel confused and are fearful of what's going to be . . . Artistic development in the midst of difficult times seems a contradiction . . . [But] when people feel completely lost, that lack of faith in reality creates a need for artificial realities, fictitious realities, in order to have something to believe in. But even if you accumulate all these reasons, there is still some factor that is mysterious, that belongs to individual creativity and can never be totally explained.

Interview/
U.S. News & World Report, 5-9:69.

Kurt Vonnegut
Author

5

I think I succeeded as a writer because I did *not* come out of an English department. I used to write in the chemistry department. And I wrote some good stuff. If I had been in the English department, the prof would have looked at my short stories, congratulated me on my talent, and then showed me how Joyce or Hemingway handled the same elements of the short story. The prof would have placed me in competition with the greatest writers of all time, and that would have ended my writing career.

Interview/
Writer's Digest, December:25.

Andrei Voznesensky
Soviet poet

6

Russian poetry tells the best things and gives an indication of the instincts of our nation. It is

423

WHAT THEY SAID IN 1988

(ANDREI VOZNESENSKY)

the poetry of religion . . . You know, in America you have the best computers in the whole world, and technology. But we have Russian poetry and something strange—the Slavic soul. You learn about this with poetry.

To reporters, Peredelkino, U.S.S.R./
Los Angeles Times, 5-31:(I)9.

John Edgar Widemon
Author

1

The best writers use language as a tool for discovery, for perception. They also invent and do things with words that haven't been done before. It's also a trap. Most readers respond to such virtuosity to an extent, but a reader of fiction wants narrative drive. My love of language is a strength but also a weakness. It's true of all writers. The thing they do best can also scuttle them. You start to read Faulkner: The long sentences are powerful—they draw you in. But they can also cause you to drift off. Then the lines draw you back in.

Interview,
Philadelphia/
Writing!, December:29.

Richard Wilbur
Poet Laureate of the
United States

2

I write in meters, stanzas and rhymes at a time when the new form [of poetry] is prosaic free verse. It is counter to the times. Sometimes I feel self-doubtful, a stick in the mud.

Interview/
Los Angeles Times,
7-31:(Book Review)6.

Richard Wilbur
Poet

3

I have no facility or speed in writing, and so my secret must be patience. It has always been clear to me that I am slow-witted and slow to please myself, but that a willingness to brood for hours over a phrase or line can result in presentable work. The Spirit in *Comus* talks about "meditating"—that is, composing—his "rural minstrelsy." Well, I am meditative to a fault, but I've accepted the fact that there is no other way for me.

Interview/
Writer's Digest, December:31.

Paul Zindel
Author

4

The advice I give my own [writing] students is this: "Forget about the spelling; forget about the grammar. Just tell me your story. Tell me how you *feel* about it." When I was in school, the least interesting things about writing, the mechanics, were emphasized. *Everybody* is really a well of tremendous stories. Get in touch with the most interesting, most difficult part—the emotional side of a story. If you can first get away from worrying about spelling and following grammar rules, you'll find that your imagination is free to write. First, you have to get the story out, in any shape or form. *Then,* you go back to the structure.

Interview/Writing!, March:20.

William Zinsser
Author, Editor

5

The novelist in his or her fictional journey is seldom far from the world of politics, if by politics we mean established authority of some kind—state or church, for instance, or social convention. More than most writers, the political novelist is interested in the rise and fall of ideas.

The New York Times, 2-4:16.

Medicine and Health

Brock Adams
United States Senator,
D-Washington

1

AIDS is a difficult issue for all of us to discuss. It forces us to discuss many issues that we would rather not talk about. But AIDS is going to be with us for a long time, and we have a responsibility to ensure that the Federal government provides leadership and fights many of the battles in this epidemic.

Before the Senate, Washington/
The Washington Post, 5-2:(A)19.

John Bailar
Professor of epidemiology,
McGill University (Canada)

2

[On the shortage of cancer patients willing to take part in testing new anti-cancer drugs]: People worry about not getting enough money or staff for cancer research, but when it comes right down to it, the ultimate problem is almost always the availability of patients . . . Doctors often feel a trial is not appropriate for their patient. And sometimes they think the treatment answer is clear and they shouldn't gamble. But they are often wrong about that. The state of the art changes very quickly in this business, and too many physicians are not keeping up.

The Washington Post, 7-25:(A)6.

Karst Besteman
Executive director, Alcohol
and Drug Problems
Association, Washington

3

[On the "just say no" campaign to fight drug abuse]: Its greatest efficacy is that it says, "This is our social expectation" . . . We knew from the beginning it was just a simple slogan, like "an apple a day" or "brush your teeth after every meal." Have you ever known a kid who does

that? But that's what we tell kids in hopes they will brush once a day.

Los Angeles Times, 8-10:(I)20.

Rodrigo Botero
Journalist; Former Minister
of Finance of Colombia

4

Lowering the infant mortality rate means much more to the ordinary man and woman of a developing country than obtaining an X percentage of growth in the GNP per capita, which to the majority of [those] people is an absolutely abstract and mysterious concept . . . You cannot lower the infant mortality rate unless you offer to *all* of the population a minimum of medical service—instead of offering it to the 10 per cent wealthy urban elite. You cannot achieve 70 years of life expectancy at birth unless you extend to *all* of your population, to all social classes, minimum conditions of hygiene, nutrition, education and literacy.

At Wingspread Conference,
Racine, Wis., April/
The Christian Science Monitor,
7-25:(B)7.

Otis R. Bowen
Secretary of Health and
Human Services of the
United States

5

Many of you [business executives] have already instituted programs to persuade your employees to stop smoking, to eat properly, to exercise more regularly, to drink moderately or not at all and to avoid drugs. To add to this persuasion on the wisdom of avoiding AIDS isn't such a quantum leap.

At forum sponsored by
Allstate Life Insurance Co.,
Washington, Jan. 20/
Los Angeles Times, 1-21:(I)21.

Daniel Callahan
Author,
Ethicist

1

What do we owe each other as we grow old? I think we would be justified in saying that beyond a certain age we will simply not provide expensive, life-extending care. We will always relieve your pain and suffering, but we will not give you organ transplantations, we will not give you access to open-heart surgery, or even possible access to an intensive-care unit. We will really say: "Look, we have already done justice to you in our society by getting you this far. And we cannot be asked to indefinitely extend your life." We've got a whole range of social problems that we are not adequately addressing—inadequacies in our public-school system, in our transportation system, in our urban ghettos, for example. So we need to stand back and ask, "What's really good for our society?" The provision of health-care for the elderly is a kind of endless frontier. Because the body always decays, there will always be more things to do. We now have a situation where the elderly have become very fearful about what their old age is going to be—fearful on the one hand of excessive technological interventions when they're dying or critically ill or, on the other hand, that they'll end their years in the back room of a nursing home, demented or totally out of things.

Interview/
U.S. News & World Report,
2-22:78.

Joyce Clifford
Nurse-in-chief,
Beth Israel Hospital,
Boston

2

Our society places a lower value on nurturing and caring roles, which are very integral to the work of nurses. It's seen as women's work, and it's under-valued, just as the care of children and the elderly is under-valued.

"Ms.," June:75.

James P. Comer
Professor of child psychiatry,
Yale University Child Study
Center; Associate dean,
Yale School of Medicine

3

[On people who abuse their spouses or children]: There is a need to feel adequate by controlling somebody else or abusing somebody else. Many people in our country have a sense of inadequacy because they grow up in an exclusionary society, a competitive society, that says that anybody who doesn't go to the very top didn't work hard enough. That creates a great deal of insecurity—economic, social, psychological—and people have to exploit and abuse others in order to feel adequate.

Interview/
USA Today, 12-7:(A)11.

Robert L. Crandall
Chairman, American Airlines

4

Companies like ours pay for health care twice—once for our own employees and then again, via taxes and inflated health-insurance premiums, for the employees of those businesses who don't provide benefits for their own people.

Los Angeles Times,
7-24:(I)16.

Vincent T. DeVita, Jr.
Director, National Cancer
Institute of the United States;
Physician-in-chief-designate,
Memorial-Sloan Kettering
Cancer Center, New York

5

[On progress in the war on cancer]: I think we have the machinery of the cancer cell in our hands. I think we're in for an exciting decade. It's unstoppable. There's no chance in hell that we can fail.

Interview, Bethesda, Md./
The Washington Post,
8-22:(A)13.

Robert J. Dole
United States Senator,
R-Kansas; Candidate for the
1988 Republican
Presidential nomination

1

[Criticizing proposals that government supply needles to drug addicts to prevent the spread of diseases, such as AIDS]: Giving clean needles to addicts may prevent disease, but it also endorses addiction. We ought to be trying to raise the standards in America, not come down to the standards of those who have the problems.

At White House conference on
drugs, Washington, March 3/
The Washington Post, 3-4:(A)14.

Robert K. Dornan
United States Representative,
R-California

2

Just like we have to do something on the demand side of narcotics, we have to do something on the demand side of AIDS. We have to stop glorifying homosexuality as a life-style. Unsanitary, dirty sex and unsanitary, dirty needles have created the greatest health crisis of our time.

Interview, Dec. 13/
Los Angeles Times, 12-14:(I)30.

Michael S. Dukakis
Governor of Massachusetts (D);
Candidate for the 1988 Democratic
Presidential nomination

3

[Signing the nation's first bill providing health insurance for all Massachusetts residents and calling for similar legislation covering the entire country]: As an American, I don't want my country to stand alone with South Africa as the only two industrialized nations in the world that do not provide basic health security for their citizens. I think it's unconscionable that 37 million of our fellow citizens, most of them members of working families, do not have one dime of basic health insurance . . . From now on, when the sick land at the doorstep of our health-care system, the first question of them will be, "Where does it hurt?" not "How will you pay?"

Boston, April 21/
The New York Times,
4-22:8.

4

[Supporting a national pre-natal health-care program]: The cost of pre-natal care—care that can prevent an infant from being born with an abnormally low birth weight—can be as little as $400. But the cost of caring for that person over a lifetime of illness—illness that could and must be prevented—can reach $400,000 . . . When children and their families have needed a helping hand, [the Reagan-Bush Administration] has given them a cold shoulder. [Vice President and Republican Presidential nominee George] Bush said the other day he was "almost haunted" by the way some children live in America today, but he says that we can't solve their problems . . . I think we can, and, beginning on January 20, 1989, we're going to begin.

Brookline, Mass., Sept. 21/
Los Angeles Times,
9-22:(I)19.

5

My state just became the only state in the nation to provide for universal health care, and we did it with the support of the business community and labor and the health-care community and with virtually everybody in the state. The fact of the matter is that employers who today are insuring their employees are paying the freight because they're paying for those who *aren't*. And I think it's time that when you've got a job in this country, it came with health insurance. That's the way we're going to provide basic health security for all of the citizens of this country of ours.

At Presidential debate,
Winston-Salem, N.C., Sept. 25/
The New York Times,
9-26:10.

Pierre S. duPont IV
Candidate for the 1988
Republican Presidential
nomination; Former
Governor of Delaware (R)

1

AIDS is not a civil-rights issue; it's a severe medical problem with life-and-death moral overtones. We have to take care of people with the disease and do the research to find a cure. But our first responsibility is to stop the spread of it. If we all limit our intimate relationships to a single person, there will be no more AIDS.

Interview/
U.S. News & World Report,
1-25:15.

David Durenberger
United States Senator,
R-Minnesota

2

About 5 per cent of the U.S. population has diabetes—that's 11 million Americans, and a half a million more will be diagnosed this year. But only 6 million of the 11 million know they have diabetes. The remaining 5 million have it but don't know they do. Clearly, these individuals must be identified and given the health care they need ... Those with diabetes spend twice as many days in hospitals as those without diabetes, and diabetes is the fourth leading cause of visits to physicians' offices.

Before the Senate, March 15/
The Washington Post,
3-18:(A)24.

William Evans
Physiologist, U.S. Department
of Agriculture-Tufts University
Center on Aging

3

There is no group in our population that can benefit more from exercise than senior citizens. For a young person, exercise can increase physical function by perhaps 10 per cent. But in an old person you can increase it by 50 per cent.

Time, 2-22:79.

Marlin Fitzwater
Assistant to President of the
United States Ronald Reagan
for Press Relations

4

[On criticism that the Reagan Administration spends too little money fighting the drug problem]: We are spending billions of dollars on drugs. And we are willing to spend more. But we want to do it in a reasonable manner ... We understand everyone's concern and everyone's urge for action, but just to come up with a bill that throws more money at the problem, that isn't direct and doesn't have a good idea of what it's trying to do, is probably not the best, constructive way to do it. And you're seeing a lot of politics involved here . . . a lot of political posturing.

April 15/
The Washington Post, 4-16:(A)8.

A. Bartlett Giamatti
President, National
(baseball) League

5

While it may have a number of social causes, fan unruliness [at sports events] cannot be separated from the issue of excessive use of alcohol. I have no data, but I would say that more problems occur and more human damage is done because of excessive drinking than because of drugs.

Time, 5-23:70.

Willis D. Gradison, Jr.
United States Representative,
R-Ohio

6

Neither the public nor the private sector has figured out how to bring health-cost increases down to the level of general inflation. Medicare once again will be revisited for budget savings [in the next Congress]. The [expected] emphasis will be on the physician side—the hospital side has been getting most of the attention over the past three or four years. Of course, the alternatives for action in the physician area are not entirely clear.

The Washington Post, 11-19:(A)8.

Orrin G. Hatch
United States Senator,
R-Utah

1

[On AIDS]: I have known homosexuals that I liked and I have known homosexuals that I disliked as human beings. Some of them are just as fine human beings as anybody on this [Senate] floor . . . The fact that I disagree with their sexual orientation—and I do—does not stop me from having some compassion for the fact that AIDS is devastating that community. It does not stop me from intelligently appraising the fact that it is starting to devastate every community, not just homosexuals but heterosexuals and young children and everybody else. And it is going to be so pervasive that everybody in this country is going to be shaken by it.

Before the Senate, Washington/
The Washington Post, 5-12:(A)19.

Jesse Helms
United States Senator,
R-North Carolina

2

Let me tell you something about this AIDS epidemic. There is not one single case of AIDS reported in this country that cannot be traced in origin to sodomy . . . The point is, we should not allow the homosexual crowd to use the AIDS issue to promote and legitimize their life-style in American society. And that is what is going on.

Before the Senate, Washington/
The Washington Post, 5-2:(A)19.

Lawrence Horowitz
Physician; Former Staff
Director, Subcommittee on
Health and Scientific Research,
United States Senate

3

Organized medicine has failed to set up an ongoing monitoring system to review the quality of medical care. A doctor licensed today can practice for the next 30 years without ever having his or her competence re-evaluated . . . Very few people would get on an airplane if the pilot were

licensed in 1960 and flying the jets of 1988 without ever having to demonstrate his or her competence to fly those new jets. But many more people die on the operating table and in hospitals each year than die in airplane crashes, and yet we don't require that physicians have their competence recertified.

Interview/USA Today, 11-1:(A)11.

4

The doctor you select, and the hospital in which you're treated, can be more important in determining the outcome of your illness than the disease you have. There can be two different patients walking through two different doctors' doors and one may get better, one may not. And the difference is not the disease, but the doctor.

Interview/USA Today, 11-1:(A)11.

William C. Hsiao
Professor of economics and
health policy, School of Public
Health, Harvard University

5

[On the theory that doctors should charge what their service is worth to their patients]: Some physicians feel that they should be able to charge the patients that way. And that is something which is contrary to the free-enterprise, competitive economic system under which we live. For example, a pair of eyeglasses is worth tens of thousands of dollars to me. But the cost of that pair of eyeglasses is maybe $80. We do not let the eyeglass-makers charge us $20,000 for a pair of eyeglasses. Because that would be unfair practice. In medicine, that may not work very well, because when you and I become seriously ill, if our life is threatened, we're not going to shop around. So, in that sense, medicine holds some monopolistic power.

Interview/USA Today, 9-29:(A)7.

Derek Humphry
Founder, Hemlock Society

6

We are not an anti-medical group, but we see dramatic advances in medical technology as a

(DEREK HUMPHRY)

two-edged sword. It saves our lives and does wonders for us, yet it can also make our deaths miserable . . . People should not have to die in a hospital bed with pipes in their noses and mouths, if they don't want to.

The Christian Science Monitor,
1-15:4.

Betty Jackson
Assistant director of nursing
research, Montefiore Medical Center,
New York

1

I've been advised to tell people I'm an educator, not a nurse. It makes me angry when people say that. Don't they know that when you're in a hospital what you need is a damn good nurse?

"Ms.," June:76.

C. Everett Koop
Surgeon General of the
United States

2

If we could conquer AIDS in this century, the problems that are ancillary to AIDS that are not medical would go on for another 25 to 50 years. There's going to be nobody in this country that's untouched by the economics of it. For example, they're going to run into problems with health-care delivery. In New York, which has the largest number of AIDS patients, people are already finding it hard to find hospital beds.

Interview/USA Today, 5-5:(A)7.

3

[Criticizing tobacco products]: Is it appropriate for tobacco products to be sold through vending machines, which are easily accessible to children? Is it appropriate for free samples of tobacco products to be sent through the mail or distributed on public property, where verification of age is difficult if not impossible? Shouldn't we treat tobacco sales at least as seriously as the sale of alcoholic beverages, for which a specific license is required—and revoked for repeated sales to minors?

News conference,
Washington, May 16/
Los Angeles Times, 5-17:(I)1.

4

For the next 15 years, everything you and I will look at, worry about and talk about in reference to health will be a symptom of the overriding tension between our aspirations and our resources. The things that fascinate Americans are Teflon hips and artificial hearts and separating Siamese twins and transplants and so forth. They're all marvelous and fine—I've been part of them, I made the problem—but with the need we have for so many other things, the competition for funding is going to be great. There are going to be some tough choices down the road.

Interview/Esquire, June:156.

5

We can say today, with greater certainty than ever before, that cigarettes are the most important individual health risk in this country, responsible for more premature deaths and disabilities than any other known agent.

USA Today, 7-26:(A)8.

6

If you are among the two out of three Americans who do not smoke or drink excessively, your choice of diet can influence your long-term health prospects more than any other action you might take . . . Nutritional problems for most Americans have shifted to those created by overconsumption of certain dietary components. Of greatest concern is our excessive intake of dietary fat and its relationship to risk for chronic diseases, such as coronary heart disease, some types of cancers, diabetes, high blood pressure, strokes and obesity.

News briefing,
Washington, July 27/
The New York Times, 7-28:1.

(C. EVERETT KOOP)

1

[Saying the anti-smoking campaign in the U.S. has not adversely affected the finances of tobacco companies]: Although they must notice a change in American sales, they more than make up for it in what they do overseas, which is of real concern to me because they are exporting cigarettes to the Third World. Another factor that is of great concern to me is that as cigarette companies diversify more and more, they get more and more clout, because they control and own practically everything. It would be impossible, I think, to live in Washington for two weeks and not patronize either Philip Morris or RJR Nabisco.

Interview, Oct. 21/
The New York Times, 10-22:5.

Charles LaPorte
Deputy Commissioner for
Substance Abuse Services
of New York State

2

The vast majority of opiate-addicted individuals are abusing a second-substance—cocaine, alcohol. A good percentage have a tremendous need for social programs. A number of them have mental problems. If it's only heroin addiction we're dealing with, it's easy. But I see people who come in, get their dose [of methadone to control their heroin problem], then go outside and commit crimes for their secondary drug, for their housing, for their food. I see them hanging out, dealing other drugs. If we can't control them, if we can't service them, they're the ones who make it impossible to site clinics in a community.

The New York Times, 12-5:(A)13.

Bonnie Liebman
Director of nutrition, Center
for Science in the Public
Interest, Washington

3

Instead of teaching good nutrition in schools, we subject our kids to television commercials that push fast foods, soft drinks, candy bars and sugary cereals. And then we wonder why kids don't ask for fruits and vegetables. I'm not sure there's anything a teacher could do in a classroom to overcome TV commercials, but we're not even trying.

The New York Times, 1-6:15.

Mack Lipkin, Jr.
Associate professor, Medical
School, New York University;
Director, National Task Force
on Medical Interviews

4

[On doctors' interviewing their patients before treatment]: Interviewing is a core clinical skill, one that determines a physician's competence; except for a minority of physicians, most are not doing this well . . . If you feel your doctor is not listening to you, don't be hesitant. Make your concerns explicit. Try to ask the questions that are on your mind anyway. You can say, "These are my concerns, doctor; what would you like to know" . . . One of the most common errors by physicians is the failure to use questions that get the best information. The best strategy is to begin with open-ended questions that let the patient say what is on his mind, then proceed to more focused questions that medical decision-making requires. If the physician uses only closed questions, what he learns will be restricted only to what he can think of. He can miss crucial information that way.

The New York Times, 1-21:12.

H. E. Lister
Chairman, Allstate Life
Insurance Company

5

As a society, we simply cannot afford—emotionally or economically—to give in to AIDS. We have to fight it at every turn, with every weapon at our disposal. And corporations have every legitimate reason to be out front leading the charge.

At forum sponsored by Allstate Life
Insurance Co., Washington,
Jan. 20/Los Angeles Times, 1-21:(I)21.

431

George Lundberg
Pathologist; Editor,
"The Journal of the
American Medical Association"

1

[On euthanasia]: There are many physicians, myself included, who believe that the place where life and death decisions should be made is at the bedside, between the patient, family, doctor and, if appropriate, a religious representative, and that there's no place for the courts in this decision.

Time, 2-15:88.

2

[On the sharp decline in the number of autopsies being performed]: By far the most important effect of this decline of the autopsy is the lack of assurance of control of the quality of medical care. At a time of profound erosion of public trust in the medical profession, nothing could be worse than bringing up the old image of a cover-up.

The New York Times, 7-21:23.

Maurice Maisonnet
Chairman, International
Association for Hospital
Hygiene

3

[On infections contracted by patients in hospitals]: We generally talk about an infection rate of about 12 per cent. Actually, these incidents occur in an uneven pattern. There are "good" and "bad" hospitals, and "good" and "bad" wards. We know, for example, that with orthopedic surgery, there is generally a very low infection rate—about 0.3 per cent or 0.4 per cent. We also know that the figures for recovery rooms can be much higher than average.

World Press Reveiw, August:55.

Carol McCarthy
President, American Hospital
Association

4

[On the importance to hospitals of Medicare payments]: Medicare is very important. That's the program that takes care of the elderly and the disabled. Medicare provides for hospitals, on average, about 40 per cent of all revenues, because most of those over 65 are those who find themselves frequently in need of hospitalization. So when the Medicare program under-pays, it has a significant impact on our hospitals. It's most easily expressed as the result of the Federal government's efforts to deal with its budget deficits by reducing the outlays for the Medicare program.

Interview/USA Today, 8-31:(A)9.

Edwin Meese III
Former Attorney General of
the United States

5

I think we have a strong possibility of making major reductions in [illegal-] drug use if we continue even more aggressively in some of the things that have been started by this [Reagan] Administration. And that is, prevention and education activities starting from the lowest grades, major efforts by employers to establish drug-free work places, including the use of drug testing. Additional steps to make it clear that in no part of society will drugs be tolerated. These are the things that are necessary. We have the means to reduce considerably the drug problem. What we need is will and the individual commitment to do it.

Interview/
USA Today, 12-12:(A)11.

Lynette Mundey
Medical director,
MASS Clinic, Alcohol and
Drug Abuse Services
Administration of the
District of Columbia

6

We who do not use [illegal] drugs cannot understand why people can't just stop—like that—using drugs. After you've lost your job, your home, your family, why can't you just stop? But that's the nature of the beast. This is a disease. It's a chronic disease, just like diabetes

(LYNETTE MUNDEY)

or hypertension. It's a progressive disease, which means that if you do nothing about it, just like diabetes or hypertension, it can be fatal.

The Washington Post,
12-27:(Health)6.

Ronald Reagan
President of the United States

1

[On the new catastrophic-illness coverage for Medicare beneficiaries]: [This new coverage] will help remove a terrible threat from the lives of the elderly and disabled Americans, a threat of an illness requiring acute care, one so devastating it could wipe out the savings of an entire lifetime . . . We have no real way of knowing how much these services will cost. [An increase in costs] could be more than a budget problem; it could be a tragedy. The program, after all, is to be paid by the elderly themselves. So we must control the costs of these new benefits, or we'll harm the very people we're trying to help.

Signing bill authorizing the new
coverage, Washington, July 1/
Los Angeles Times, 7-2:(I)20.

William L. Roper
Administrator, Health Care
Financing Administration of
the United States

2

[On the reports issued by his agency that indicate death rates for Medicare patients at the nation's hospitals]: I am confident that it has had a profound impact on focusing attention on the actual care that is delivered in hospitals. I believe information is power and information drives change. The more of this kind of information, appropriate information, we can publish, the better informed the decisions will be that are being made.

News conference,
Washington, Dec. 15/
Los Angeles Times, 12-16:(I)44.

Robert C. Schlant
Professor of cardiology,
School of Medicine,
Emory University;
Former president, Association
of University Cardiologists

3

Sometimes it's rather discouraging to see how [former heart patients] are living after their recovery. They may stop smoking for a while but then, a year later, they are back on cigarettes. We're doing rather miserably in getting people to alter their life-styles. In an ideal world [we would] get some people to alter their lives before anything happens. After all, everything we do— bypassing, other surgeries, after-care treatment— is secondary and palliative. It's primary prevention that is needed.

Los Angeles Times, 12-25:(I)3.

Mervyn Silverman
President, American
Foundation for AIDS Research

4

[On his organization's awarding a grant to a Portland, Oregon, clinic to distribute clean needles to drug addicts as a way of preventing the spread of AIDS]: The feeling of a lot of people who work in AIDS is that we're engaged in a war, and in wartime we do things—hopefully good things—we wouldn't normally do. I never heard of anybody starting to use drugs because needles were available, or stopping because they couldn't find a clean one. Sure, it's a mixed message, but if we want to keep people alive to give them the straight [anti-drug] message, we've got to do it.

June 9/
The Washington Post, 6-10:(I)1.

Fortney H. (Pete) Stark
United States Representative,
D-California

5

The cost of health care to the [U.S.] economy needs to be immediately addressed. The Japanese are healthier, while spending about half as much of their GNP on health care. It is no wonder we are not competing in world markets. Doctor costs in particular need to be addressed.

The Washington Post, 11-19:(A)8.

B. J. Stiles
President, National
Leadership Coalition on AIDS

1

[Saying most companies have remained un-involved with the AIDS issue]: As yet it is still very sensitive for most national airline carriers, hotel chains and fast-food enterprises to make known publicly what their commitment to AIDS might be. The fear is that you and I as consumers may still be skeptical that when a corporation commits itself on AIDS, that may imply that they may have cases of AIDS in their work-force or a special interest in the disease . . . [But] even with the most conservative projections, we will have 300,000 cases of AIDS in this country within three years, compared with 55,000 now. So the experience of many companies with the epidemic will likely change—and with it their policies.

The New York Times, 3-22:28.

Louis W. Sullivan
Secretary of Health and
Human Services-designate of
the United States

2

[On public-health priorities for the U.S.]: First, we must develop new initiatives and oppor-tunities to improve the efficiency, the effective-ness and equity of our nation's health-care system. Two, we must bring runaway health-care costs under control without compromising quality health care or access to health care. We must address the disparities that exist in the avail-ability and the quality of health care for Ameri-cans of all economic means, especially finding ways to improve this care for the nation's minori-ties and our disadvantaged citizens. And four, we must work tirelessly to find cures and better treat-ment for dreaded diseases like cancer, heart

disease and AIDS through strengthening our efforts in biomedical research.

News conference,
Washington, Dec.22/
The New York Times, 12-23:(A)10.

James D. Watkins
Admiral, United States Navy (ret.);
Former Chairman,
President's Commission
on AIDS

3

[On current health-care problems]: We have a burgeoning problem of delivering health care to the elderly. We have a hardening of an under-class, as many have called it, from single parent-ing, usually a mother; poverty; school dropout rates; all of the things that go with a growing sense of hopelessness among too many in the popula-tion. We see an insidious drug-abuse specter over the nation. And the unwillingness of people to come into health-care professions because they're very worried about liability—"What are the [in-surance] premiums I'm going to have to pay? Look at the threats against me. Look at the court cases."

Interview/USA Today, 6-28:(A)11.

4

[On Vice President, and now President-elect, George Bush's endorsement last summer of the AIDS Commission's report that advocated anti-discrimination and confidentiality legislation in dealing with AIDS patients]: I called him up in Maine a few days later and I said: "Mr. Vice President, I'm calling you to tell you what a courageous act you just performed. I wasn't anticipating that." I said: "You're going to lose a lot of right-wing votes because of this." He said: "Jim, I know it. But it was the right thing to do." When he said that, I broke down. It was such an important statement to me, personally, that I had not heard from anyone in the Executive Branch, that I was overwhelmed by it. I knew then there was hope.

Los Angeles Times,
12-12:(I)14.

James Watson
Molecular biologist;
Co-winner, 1962 Nobel Prize
for Medicine and Physiology

1

DNA provides the information that makes possible our existence and the existence of every other form of life. If you want to understand human beings in this very complete sense, you've got to understand the nature of DNA, how complicated it is, what sorts of instructions it carries ... There are really two basic forms of diseases that human beings suffer. One is infectious disease, and the other is genetic disease—a disease which results from imperfections in our genetic [DNA] instruction. Working out the genetic instructions for human existence will make it much easier for us to understand the nature of all these genetic diseases.

Interview/USA Today, 6-13:(A)11.

Henry A. Waxman
United States Representative,
D-California

2

[On ways to discourage people from smoking]: We can license cigarette sales, we can make sure they're not sold to minors, we can say more about the advertising of cigarettes, especially the promotion of cigarettes to children and women. We can increase taxes on cigarettes, which would make them more expensive, so that many young people won't get started with a habit that's going to be so expensive. These are some of the things we can do legislatively to discourage people from smoking and, hopefully, get the clear message out that people who don't smoke shouldn't start, and those who are smoking should be aware that, notwithstanding the fact that it's addictive, they can still quit.

Interview/USA Today, 6-15:(A)9.

3

[Criticizing the Reagan Administration for proposing to ban research using tissue from aborted fetuses]: The reason more premature infants survive now is fetal research. The reason we have safe vaccines for children is fetal research. Only in an election year could even this White House propose something so far-reaching and so short-sighted.

The Washington Post, 9-9:(A)4.

4

[On House-passed legislation to fund the fight against AIDS]: The large margin of passage shows that the House believes common sense and good medical judgment is the right course for our nation in dealing with this epidemic. By protecting confidentiality, we've created a real incentive for people to come forward, to be tested and to learn how to stop the spread of the disease. There's nothing to be gained by frightening people away.

Washington, Sept. 23/
Los Angeles Times, 9-24:(I)1.

Robert Windom
Assistant Secretary for Health,
Department of Health and Human
Services of the United States

5

It took years to educate people to stop smoking to prevent cancer. Even today, people continue [to smoke], or they don't want to accept the anti-smoking message. They ignore it, they don't listen to us, and it takes a long time for many people to get that message. It's like going to school: you've got to hear the lesson several times before you learn what the teacher's saying. The educational process is repetition, day in and day out, so that's why a lot of people might say it takes so much information over and over before they get hit with the reality.

Interview/USA Today, 5-5:(A)7.

Sidney Wolfe
Co-founder, Public Citizen
Health Research Group,
Washington

6

... there are too many people making too much money from health care. Without adequate regulatory restraints, there's bound to be a lot of

WHAT THEY SAID IN 1988

(SIDNEY WOLFE)

unnecessary services rendered. I have a whole box sitting there that contains item after item mailed to me, as a doctor, asking me if I'd like to open up a new profit center in my office. "Buy our testing machine, buy this, buy that—it will pay for itself in two months." Hospitals with empty beds—something like a third of all beds are unoccupied—are doing the same thing, opening eating centers, sleeping centers, burping centers— all to generate more revenue to justify their existence. Who's paying for this expensive care?

Interview, Washington/
The Wall Street Journal,
4-22:(R)30.

The Performing Arts

BROADCASTING

Jay Presson Allen
Television writer

1

[TV writing] isn't like making movies. Your rewards are immediate; your punishments are immediate. You have no hope of getting it right. You *don't* get it right. And yet every day you start all over again. It's fascinating.

Interview/
American Film, March:43.

Michael Checkland
Director general, British
Broadcasting Corporation

2

A distinguished newspaper columnist in Britain talked about the BBC last week as one of three national assets that he was urging the government not to destroy. He said, "After the monarchy, the BBC is probably our most renowned institution. Our television, both commercial and public, is the envy of the world, and justly so" . . . This sense of ownership which people feel about the BBC makes them especially critical about its programming. All [their letters] include a phrase like, "It's my money you're spending"—and, of course, they're right.

Before Academy of Television Arts
and Sciences, Los Angeles/
Emmy Magazine, May-June:53.

Dan R. Coats
United States Representative,
R-Indiana

3

[On young viewers who are exposed to violence on TV]: Ultimately, it is the responsibility of parents to deal with these concerns . . . not the government and not the broadcasting industry. We're kidding ourselves if we think otherwise.

USA Today, 10-24:(A)10.

Joan Ganz Cooney
President, Children's
Television Workshop

4

We want kids to read, and we know TV is a thief of time. But we can't keep moaning about the fact that not only kids, but all of us, are getting more and more of our information from TV. And if we're honest about it, we know that TV is often the catalyst that drives us to read more about something we only learn in sketch from the tube. But even if TV isn't a back door into books, as we hope it can be, if you can only teach with television, isn't that better than not teaching at all? What we most need is moral leadership to reverse our predisposition against TV—which is something politicians are uniquely suited to provide. If only they would.

Interview/
U.S. News & World Report,
6-13:19.

Barbara Corday
Executive vice president,
CBS Entertainment

5

Keep the talented writers from leaving the weekly shows. That's the name of the game. There is no substitute for wonderful writing, but a lot of the best writers burn out in series television.

Interview/"Ms.," October:67.

Fred W. Friendly
Professor emeritus of journalism,
Columbia University;
Former president, CBS News

6

Commercial TV makes so much [money] doing its worst that it can't afford to do its best . . .

437

(FRED W. FRIENDLY)

You can't go on letting the public airwaves be raped by people who don't give a damn about content but only care what they can sell the station for in two or three years.

Before Senate Communications Subcommittee, Washington, April 27/Los Angeles Times, 4-28:(IV)14.

Don Hewitt
Producer, CBS-TV

1

Sometimes the television set is a theatre. Sometimes it's a sports arena. Sometimes it's a newspaper. And sometimes it becomes a chapel. And that's what it was at the time of the [President John] Kennedy assassination [in 1963]. Americans went to church in front of their television sets, and the whole country held hands. That weekend we got the assignment we never asked for—ministering to the country in times of national trauma. J. F. K. Martin Luther King. Bobby Kennedy. The [space-] shuttle disaster. From that day on, if . . . a plane is taken hostage or there's a baby in a well, the country goes to their television. And it started that day in Dallas [when John Kennedy was assassinated].

Interview/TV Guide, 11-19:8.

Robert Hughes
Art critic; Author

2

Television tends to favor a particular kind of simple-mindedness in a particularly insistent way, and it has shown that it is capable of debasing the manners and morals of an immense population of what was once the greatest democracy in the world [the U.S.]. It has done this so definitively that almost no further degradation is possible. I think there's an excellent case to be made for the abolition of the television, and were I the benevolent dictator of the world, that would be high on my list.

Interview/Esquire, June:223.

Glenda Jackson
Actress

3

The one medium I really dislike intensely is television. The thing I loathe about television is that those cameras are just as happy photographing each other as they are looking at you. And there's absolutely no sense of anything in a television studio . . . I hate working for it. It doesn't teach you anything.

Interview, New York/ The Christian Science Monitor, 5-18:22.

Pierre Juneau
President, Canadian Broadcasting Corporation

4

Increased Canadian content in English-language [Canadian] television is imperative. As competition from American programs constantly increases, maintaining adequate levels of service means investing sufficient resources in [domestic Canadian] programs.

Emmy Magazine, Jan.-Feb.:6.

Larry King
TV-radio talk-show host

5

. . . all people who really make it in radio and television break rules. Like, always be yourself. The great ones are always themselves—like [Jackie] Gleason and [Arthur] Godfrey. What you see is what they are. The problem is that 98 per cent of the people try to be somebody else, so when the camera comes on or the light goes on over the microphone, their voices change or the way they talk changes. They begin to think, "What does the audience want to hear?" They forget just to be themselves.

Interview, Virginia/ Cosmopolitan, November:176.

Linda Lavin
Actress

6

I think people do want to see themselves as they are [in TV programs]. That's the kind of

(LINDA LAVIN)

feedback that I got in the nine years [her show] *Alice* was on television and that I get even now because it's in syndication. People say, "Thank you for showing me how to laugh, for showing me that I'm not alone in my plight." I think that television can be extremely powerful in showing us as we are and freeing us to feel good about ourselves and our struggles. I think that's the reason for the success of *All in the Family* and *Cagney and Lacey*. It isn't just the drama. It's the relationships and the reality of the people that audiences connect to.

Interview/USA Today, 12-14:(A)7.

Lindsay Law
Vice president and executive producer, "American Playhouse," PBS-TV

1

I like the harmonious environment of working in public television. I'm not one who thinks that art comes out of maximum strife. But aside from that, and on a larger scale, having grown up learning the variety of experience through reading, I'm concerned that the art of storytelling doesn't come naturally to young film-makers these days. [TV has] standardized and reduced experience in our culture. And we're growing out of touch with history . . . I work in a small world, but the projects are sustaining, whether they're successful or not. It means a lot to me that our conversations center on how to make what we're doing better, and that doing our best is our main criterion.

Interview/Los Angeles Times,
12-25:(Calendar)62.

Sheldon Leonard
Director

2

Television today is conditioned by how much product it sells. A show's survival is not based on whether it's good, but on how well it sells. That's the wrong sort of standard, but there's nothing you can do about it.

Interview/
Emmy Magazine, July-Aug.:36.

Jim Mooney
President, National Cable Television Association

3

Cable [TV] is reaching critical mass both as a force in television programming and in the consumer's perception of what constitutes a full menu of television choices. Today, watching only broadcast television is like eating at McDonald's every night. Viewers are now aware of the possibilities.

Los Angeles Times, 1-7:(VI)6.

Geraldo Rivera
TV discussion-show host

4

So much of the TV business, if it's done right, is improvisational. That's what people are afraid of now. That's why the network news divisions never do live shows unless they're set pieces: the [U.S.-Soviet] summit, the [political] convention. They never go "live" to a drug bust or anything as uncontrollable as that—which is really [discussion-show host Phil] Donahue's genius in the talk-show arena: He's unscripted. You go in and synthesize a reality, and then you let it roll. That's the formula: You bring the forces to bear where they can act and react, and, using your wit and your research, try to convert heat to light.

Interview, New York/
Cosmopolitan, October:226.

Howard Rosenberg
Pulitzer Prize-winning television critic, "Los Angeles Times"

5

The problem with most of the critics I've read is that they define their jobs too narrowly. They treat TV only as an art-form, not as a social form. The TV critic is really the decathlete of critics. Because TV is so eclectic, you can write about everything. That includes being a social commentator . . . Since I've been doing this job, critics have gotten a lot tougher. Back in 1971, when I started, most of the television critics were old geezers near retirement. The papers put them

(HOWARD ROSENBERG)

in a corner and let them rewrite press releases. They did that until they melded into their desks, and then somebody would come along and throw out the desk and the person sitting at it. But in the mid-'70s, as newspapers became more aware of the reality of TV—that it was here to stay, that "Hey, I gotta cover it because it's *powerful*"— there was an emergence of a different kind of critic—younger, with a news background and reporting instincts.

Interview/
Emmy Magazine, Jan.-Feb.:18.

John H. Savage
Producer

1

The major difference between Soviet television and ours [U.S. TV] has been that their TV is supposed to teach people to think correctly; our TV is supposed to gather an audience, so it can be sold to an advertiser.

Interview/
The Christian Science Monitor,
11-29:24.

Tom Shales
Television critic,
"The Washington Post"

2

I think the critic in any medium should be someone who loves that medium. I do love TV, and I see a lot of critics out there who seem not to. They're more inclined to assert superiority over the medium. I don't feel superior to it at all.

Emmy Magazine, Jan.-Feb.:18.

Grant Tinker
President, GTG Productions;
Former chairman, National
Broadcasting Company

3

The only talent I have is in knowing talent when I see it. I don't have one creative bone in my body. I've never had an original thought. But, and

this is a big but, I do know creativity when I see it, and I know that it's important to let creative people have their go at things.

USA Today, 2-29:(D)2.

Laurence A. Tisch
President, CBS, Inc.

4

There's always room on the [TV] schedule for anything that's good. I have a very simple philosophy: If it's good, if it represents quality, eventually people will come around to it. You can't look at it just from a money standpoint. That's a trap. Because if you wanted to program your network with low ratings, maybe you could make much more money than programming it with decent ratings. But that's not our intention. Our intention is to program it for the most consumer satisfaction and to build up a certain loyalty to a program. A [documentary news] program like *West 57th*, if it's right, can last for 10 or 15 years. *60 Minutes* is on for 20 years. Then you have a real franchise. It's not a sitcom that may be in for two years or three years, and then gone. I think there's a difference in the franchise value of a program of this type, and we don't want to say we're going to put on a program that doesn't cost much, and we'll accept a low rating. I'd rather spend much more money on the program and get the rating.

Daily Variety, 1-15:79.

Ted Turner
Chairman, Turner
Broadcasting System

5

[On the TV networks' loss of audience to such alternatives as cable-TV, pay-TV and videocassettes]: The networks are not doing anything wrong. It's like AM radio. They weren't doing anything wrong either, but FM radio was better.

Time, 10-17:57.

Garrick Utley
Correspondent, NBC News

6

[Criticizing "tabloid TV" shows, discussion programs that cover controversial topics in a sen-

(GARRICK UTLEY)

sationalist manner]: The very presence on the television screen, coming out of that box into television homes, gives these programs and the subjects and the behavior a certain legitimacy . . . These are entertainment programs posing as news programs, posing as documentary programs, posing as investigative journalism. [And worse,] they are feeding off the lifeblood of news itself.

Before Radio-Television News
Directors Association, Las Vegas, Nev./
Daily Variety, 12-5:22.

Fritz Weaver
Actor

1

Television is junk—situation comedies, turned out like ground meat, and the cynical manipulation of the audience.

Interview, Washington/
The Christian Science Monitor,
9-29:19.

Edward Woodward
British actor

2

There's absolutely no difference between doing McCall [the character in his TV series] and Richard III. No difference whatsoever. You are presenting to the audience a character and a story that have to be as honest and believable as they are interesting. It's just a different approach. You use as much energy for TV, but you channel that energy differently. In England, in the early days of live television, there was this thing called natural acting, which was a lot of foolishness. Acting's acting. The net result was that the

soundman always looked as though he were going deaf trying to hear what the actors were saying. In American TV there are actually divisions between the times of day you work. Actors who work the morning programs are desperately trying to get into [the afternoon] soaps to show that they're really actors, and the big soap stars are desperately trying to get into prime-time. It's ridiculous. You're judged by the time of day you work. And this thinking is being perpetuated for the most part by the actors themselves.

Interview, New York/
Emmy Magazine, March-April:10.

Timothy E. Worth
United States Senator,
D-Colorado

3

Something is wrong with the state of children's television in this country. I have been saying that ever since I was first elected to Congress in 1974. Back then, broadcasters' service to children was merely considered unsatisfactory. Today it is little short of a national disgrace. There is virtually no programming offered to serve the educational or informational needs and interests of youngsters. Children spend more time watching television—an estimated 1,500 hours each year—than they do attending school or engaging in any single activity except sleeping. However, with the notable exception of some very good public-broadcasting programs, such as the now-legendary *Sesame Street,* the medium of broadcast television has largely failed to deliver any worthwhile educational content for youngsters. As a result of the FCC's neglect of this problem, a troublesome situation has grown much worse.

Before the Senate,
Washington, Oct. 19/
The New York Times, 10-20:(B)2.

MOTION PICTURES

Pedro Almodovar
Spanish director

1

I always loved the artificiality of Hollywood. In my own films, I try to find the artifice which works best with the story I'm telling. It doesn't take away from the film. In fact, the more artificial it is, the more the emotions of the characters can shine through.

Interview, Los Angeles/
Los Angeles Times, 12-20:(VI)8.

Don Ameche
Actor

2

By 1949, my picture career was all over. I turned down an offer to renew my contract with Fox because I thought I could choose my own films. It was a brutally bad mistake. It's not just difficult, it's impossible, for an actor to choose his own properties.

Newsweek, 10-31:72.

Alexander Askoldov
Soviet director

3

It stupefies me that after 2½ years of *perestroika* [reform in the Soviet Union] not a single deep, authentic, intellectual film has been shot in the Soviet Union. Sure, you can do as much reconstruction as you like. You can buy nice film, you can cooperate with Hollywood, but if you don't have anything inside you, then nothing will happen. So many directors are traveling to America, but they don't have any ideas. They're coming here because they're running around shopping!

Interview, California/
The Wall Street Journal, 5-24:32.

Bernardo Bertolucci
Director

4

Cinema is living in a moment of shyness and fear of the challenge of television. Too many movies have been intimidated by TV. They are trying to imitate the rhythms and language of television. Maybe I'm an idealist, but I still see [movie] theatres as big cathedrals where we all go to dream the same dreams together. I really believe in the spirit of cinema.

Accepting Directors Guild of
America Award, Beverly Hills, Calif./
Daily Variety, 3-14:27.

Tony Bill
Producer, Director; Former actor

5

My feeling is that the greatest single problem with every actor—maybe even more so for the stars—is the compulsion to be good: the feeling, sometimes subconscious, that every moment of every job is an audition for the next one. I don't know how to get rid of that. When I was an actor, I got rid of it because I didn't *need* to act; I didn't have that financial or emotional need. Most actors are inherently desperate to be good, to protect an image, to secure a position. One advantage of using non-actors or new people is that they don't come in with such desperate baggage.

Interview/American Film, April:12.

John Boorman
Director

6

Real cinema is metaphor. It expresses more than you see. Images and action and words all coincide to tell more than the surface, which so much of the time is flat.

Interview/Daily Variety, 2-2:12.

James L. Brooks
Director, Screenwriter

1

[On a screenwriting conference he attended several years ago]: I love dialogue, and I think it has a place in film, and it surprised me to find that was a debatable point. The others all felt the dialogue had to be subordinated. The seminar ended up with criticism of Paddy Chayefsky, who I think is one of the great writers in the language. Some of these film buffs were saying that Chayefsky's gorgeous speeches about the human experience were heresy in film. I understand more visual films, but I can't understand the people who don't appreciate dialogue.

Interview, Los Angeles/
The New York Times, 1-7:18.

Frank Capra
Former director

2

[Criticizing the colorizing of old black-and-white films, such as his *It's a Wonderful Life*]: *It's a Wonderful Life* was filmed in black-and-white. The makeup, the sets, the costumes, the camera and laboratory work were all designed for black-and-white film, for a black-and-white palette, not color. It's a different technique. The male actors wore no makeup and the actresses, only that which they wore every day. I wanted everyone to look natural. Then came Colorization Incorporated and poured their pastels over everything so that everyone looks the same. Even the villain looks pink and cheerful. The story has, therefore, been changed. This monstrosity is an embarrassment to me and my friend, [the star of the film] James Stewart. I appeal to you for the chance for redress and justice, not only for myself but for colleagues who are no longer here to defend their reputations for themselves. For if they have not already been under attack by insults of shortening and lengthening, electronic speeding up and slowing down, by editing, colorization, re-scoring and other electronic revisions, they will be shortly.

Letter to House Appropriations
Committee/Daily Variety, 6-16:2.

John Cleese
Actor, Screenwriter

3

There is a well-established tradition of fairly cruel humor in film, starting with Chaplin and the Marx Brothers, right through to the manipulativeness of [TV's] Bilko, the gentle cynicism of George Burns and up to the very tough comedy you get from the modern comics in the 1980s. I think comedy that doesn't have that streak is essentially mediocre, safe and uninteresting. The question then is, is it really cruel; but I think, for example, when [cartoon character] Tom is run over by Jerry on a steamroller, you laugh, but you don't think, "God, that poor cat must have suffered dreadfully." You can see that it is an idea. Literal-minded people cannot see the difference between what happens on screen and what happens in reality; but more intelligent people understand that they can laugh at an idea which would not be funny in real life. They can make that jump between pretend and real, and they can laugh at the dark side of life when it is pretend.

Interview/
Films & Filming, October:7.

Claude Chabrol
French director

4

[On what he would like to take from directors Ernst Lubitsch, F. W. Murnau, Fritz Lang and others]: I would have liked to take Lubitsch's irony, his ability to treat things in a funny way. If you don't know how to laugh at yourself, others may laugh at you. From Murnau, I'd like the capacity to single out an esthetic force in everything. From Lang, I'd take the ability to identify and dismantle the mechanisms of human existence at the very moment when it is being described. Roberto Rossellini also influenced me regarding timing and rhythm, with his way of cutting things short and turning chance to his advantage. "Everything in life is worth making complicated," he said to me, "except directing."

Interview/
World Press Review,
October:61.

Julie Christie
Actress

1

[On the few films she has made in the past several years]: They haven't exactly been [commercial] blockbusters. But the kinds of films I'm interested in these days will never reach a huge audience. I know that going in. I'm not at all discouraged by the number of films offered to me. I'm pleased that things do not turn up more often.

Interview, Sydney, Australia/
The New York Times, 7-12:18.

Sean Connery
Actor

2

I don't take my so-called image too seriously. That's the kiss of death for any actor. You know, the reason Burt Lancaster has had a more varied career than Kirk Douglas is because he's refused to allow himself to be limited. He was always ready to play less romantic parts and was more experimental in his choice of roles. That's the way I've tried to be. I don't mind being older or looking stupid on-camera. I've had great roles that were totally opposite of [his long-running secret-agent role] of James Bond . . . I've tried to be guided by what was different, what was refreshing and stimulating. But somehow, producers and directors always think of me when they want a strong law-and-order man!

Interview/50 Plus, August:61.

Martha Coolidge
Director

3

[On the hardest lesson she has learned in over 20 years of film-making]: I think the biggest lesson was realizing what a director really is. The image I had, the image most people have, is that the director is completely in control of the film. You're the creative person. But that's not exactly it. The director is the sandwich person. On the one hand, you're the leader, the inspiration and guide to everyone on the set. But on the other hand, you're under all these other people you're working for, and they have their ideas about what

they expect you to do. You're the big person in one arena, but you're the employee in the other. It varies from job to job, but the biggest lesson was discovering how to find the most effective avenue of expression and creativity in the areas where you as the director have no control and no power.

Interview/
American Film, December:19.

Francis Ford Coppola
Director

4

You're limited in the kind of movies you can make. There are only types: the thriller and so on. And the economics of film-making are so tough. The director's in the position of being a point man and you can be behind the 8-ball in two days. For all the grief, what you do make may not be what people want to see, but it eats up incredible amounts of your life.

Interview, Rutherford, Calif./
Los Angeles Times,
8-7:(Calendar)5.

5

If you look at the criticism of my films, they always say, "It fails to reach me or fulfill me because it doesn't do this, this, this or this," and my feeling is that this, this, this or this is precisely what I avoid. It's a well-known fact that if you string all the chestnuts together, then everyone will like it. But making a film isn't just stringing all that obligatory stuff together; it's trying to take a little of your own way of seeing the world and putting it out so they can see that, too. The things that I really like are not successful, and I don't particularly expect them to be any more.

Interview, New York/
Mother Jones, September:23.

Constantin Costa-Gavras
Director

6

In the movie industry . . . we have a gift of vision. It's not a vision to tell people what's right or wrong, [but] an ability to help people to think, to feel, to experience the past and future, the good and the bad in a way that no one else can. Through our art we can help people understand what it feels like to be persecuted and denied justice, what it feels like to be judged by the color of our skin, not by the beliefs in our heart.

At ceremony upon receiving Torch of Liberty Award of American Civil Liberties Union, Beverly Hills, Calif., Aug. 23/Daily Variety, 8-25:3.

Jonathan Demme
Director

1

[Directing is] not about "How can I make this my own?" It's about "How can I make this interesting?" I do bring the conceit to it that if I find certain things deeply interesting or deeply amusing, then others will, too. And you've got to have that conceit or else you'll never be able to make a choice.

Interview, New York/ The Washington Post, 8-20:(C)6.

Colleen Dewhurst
Actress

2

Acting is the arena in which, once I enter it, I am wholly self-disciplined. Acting gives me pride. The emotional, mental, spiritual concentration becomes fully a reason for my being. Anything that invades, I will throw off. It is a quiet place in the storm.

Interview/Lear's, Nov.-Dec.:155.

Kirk Douglas
Actor

3

An actor becomes an actor to escape. It's a form of overcoming shyness, overcoming insecurity. You hide behind characters you play. So you become Spartacus, big and strong, or you can become weak, like in my very first picture.

There's nobody who can play weakness as well as I can. And everybody thinks of me as a tough guy. I understand weakness. I'm not afraid to play it. I know you have to be strong in order to be weak.

Interview, Washington/ The Washington Post, 9-29:(B)1.

Clint Eastwood
Actor, Director, Producer

4

[On whether he has a sense of his audience when he makes a film]: No, I don't. I just see the project. I don't like to think in those terms. I don't see the audience. I make the film, and that's it. And they like it, or they don't. That's up to them. You're always hoping they're going to see in the story what you saw, but you have to make it, then let it go. You have to make it for yourself, otherwise you're not true to what you're doing. If you make it with an audience in mind or a reviewer in mind, you'll get fooled every time.

Interview/ American Film, September:29.

5

I never had the pleasure of working on huge-budget films, though I have been in a few, along the way. And I didn't see the huge budgets transmitted to the screen that much. So maybe, all that lumped together, left me with a certain philosophy. You have to be realistic: Look at a film and know what it's going to cost, and then have the pride in making it for that. If you go over, it should be for reasons beyond your control, not for poor workmanship or a lack of decision-making ability.

Interview, New York/ The Washington Post, 10-17:(B)2.

Blake Edwards
Director, Screenwriter

6

[Saying film executives too often try to give the audience what they think it wants]: You put the ingredients together, but it's not enough. You put

(BLAKE EDWARDS)

Rambo III together and suddenly the audience doesn't want Rambo any more. That's the mistake executives always make—looking forward to the past.

Interview, Los Angeles/
Los Angeles Times, 7-26:(VI)3.

Harlan Ellison
Author, Screenwriter

1

Most of the directors who have genuine talent and ability like to have writers around [while filming]. It is the hacks who object. The less secure they are, the less they want the writer around, because the writer will point out they're doing it wrong . . . It's possible for hot writers to negotiate control but, in the final analysis, they don't have it. Robert Towne is about the best [writer] we have produced, and he has had to denounce films made from his own scripts.

Los Angeles Times, 1-20:(VI)4.

Michael J. Fox
Actor

2

. . .the more you do [as an actor], the better you get. As my father would say, if you set a full plate in front of yourself, make sure you eat it neatly, quickly and completely. And then you belch.

Interview, Los Angeles/
Los Angeles Times, 3-31:(VI)13.

George MacDonald Fraser
Author, Screenwriter

3

Critics [of historical films] tend to dwell on Hollywood's mistakes. One small blunder, one bad line, one piece of miscasting, and they dismiss a movie as junk. The critics seldom give the film industry credit for the vast amount of history it has gotten right. Sergei Bondarchuk's *Waterloo* and John Ford's *Drums Along the Mohawk* give, in a few frames, a living picture of the past that could not be obtained from volumes of written history.

Interview/People, 10-24:114.

Dustin Hoffman
Actor

4

[Saying he recently lectured at a college film class and none of the students had ever heard of *The Graduate,* one of his most famous films]: Nobody'd seen it. And a chill went through me. I went blank for 10 minutes; I started sweating. My wife, who was sitting in the back of the class, later told me I was saying things like, "Gee, it was kind of a big movie for its time. I think you'd like it. You might connect with it." But they'd never heard of it. I went home that day kind of shaking. And thinking, it's over. Twenty years. You just wake up one day and it's over.

Interview, Los Angeles/
American Film, December:61

Glenda Jackson
Actress

5

I love working for a film camera, because it is totally obsessed with what you're doing. You never have to work for its attention.

Interview, New York/
The Christian Science Monitor,
5-18:22.

Erland Josephson
Swedish actor

6

The actor himself—the art of acting—reminds people about their own possibilities. It reminds people that they [choose] a few parts in their personal lives out of a thousand possibilities. If this "secondary" art didn't exist, I think a lot of windows would be closed forever. It opens a lot of experiences and knowledge about human beings. It's also a very [fundamental] form of expressing yourself: to pretend, to lie, to show you have the possibility of being someone else if the circumstances are different.

Interview, New York/
The Christian Science Monitor,
3-23:21.

Elia Kazan
Director

1

I have a reputation as a very strong director, but I hardly raise my voice. There's nothing to raise your voice about. We're partners in an enterprise. You just talk to the actors and hope for agreement. I never bullied people the way a lot of old-time film directors did. John Ford and Howard Hawks had a slightly bullying way. Ford would ask an actor what he or she thought about a scene and then do the opposite. He once slugged somebody, but nobody had the nerve to slug him back. They could have killed him. He was just a rickety old Irishman.

Interview/
U.S. News & World Report, 6-6:55.

2

Women . . . are better actors than men. Women are always in a sense—I don't mean in a bad sense—acting. A woman who is going out asks herself, "Who am I going out with? And how do I dress to go out with that person?" Life is full of drama for them. Men aren't like that. They go out wearing the same damn suit and have a drink or two while they worry about business. That's a terrible generalization, but something like that happens. Acting fulfills women in some way that it doesn't a man.

Interview/
U.S. News & World Report. 6-6:55.

Jack Lemmon
Actor

3

[On his being chosen to be honored with the Life Achievement Award of the American Film Institute]: After I got over the initial shock and the great joy, I began to think . . . I'd better be damn careful about what I do in the future, and try not to lay too many eggs. Oy! . . . I think it does make one aware. Hey, listen, if you have done a body of work they think is this deserving, then you'd better damn well try to keep the rest of your work on as high a level—as much as you can . . . I'm in a fortunate position, yes. I pick and

choose, so to speak. But, God knows, so do dozens and dozens of other people. Sometimes we're right and sometimes we're wrong. I think the longevity of my career—and many others—is only that you're right often enough . . . Even if the film may be very good, it just may not be that pertinent to the movie-going public by the time it gets out a year-and-a-half later. So it's really very often by guess and by God.

Interview, Feb. 16/
Daily Variety, 2-18:24.

4

I don't believe you can be dumb and be a good actor. Actors have to be able to perceive human behavior and not just work from instinct. Actors are often messed up emotionally, but that shouldn't be confused with stupidity.

Interview/
American Film, March:36.

5

If once, twice in your life, an actor can get a part with more depth, he can go beyond entertaining. He can make people think. It is a noble profession, and I'm damn proud to be part of it.

Upon receiving Life Achievement
Award from American Film
Institute, Beverly Hills, Calif.,
March 10/Daily Variety, 3-14:8.

John Lithgow
Actor

6

Me and self-doubt are real good friends. But the real danger in acting is worrying about how you're going to come off, which isn't quite the same thing as how well you're going to do the role. My successes have come in roles I didn't think I was capable of playing. The only thing you have to fear is fear itself.

Interview, New York/
Los Angeles Times,
5-1:(Calendar)21.

447

Gina Lollobrigida
Actress

1

Some of today's films are made without real actors and without acceptable scripts. [As for sex in films, years ago] they restrained my dance movements in *Solomon and the Queen of Sheba,* and they made me put a diamond in my belly-button. [Today,] what can I say about films in which actresses show their behinds even before they show their faces?

World Press Review, March:53.

George Lucas
Director

2

A film-maker is working out of his own personal psychology. I like the rogue with a heart of gold. That self-centered character who eventually enters the fray ends up in everything I've ever done. But [former directors] John Ford, Howard Hawks, John Huston and Frank Capra had the same character in many of their movies. Capra had the naive, idealistic young man with a strong moral character. Ford had the lovable, hard-drinking, true-blue, loyal rogue. Art is the retelling of certain themes in a new light, making them accessible to the public of the moment.

Interview, Nicasio, Calif./
The New York Times, 6-9:17.

Sidney Lumet
Director

3

I call them "movies." I won't even use the word "film," I'm in such protest against it. And the word "cinema" won't pass my throat.

At symposium sponsored by First
New York International Festival of
the Arts and Tisch School of the
Arts, New York University,
June 21/The New York Times,
6-23:18.

4

I don't like "technique" to show [in a film]. I think it's an interruption for an audience. It certainly is for me; when I see the wheels working, that's when I cut out. But that doesn't mean that I'm against stylization. But I want it to be done with such subtlety that you can't see it happening.

Interview/
Film Comment, August:37.

Norman Mailer
Author

5

Film, to me, is vastly different from writing [novels], it's truly a different art. Theatre and novel-writing are actually closer to one another than novel-writing and film. To me, film lives somewhere in the psyche in a way that writing doesn't. It's like memory and dreams.

Interview/
Films and Filming, January:6.

Louis Malle
Director

6

. . . I don't think the cinema, as a medium, is a very good vehicle for messages or even ideas. What cinema does really extraordinarily well is emotions. It's good at sensing and discovering and evoking, a lot more like what I call the sensual arts, like painting or music. It always deals very clumsily with ideologies. It can show them, but when it really tries to demonstrate them, it's always in trouble.

Interview, Paris/
U.S. News & World Report,
2-15:69.

7

[Saying he decides what films to make based on his "curiosity"]: That's what I always keep coming back to. That's the thing that keeps you going. I was stunned, for example, by [director] John Huston, coming up at his age with something that is as young—and I mean young in the best sense—as *The Dead.* You could see the amount both of control and enthusiasm. A lot of aging directors just repeat themselves, and lose touch with what's going on. If you follow your

(LOUIS MALLE)

curiosity, though, you keep fresh. And for me, it's great each time to feel that it's the first one.

Interview, Washington/
The Washington Post, 3-4:(D)3.

1

You think of a project, a film that you want to do. And you have this dream of the film as it's going to be once it's finished. Of course, when you dream it, it's wonderful! And then you have to go through a year [of] different phases: the writing, the pre-production, shooting, editing, talking about it. And this involves a lot of people. There's a public stance that you have to take. You have to explain to your actors, your crew, your collaborators. It's very hard . . . I think that's what makes the film medium so fascinating, and so difficult. It also explains why, in the history of cinema, there's been so few really personal statements which have stayed away from becoming spectacular or show business, or which haven't lost a part of their intimacy in the process.

Interview, New York/
The Christian Science Monitor,
4-22:21.

Paul Newman
Actor

2

[On acting]: There are things to be learned from make-believe. You can do things in make-believe and then translate them into real-life behavior. I think make-believe rubs off. I think bravery can rub off. I think humor can rub off. I've incorporated little things from certain characters I've played. A way of walking, say, or a way of listening. Just fragments really, never the whole.

Interview, New York/
Esquire, June:104.

Mike Nichols
Director

3

[On the old-time movie moguls]: I defy you to say what it was that the barracudas *knew*. And

while I'm loathe to quote Bill Goldman favorably, he rightly said, "The thing about Hollywood is that nobody knows anything." But what those guys knew had something to do with the public, with having *absorbed* the public. I don't want to idealize them, but they had powerful appetites. They wanted a lot of everything—power, houses, girls, food, money. Power. And this led them to want movies to deliver powerful experiences. What we've seen since is the "committee approach" which gives you homogenized experiences.

Interview, Los Angeles/
Los Angeles Times, 12-27:(VI)8.

Nick Nolte
Actor

4

Producers produce, writers write, actors act. Actors, unless they're operating purely as producers, shouldn't take producing credits. If an actor contributes to a script, even a large hunk of it, he's still not a writer. Every film's a collaboration; usually everbody slops over into others' jobs, and that includes the people I call mentors—guys from outside the production who provide a support system . . . I can contribute to scripts; sometimes I can see why a scene is wrong, maybe add a speech. But I can't, except at the very start of production, carry the film's whole story in my mind. I get totally isolated in my character; everything comes from that one point of view.

Interview, Malibu, Calif./
Cosmopolitan, January:145.

Yuri Norstein
Soviet animated-film maker

5

My problems stem from the fact that most producers and film people and critics have a very mechanistic impression of animated film. They're very conscious of the boundaries and they don't take it seriously. But in the last few years throughout the world there's been a growth of self-esteem within the animated-film industry and a growth of

(YURI NORSTEIN)

consciousness that animated film can be an art-form just as great as any other.

Interview, Washington/
The Washington Post, 4-30:(C)13.

Alan Parker
Director

1

Pragmatically, if you want to reach the largest possible world audience, [the U.S. is] the only place to work. But you do get absorbed into a system that can gobble you up if you're not careful. Because ultimately this film industry is about the pursuit of the dollar, and so a great deal of art has been lost. A lot of people scoff if you say it's an art-form; they say it hasn't been an art-form for 60 years. The more asinine the bulk of films become, the more ashamed I am of being a film director. In a way, I think many of my generation have sold out. But every so often, you see a film and it's wonderful—and it still reaches a large audience—and you know that it's possible for us to do more responsible work . . . It's great to think you can reach a large audience, but it's also nice to think that you can affect people's lives in some way. So when they write the three-line biography of me in *The London Times* when I'm 83, they can say I tried, even if sometimes I didn't succeed. I'd be happy with that.

Interview/
American Film, Jan.-Feb.:15.

2

The *auteur* theory holds that the director does everything. The truth is, no director in history ever did everything. Film is a collaborative art, but not too many people own up to that—mainly because the directors get to do the interviews . . . If you look at *Fame,* some of the musical numbers—such as "Hot Lunch" in the lunch-room—have extraordinary energy and could only have been created on the Moviola [during editing]. So, in the end, you can have your film mucked up by a really bad editor, or have your ideas taken further by a really great one.

Interview/
American Film, Jan.-Feb.:14.

3

I think all films in a way are manipulative. You have a point of view, you know what you want to say. It's my responsibility—or my duty—to make that as powerful as possible. Also, it's a cinematic experience. Sometimes you do have to shake people up a little.

Interview, Washington, Dec. 4/
The Washington Post, 12-9:(C)6.

Gregory Peck
Actor

4

[On whether it was easier in the old days to make a film than it is today]: No. It was always difficult to make a fine picture. Of course, you could try more often [back then], make more movies because they cost so much less than they do now. The big difference, though, is that in those days there was more of a sense of raucous fun of making movies. Producers like [David] Selznick were on the set all the time; studio executives were involved in every step of production. It wasn't a job to them; they just loved making movies. I really don't care for executives now. They think differently than I do. They think more of power; they get their kicks when the stock goes up, when they make a certain deal, when they open a new amusement zone at the studio. They really have no idea what it is to create a film, to love it, to know that you have a really good scene on film that you prepared for months ahead just for that moment when the camera would turn. You get it right, and you feel so good driving home at night.

Interview, New York/
TWA Ambassador, April:67.

5

[As an actor,] you have to recapture your confidence every time you arrive on a film set. I don't know anybody who doesn't. You're never quite sure if you can step up there and do it again. Each time you have to prove to yourself that you can.

Interview, Los Angeles/
Ladies' Home Journal,
November:234.

Arthur Penn
Director

1

We can't leave you a legacy of this "shrinking" medium [motion pictures]. Somehow it's going to survive. It's a fierce, penetrating, outrageously truth-telling medium, and somehow it's going to survive being shrunk and commercialized and beaten down.

At First New York International
Festival of the Arts Film Symposium/
Film Comment, August:8.

David Puttnam
Producer;
Former chairman,
Columbia Pictures

2

The talent base isn't narrow because there are not enough gifted people around. It's narrow because the insecurity of the industry makes it that way. People would rather give a movie to the wrong director who has a good name which they can hide behind. They'll do that rather than take a chance on the person who might be exactly the right director . . . This is kind of an ongoing neurosis in the business. It is fear of blame, fear of getting it wrong, fear of failing. But . . . a creative environment cannot be dominated by a fear of failure. It is not possible if our industry is to creatively develop . . . What comes with fear, what fear does, is place power in a very few hands. It allows very few people to take control . . . In an environment in which there is no fear, power becomes devolved from the center and more people are answerable for the quality of their work.

Interview/Daily Variety, 2-1:29.

3

The [film] medium is too powerful and far too important an influence on the way we live, the way we see ourselves, to be left solely to the tyranny of the boxoffice or reduced to the sum of the lowest common denominator of public taste—this public taste or appetite being conditioned by a diet frequently capable only of producing emotional malnutrition. Movies are powerful. Good or bad, they tinker around inside your brain. They steal up on you in the darkness of the cinema to form or confirm social attitudes. They can help to create a healthy, informed, concerned and inquisitive society, or, in the alternative, a negative, apathetic and thoroughly ignorant one. To an almost alarming degree, our political and emotional responses rest, for their health, in the quality and integrity of the present and future generation of film and television creators. Accepting this fact, there are only two personal madnesses that film-makers must guard against. One is the belief that they can do everything, and the other is the belief that they can do nothing. The former is arrogant in the extreme. But the latter is plainly irresponsible and wholly unacceptable.

At Entertainment Law Symposium,
University of Southern California,
April 23/Daily Variety, 4-27:10.

4

Hollywood plays to your weaknesses. Whatever you are, it makes you more than you want to be . . . It's literally a godless place.

Daily Variety, 5-25:18.

Martin Ransohoff
Producer

5

The studio is like a train that steams along. If you want to talk about social consequences, what are the social consequences if the train stops? It's very easy to make heavies out of a few guys on the inside who have the responsibility of turning a buck. What about the jobs they are responsible for? What about the banks? Stockholders? People who invested their life savings in good faith? This in itself indicates social responsibility. Where are artists going to flourish if these institutions [the major studios] go down the tubes? Where is the cultural flowering going to come from if you can't make money to keep the train going?

Daily Variety, 5-25:16.

Robert Redford
Actor

1

Less than 10 years ago, a major [film] studio casually burned all its [musical] scores and orchestra parts—music from *The Wizard of Oz* and *Ben Hur*—all in order to free up some valuable storage space. That's the equivalent of tearing down an impressive piece of architecture in order to park 50 cars.

USA Today, 1-14:(D)2.

2

The shifting sands of major-studio leadership, which seem to be moving more and more toward lawyers and accountants and people of a different trade, raise a great voice for independent film. Which is one of the reasons that, five or six years ago, we were talking about the business moving more in this direction as the product became more centralized and real knowledge about the art of film became more foreign to the leadership. Those two things running concurrently, it seemed to me a good time to start looking for alternatives. Pretty soon it would be such a costly business.

Interview, Truchas, N.M./
Film Comment, February:38.

3

There are too many [motion-picture] directors whose entire frame of reference is television. And the movies, as a result, look more and more like commercials. All sizzle and quick cuts. Not much reliance on dialogue, and that's what a good actor relies on: words, sentences. The line. A good actor—the best actors—all have a great ear that helps them say, "Hey, I can't say that line. It doesn't sound right. It's not the way this guy would talk." Stuff like that is disappearing.

Interview/Esquire, March:122.

4

Today, the movie business is run on fear and gossip and ego. Not many people know how to tell a good story any more. And that's what great movies are all about: good stories, with a beginning, a middle and an end. Now though, if someone makes $10-million selling venetian blinds, next thing you know they've bought a [movie] studio. Everybody wants to be in the movies.

Interview/Esquire, March:122.

Lee Remick
Actress

5

[Acting] is a strange business. You can train for something that never happens, or you can get discovered and turned into a star because you happen to be in the right place at the right moment. There's really no way to prepare for anything. Certainly, you cannot plan or map out a career.

Interview, New York/
Films in Review, November:530.

Tom Selleck
Actor

6

[On the high salaries he receives as an actor]: I don't apologize for making it. People say, "Don't you feel guilty, when so many are starving?" Well, I strongly believe that my success has created lots of jobs. I don't stick the money in a mattress; I spend it, I directly employ a lot of people. The fact that I'm hired for a movie gets it financed, creates work. It's not that I take a bigger slice of the pie—I make the pie bigger.

Interview/
Cosmopolitan, December:169.

Omar Sharif
Actor

7

Actors need to have a passion outside of their work. You know, as celebrities, we get so much adulation at certain times in our lives that we don't live realistically. We become a little bit above the clouds, and we forget that we are human persons who can adjust to living a normal life. On the other hand, when you're an actor you're unemployed for long periods of time. You

(OMAR SHARIF)

don't know when your next job is coming, and you begin to think, gee, they don't want me any more. I might never get a job again. And if you don't have something to keep your mind occupied during the day, you tend to become neurotic.

Interview/50 Plus, September:32.

Melville Shavelson
Screenwriter

1

Without what writers write, directors, producers, even actors, would be speechless.

Emmy Magazine, March-April:16.

Stirling Silliphant
Screenwriter

2

[On how he deals with the lack of public recognition of most screenwriters]: Smile a lot—and cry in private. You just have to accept the fact that you are "only the writer." It was an exhilerating, wonderful experience when I won the Academy Award for *In the Heat of the Night.* We also got Best Picture, Best Actor, Best Editing, best this, and best that. But, when I got backstage with all the photographers, they weren't taking my picture. They were all taking [actor] Rod Steiger's picture. So be it! When you don't get invited to the premieres, the parties, console yourself with having the spiritual knowledge that you created this thing. You know that without you in the beginning, all the rest of the people taking bows wouldn't be there now. They, like the work, are simply your [the screenwriter's] creatures, the population of your private dreams. And *that* is heady stuff.

Interview/
American Film, March:15.

James Stewart
Actor

3

People come up to me—it's happened so many times—and they say, "I remember something

you did in a movie . . ." and they can't remember what the picture was about, or when they saw it, or even its title. What they remember is something that happened, something that *moved* them. I guess I just want to know I've given people a small piece of *time* they'll never forget.

Interview, Beverly Hills, Calif./
The Saturday Evening Post,
May-June:111.

Dean Stockwell
Actor

4

I think that my acting was strictly intuitive, from the beginning, and has always remained that way. I resisted any attempts by anyone to assist me. Even when I first started acting, when I was six or seven, I always knew, when I was doing a scene, if it was right. I don't know how I knew, but I knew . . . When it's intuitive, that's a bypassing, really, of the thought process. It's a source that's just prior to or more original than the thought process. When I did think about it, I thought about it in terms of honesty or truth or self, or how *I* would react, how *I* would feel, what *I* would do, and what *I* would say.

Interview, Santa Monica, Calif./
Film Comment, August:28.

Elaine Stritch
Actress

5

[Saying she doesn't like to talk about her acting method]: I find it impossible. I don't know what the hell I'm doing up there half the time. These performers who go on about their technique and craft—oh, *puleeze!* I don't know what technique means. But I do know what experience is. I know in my gut when I've done a scene right.

Interview, New York/
People, 1-11:76.

Cicely Tyson
Actress

6

To me, the epitome of a director is someone who surrounds himself with a brilliant talent . . .

453

(CICELY TYSON)

and allows him to do his job. If he places you on the track and you veer a little to the right or to the left, he [the director] is able, just by the touch of a hand, to straighten you up.

At presentation of Jean Renoir
Humanitarian Award to Richard
Attenborough, Los Angeles/
Daily Variety, 1-25:2.

Wim Wenders
West German director

1

I always like . . . films that have an idea and an ideal. I think that's a force and a power that movies can have, and that it's being used less and less. Things have become very cynical and very opportunistic. The very idea of entertainment has become rather cynical—as if any moral views were not entertaining enough.

Interview, Los Angeles/
Los Angeles Times, 5-17:(VI)6.

Haskell Wexler
Cinematographer

2

A "political" film is a film whose ideas or politics or philosophy is contrary to the status quo, contrary to the system, contrary to what is fed to us every day. All films and all media are political. They present certain ideas, most of which we've been conditioned to accept. When I was growing up, black people in movies were presented as ignorant and obsequious. Films created and perpetuated stereotypes. Even cowboy-and-Indian movies, when you think about it, are political.

Interview/
American Film, October:14.

Billy Wilder
Director, Writer, Producer

3

If you show [the audience] a picture, they must forget there was a crew and a dolly and all kinds of technical people in back. You must suck them into what's happening on the screen. I don't do those crazy setups—that's what they call "directing the director." However, I try to be as elegant and smooth and novel, if you want, without them noticing the technique.

Interview, Los Angeles/
The Christian Science Monitor,
4-12:22.

4

How do you become a producer today? You buy a book. Since there are no writers or directors under contract, studios are used now like Ramada Inns. The dastardly thing is that a year and a half will be spent on the contract. People never meet to discuss a script. It's all who's going to get credit and what percentage of the gross.

Interview, Beverly Hills, Calif./
The New York Times, 10-3:(B)1.

Robin Williams
Actor

5

[In the film industry, a big success] moves you up in the food chain. It's like life in the Precambrian sea. There is a food chain of scripts, and success can give you access to *better* scripts.

Interview, New York/
The New York Times, 1-25:21.

Edward Yang
Taiwanese director

6

Film is 100 per cent commitment. Even when I'm asleep and I wake up, I think of ideas. I relax when I'm inspired. I get excited to tell my scriptwriter or friends about my idea. That's rewarding. That's the most relaxing thing for me.

Interview, Washington/
The Christian Science Monitor,
12-21:19.

MUSIC

Hildegard Behrens
Opera singer

1

I'm not convinced about planting [operas] into different periods [of time]. I like to work from the precise thing rather than to make analogies, and nothing can get more precise than as the composer has written it. Then everything fits, no matter what—the fashion of clothes, the language, the problems between people. If you set *Fidelio* in the French Revolution, where it belongs, you can understand what it meant at that time for a woman to dress like a man and work like a man, something so totally self-denying. It stresses the enormous sacrifice she makes to find her husband. Then everyone can draw his own analogies.

Interview/Opera News, 2-27:29

Leonard Bernstein
Composer, Conductor

2

When I'm conducting, sometimes I become a kind of surrogate composer. When I really study a score, I re-compose it along with the composer. Sometimes, in fact, I feel like I've just written the work myself. Or sometimes, in a performance, if the orchestra is really playing well, it seems like I'm making the work up on the spot as we go along. I'll say to myself, "Let's bring the horns in there," or "Let's add a flute there." There are also times, conducting, when the performance stops—you come to the end of a work—and it takes you minutes to even remember where you are. Those times you are immortal. There are times when I definitely feel immortal—love-making and music-making. But when you *write* music, you are definitely immortal—there's no question about that. You're not even on this earth. Time ceases, space ceases. Often, you know this only in retrospect.

When you come back, you realize that you've been away. That place is immortal. It's very different than sharpening pencils.

Interview, Fairfield, Conn./
TWA Ambassador, December:63.

Edward Bradberry
General director, Augusta (Ga.)
Opera Company

3

[On the Augusta Opera]: [In terms of cities nationally,] most places that have opera are burgeoning metropolises compared to Augusta, so it's surprising to people that we even have a company here, let alone a fine one. There are certain variables, such as geography, population and the attitude of one's constituency, but what's on your stage shouldn't be affected by those. Artistically, the standard is the standard.

Interview, Augusta, Ga./
Opera News, 4-9:32.

William Broughton
Conductor, English String
Orchestra (Britain)

4

One of the things slowly moving in the right direction is that we're moving back to the situation of orchestras having music directors who work with their own orchestras. I think this idea of superstars flying in and out of cities is not going to be acceptable to audiences for much longer. It's music that suffers in the end, the whole of the artistic enterprise. And programs, of course, are just designed around these superstar conductors and soloists, which must be a very, very unhappy lot for orchestras. I hope that America and London—where this has been particularly appalling—have realized this and have begun to ask much more of their music directors.

Interview, New York/Ovation, October:12.

John Cage
Composer

1

There are composers, like myself, who continue to write out music. But there are also composers who make music by making records. There are also those who make their own instruments or, in electronic music, they make their own circuits. They become musicians like troubadours, where they take their equipment from one place to the other, set it up and simply play music. When they change the instrument or circuit, it ends a certain "composition."

At "Music in Post-Modern America"
symposium sponsored by Pomona (Calif.) College/
Los Angeles Times, 2-13:(VI)11.

Sammy Cahn
Songwriter

2

There's no more rewarding career than successful songwriting. You walk on the streets, someone's humming your song. You get in a cab, they're playing your song on the radio. You go to a restaurant, they're playing your song. If a man in 50 years has written five songs that are immediately identifiable, he's done well. So you have some notion of my pride.

Interview, New York/
The Washington Post, 9-19:(B)4.

Bruce Crawford
General manager,
Metropolitan Opera,
New York

3

[On his decision to leave the Metropolitan Opera]: I don't want to seem naive, but coming from the subculture, I hadn't perceived how much the classical music business—the whole trade-off between entertainment and art—how crass it really is. It is something to behold. With 52-week contracts and a 4,000-seat house, well, you are not going to be a temple of art.

Interview, New York/
The Wall Street Journal,
11-8:(A)14.

Edo de Waart
Conductor

4

I'm a performer. I feel a performer—almost like a photographer—should record not only what has been in the past, but what is going on in his own time. You show these pictures of the moment: This is *now* . . . There are all kinds of possibilities. But we just record. We give it our everything: We rehearse them well; we play them with our whole hearts and leave time to judge it. And the critics!

Interview, New York/
The Christian Science Monitor,
9-20:19.

Ghena Dimitrova
Opera singer

5

Conditions today are much less pleasant than before. The music business is ferocious. Art should not be business—it should be cultivated to convey emotions. Voices are delicate things, and our world is all about stress. Voices have to be treated like flowers, living things to be handled with care. But now everything is done fast, ready-made, especially in America. Everything is supposed to happen at once. A young singer is either hailed as a new Callas or a new Del Monaco, described as having the biggest voice—what does that mean, watts? kilowatts?—and they have a three-or-four-year career, or if they have a sore throat or sing a role that is not for them, they are never forgiven. The young artist suffers a lot. Art has to be learned slowly, through training and experience and understanding tradition.

Interview, New York/
Opera News, 2-13:29.

Veronika Dudarova
Conductor, Moscow
Symphony Orchestra

6

Classical music is eternal. Whatever the fashion of the times, the music of the masters endures in the same way that the art of Leonardo da Vinci and Michelangelo remains alive.

Interview/World Press Review,
October:40.

Charles Dutoit
Conductor

1

Unfortunately, few [opera] singers care enough about words. I admire Dietrich Fischer-Dieskau's emphasis on verbal clarity, as well as his intelligence. But then on the whole, I must say, I prefer to deal with intelligent people . . . Right now, it's not easy to cast operas. We are faced with a shortage of first-class singers. They exist, of course, but are busy all the time. The moment they make any reputation, they are over-booked.

Interview/Opera News, 1-2:17.

Dietrich Fischer-Dieskau
Lieder singer

2

[On lieder singing]. If I have done something, not to change the way of singing, but to build up a new kind of value for this art-form, then that would be much. It was a dying form, I think, when I started. Maybe it's still dying; not many new things of worth have appeared . . . When Schoenberg begins to write real 12-tone music, that's a frontier. From then on, the singer is a slave to written notes. I always try to bring some un-said things into this music, mostly from the poem, but it's very difficult. My own opinion is that the only possibility for approaching modern music is to combine these wide leaps, these dissonant intervals, into a line—to bind them together. This is a very Romantic idea; it may very well be wrong.

Interview, New York/
The New York Times, 3-22:20.

Stan Getz
Jazz saxophonist

3

[Jazz] is more than light entertainment. [But] it has suffered an unusual fate—misunderstood in the land of its birth; too often its buoyancy and rhythmic thrust have been confused with pushiness and arrogance. The value of jazz still has to be clarified. People involve themselves with its superficialities without digging for its soul. Fortunately, a beginning has been made, through the rapid growth of jazz programs in our schools.

Interview/
Los Angeles Times, 8-3:(VI)9.

Dizzy Gillespie
Jazz musician

4

[Saying he believes in instruction in jazz]: I love it. It prepares our musicians for a job. They take harmony, they take composition, oh man, and they know it. We've got many young musicians that know the music. And they give you such respect, these young musicians. When the young guys come out and play your licks, that's their way of toasting you when they do that; so you say, okay, go right ahead. It doesn't matter, because everybody is a thief in this business.

Interview, New York/
The Christian Science Monitor,
2-22:23.

Philip Glass
Opera composer

5

Just recently, somebody asked me how long it took me to write one of my pieces he'd just heard. And I said about forty years. I know it sounds like a cynical answer, but I've been working at this business of composing since I was eight. And everything adds to the whole—everything I've learned influences the music I write.

Interview, New York/
Opera News, June:12.

Herbie Hancock
Jazz musician

6

For musicians, music education is very important, first of all for very practical reasons. There is the dazzle of being a rock star; but if you become a rock star, what are you going to do when that's over? There are very few Mick Jaggers or Tina Turners. You've got to do something. If you have some kind of formal education, you can read, which means you can play anybody's music and play it quickly. If you can carry it further into composing, orchestration and arranging, then you might have the opportunity to do a movie score, to do writing for several instruments. There are so many opportunities where education might really come in handy if any of

457

(HERBIE HANCOCK)

these things are a dream of yours. In an immediate sense, there's something about education that builds confidence. If anything, that may be the strongest force—the confidence that you feel when you've got some background and education. You need confidence to play. That's what's behind the power of projection. If you don't have the power of projection, you might as well get off the stage, stay home and play for yourself.

Interview, Los Angeles/
Down Beat, June:18.

Margaret Hillis
Conductor

1

If a male conductor gets up on the podium and makes a mistake, the perception is "he's no good." If a woman gets up and makes a mistake, it's because "she's a woman."

Panel discussion
at Juilliard School, New York/
The Christian Science Monitor,
11-28:21.

Mariss Jansons
Soviet conductor

2

The Soviet way of playing Tchaikovsky is different than what is played in the West. It is more dramatic, more classical, not too sentimental. The music is written with big, emotional feelings. If you exaggerate those feelings, it becomes too agitated and sentimental. You must not put sugar in honey—the music speaks for itself. It's a matter of balance, how far you can go. You must not play too dry, or one tempo. I can't say that everyone from the West does that, but many do.

Interview, Montreal/
Los Angeles Times, 3-24:(VI)5.

3

Everyone understands music, because there are no words, only feelings. All people have souls and hearts, so all people can feel.

Interview, Montreal/
Los Angeles Times, 3-24:(VI)5.

Anthony Rolfe Johnson
Opera singer

4

In this business, you're surrounded by people who do things for you—agents, secretaries, financial people—down to the nanny for your children. When your way of life is the least bit threatened, you start to realize how little you actually do yourself. [But now] I question everything. I look to see if three days before a major recital for a broadcast in London are really enough. If I've done those things and it goes wrong, I have only myself to blame. I'm much more in control of my own life now, and I feel infinitely better for it.

Interview/Opera News, 1-30:21.

Harvey Lichtenstein
President and executive
producer, Brooklyn (N.Y.)
Academy of Music

5

Opera isn't just something you listen to. It is a theatrical medium, and the idea is to make [it] interesting and exciting theatrically. And you don't do that by putting on the same production year after year after year [or] getting uninteresting directors or directors who have no ideas or no imagination, either intellectually, philosophically or visually.

Interview, Brooklyn, N.Y./
Los Angeles Times,
12-25:(Calendar)8.

Witold Lutoslawski
Polish composer

6

I cannot say that the need to communicate with an audience is the foundation of my style. In principle, I write music that *I* would like to hear, music that is an expression of my own tastes, wishes and desires. I am offering audiences my own internal truth; but I believe that other people have similar tastes, and that they will find something for themselves in my music.

Interview, Oslo, Norway/
The New York Times, 6-25:12.

Gary Karr
Bassist

1

There's a flaw in human perception. We believe that for something to be virtuosic, it has to be high [in tone]. I think that's unfair; it seems to me that we're missing out. It's real negligence and stupidity to say that a soprano is more exciting to hear than a basso profundo. I think every human being could be more moved, in the gut, by low sounds than high. The low sounds—in the register of the human voice, or even lower—really grab you in a way that is special. That we've ignored that fact is incredible.

Interview/Ovation, March:13.

Erich Leinsdorf
Conductor

2

[The late conductor Arturo Toscanini] placed great value on whether a [opera] singer had a natural smile. Even for a serious role. I found that puzzling until much later, when I realized that a singer who couldn't smile easily probably didn't have many other expressions either.

Interview, New York/
The Wall Street Journal, 1-21:28.

Waltraud Meier
Opera singer

3

To exploit the privilege of being a [opera] singer to promote oneself, I find that horrible. To serve the music with all the means one has, that is truly fun. As long as one tries to trace the truth that lies in the music—how far one succeeds is another question—and keeps the eyes open, then one doesn't become blinded by a certain degree of success. It's exciting for me to sing in big houses, but that's not a goal. My goal is to work at the highest level, with a super orchestra, marvelous colleagues, a wonderful conductor. And that could be in the provinces.

Interview/
Opera News, 3-12:46.

Riccardo Muti
Music director, La Scala Opera
(Italy)

4

I believe that the government in the United States should give much more [money] to the orchestras. There are so many orchestras in this country [the U.S.], from a very high level to—well, you know. But every one is essential for the cultural education of the people. A community orchestra in a small town may not be a great orchestra. Non-professional musicians get together and play music for an audience. They don't do this for entertainment, but for cultural reasons. Everybody knows that if you have better-educated people, you have better people. So the fact that orchestras can collapse in this country is, of course, a negative sign. In Italy, culture is something that belongs to the state. It is the duty of the state to take care of it. It is not a luxury, culture. It's something that the people must have. And if they cannot collect the money, the state must provide.

Interview, New York/
Ovation, December:14.

Anne-Sophie Mutter
West German violinist

5

Playing with the greatest musicians only makes you better . . . As long as we understand each other in music, age is of no interest. I think the whole age thing is crazy. Musical maturity is not a question of being around a long time.

Interview/Ovation, April:27.

6

Violinists have every evening a different instrument to respond to. My violin's sound is always changing in response to different temperatures and levels of humidity and everything else, and because it's in a constant process of development, it is never the same. It is not like a lamp, which looks the same today and tomorrow. My relation with my violin is something I re-create every day.

Interview, New York/
The Washington Post, 12-10:(G)1.

(ANNE-SOPHIE MUTTER)

1

I think of myself as just one of the performers. I don't think of myself as a star—that's a very empty word, "star." When I play a concerto, I am simply the composer's interpreter—Beethoven is the star, not me.

*Interview, New York/
The Washington Post,
12-10:(G)11.*

Hermes Pan
Choreographer

2

I don't know what happened to good musicals, good dancing, good songs, good lyrics. I blame it all on the Beatles, and on the drug experience, the Janis Joplin-types, the screamers, hard rock, metal rock. That music drives me out of my mind with its un-understandable, meaningless, repetitive lyrics. But I think things will return, eventually, to sanity.

*Interview, Beverly Hills, Calif./
Daily Variety, 4-5:11.*

Murray Perahia
Pianist

3

[On playing for recordings]: To a certain extent, the recording process inhibits risk-taking in a performance. But a recording session and an actual concert performance are two entirely different things. Wrong notes at a concert can be ignored if a performance catches fire. Wrong notes repeated over and over in a recording, however, are a problem . . . Too often, modern recording techniques emphasize very close miking of the piano. This produces a piano image that is sometimes metallic, larger-than-life—and artificial.

Interview/Ovation, February:16.

Maurice Peress
Conductor

4

[On jazz musician Duke Ellington's less-known classical compositions]: It's my hope that this music will find its way into the standard repertoire, just as other American composers' music has. Ellington's extended works scored for symphony are masterful . . . and you're talking to someone who is a symphony conductor and who spends all his spare time unearthing editions of Americana—George Antheil, Gershwin operas, Will Vodery. Ellington ranks with Ives and Copland, and I feel that because Ellington never identified himself with the so-called serious musical world, he gave himself, as us, a gift because he was able to develop skills while never losing sight of his Afro-American roots.

The New York Times, 6-24:13.

Trevor Pinnock
Director, English Concert (orchestra)

5

[On his group's specializing in "early music"]: I consider it part of my mission to work with conventional instruments, to work uninhibitedly but stylishly. The orchestra will never sound like an old instrument, nor should it; but some essential core of truth can come through, as it were, in translation. There are two sorts of music-making, good and bad, and that is more important than any choice of instrument.

Interview/Newsweek, 10-3:54.

Simon Rattle
*Conductor, City of Birmingham
(England) Symphony Orchestra*

6

It's a vocation, like nursing, to be a musician in England. It's something you do for love—you cannot consider it a serious profession in terms of financial rewards or comforts . . . In the best English audiences, there is a kind of communion with the music and intent, active listening one very rarely finds in America. Here [in the U.S.] it's much more passive.

*Interview, San Marino, Calif./
Los Angeles Times, 3-29:(VI)4.*

Steve Reich
Composer

7

I hate opera. The conventions—aria recitatives, the whole vocal style—are from another

(STEVE REICH)

time. To change the musical language or the subject matter doesn't set it up for me as a music drama. You get composers today who are trying to create something contemporary and immediate, yet once the singers open their mouths, you're back into 17th-, 18th-, 19th-century Italy. It grinds my gears and it hurts my ears.

Interview, New York/
The Wall Street Journal, 2-3:20.

Ned Rorem
Composer

1

The force of music over all the other arts is that it can't be proved to mean anything. Tradition has it that it can mean storms or nice weather or love or sometimes death. Those are vague, general terms. It can't mean purple, it can't mean knife and fork, and it can't mean unrequited or unfulfilled love. And besides, what is love? What love was to Wagner is something quite different from those trombone bumps and grinds Shostakovich wrote in *Lady Macbeth of Mtsensk*. Nonvocal music has no concrete meaning.

Interview/
Opera News, October:25.

Peter Sellars
Opera director

2

My life has been full of interesting phases where I have gone from being *persona non grata* to the Great White Hope when I can't even get arrested when I try. I plunge from the top of the heap to the bottom of the birdcage! I see myself as an entrepreneur who works to achieve the best working conditions possible, and I know that my basic job is to surround myself with the most interesting people possible and put them together on a project and allow it to happen. I push them, they push me.

Interview/
Ovation, September:22.

Robert Shaw
Music director and conductor,
Atlanta Symphony Orchestra

3

The arts are too important to be left to the professionals . . . Professionals untouched by amateurs lose the reason they went into music in the first place.

Interview/Ovation, May:9.

Leonard Slatkin
Music director, St. Louis
Symphony Orchestra

4

The great thing about music is that there's no wrong approach and no right approach. As long as people don't stray too far out of parameters established by the composer, I'm relatively comfortable.

Interview/Opera News, 12-10:26.

James Taylor
Singer, Songwriter

5

There are a number of currents that happen in my music. There are some types of song that I write that evolve very slowly; they're sort of glacial. And then there are other ones that represent a wide range of influences, where I'm influenced by drastically changing things. But they all distill themselves down to my vocal and guitar technique, which is like a lens or filter system, through which they are rendered in many ways the same.

Interview/
The Christian Science Monitor,
3-22:32.

Frederica von Stade
Opera singer

6

I didn't realize I wanted to be a professional performer until I was in my 20s. Or rather, I pretended I didn't want it, because it was so important I could not bear the thought of trying and failing. Then, little by little, I won competi-

461

WHAT THEY SAID IN 1988

(FREDERICA VON STADE)

tions and took singing lessions; I auditioned at the Met and they gave me small parts and gradually the parts got bigger. But all through the first 10 years of my career, I had the feeling: "Someone will find out I can't do this, and my career will end."

Interview, Washington/
The Washington Post, 2-27:(D)7.

Andre Watts
Pianist

1

[On whether he ever plays alone, just for his own enjoyment]: No. I think that's something you lose. You strive to develop that critical faculty, to perfect your craft, and once you've gotten some reasonable measure of that critical faculty implanted, you never shut it off.

Interview/
TWA Ambasador, April:61.

Dolora Zajick
Opera singer

2

An audience comes to an opera to get lost in it. A successful production is one that people get wrapped up in. That happens only when everyone works together, when nobody involved—director, conductor or singer—is out there using "applaud me" techniques or is on an ego trip. Oh, celebrities are good, and they should be encouraged, but the important thing is making the *piece* work, not ego. I don't mind being in the background it it's appropriate. Singers, like jewels, work better in a good setting. Who cares about being center stage? If the piece is done the way it's intended, audiences will love it *and* you.

Interview/Opera News, July:12.

Ellen Taaffe Zwilich
Pulitzer Prize-winning
composer

3

No work by an American composer could truly represent all that is going on in American composing today. Individual American composers are putting things together that reflect their own experiences and likes and training. We all get completely different musical educations that result in the widest range of composition, from Minimalism to total serialism. So that I'm not representing all that's in American music today; I'm representing all that's in me. And that is very much the state of American composing . . .

Moscow/
The New York Times, 6-6:19.

THE STAGE

Stella Adler
Teacher of acting

1

The need for help grows stronger in the theatre as producers and directors have less and less to do with the career of the actor. Actors have been stranded. They get very little help. The director is there for the ideas of the play and the ensemble, and doesn't always see that the actor is capable of growth and change. It happens now that the director will simply fire the actor he doesn't like.

Interview, Los Angeles/
Los Angeles Times, 9-6:(VI)1.

Alvin Ailey
Choreographer

2

I always think that the best ballets are those that are the most personal—at least those of mine that endure, ones that hurt a little bit to get out, where you give a real chunk of yourself to make this happen.

Interview, New York/
The Christian Science Monitor,
12-5:22.

Jane Alexander
Actress

3

[On the high price of Broadway theatre tickets]: As an actor, the high prices make you feel you have to be a performing seal to justify the costs. Theatre-going has become a commodity rather than food for the soul. But then I think about those $40 and $50 prices and realize that I pay that much for a plumber to come and fix a faucet.

The Christian Science Monitor,
9-26:1.

Gerald Arpino
Artistic director,
Joffrey Ballet

4

The fact that [Joffrey Ballet founder the late Robert Joffrey and I] were two Americans is crucial when you compare us to others. Peter Martins of the New York City Ballet is trained in the Academy of Dance in Denmark, not the school of American ballet. He came full-blown from a tradition where you start at seven years old. Then you have [Mikhail] Baryshnikov, who comes from a Russian academy of dance—where you are chosen and nurtured for a lifetime— filling in for [the late head of the New York City Ballet] George Balanchine, who was also Russian. But when you look at me as artistic director, here is a pure American, who had to work as a waiter on weekends for 2½ years to pay for his lessons, to fight off his brothers, his church, his family, etc., because the word "ballet" was such an esoteric, elitist word that had no meaning for the baseball and football players and all my associates.

Interview, Los Angeles/
The Christian Science Monitor,
5-4:21.

Emanuel Azenburg
Producer

5

You have to be pessimistic about the future of Broadway, because it's not doing anything about its problems. It has union problems, over-priced-ticket problems, the problems of television and film drawing away all the actors, directors and writers. I don't think the theatre will go away, but it will continue to diminish.

Interview/
Horizon, September:63.

463

WHAT THEY SAID IN 1988

Victor Barbee
Principal dancer, American Ballet Theatre

1

[On ballet]: It's the portrayal that makes the character, not the character that makes the portrayal. Some dancers look across the stage at their partners with a pained expression and think they're acting. That's rubbish. That doesn't touch people's emotions. And if you are doing dramatic ballets and you don't touch people, what's the point? For me, that's what it's all about.

*Interview/
Dance Magazine, September:52.*

Philip Bosco
Actor

2

The importance of language is why I've stressed for many years, to a lot of people's annoyance, that one of the terrible problems we have in the American theatre is the inability of many of our leading players—who are extremely talented in all those qualities that you would assume would be part of any good actor's makeup—to speak the language. That's the only thing we really miss, and why the English are forever being imported to play parts where some kind of decent speech is required. It's a tragedy that we've had to suffer that. We've been intimidated for so long by the English—not all of the English, of course—but a significant number of them who really do handle language beautifully. It's because of their tradition and their training. It's a pity. And I blame it on the Actors Studio [in the U.S.]. We've been overemphasizing that kind of gut-sincerity thing, and we've lost sight of the other.

*Interview, New York/
The New York Times, 11-17:(B)3.*

John Butler
Choreographer

3

I think dancers are the same all over the world. They're funny, magical, disciplined, beautiful people. They're not happy unless they're *kvetching,* but God bless them, they'll kill themselves for you. If they like you and what you do, they'll love you to death. They'll rehearse seven days a week without a break, and that's really your return. That's what it's all about.

Interview/Horizon, April:35.

Martha Clarke
Performance artist

4

There's an understanding I have of things that's not logical and that seems inexplicable to me. I try to figure it out in these theatre works. And what I've figured out is that there aren't any answers for anything. There's no way to go about finding things out—except one can only be true to oneself. My subject matter is too huge to contain an answer. It's cosmic. But it's an interesting way to spend one's time, probing about it through imagery.

Interview/Horizon, May:40.

Merce Cunningham
Choreographer

5

I think *movement,* to me, is, always has been and remains the same. It has a life of its own. I don't think that it needs an explanation—you can, but I don't think it needs it. It has a spirit—if you can get it out, if you can find a way to let it come out. And it certainly is a part of what anybody does in life, whether they are dancers or not dancers, because it is part of the world.

*Interview/
Dance Magazine, March:61.*

Gordon Davidson
Artistic director, Mark Taper Forum, Los Angeles

6

Everyone's doing new plays now. That's where the money is; that's where the excitement is. As theatres, we have a responsibility to try to understand what each writer is struggling with, and if we're in a position to help, to make some

464

kind of process available whereby plays can grow.

*Panel discussion sponsored by
Los Angeles Theatre Center/
Daily Variety, 3-9:8.*

Brian Dennehy
Actor

1

[Comparing acting on stage with acting in films]: I have a little apartment in Los Angeles. I'm borrowing an apartment here in New York [while he does *The Cherry Orchard* on stage]. I ride the subway every day—no cabs. I'm glad to be a half-assed movie star. But what makes me happiest is challenging myself as an actor. I want to do [*King*] *Lear.* If that means Chicago at $400 a week, fine . . . Don't get me wrong. I like being in movies. I like making money. But it ain't Chekhov.

*Interview, New York/
Newsweek, 2-22:72.*

John Gielgud
Actor

2

[On stage acting]: If you do only films and television in short takes, the concentration starts to go. It's very important to learn whole plays instead of brief scenes. Sybil Thorndike kept her memory perfect well into her 90s by doing plays. Edith Evans gave up the theatre, and then couldn't remember a thing.

Newsweek, 3-21:75.

John Guare
Playwright

3

Theatre is deep in our bones. Cavemen sitting around together. A storyteller says, "I'm going to tell you this." Someone decides it would be better if two people were telling the story. Then someone else suggests that three people act it out. And so you have theatre. Strangers sitting together in the dark, trying to figure out who we are, how we fit into things.

Esquire, September:122.

Helen Hayes
Actress

4

On stage I think in some ways I've always had a magic connection with audiences. I don't know how it is, but I get on there and manage to reach across and get them to join me in whatever we're doing . . . We actors, you see, are there to serve, and when we serve up something the world enjoys and responds to, then we feel gratitude and feel we've done something.

*Interview, Nyack, N.Y./
The Christian Science Monitor,
8-10:19.*

Gregory Hines
Dancer

5

I believe if you took a poll, our image of the tap dancer would be one of a slight person wearing tails. But we need to shake that up. One of the things that attracts people to ballet and modern dance is the fact that the bodies are so beautiful, and they are seen in tights. But in the instance of the tap dancer, he is completely shrouded in a tuxedo.

*Interview/
Dance Magazine, December:48.*

Al Hirschfeld
Theatrical cartoonist

6

I enjoy doing drawings of people like Carol Channing and Zero Mostel—the explosive actors, the glandular actors. The ones with the bulging eyes who don't close the doors—they slam them. They communicate to the last row of the balcony. That kind of actor is disappearing. It's understandable, because of the economics. They have to make their living in television and the movies, where they don't have to project.

*Interview, New York/
The New York Times, 6-21:22.*

Eugene Ionesco
Playwright

1

Theatre doesn't exist at the moment. It's bad everywhere. Between 1950 and 1960 it was good. Beckett, Genet, Adamov, *moi.* It was theatre where you posed a problem, the most important problem of all: the problem of the existential condition of man—his despair, the tragedy of his destiny, the ridiculousness of his destiny, the absurdity of his destiny.

Interview, New York/
The New York Times,
6-15:19.

Glenda Jackson
Actress

2

[Saying she isn't made for the glamorous side of the theatre and rarely goes to high-profile parties]: Those events make us [actors] look like idiots. The glitzy side of the theatre presupposes that we actually do nothing of any value, so we have to curry favor with audiences. It reduces ourselves to the level of popularity contests. I don't regard the theatre as something that has to beg for its existence, or acting as something that only the emotionally crippled enter.

Interview/
USA Today, 4-25:(D)5.

Garson Kanin
Playwright

3

When one writes—especially with plays, not so much with short stories or novels—the piece starts developing a personality of its own, a drive of its own, an intellect, sometimes, of its own. If you're wise, you go with it. You don't try to press it or push it into the direction that you originally intended. You just find out what runs down your sleeve and test it. Thornton Wilder once said, "Writing is a coy game that you play with your unconscious."

Interview/Playbill, December:8.

Robert La Fosse
Principal dancer,
New York City Ballet

4

... the art of dancing is the art of pleasing—it's pleasing the teacher, the ballet master, the director, the audience, the critic. Your whole life [as a dancer] is subject to pleasing other people. Well, I came to understand that, first and foremost, I had to please myself.

Interview/
Dance Magazine, March:55.

John Lithgow
Actor

5

... stage acting feeds you immediately. It stays fresh because you have the feeling every night that the audience is seeing the play for the first time. They're starting fresh and so are you. It's different every night.

Interview, New York/
Los Angeles Times,
5-1:(Calendar)21.

Yekaterina Maximova
Ballerina, Bolshoi Ballet
(U.S.S.R.)

6

[As a ballerina] I was always questioning, always asking: Why was such a movement done here? For example, arabesque, failli, glissade, assemblé—why? For what reason? When I knew, then I could interpret the mood. So many dancers today think that to have technique and control, like those of sportsmen, is all that's necessary. It's not! It's the technique together with the musicality and phrasing, plus acting, mime, expression, that makes a ballerina. Also, it's about studying and appreciating art, music, literature.

Interview, Naples, Italy/
Dance Magazine, October:48.

Anne Meara
Actress

7

I'm always happy to read or audition for any theatre project. It doesn't matter what kind of

(ANNE MEARA)

theatre it is. It could be a theatre in a storefront or a theatre in a closet . . . I'm not waiting . . . for the blue fairy to come down and say I'm another Helen Hayes. Quite simply, I've sifted down to doing a job and feeling good about it.

Interview, New York/
The New York Times, 11-11:(B)2.

Arthur Miller
Playwright

1

The theatre in New York today is very hostile to straight plays of any kind, even those that get good reviews. Broadway is a show shop—musicals, light entertainment. I go to the movies to see something serious.

Interview/
U.S. News & World Report,
1-11:55.

2

I don't think any of my plays would be done today and, if they were done, I think they would be condemned. I think there used to be a different conception of what was legitimate and what wasn't. I think that there's a kind of suspicion now that if a play engages, even peripherally, in moral or social issues, that it's less than art.

At symposium sponsored by First
New York International Festival of
the Arts, June 16/
The New York Times, 6-18:12.

Arnold Mittelman
Producing director, Coconut
Grove Playhouse, Miami

3

Theatre is a literal art-form. We speak words, and we show human behavior as it is. Ballets, symphonies, operas, museums are not like theatre. Some of them are symbolic art-forms, some impressionistic. Theatre is actual. So you can reflect human behavior, and put philosophical questions in literal terms.

Interview/Horizon, April:25.

Graeme Murphy
Artistic director, Sydney (Australia)
Dance Company

4

[On dance audiences]: I want them to go into the theatre wondering what's going to come next, to get a buzz from seeing something new. That's a happy ecology, the balance between a risk-taking [dance] company and its audience. It doesn't happen often enough.

Interview/
Dance Magazine, May:64.

Marsha Norman
Pulitzer Prize-winning
playwright

5

I have a little piece of paper at home that says, "Have I written something that will humiliate me?" This is a note I wrote to myself after I finished *'night, Mother.* I thought it was a very strong possibility, since the play is so risky. I had no idea who would want to read it, or direct it, or even see it. But this is exactly the kind of abandon you must write with. You must not care if anyone wants to see your play. You must write it for yourself. That way, there's a force, a drive behind your writing that gets into the script . . . [Talking about scripts while they're being written is] dangerous, because you are apt to take people's opinions so seriously, so personally. You can be diverted from your purpose if someone you care about says he doesn't like what you're doing. Plays should be the product of a single point of view, and if you can talk about a play, you shouldn't be writing it. Save writing for only those things you can't talk to anyone about.

Interview/
Writer's Digest, September:37.

Bernadette Peters
Entertainer

6

[On her being considered by some to be the Number 1 musical-comedy performer]: If I let it go to my head, it would prevent me from doing a good job. In *Song And Dance,* I'd arrive [at the

(BERNADETTE PETERS)

theatre] every night and re-prepare the role, because I'm a human being and I'm different every day. If I tell myself, "Okay, if I push these buttons, certain things are going to happen," I have a performance where I'm just pushing buttons. But if I think about how am I feeling today, how can I make it personal tonight, then it becomes fresh, and I love to surprise myself on stage.

Interview/Horizon, Jan.-Feb.:28.

Harold Pinter
Playwright

1

My attitude toward my own playwrighting has changed. The whole idea of a narrative, of a broad canvas stretching over a period of two hours—I think I've gone away from that forever. I can't see that I could ever encompass it again. I was always termed—what is the word—"minimalist." Maybe I am. Who knows? But I hope that to be minimal is to be precise and focused. I feel that what I've illuminated is quite broad— and deep—shadows stretching away.

Interview, New York/
The New York Times, 12-6:(B)3.

Gerald Schoenfeld
Chairman,
Shubert Organization

2

[On what could bring down Broadway theatre-ticket prices]: Concessions from unions would help. Investment tax credits, such as motion pictures have had, would help. We would like some flexibility in developing the air rights over theatres and a change in the method of taxation in the city, which would reflect time when the theatres are dark. Theatre owners are already reducing rental prices in cases of theatres not doing well. But as long as labor, scenery, costume and advertising costs rise, we have no alternatives. We are not like sports; nobody builds us stadiums . . . The Shubert Organization feels a responsibility to bring good product to the public, and often we produce or co-produce plays which are worthwhile but not necessarily great money-makers. But we are not Fort Knox and have to make sound business judgments, because, if we don't, we would not be able to indulge the artistic side.

Interview/
The Christian Science Monitor,
9-26:23.

Sam Shepard
Playwright

3

I'd been writing for 10 years in an experimental maze—poking around, fishing in the dark. I wasn't going anywhere. I felt I needed an aim in the work versus just the instinctive stuff, which is very easy for me to do. I started with character, in all its complexities. As I got more and more into it, it led me to the family. I always did feel a part of that tradition, but *hated* it. I couldn't stand those plays that were all about the "turmoil" of the family. And then all of a sudden I realized, well, that was very much a part of my life, and maybe that has to do with being a playwright, that you're somehow ensnared beyond yourself.

Interview, Virginia/
Esquire, November:148.

Roslyne Paige Stern
Publisher,
"Dance Magazine"

4

Although the standards and the level of American dance remain high, it is not without cost. These are hard times. Economic difficulties have beset the dance world with the serious shortage of very necessary funding. The ravages of drugs on the dance world have, unfortunately, become an all-too-popular topic in the press every day, casting a pall over our environment, challenging our dignity, and causing us constant anxiety. And we are not only losing some of our best dancers, we're losing some of our best spaces for dance— those studios in which we work, create and live. Because of painful economic realities—and more specifically, because of greed among spe-

(ROSLYNE PAIGE STERN)

cial interests in this city [New York]—we have experienced a dramatic decline in available, attractive places in which to work. And, unfortunately, there is an even worse enemy now, too, one that haunts us all and has burdened the entire arts community with its tragic weight of sadness and loss and needless waste of human life. The heroic fight against AIDS is also a part of what we are affirming here tonight—an essential, integral battle that involves us all to use those life-affirming skills that have sustained us all for so long—the ability to dance in the face of death.

At "Dance Magazine" awards
ceremony, New York, April 25/
Dance Magazine, October:55.

Roger L. Stevens
Chairman, Kennedy Center
for the Performing Arts,
Washington

1

[On a new fund he heads which will donate money to regional theatre companies]: We're making these grants because the theatre badly needs new material and new playwrights. Everyone admits there's a shortage. I'm talking about theatre in the whole country, not just the commercial world of Broadway. These regional companies may not have enough money for rehearsals or hiring a director of choice. They may want to spend time afterward analyzing what went right or what went wrong. We're giving money for specific things like that.

Interview, Washington/
Los Angeles Times, 6-28:(VI)3.

Isabelle Stevenson
President, American
Theatre Wing

2

[On the high price of Broadway theatre tickets]: For many people, buying tickets has become practically an investment decision. They spend more than $150 for a night out on Broadway. It wipes out the sheer joy of theatre-going.

The Christian Science Monitor,
9-26:1.

Fritz Weaver
Actor

3

. . . when you play the great roles, you get spoiled and think you'll have a whole career playing nothing but great roles, and of course you can't. It's the wrong thing to start on, because it gave me the false idea of the circumstances of our profession. You play a lot of junk most of the time.

Interview, Washington/
The Christian Science Monitor,
9-29:19.

Edward Woodward
Actor

4

My greatest ambition is to be an old man in the theatre—to die on the stage in the middle of the most fantastic death scene, and then have the curtain come down. To die beautifully and gently in harness would be absolutely lovely.

Interview, New York/
Emmy Magazine, March-April:12.

Philosophy

Morris B. Abram
*Chairman, President's
Commission for the Study of
Ethical Problems in Medicine*

1

We must begin to comprehend that death is not always to be fended off. I had begun to understand that when I fell ill with myelocytic leukemia 15 years ago. During my treatment, I reflected that death is the frame around the painting of life. A painting on a canvas of infinite size, worked on eternally, would be without focus, meaning and probably without beauty. A painting, as life, needs limits. While I have an almost insatiable craving for knowledge, I believe death to be the final and perhaps greatest teacher—the one that provides the key to the ultimate questions life has never answered. In my darkest hours I have been consoled by the thought that death at least is a payment for the answer of life's haunting secrets.

*Before Congressional Joint
Economic Committee,
Washington, June/
The Wall Street Journal,
11-28:(A)14.*

Isaac Asimov
Science-fiction writer

2

A hundred years ago, 95 per cent of the labor force was involved in food production or distribution. Experts predicted that once the farms went, the world would be put out of work. If you had told them that in the next century their descendants would be, say, flight attendants or television cameramen, they would have thought you were crazy. The future is full of impossible possibilities. The irony is, those who predict it best are the historians.

*Interview,
New York/
Time, 12-19:82.*

Milton Berle
Comedian

3

Jokes should work at any time. When they pay to come and see you, or they turn on the television set, they're either going to laugh at you or not. I don't believe in "seasonal" humor, like the idea that during a stock-market crash people want to laugh and forget themselves. That's quite true, but funny is funny.

*Interview, New York/
The Christian Science Monitor,
1-21:4.*

David Birney
Actor

4

There's a fantasy that you fall in love, get married and everything will automatically be all right. But in reality, falling in love is like a vacation on a Caribbean island. Marriage, on the other hand, is like scratching a living from the steep, stoney slopes of Sicily. They are two separate events.

*Interview/Ladies' Home Journal,
February:80.*

Ernest Borgnine
Actor

5

There's one memory which goes back to my days as a struggling actor in New York that sums it up for me. I was walking the streets; it was winter; I had a family and needed a job. Then, I was drawn to the smell of chestnuts in the air and it drew me like a magnet. Then I saw it—a sign on a cart that read: "I don't want to set the world on fire, I just want to keep warm." That's the story of my life.

*Interview/
Los Angeles Times, 11-12:(V)10.*

William Boyd
Author

1

... things are crazy and totally unpredictable and nobody knows what's going to happen, so what sort of attitude do you have in the face of this kind of indifferent and random universe? I think that the comic absurd is the only way to cope with it, because if things don't make any sense, then sensible interpretations are some sort of smokescreen. In my [book] heroes' case, it's usually to do with recognizing that the universe is utterly indifferent to the fate of individuals. Once you realize that, all sorts of choices and dilemmas don't come any easier, but there's some sort of perverse logic there working.

Interview/
Publishers Weekly, 4-29:57.

Warren Buffet
Chairman,
Berkshire Hathaway

2

I don't have a problem with guilt about money. The way I see it is that my money represents an enormous number of claim checks on society. It's like I have these little pieces of paper that I can turn into consumption. If I wanted to, I could hire ten thousand people to do nothing but paint my picture every day for the rest of my life. And the GNP would go up. But the utility of the product would be zilch, and I would be keeping those ten thousand people from doing AIDS research, or teaching, or nursing. I don't do that, though. I don't use very many of those claim checks. There's nothing material I want very much. And I'm going to give virtually all of those claim checks to charity when my wife and I die.

Interview/Esquire, June:159.

George Burns
Entertainer

3

People *practice* to get old. The minute they get to be 65 or 70, they sit down slow, they get into a car with trouble, they start taking small steps.

Time, 2-22:79.

John Chaney
Basketball coach,
Temple University

4

It's ridiculous to think that you can pick out one guy and say, "That's what I want to be like." If a teacher has something you like, then great, pick up that piece. If your mailman has a great personality, then add that to your total person. A role model is not a person. It's a behavior.

The Christian Science Monitor,
10-31:18.

Noam Chomsky
Author, Philosopher

5

... intellectuals are the most indoctrinated part of the population. In fact, there are good reasons for this. First, as the literate part of the population, they are the ones most susceptible to propaganda. Second, they are the ideological managers, so they have to internalize the propaganda. They have to believe it.

At town hall, Keene, N.H./
Mother Jones, October:37.

Daryl Chubin
Senior analyst, Office of
Technology Assistance,
United States Congress

6

One of the things we know about attentive publics is that when they personalize or identify with the risks, it's then that they are moved to act.

The Christian Science Monitor,
9-14:6.

John Cleese
Actor, Screenwriter

7

... as you get older, you realize that it is an absolute miracle that anything works at all in this world. Instead of seeing it, as you do when you are young, as a place which is basically rational with small areas of insanity, you see it quite the other way around; the whole place is a complete

(JOHN CLEESE)

madhouse. Billy Connolly says it gets harder to make jokes as you get older because life gets much funnier than any material you can dream up, and I find this is happening to me all the time.

Interview/
Films & Filming, October:8.

John B. Connally, Jr.
Former Governor of Texas (D);
Former Secretary of the Treasury
of the
United States

1

I don't believe in retiring. I don't intend to retire. I don't think anyone should. People start withering. The mind is like a muscle. Unused, it begins to atrophy.

Interview, Houston/
Los Angeles Times, 1-22:(I)24.

Sean Connery
Actor

2

I had fame and fortune as a young man, and now, at 57, I wouldn't want to be that young again for anything in the world. I loved turning 50—it meant I was a true survivor, as an actor and as a human being. I'm not looking for a fountain of youth, as some actors are. Some of them, poor things, are contantly trying to look and act young, young, young. Instead, they wind up immature.

Interview/50 Plus, August:60.

Alistair Cooke
Journalist, Commentator

3

. . . I think of Isaiah Berlin's great distinction taken from the Greek poet Archilochus about the difference between a hedgehog and a fox. The hedgehog, Berlin said, wants to see the world ordered the way it ought to be, and Berlin quotes Plato, Dante and Bernard Shaw as typical examples of that. Then Berlin cites Pushkin, Tolstoy and Shakespeare as foxes who are more

excited by the way life is, with all its contradictions. I'm with the foxes.

Interview, San Francisco/
The New York Times, 11-19:12.

Francis Ford Coppola
Motion-picture director

4

The meaning of life seems to be easier to come to when you're sitting in the country. Looking out at what seems to be the world around me, the evidence of incredible creativity is so abundant, so alive in the creation that created us that it must be right for us to be creative, too. That's what we should be doing. The important thing is not so much the facts of the world around us. I am a person who puts a lot of stock in intuition and love and feelings. I know for sure that's really me; whereas the fact that I'm sitting in this place with you and talking, and there's a couch over here—well, that's just a lot of molecules. I don't take as so important the actual physical life, much less who's the President or whether [film critic] Roger Ebert didn't like my film. Those things seem like little details compared to what I do know, which is that there is such a thing as passionate feeling.

Interview, New York/
Mother Jones, September:24.

Bette Davis
Actress

5

I think for me the golden years are not now. Recent years have not been very pleasant. I've always roared with laughter when they say life begins at 40. That's the funniest remark ever. The day I was born was when life began for me.

Interview, New York/
Ladies' Home Journal,
February:40.

Ghena Dimitrova
Opera singer

6

What I got from my heritage is the knowledge that anything worthwhile—anything in life, not

(GHENA DIMITROVA)

only music—does not grow out of thin air. It comes from the ground. That means preparation and a sense of professional responsibility. One goes carefully up the ladder, one rung at a time. You work and work some more, go back and study again. I've lived 20 years in the West, but because of my heritage I've never come to believe in things that are easy and fleeting.

Interview, New York/
Opera News, 2-13:29.

Michael S. Dukakis
Governor of Massachusetts (D);
Candidate for the 1988 Democratic
Presidential nomination

1

Life moves so fast these days—particularly here in the U.S.—that people don't have a sense of history. One of the great strengths that a Harry Truman or a John Kennedy had was that they were students of history. They knew the kinds of issues or challenges that they were confronting were not original with them. You go back and read the ancient Greeks, and you have a pretty good sense of the same kinds of ethical, moral and political challenges being faced.

Interview, Brookline, Mass./
U.S. News & World Report, 2-1:25.

Freeman Dyson
Physicist

2

The game of status-seeking, organized around committees, is played in roughly the same fashion in Africa, in America and in the Soviet Union. Perhaps the aptitude for this committee game is part of our genetic inheritance, like the aptitude for speech and for music.

At College of Wooster (Ohio)
commencement/Time, 6-13:74.

Umberto Eco
Italian author

3

In the United States, there's a Puritan ethic and a mythology of success: He who is success-

ful is good. In Latin countries, in Catholic countries, a successful person is a sinner. In Puritan countries, success show's God's benevolence. In Catholic countries, your God loves you only when you've suffered.

Interview, Bologna, Italy/
The New York Times, 12-13:(B)1.

Seymour Epstein
Psychologist, University
of Massachusetts

4

I.Q. and success in living have little to do with each other. Being intellectually gifted does not predict you will earn the most money or achieve the most recognition, even among college professors . . . How well people manage their emotions determines how effectively they can use their intellectual ability. For example, if someone is facile at solving problems in the quiet of her office, but falls apart in a group, then she will be ineffective in a great many situations.

The New York Times, 4-5:17.

Amitai Etzioni
Sociologist; Director,
Center for Policy Research,
George Washington University

5

We need to recognize that both the society and the individual are essential to a morality which we can use in the next century. If we could enter the next century with a wider recognition of that balance—and get away from either collectivistic excesses or the celebration of radical individualism—I think we'd be better for it.

At Wingspread Conference,
Racine, Wis., April/
The Christian Science Monitor, 7-25:(B)11.

Fang Lizhi
Former vice president,
University of Science and
Technology (China);
Former member, Communist Party
of China

6

Marxism is useless. Philosophically, it's very backward. As for socialist theory, experience has

473

(FANG LIZHI)

proven it a failure . . . Going abroad had a great influence on me. I saw what it was like to conduct research free from Marxism. Chinese leaders say that without the guidance of Marxism one cannot arrive at correct results. Overseas, I found people achieving striking results, and they were not guided by Marxism!

Interview/
The Christian Science Monitor,
11-18:36.

Stephen Jay Gould
Professor of geology,
Harvard University

1

The only thing we have as human beings that is distinctive is rational thought. But it's so fragile. It's so easy to let any kind of emotionalism overwhelm it. You can undo in a microsecond what it took years to build up.

U.S. News & World Report,
2-8:64.

Gilbert M. Grosvenor
Chairman and president,
National Geographic Society

2

The pencil is a classic example of interdependence. There are 15 to 18 ingredients in it, among them graphite, which comes from Sri Lanka; zinc, which comes from, among other places, the U.S.S.R.; a wax which comes from Mexico; pumice which comes from Italy. Then it gets into ships that are registered in Liberia that carry all these materials which are made in Japan. You think of a pencil as just a piece of wood with lead in it, but there's more to it. It is the whole story of working together with different nations in the world.

Interview,
Washington/
The Christian Science Monitor,
1-25:17.

Edward Harrison
Professor of physics and
astronomy, University of Massachusetts,
Amherst

3

By equating God and the universe, we give back to the world what long ago was taken away. The world we live in, with our thoughts, passions, delights, and whatever stirs the mortal frame, must surely take on a deeper meaning. Songs are more than longitudinal sound vibrations, sunsets more than transverse electromagnetic oscillations, inspirations more than the discharge of neurons, all touched with a mystery that deepens, the more we contemplate and seek to understand.

Interview, Amherst, Mass./
The Christian Science Monitor,
8-31:17.

Gary Hart
Candidate for the 1988
Democratic Presidential
nomination; Former United
States Senator, D-Colorado

4

Very little in human life that is worthwhile happens by luck or by accident. Achievement requires commitment and investment of time and money and energy. No national athletic team wins a national championship by accident, and no nation triumphs that way, either . . . Albert Schweitzer said: Anyone who proposes to do good must not expect people to roll stones out of his way, but must accept as his lot, calmly, if they roll a few more upon it. A strength which becomes clearer and stronger through its experience of such obstacles is the only strength which can conquer them.

Campaign speech/
The New York Times, 1-26:13.

Jesse L. Jackson
Civil-rights leader;
Candidate for the 1988
Democratic Presidential nomination

5

When we turn *to* each other, and not *on* each other, that's victory. When we build each other,

(JESSE L. JACKSON)

and not destroy each other, that's victory. Red, yellow, brown, black and white—we're all precious in God's sight. Everybody is somebody.

Campaign speech/
Los Angeles Times, 4-2:(I)19.

1

Nothing hurts me quite so much as to see people surrender because their hopes have been dashed, to see grapes of potentiality, sweet with juice, become raisins of despair.

Campaign speech,
New York, April 15/
The New York Times, 4-16:9.

Jesse L. Jackson
Civil-rights leader;
Former candidate for the
1988 Democratic
Presidential nomination

2

Blacks and Hispanics, when we fight for civil rights, we are right—but our patch isn't big enough. Gays and lesbians, when you fight against discrimination and for a cure for AIDS, you are right—but your patch isn't big enough. Conservatives and progressives, when you fight for what you believe, you are right—but your patch isn't big enough. But don't despair. When we bring the patches together, make a quilt, and turn to each other and not on each other, we the people always win.

At Democratic National Convention,
Atlanta, July 19/
The New York Times, 7-20:12.

Norman Lamm
President,
Yeshiva University

3

Moderation should never be confused with indecisiveness. On the contrary, a lack of self-confidence in one's most basic commitments is often expressed in extremism. Only one who is sure of what he stands for can afford to be moderate. A strong heart can risk being an open heart.

Speech at Fifth Avenue Synagogue,
New York, March 22/
The New York Times, 3-24:9.

Lewis Lapham
Editor, "Harper's" magazine

4

We need to realize that money is not the ultimate power of the world. It is not money itself, but the *love* of money that is the root of all evil. If you let this love blot out courage, work, art, romance—then you are closing yourself into a narrower and narrower cage.

Interview, New York/
Publishers Weekly, 2-5:76.

Lee Kuan Yew
Prime Minister of Singapore

5

. . . there is hope in the world. There is no reason for poverty, misery, anger, frustration, quarrels and war. There is enough in this world to feed, clothe and satisfy everybody if we are prepared to make adjustments, and if conditions are such that you have capital coming across to help under-developed people . . .

Interview, Singapore/
USA Today, 5-13:(A)11.

Dan Lewis
Urbanologist,
Northwestern University

6

The ultimate issue of "community" is, What do we owe other people? In our society, where individualism plays such an important role, we don't have a public ethic about what we owe others.

Time, 6-27:47.

George Lucas
Motion-picture director

7

Success is insidious. You think you can manage it but it creeps up on you. It tests you and

475

(GEORGE LUCAS)

everyone around you. I thought maybe because I'd got it in increments I could handle it. But . . . it's hard.

Interview, San Rafael, Calif./
Los Angeles Times,
5-15:(Calendar)39.

Robert S. McNamara
Former Secretary of Defense
of the United States

1

We don't bring to a consideration of public-policy issues a moral foundation. My experience in public-policy debates has been that you are thought to be rather naive if you introduce the moral dimension.

At Wingspread Conference,
Racine, Wis., April/
The Christian Science Monitor,
7-25:(B)10.

Arthur Miller
Playwright

2

I'm convinced that time has no existence in the mind at all. We partition time out of necessity, so that if I say I will be somewhere at 1 o'clock, we agree on what 1 o'clock is. Civilization couldn't function otherwise. But our minds are a swirling mass of images and recollections that are connected, and it's the connections that count.

Interview/
U.S. News & World Report,
1-11:54.

Francois Mitterrand
President of France

3

Politicians should be modest when faced with the man of knowledge. Tomorrow will be less like today, because we're seeing a transfer of power from politics to science. The century of a scientific and technical leap forward was also that of the [concentration] camps and bestialities, the century of Auschwitz and penicillin, where one saw, where one sees, doctors torture. Century of the green revolution and the brown-shirts, of the conquest of the cosmos and the desertification of the earth, where life expectancy has doubled in the industrialized countries, while genocide and fanaticisms of all kinds have redoubled.

At conference of Nobel laureates,
Paris, Jan. 18/
The New York Times, 1-19:7.

4

I believe in the virtue of traditions, and I recall having often spoken this phrase: "Memory is revolutionary." If one has the ambition of preparing the century to come, breaking with the past or being ignorant of it amounts to cutting one's own roots and drying up on the spot.

Interview/
U.S. News & World Report,
3-7:45.

5

Personally, I believe that nothing better defines the modern democracy we practice today than the synthesis that must constantly be reinvented between liberty and equality . . . I think that there are few in our two countries [the U.S. and France] today who would contest the notion that "Men are born and remain equal," or that the state must be run by laws. Nor does anyone question the separation of powers, universal suffrage, public education or the abolition of slavery; in sum, all that forms the foundation of a republic and a democracy, and, I would add, even civilization. But we must relentlessly strive to see that these principles do indeed become facts . . . We must work to end oppression, humiliation, segregation and the disrespect of human rights . . . I can assure you that this can only happen when one is willing to break away from what the established order may contain in terms of false traditions.

At New York University, Sept. 28/
The Washington Post,
10-11:(A)18.

Bill Moyers
Broadcast journalist

1

In the last 30 years, I've discovered that bread is the great reinforcer of the reality principle. Bread equals life. On the frontier they had to produce this themselves. But if you're like me, you have a thousand and more times repeated the ordinary experience of eating bread without a thought for the process itself. This was brought to me the other day by a friend who said: "I depend for bread on hundreds of people I don't know and will never meet. If they fail me, I starve. If I cannot give them something of value in exchange for this, I fail them." Bread and life are shared realities. No one prays the Lord's Prayer in the first-person singular. It is always, "Give *us* this day *our* daily bread." Our very lives depend on the ethics of strangers, and most of us are always strangers to other people. If you want to see a monument to this, look around. Literally, look around. Think of all the people you will never know and will never meet who raised this university up from just a high spot in Austin.

At University of Texas at Austin
commencement/The Christian
Science Monitor, 7-27:26.

Howard Nemerov
Poet Laureate of the
United States

2

The secrets of success are a good wife and a steady job. My wife told me.

Interview/
Writer's Digest, December:31.

Paul Newman
Actor

3

Everything I ever tried to do I started badly. Take politics. Started out making a real ass of myself. I did the same as an actor. And it was the same with [racing] cars. I come very, very slow to things. Everything I have ever tried to do I entered with a sense of confusion and, "Well, why not?" Then, once the decision got made, and

I was stuck with it, I had to *bleed* commitment into it. Like filling up a tire.

Interview, New York/
Esquire, June:107.

4

The trick of living is to slip on and off the planet with the least fuss you can muster. I'm not a professional philanthropist, and I'm not running for sainthood. I just happen to think that in life we need to be a little like the farmer who puts back into the soil what he takes out.

Interview/
Ladies' Home Journal, July:161.

Randy Newman
Singer, Songwriter

5

We should all be smart enough to know that money doesn't make us happy. The trouble is that in America the smart people who opt for a life that isn't based on getting rich—who decide to teach chemistry or work for a public-radio station—get their faces rubbed in it. Through television, people in this country who don't have a lot are constantly reminded that life could be more comfortable.

Interview/
The New York Times, 9-28:20.

Louis Nizer
Lawyer

6

While we cannot control the length of our lives, we can control the width and the depth of our lives. Versatility should be the rule, not the exception.

Interview/USA Today, 6-8:(A)2.

Miguel Obando y Bravo
Roman Catholic Archbishop
of Managua, Nicaragua

7

In the life of great men, there are moments of light and darkness, moments of power and of

(MIGUEL OBANDO Y BRAVO)

uncertainty. There are moments when one is exalted, and moments when one sees one's obligations.

At Mass, Managua, March 27/
The New York Times, 3-28:4.

Norman Vincent Peale
Author, Clergyman

1

[On a forthcoming tribute to him on his 90th birthday]: What is the point of a testimonial for the fact that you've reached 90 years? You just haven't died, that's all.

Time, 6-6:75.

T. Boone Pickens
Industrialist

2

Be willing to make decisions. That's the most important quality in a good leader. Don't fall victim to what I call the "ready-aim-aim-aim-aim syndrome." You must be willing to fire.

At George Washington University
commencement/Time, 6-13:74.

Sidney Poitier
Actor

3

You spend the better part of your life trying to put your life within the bounds of safety, security. You build a fortress around your life. And you begin to find, as I did when I stepped away, that it's not always that necessary . . . Therefore, I'm living in a way that isn't dictated by my pocketbook. I want to read more, travel some, go to weird places.

Interview, New York/
Newsweek, 2-22:73.

Ronald Reagan
President of the United States

4

Freedom is the right to question and change the established way of doing things. It is the con-

tinuing revolution of the marketplace. It is the understanding that allows us to recognize shortcomings and seek solutions. It is the right to put forth an idea, scoffed at by the experts, and watch it catch fire among the people. It is the right to stick—to dream—to follow your dream, or stick to your conscience, even if you're the only one in a sea of doubters. Freedom is the recognition that no single person, no single authority or government, has a monopoly on the truth, but that every individual life is infinitely precious, that every one of us put on this world has been put there for a reason and has something to offer.

At Moscow (U.S.S.R.) State University,
May/
The Wall Street Journal, 9-2:10.

5

Just as democratic freedom has proven itself incredibly fertile—fertile not merely in a material sense, but also in the abundance it has brought forth in the human spirit—so, too, utopianism has proven brutal and barren . . . In Western Europe, support for utopian ideologies, including support among intellectuals, has all but collapsed. While in the non-democratic countries, leaders grapple with the internal contradictions of their system. And some ask how they can make that system better and more productive. In a sense, the front line in the competition of ideas that has played in Europe and America for more than 70 years has shifted east. Once, it was the democracies that doubted their own view of freedom and wondered whether utopian systems might not be better. Today, the doubt is on the other side.

Speech, Helsinki, Finland,
May 27/The New York Times,
5-28:5.

6

If future generations do say of us that, in our time, peace came closer, that we did bring about new seasons of truth and justice, it'll be cause for pride. But it shall be a cause of greater pride still if it is also said that we were wise enough to know that the deliberations of great leaders and great

(RONALD REAGAN)

bodies are but overture; that the truly majestic music—the music of freedom, of justice and peace—is the music made in forgetting self and seeking in silence the will of Him who made us.

At United Nations,
New York, Sept. 26/
The New York Times, 9-27:6.

Robert Redford
Actor

1

[On being famous]: The bad part is that you become an object. And there are three dangerous stages to that: One, people start treating you like an object. Two, you start behaving like an object. And three, you become one. That's terminal. You start walking around saying, "Gee. It's tough to be famous and have all this money." Really?

Interview/Esquire, March:122.

William H. Rehnquist
Chief Justice of the
United States

2

When you are young and impecunious, society conditions you to exchange time for money, and this is quite as it should be. Very few people are hurt by having to work for a living. But as you become more affluent, it somehow is very, very difficult to reverse that process and begin trading money for time.

At Marquette University
commencement/Time, 6-13:74.

Pat Riley
Basketball coach,
Los Angeles "Lakers"

3

If you go about living your life as you choose, and you're happy with it, and you're on a mission, then the opinion-makers will never really affect you. I think it comes down to defining the discipline in your life, the character in your life,

the quality of your life. After we [the *Lakers*] lost in '84, I went through torment that summer, being publicly mocked and humiliated by the media. But I realized then that it didn't make any difference what had happened. What matters is how you deal with it. It's how you take it. It's how you come back from it.

Interview/Esquire, June:111.

Kenny Rogers
Singer

4

Part of success for a man is knowing when you've done your best and it's time to move on. I've always been more afraid of stagnation than failure. At least you can learn from failure. To me, nothing is sadder or more pathetic than an ex-anything.

Interview/
McCall's, November:14.

Felix G. Rohatyn
Senior partner,
Lazard Freres;
Chairman, Municipal
Assistance Corporation of
New York

5

Money is the standard now. It's the new religion. We have two religions in this country, fundamentalism and money, and I don't know which is worse. I don't see the death of greed. I see people worried that they may have come along a couple of years too late.

Interview/Esquire, June:185.

Carlos Salinas de Gortari
Economist;
Institutional Revolutionary
Party candidate for
President of Mexico

6

Reform implies risks, but risks are better than not doing anything. I prefer the risk of reform to the risk of inactivity.

Interview, May 9/
The Washington Post, 5-12:(A)23.

Jose Sarney
President of Brazil

1

[On his being a poet who became President of Brazil]: I was never attracted by power. But in this life, there are two parallel paths, one of which is the path of politics, which brings you to power; the other is literature. I must accept fate and destiny and put up with the political.

Interview,
Brasilia, Brazil/
USA Today, 3-4:(A)9.

Poul Schlueter
Prime Minister of Denmark

2

Socialist ideas are becoming more and more outdated, and if Karl Marx had lived today he would probably not have been a Marxist. He was far too clever for that. I think he would have been a modern conservative, just like me.

Los Angeles Times, 4-28:(I)2.

Vincent Scully
Architectural historian,
Yale University

3

One of the big things that . . . distinguishes me from artists is that I hate death more than anything. It infuriates me, and that's the death of anything—people, things, a piece of furniture, a glass. It's absolutely a fact—psychotic, I know—but I do want to conserve, to save everything. That's really basic; it transcends belief in anything else because out there is a terrible void, nothing.

Interview/
Publishers Weekly,
9-30:48.

Erich Segal
Author

4

The limelight is like sunshine at first, and then eventually you can get sunstroke from it.

USA Today, 8-25:(D)2.

Maurice Sendak
Author, Designer

5

Of course we're going to die. Doesn't everybody know that? And is that still something that is frightening? Of course, of course. It's less frightening as you get older, if you put any thought into it, or any time. For a person like myself, who has suffered serious ill health, it becomes part of your tissue; you think about it all the time. I don't say it's easy, and I don't mean to sound fatuous about it, but it doesn't make me unhappy. Life-things make me unhappy, like getting through a day in New York.

Interview, New York/
The New York Times, 10-19:(B)6.

Omar Sharif
Actor

6

Ideally, I would love to find a woman who would be my girlfriend, always. I could call her on the phone and say, "Shall we have dinner?" And we have dinner, go back together; but then she has her apartment and I have mine. We have our own lives, our own friends. We can share friends or not, it doesn't matter. But we have this courting relationship forever. It never gets into a rut. You see, when you're dating someone, when you meet them you're dressed right, you've had your bath, you don't belch or do things like that—it's rude to say, but it's the truth. Once you get married, you start living in the same room, and I guess you can't keep yourself from belching forever, you know? And you also have to be uncombed sometimes; you have to put cream on your face, curlers on your hair. You have to go to the toilet, and flush, and you've got to hear that.

Interview/50 Plus, September:36.

Karlheinz Stockhausen
Composer

7

. . . this is the meaning of life—continuously to add something we haven't known so far. That, anyway, is the meaning of all existing things. Existence is built upon the idea of the creative—

(KARLHEINZ STOCKHAUSEN)

that there is always something unknown to be discovered, which causes and motivates new perception, new studies, the energy to go on.

Opera News, May:16.

Anthony Storr
Psychiatrist,
Oxford University

1

I'm surprised at the number of people who have told me that they used to feel guilty because they enjoyed solitude, but now, after hearing what I have to say, they understand that it's okay to take pleasure in being alone. I believe that the happiest lives are probably those in which neither interpersonal relationships nor impersonal interests are idealized as the only way to salvation. The desire and pursuit of the whole must comprehend both aspects of human nature.

Interview/
U.S. News & World Report,
9-12:62.

Richard Taub
Professor, division of social
sciences, University of Chicago

2

Often communities that are the most cohesive are also hostile and fearful of outsiders. Community spirit says, "Take care of your own." The ethical challenge is to make people see that the world is their community.

Time, 6-27:47.

Nguyen Co Thach
Foreign Minister of Vietnam

3

We have taught that everything from capitalism is corrupt. This is false. Without some capitalism, there can be no socialism.

Interview/
USA Today, 9-9:(A)2.

Margaret Thatcher
Prime Minister of the
United Kingdom

4

The great battle now is to prevent the smaller minority ruining the lives of the majority by violence, by dirtiness, by graffiti, by everyday surliness . . . Graciousness has been replaced by surliness in much of everyday life.

Interview/
The Washington Post, 5-25:(A)25.

5

Battles in life are never won. I mean, you don't have your household budget permanently balanced; you have to balance it every year. Life's a continuous business, and so is success, and requires continuous effort.

Interview, London, Sept. 27/
The New York Times, 9-28:9.

6

. . . there are two fundamental creeds guiding the world's political, philosophical, personal future. One is the Marxists' [idea of] central control and [that] the citizen has to conform. The other [is embodied in] the Constitution of the United States: The people came here because they believed in certain fundamental liberties . . . We've got two theories. We've got two practical results. And Marxism's had it. You cannot deny the fundamental essence of human nature and expect to succeed.

Interview, Washington/
Newsweek, 11-28:52.

Tatiana Tolstaya
Soviet author

7

Here [in the U.S.], everyone is offended if he suffers. You go to a psychiatrist. I think that's nonsense. If you go to a psychiatrist, then you spoil your soul. If you feel awful, if you feel just irritated, if you feel depressed, Americans run to the doctor. But we [Soviets] never [do] because I think if you feel that state of mind, your soul is

(TATIANA TOLSTAYA)

growing . . . when you feel pain, something is growing.

Interview, Beverly Hills, Calif./
Los Angeles Times, 1-25:(V)1.

John Updike
Author

1

A good relationship is one in which it's understood that there's a limit to what can be communicated and what can be shared. All of our earthly signals are just, well, they're gestures, and hints, but there's always going to be a lot that can't be said, a certain amount that shouldn't be said. I think that tact, which operates in our superficial social relations, also really has to operate at the most intimate level, that one is tactful even in the paroxysms of amorous bliss, that there's a certain large amount of the unsaid. But one can feel that and still try to communicate.

Interview/
The New York Times, 3-2:20.

Brian Urquhart
Former Under Secretary General
of the United Nations
for Special Political Affairs

2

I am an idealist, I have to admit it. I think human nature is self-interested. But there is such a thing as enlightened self-interest. The trick is to engage self-interest at the point where it touches other people's self-interest . . . I maintain that my idealism, which is based on some fairly rough experience, is a great deal more realistic than the totally defeatest notion that human beings are born to suffer and kill each other. If one believes that, one should go dig a deep hole and jump into it.

Interview, New York/
Time, 12-5:52.

Peregrine Worsthorne
Editor, "The Sunday Telegraph,"
London

3

In a democracy, almost nothing important can be talked about truthfully except in private, for fear of being misunderstood by a mass electorate. Race cannot be spoken about openly. AIDS cannot, either. Nor, for the most part, can foreign affairs . . . I mean, simply, that the element of frankness and truthfulness in public discourse is very small, and only when you actually get them in private do people ever speak truthfully. In private, an Irish politician will say, "It will be the end of the world if we were actually to have Northern Ireland incorporated in the Republic." But can you get an Irish politician to say that in public? Of course you can't. Likewise, in many ways, the British would be glad to be rid of Northern Ireland, but can't say so. It is in these areas that I think private discourse is truthful and public discourse is hypocritical. It has been true since democracy took over. Once people depend upon not offending the voter, public discourse becomes hypocritical.

Interview, London/
The New York Times, 12-7:(A)6.

Religion

Nancy Ammerman
Professor of sociology of religion,
Emory University

1

For conservatives, the Bible contains scientific as well as spiritual facts about the world. To admit any doubt about details in Scripture is to begin the process that could lead to total doubt. It's the slippery-slope argument, and at the bottom of the slope is the deity of Christ itself, which conservatives fear could be doubted . . . [On the other hand,] a moderate has more of a seat-of-the-pants belief in the Bible. Did Jonah really spend three days in the belly of the whale? For a moderate, it may not matter. The question is, what can we learn from this story?

Interview/USA Today, 6-16:(A)7.

Oscar Arias
President of Costa Rica

2

We should no longer be ashamed of feelings, of piety. It is not true that they degrade reason and science. Piety is no less than the intelligence of the soul and we need heart and brains to recover the world in our hands, for the values we cherish.

At Harvard University
commencement/The Christian
Science Monitor, 7-27:26.

Yuri Aslanov
Inspector of Religious Affairs
of the Soviet Union

3

My generation grew up with the conviction that religion would never cease to be a reactionary force. Now we are being told that believers, too, can be good citizens, and I can see that their moral standards are often better than those of many atheists.

World Press Review,
September:57.

Edmond L. Browning
Presiding Bishop, Episcopal Church
of the United States

4

The issue of the ordination of women [in the Anglican Church of Britain] is so potentially divisive here [in Britain], so difficult. We are committed to it but, here, it's not a question of right or wrong. It's a question of time. The key is diversity—we're a diverse communion and we must live together as a communion.

Interview, Canterbury, England/
The New York Times, 7-20:5.

John Buchanan
Chairman, People for the
American Way

5

[On the controversy over teaching about religion in public schools]: You can't have an accurate portrayal of history and leave out religion.

U.S. News & World Report, 7-4:57.

George Bush
Vice President of the United States;
1988 Republican
Presidential nominee

6

It is important that we all respect the separation of church and state, just as we are meticulous in defending the right of all people, including evangelicals, to participate in the process without intimidation or ridicule. Separation of church and state? Yes. One nation under God? Yes, transcending even political-party lines. Evangelicals, as all other Americans, have the right, and even a responsibility, to participate in the process, advocating their values. I support them. I think their involvement is healthy for America.

Interview/
Christianity Today, 9-16:40.

(GEORGE BUSH)

1

I know it's controversial but I don't think it's wrong for kids to have a voluntary prayer, a minute of silent prayer, in our schools. I think that it's right. I think that it's good for the moral fiber of our country.

*Campaigning,
Wenona, Ill., Sept. 28/
Los Angeles Times, 9-29:(I)20.*

G. Raymond Carlson
*General superintendent,
Assemblies of God*

2

[On his church's recent sex scandal involving evangelist Jimmy Swaggart]: . . . right now we feel it's the biggest problem . . . [but] out of this I think there's coming a purification of the church . . . Many people are looking introspectively, looking into their own lives: What are our priorities? What is our relationship to Christ? What about our life? As grievous as the difficulties of these days, the church is going to be a better church, and that's because of the grace of God.

Interview/USA Today, 3-28:(A)11.

Harvey Cox
*Professor of divinity,
Harvard Divinity School*

3

[The revival of religion in America is part of] a global phenomenon that has to do with the unraveling of modernity and all the different components that went into that, a kind of faith that science would master all of our problems, or the kind of individualism which was part of the modern ethos and which has now resulted in isolation and loneliness . . . When I first came to teach here 22 years ago, other than at the Divinity School, it would be hard to find people who would admit to being both serious intellectuals and also personally concerned or involved in a religious tradition or practice. Now the interest in religious studies is growing, and it's hard to find people to staff all the courses.

*Interview/
Publishers Weekly, 10-7:97.*

Carl Gershman
*President, National
Endowment for Democracy*

4

. . . it should be possible to acknowledge and reaffirm the inter-relationship between democracy and human rights. It should also be possible to embrace a new understanding of the way in which efforts to advance democracy and to protect human rights reinforce and strengthen each other. People working for democracy, after all, often face harassment, arrest, even torture and death. They need the protection of human-rights activists. At the risk of over-simplifying the relationship, it may be said that human-rights advocacy has to do with the protection and enlargement of political, intellectual and cultural space. Efforts to advance democracy have to do with the use that is made of that existing space. To the extent that these efforts succeed, they will establish a legal framework and institutional infrastruture that will ground human rights in everyday practice and procedure so that these rights become a living reality for each individual.

*At Georgetown University, Dec. 9/
The Washington Post,
12-29:(A)22.*

Mikhail S. Gorbachev
*General Secretary,
Communist Party of
the Soviet Union*

5

[On his policy of *perestroika,* reform, in the Soviet Union]: Mistakes made with regard to the church and believers in the 1930s and the years that followed are being rectified. A new law on the freedom of conscience, now being drafted, will reflect the interests of religious organizations . . . The believers are Soviet people, workers, patriots, and they have the full right to express their conviction with dignity. *Perestroika,* democratization concern them as well— in full measure and without restriction.

*To Russian Orthodox Church
leaders, Moscow, April 29/
The Washington Post,
4-30:(A)1.*

(MIKHAIL S. GORBACHEV)

1

All believers, irrespective of the religion they profess, are full-fledged citizens of the Soviet Union. [The Communist Party's own atheism is] no reason for a disrespectful attitude to the spiritual mindedness of the believer, and still less for applying any administrative pressure to assert materialistic views.

At Soviet Communist Party
conference, Moscow, June 28/
Los Angeles Times 6-29:(I)9.

Billy Graham
Evangelist

2

[On the sex and money scandals that have hit TV evangelists recently]: I don't have the answers to that. A couple of big names have crashed. But it's like the thousands of flights at O'Hare [Airport] in Chicago. The overwhelming majority don't crash . . . I think there has been a wound, but I don't think it's a deadly wound. It may be a cleansing wound. A cleansing is taking place. It's making everybody look to their financial integrity and responsibility. And to their personal life-styles. Public evangelists must watch themselves very carefully.

Interview, Asheville, N.C./
Christianity Today, 11-18:20.

David Hartman
Director, Shalom Hartman Institute
for Jewish Study,
Jerusalem

3

[On proposed Israeli legislation defining "who is a Jew"]: This is a real test of Israel's respect and concern for diaspora Jewry. Personally, I hope the amendment is always debated but never passed, because its presence on the table allows us to argue about some of the most important questions that we face about ourselves. But if it passed, it would be a terrible, terrible blow.

The Washington Post,
12-12:(A)19.

Jesse L. Jackson
Civil-rights leader;
Candidate for the 1988
Democratic Presidential
nomination

4

We have this interesting combination here in America of religious freedom without religious domination. We do not have leaders who come from heaven down, but from the people up.

Interview/
Los Angeles Times, 5-27:(I)31.

Immanuel Jakobovits
Chief Rabbi of the United
Hebrew Congregation of
Britain and of the
Commonwealth

5

[On his becoming the first rabbi in the British House of Lords]: Nobody today thinks that, by dropping their Jewishness, they will find it easier to be accepted in society. My elevation is the best example of that. I have been elevated not because I renounced my Jewish beliefs or modified them or made concessions, but on the contrary, because I held strictly to them and proclaimed them without adulteration and without concessions.

Interview, London/
The New York Times, 2-10:7.

Eugene Antonio Marino
Roman Catholic Archbishop-
designate of Atlanta

6

[On his becoming the first black U.S. Archbishop]: Blacks have a rich tradition of spirituality, but it is not a tradition which enriches the Catholic Church, unfortunately. I would see my appointment as a great sign of hope to black Catholics in our country and to all people of good will. It means that the Church recognizes the wealth within its own ranks, that it is a church of many significant minorities.

News conference,
Atlanta, March 15/
The New York Times, 3-16:1

Brian John Masters
Anglican Bishop of Edmonton,
London, (England)

1

Women certainly can make a contribution, and do make a contribution, to the [Anglican] Church. But women in the priesthood will divide the Church and hamper its mission. There is little evidence from the Episcopal Church in the U.S. that that particular body has been strengthened by the ordination of women.

The Christian Science Monitor,
7-20:9.

Eric M. Meyers
Director, Center for Judaic Studies,
Duke University

2

[Criticizing the effort by Orthodox Jews in Israel to redefine "who is a Jew"]: There is great concern in the [American Jewish] community, great malaise, great fear that this is going to go into law. You can judge the latest news from Israel by the tumult in the lunchroom [at the university] . . . If the [Orthodox] amendment goes through, it will create a barrier between Israel and the diaspora. I would see this as creating a rift in Jewish life, something fundamental and divisive . . . To see the Orthodox wield that much power is frightening.

Interview/
The New York Times,
11-21:(A)6.

Eugene Mihaly
Vice president, Hebrew
Union College, Cincinnati

3

Any way you look at it, intermarriage [between Jews and non-Jews] is an inevitable consequence of an open society. A very high percentage of Jewish young people go to college and at a marriageable age come in contact with non-Jewish students. It's only natural that some of them should fall in love.

Time, 10-3:82.

Richard John Neuhaus
Director, Rockford Institute
Center on Religion and
Society, New York

4

There may yet emerge an American way of being Roman Catholic, and a Roman Catholic way of being American, that bear witness to what is authoritative for all of us . . . [But] the era of simply welcoming change has to give way to a more disciplined discernment of what changes are authentic and which are alien to the Christian gospel.

U.S. News & World Report,
4-11:60.

George W. Paterson
Associate professor,
School of Religion
University of Iowa

5

[On the recent sex scandals involving TV evangelists]: There is a strong body of opinion that the emotional wellsprings of religious experience and sex are very close to one another.

USA Today, 3-1:(A)10.

Oral Roberts
Evangelist

6

[On the recent sex scandals involving TV evangelists]: Right now, this old world, the media and certain church people are dragging the name of evangelists in the mud.

USA Today, 3-1:(A)10.

Robert Runcie
Archbishop of Canterbury
(England)

7

[On the disagreement in the Anglican Church over the ordination of women clergy]: Until there is a decisive, ecumenical, Christian answer to this question, there will inevitably be the risk of broken, or at least impaired, communion between the provinces of the [Anglican] Com-

(ROBERT RUNCIE)

munion, where some have advanced while others have held back. If a thing is of God, it will flourish. If not, it will eventually wither. In the meantime, we have to endure the pain felt by protagonists and antagonists alike.

At Lambeth Conference, London/
Los Angeles Times, 1-12:(I)3.

Avraham Shayevitz
Chief Rabbi of Moscow

1

Things are much better now [for Jews in the Soviet Union] since [Soviet leader Mikhail] Gorbachev [came to power]. There is a difference. We are definitely on the way to democracy, of course not only for the Jews. Up to now we have lived in an empty religious state.

To reporters, Tel Aviv, Israel/
The Washington Post, 12-28:(A)15.

Alexander M. Schindler
President,
Union of American
Hebrew Congregations

2

[Criticizing the effort by Orthodox Jews in Israel to redefine "who is a Jew"]: Israel was to be a country where a Jew didn't need a visa. The first piece of legislation after independence was the Law of Return, that any Jew from anywhere could enter and claim citizenship. Now, 40 years later, we find a minority trying to narrow it. In a practical sense, true, how many [Jewish] converts come to Israel? But the symbolic impact is very, very great. A great many Jews feel they are being excluded in the eyes of Israel, and there is a sadness, an alienation.

The New York Times, 11-21:(A)6.

Chaim Seidler-Feller
Rabbi; Director, Hillel
Society, University of
California, Los Angeles

3

[Criticizing the effort by Orthodox Jews in Israel to redefine "who is a Jew"]: The central question the [world] Jewish community is facing is what kind of Israel are we going to have. This new legislation runs contrary to the humanistic, open and tolerant Israel that we love. This is an obvious attack on modernity, a *kulturkampf* . . . This conflict has been brewing beneath the surface. It is sewn into the very fabric of Israel. The Israel that we have come to love and respect will be so different. A deep and maybe irreparable alienation will set in.

Interview/
The New York Times,
11-21:(A)6.

Paul Simon
United States Senator,
D-Illinois;
Candidate for the
1988 Democratic
Presidential nomination

4

I'm a Lutheran by background. We do not generally use the phrase "born again," so I cannot say that I experienced any sudden, dramatic, cataclysmic change in my life that way . . . I instinctively know that there is something beyond. There is more meaning to life than what you and I now perceive. I think I have felt the presence, but not in a dramatic way like a lot of people feel they have a message from God.

Interview, Makanda, Ill./
U.S. News & World Report,
1-18:27.

John Shelby Spong
Bishop of Newark, N.J.

5

[On the opposition in the British Anglican Church to the ordination of women]: It's particularly strange here in Britain where they oppose ordination. It's anachronistic. They have Margaret Thatcher as Prime Minister, and Queen Elizabeth. And they say a woman can't be in the clergy!

Canterbury, England/
The New York Times,
7-20:5.

WHAT THEY SAID IN 1988

Barbara Thiering
Theologian, University of Sydney
(Australia)

1

To see God as male is idolatry. It is like the worship of images in man's own shape. God as male, as the father, is only a metaphor, but . . . the church has forgotten this and has taken it literally.

World Press Review, January:57.

Jack M. Tuell
Methodist Bishop of
Los Angeles

2

The time has come to say the last rights over the notion that the defining characteristic of United Methodist theology is pluralism. [Methodists] have many differing perspectives and interpretations of Christian faith, [but the word "pluralism" has] philosophical overtones which contradict our understanding of Christian faith . . . There is no evangelical appeal to join a group whose principal identifying mark is that everyone disagrees with everyone else.

At United Methodist General
Conference, St. Louis, April 26/
Los Angeles Times, 4-27:(I)3.

Jerry Vines
President, Southern Baptist
Convention

3

The issue with which Southern Baptists have been grappling is not the interpretation of the Bible, but the nature of the Bible. It is not so much what the Bible says as what the Bible is. I believe that the Bible does not merely contain the word of God, but that it *is* the word of God. And Southern Baptists have gone on record unmistakably as affirming that the Bible has truth without any mixture of error.

Interview/
USA Today, 6-16:(A)7.

Andrew Young
Mayor of Atlanta

4

Black preachers start out not intending to make sense. They create a kind of psychological connection. You end up crying. You end up feeling good. You end up thinking about your mama, and you go away fulfilled. But you're not a bit better off.

Newsweek, 2-29:13.

Science and Technology

Joseph Allen
Executive vice president,
Space Industries, Inc.;
Former American astronaut

1

In certain [space] activities, the Soviets are definitely ahead of us [the U.S.]. That leaves one with a lot of emotion. One is congratulations to a hard-working team of competitors who have, through some tough times, persevered. At the same time, there is a certain amount of chagrin in that our own program has started and stopped, started and stopped. A third is perhaps a nervousness that, to the degree of long-term experience in a permanently occupied space station, it will clearly lead to lots of knowledge. In this case, it's not American knowledge.

Interview/USA Today, 1-19:(A)13.

Lew Allen
Director, Jet Propulsion
Laboratory, National
Aeronautics and Space
Administration of the
United States

2

[On whether, due to problems with U.S. launch vehicles, the U.S. might use European launchers to loft space missions]: There could be [a possibility of that]. My own view is that technology transfer and other issues are not so great as to preclude it. If there are opportunities to do good science, and it can be done using other people's vehicles, we should not shy away from that . . . [But] one doesn't want to shift too many payloads off to somebody else's launch vehicle.

Interview, Pasadena, Calif./
The Christian Science Monitor,
1-6:3.

3

NASA should consider its mission to accomplish space science as a mission to be accomplished by the most effective means that it can, whether or not that involves a manned spacecraft. And in most cases it won't. The budgets and allocations of resources to that should stand on their own, in contrast to being a percentage of the manned flight endeavor. Similarly, the technology programs of NASA, which have over recent years been limited to the development of technologies that are most important for the manned missions, should be expanded to have a characteristic closer to the aeronautics activities of NASA.

Interview, Pasadena, Calif./
The Christian Science Monitor,
1-6:4.

Isaac Asimov
Science-fiction writer

4

[On a solution to the earth's over-population]: Colonize the moon. Build space stations. Then go on to populate Mars and the other planets. There is unlimited solar energy out there, and a plethora of minerals and acres of land. Going into the galaxy is not nearly so fantastic as it seems. We are already more informed about outer space than the early explorers ever were about the oceans they sailed on or the lands they discovered.

Interview, New York/
Time, 12-19:82.

James Beggs
Former Administrator,
National Aeronautics and
Space Administration
of the United States

5

The competitive posture of the United States is based on our progress in science and technology. What the American people are not aware of is the fact that this nation, for the last 20 years, has been cutting its investments in that progress.

WHAT THEY SAID IN 1988

(JAMES BEGGS)

And that's tragic. It's a national disgrace and it needs to be redressed.

Panel discussion/
USA Today, 9-28:(A)9.

Erich Bloch
Director, National
Science Foundation

1

[Saying the U.S. is losing the technology race to Japan]: The deadly aspect is that we are losing whole sectors of industry and therefore the competence to do something. To give an example, the whole video and television area. If you wanted to start an industry to design television sets, you wouldn't have the knowledge base in place any more. You'd have to build it from scratch . . . The problem that we have as a country is that we aren't as fast on our feet in getting something from basic research into a product in the marketplace. The Japanese are beating us at the game. The second problem is, we don't have the staying power. The VCR took 20 years to develop. Well, who stayed in it? The Japanese, not RCA. That's one of hundreds of examples.

Interview/
The Wall Street Journal,
11-14:(R)32.

William D. Carey
Science analyst,
Carnegie Corporation

2

[Saying recent increases in the U.S. Federal budget for science expenditures are not adequate to make up for past budget cuts]: The total expenditures for basic research declined from 1969 and rose to equal that same figure only in 1978 . . . This is to be compared with the decade of the '60s, in which there was more than a doubling of Federal funding of basic research expenditures. And if we go to R&D as a whole, the Federal investment had even a longer period of stagnation—16 years from 1966 to 1982—before it started upward again. And since, in both cases, the professional personnel had been growing at a rate of 5 or 6 per cent a year, the support per worker had clearly declined and the improvement in the 1980s has not yet provided a compensation. So, in addition to the inevitable squeeze in budgets which we face, the possibility of continued improvement in the basic research area— or in the R&D area—is by no means going to be adequate to recover our earlier position.

The Christian Science Monitor,
2-23:17.

Michael Collins
Former American astronaut;
Former Director, National
Air and Space Museum

3

The American people have not made up their minds about space. They're intrigued by the idea of space exploration; they're just not too keen on paying for it. The funding pendulum swings back and forth, and it makes planning a lot more difficult in this country than it does in the Soviet Union. I believe in exploration. I believe in peering through microscopes, looking out through telescopes. And beyond looking, I believe in going. To have some unknowns out there, things that you just can't figure out, places you've never been—this is what human beings are all about . . . What we're talking about fundamentally is exploration and the human spirit.

Interview/
U.S. News & World Report,
5-16:55.

4

A playwright once said, "If you can't write the plot of a play on the back of a matchbook, it's not going to be a successful play." You could apply that to the space program. If you ask what our next goal is, NASA will pull out a fact sheet four pages long. The problem is most people fall asleep before they've read the first page.

Interview/
U.S. News & World Report,
5-16:55.

James C. Fletcher
Administrator, National
Aeronautics and Space
Administration of the
United States

1

[On whether a joint U.S.-Soviet mission to Mars would be desirable]: There are a lot of things to be gained. There's the political gain, reconciling some of our differences. It might even save money, but that's questionable. But there are a lot of minuses, too. If they invade some other country and we get upset, you've wasted a lot of effort. So we're moving in that direction slowly but carefully.

Interview/
USA Today, 9-26:(A)5.

2

The bottom line is that NASA is in pretty good shape right now. I expect the nation will applaud us until we have another accident [like the shuttle *Challenger* blowing up in 1986]—and, believe me, there will be some day. But I am hoping it is much longer than 10 years from now, way out in the future.

Before National Press Club,
Washington, Oct. 18/
The Washington Post, 10-19:(A)21.

Konstantin V. Frolov
Vice president,
Soviet Academy of Sciences

3

. . . in the spirit of *perestroika* [the new Soviet policy of reform], we are decentralizing scientific administration, giving much greater autonomy to subordinate institutes and regional research facilities. We're also forcing administrators to resign at the age of 65, bringing in 5 per cent of new scientists every year, and thereby assuring Soviet science of new blood.

Before American Society for the
Advancement of Science, Boston,
Feb. 14/The New York Times,
2-15:9.

Jake Garn
United States Senator,
R-Utah

4

It's absolutely impossible to guarantee safety in space, because space is not a normal activity. You have tens of thousands dying on the highways each year, and people say "ho hum." Then, seven die in space [in the space-shuttle *Challenger* disaster in 1986], and the world stops for two years. If people think there's not going to be another accident in space, they're kidding themselves.

USA Today, 7-5:(A)2.

Sheldon Glashow
Professor of physics,
Harvard University;
Winner, 1979 Nobel Prize in
physics

5

What's obvious to me is that we're not having a crisis [in U.S. science education]; we're having a disaster. We're not teaching kids science and mathematics at all. The reason is that they're usually taught by teachers who don't know the subject. I don't see a solution. But as long as our country remains a wealthy one, we can import them; more than half the graduate students in science, math and engineering are foreigners. They're the solution.

Interview/USA Today, 5-2:(A)11.

Ralph E. Gomory
Senior vice president for
science and technology,
International Business
Machines Corporation

6

Although I don't know how many people need to understand science, my guess is that it's a minority. What we really need, in my opinion, is to educate everyone in the three R's, which we clearly don't do well enough today.

The Wall Street Journal,
9-27:30.

491

Earle Harbison, Jr.
President,
Monsanto Company

1

The benefits of biotechnology to our health, to our environment and to our economy become more clear with every new research article published, every new field test begun, every new therapeutic tool submitted for approval . . . It is not surprising, therefore, that many governments have formally recognized biotechnology and genetic engineering as important to the future of their nations. They have targeted the disciplines involved, organized for progress, and in some cases, taken a major role in directing research, development and commercialization. In this country [the U.S.], by contrast, biotechnology is still perceived primarily as a regulatory and legal problem, not an economic opportunity. A regulatory structure has been fashioned that is functioning quite well in assuring the public that the science of biotechnology is safe. Beyond the regulatory concerns, however, there is a political vacuum. Historically, I think it is fair to say that our country rarely charts a long-term strategy for emerging technologies in order to assure they are properly recognized and supported, let alone to assure that they deliver the economic benefits they offer. In other words, much effort is being expended to see that nothing goes wrong, but little effort is being expended to see that things go right.

Before Senate Agriculture,
Nutrition and Forestry Committee,
Washington/The Wall Street Journal,
1-6:16.

David C. Hilmers
American astronaut

2

[On the recent successful flight of the U.S. space shuttle *Discovery,* of which he was a crew member, the first shuttle flight since the shuttle *Challenger* blew up in 1986 killing seven astronauts]: I want you to remember what this flight meant to America. I want you to remember what America can do when it pulls together and works for a goal. I want you to remember how hard a setback we had and how we can bounce back

from adversity. I want you to remember that America should continue to have dreams.

At Discovery *post-landing ceremony,*
Edwards Air Force Base, Calif.,
Oct. 3/Los Angeles Times, 10-4:(I)1.

Noel W. Hinners
Associate Deputy
Administrator for Strategic
Planning, National Aeronautics
and Space Administration of
the United States

3

[On the current successful mission of the U.S. space shuttle *Discovery,* the first shuttle launched since the shuttle *Challenger* blew up in 1986, killing seven astronauts]: Everyone is being so damned careful with this launch. But I don't worry about this launch. I worry about 20 launches down the line. How do you keep up a sustained effort? You can't legislate human error out of the system. You just have to keep working at it.

Los Angeles Times, 10-3:(I)14.

Roald Hoffmann
Professor of physical science,
Cornell University; Winner,
1981 Nobel Prize for chemistry

4

Every citizen, whether in science or not, ought to know chemistry, physics and biology at some level. People should have the right to decide technical questions; with that right comes a responsibility to learn enough science to be able to judge the basic issues. Science is an essential part of our *culture.* To deal with the complicated, technological world of tomorrow, one needs the lessons of both science and the humanities.

Interview/
U.S. News & World Report,
3-14:58.

James Kaler
Professor of astronomy,
University of Illinois

5

[On revelations that President and Mrs. Reagan utilize astrology in some of their de-

(JAMES KALER)

cision-making]: How can you control a science budget of billions of dollars when you believe in nonsense of this magnitude. It is painful for me to think about it.

Newsweek, 5-16:20.

Shuichi Kato
Japanese philosopher

1

The major question is not how to *develop* technology but how to *use* technology. [Since] technology doesn't teach us how to *use* the technology, the principle of schooling should be shifted from an increasingly strong emphasis on scientifically technological education to something else. You might call it humanities, but I would call it poetry or arts.

At Wingspread Conference,
Racine, Wis., April/
The Christian Science Monitor,
7-25:(B)11.

Christopher Kraft
Former Director of Flight
Operations, Johnson Space
Center, Houston

2

[On the 2½-year waiting period between the *Challenger* space shuttle disaster and the next shuttle flight later this year]: If we see space flight as a necessary element in our formula for national survival, then a 2½-year hiatus is totally unacceptable. [This comment is] not to necessarily criticize what has transpired but to prepare for what is likely to happen again. More specifically, if every time there is a fatal accident in space, the result is a long and frankly unnecessary delay before continuing, then we should re-evaluate our objectives. Flying in commercial airplanes, driving on the freeway, or walking across the street have their risks, but we have all accepted the gains commensurate with these risks. Why should space flight be treated in any other way?

Before National Geographic Society,
Washington, Jan. 27/
The Washington Post, 1-28:(A)3.

Patrick J. Leahy
United States Senator,
D-Vermont

3

Small firms have been a remarkable catalyst for technological advances in this country. We cannot afford to lose their innovative contribution in biotech. It is critical for America to have a variety of small and large firms [in biotech work].

Nation's Business, February:14.

John Logsdon
Director, Space Policy Institute,
George Washington University

4

You can't justify a Mars visit on the basis of scientific benefits, or any other benefit. The balance sheet doesn't work out. Man will go to Mars for the same reason he crossed the ocean looking for new lands. He wants to go there and stay, to inhabit a new place.

Los Angeles Times, 9-6:(I)16.

Mike Lounge
American astronaut

5

[On the imminent launching of the space shuttle *Discovery*, of which he is a member of the crew]: We'll get up, put on our new spacesuits, get in the van and go to the [launching] pad. It will be a very lonely thing, the five of us in this huge steaming machine. It's you and this tremendous machine and a couple of technicians who strap you in. The real world is a voice on the radio.

The New York Times, 9-27:24.

Bill Nelson
United States Representative,
D-Florida

6

[Arguing against cutting financing for the U.S. space program in order to provide more funds for social programs]: We cannot fall victim to financial myopia and emotional appeals about priorities. We must remain competitive in outer space, because that is truly the future of this country.

Washington, June 22/
Los Angeles Times, 6-23:(I)13.

William C. Norris
Former chairman, Control
Data Corporation

1

The U.S. competitive position in high technology is eroding, and what we need are new competitive products to get us back into the leadership position. I believe that we can find many of those products in Soviet laboratories where a great deal of research is not fully utilized ... I am talking about a very large program based on Soviet technology and American entrepreneurship. There are opportunities—I can see them already—in virtually every field of high technology, from computers to communications to medical instruments. Ten years from now, we should be forming 200 of these joint high-tech companies a year.

Interview, Moscow/
Los Angeles Times, 6-16:(IV)1.

Michael Oppenheimer
Senior scientist,
Environmental Defense Fund

2

Scientists pay a price for becoming advocates. Most scientists are satisfied to pursue their research without the question of whether it's socially relevant. They don't have the time or inclination to pursue their findings. But if scientists don't explain the meaning of their work in a political context—who will?

Los Angeles Times, 7-14:(I)19.

Frank Press
President, National
Academy of Sciences

3

We scientists, who recommend the rationality and orderly process of our profession to government policy-makers, are fast losing our credibility for being balanced, fair and analytical. Our internal dissension and the mixed, conflicting and self-serving advice emanating from our community are threatening our ability to inform wise policy-making ... At a time when we should revel in dazzling progress in almost every field of science, this sniping and carping among scientists is disturbing and destructive.

At National Academy of Sciences
meeting, Washington, April 26/
The Washington Post, 4-27:(A)19.

Ronald Reagan
President of the United States

4

[On the opposition he has faced in trying to proceed with a U.S. space defense system]: If we've learned anything in five years, it's that it's sometimes easier to bring into being new technologies than it is to bring about new thinking on some subjects. Breakthroughs in physics are sometimes easier than breakthroughs in psyches.

At conference sponsored by
Institute for Foreign Policy Analysis,
Washington, March 14/
Los Angeles Times, 3-15:(I)5.

5

[Supporting the U.S. construction of a super collider particle accelerator]: I know that some people may question the practical applications of the superconducting super collider. The strange world of subatomic particles, they may think, will never be more than an arcane interest to a few highly specialized scientists. But the truth is, the practical applications of this new technology are already changing the way we live. Every time someone turns on his desk computer, makes a phone call or plays a video game, he is plugging into that mysterious world of quantum physics. The superconducting super collider is the doorway to that new world of quantum change.

To science students,
Washington, March 30/
Los Angeles Times, 3-31:(I)4.

6

Mankind's journey into space, like every great voyage of discovery, will become part of our unending journey of liberation. In the limitless reaches of space, we will find liberation from tyranny, from scarcity, from ignorance and from

(RONALD REAGAN)

war. We will find the means to protect this Earth and to nurture every human life, and to explore the universe . . . This is our mission, this is our destiny.

At Johnson Space Center,
Houston, Sept. 22/
The Washington Post, 9-23:(A)3.

Yuri Romanenko
Soviet cosmonaut

1

[On his recent 326 days in space]: We don't feel loneliness, even though we are separated by large distances from our country and our family. We are tied to earth with invisible strings.

To reporters, Moscow, Jan. 20/
Los Angeles Times, 1-21:(I)6.

Robert Rosenzweig
President, Association of
American Universities

2

Our problem is not that we have too much science and too little technology—or the reverse of that—but that we have developed a marvelous system for mobilizing bureaucratic and Congressional support for generating funds for research programs that are dispersed throughout a large number of agencies, with no compensating capacity for imposing intellectual order on it. That has been, at most, a minor problem until now; it is becoming a major one. At the risk of over-simplifying a complicated problem, I would suggest the best approach is through the Presidency . . . [A] strong advisory apparatus, closely connected to the points of influence in the White House and deeply involved in budgetary decisions, is the best and perhaps the only way to bring the disparate and competing elements of the scientific community to the table . . . to make choices under conditions of scarcity.

Before Consortium of Social Science
Associations, Dec. 13/
The Washington Post,
12-20:(A)24.

Roald Z. Sagdeyev
Director, Soviet Institute of
Space Research

3

[Saying there is too much bureaucracy in the Soviet space program and not enough scientific expertise]: Unfortunately, one must admit that for the most part, in the [Soviet] Academy of Sciences, space research is now conducted at the level of figureheads. Thus we are now losing our leading position in space, to a significant degree, and not only in the Academy of Sciences.

Speech,
Moscow, October/
The New York Times,
11-5:3.

4

[Saying the Soviet space-shuttle program is a mistake]: It went up; it came down. But it had absolutely no scientific value. My personal view is that American experience with the shuttle indicates that, from the point of view of cost efficiency, the shuttle is in deep trouble. It is much simpler and cheaper to fly a payload with any kind of *expendable* vehicle.

Interview/
The New York Times,
11-22:(B)7.

Patricia Schroeder
United States Representative,
D-Colorado

5

We must reverse our current research-and-development priorities. In 1980, the Federal government's basic research budget was split 50-50 between military and civilian applications. This year, it's split 80-20 in favor of the military. We were the leaders in science and medical and energy research. We cancelled all of that, and threw our money into space on SDI. To compete in the world and retain our middle class, we must retain research and education. That is what creates jobs. And recycling water is a better job than burger-flipping.

"Ms.," February:52.

Morris Shamos
Professor emeritus of physics,
New York University

1

Well over 95 per cent of [U.S.] society is totally ignorant of science and shows no signs of being any worse off. You don't have to know anything about quarks or the second law of thermodynamics to be a successful banker, lawyer or Wall Street broker.

U.S. News & World Report,
11-14:61.

Vladimir Shatalov
Commander, Soviet
cosmonaut training center

2

[On Soviet cosmonaut Yuri Romanenko's recent 326-day stay in space]: For one year, a person can work in outer space. This doesn't lead to serious changes, biologically or physiologically. Maybe we can extend the duration gradually. Sooner or later, man will fly to Mars, and Yuri Romanenko's example gives us hope that, after getting there, people will be able to walk on the surface of Mars unassisted, and conduct studies there.

To reporters, Moscow, Jan.20/
Los Angeles Times, 1-21:(I)6.

Marcia Smith
Space analyst,
Congressional Research
Service of the United States

3

. . . the American taxpayers want everything, and they aren't willing to pay the taxes to bear the cost. If you give NASA all the money it needs, where are you going to get it from? The major difference between the Soviet and American [space] programs is their [Soviets'] commitment, which they have had since they launched the very first satellite.

Panel discussion/
USA Today, 9-28:(A)9.

David Webb
Chairman of space studies,
University of North Dakota;
Member, National
Commission on Space
of the United States

4

[Saying NASA is facing a technological "brain drain"]: The agency has lost its expertise and technological edge in very vital areas that are going to be required for future [space] exploration. The President may make policy, but the agency is totally unprepared to fulfill it.

USA Today, 9-27:(A)5.

Albert Wohlstetter
Co-Chairman, Federal
Commission on Integrated
Long-Term Strategy

5

It's silly to think [this] Commission is calling for the militarization of space. Space has been militarized from the start. The first man-made system [*Sputnik*] was launched on a Soviet ICBM, and both sides have put satellites with military purposes in orbit ever since. And the Commission does not want to start a space race. We are just recognizing the reality that space systems, as with other military systems, must be able to function in wartime to deter attack.

Interview, Washington, Jan. 21/
Los Angeles Times, 1-23:(I)18.

Shoshana Zuboff
Assistant professor of
business administration,
Harvard Business School

6

Quite simply, information technology is altering both the nature and experience of work. It used to be that work was very much a bodily experience. People, especially in certain segments of manufacturing, knew how well they were doing their jobs based on touch, sight, even smell. A worker on a paper machine in a pulp mill, for example, could judge the moisture content of a roll by slapping it and literally getting the

(SHOSHANA ZUBOFF)

feel in his fingers. But with the advent of computer technology, abstract cues are coming to predominate over physical ones. Many of the tasks of both blue-collar workers and managers are now done through the medium of symbolic electronic information. Workers and managers have to be able to understand that information and manipulate and use it in creative and innovative ways. That requires analytical, problem-solving and conceptual skills that are very different from the more physical forms of knowledge.

Interview/
U.S. News & World Report,
5-30:52.

497

Sports

Muhammad Ali
Former heavyweight boxing
champion of the world

1

[On boxing fans]: People love to be amused, love to try to understand that which they can't understand. They love to be mystified. Who's going to win the fight? What round? They're all there; they're all excited. Waiting. First they talked about me and [Sonny] Liston, and then me and [Joe] Frazier. Now [Michael] Spinks and [Mike] Tyson. And when [their championship fight is] over, then it's something else they want, something else that'll amuse them, and mystify them.

Interview,
Atlantic City, N.J., June 27/
The New York Times, 6-28:53.

Sparky Anderson
Baseball manager,
Detroit "Tigers"

2

I love to go to the [ball] park. I always feel safe there; it's my comfort zone. I know everyone that works in the stadium, in the front office, down on the field; I know all the people. Coming to the ballpark, that's my relaxation. I get out of the house as fast as I can; I don't like to hear the phones ringing . . . It's a tremendous life. I feel bad for players because, when they're done, it's got to be a lonesome feeling. I couldn't do it [live away from the game]. I know when they're done, they're going to wish they were back. It never fails. I know guys who make big, big money [outside] of baseball—they'd drop everything to come back. It's almost like a disease. No way in the world I would be happy without it. Money will let you acquire a house and car and clothes but, as you acquire them, they don't mean nothing to you. It's the war, the battle, *that's* what gets you.

Interview/
Los Angeles Times, 7-19:(III)3.

3

It helps if you [as a manager] can motivate, and it helps if you know when to change pitchers. But if the [player] talent isn't there, it doesn't make any difference what a manager does.

Interview/
The Christian Science Monitor,
8-1:16.

Mario Andretti
Auto-racing driver

4

I can't talk for other people, but I still enjoy getting into the race car and competing. And I think perhaps experience works for you. If a person is physically fit and keeps a certain edge, there's no reason he can't keep on driving. After all, we're not all total wrecks in our late 40s. The guys who do retire earlier usually just get their belly full of it and get out. It's really an individual situation.

Interview/
Los Angeles Times, 5-15:(III)16.

Don Baylor
Baseball player,
Oakland "Athletics"

5

[Saying more blacks should be hired for high-level positions in baseball]: I look around and I see one hiring here, one there, another one there. But these aren't on the field. There are no black managers, still no third-base coaches. There are a few hitting coaches, a few office jobs and some scouts, but everything else remains the same. They say that minorities aren't qualified, but they're not taking a person who is qualified and training him to do the job. Those numbers are just numbers. They satisfy the argument that things are being done.

The New York Times,
4-6:46.

(DON BAYLOR)

1

A baseball season is not a sprint, it's a marathon. Baseball is all about staying power and endurance.

Los Angeles Times, 5-12:(III)8.

Elgin Baylor
Vice president and general manager, Los Angeles "Clippers" basketball team; Former player

2

What people don't seem to realize is that you play basketball with your head as well as your body. Even though instincts are important when a certain play has to be made or the clock is running out, if the fundamentals aren't already there, you're probably not going to be successful. There is a right way and a wrong way to do things in basketball and, without having learned the basics, no player is able to fit completely into a team concept. Most rookies I see today rely too much on their natural ability and not enough on making the game's fundamentals work for them. I'm not arguing the fact that today's player is stronger, can run faster, jump higher and probably shoot better than the majority of men I played with and against. But most rookies don't know how to run a fast break or finish off a play, and not too many of them have a very good overall knowledge of the game. Often they don't even take good percentage shots, and there's no excuse for that.

Interview, Los Angeles/
The Christian Science Monitor,
11-28:18.

William J. Bennett
Secretary of Education of the United States

3

[On the recent Washington *Redskins* victory over the Denver *Broncos* in the Super Bowl]: Not only am I a *Broncos* fan, I'm a dumb *Broncos* fan. After the first quarter [when Denver held a short-lived lead], I called all my friends who were

Redskins fans and said, "How do you like it?" As a historian, I should know that after a first quarter comes a second quarter.

At Washington Quarterback's
Club awards gala, Feb. 27/
USA Today, 2-29:(C)2.

Yogi Berra
Baseball coach, Houston "Astros"; Former player

4

What you always need [in baseball nowadays] is a lot of pitching, and today you've also got to have three good arms in the bullpen. In the old days, starting pitchers used to go eight or nine innings at a time. If a manager wanted to take his starter out, he had to fight him for the ball. Now you look at the mound when trouble starts, and except for a few guys, they all want to come out in the sixth inning.

Interview/
The Christian Science Monitor,
8-8:16.

Raymond Berry
Football coach, New England "Patriots"

5

[Saying he recently saw the Boston Pops Orchestra]: Their execution was flawless. I appreciated all the work that went into it and said how nice it must be to be in a business where people don't try to screw things up by hitting you over the head . . . Football is a massive effort to make the other guy screw up.

USA Today, 9-22:(C)3.

Matt Biondi
American gold-medal Olympic swimmer

6

[On being a champion swimmer]: The burden of public expectation is tremendous. It's like a ladder. When you start out, you're at the bottom and work up. There's satisfaction every time you

(MATT BIONDI)

climb one more rung. You see your accomplishments. The people keep getting smaller and smaller at the bottom. But when you reach the top, there's nowhere to go, only down. You feel stagnant. You look down and you have to fight people off. You lose a race and people sound as if you let them down. How could you do this to them?

Interview, Orlando, Fla./
The New York Times, 3-25:44.

Larry Bird
Basketball player,
Boston "Celtics"

1

I'd love to play in the Olympics and win a gold medal. But after the success I've had, I wouldn't want to take away the biggest moment an 18-year-old or 20-year-old kid might ever have.

The Christian Science Monitor,
5-12:18.

Jim Boeheim
Basketball coach,
Syracuse University

2

[On player brawls in college basketball]: If it's a physical game, you have to be physical. If someone's pushing you, you've got to push back. But if it gets to the point where it gets past that, we tell our players that we don't want to be involved in a fight. But they don't always walk away. I don't think, in the heat of an intense game, that players can walk away.

The New York Times, 2-23:50.

Pat Bowlen
Owner, Denver "Broncos"
football team

3

It's an extremely significant thing to win the Super Bowl. I don't think it's a boasting kind of thing, just the knowledge that you were part of a team that was good enough to be the best. That

travels with you, and I think it has a lot of significance on the future of your life.

Interview, San Diego/
The Washington Post, 1-29:(D)6.

Bobby Breathard
General manager, Washington
"Redskins" football team

4

After college, everybody [who wants to be a professional athlete] should have to serve two years, either in the military or getting a real job. Then they'd really see what real life is like. I've never seen so many unhappy guys in their jobs as professional athletes. All they're concerned about is what the next guy's making [in salary].

USA Today, 9-28:(C)3.

Tom Brookens
Baseball player,
Detroit "Tigers"

5

This is not a spectacular team. We're kind of blue-collar. We have some good days and we have some bad days. We punch the clock on the way in and we punch it again on the way out.

Interview,
Detroit, June 20/
Los Angeles Times, 6-21:(III)3.

Jim Brown
Former football player,
Cleveland "Browns"

6

[Saying black athletes share in the blame for sports' racial problems]: The black athlete is as much responsible as anyone. The black athlete has no social concern. His only concern is economics. He is playing the game with the major corporations by being the good guy and not speaking out. He is the high-paid guy who doesn't mind being used that way. He doesn't care or know that the guy suffered before him.

USA Today, 1-19:(C)2.

James H. Burnley
Secretary of Transportation
of the United States

1

Athletes, like the millions of ordinary Americans who look up to them, should be made to suffer real-life consequences for drug use. The policy for athletes should be straightforward: If you are using drugs and come forward to enter rehabilitation, fine; the leagues will be there to help. But if you use drugs and get caught, you're out permanently.

Before International Narcotics
Enforcement Officers Association,
New Orleans/
Los Angeles Times,
9-7:(III)2.

Jerry Burns
Football coach,
Minnesota "Vikings"

2

[Saying that having to release players is an unpleasant task]: Nobody likes to be the guy that kicks Santa Claus out of the house.

USA Today,
8-19:(C)13.

Brett Butler
Baseball player,
San Francisco "Giants"

3

As a kid, I had to be flamboyant because I wanted to be noticed. I was always the last one to be picked when they chose up sides. Then we'd play and I'd be the first one picked the next time. Now I have to be the spark of the club, the table setter. If I can get on, steal and score in the first inning, it gives our pitcher a tremendous lift. If arrogance plays a part in it, then I guess I'm arrogant, though I prefer to call it desire. There are guys with more talent, but no one has more desire.

Interview,
Scottsdale, Ariz./
Los Angeles Times, 3-27:(III)5.

Connie Carpenter-Phinney
Member, United States
Olympic Committee Advisory
Committee on Substance
Abuse, Research and Education

4

[On track star Ben Johnson's losing his gold medal in the current Olympic Games, because of his testing positive for steroid use]: The one really good thing that's coming out of the Olympics regarding the positive test is that it will serve as a deterrent in the future. Drug use is a problem in sports. Hopefully, this will provoke a public outcry against drug use in sports. Maybe there's a certain apathy on the part of the public, coaches and athletes that becomes a quiet acceptance of drug use. It can't be that way.

USA Today,
9-27:(E)2.

Pete Carril
Basketball coach,
Princeton University

5

Some guys, they take a look at an automobile and their eyes light up like you can't believe. They slam the doors, they check this, they do everything. When they go to wash that car, it's unbelievable what they do. Some guys take a look at a girl—all the way down the street. Unbelievable. I take a look at a basketball player that's got some innocence in his face, where, with his eyes, he's telling you that he wants to be good—that turns me on. I haven't seen enough of that lately. But when I see it, I know it. And I get excited.

Interview/
Esquire, January:103.

Pat Cash
Tennis player

6

[On his losing the Australian Open after winning Wimbledon in 1987]: I'm not greatly disappointed, although I obviously wanted to win. You cannot play the best tennis of your life every day. There are only a few points between the top

(PAT CASH)

players in the world, and one day it will go one way, another day the other.

Interview,
Melbourne, Australia, Jan. 24/
The New York Times, 1-25:39.

Stanley Cheren
Sports psychiatrist

1

[On New York *Yankees* manager Billy Martin twice recently kicking dirt on umpires during baseball games]: Kicking dirt and throwing dirt are obvious simple displacements from kicking the person and hitting the person. Dirt adds another quality, filth, ultimately meaning contempt. It's an expression of contempt. As you get older, when you feel that something is being unfairly imposed by authority, you fight back more readily than you would as a younger person. In this situation, it really is an extension of a long-standing conflict with authority. This guy [Martin] is legendary for his conflict with bosses, and I'm equating umpires with bosses.

Interview/
The New York Times, 6-2:49.

Anwar Chowdhry
President, International
Boxing Association

2

Our main purpose is to bring boxing back to what it should be: the noble art of self-defense. We want to have a clean, scientific sport, based on good footwork and scoring punches. We want to eliminate blood from the ring completely.

Interview, Vienna, Dec. 6/
The New York Times, 12-7:(B)11.

Jack Clark
Baseball player,
New York "Yankees"

3

I'm looking to drive runs in, and I've learned you don't need to hit homers to do that. I'm a line-

drive hitter, not a home-run hitter. I'm trying for line drives. A home run for me is a ball I miss a little.

Interview, Fort Lauderdale, Fla./
The Washington Post, 3-5:(D)3.

Willie Clark
Jockey

4

I raced at the big tracks when I was younger— Mountain Park and Atlantic City, all over Florida, Sportsman's Park in Chicago. That Sportsman's Park used to be something. There'd be about 75 people in the stands, and $3-million [would] be bet. Bookies [would] bring in money in suitcases. But I never did like the big tracks. Too much competition for rides, and too much bull. Give me a nice, quiet little pond . . . anytime. Better for the digestion.

Interview, Charles Town, W.V./
The Wall Street Journal, 3-25:17.

Roger Craig
Baseball manager,
San Francisco "Giants"

5

Will there ever be [a female major-league baseball umpire]? I don't know. But *should* there be a woman umpire in the majors? My answer is no, and I'll tell you why. The abuse you have to take as an umpire is terrible, and I just don't think women should have to take that kind of abuse.

Interview/
Los Angeles Times, 8-27:(III)7.

Ron Darling
Baseball pitcher,
New York "Mets"

6

[On the fact that he went to Yale]: I heard someone say, "How can a guy that intelligent play baseball?" I say, "How can a guy that intelligent *not* want to play baseball?"

Los Angeles Times, 3-29:(III)2.

Anita DeFrantz
*United States representative
to the International Olympic
Committee*

1

Sports is about risk-taking. People who compete in sports know this. A person can train for years in the hope of winning an Olympic medal, and not make it. They can lose because of an injury or because they had a subpar day or because one of their rivals exceeded his or her best times ever. But those with talent and a dream are going to take that chance anyway, regardless of the physical risks or the financial costs.

*Interview, Los Angeles/
The Christian Science Monitor,
8-16:16.*

Chris Evert
Tennis player

2

To me, Wimbledon stands for prestige, quality and tradition. It's the most famous [tennis] tournament in the world, and the Centre Court is the most famous court in the world. When I think of Wimbledon, I think of the All England Club, the grass courts, royalty and the ivy on the walls. The whole thing is so dignified. You always want to be at your best when you play Wimbledon, because it's the best tournament in the world.

Newsweek, 6-27:48.

Manfred Ewald
*President, East German
Olympic Committee*

3

We're in full accord with [the Canadian Sports Minister] as far as doping, unfairness, brutality and cheating [in the Olympics] is concerned. In other words, we're against all of that. But by fighting against that, you're fighting only against the blooming flower. The fight has to be carried out against the roots of the evil, such as professional sports and misuse of commercialism. When the money enters the picture at that level, athletes start cheating and poisoning themselves. I'm not accusing all athletes of that, but some of

them. We should also fight against their bad advisers, agents and coaches who think only of themselves and the money they can make off the athletes.

Los Angeles Times, 2-19:(III)7.

4

There's no secret to the success of GDR [Olympic] athletes. It's the result of years of planning and working toward it. What we do is give young people a chance to develop in certain sports, and we support their ambition. But don't call it a farm for athletic talent. We give young people the same opportunity in economics, science, singing, dancing or ballet. We find the talent and then help them further their careers. This doesn't work in all countries. It depends on the economic, social, traditional and political structure of each country.

Los Angeles Times, 2-19:(III)7.

Donald Fehr
*Executive director, Major League
(baseball) Players Association*

5

There are numerous metropolitan areas currently without big-league baseball . . . which appear fully capable of supporting such teams. In the players' view, if a city can support a major-league quality team, it should have one. Baseball's owners, whose actions speak far louder than their words, do not share this goal. On the contrary, relying on their immunity from the antitrust laws, baseball's owners artificially restrict the number of franchises and deliberately leave potential markets vacant, forcing cities to compete with one another for the very rare, and therefore very expensive, opportunity to have a big-league club. The owners' monopoly control over the number and location of franchises pits potential expansion cities against one another and against cities currently having clubs, disadvantaging cities and fans but benefiting baseball's owners, who thus profit handsomely from their monopoly.

*Before District of Columbia
Committee on Baseball,
Washington, May 18/
The Washington Post, 5-19:(B)3.*

503

George Foreman
*Former heavyweight boxing
champion of the world*

1

You don't need killer instinct to be a fighter. If I can't whip a man cleanly and competitively, I don't want to fight . . . Before, I had to work up dislike against the men I fought. Now I can appreciate the plain athletic side, and look on my opponents as brothers.

*Interview,
Las Vegas, Nev./
The Wall Street Journal,
3-21:20.*

Jeff Francis
*Football player,
University of Tennessee*

2

I've learned that you have Saturday night and Sunday friends, and then you have real friends. After a win, everybody wants to hang around with you on Saturday night and Sunday, so they can feel like they're a part of it. When you lose, you find out who your friends really are.

USA Today, 9-22:(C)15.

Joe Garagiola
*Baseball announcer,
NBC-TV; Former player*

3

I have seen [baseball] umpires on the field today who bait managers, follow them back to the dugout and purposely prolong arguments. Basically, I'm all for umpires. They have a tough job and most of the time they handle it well. Players and managers should be fined or suspended when they curse an umpire, bump him physically or put their hands on him. But umpires aren't supposed to dominate the game either. Their job is to control it in as dignified a way as they can. Not all of them now seem to recognize this.

*The Christian Science Monitor,
6-15:18.*

A. Bartlett Giamatti
*President, National
(baseball) League*

4

[On the recent incident involving Cincinnati manager Pete Rose's alleged shoving of an umpire]: The extremely ugly situation that developed in Cincinnati in the ninth inning on Saturday, April 30th, was one of the worst in baseball's recent memory. Such disgraceful episodes are not business as usual, nor can they be allowed to become so. For forcefully and deliberately shoving an umpire, the manager of the *Reds,* Mr. Pete Rose, is suspended for 30 days and fined a substantial amount. Inciting the unacceptable behavior of some of the fans were the inflammatory and completely irresponsible remarks of local radio broadcasters . . . The National League will not tolerate the degeneration of baseball games into dangerous displays of public disorder, nor will it countenance any potentially injurious harassment, of any kind, of the umpires. A tiny minority of fans, or others, cannot be allowed to disgrace the vast majority of decent individuals who truly care for the game.

New York, May 2/
Los Angeles Times, 5-3:(III)5.*

A. Bartlett Giamatti
*President, National (baseball)
League; Commissioner-
designate of Baseball*

5

What always intrigued me about baseball is the relationship of the individual to the group. It's very much an individual sport that you play as a team member, but it isn't a team sport the way football is, where 11 men move on a pre-arranged signal. Baseball has a random, serendipitous nature.

*Interview, New York/
The New York Times, 12-28:(B)3.*

Mike Gottfried
*Football coach,
University of Pittsburgh*

6

[On football agents who try to sign up college players for the pro teams]: There are no rules

(MIKE GOTTFRIED)

governing agents. The only qualification for an agent is a pulse.

USA Today, 8-29:(A)8.

Bud Greenspan
Sports-film producer

1

[On TV coverage of the current Olympic Winter Games in Calgary]: Network TV coverage is a product of the electronic revolution, and there are no writers. There are no creative persons in the field. They're tracking stories from the [production] truck. It sounds egomaniacal, but they're not in my league. I think that I'm the best. They're not equipped to tell stories. They spend so much money inventing some gadgetry, I guess it would be sacrilegious not to use it. But they get lost in the technology . . . The unfortunate part is the networks' belief that the attention span of people is such that they have to go, "Here, here, here," just like that.

Interview, Calgary, Canada/
Los Angeles Times, 2-28:(III)4.

Wayne Gretzky
Hockey player,
Edmonton "Oilers"

2

The only thing talented teams or talented people don't get enough credit for is their work ethic. A lot of times people say they should win because they have the most talent. Ability and talent are fine, but if you don't work hard in the playoffs, you're not going to accomplish anything.

Boston, May 23/
The Washington Post, 5-24:(D)2.

Calvin Griffith
Former owner,
Minnesota "Twins"
baseball club

3

Certainly the ballplayers are over-paid. They say they only have a short [career], but the way I look at it, the ballplayer's work is what he has brought through the gate. To be a star, a ballplayer has to be a personality and produce on the field, so people will enjoy coming out to see him. There are not too many ballplayers of that stature. A fellow like Babe Ruth or Sandy Koufax, Bob Gibson, Ted Williams, Stan Musial, Pete Rose—they are entitled to a lot of money . . . [But] Jim Rice, with the Boston *Red Sox*—he's way, way down in hitting and everything else, and he's getting over $2-million a year.

Interview/
Los Angeles Times, 5-22:(IV)7.

Thomas R. Heitz
Historian, National Baseball
Hall of Fame and Museum,
Cooperstown, N.Y.

4

[On the spreading world-wide interest in baseball]: A few years ago when the first calls came in for information about the game, I was mildly amused that baseball was expanding its horizons internationally. But what was a curiosity a couple of years ago has turned into a flood of requests for information about baseball from dozens of teams, amateur associations and national sports groups . . . When I first came here, I fully expected to field requests for information about baseball play and baseball history from predictable places such as Latin America. But Switzerland? Switzerland!

Interview, Cooperstown, N.Y./
The New York Times, 8-1:35.

Robert Helmick
President, United States
Olympic Committee

5

It is simply no longer possible for a world-class athlete to compete successfully and at the same time earn a living in a full-time job. Our goal is to provide our top-level athletes with sufficient support for living and training expenses so that they may spend the time necessary to train and compete internationally.

Colorado Springs, Colo., July 21/
The Washington Post, 7-22:(F)1.

WHAT THEY SAID IN 1988

Frank Jobe
Team physician,
Los Angeles "Dodgers"
baseball club

1

[On the importance of physical fitness in the development of top athletes]: The age group where you begin to see the change is after they pass their teens. A world-class athlete can beat anybody in his city, his state, his region. Then he gets into national and international competition, and sees there are people as good as he is. In their 20s they begin to realize that you have to be more than good, you have to be in peak condition, at the top of your game, to win.

USA Today, 9-8:(C)2.

Ben Johnson
Canadian track-and-field
athlete

2

[On his being stripped of his gold medal in the 1988 Olympics due to tests showing he had steroids in his system]: I won a gold medal and then had to give it back because they said I tested positive. When I was a kid, I never took drugs. People who knew me in Jamaica and people who know me here know I wouldn't take drugs. I have never ever knowingly taken illegal drugs, and I would never embarrass my family, my friends, my country and the kids who love me.

News conference, Toronto, Oct. 4/
The Washington Post, 10-5:(B)4.

Jim Kaat
Former baseball pitcher

3

Pitching is not as much a game of strength as it is a skill. Pitching is not so much a science as it is an art. Mike Cuellar, Tommy John—their art is to destroy a hitter's timing. Sure, you're always going to have your Nolan Ryans and Roger Clemenses, but they're like the guys who cork their bats or scuff the balls—a very small percentage.

Los Angeles Times, 5-15:(III)5.

Dick Kazmaier
Former football player and
Heisman Trophy winner,
Princeton University

4

Being a [college] football player is very hard work. It's physically hard, as well as being quite demanding, both mentally and emotionally. If you're playing football and being a student, then you're really giving of yourself. And when you give of yourself, you're the beneficiary of all the hard work. Anyone who learns that process will have the sustenance to carry him forward in his life beyond the field.

The Christian Science Monitor,
11-22:20.

Billie Jean King
Tennis player

5

One thing I detest from the media is how they try to get you over the hill as quickly as they can, asking you when you're going to retire. The first time they asked me when I was going to retire I was 23. I finally had won Wimbledon a couple of times, and I'm looking at them like, jeez! I had started playing full-time tennis at 21 and had finally accomplished a couple of things I wanted. Chris [Evert] and Martina [Navratilova] have to deal with that all the time. I feel like saying, "Why don't you leave these guys alone? They'll tell *you* when they're ready to retire. Believe me, they'll tell you."

Interview/"Ms.," February:58.

Bob Knepper
Baseball pitcher,
Houston "Astros"

6

[On women as major-league umpires, such as the one who umpired at a recent pre-season game he pitched in]: As far as her ability for umpiring, she seems fine, but I don't think a woman should be an umpire. There are some things that men shouldn't do and some things that a woman shouldn't do. I think umpiring is one of them . . . I have a belief that God has intended man and

506

(BOB KNEPPER)

woman to be different. It's a physical thing. I don't think women were created by God to be a physical, hard person. I think God created women to be feminine.

March 14/
Los Angeles Times, 3-16:(III)1,7.

Tom Lasorda
Baseball manager,
Los Angeles "Dodgers"

1

[On the 30-day suspension given Cincinnati manager Pete Rose for pushing an umpire during an argument on the field]: It's pretty steep. But managers and ballplayers must realize that umpires are like sacred cows in India—you can't touch them.

Los Angeles Times, 5-4:(III)5.

2

[On managing]: When you don't have a lot of [player] power, you can't sit back and wait. You have to manage more and create the opportunities. I've said it before: A manager is only as good as the players he has. But the responsibility of the manager is to get the most out of his players.

Los Angeles Times, 10-3:(III)20.

Frank Layden
Basketball coach,
Utah "Jazz"

3

[On his days as Niagara University coach]: When I took over, my predecessor told me he had left three envelopes in the top right desk, and if things got tough I should open them, one at a time. The first year we went 2-25, and I opened the first envelope. It said, "Blame me." So I told everyone the previous coach had let the program deteriorate. The next year wasn't much better, so I opened the second envelope. It said, "Blame the alumni." So I told everyone the alumni weren't helping enough. The third year, it didn't go much better, so I opened the third envelope. It said, "Prepare three envelopes."

Los Angeles Times, 5-10:(III)2.

Sugar Ray Leonard
World Boxing Council
middleweight champion

4

When a fighter looks into his corner for instructions, he should give up. That's not going to work. What are they going to tell him? To keep running? Keep your hands up? A fighter should know what to do.

Interview, Scotrun, Pa./
The Washington Post, 10-26:(C)10.

Taras (Terry) Liskevych
Women's volleyball coach,
University of the Pacific;
Coach, 1988 U.S. women's
Olympic volleyball team

5

Coaches tend to lump a team together as a whole. They give group commands, like concentrate, get tough—and expect each athlete to respond to those words the same way. It'll never happen. To reach a player, you've got to know her as an individual—her strengths, weaknesses, response under pressure and her ability to meet the challenge.

Time, 9-19:26.

James Loehr
Sports psychologist

6

Of all the sports I've worked with, tennis is by far the toughest, mentally. In pro tennis, you're all alone out there. There are no substitutions. There is no clock. There is no coach with you. Sometimes you have to concentrate intensely for more than three hours. You've got an opponent staring at you. Plus the amount of money at stake is enormous. I've had some players tell me the pressure got so bad they couldn't even lift their arms.

The Wall Street Journal, 2-26:(D)20.

Fred Lynn
Baseball player,
Baltimore "Orioles"

7

[On his team's so far losing the first 15 games of the season]: I feel as much pressure as I've ever

(FRED LYNN)

felt. I feel the kind of pressure I felt on clubs in pennant races. You say, "You're in last place, how can there be pressure?" There's tremendous pressure. It's not a monkey on our backs anymore. It's Godzilla.

Milwaukee, April 21/
The Washington Post, 4-22:(D)1.

John Madden
Sports commentator; Former
football coach, Oakland "Raiders"

1

[On player specialization in pro football]: Today there is an offensive package for every down, whether it's short yardage, long yardage, or simply trying to have your kicking team put three points on the scoreboard. Then the defense counters with its blitzes, double coverage and extra linebacker, and it becomes difficult to keep track of all the changes. To me, the weakness of specialization is that too many of a team's best athletes play fewer minutes. Also, specialists tend to lose skills in other areas.

The Christian Science Monitor, 10-26:18.

Carol Mann
President, Women's
Sports Foundation

2

Beyond college, we have had a diminishment in the number of women holding coaching and sports-administration positions in the past 10 years by over 50 per cent. As women's sports have increased in their importance and visibility, more men are being selected for those leadership positions. In the pros, the two major sports are still golf and tennis for women.

Interview/USA Today, 2-4:(A)9.

Mark Marquess
Baseball coach,
Stanford University;
Coach, 1988 U.S. Olympic
baseball team

3

[On the difference between coaching in college and in the professional leagues]: [As a college coach,] you spend so much more time with your players, as people, that it's almost like being a parent. A pro coach has to deal with his players' individual problems only if they relate to the business of playing baseball, on an adult and business basis. But with college players, you're closer to other facets of their lives, schoolwork and growing up. Even the ones who think they're only looking ahead to playing baseball after college, really have more than just baseball on their minds. And most look forward to some other kind of life. Then you come across them years later, or they come back for a visit, and you see what they've become. That's the real reward, not just success on the field. That's the satisfaction all teachers get, and that's why I love doing what I'm doing.

Interview/
The New York Times, 7-21:46.

Billy Martin
Baseball manager,
New York "Yankees"

4

[On his relationship with *Yankee* owner George Steinbrenner, with whom he has had frictions in the past which resulted in his being fired four times]: Everybody's wondering when Billy is going to explode, when he's going to do something. I hope you have a long wait. But something will happen [during the coming season when he starts his fifth time as manager], you can guarantee that. It's inevitable. We're going to disagree. But we're friends. We'll stay friends. And we're not going to let the press come in between us this time. It won't last long if we disagree. We have agreed we are friends and won't let the media get in between us. I've got to try not to get mad and yell back. He has my heart, and I have his bank.

Interview/
Los Angeles Times, 1-6:(III)2.

5

When you talk about a manager like myself, you're talking about someone with the ability to change the outcome in anywhere from 20 to 50

(BILLY MARTIN)

games a season. A lot of managers rely too much on their coaches. Let them, because those are the guys I'm always going to have an edge against. The thing is, I do everything myself. I'm the guy who decides when to bring the infield in, where to position the outfielders, whether to steal or bunt or go for the big inning. Somebody out there on the field is getting a signal from me before every pitch. But the big thing is that I never stop teaching.

Interview/
The Christian Science Monitor,
6-9:18.

Willie Mays
Former baseball player,
San Francisco "Giants"

1

I played [baseball] for two reasons: for fun, and for the fans. I entertained them. That's why I get jobs now. The people I entertained want to see me. They say, "Willie, will you sign this for my little boy?" Those things make me feel good.

Interview, Atlantic City, N.J./
USA Today, 5-6:(A)2.

Tim McCarver
Former baseball catcher,
St. Louis "Cardinals" and
Philadelphia "Phillies"

2

[On umpires]: Umpires are arbiters. I was friends with some. I liked some more than others. A catcher's got to be the conduit between the pitcher and the umpire. I tried to do that. I don't make light of their profession.

USA Today, 4-7:(A)7.

John McEnroe
Tennis player

3

[On his reputation for being a temperamental player]: It is time to be an adult. Blowing up on court just doesn't give the same thrill as when I

was a kid. As a father it just doesn't appeal to me anymore.

Tokyo/USA Today, 4-14:(C)8.

Mark Messier
Hockey player,
Edmonton "Oilers"

4

As a team and as a player, you've got to prove yourself over and over again. I find it a challenge to go out there and try to finish in first place every year and to try to win every playoff series and to try to win Stanley Cups. We're all out there going after the same thing. Hockey is a physical game and it's an intense game. And if you're not as sharp and intense as you can be, you're going to get beat. It's as simple as that.

Los Angeles Times, 5-22:(III)5.

Ron Meyer
Football coach,
Indianapolis "Colts"

5

I want my teams to be unpredictable, but I want to be able to get that one yard whenever we need it. I want my offense to be exciting and thrilling, and thrilling comes with winning.

Interview/USA Today, 1-8:(E)10.

Rick Monday
Former baseball player,
Los Angeles "Dodgers"

6

No good hitter ever wants to admit to himself that he can't go up to the plate and rip a pitcher any more. In fact, anything less than complete confidence in your ability to hit the ball can lead to disaster. What happens late in your career is this: Home plate stays the same but the effectiveness of your personal strike zone begins to shrink. Suddenly pitches you used to hit with ease, you can't handle any more. You're not exactly through, because if a pitcher makes a mistake, you might still hit that mistake occasionally for a home run; but you definitely know you've lost something.

Interview/
The Christian Science Monitor,
6-29:16.

Edwin Moses
Former Olympic gold
medalist in hurdling;
Member, athletes' commission,
International Olympic Committee

1

The main belief is that the Olympics should be a forum for the best athletes in the world . . . Amateurism, as we knew it five of six years ago, does not exist today. There are pros in the Olympic Games.

The Washington Post, 2-26:(G)5.

Dale Murphy
Baseball player,
Atlanta "Braves"

2

Winning is important, but giving your best and realizing that sometimes you are not going to win is even more important.

Newsweek, 10-31:65.

Martina Navratilova
Tennis player

3

Comparing Steffi [Graf] with me at 18 is like comparing apples and oranges. She is a better player than I was at 18, but I was a better player at 18 than Billie Jean King was at 18, and Billie Jean was a better player than Althea Gibson. Every generation is better than the last one, and that's what's keeping me in the game and keeping me excited.

The Christian Science Monitor,
5-3:18.

4

[On the Wimbledon tennis tournament]: That place will probably motivate me until I'm 50. I think I could lose all my other matches throughout the year but, if I still won Wimbledon, I'd be happy. It's that important. It's always been the most important one for me—for all it stands for, and for all the other great champions who have been there. Maybe one out of 100 players would say they would rather win the U.S. Open, but I doubt that.

Newsweek, 6-27:48.

Mac O'Grady
Golfer

5

I love the game. To be out there and see all those people, eyes focused on the golf ball as we send it towards the heavens, silhouetted against the horizon—to roll it on this topographical surface—to watch the ball get near the hole, and half of the people are pulling for it to go in the hole and the other half are rooting for it not to go in. And none of them realize the ball has a consciousness of its own. It's like the Jimmy Stewart movie, *It's A Wonderful Life.* It's priceless.

News conference, Carlsbad, Calif.,
Jan.12/Los Angeles Times,
1-13:(III)11.

Brian O'Neill
Executive vice president,
National Hockey League

6

[On his ordering suspensions for hockey players who engage in violence against other players during the game]: It's not easy to sit in judgment of hockey players who are making their living at this game. But it's always been my belief that it's a necessary part of the game. We have a very violent, emotional game and things are going to happen. It's necessary to maintain some kind of order. It's an important job. It's just not a very pleasant one.

Interview, Montreal/
The New York Times, 11-21:(B)7.

George Perles
Football coach,
Michigan State University

7

[On criticism of his conservative offensive approach]: You know, I met [Georgia coach] Vince Dooley Monday night at a Gater Bowl party, and he runs a conservative offense and is retiring after 25 years. It seems to me Bo Schembechler at Michigan was criticized for being too conservative. So was Woody Hayes at Ohio State. Why is it that all of these guys who are criticized last so long and win so much? Maybe I'm on the right track.

USA Today, 12-28:(C)11.

Richie Phillips
Executive director,
Major League (baseball)
Umpires Association

1

[On TV instant replays which sometimes show umpires making a wrong call]: The problem with instant replay is we don't have sufficient technological sophistication to ascertain with any degree of certainty whether a runner is safe or out, or a ball is fair or foul. The one dimension isn't sufficient and the cameras are subject to distortion. We have to stick with the umpire's call and I applaud them for trying to get it right.

USA Today, 7-1:(C)4.

Lou Piniella
Baseball manager,
New York "Yankees"

2

[On high player salaries]: Once a game starts, money doesn't enter into it. A player is getting his salary because he's done a little more than others, had a little more success. You expect more, because he's produced in the past, but they're subject to human frailties, too. All you can do is expect, and then you have to respect that effort.

The New York Times,
8-25:42.

Dan Reeves
Football coach,
Denver "Broncos"

3

I think even a winning team has to set goals for itself to improve. I also believe that you've got to have an offense with a lot of flexibility to combat the kind of sophisticated defenses that are in use today. I'm not talking about just a complicated offense, but one where you can do a lot of different things from a lot of different formations.

The Christian Science Monitor,
1-28:18.

Frank Robinson
Baseball manager,
Baltimore "Orioles"

4

[On his team's losing the first 21 games of the season]: It's a test. It's a real test. But we have to keep going. There's only so much you can say. You can say things 15 times, and it doesn't mean a lot. Each loss is tougher and tougher. The longer we're in it, the more each individual tries to do. That's not the way to play this game. You have to go up and try to get a hit, not try to win a game.

The Washington Post, 4-29:(C)1.

Pete Rose
Baseball manager,
Cincinnati "Reds"

5

[On the recent incident involving his alleged shoving of an umpire and the resultant 30-day suspension and fine he received]: No player or manager has greater respect for the umpires than I do, and I have demonstrated that over the years. But I am shocked at the length of the suspension I received. While I expected to be suspended, I feel that this unprecedented 30 days is excessive. I also feel that I should have been given the right to give my side of the matter to the league president. The umpire certainly presented his side. In light of this, I have no choice but to appeal the decision.

Cincinnati, May 2/
Los Angeles Times, 5-3:(III)5.

6

It's important to communicate with players. One may need a pat, one may need a kick, one may need to be left alone. It's up to me to know who needs what.

TV Guide, 10-8:13.

Juan Antonio Samaranch
President, International
Olympic Committee

7

[Condemning illegal drug use by Olympic athletes]: Yes, doping equals death. Death

511

(JUAN ANTONIO SAMARANCH)

psychologically, with the profound, sometimes irreversible alternation of the body's normal processes through inexcusable manipulation. Physical death, as certain tragic cases in recent years have shown. And then, also death of the spirit and intellect, by the acceptance of cheating. And, finally, moral death, by placing oneself de facto outside the rules of conduct demanded by any human society.

Before International Olympic
Committee members,
Seoul, South Korea, Sept. 12/
The New York Times, 9-13:48.

Juan Samuel
Baseball player,
Philadelphia "Phillies"

1

[On being in a hitting slump]: You can't tell [why it happens]. When you're in a slump, you swing at "balls," and take "strikes." You sit and guess, and you guess wrong. You guess fast ball, and get a breaking ball. You're always guessing wrong when you're in a slump.

Interview, Philadelphia/
Los Angeles Times, 6-5:(III)15.

Dave Schmidt
Baseball pitcher,
Baltimore "Orioles"

2

[On his team's losing the first 21 games of the season]: I realize that we've been setting records that have been on the books for a long time, but it's just baseball. I don't even think the World Series belongs on page one [of the newspapers]. There's war in the Middle East, war in Central America, trade bills, a Presidential race . . . and there we were, right next to all of that. I mean, it hurt to take the abuse from the media that we have. It hurt to have fans call us names and to have to answer the same questions every day. We're professionals. We take pride in what we do.

Chicago, April 29/
Los Angeles Times, 4-30:(III)9.

Bill Shoemaker
Jockey

3

You can't take too much hold of a horse. Most horses don't like it, and some have run off with jocks. I learned to kind of gallop along with them. You want them to relax and take hold of the bit, and not spit it out. I've never been much of a whip jockey, so I have to rely on my hands, on finessing the horse—more so as I've gotten older—and keep the touch light, like putting in golf.

Interview, New York/
The New York Times, 4-9:31.

Pam Shriver
Tennis player

4

[On the fact that the Olympic Games are basically for amateurs in sport, not professionals]: What struck me about this place is that there are so many unbelievable athletes who don't receive big rewards for their sport. This [the Olympics] is their ultimate. There is no comparison to what I do [as a paid professional]. And it will be four years before the Olympics are held again [while professional athletes are constantly playing, improving and reaping the rewards].

Interview at Olympic Games, Seoul,
South Korea/The New York Times, 9-28:52

Don Shula
Football coach,
Miami "Dolphins"

5

[Great quarterbacks need] skill, mental toughness, self-confidence, patience, perseverance, concentration and the killer instinct. And an ability to rise to the occasion and make others believe in him.

TV Guide, 1-16:8.

John Silva
Sports psychologist;
Former president, Association
for the Advancement of
Applied Sports Psychology

6

[On why New York *Yankees* manager Billy Martin would, as he did recently, twice kick dirt

(JOHN SILVA)

on umpires during baseball games]: I've asked myself that same question. What possesses a person to do such a thing, and why would a league allow a person who is in such an influential position with fans and youngsters and other people in the game to exhibit such infantile behavior? . . . He obviously wasn't that concerned about the impression that people are going to have, because he didn't make any attempt to restrain himself. This is essentially an assault behavior. If you spit on somebody, they can charge you with assault. If you throw dirt on somebody, certainly you can be charged with assault.

Interview/
The New York Times, 6-2:49.

Jimmy (The Greek) Snyder
Commentator, CBS Sports

1

[If blacks] take over the [basketball] coaching jobs like everybody wants them to, there's not going to be anything left for the white people. I mean, all the players are black. The only thing that the whites control is the coaching jobs. Now, I'm not being derogatory about it, but that's all that's left for them. Black talent is beautiful, it's great, it's out there. The only thing left for the whites is a couple of coaching jobs . . . There's 10 players on a basketball court; if you find two whites, you're lucky. Four out of five or 9 out of 10 are black. Now, that's because they practice and they play and practice and play. They're not lazy like the white athlete is.

Broadcast interview/
WRC-TV, Washington, 1-15.

Michael Spinks
Former heavyweight boxing
champion of the world

2

Fighting another man is like having all 32 of your teeth pulled. Anybody who tells you he enjoys it is crazy.

Interview, Kiamesha Lake, N.Y./
The Wall Street Journal, 5-13:15.

Willie Stargell
Former baseball player,
Pittsburgh "Pirates"

3

You come into this game without ulcers. You ought to go out without ulcers. You can't be tied up in knots all the time; it's something to cherish, something to enjoy.

Los Angeles Times, 1-13:(III)7.

Marlon Starling
World Boxing Association
welterweight champion of
the world

4

I hate [boxing]. I particularly hate to look like a loser even if I'm a winner. I don't want to sit there with an ice pack on a split lip and two swollen eyes and bleeding God knows where, and have somebody congratulating me.

Los Angeles Times, 7-1:(III)1.

George Steinbrenner
Owner, New York "Yankees"
baseball club

5

[On the increasing length of professional sports seasons]: When [a player is] making $800,000 a year, there's no such thing as battle fatigue.

USA Today, 6-22:(A)8.

Darryl Strawberry
Baseball player,
New York "Mets"

6

Sometimes I think people don't take the trouble to understand our status, being in the limelight at such a young age. You can't judge a young man at 21. You're still a kid at heart. Nothing prepares you for it. Fame is special in the world. Once you are in the situation of being out in the world, there are different expectations. You're so young. You have to know yourself, what you can do in your career. Don't let other things destroy you.

Interview, New York, April 20/
The New York Times, 4-22:25.

Lawrence Taylor
Football player,
New York "Giants"

1

[On his being suspended for drug use]: They say "just say no to drugs." Great. But you don't realize it until you've been there. The first time you say no to drugs, great. The second time it comes a little easier. But hell, the first time you say "yes" to it, every other time after that, you're a goner. It's not just one instance. You do drugs one time and you do the second time, you've passed from casual use. You're an addict.

Interview, Aug. 31/
The New York Times, 9-1:41.

Daley Thompson
British Olympic gold-medal-
winning decathlete

2

I think [the Olympics is] one of the most genuinely humanitarian thoughts that man has ever had. The youth of the world coming together to play—it's a wonderful dream. I'm a Village person. I like to go around and meet gymnasts and weight lifters, every kind of athlete. We share a special understanding. All sports are the same; it's just the rules that are different. Were [basketball star] Michael Jordan and I to meet, I honestly think we could communicate without sentences, with just the start of words, maybe with knowing nods alone. At the Olympics, I love watching almost anything at all that's special, as long as it doesn't have a horse in it.

Interview/Time, 9-19:51.

Tom Trebelhorn
Baseball manager,
Milwaukee "Brewers"

3

[Saying there are too many balks being called by umpires]: Maybe we haven't instructed our pitchers properly, but I'm also seeing balks called that aren't balks. We don't want the runner to be deceived by the pitcher's motion, but we're only deceiving ourselves and ruining the game. A few guys cheated for 25 years and were allowed to cheat. Now we're taking cheaters, semi-cheaters and guys with no reason to cheat, and calling balks on them all. The umpires are on center stage and making a show of it as if the fans came to see them instead of the players. I saw a guy call one as if he was leading a Tchaikovsky symphony. The whole thing is out of whack. I mean, I could put 10 players on the field and the umpires might not see it because they're looking for the balk.

Los Angeles Times, 4-17:(III)3.

Billy Tubbs
Basketball coach,
University of Oklahoma

4

If you want good defensive stats, then hold the ball. Our philosophy is different. We want to cover 100 per cent of the floor 100 per cent of the time. Our defense is our offense. People don't understand that, because they just look at the stats.

Interview/USA Today, 3-28:(C)6.

Ted Turner
Owner, Atlanta "Braves"
baseball club

5

[Arguing against basic changes in baseball rules]: Some things don't need changing—the sunrise doesn't need changing, moonlight doesn't need changing, azaleas don't need changing, baseball doesn't need changing.

The Washington Post, 10-15:(A)27.

Peter V. Ueberroth
Commissioner of Baseball

6

[Saying he would not permit non-major-league players to be used as replacements if there is a baseball-player strike in 1990]: It's obviously been discussed because it's been done in other sports. But be careful not to mention the other sports because they're not really comparable [to baseball]. This one is really an institution. I don't want to make it sound sacred, but it has a special nature amongst the people in the country. It's a love affair.

Interview/
Los Angeles Times, 1-25:(III)11.

(PETER V. UEBERROTH)

1

[On the hiring of minorities for high-level positions in baseball]: I've found that people do not leap into decision-making positions; they earn them. You first have to have people in the system, and that's what we have now. I'm not ready to claim a victory, to say the job is finished, but we've made great strides, great progress. We have two or three clubs which now have a minority as chief financial officer, and those are the type positions from which club presidents evolve. Some people, in fact, say we now have too much of an open policy, but maybe that's the result of the door having been closed for too long. It's a sensitive subject. We don't want to be unfair to non-minorities, but I think it's being done well. I don't see any tokenism, and that's important. I think we're a good example to media companies, business companies, any type companies.

Interview/
Los Angeles Times, 4-6:(III)6.

2

[On a future expansion program for the major leagues in which cities would be selected, farm teams established, then major-league teams activated a year or two later]: These ideas are not mine. I'm following the owners. At our last meeting [about expansion], we asked, "How could we do this if we wanted to do it perfectly, not the herky-jerky way it's been done in the past?" Baseball doesn't have the luxury of getting players who are the "finished product" out of college, the way football and basketball do. In the past, expansion teams have been made up of other teams' [castoffs]. It would be better if we gave our next expansion teams—and we definitely think baseball is going to expand—an equal shot at the youngsters in the draft for a year or two. If you have 80 kids playing down there on the farm, it creates interest in home-grown players before a franchise ever plays its first major-league game. Also, it means an expansion team could start off with credible chances to make trades if it wanted. We just want to get expansion right this time.

Interview, July 5/
The Washington Post, 7-6:(C)6.

3

[On whether instant replay will be used in major-league baseball to determine the accuracy of umpires' calls]: There will not be instant replay of any sort. We're just not going to do it. The umpires making split-second decisions is part of the flavor of the game. We don't want to lose that flavor. You can make a dish so bland that it's not worth sitting down at the table.

July 5/
The Washington Post, 7-6:(C)6.

4

[On the paucity of black managers in baseball]: We've made progress. But I've hammered and hammered and hammered at every single owner: "Do not hire anybody who you don't believe in. I don't want any tokenism in this game. Do not let that happen."

Before National Association of
Black Journalists, St. Louis/
The New York Times, 8-27:7.

5

[On the readjustment of the starting times of this year's baseball play-off games to accommodate broadcasting of the U.S. Vice-Presidential debate]: The election of leaders of this country is far more important than a baseball game. Having said that, I'd rather watch a baseball game.

USA Today, 9-30:(C)15.

Jim Valvano
Basketball coach,
North Carolina State
University

6

[On college administrators]: Monday through Friday they want you to be like Harvard. On Saturday, they want you to play like Oklahoma.

Los Angeles Times, 1-18:(III)2.

7

Obviously, the most important thing [in winning the NCAA tournament] is talent. But let's

(JIM VALVANO)

get past the obvious, okay? Since you've got so many talented teams, to win the whole thing you need to be lucky.

Interview/TV Guide, 4-2:12.

Andy Van Slyke
Baseball player,
Pittsburgh "Pirates"

1

I'm not a masochist. I don't like pain. But I don't fear doing something on the field. I don't fear any aspect of the game, whether it's in the field, hitting, diving for a ball or trying to break up a double play. You can't play this game with fear. There's only one way to play this game—with fun. And getting dirty, getting a little bit of dirt or a little bit of blood on you now and then, is part of the fun.

Interview, Pittsburgh/
Los Angeles Times, 7-31:(III)8.

Dick Vitale
Commentator, ABC Sports

2

[To win the NCAA tournament,] you better have the common denominator of being an excellent team defensively. Take a look at Indiana, Georgetown, Villanova. The other ingredient is the star player—somebody who can make the big play. Steve Alford for Indiana last year, "Never Nervous" Pervis Ellison the year before. Prime-time players; the pressure's on and they want the ball. So here's the formula: defense plus star player equals NCAA title.

Interview/TV Guide, 4-2:13.

John Walker
1976 Olympic gold-medal
winning runner from
New Zealand

3

[On the absence of Australian and New Zealand winners in recent running contests]: The same thing has happened to American milers.

Greed, laziness, unwillingness to sacrifice. Fondness for sitting in front of the video 16 hours a day. Partiality toward the automobile. Who wants to go out on a hill in the rain and wind and run 20 miles when he could be home with a sweet and a warm fire? Who wants to work hard for anything? I think they want to win an Olympic medal in a lottery. Or maybe the government will give it to you.

Los Angeles Times, 1-19:(III)1.

Bill Walton
Former basketball player

4

[On why he loves basketball]: Everyone has to do everything—rebound, score, pass, play defense. There aren't any placekickers or relief pitchers.

The Christian Science Monitor,
11-22:20.

Doug Williams
Football player,
Washington "Redskins"

5

Winning is the greatest thing in the world, whether it is hopscotch or football, marbles or political elections. The bottom line is winning, but you also have to put losing into perspective. When you lose, you have to say, "One day I will win." Over the 10 years of my career, I have had so many downs that I knew the law of averages said something would bring me up.

Interview/USA Today, 6-14:(A)11.

Jimy Williams
Baseball manager,
Toronto "Blue Jays"

6

When [star players] make $2-million a year, they think they're bigger than the ball club. Well, they're not. When they get a base hit and drive in a run, everything is fine. But none of them can handle constructive criticism.

To reporters/
The Christian Science Monitor,
8-8:16.

John Wooden
Former basketball coach,
University of California,
Los Angeles

1

I'm certainly not for any more games. I think they're playing too many games now for college students. They play every day of the week, every time of the day, whenever television wants. And all the timeouts—sometimes it takes 10 minutes to play the final two minutes—destroy the flow of the game. I think all that is bad for the game.

Interview/
Los Angeles Times, 3-27:(III)10.

2

Television has brought about games being played almost every hour of the day. Television has taken over a lot of the play in the games by demanding, and getting, extra timeouts. That interrupts the flow of the game oftentimes. But there's always another side. Maybe television has been the best thing that's ever happened to the non-income producing sports [like college basketball]. Maybe it has been the best thing that's ever happened to women's athletics. So it has served a good purpose in many ways, too. But I think television has hurt the team play in basketball. It has brought on more individual, fancy showmanship . . . There are greater players today—individual players—than ever. And they're amazing in their individual ability. But I don't think you see nearly as good a team play as you used to have.

Interview, Encino, Calif./
The New York Times, 3-28:34.

John Ziegler
President, National
Hockey League

3

Violence will always be with us in hockey. It is a game of frustration. Just think about it: A player starts something. He starts to skate with the puck and somebody gets in his way. Somebody pushes him. Somebody jabs at him . . . Anytime you get a situation of high anxiety and frustration in any walk of life, you get violence.

Los Angeles Times, 5-15:(III)3.

Index to Speakers

A

Aaron, Henry, 253
Abalkin, Leonid I., 329
Abed Rabbo, Yasir, 358
Abernathy, Ralph David, 19
Abou Samra, Youssef, 358
Abram, Morris B., 358, 470
Abrams, Elliott, 281
Abramson, Mark A., 174
Abu Sharif, Bassam, 358
Adamishin, Anatoly L., 271
Adams, Brock, 359, 425
Adler, Allan, 68
Adler, Stella, 463
Adley, Robert, 329
Afanasyev, Yuri F., 329
Aganbegyan, Abel, 90, 253, 329
Aho, C. Michael, 34
Ailey, Alvin, 399, 463
Akers, John F., 90
Akgiray, Vedat, 34
Akhromeyev, Sergei F., 68
Aldridge, Edward C., 68
Alexander, Jane, 463
Alfonsin, Raul, 281
Ali, Muhammad, 498
Allen, Jay Presson, 437
Allen, Joseph, 263, 489
Allen, Lew, 489
Allende, Isabel, 413
Almodovar, Pedro, 399, 442
Alston, Philip, 142
Ameche, Don, 442
Amital, Yehuda, 359
Ammerman, Nancy, 483
Anderson, Donnald K., 174
Anderson, Sparky, 498
Andretti, Mario, 498
Antinori, Piero, 266
Aquino, Corazon C., 309
Arafat, Yasir, 359-360
Araka, John, 393
arap Moi, Daniel, 142, 159, 276
Arbatov, Georgi A., 142, 330
Ardebili, Abdul Karim Musawi, 360
Arens, Moshe, 360
Arias, Luis Alberto, 282

Arias, Oscar, 68, 282-283, 393, 483
Arledge, Roone, 206
Armacost, Michael H., 142, 361
Armitage, Richard L., 310
Arpino, Gerald, 463
Ashcroft, John D., 90, 117
Ashe, Victor, 266
Asimov, Isaac, 133, 413, 470, 489
Askoldov, Alexander, 330, 442
Aslanov, Yuri, 483
Aspin, Les, 68-69
Assad, Hafez al-, 361
Astin, Alexander W., 117
Atherton, Alfred L., 143
Atkins, Chester G., 310
Atwater, Lee, 206
Atwood, Margaret, 413
Austin, Gerald F., 207
Austin, James, 51
Avineri, Shlomo, 361
Avril, Prosper, 283
Azenburg, Emanuel, 463

B

Babangida, Ibrahim B., 271
Babbitt, Bruce, 34, 90-91, 174, 207, 406
Backa, Wladyslaw, 330
Baer, M. Delal, 283
Bailar, John, 425
Baker, James A., III, 91
Ball, George W., 361
Balz, Dan, 207
Banda, Hastings Kamusu, 271
Bandar Bin Sultan Bin Abdulaziz, 361
Bani-Sadr, Abolhassan, 361
Barbee, Victor, 464
Barber, James David, 174-175
Barnard, William, 207
Barron, Stephanie, 399
Batra, Ravi, 34, 91
Batts, Lana, 263
Baucus, Max, 284
Baylor, Don, 498-499
Baylor, Elgin, 499
Bays, Karl D., 34
Bazin, Marc, 284

519

Beals, Alan, 266
Beattie, Mollie, 133, 175
Beckel, Robert, 208
Beggs, James, 489
Behrens, Hildegard, 455
Bein, Johanan, 362
Bell, Terrel H., 117
Belli, Melvin, 199
Bellow, Saul, 414
Belous, Richard, 91
Bendjedid, Chadli, 271
Bennett, Georgette, 51
Bennett, William J., 117-118, 175, 208, 499
Bentsen, Lloyd, 19, 34-35, 92, 118-119, 143, 175, 208-210, 284
Benvenisti, Meron, 362
Bere, James, 35
Berle, Milton, 470
Bermudez, Enrique, 284-285
Bernas, Joaquin, 310
Bernstein, Leonard, 455
Berra, Yogi, 499
Berry, Raymond, 499
Bertolucci, Bernardo, 442
Besharov, Douglas, 253
Bessmertnykh, Alexander, 362
Besteman, Karst, 425
Bhutto, Benazir, 310
Biden, Joseph R., Jr., 51, 175
Bikkenin, Naili B., 330
Bill, Tony, 442
Biondi, Matt, 499
Bird, Larry, 500
Birney, David, 470
Black, Conrad M., 406
Black, Earl, 210
Blaker, James R., 69
Blinder, Alan S., 92
Bloch, Erich, 311, 490
Bloom, Allan, 13, 119
Boeheim, Jim, 500
Bogdanov, Pyotr S., 331
Boguslavskaya, Zoya, 19
Bond, Christopher S., 285
Bookbinder, Hyman, 362
Boorman, John, 442
Boorstin, Daniel J., 35
Boren, David, 69
Borge, Tomas, 285
Borgnine, Ernest, 470
Bork, Robert H., 19, 199
Bosco, Philip, 464
Boskin, Michael J., 92

Bosworth, Barry, 253
Botero, Rodrigo, 425
Botez, Mihai, 331
Botha, Adriaan, 271
Botha, Pieter W., 271-272
Bowen, Otis R., 51, 425
Bowlen, Pat, 500
Boyd, Aquilino E., 286
Boyd, William, 414, 471
Boyer, Ernest L., 119
Bradberry, Edward, 455
Bradley, Bill, 92, 175, 311
Brady, Nicholas F., 35-36
Brand, Stanley, 143
Brandt, Willy, 331
Breathard, Bobby, 500
Breed, Allen F., 52
Bremer, L. Paul, III, 143, 362
Brenner, Daniel, 406
Brill, Steven, 199
Brinkley, David, 210, 406
Brinner, Roger E., 92
Broadbent, John Edward, 286
Brock, William E., 93, 210
Brogan, Hugh, 211
Bronfman, Edgar M., 331
Brookens, Tom, 500
Brooks, James L., 443
Broughton, William, 455
Brown, Harold, 69, 143
Brown, Jim, 500
Brown, Lester, 133
Brown, Willie, 211
Browning, Edmond L., 483
Brundtland, Gro Harlem, 133
Brzezinski, Zbigniew, 331, 363
Buchanan, John, 483
Buchanan, Patrick, 211
Buffet, Warren, 471
Bukovsky, Vladimir, 332
Bumpers, Dale, 176
Burgess, Anthony, 119, 414
Burgin, Richard, 414
Burke, James, 36
Burlatsky, Fyodor M., 332
Burnett, Jim, 263
Burnley, James H., 263, 501
Burns, Arnold I., 199
Burns, George, 471
Burns, Jerry, 501
Burns, Robert L., 399
Busby, Horace, 211
Bush, George, 13-14, 19-21, 36-37, 52-54, 69-71, 93-

95, 119-120, 133-134, 144-147, 176-178, 199-200, 211-216, 253-254, 286-287, 332, 363-364, 483-484
Butler, Brett, 501
Butler, John, 464
Byrd, Robert C., 37, 72, 95, 147, 200

C

Cage, John, 456
Cahn, Sammy, 456
Caldwell, Sarah, 399
Calero, Adolfo, 287
Callahan, Daniel, 426
Capra, Frank, 443
Cardenas, Cuauhtemoc, 287
Carey, William D., 490
Carlson, G. Raymond, 484
Carlson, Richard, 333
Carlucci, Frank C., 72-73, 148, 364
Carnes, Bruce M., 120
Carnevale, Anthony, 95
Carpenter-Phinney, Connie, 501
Carril, Pete, 501
Carrington, Lord, 333
Carter, Jimmy, 21, 216-217, 287, 364
Carter, Rosalynn, 21, 178, 200, 406
Cash, Pat, 501
Castro, Fidel, 14, 148, 288
Cavazos, Lauro F., 121
Cerezo, Vinicio, 288
Cesar, Alfredo, 288-289
Chabrol, Claude, 443
Chafee, John H., 96
Chain, Beverly, 37
Chancellor, John, 217
Chandler, Robert F., Jr., 148
Chaney, John, 471
Charles, Prince, 134
Chase, William M., 121
Chebrikov, Victor, 333
Checkland, Michael, 179, 437
Cheren, Stanley, 502
Chiles, Lawton, 96
Chirac, Jaques, 333-334
Chisholm, Shirley, 21
Chissano, Joaquin A., 272
Chittipeddi, Kumar, 37
Choi Seh Hyung, 311
Chomsky, Noam, 471
Chowdhry, Anwar, 502
Christie, Julie, 444
Chubb, John, 121, 217
Chubin, Daryl, 471
Clancy, Tom, 415

Clark, Jack, 502
Clark, Joe, 365
Clark, Manning, 311
Clark, William C., 135
Clark, Willie, 502
Clarke, Martha, 464
Clarke, Robert L., 37
Cleese, John, 443, 471
Clifford, Clark M., 148
Clifford, Joyce, 426
Climaco, John, 54
Cline, Ray, 311
Clinton, Bill, 96
Clouthier, Manuel J., 289
Coats, Dan R., 437
Cochran, J. Thomas, 266
Cockburn, Leslie, 289
Coelho, Tony, 179, 217, 289, 365
Coffin, Frank M., 200
Cogan, John, 254
Cohen, William S., 54
Collins, Michael, 490
Comer, James P., 121, 426
Commager, Henry Steele, 14
Conable, Barber B., 148
Connally, John R., Jr., 217, 472
Connery, Sean, 444, 472
Conover, David, 55
Cony, Edward, 407
Cooke, Alistair, 407, 472
Coolidge, Martha, 444
Cooney, Joan Ganz, 437
Cooney, Stephen L., 38
Coppola, Francis Ford, 399, 444, 472
Corday, Barbara, 437
Cordovez, Diego, 311
Cornish, Edward, 96
Corrigan, Robert, 121
Costa-Gavras, Constantin, 444
Cox, Harvey, 484
Craft, Christine, 407
Craig, Roger, 502
Crandall, Robert L., 426
Cranston, Alan, 55, 73, 273, 365
Crawford, Bruce, 456
Crigler, Ann, 218
Cronkite, Walter, 218
Crowe, William J., Jr., 73, 365, 393
Crutzen, Paul Josef, 135
Cruz, Arturo, 290
Cunningham, Merce, 464
Cuomo, Mario M., 96, 179, 218-219, 254, 407
Curtis, Gerald L., 312

Cushing, Frank M., 135
Cussler, Clive, 415

D

Dalai Lama, 312
D'Amato, Alfonse M., 55
Darling, Ron, 502
Darman, Richard G., 96
Daschle, Thomas A., 179
Dash, Sam, 179
D'Aubuisson, Roberto, 290
Davidson, Gordon, 464
Davies, Dennis Russell, 400
Davies, Robertson, 415
Davis, Bette, 472
Dean, John Gunther, 312
Deardourff, John, 219
DeConcini, Dennis, 273
DeFrantz, Anita, 503
Degler, Carl N., 14
de la Madrid, Miguel, 290, 393
DeLillo, Don, 415
Dellinger, Walter, 219
Dellums, Ronald V., 73
Delvalle, Eric Arturo, 290
De Mita, Ciriaco, 334
Demjan, Sandor, 97
Demme, Jonathan, 445
DeMott, Margaret, 400
Dempsey, Paul, 264
Dennehy, Brian, 465
Deressa, Yonas, 273
Derrick, Butler, 55
Dershowitz, Alan, 55
Deukmejian, George, 219
DeVita, Vincent T., Jr., 426
de Waart, Edo, 456
Dewhurst, Colleen, 445
DiBona, Charles, 135
Dickinson, William L., 74
Dicks, Geoffrey, 97
Dimitrova, Ghena, 456, 472
Djilas, Milovan, 149, 334
Doanh, Le Dang, 312
Dodd, Christopher J., 290
Dole, Robert J., 38, 74, 97, 149, 220-221, 254, 291, 365, 407, 427
Donahue, William, 221
Donatelli, Frank, 221
Doran, Charles F., 291
Dornan, Robert K., 427
Douglas, Kirk, 445
Douglass, Joseph, Jr., 74
Dove, Rita, 415

Duarte, Jose Napoleon, 291
Dubcek, Alexander, 334
Dudarova, Veronika, 456
Duhamel, Alain, 334
Dukakis, Michael S., 15, 21-22, 38-39, 55-56, 75-77, 98-100, 122, 135-136, 149-151, 179-180, 200-201, 221-224, 254-255, 273, 291-292, 335, 366-367, 427, 473
du Plessis, Fred, 274
du Pont, Pierre S., IV, 180, 428
Durenberger, David, 428
Durr, Kent, 274
Durrell, Lawrence, 415
Dutoit, Charles, 457
Dymally, Mervyn, 22
Dyson, Freeman, 473

E

Eads, Arthur Coleman, 57
Easterbrook, Frank H., 201
Eastwood, Clint, 445
Eban, Abba, 367
Eckart, Dennis E., 181
Eco, Umberto, 473
Edwards, Blake, 445
Edwards, Mickey, 57
Eisenberg, Warren W., 367
Eizenstat, Stuart E., 181
Ekpu, Ray, 274
Ellison, Harlan, 446
English, Glenn, 57
Epstein, Seymour, 473
Eskew, Carter, 224
Esquivel, Roderick, 293
Etzioni, Amitai, 473
Evans, Daniel J., 57, 181
Evans, William, 428
Evert, Chris, 503
Ewald, Manfred, 503

F

King Fahd, 367
Fahrenkopf, Frank J., Jr., 225
Falwell, Jerry, 22, 408
Fang Lizhi, 317, 473
Fanning, Katherine, 408
Fasheh, Munir, 368
Fazio, Vic, 181
Fehr, Donald, 503
Feingold, S. Norman, 100
Fergusson, Frances D., 15, 39
Ferraro, Geraldine, 22
Field, Mervin, 100
Fienberg, Linda D., 22

Finn, Chester E., Jr., 122-123
Fischer, Oskar, 335
Fischer-Dieskau, Dietrich, 457
Fitzpatrick, Beatrice, 23
Fitzsimmons, William, 123
Fitzwater, Marlin, 293, 312, 368, 428
Flanagan, Thomas B., 416
Fletcher, James C., 491
Foley, Thomas S., 225
Ford, Betty, 182
Ford, Gerald R., 182, 225, 408
Foreman, George, 504
Fowler, Donald L., 225
Fowler, Wyche, 182
Fox, Michael J., 446
Foxman, Abraham, 23
Francis, Jeff, 504
Frank, Anthony M., 182
Frank, Barney, 97
Frankenthaler, Helen, 400
Fraser, Douglas A., 100
Fraser, George MacDonald, 446
Freedman, Monroe H., 182
Freij, Elias, 368
Friedman, Milton, 57
Friendly, Fred W., 437
Frolov, Konstantin V., 491
Fuentes, Carlos, 183, 293, 416
Fulwood, Isaac, 57
Futrell, Mary Hatwood, 23, 123
Futter, Ellen, 23, 123

G

Gal, Reuven, 368
Galbraith, John Kenneth, 39
Gale, Robert, 136
Galvin, John R., 77, 336
Gandhi, Rajiv, 151, 313
Garagiola, Joe, 504
Garcia, Alan, 293
Gareyev, Makhmut A., 77
Garn, Jake, 183, 491
Gartner, Michael, 226
Gates, Daryl, 57
Gates, Robert M., 151
Gejdenson, Samuel, 183
Geldenhuys, Deon, 274
Gemayel, Amin, 368
Genscher, Hans-Dietrich, 336
Gephardt, Richard A., 39, 100-101, 183, 226
Gerasimov, Gennadi I., 152, 368
Gershman, Carl, 484
Gerstner, Lou, 101
Getz, Stan, 457

Gewirtz, Paul, 183
Giamatti, A. Bartlett, 124, 416, 428, 504
Gielgud, John, 465
Gillespie, Dizzy, 457
Gingrich, Newt, 226
Giovanni, Nikki, 416
Giuliani, Rudolph W., 57
Glashow, Sheldon, 491
Glass, Philip, 457
Glasser, Ira, 226
Gluckstern, Norma B., 58
Goddard, Terry, 266
Godson, Roy, 152
Goering, Curt, 152
Golan, Galia, 153
Goldstock, Ronald, 58
Goldwater, Barry M., 183, 226
Golodner, Jack, 400
Gomory, Ralph E., 491
Gonzalez, Felipe, 153, 336
Gorbachev, Mikhail S., 78, 136, 153-155, 201, 313, 336-339, 369, 408, 484-485
Gore, Albert, Jr., 24, 78, 155, 226-227, 264
Gostev, Boris I., 339
Gotlieb, Allan E., 136, 183
Gottfried, Mike, 504
Gould, George, 40
Gould, Stephen Jay, 474
Gradison, Willis D., Jr., 101, 428
Graham, Billy, 485
Graham, Bob, 293
Gramm, Phil, 227
Grant, Gerald, 124
Gray, Alfred M., 78
Gray, William H., III, 24, 184
Grayson, George W., 227
Green, Richard R., 124-125
Greene, Graham, 416
Greenfield, Jeff, 417
Greenspan, Alan, 40, 101-102
Greenspan, Bud, 505
Greenstein, Fred I., 227
Greenstein, Robert, 255
Greenwald, Gerald, 339
Greider, William, 40
Gretzky, Wayne, 505
Griffith, Calvin, 505
Grinspoon, Lester, 58
Grossman, Lawrence, 227
Grosvenor, Gilbert M., 125, 474
Grosz, Karoly, 340
Groves, Lawrence A., 125
Guare, John, 465
Guest, Lawrence A., 102

Guinan, James M., 41
Gurdian, Ramiro, 294

H

Haayen, Richard J., 41
Hagen, Carl, 340
Haig, Alexander M., Jr., 15, 58, 79, 102, 125, 155-156, 228, 313
Hailsham, Lord, 340
Haley, Alex, 417
Hall, Donald, 417
Hallaj, Mohammad, 369
Hambrick, Margaret, 59
Hamilton, Lee H., 294
Hammer, Armand, 340
Han Xu, 314
Hancock, Herbie, 457
Handel, William, 255
Hanson, Lord, 41
Harbison, Earle, Jr., 492
Hardy, Dorcas R., 256
Harkabi, Yehoshafat, 369-370
Harkin, Tom, 294
Harris, David A., 228
Harrison, Edward, 474
Hart, Gary, 15, 79, 184, 228-229, 295, 474
Hart, Peter, 229
Hartman, Arthur A., 340-341
Hartman, David, 370, 485
Hatch, Orrin G., 59, 102, 230, 429
Hatfield, Mark O., 59, 156
Haughey, Charles J., 341
Hawke, Robert, 41, 103, 314
Hayes, Helen, 465
Hays, Ronald, 314
Healey, John, 156
Hecht, Anthony, 417
Hechter, Daniel, 400
Heisbourg, Francois, 341
Heitz, Thomas R., 505
Helmick, Robert, 505
Helms, Jesse, 24, 59, 79, 429
Herrington, Lois, 59
Hess, Stephen, 230
Hewitt, Don, 438
Higgins, Stephen E., 60
Hillis, Margaret, 458
Hilmers, David C., 492
Hines, Gregory, 465
Hinners, Noel W., 492
Hirschfeld, Al, 465
Hobson, Julius W., Jr., 184
Hodsoll, Frank, 401
Hoffman, Dustin, 446

Hoffman, Martin, 256
Hoffmann, Roald, 126, 492
Hohorst, James, 41
Hollings, Ernest F., 295
Holm, Jeanne, 79
Holwill, Richard N., 295
Honig, Bill, 60
Hooker, Michael, 136
Hooks, Benjamin L., 230
Horan, Hume A., 156
Hormats, Robert, 41
Horner, Constance, 103
Horowitz, Lawrence, 429
Hospers, John, 60
Houderi, Ahmed, 274
Hough, Jerry R., 184
Howard, Dan, 60
Howe, Geoffrey, 370
Hsiao, William C., 429
Hudiburg, John J., 103
Hughes, James W., 266
Hughes, Robert, 438
Hume, John, 341
Humphrey, Gordon J., 156, 341
Humphry, Derek, 429
Hussein I, 370-371
Husseini, Faisal, 371
Hyde, Henry J., 184, 201, 372
Hyun Hong Choo, 314

I

Iacocca, Lee A., 41-42, 103, 264
Ideman, James M., 201
Ikle, Fred C., 80, 185
Inoguchi, Kuniko, 314
Inouye, Daniel K., 24
Ionesco, Eugene, 466

J

Jackson, Betty, 430
Jackson, Glenda, 438, 446, 466
Jackson, Jesse L., 15, 25, 42, 60, 80, 103-104, 126, 156-157, 230-233, 256-257, 275, 295-296, 341, 372, 474-475, 485
Jacob, John E., 25, 257
Jakes, John, 417
Jakes, Milos, 341-342
Jakobovits, Immanuel, 485
James, Kay, 26
Jamieson, Kathleen Hall, 233
Jansons, Mariss, 458
Jaruzelski, Wojciech, 342
Jarvis, Sonia, 233
Jenkins, Brian, 157

Ji Shaoxiang, 315
Jobe, Frank, 506
John Paul II, 60, 275, 296, 342
Johnson, Anthony Rolfe, 458
Johnson, Ben, 506
Johnson, Lady Bird, 137
Johnson, M. L., 264
Johnston, J. Bennett, 104, 137
Johnston, Lloyd D., 61
Jordan, Barbara, 26
Josephson, Erland, 446
Josephson, Michael, 157, 185
Jugnauth, Aneerood, 275
Juneau, Pierre, 438
Jungkuntz, Richard, 126

K

Kaat, Jim, 506
Kabakov, Ilya, 342
Kadar, Janos, 342
Kahn, Wolf, 401
Kalb, Marvin, 408
Kaler, James, 492
Kamber, Victor, 104
Kanaga, William S., 42
Kane-Berman, John, 275
Kanin, Garson, 466
Karp, Walter, 185
Karpov, Vladimir V., 418
Karr, Gary, 459
Kato, Shuichi, 493
Katz, Barry M., 126
Kaufman, Paula T., 418
Kazan, Elia, 401, 447
Kazmaier, Dick, 506
Kean, Thomas H., 26, 104, 126, 157, 185, 233-234
Keene, Karlyn, 234
Keller, George M., 137
Kellerman, Jonathan, 418
Kemp, Geoffrey, 157
Kemp, Jack, 42, 105, 158, 185, 234, 257
Kennedy, Anthony M., 16
Kennedy, Edward M., 26, 105, 235
Kennedy, Joseph P., III, 235
Kennedy, Paul, 16, 105
Kennedy, William, 418
Kerrey, Bob, 235
Kertzer, David, 16
Kesey, Ken, 419
Khair Allah, Adnan, 373
Khalaf, Salah, 373
Khameini, Ali, 373
Khomeini, Ruhollah, 374
Kim Dae Jung, 315

Kim Young Seok, 315
King, Billie Jean, 506
King, Larry, 438
King, Tom, 343
Kinnock, Neil, 343
Kirk, Paul G., Jr., 235
Kirkland, Lane, 105
Kirkpatrick, Jeane J., 158
Kirshbaum, Laurence J., 419
Kissinger, Henry A., 158, 235, 296, 315, 343, 374
Kleiman, Mark, 61
Knepper, Bob, 506
Koch, Edward I., 61, 257-258
Koch, Noel, 374
Kohl, Helmut, 343-344
Kohut, Andrew, 236
Kollek, Teddy, 375
Kondrashov, Stanislav, 344
Koop, C. Everett, 430-431
Koppel, Ted, 236
Korb, Lawrence J., 81
Kraft, Christopher, 493
Kramer, Andrew, 402
Kramer, Hilton, 402
Kristol, Irving, 236
Kropp, Arthur J., 201
Kunstler, William M., 202
Kuntsevich, Anatoly, 81
Kuprianov, Vyacheslav, 419
Kutscher, Ronald E., 127
Kyvig, David E., 61

L

La Fosse, Robert, 466
Lam, Conrad, 315
Lamm, Norman, 475
Lamm, Richard D., 258
Lancaster, H. Martin, 236
Lance, Bert, 236
Lanfang, Yevgeny, 409
Lang, Jack, 402
Lapham, Lewis, 186, 419, 475
LaPorte, Charles, 431
Larijani, Muhammad Javad, 315
Larrain, Luis, 296
Lasley, R. Paul, 266
Lasorda, Tom, 507
Latta, Delbert, 186
Lattes, Jean-Claude, 419
Lautenberg, Frank R., 137, 236
Lavin, Linda, 438
Law, Lindsay, 439
Lawn, John, 61
Layden, Frank, 507

Leahy, Patrick J., 81, 137, 258, 493
Leath, Marvin, 186
Lee Kuan Yew, 158, 316, 475
Lee Teng-hui, 316
Leinsdorf, Erich, 459
Leland, Mickey, 237
Lelyveld, Arthur, 26
Lemmon, Jack, 447
Lenihan, Brian, 344
Leonard, Sheldon, 439
Leonard, Sugar Ray, 507
Le Pen, Jean-Marie, 344
Lesher, Richard L., 106
Lesser, Wendy, 419
Levchenko, Stanislav A., 158
Levin, Carl, 61
Levin, Henry, 127
Levine, Irene, 258
Levinger, Beryl, 258
Levitt, Arthur, Jr., 42
Lewis, Bernard, 375
Lewis, Dan, 475
Lewis, R. W. B., 420
Lewis, Samuel W., 375
Lewis, Stephan, 159
Lewis, Stephen R., Jr., 127
Li, David, 316
Li Peng, 316-317
Lichtenstein, Harvey, 458
Lifton, Robert, 375
Liebman, Bonnie, 431
Lilley, James, 317
Liman, Arthur, 186
Lincoln, C. Eric, 26
Linh, Nguyen Van, 317
Linowes, Robert F., 186
Linowitz, Sol M., 202, 296
Lipkin, Mack, Jr., 431
Lipton, Martin, 43
Liskevych, Taras (Terry), 507
Lister, H. E., 431
Lithgow, John, 447, 466
Lizichev, Alexei D., 81, 318
Loehr, James, 507
Logsdon, John, 493
Lollobrigida, Gina, 448
Lord, Winston, 318
Lounge, Mike, 493
Lucas, George, 402, 448, 475
Lucas, Grenville, 138
Lugar, Richard G., 275
Lumet, Sidney, 448
Lundberg, George, 432
Lutoslawski, Witold, 458

Luttwak, Edward, 81, 393
Lyng, Richard E., 43
Lynn, Fred, 507

M

Ma Ying-chiu, 318
Mabus, Ray, 186
MacDonald, David, 275
MacNeil, Robert, 402
Madden, John, 508
Mahe, Eddie, 237
Mahoney, Michael A., 81
Mailer, Norman, 448
Maingot, Anthony P., 297
Maisonnet, Maurice, 432
Maksoud, Clovis, 375
Malamuth, Neil, 62
Malle, Louis, 448-449
Manglapus, Raul, 318-319
Manheim, Jarol, 237
Manigat, Leslie F., 297
Mankiller, Wilma, 27
Mann, Carol, 508
Mann, Theodore R., 376
Mann, Thomas E., 106, 187
Mansfield, Mike, 319
Marcos, Ferdinand E., 319
Marino, Eugene Antonio, 485
Marker, Jamsheed K. A., 319
Markman, Stephen, 62
Markus, Greg, 237
Marquess, Mark, 508
Marshall, Thurgood, 27
Martin, Billy, 508
Masters, Brian John, 486
Matamoros, Bosco, 297
Matlock, Jack, 159
Matsunaga, Spark M., 420
Matthews, Frank, 27
Maximova, Yekaterina, 466
Mayor Zaragosa, Federico, 159
Mays, Willie, 509
Mbeki, Thabo, 276
McCain, John, 187, 237
McCarry, Charles, 420
McCarthy, Carol, 432
McCarthy, Eugene J., 187
McCarver, Tim, 509
McCloskey, Paul N., Jr., 237
McCollum, Bill, 62
McElvaine, Robert, 238
McEnroe, John, 509
McGovern, George S., 159, 238, 297
McGuire, E. Patrick, 187

McLaughlin, Ann Dore, 106
McLaughlin, John, 187
McNamara, Robert S., 394, 476
Meara, Anne, 466
Medvedev, Roy, 344-345
Meese, Edwin, III, 62, 187-188, 202, 409, 432
Meier, Waltraud, 459
Mengistu Haile Mariam, 276
Mercer, Robert E., 107
Messier, Mark, 509
Metzenbaum, Howard H., 188
Meyer, Ron, 509
Meyers, Eric M., 486
Michel, Robert H., 27, 188
Michelman, Kate, 28
Mihaly, Eugene, 486
Mikulski, Barbara A., 189, 238
Miller, Arthur, 467, 476
Miller, George, 107
Miller, James C., III, 189
Miller, Samuel C., 402
Millett, Richard L., 298
Mills, Kay, 409
Mineta, Norman Y., 28
Mitchell, George J., 82, 138, 202
Mittelman, Arnold, 467
Mitterrand, Francois, 82, 107, 345-346, 376, 476
Modigliani, Franco, 107
Mohammad Ibn Fahd, 376
Mondale, Walter F., 238
Monday, Rick, 509
Moody, Charles, 28
Mooney, Jim, 439
Moore, Allen, 346
Moore, Jonathan, 159
Morales Carazo, Jaime, 298
Moran, James P., 62
Morgan, Charles, 28
Morgenthau, Robert M., 202
Morita, Akio, 43
Morley, John David, 319
Moroi, Ken, 107
Morris, Frank, 107
Morris, Jay F., 259
Morris, Milton, 29
Morris, Norval, 63
Morrison, Alan B., 189
Morton, E. James, 43
Moses, Edwin, 510
Moss, Ambler, 298
Mott, William Penn, 138
Moyers, Bill, 409, 477
Moynihan, Daniel Patrick, 108, 138, 238, 259, 264
Mubarak, Hosni, 376-377

Mudd, Roger, 409
Mulch, William, 259
Mulroney, Brian, 138, 238, 298-299
Mundey, Lynette, 432
Murdoch, Iris, 420
Murdoch, Rupert, 43, 108
Murphy, Dale, 510
Murphy, Graeme, 467
Murphy, Richard W., 377
Muskie, Edmund S., 189
Muti, Riccardo, 459
Mutter, Anne-Sophie, 459-460

N

Nasser, Hanna, 377
Nauman, Bruce, 402
Navratilova, Martina, 510
Neas, Ralph G., 29
Needham, James J., 44
Nelson, Bill, 493
Nemerov, Howard, 420, 477
Netanyahu, Benjamin, 394
Neuhaus, Richard John, 486
Neuman, Nancy M., 239
Neumann, Robert, 377
Newman, Paul, 449, 477
Newman, Randy, 477
Nichols, Mike, 449
Nixon, Richard M., 82, 160, 239, 299, 320, 377
Nizer, Louis, 203, 477
Nofziger, Lyn, 189
Nolte, Nick, 449
Noonan, Peggy, 239, 420
Nordlinger, Gary, 240
Noriega, Manuel Antonio, 160, 299
Norman, Marsha, 420, 467
Norris, William C., 494
Norstein, Yuri, 403, 449
Norton, Eleanor Holmes, 29, 189
Nujoma, Sam, 276
Nunn, Sam, 82, 160, 240, 299
Nusseibeh, Sari, 378
Nyerere, Julius K., 276

O

Oakley, Phyllis, 346
Obando y Bravo, Miguel, 299, 394, 477
O'Brien, David, 203
O'Connor, Sandra Day, 29
O'Dell, Jack, 29
O'Donnell, Kirk, 240
O'Grady, Mac, 510
O'Hare, Hugh, 160
O'Neill, Brian, 510

Oppenheimer, Michael, 494
Orasin, Charles, 63
Oreffice, Paul F., 108
Orfield, Gary, 127
Ornstein, Norman J., 30, 160, 190, 240
Ortega, Daniel, 300
Ortega, Humberto, 300
Orton, Robert, 82
Owen, Gary, 240
Oyelakin, Lawrence, 276

P

Packard, David, 83
Packwood, Bob, 108, 190
Pahlavi, Reza, II, 378
Pan, Hermes, 460
Panetta, Leon E., 190, 259-260
Panto, Sal, Jr., 267
Papandreou, Andreas, 348
Pappas, Ike, 410
Parejo Gonzalez, Enrique, 63
Parker, Alan, 450
Parker, Maynard, 240
Parkinson, Cecil, 347
Parton, Dolly, 30
Pastora, Eden, 301
Paterson, George W., 486
Patrick, Dennis, 240
Payne, Donald M., 241
Peale, Norman Vincent, 478
Peck, Gregory, 450
Peck, Robert A., 320
Pell, Claiborne, 301, 378
Pendleton, Clarence M., Jr., 30
Penn, Arthur, 451
Perahia, Murray, 460
Peres, Shimon, 378-379
Peress, Maurice, 460
Perez de Cuellar, Javier, 394
Perle, Richard N., 83
Perles, George, 510
Perot, H. Ross, 16, 44, 260
Perry, Carrie Saxon, 267
Peters, Bernadette, 467
Peters, Charles, 30, 190
Petersen, Donald E., 16
Peterson, Peter, 44, 260
Petrovsky, Vladimir F., 161
Phillips, Kevin P., 241
Phillips, Richie, 511
Pickens, T. Boone, 478
Pickering, Thomas, 161
Pierce, Samuel R., Jr., 260

Pilcher, Rosamunde, 421
Piniella, Lou, 511
Pinnock, Trevor, 460
Pinochet, Augusto, 301
Pinter, Harold, 468
Pipes, Daniel, 380
Pitt, Theo H., Jr., 44
Poehl, Karl Otto, 44, 108
Poitier, Sidney, 478
Porath, Uri, 410
Powell, Colin L., 161, 190
Powell, Jody, 410
Powell, Lewis F., Jr., 63
Pozsgay, Imre, 347
Press, Frank, 494
Prestowitz, Clyde, 45
Price, Charles H., II, 347
Price, Reynolds, 421
Proxmire, William, 45, 108, 190, 241
Pryde, Paul, 242
Pryor, David H., 108, 191
Puttnam, David, 17, 451

Q

Qaddafi, Muammar el-, 162, 277, 380
Qian Qichen, 162, 320
Quayle, Dan, 17, 30, 45, 63-64, 109, 139, 162, 191,
242-244, 260-261, 301, 347, 410
Quinlan, Pierce, 109

R

Rabbani, Burhanuddin, 321
Rabin, Yitzhak, 380
Rafsanjani, Hashemi, 380-381
Rahn, Richard, 109-110
Rakowski, Mieczyslaw, 347
Ramirez, Eric, 302
Ransohoff, Martin, 451
Rather, Dan, 410-411
Rattle, Simon, 460
Ray, Randy, 403
Reagan, Maureen, 30
Reagan, Nancy, 64, 191
Reagan, Ronald, 3-9, 17, 30, 45-46, 64, 83-84, 110-111,
127, 162-164, 191-193, 244-245, 261, 277, 302-
303, 321, 348-349, 381, 394, 403, 433, 478, 494
Redford, Robert, 403, 452, 479
Redman, Charles E., 277, 303, 349, 382
Reeves, Dan, 511
Regan, Donald T., 46, 245
Rehnquist, William H., 203, 479
Reich, Robert B., 46, 111
Reich, Steve, 460

Reid, Harry M., 193
Reischauer, Edwin O., 321
Reitman, Alan, 31
Remick, Lee, 452
Restic, Joe, 127
Reynolds, William Bradford, 31
Rhodes, Frank H. T., 31
Rice, Anne, 421
Richards, Ann, 64, 111, 246
Richardson, Elliot L., 203
Richter, Richard P., 128
Ridgway, Rozanne L., 349
Riesman, David, 128
Rifai, Zaid, 382
Rifkin, Jeremy, 84
Riley, John, 265
Riley, Pat, 479
Risser, James, 411
Rivera, Geraldo, 439
Roa Bastos, Augusto, 421
Robb, Charles S., 111, 164, 193, 246
Robbins, Tom, 421
Roberts, Clayton, 112
Roberts, Cokie, 246
Roberts, Oral, 486
Roberts, Roy S., 31
Robertson, Don, 422
Robertson, Pat, 193, 246
Robinson, Frank, 511
Robinson, James D., III, 112
Robinson, Michael J., 246
Robinson, Thomas W., 321
Rocard, Michel, 193, 350
Roett, Riordan, 303
Rogers, Bernard W., 350
Rogers, Kenny, 479
Rogers, William P., 84, 164
Roh Tae Woo, 321-323
Rohatyn, Felix G., 112, 479
Rollins, Ed, 247
Romanenko, Yuri, 495
Roper, William L., 433
Rorem, Ned, 403, 461
Rose, Frank, 128
Rose, Pete, 511
Rosenberg, Howard, 439
Rosenthal, Jack, 411
Rosenthal, Mitchell, 65
Rosenzweig, Robert, 194, 495
Rosow, Jerome, 112
Rostenkowski, Dan, 112
Roth, Philip, 422
Roth, William V., Jr., 85

Rothstein, Paul F., 165
Rousakis, John, 267
Rovensky, Dusan, 350
Rowny, Edward L., 85, 165, 350
Rubinstein, Elyakim, 382
Ruckelshaus, William D., 139
Ruder, David S., 47
Rudman, Warren B., 247
Ruenes, Pelayo, 303
Rule, Charles F., 47
Runcie, Robert, 486
Runyon, Marvin, 139
Rycroft, Robert, 139

S

Saadawi, Nawal, 31
Sabato, Larry J., 247
Sachs, Jeffrey, 303
Sagdeyev, Roald Z., 495
Saguisag, Rene, 323
Sakharov, Andrei D., 18, 85, 139, 165, 350-351
Salinas de Gortari, Carlos, 304, 479
Samaranch, Juan Antonio, 511
Samuel, Juan, 512
Samuels, Paul N., 65
Sarbanes, Paul S., 247
Sarney, Jose, 304, 480
Sasser, James R., 85, 194, 305
Savage, John H., 440
Savage, Thomas, 422
Savimbi, Jonas, 248
Scalia, Antonin, 194, 204
Scammon, Richard, 248
Schaefer, William Donald, 65, 194, 248
Schick, Allen, 113
Schifter, Richard, 351
Schindler, Alexander M., 383, 487
Schlant, Robert C., 433
Schlesinger, Arthur M., Jr., 128, 403, 422
Schlesinger, James R., 86, 351
Schlueter, Poul, 480
Schmidt, Dave, 512
Schmidt, Helmut, 47, 113, 248
Schmoke, Kurt, 65
Schoenfeld, Gerald, 468
Schorr, Daniel, 165, 194
Schorr, Lisbeth, 261
Schott, Jeffrey L., 47
Schroeder, Patricia, 128, 139-140, 195, 261-262, 495
Schuh, Edward, 165
Schumer, Charles E., 195
Scowcroft, Brent, 166
Scully, Vincent, 404, 480

Sears, John, 248, 411
Segal, Erich, 480
Segal, Martin, 404
Seidler-Feller, Chaim, 487
Seligmann, Peter, 140
Sellars, Peter, 404, 461
Selleck, Tom, 411, 452
Sendak, Maurice, 480
Sessions, William S., 65, 195, 204
Sewall, Gilbert, 128
Shahani, Leticia Ramos, 323
Shalala, Donna, 129
Shales, Tom, 440
Shamir, Yitzhak, 383-385
Shamos, Morris, 496
Shanker, Albert, 129
Shao Yu-ming, 323
Shapiro, Harold, 129
Sharansky, Natan, 166, 352
Shareh, Farouk, 385
Sharif, Omar, 452, 480
Sharon, Ariel, 386
Shatalov, Vladimir, 496
Shavelson, Melville, 453
Shaw, Robert, 461
Shawa, Rashad, 386
Shayevitz, Avraham, 487
Sheets, Wayne, 65
Shepard, Sam, 468
Shestack, Alan, 404
Shevardnadze, Eduard A., 166, 323, 352
Shishlin, Nikolai V., 86, 166, 324
Shmelyev, Nikolai, 352
Shoemaker, Bill, 512
Shriver, Pam, 512
Shula, Don, 512
Shultz, George P., 48, 66, 86-87, 167-168, 277, 305, 324-325, 386-388
Sidey, Hugh, 404
Sidorsky, David, 389
Siegman, Henry, 389
Sigur, Gaston J., 168
Silber, John R., 168
Silliphant, Stirling, 422, 453
Silva, John, 512
Silverman, Mervyn, 433
Silverstein, Josef, 325
Simon, Paul, 113, 248, 487
Simpson, Alan K., 249
Sims, Nicholas, 87
Sinai, Allen, 113
Slatkin, Leonard, 461
Smeal, Eleanor, 32
Smilow, Joel E., 129

Smith, Adam, 18, 48
Smith, Hedrick, 352
Smith, Lawrence J., 389
Smith, Marcia, 496
Snowe, Olympia, 32
Snyder, Jimmy (The Greek), 513
Solis Palma, Manuel, 306
Sonnenfeld, Jeffrey, 48
Specter, Arlen, 66, 168, 389
Spencer, Elizabeth, 422
Spencer, Stuart, 249, 267
Spinks, Michael, 513
Spong, John Shelby, 487
Squadron, Howard, 390
Srinivasan, M. R., 325
Stanley, Harriet, 265
Stargell, Willie, 513
Stark, Fortney H. (Pete), 433
Starling, Marlon, 513
Steel, Danielle, 423
Steelman, Deborah, 262
Steinbrenner, George, 513
Steinbrenner, John, 168
Steinhardt, Ralph, 204
Steisel, Norman, 140
Stelmachowski, Andrzej, 352
Stepp, John R., 113
Stern, Philip, 195
Stern, Roslyne Paige, 468
Sterns, Monteagle, 169
Stevens, Roger L., 404, 469
Stevens, Ted, 195, 325
Stevenson, Isabelle, 469
Stewart, James, 453
Stewart, James K., 66
Stiles, B. J., 434
Stockhausen, Karlheinz, 480
Stockman, David A., 114
Stockwell, Dean, 453
Stolz, Preble, 66
Stone, I. F., 390, 411-412
Storr, Anthony, 481
Strauss, Robert S., 114, 169, 249
Strawberry, Darryl, 513
Stritch, Elaine, 453
Stroessner, Alfredo, 306
Sturdivant, John N., 195
Subramanian, R. R., 326
Sullivan, Louis W., 434
Sulzberger, Arthur O., 129
Summers, Clyde, 114
Sununu, John H., 114, 196, 390
Sverdlov, Yevgeny, 87
Sweitzer, Thomas, 48

Sykes, Charles, 130
Symms, Steven D., 49, 87

T

Taddei, Giuseppe, 405
Taft, William H, IV, 87
Takeshita, Noboru, 326
Talese, Gay, 423
Tamari, Meir, 49
Tambo, Oliver, 278
Tamir, Avraham, 390
Taub, Richard, 481
Taylor, Arthur A., 115
Taylor, James, 461
Taylor, Lawrence, 514
Terkel, Studs, 18, 169, 250
Thach, Nguyen Co, 326, 481
Thatcher, Margaret, 169-170, 250, 353-354, 394, 412, 481
Thayer, Nathaniel, 326
Thiering, Barbara, 488
Thomas, Cal, 196
Thomas, Helen, 412
Thompson, Daley, 514
Thompson, James R., 250
Thornburgh, Dick, 66, 196, 204-205
Thornton, Dean D., 265
Thurmond, Strom, 196
Timpane, P. Michael, 130
Tinker, Grant, 440
Tinoco, Victor Hugo, 306
Tisch, Laurence A., 440
Tisch, Preston Robert, 196
Toffler, Alvin, 49
Tolchin, Susan, 49
Tolstaya, Tatiana, 481
Torricelli, Robert G., 390
Towell, Timothy L., 170
Tower, John G., 87-88
Trachtenberg, Stephen Joel, 130
Train, Russell E., 140
Travisono, Anthony P., 66-67
Trebelhorn, Tom, 514
Trible, Paul S., Jr., 197
Trice, Carolyn, 130
Trost, Carlisle A. H., 354
Trowbridge, Alexander, 50
Tsiang, S. C., 326
Tubbs, Billy, 514
Tuell, Jack M., 488
Turner, John N., 306
Turner, Maurice T., Jr., 67
Turner, Robert, 170
Turner, Ted, 440, 514

Tutu, Desmond M., 278-279
Tyson, Cicely, 453

U

Ueberroth, Peter V., 514-515
Uno, Sosuke, 327
Untermeyer, Chase, 197
Updike, John, 423, 482
Urban, Jerzy, 354
Urquhart, Brian, 171, 482
Usdan, Michael, 130
Utley, Garrick, 440

V

Valdez, Gabriel, 307
Valvano, Jim, 515
Vance, Cyrus R., 88
Van de Kamp, John, 115
van der Merwe, Stoffel, 279
Van Slyke, Andy, 516
Vargas Llosa, Mario, 250, 423
Vassiliou, George, 354
Verity, C. William, Jr., 50, 250
Vest, George S., 171
Vick, Kathy M., 250
Viguerie, Richard, 250
Villalobos, Joaquin, 307
Vines, Jerry, 488
Vitale, Dick, 516
Volcker, Paul A., 197
Von Bernuth, Rudy, 327
Vonnegut, Kurt, 423
von Raab, William, 67
von Stade, Frederica, 461
Voznesensky, Andrei, 423
Vuono, Carl E., 88
Vyshinsky, Mikhail P., 354

W

Wagner, Bill, 205
Wagner, Carl, 251
Waldheim, Kurt, 355
Walesa, Lech, 355-356
Walker, John, 516
Walker, William G., 307
Waller, Robert D., 356
Walters, Vernon A., 390
Walton, Bill, 516
Walz, Gary, 131
Warch, Richard, 131
Ward, Benjamin, 67
Warner, John W., 88
Warren, Alfred S., Jr., 115
Watanabe, Michio, 115

Watkins, James D., 434
Watson, James, 435
Wattenberg, Ben, 262
Watts, Andre, 462
Waxman, Henry A., 140, 435
Weaver, Fritz, 441, 469
Webb, David, 496
Webb, James H., Jr., 88-89
Weber, Vin, 251
Webster, William H., 171, 395
Weicker, Lowell P., Jr., 32
Weithas, William V., 50
Weizman, Ezer, 391
Welsh, David, 279
Wenders, Wim, 454
Wertheimer, Fred, 171, 197, 251
Wexler, Haskell, 454
Whalen, John P., 131
Wharton, Clifton R., Jr., 131
Wheelock, Jaime, 307
White, John, 251
Whitehead, Charles, 251
Whitehead, John C., 171, 356
Whitehead, Ralph, 18
Wick, Charles Z., 172
Widemon, John Edgar, 424
Wiesel, Elie, 279
Wilbur, Richard, 424
Wilder, Billy, 454
Wiley, Richard E., 412
Wilkinson, Paul, 391
Williams, Doug, 516
Williams, Franklin, 205
Williams, Jimy, 516
Williams, Pat, 115
Williams, Robin, 454
Williamson, Richard S., 172
Wilmerding, John, 405
Wilson, Jean Gaddy, 412
Windom, Robert, 435
Winpisinger, William, 116, 252
Wise, David, 172
Wiseberg, Laurie, 172
Wittrock, Merlin, 131
Woerner, Fred W., 307

Woerner, Manfred, 172, 356
Wohlstetter, Albert, 89, 496
Wolf, Stephen, 265
Wolfe, Sidney, 435
Wolfe, Tom, 412
Wolpe, Howard, 280
Wooden, John, 517
Woodward, Edward, 441, 469
Woodwell, George M., 141
Worsthorne, Peregrine, 482
Worth, Timothy E., 441
Wright, Jim, 18, 50, 116, 132, 197-198, 252, 307-308
Wu Xueqian, 327
Wuerthner, J. J., Jr., 262

Y

Yaacovson, Zvi, 391
Yakovlev, Aleksandr N., 173, 356-357, 395
Yamamoto, Tadashi, 327
Yang, Edward, 454
Yankelevich, Daniel, 252
Yard, Molly, 32
Yeltsin, Boris, 357
Yerxa, Rufus, 308
Yeutter, Clayton K., 173
Young, Andrew, 33, 252, 488
Yzaguirre, Raul, 32

Z

Zajick, Dolora, 462
Zaslavskaya, Tatyana, 357
Zelinsky, Wilbur, 18
Zhao Ziyang, 327-328
Zhurkin, Vitaly, 357
Zia ul-Haq, Mohammed, 328
Ziegler, John, 517
Ziegler, Ron, 198
Zigler, Edward F., 132
Zindel, Paul, 424
Zinsser, William, 424
Zogby, James, 391
Zuboff, Shoshana, 496
Zumwalt, Elmo R., Jr., 392
Zwilich, Ellen Taaffe, 462

Index to Subjects

A

Abbas, Abu al-, 374:5
Abortion—*see* Women
Achievement, 474:4
Acid rain—*see* Environment
Acquired immune deficiency syndrome
  (AIDS)—*see* Medicine
Acting/actors, 403:4, 447:1, 453:1, 453:6
  Actors Studio, 464:2
  audience, 465:4, 466:5
  career, 452:5
  celebrities, 452:7
  choice of roles/properties, 442:2, 444:2, 447:3
  confidence, 450:5
  depth, part with, 447:5
  dialogue, 452:3
  doubt, self-, 447:6
  escape, 445:3
  experience/knowledge about human beings, 446:6
  good, compulsion to be, 442:5
  great roles, 469:3
  image, 444:2
  intuitive, 453:4
  longevity, 447:3
  make-believe/real life, 449:2
  more, doing, 446:2
  in motion pictures, 446:5, 465:1, 465:5, 465:6
  moving people, 453:3
  natural acting, 441:2
  noble profession, 447:5
  past roles forgotten by audience, 446:4
  quiet place in the storm, 445:2
  salaries, 452:6
  sexy roles, 448:1
  in stage/theatre, 463:1, 463:3, 464:2, 465:1, 465:2, 465:4, 465:6, 466:2, 466:5, 466:7, 469:4
  stupidity, 447:4
  success, 454:5
  technique, 453:5
  in television, 438:3, 441:2, 465:2, 465:6
  weakness, playing, 445:3
  women/men aspect, 447:2
  writing, actors doing, 449:4
  young, looking/acting, 472:2
Adversity, 479:3

Advertising—*see* Commerce
Affluence/wealth/prosperity, 14:2, 253:5, 254:1, 471:2, 475:4, 477:5, 479:1, 479:2, 479:5
Afghanistan:
  Communism, 311:5
  dictatorship, 164:3
  independence, 311:6
  mujahideen rebels, 146:1, 146:2, 315:6, 318:1, 319:5, 320:4, 321:1, 323:6, 324:2, 328:3
  Najibullah, 311:5, 315:6, 323:6
  non-aligned, 324:1
  foreign relations/policy with:
    Iran, 315:6
    Pakistan, 311:5, 328:3
    Soviet Union, 146:1, 146:2, 152:1, 155:5, 158:2, 244:5, 323:6, 328:2, 350:5
      troop withdrawal, 311:6, 312:5, 313:3, 315:6, 318:1, 319:5, 320:4, 320:5, 321:1, 321:2, 321:3, 324:1, 324:2
    U.S., 146:1, 146:2, 164:1, 164:2, 244:5, 319:5, 320:4, 321:2, 324:2
Africa, pp. 271–280
  colonialism/independence, 274:3, 278:2
  contrasts, continent of, 274:3
  democracy/freedom, 271:3, 278:2
  hunger, 259:1
  leaders, 274:3
  nationalism, 276:5
  Organization of African Unity (OAU), 276:5
  poverty, 274:3, 275:2
  foreign relations/policy with:
    Britain, 271:3
    South Africa, 276:6
    U.S., 150:3
  See also specific African countries
Age/youth, 471:3, 471:7, 472:2, 472:5, 478:1
Agriculture/farming:
  Dukakis, Michael S., 36:4, 45:4
  economic aspect, 99:2, 104:1, 231:2
  environmental aspect, 137:7
  exports/foreign markets, 35:1, 36:4, 43:2, 48:3, 101:1
  family-farm auctions, 256:3
  program/policy, farm, 35:1, 36:4, 45:4
  subsidies, 91:1
  supply controls, 36:4

AIDS (acquired immune deficiency syndrome)—
see Medicine
Air transportation—see Transportation
Albany, N.Y., 418:4
Alcohol—see Medicine: drug abuse
Alford, Steve, 516:2
Algeria:
    education, 271:4
    open society, 271:4
    foreign relations/policy with:
        France, 363:1
Ali, Muhammad, 169:3
Allen, Woody, 169:3
Alone, being, 481:1
Ambition, 470:5
American scene, the, pp. 13-18
America/U.S.:
    adolescence/maturity, 14:6
    affluence, 14:2
    banality, 18:3
    "Can I help you?", 18:1
    century, American, 13:4
    citizenship, 14:2
    communities, 14:3
    confidence/optimism/"can-do" attitude, 16:2,
       16:5
    criticism, self-, 18:1
    culture, Western, 14:7
    decency, 13:2
    democracy/freedom, 13:2, 13:3, 13:5, 16:3,
       17:2, 17:4, 17:5, 18:1
    disillusionment, 17:1
    diversity, 13:1, 13:3, 14:3, 15:1, 15:6
    dream, American, 15:2, 17:1, 222:3, 255:2
    entrepreneurial spirit, 250:5
    ethnicity, 13:1, 13:3
    excellence in, 15:4
    exceptionalism, 18:4
    fabulous country, 17:2
    fat and happy, 14:1
    the flag, 13:6
    Fourth of July, 18:6
    granted, taking for, 14:2, 16:4
    greed, 17:3
    immigrants, 13:1, 15:1
    inventiveness, 14:6
    limits, no, 222:4
    little guy, country of, 13:5
    materialism, 14:2, 15:5
    miracles happen in, 17:2
    Number 1, no longer, 14:5
    opportunities, 17:5
    patriotism/nationalism, 18:5, 18:6, 208:3,
       218:2

America/U.S.: *(continued)*
    patriotism/nationalism *(continued)*
      see also Dukakis, Michael S.
    Pledge of Allegiance, 16:3, 17:6, 18:4
      see also Dukakis, Michael S.
    political vs. people aspect, 18:2
    pollution, 18:3
    service to, 15:3
    social experimentation, 14:4
    thousand points of light, 14:3
    unity, 15:6
    winners, 16:5
American Bar Association (ABA)—see Law
American Civil Liberties Union (ACLU)—see
    Civil rights
American Federation of Labor-Congress of
    Industrial Organizations (AFL-CIO)—see
    Labor: unions
American Film Institute—see Motion pictures
Americas/Latin America/Central America, pp.
    281-308
    Communism, 302:3
    defense/military, 307:5
    democracy/freedom, 281:4, 281:5, 287:4,
      292:4, 294:3, 302:4, 303:5, 305:3, 305:5,
      307:5
    destabilization/subversion, 305:3
    drugs, 66:1, 292:5, 292:6, 293:3, 294:3
    economy/debt, 281:4, 281:5, 287:4, 293:3,
      294:3, 296:2, 303:5, 304:6
    government, self-, (Caribbean), 297:1
    literature/books aspect, 421:4
    Organization of American States (OAS), 305:4
    violence, 292:6
    foreign relations/policy with:
      Canada, 304:6
      Chile, 303:3
      China, 304:6
      Europe, 304:6
      Japan, 304:6, 312:1
      Soviet Union, 146:2, 149:3, 153:1, 155:3,
        155:5, 292:2, 292:3, 293:3
      U.S., 148:2, 164:2, 281:4, 281:5, 287:4,
        290:3, 292:2, 292:3, 292:4, 292:5,
        293:3, 293:5, 294:3, 296:2, 296:6,
        299:5, 303:5, 304:6, 305:3, 305:5,
        307:5, 312:1
        drugs, 66:1
      Monroe Doctrine, 149:3
      overthrowing governments, 222:4
    See also specific countries of the Americas
Anglican Church—see Religion: Christianity
Angola:
    UNITA, 162:1, 273:2, 273:4, 278:5

Angola: *(continued)*
  foreign relations/policy with:
    Cuba, 272:5, 273:4, 278:5
    South Africa, 272:5, 276:6, 278:5
    Soviet Union, 153:1, 155:5, 157:1, 158:1
    U.S., 145:2, 157:1, 159:4, 162:1, 164:2,
      273:2, 273:4, 278:5
Antheil, George, 460:4
Aquino, Corazon C.—*see* Philippines
Arabs—*see* Israel: foreign affairs; Middle East
Arafat, Yasir—*see* Palestinians: PLO
Archilochus, 472:3
Architecture—*see* Arts
Argentina, 298:1
Arts/culture, pp. 399-405
  aloneness of artist, 400:3
  amateur/professional aspect, 461:3
  architecture, 134:6, 402:1, 404:1
  black aspect, 402:6
  business aspect, 456:5
  censorship, 399:2
  children aspect, 403:5
  commitment to, 400:1
  competition, 404:4
  controversy, 402:3
  creative people, 399:6
  education/schools aspect, 401:1, 401:2
  exchanges, cultural, 399:5, 402:2
  exploitation/copying, 400:4
  "extras," seen as, 399:4
  fashion design, 400:5
  focuses things for people, 401:4
  freedom aspect, 403:3
  funding/support aspect, 399:1, 400:1, 403:6
  government/Federal aspect, 399:1, 403:6
  hard to look at, 404:3
  ideal which cannot be achieved in real life,
    403:1
  ideas, 405:2
  imagination snared, 403:5
  Italy, 459:4
  Kennedy Center (Washington), 404:6
    Kennedy Center Honors, 399:1
  lie, art doesn't, 400:3
  literacy, cultural, 401:2
  machismo aspect, 402:5
  "making it" as artist, 403:4
  museums, 399:3, 402:6, 403:2, 404:4, 467:3
  one person's vision, 401:5
  originality, 401:3
  painting, 401:3, 401:4, 448:6
  peace aspect, 404:2
  photography, 456:4
  Presidency (U.S.) aspect, 402:5, 404:5

Arts/culture *(continued)*
  public/outdoor art, 400:2
  relevancy, 402:6
  sanitized, 404:3
  Soviet Union, 342:5, 403:3
  straightforward ideas, 402:7
  strife, art from, 439:1
  success, 405:1
  themes, retelling of, 402:4, 448:2
  university aspect, 339:4
Asia/Pacific, pp. 309-328
  century of the Pacific, 319:2
  changes, 325:4
  defense/military, 322:2
    nuclear weapons, 313:5
  democracy, 325:4
  imperialism/colonialism, 313:2
  science/industry, 311:1
  socialism, 325:3
  trade, 316:5, 319:2
  foreign relations/policy with:
    Europe, 313:2
    Japan, 316:5
    Persian Gulf, 365:2
    Soviet Union, 153:1, 313:4, 313:5, 314:3,
      322:2
    U.S., 311:1, 313:4, 313:5, 316:5, 319:2,
      322:2, 325:3, 325:4
  See also specific Asian/Pacific countries
Assad, Hafez al-—*see* Syria
Astrology—*see* Reagan, Ronald; Science
Atlantic City, N.J., 266:6
Attorney General (U.S.)—*see* Judiciary: Justice,
  Dept. of
Augusta, Ga., 455:3
Austen, Jane, 420:4
Australia:
  isolationist, 314:2
  silence, Australian, 311:4
  sports (running), 516:3
  foreign relations/policy with:
    China, 314:2
Austria, 355:1, 355:2, 355:3
Auto racing, 498:4
Automobiles—*see* Transportation

B

Bahrain:
  foreign relations/policy with:
    U.S., 168:4
      arms sales, 366:4
Baker, Howard H., Jr., 247:2
Baker, James A., III, 169:2
Balanchine, George, 463:4

Bangladesh, 327:2
Banking—*see* Commerce
Baryshnikov, Mikhail, 463:4
Baseball:
  blacks/minorities, 498:5, 513:1, 515:1, 515:4
  blue-collar aspect, 500:5
  cities without, 503:5
  coaching 508:3, 513:1
  college, 508:3, 515:2
  expansion/new cities, 515:2
  fans, 509:1, 512:2
  football compared with, 504:5
  hitting, 509:6
    home runs, 502:3
    slumps, 512:1
  importance, 515:5
  individual/team sport, 504:5
  managing/managers:
    black, 498:5, 515:4
    do everything, 508:5
    love of game, 498:2
    owners aspect, 508:4
    players aspect, 498:3, 507:2, 511:6
    umpires, arguments/abuse, 502:1, 504:3, 511:5, 512:6
  monopoly/antitrust aspect, 503:5
  owners, 503:5, 508:4, 512:2
  pitching/pitchers, 509:2, 509:6
    an art, 506:3
    balks, 514:3
    bullpen, 499:4
    changing pitchers, 498:3
    starting pitchers, 499:4
  players:
    arrogance, 501:3
    desire, 501:3
    endurance/staying power, 499:1
    fame, 513:6
    fear, 516:1
    fun, 516:1
    intelligence, 502:6
    managers aspect, 498:3, 507:2, 511:6
    motivation, 498:3
    retirement, 498:2
    salaries, 123:4, 505:3, 511:2, 516:6
    stars, 516:6
    strikes, 514:6
    talent/ability, 498:3, 507:2
    ulcers, 513:3
    umpires aspect, 504:3
  press/media, 508:4, 512:2
  rule changes, 514:5
  Switzerland, 505:4
  television instant replays, 511:1, 515:3

Baseball: *(continued)*
  umpires:
    accuracy of calls, 511:1, 515:3
    arbiters, 509:2
    arguments/abuse, 502:1, 504:3, 504:4, 511:5, 512:6
    balks, calling of, 514:3
    dominate game, 504:3
    female, 502:5, 506:6
    players aspect, 504:3
  a "war," 498:2
  winning/losing, 507:7, 510:2, 511:4, 512:2
  World Series, 512:2
  world-wide interest, 505:4
  teams:
    Baltimore *Orioles,* 507:7, 511:4, 512:2
    Boston *Red Sox,* 505:3
    Cincinnati *Reds,* 504:4, 507:1
    Detroit *Tigers,* 500:5
    New York *Yankees,* 123:4, 502:1, 508:4, 512:6
Basketball:
  college, 500:2, 515:2, 516:6
    NCAA tournament, 515:7, 516:2
    star players, 516:2
    team/individual play, 517:2
    television aspect, 517:1, 517:2
    timeouts, 517:1, 517:2
    too many games, 517:1
  defense—*see* offense, *this section*
  fundamentals, 499:2
  offense/defense, 514:4, 516:2
  players:
    brawls, 500:2
    desire, 501:5
    do everything, 516:4
    rookies, 499:2
    stars, 516:2
  television aspect, 517:1, 517:2
  winning/losing, 507:3, 515:7, 516:2
  teams:
    Georgetown University, 516:2
    Los Angeles *Lakers,* 479:3
    University of Indiana, 516:2
    University of Oklahoma, 515:6
    Villanova University, 516:2
Beatles, the, 460:2
Beckett, Samuel, 466:1
Beethoven, Ludwig van, 460:1
Bellow, Saul, 418:4
Ben-Gurion, David, 379:5
Bennett, William J., 123:3, 124:2
Bentsen, Lloyd, 109:1, 109:2, 122:3
  fund-raising, 243:3

Bentsen, Lloyd *(continued)*
  Middle East, 366:4, 367:1
  vanilla, pure, 211:3
Berlin, Isaiah, 472:3
Bermudez, Enrique, 289:4
Bernbach, William, 50:4
Bible, the—*see* Religion: Christianity
Bill of Rights—*see* Constitution (U.S.)
Blacks—*see* Civil rights
Boeing Co., 265:3
Boesky, Ivan, 15:5
Bolivia:
  economy, 140:2
  environment aspect, 140:2
  foreign relations/policy with:
    Panama, 298:1
Bondarchuk, Sergei, 446:3
Books—*see* Literature
Bork, Robert H., 19:4, 223:4
Boston, Mass., 134:2, 139:1
Boston Pops Orchestra, 499:5
Boxing:
  enjoyment by boxer, 513:2, 513:4
  fans, 498:1
  killer instinct, 504:1
  knowing what to do, 507:4
  self-defense, art of, 502:2
  winning, 513:4
Brazil, 480:1
  foreign relations/policy with:
    U.S., 304:7
Brezhnev, Leonid I.—*see* Soviet Union
Britain—*see* United Kingdom
Broadcasting/television, pp. 437-441
  abolition of, 438:2
  acting in, 438:3, 441:2, 465:2, 465:6
  art-form, 439:5
  as we are, showing us, 438:6
  audience, 438:6, 441:1
    loss of, 440:5
  baseball instant replay, 511:1, 515:3
  baskeball (college) aspect, 517:1, 517:2
  Britain/BBC, 437:2, 441:2
  cable/pay TV, 439:3, 440:5
  Canada, 438:4
  children/young viewers, 437:3, 437:4
  choices, 439:3
  commercial TV/product-selling, 437:6, 439:2, 440:1
    commercials, 431:3
  Congress/Senate, televising of, 175:5, 194:5
  courtroom dramatizations, 205:2
  critics, 439:5, 440:2
  evangelists—*see* Religion

Broadcasting/television *(continued)*
  Fairness Doctrine, 412:4
  Federal Communications Commission (FCC), 240:7, 412:4, 441:3
  improvisational, 439:4
  information source, 437:4, 438:1
  "live" TV, 439:4
  money aspect, 437:6
  motion pictures compared with, 437:1, 442:4, 452:3
  National Broadcasting Co. (NBC), 42:2
  news—*see* Journalism: broadcast
  politics/elections, 226:1
    advertising, political, 215:4, 216:2, 218:1, 233:3, 240:7, 248:6, 250:1
  public TV, 439;1, 441:3
  quality, 440:4, 441:1
  radio, 440:5
  ratings, 411:5, 440:4
  reading, effect on, 437:4
  simple-minded, 438:2
  social form, 439:5
  Soviet Union, 440:1
  sports coverage, 505:1
    See also specific sports, this section
  stage/theatre compared with, 465:2
  standardized culture, 439:1
  stations, sale of, 437:6
  "tabloid TV," 440:6
  talent/creativity, 440:3
  teaching aspect, 437:4
  violence, 437:3
  war aspect, 394:3
  wealth, protrayal of 477:5
  writing for, 437:1, 437:5
  be yourself, 438:5
  programs:
    ABC News Nightline, 406:3
    Alice, 438:6
    All in the Family, 438:6
    Amos 'n' Andy, 27:4
    Cagney and Lacey, 438:6
    Sesame Street, 441:3
    60 Minutes, 440:4
    Today, 420:3
    West 57th, 440:4
  See also Journalism: broadcast
Broadway—*see* Stage
Brokaw, Tom, 150:1
Bronx, N.Y., 258:3, 266:6
Budget deficit, government—*see* Economy
Bulgaria, 158:1
Burma, 325:5
Burns, George, 443:3

Bush, George, 220:1, 220:4, 224:2, 224:3, 229:5, 231:2, 249:1
  abortion, 30:1, 244:6
  accomplishments, 228:1
  ACLU, 226:4
  appointments, 197:3
  arms sales to Arabs, 366:4
    to Iran, 246:1, 367:1
  black aspect, 211:4, 233:2
  campaign tactics, negative, 210:2, 216:2, 222:5, 224:4, 232:5, 233:3, 238:4, 241:3, 247:1
  caring, 212:2
  charisma, 217:2
  crime, 63:6
  defense/military, 76:4, 76:5
  Dole, Robert J., aspect, 247:2
  driven, 213:3
  drugs, 55:6, 56:5, 209:1, 212:5, 244:6
  economy, 90:4, 99:3, 99:4, 99:5, 100:2, 100:3, 104:3, 223:6, 246:1
  education, 118:7
  elite image, 250:3
  eloquence/articulation, 212:1, 214:1
  Europe, 170:1, 354:1
  fears, playing on people's, 218:1
  foreign affairs, 150:4, 157:5, 166:7, 249:2
  government aspect, 179:2
  image, 237:5
  Iran, 143:2, 150:5, 236:1, 246:1, 367:1
  leadership, 217:5, 222:1, 236:3
  mandate, 224:5
  medicine/health aspect, 427:4
    AIDS, 434:4
  Panama/Noriega, 209:1, 212:5, 236:1
  perception, public, 247:1
  personality, 212:3, 214:1, 249:3
  Pledge of Allegiance, 162:5, 219:4, 223:1, 244:6
  prayer, school, 244:6
  qualifications/experience, 211:1, 211:5, 212:3, 218:3, 219:6, 241:3, 245:2
  Quayle, Dan, aspect, 209:3, 223:3
  tolerant, 206:4
  trade, foreign, 39:1
  women voters, 225:1, 247:1
  women's rights, 32:4
Business—see Commerce

C

Cable News Network—see Journalism: broadcast
Calder, Alexander, 400:2
Calero, Adolfo, 289:4

California, 134:1
Callas, Maria, 456:5
Cambodia (Kampuchea):
  foreign relations/policy with:
    China, 326:4
    Soviet Union, 153:1, 155:5, 158:1
    U.S., 164:2, 326:4
    Vietnam, 310:2, 320:5, 326:4
Camus, Albert, 418:4
Canada:
  acid rain, 136:4, 138:5, 284:1
  community, sense of, 286:3
  economy, 110:3, 286:2
    See also trade, this section
  elections, 298:4, 298:6
  literature/books, 415:3
  Mulroney, Brian, 306:6
  social democratic parties, 286:2
  socialist monarchy, 415:3
  television, 438:4
  trade, foreign, 304:6
    See also U.S., this section
  foreign relations/policy with:
    Americas, 304:6
    U.S., 284:1, 286:3, 291:2, 298:5, 298:6, 299:1, 304:6
      acid rain, 136:4, 138:5
      trade agreement, 284:1, 286:3, 291:2, 298:5, 298:6, 306:5, 306:6, 308:2
Cancer—see Medicine
Capital punishment—see Crime
Capitalism/free enterprise, 37:4, 49:2, 106:1, 108:4, 151:5, 286:3, 307:2, 331:2, 374:2, 481:3
  See also specific countries
Capra, Frank, 448:2
Caribbean—see Americas
Carlucci, Frank C., 89:1
Carter, Jimmy:
  criticism, taking of, 186:3
  defense/military, 69:5
  economy/debt, 99:5
  election, 1988, 246:5
  failures, 227:5
  Federal system, 179:2
  human rights, 251:5
  Nicaragua, 330:3
  outsider, 220:3
  Panama, 281:3
  Vice-Presidential aspect, 178:3
Casey, William J., 152:2
Castro, Fidel—see Cuba
CBS News—see Journalism: broadcast
Ceaucescu, Nicolae, 331:2, 394:7

Censorship—*see* Arts
Central America—*see* Americas
Central Intelligence Agency (CIA), U.S.—*see* Foreign affairs: intelligence
Century, 20th, 476:3
Chad, 162:1
Channing, Carol, 465:6
Chaplin, Charles, 443:3
Chaucer, Geoffrey, 126:1
Chayefsky, Paddy, 443:1
Chekhov, Anton, 465:1
Chiang Ching-kuo—*see* Taiwan
Child care—*see* Social welfare
Chile:
  democracy, 303:3, 307:1
  economy, 296:5, 301:3
  isolation, 303:3
  Pinochet, Augusto, 307:1
  foreign relations/policy with:
    Americas, 303:3
    U.S., 303:3
China:
  Communism/Marxism, 149;1, 317:5, 323:5, 327:5, 473:6
  defense/military, 320:1
    arms sales, 327:3
  democracy, 316:4, 317:5
  economy, 106:1, 168:5, 317:1, 320:1
  foreign affairs, 320:1
  political parties, 317:5
  reform, 316:6
  Tibet, 312:2
  trade, foreign, 314:1, 318:2
  foreign relations/policy with:
    Americas, 304:6
    Australia, 314:2
    Cambodia, 326:4
    Europe, 320:1
    Hong Kong, 315:1, 315:5
    India, 321:6, 326:1
    Japan, 304:6, 320:1, 321:6
    Korea, North, 322:2
    Pakistan, 326:1
    Soviet Union, 153:1, 321:6, 324:5
    U.S., 303:4, 314:1, 318:2, 320:1, 321:6, 326:2, 328:2
    Vietnam, 321:6
Christ, Jesus—*see* Religion: Christianity
Chrysler Corp., 48:6
Chun Doo Hwan—*see* Korea, South
Churchill, Winston S., 171:1, 234:3
Cinema—*see* Motion pictures
Cities—*see* Urban affairs
Civil rights/blacks/racism/minorities, pp. 19-33

Civil rights/blacks/racism/minorities *(continued)*
  affirmative action, 22:2, 24:2, 27:3, 30:3, 214:3, 215:3, 221:2, 226:4
  American Civil Liberties Union (ACLU), 20:6, 21:5, 31:1, 52:6, 53:2, 57:7, 63:6, 214:3, 215:3, 221:2, 226:4
  Amos 'n' Andy (TV show), 27:4
  arts aspect, 402:6
  Attorney General, U.S., 20:2, 27:3
  baseball, 498:5, 513:1, 515:1, 515:4
  Bork, Robert H., aspect, 19:4
  Bush, George, aspect, 211:4, 233:2
  business aspect, 31:4
  Civil Rights Commission, U.S., 22:2
  Congress (U.S.) aspect, 31:2, 32:3
  conservatism (political), 30:5
  crime, 51:1, 54:1
    FBI, 65:5
  democracy, true, 27:2
  Democratic Party (U.S.) aspect, 21:2, 22:2, 24:3, 206:6, 211:4, 219:2, 220:2, 230:4, 233:2
  Dukakis, Michael S., aspect, 24:3, 233:4
  economy, 26:6, 115:4
  education —*see* Education: blacks
  employment/jobs, 93:6
  enforcement, 201:6
  equality, civil, 39:5
  foreign affairs, black aspect of, 157:1
  Georgia, 33:1
  government/politics aspect, 29:1
  Hispanics, 20:1, 32:6, 51:1
  history, rewriting of, 27:4
  Indians, American, 27:1
  Jackson, Jesse L.—*see* Democratic Party, U.S.; Politics
  Japanese-American internment, 24:4, 24:5, 28:3
  judiciary/courts aspect, 205:3
    Supreme Court, minorities on, 200:3
  King, Martin Luther, Jr., 19:1, 23:3, 24:3, 26:5, 28:5, 29:3, 438:1
  Massachusetts, 33:1
  middle-class blacks, 26:6
  movement is alive, 23:3
  neighborhoods, 26:6
  poets, black, 415:5
  politics/elections, 21:2. 24:3, 216:4, 219:2, 227:2, 230:3, 230:4, 230:5, 230:6, 233:1, 233:4, 234:2, 244:2, 250:7, 252:3
    See also Jackson, Jesse L.
  pornography/obscenity, 20:6, 21:5, 420:1
  poverty/poor, black aspect of, 25:5, 255:4, 257:2

Civil rights/blacks/racism/minorities *(continued)*
  prejudice, 25:4
  Presidential Cabinet, 20:1
  press/media, 25:3, 32:6
    newspaper staffs, minorities on, 408:2
  progress/retreat/present vs. past, 21:1, 27:2, 31:3, 32:3
  Reagan, Ronald, aspect, 22:2, 25:5, 26:4, 27:3, 28:4, 29:2, 31:2, 223:4
  Republican Party (U.S.) aspect, 22:2, 26:3, 30:5, 206:6, 211:4, 220:2, 220:5, 220:6, 230:4, 233:2, 233:5, 234:5
  segregation, 25:1
  Semitism, anti-, 23:2
  South, the U.S., 24:1, 29:1, 32:6, 33:1
  sports aspect, 500:6
    See also baseball, *this section*
  turning back the clock, 209:1
  violence, non-, 19:1
  See also Namibia: apartheid; South Africa: apartheid
Clemens, Roger, 506:3
Coal—*see* Energy
Cocaine—*see* Crime: drugs
Collectivism, 473:5
Colleges—*see* Education
Collins, Jackie, 423:1
Commerce/business/industry/finance, pp. 34-50
  advertising, 50:4
    See also Politics
  banking:
    deregulation, 43:4
    failures, 43:4
    management, 37:6
    savings and loans, 44:5
  Big Business, 45:3
  buyer beware, 49:2
  capital-gains taxes, 37:2, 92:6, 99:5, 100:3
  civil-rights aspect, 31:4
  competition, 45:3
    foreign, 34:1, 38:3, 91:4, 92:3, 105:4, 167:4
      education aspect, 121:1, 128:5, 132:1
  Consumer Product Safety Commission, U.S., 187:4
  consumers, 37:4
  deal-making, 39:3
  debt, foreign, 47:4
  designer labels, 35:3
  diversification, 36:3
  education/schools aspect, 50:2, 118:4, 119:1, 121:1, 128:5, 132:1
    college/university aspect, 42:3
  ethics, 42:3
  executives/management/CEOs, 36:3

Commerce/business/industry/finance *(continued)*
  executives/management/CEOs *(continued)*
    bureaucrats, 49:3
    departure of, 48:5
    ethics, 42:3
    losing jobs, 96:1
      golden parachutes, 34:3, 103:5
    moving around, 43:5
    paid, over-, 34:4
    perks, 37:5
    selfishness, 35:2
  Federal Reserve Board (U.S.), 40:4, 45:2, 92:4, 92:7
  foreign investment in U.S.—*see* investment, *this section*
  government/regulation aspect, 38:4, 40:3, 41:3, 49:2
    See also Economy: government
  greed, corporate, 48:6
  interest rates, 48:4, 92:2, 99:2, 105:1, 107:3, 108:5, 113:4
  investment, 37:3, 38:6, 96:6, 112:3
    foreign investment/ownership in U.S., 37:1, 38:1, 38:5, 39:2, 44:4, 45:1, 47:4, 49:1, 49:4, 50:1, 107:4, 109:2, 111:4
  involvement outside work-place, corporate, 106:4
  language, knowledge of foreign, 50:2
  loans, character, 36:1
  loyalty to America, 48:6
  market forces, 41:6
  medicine/health aspect:
    AIDS, 425:5, 431:5, 434:1
    insurance, employee, 426:4, 427:5
    smoking, attitude toward, 425:5
  mergers/takeovers/raiders, 34:5, 35:2, 38:3, 38:5, 46:4
    antitrust, 37:4, 47:3, 50:6
    leveraged buyouts (LBOs), 36:3, 43:1, 47:2
  monetarism, 102:4
  monetary policy, 92:7
  monetary system:
    dollar, U.S., 42:4, 44:6, 105:4
    foreign-exchange trading, 41:5
    gold standard, 90:4
  Number 1, U.S. as, 34:1, 37:3
  private/public financial risk, 36:2
  profit as sole goal, 41:2
  psychological product satisfaction, 35:3
  quality aspect—*see* Economy
  retailing, 41:1
  risk-taking, 37:2
  stability, 108:3

Commerce/business/industry/finance *(continued)*
  stock/securities market/Wall Street, 38:5, 44:3,
    47:5
    a casino, 34:2, 34:3
    clearing system, unified, 35:4
    computer-directed trading, 44:1
    crash of 1987, 40:2, 45:5, 47:1
    greed, 177:3
    insider trading, 222:4
    Japanese influence, 48:4
    junk bonds, 43:1
    a mirror, 39:4
    non-productive, 41:7
    program trading, 46:3
    short-term/long-term aspect, 34:2, 47:1
    small investor, 34:2, 47:1
    sounds of, 42:5
    speculating, 34:3
  taxes:
    capital-gains, 37:2, 92:6, 99:5, 100:3
    corporate, 108:4
  tobacco companies, 431:1
  volatility of markets, 40:1
  women aspect, 23:1, 23:4
  world market, 50:2
Commitment, 477:3
Committees, 473:2
Common Cause, 197:5
Common sense, 14:4
Communism/socialism, 97:1, 145:2, 149:1, 149:2,
  149:3, 150:2, 151:5, 158:1, 159:4, 163:4,
  164:1, 164:2, 164:5, 171:5, 412:2, 480:2,
  481:3
  See also Marx, Karl, *and specific countries*
Confidence, self-, 475:3
Conformity, non-, 18:5
Congress, U.S.:
  accountability, 188:3
  civil-rights, 31:2, 32:3
  committee chairmen, 184:1
  constituencies, narrow, 184:5
  constituents, 195:4
  Constitution (U.S.) aspect, 179:5
  contributors, financial, 195:4
  decision-making, 176:3
  defense/military aspect, 70:1, 72:1, 82:1, 86:3,
    87:6, 143:3, 170:5
  Democratic Party aspect, 224:5
  economy, 91:2, 93:2, 93:3, 94:1, 95:2, 104:2,
    106:2, 107:1, 109:3 111:1, 113:2
  environment aspect, 137:4, 137:7
  ethics, 177:1, 188:1, 189:5
  evaluating proposals, 190:4
  followers, 176:3

Congress, U.S. *(continued)*
  foreign affairs, 143:3, 144:1, 160:5, 160:6,
    170:5, 176:2
  intelligence/CIA aspect, 172:3
  law-making, 174:2
    See also Government
  members:
    being a, 180:4, 190:1
    election, re-, 184:5
    honoraria, 197:5, 198:1
    important, wanting to be, 197:2
    laws, immunity from, 197:7
    lobbying after leaving office, 188:2, 196:4
    salary, 197:5
    trained/educated, better, 197:2
  powers, 179:5
  Presidency (U.S.) aspect, 72:1, 82:1, 160:6,
    170:5, 179:5, 180:1, 186:3, 190:4, 194:1
    being in Congress, 176:2
  Social Security, 254:2
  special interests, 176:3, 193:1, 197:5, 198:1,
    212:4
  spending, 186:2
  television coverage of, 175:5, 194:5
  trust, public, 193:1
  Washington, D.C., aspect, 184:3
  women aspect, 32:5
  House of Representatives:
    debate, 187:2
    Democratic Party aspect, 188:5, 252:2
    incumbents, 251:4
    legislative aspect, 179:4
    productivity, declining, 188:5
    Republican Party aspect, 187:1, 235:4, 244:3
    Senate compared with, 179:4, 182:3, 187:2,
      193:2
    Speaker, 195:2, 226:3
    whips through bills, 193:2
  Senate:
    analytical aspect, 179:4
    consensus, 197:1
    debate, 181:4, 187:2, 190:7, 193:2, 194:2
    Democratic Party aspect, 245:4, 252:2
    discourtesy, 181:4
    filibusters, 194:2
    House compared with, 179:4, 182:3, 187:2,
      193:2
    policy-making, 197:1
    relations with other Senators, 191:2
    Republican Party aspect, 235:4
    running for, 207:3, 238:3
    Senator, being a, 176:1, 179:4, 182:3, 193:2
    television coverage of, 175:5
Connolly, Bill, 471:7

Conservatism—*see* Politics
Constitution, U.S., 71:6, 102:6, 192:1, 481:6
  apart, sets U.S., 16:1
  Bill of Rights, 226:4
  Congress/Presidency aspect, 179:5
  judges' interpreting of, 200:1
  separation of powers, 189:3
  Amendments:
    First, 408:1, 411:6
    Second, 63:5
Cooperation, 474:5, 475:2, 475:6, 477:1, 481:2
Copland, Aaron, 460:4
Costa Rica:
  Arias, Oscar, Nicaraguan peace plan, 284:3,
    292:1, 294:2
  Communism, 291:1
  economy, 282:3, 283:3
  education, 282:3
  social welfare, 282:3
  foreign relations/policy with:
    Nicaragua, 301:4
    See also Arias, Oscar, *this section*
    Panama, 298:1
    U.S., 291:1
Courts—*see* Judiciary
Creativity, 472:4, 480:7
Crime/law enforcement, pp. 51-67
  ACLU aspect, 52:6, 57:7, 63:6
  Bush, George, aspect, 63:6
  capital punishment/death penalty, 56:3, 57:1,
    59:3, 61:6, 63:4, 66:4, 203:4
    See also drugs, *this section*
  civil-rights/black aspect, 51:1, 54:1
  criminal-justice system, 63:1
  drugs, illegal, 51:4, 56:1, 56:4, 59:6, 60:5, 61:3,
    62:6, 67:3, 249:4, 267:3
    capital-punishment aspect, 53:3, 53:5, 55:3,
      57:4, 59:4, 62:3, 64:1, 64:4
    cocaine/crack, 57:2, 57:5, 60:5, 61:2, 65:1, 66:1
    criminal activity, involvement in, 62:5, 65:2
    "czar," government/one-man, 51:3, 55:6
    demand/supply aspect, 51:4, 52:2, 59:7,
      60:4, 61:1, 62:3, 66:1, 67:2
    heroin, 55:5, 57:2, 60:5
    international aspect, 56:5, 57:8, 58:4
    legislation, 51:2, 53:4, 55:5, 57:5, 58:3,
      61:5, 65:1, 65:4
    liberty aspect, 60:6
    marijuana, 53:4, 57:2, 64:2
    market, knowledge of, 61:2
    Mexico, 304:1
    military, use of, 54:6, 55:2, 57:3, 64:1
    Nicaraguan contras, 56:2
    Panama, 56:2

Crime/law enforcement *(continued)*
  drugs, illegal *(continued)*
    source, destroy at, 52:4
    South America, 66:1
    State Dept. (U.S.) aspect, 57:8
    terrorists, dealers are, 52:3
    testing, 52:5
      government employees, 194:3, 195:6
    users, 57:2, 64:2, 66:5
    values, 53:4, 56:2
    "victimless," 64:3
    in workplace, 64:3
    youth aspect, 57:6
    See also Medicine: drug abuse
  Dukakis, Michael S., aspect, 53:1, 53:3, 57:7,
    63:6, 64:1, 244:6
  education aspect, 51:1, 60:2
  Federal Bureau of Investigation, U.S. (FBI)
    289:4, 418:3
    women/minorities aspect, 65:5
  gun control, 54:3, 55:1, 55:4, 55:7, 60:1, 60:5,
    61:4, 63:5, 65:6
    National Rifle Association (NRA), 63:2,
      63:6
  honesty, 60:3
  international aspect, 59:5, 63:3
    See also drugs, *this section*
  judges, 53:2, 53:6, 59:6
  liberalism/left aspect, 53:6, 54:2
  medical aspect, 51:1
  Miranda rule, 62:2
  neighborhood aspect, 67:4
  older offenders, 51:1
  organized crime, 54:5, 58:2, 104:4, 202:3
  police, 53:2, 62:2
  prisons, 60:2, 65:3
    cost, 66:3
    crowding, 51:1, 52:1, 54:4, 62:4, 66:6
    furloughs/week-end passes, 53:1, 53:3,
      53:6, 58:1, 59:2, 63:6 67:1, 224:2, 244:6
    rehabilitation, 59:1
  Prohibition, 61:4
  rights of criminals, 52:6, 53:2
  sentencing, 53:3, 53:6, 59:6, 201:5
  sexual violence, 62:1
  State Dept. (U.S.) aspect, 59:5
  unions, labor, 54:5, 58:2, 104:4, 185:6, 202:3
  vengeance against criminals, 59:4
  victims, 52:6, 53:6, 54:1, 64:4, 66:3
  violent crime, 54:1, 56:3, 58:1, 67:2
  welfare aspect, 60:2
  white-collar, 176:6
  women, sexual crimes against, 62:1
Crocker, Chester, 278:5

Cuba:
    armed population, 288:1
    Castro, Fidel, 155:5, 286:5, 293:6, 301:2, 302:6
    Communism, 286:5, 291:1, 302:6
    defense/military:
        missiles, 288:2
    freedom, 286:5, 302:6
    human rights, 293:6
    one-party system, 288:3
    foreign relations/policy with:
        Angola, 272:5, 273:4, 278:5
        El Salvador, 285:2
        Nicaragua, 158:1, 296:4, 302:4
        Soviet Union, 151:1, 288:2
        U.S., 14:5, 151:1, 159:4, 286:5, 288:2,
            289:3, 291:1, 301:2, 302:6, 303:4
Cuellar, Mike, 506:3
Culture—*see* Arts
Cuomo, Mario M., 407:4
Cyprus, 346:6, 354:5
Czechoslovakia:
    Communism, 149:1, 334:5
    democracy, 334:5, 342:1, 350:3
    economy, 341:7
    reform, 350:3
    foreign relations/policy with:
        Soviet Union, 334:5, 350:3

D

Dana, John Cotton, 402:6
Dance/ballet, 401:1, 402:5, 463:2, 464:1, 464:3,
    464:5, 465:5 466:4, 466:6, 467:3, 467:4
    AIDS aspect, 468:4
    Denmark, 463:4
    drug abuse, 468:4
    elitist, 463:4
    Joffrey Ballet, 463:4
    New York City Ballet, 463:4
    Soviet Union, 463:4
    U.S., 463:4
Dante Alighieri, 416:4, 472:3
Da Vinci, Leonardo, 456:6
Death, 470:1, 480:3, 480:5
Decisions, making, 478:2
Defense/military, pp. 68-89
    absense of arms, 394:7
    Air Force, U.S.—*see* bombers, *this section*
    air shows, public, 73:1
    aircraft carriers, 77:2, 80:2, 84:3
    anti-ballistic missile (ABM)—*see* defensive
        systems, *this section*
    arms control/disarmament/arms race, 68:3, 71:1,
        71:2, 73:3, 74:4, 75:5, 76:3, 78:1, 82:2, 82:3,
        84:3, 87:2, 147:2, 147:5, 158:1, 218:2, 393:4

Defense/military *(continued)*
    arms control/disarmament/arms race *(continued)*
        agreement for agreement's sake, 83:2, 155:4
        INF treaty, 69:4, 71:3, 73:2, 73:4, 79:4,
            83:8, 84:5, 85:2, 86:1, 86:2, 86:5, 86:6,
            88:2, 164:7, 341:5, 343:3, 343:4, 343:5,
            350:2, 351:6
        SALT II, 88:2
        START, 69:4, 74:2, 81:1, 86:1, 146:4
        verification/inspection, 69:4, 77:4, 84:5,
            85:2, 86:1, 86:6, 87:4
        See also Soviet Union: defense
    arms sales/trafficking, 87:1, 157:5, 366:4
        See also Iran: U.S.; Saudi Arabia: defense
    balance of power/parity/superiority, 77:5, 78:2,
        85:4, 92:3, 158:4
    bases, overseas, 69:2, 89:3
    bases, unneeded, 85:1
    "bean count," 77:5
    bombers:
        B-1, 69:6, 74:1, 84:3
        B-52, 74:1
        Stealth, 68:4, 69:6, 71:1, 76:3, 76:5
    Bush, George, aspect, 76:4, 76:5
    careerism, 78:5
    chemical weapons, 71:5, 75:5, 81:2, 82:6, 84:2,
        87:2, 395:1
        biological weapons, 84:4, 87:3
    choice between rifles and bread, 68:5
    comparable to Soviet equipment, U.S. equip-
        ment is, 68:3
    Congress (U.S.) aspect, 70:1, 72:1, 82:1, 86:3,
        87:6, 143:3, 170:5
    Constitutional protection for members, 68:1
    conventional arms, 70:2, 73:6, 75:2, 75:3, 76:5,
        77:4, 85:4, 99:3
        See also Europe: defense
    Defense, U.S. Secretary of, 75:5, 77:3, 81:1,
        89:1, 161:3
    Defensive systems, 80:1
        anti-ballistic missile (ABM), 75:1, 76:2
        space defense/strategic defense initiative
            (SDI)/"Star Wars," 69:3, 69:5, 70:3,
            70:4, 75:1, 75:3, 76:2, 76:3, 76:5, 77:2,
            82:4, 83:3, 83:4, 83:6, 83:8, 84:3, 85:3,
            122:3, 218:2, 494:4, 495:5
    Democratic Party (U.S.) aspect, 70:3, 73:6,
        79:3
    deterrence, 68:4, 70:2, 74:1, 74:2, 75:3, 76:1,
        76:3, 76:5, 77:1, 79:1, 82:2, 82:3
    development of new systems, 76:1
    discipline, 68:1, 73:1
    distrust among nations, 83:7
    draft, 79:5

Defense/military *(continued)*
  drugs, military used to fight, 54:6, 55:2, 57:3, 64:1
  Dukakis, Michael S., aspect, 69:5, 70:2, 71:1, 227:1, 227:3
  duplication among services, 88:4
  education/Army War College, 88:3
  greed, 74:3
  ideas vs. arsenals, 80:3
  industry, 86:3
    complex, military-industrial, 82:4
    contracts/procurement system, 83:1, 87:6
      fraud/scandal, 68:6, 70:1, 75:4, 76:4, 84:1, 202:3
      former Defense Department workers, employment of, 72:4, 76:4
  interrelationship between arsenals, 78:3
  leadership, 73:5, 89:1
  liberalism/left aspect, 69:6, 84:3
  loyalty/obedience, 81:6
  management, mis-, 75:1
  manpower-intensive, 88:1
  Marine Corps, U.S, 78:5, 170:5
  missiles:
    cruise, 76:3, 76:5, 146:1, 146:2
    Midgetman, 69:6, 77:2, 80:2
    MX, 69:5, 69:6, 76:5, 77:2
    Pershing, 146:1, 146:2
    Trident 2, 76:3
  modernization of forces, 76:3, 77:1
  morale, 73:1
  National Guard, U.S./Quayle, Dan, aspect, 209:2, 214:2, 235:3, 242:4
  Navy, U.S.:
    size of, 69:6, 88:5, 89:2
    See also aircraft carriers, *this section*
  nuclear aspect, 70:2, 72:2, 78:2, 79:2, 85:4, 153:5, 394:1, 395:2
    first strike/use, 75:2, 78:3, 78:4, 80:4, 83:4
    freeze, 71:1, 71:4, 83:8
    proliferation, 158:2
    testing/test ban, 69:5, 77:4, 151:1
  opposition to weapons systems, 69:5, 69:6, 71:1, 84:3
  overseas, U.S. forces, 157:5, 170:5
  policy-making, 73:5
  power/force, use of, 146:3, 150:2, 154:5, 155:2, 155:5, 171:1, 302:3, 395:2
  Presidency (U.S.) aspect, 72:1, 82:1
    Commander-in-Chief, 71:6, 143:3
    War Powers Act/Resolution, 82:1, 82:5, 170:5
  readiness, 81:5
  reform, 81:1, 81:3

Defense/military *(continued)*
  regulation of, 70:1
  Republican Party (U.S.) aspect, 76:4
  science/technology aspect, 495:5
    space aspect, 69:3, 78:1, 496:5
      See also defensive systems, *this section*
  shortages, equipment, 75:3
  space—*see* defensive systems, *this section;* science, *this section*
  spending/budget/cost, 68:4, 68:5, 69:2, 69:3, 73:5, 74:3, 75:1, 75:4, 77:1, 77:2, 77:3, 78:6, 79:3, 80:2, 80:5, 81:3, 82:4, 85:1, 85:5, 86:3, 86:4, 87:6, 88:1, 89:2, 96:5, 99:3, 100:2, 104:3, 113:3, 114:3, 122:3, 126:2
    cuts, 145:6, 168:5
  strong defense, 381:3
    strength, peace through, 69:6, 71:6, 158:3
  Third World, 70:4, 87:1, 387:5
  War Powers Act/Resolution—*see* Presidency, *this section*
  weakness, 145:5
  women aspect, 79:5
  See also specific countries and areas
De Gaulle, Charles, 353:5, 359:4
Del Monaco, Mario, 456:5
Democracy/freedom, 13:2, 13:3, 13:5, 16:3, 17:2, 17:4, 17:5, 18:1, 27:2, 102:5, 144:6, 150:2, 159:5, 162:4, 163:6, 164:6, 168:1, 170:2, 175:7, 179:1, 192:2, 192:3, 231:1, 394:3, 411:2, 476:5, 478:4, 478:5, 478:6, 481:6, 482:3, 484:4
Democratic Party, U.S., 222:4, 223:2
  abortion, 230:1
  American dream, 222:3
  caucuses, 240:5
  change, 245:1
  child care, 253:7, 260:6
  civil-rights/black aspect, 21:2, 22:2, 24:3, 206:6, 211:4, 219:2, 220:2, 230:4, 233:2
    See also Jackson, Jesse L., *this section*
  Congress (U.S.) aspect, 224:5
    House of Representatives aspect, 188:5, 252:2
    Senate aspect, 245:4, 252:2
  defense/military, 70:3, 73:6, 79:3
  earlier periods, 227:5
  economy, 93:6, 93:7, 94:3, 102:3, 104:3, 104:5, 105:2, 108:6, 110:6, 111:3, 114:1, 207:3, 241:4, 244:5
  election (1988), 15:1, 217:5, 218:1, 218:2, 222:1, 229:5, 230:3
  environment aspect, 133:6
  foreign affairs, 149:3, 149:4, 151:3, 207:3

Democratic Party *(continued)*
future, handling of, 225:5
government, privatization of, 181:1
heart and soul, 226:6
homosexual aspect, 230:1
ideology, 208:5
inclusion, politics of, 208:4
Jackson, Jesse L., aspect, 24:3, 207:1, 210:3, 211:3, 211:4, 219:2, 221:5, 222:2, 227:4, 230:4, 250:7, 251:5, 251:6, 252:1, 252:3
Jewish aspect, 228:3
leadership, 215:5
liberalism/left aspect, 215:5, 242:1, 242:2, 251:5
lost sheep, going after, 252:4
McGovern, George S., aspect, 238:2
Nicaragua, 281:1, 291:1, 300:3
prayer, school, 230:1
Presidency (U.S.) aspect, 207:3, 241:4, 244:5, 246:5, 249:5, 250:6
rank and file, 215:5
Reagan Democrats, 233:3
Republican Party aspect, 226:2
Roosevelt, Franklin D., aspect, 221:3
roots, return to, 231:3
saying nothing, 233:6
social welfare, 253:3, 257:3
Social Security, 261:2
South, the, 246:3, 252:3
South Africa, 275:1
united, 208:5, 209:1
vibrant/competitive, 235:4
weakness, 247:4
Yuppie aspect, 226:2
Denmark, 463:4
Dependence, inter-, 474:2
Dickens, Charles, 415:6
Discourse, public, 482:3
Dixon, Jeane, 196:3
Doctors—*see* Medicine
Dole, Robert J., 210:1, 220:1, 247:2
Donahue, Phil, 439:4
Dooley, Vince, 510:7
Dostoyevsky, Feodor, 418:4, 420:4
Douglas, Kirk, 444:2
Drugs—*see* Americas; Bush, George; Crime; Football; Foreign Affairs: intelligence; Labor; Medicine; Nicaragua; Panama; Republican Party; Sports; Transportation: railroads
Dukakis, Michael S., 209:1, 209:3, 210:2, 213:3, 215:2, 216:1, 217:4, 231:2, 231:4, 231:5, 231:6, 232:1, 241:4, 249:1, 249:2
abortion, 30:1, 244:6
ACLU, 214:3, 215:3, 221:2, 226:4

Dukakis, Michael S. *(continued)*
attributes, 232:2
blacks aspect, 24:3, 233:4
broad constituency, 216:4
campaign style/tactics, 211:2, 213:4, 217:6
negative campaign, 216:2, 233:3, 238:4, 241:3
charisma, 217:2
conservative aspect, 223:6
crime, 53:1, 53:3, 57:7, 63:6, 64:1
prison furloughs, 53:1, 53:3, 63:6, 224:2, 244:6
defense/military, 69:5, 70:2, 71:1, 227:1, 227:3
dullness, 175:6
economy, 90:4, 93:4, 93:5, 93:7, 94:1, 94:3, 94:4, 95:1, 95:3, 95:4, 104:5, 107:1, 109:1, 110:4, 111:6, 114:5
investment, foreign, 37:1
spending, 227:3
taxes, 37:2, 227:3
education, 120:3
environment, 134:2, 139:1
farm policy/program, 36:4, 45:4
foreign affairs, 144:3, 144:5, 145:2, 145:3, 145:4, 149:3, 149:4, 155:3, 157:1, 157:5, 158:2, 166:7, 227:1
issues/ideology/competence, 213:1, 213:5, 219:5
Jackson, Jesse L., aspect, 212:5, 227:2
leadership, 217:5
liberalism, 206:5, 213:1, 215:3, 223:6, 224:1, 244:1, 244:6, 245:3, 247:4
likability, 229:5
Nicaragua, 300:3, 301:5
patriotism, 215:1, 219:4, 223:2, 226:4, 232:5
Pledge of Allegiance, 162:5, 208:3, 214:3, 215:1, 217:1, 219:4, 223:1, 244:6
prayer, school, 244:6
qualifications/experience, 218:3, 227:1, 241:3
unknown quantity, 217:6
vanilla, pure, 211:3
Duke University, 26:6, 125:5
Duvalier, Jean-Claude—*see* Haiti

E

Eastman, George, 48:5
Ebert, Roger, 472:4
Economy, pp. 90-116
bankruptcy personal, 115:4
blacks aspect, 26:6, 115:4
borrowing, 93:1, 100:3, 101:3, 107:4, 209:1
budget/spending, government, 91:2, 92:1, 92:5, 93:2, 93:3, 94:3, 94:5, 97:3, 99:3, 100:2, 106:2, 108:1, 109:3, 110:1, 110:4, 111:1,

Economy *(continued)*
 budget/spending, government *(continued)*
   111:6, 113:1, 113:2, 113:3, 114:2, 114:3,
   193:1, 227:3
   balanced budget, 96:5, 99:1, 114:3, 223:6,
    257:4
    amendment, 111:1
   deficit/debt, 39:2, 49:1, 50:1, 90:2, 90:4,
    91:1, 92:1, 92:2, 92:4, 92:5, 93:3, 94:5,
    95:2, 95:5, 96:6, 97:2, 97:3, 97:4, 98:4,
    99:2, 99:5, 100:2, 100:3, 101:4, 101:5,
    102:1, 102:3, 102:4, 103:1, 104:3,
    105:2, 106:2, 107:1, 107:3, 107:4,
    108:1, 109:3, 110:1, 110:2, 111:1,
    111:4, 112:3, 114:2, 121:2, 193:3,
    200:6, 249:4, 327:4
   entitlements—*see* Social welfare
   process, Federal budget, 181:5
   surplus, 101:3
  Congress (U.S.) aspect, 91:2, 93:2, 93:3, 94:1,
   95:2, 104:2, 106:2, 107:1, 109:3, 111:1,
   113:2
  consolidation, 114:1
  credit cards, 115:4
  decline, 98:2
  Democratic Party (U.S.) aspect, 93:6, 93:7,
   94:3, 102:3, 104:3, 104:5, 105:2, 108:6,
   110:6, 111:3, 114:1, 207:3, 241:4, 244:5
  difference, emphasizing, 94:4
  Dukakis, Michael S., aspect, 37:1, 90:4, 93:4,
   93:5, 93:7, 94:1, 94:3, 94:4, 95:1, 95:3,
   95:4, 104:5, 107:1, 109:1, 110:4, 111:6,
   114:5
  See also Dukakis, Michael S.
  education aspect, 117:1, 119:6
  egalitarianism, 90:1
  entrepreneurship, 95:4, 110:5, 250:5
  environment aspect, 137:4, 140:2
  foreign-affairs aspect, 168:5, 169:2
  government aspect, 106:1, 113:2
   regulation, 93:7, 94:3, 102:4, 109:5, 110:4,
    110:5
    See also Commerce: government
   See also budget, *this section*
  growth/strength/expansion, 14:1, 48:2, 92:4,
   95:4, 96:2, 96:6, 101:5, 102:1, 107:6,
   108:3, 108:5, 109:5, 110:3, 110:6, 111:3,
   113:4, 213:2, 215:3
  home-buying, 105:3, 116:2
  inflation, 47:4, 48:2, 92:2, 93:6, 94:5, 102:4,
   107:6, 113:4, 220:3
  Japan-U.S. aspect, 48:4, 311:2
  liberalism/left aspect, 94:3, 102:3, 104:5,
   109:1, 110:4, 111:1, 111:3

Economy *(continued)*
 middle class, 95:3
  blacks, 26:6
 monetary policy—*see* Commerce
 Presidency (U.S.) aspect, 93:2, 94:5, 111:1
 prices, 90:1
 privatization—*see* Government
 productivity, 39:3, 90:2, 90:3, 96:6, 106:4,
  111:3
 prosperity, illusion of, 92:2
 purpose/meaning, 14:1
 quality of product, 38:3, 50:3, 103:3, 115:3
 Reaganomics, 96:5, 100:7
 recession/depression, 47:4, 91:3, 107:6, 108:6,
  113:2, 241:4
 recovery, 93:6, 93:7, 108:3, 110:3, 255:4
 Republican Party (U.S.) aspect, 99:2, 102:3,
  105:2, 110:6, 111:5
 rich/poor aspect, 94:4, 99:3, 99:5, 100:2,
  100:3, 104:1, 107:2, 108:4, 111:2
 savings, 90:2, 96:6, 101:3, 115:4
 science/technology aspect, 492:1
 service/manufacturing sector, 103:3, 107:5,
  113:5, 115:1
 standard of living, 34:1, 90:2, 92:1, 98:5, 105:5,
  115:1, 117:1, 148:6
 superiority, U.S., 14:5, 105:4, 115:1
 supply and demand, 90:1
 supply-side, 102:4
 violence, economic, 104:1
 wealth concentration, 91:3
 See also Commerce; Bush, George; Dukakis,
  Michael S.; Labor; Taxes; Trade, foreign;
  and specific countries and areas
Education/schools, pp. 117:132, 249:4
 accountability, 120:1, 123:1, 123:3, 127:5
 arts aspect, 401:1, 402:2
 basics, 118:4, 118:5, 119:1, 125:6
 blacks/minorities aspect, 127:4, 131:4
  Federal aid and discrimination, 19:5
  See also college, *this section*
 Bush, George, aspect, 118:7
 choice in, 120:2
 citizens, creation of good, 124:2
 class size, 122:5
 commerce/business aspect, 50:2, 118:4, 119:1
  competition, international, 121:1, 128:5,
   132:1
 composition/writing courses, 128:4
 creativity, fostering of, 119:4
 crime aspect, 51:1, 60:2
 deficit, educational, 121:2
 democracy, not a, 121:3
 discipline, 120:5

Education/schools *(continued)*
dispensable, not, 126:2
Dukakis, Michael S., aspect, 120:3
economy aspect, 117:1
  employment/jobs, 96:4, 119:6, 126:5, 127:1
is empowerment, 123:5
geography, teaching of, 125:4
goals, setting of, 120:1
golden thread of, 119:2
government aspect:
  Federal/state, 19:5, 120:1, 123:3, 124:3, 125:6
  spending/budget, 95:5, 113:3, 120:2, 121:4, 125:6, 126:2, 132:1
guidance counselors, 131:1
high schools, 125:6, 126:5, 127:1, 128:5
history books, 128:6
ideas, transmission of, 129:3
illiteracy/reading, 117:1, 118:4, 118:5, 119:2, 122:1, 125:6 126:5, 129:5
importance of, 124:4
vs. information, 124:2
Japan, 117:1, 125:6
key to future, 125:6
kindergarten, 132:2
learning aspect, 128;2
length of school year, 117:1
liberal arts, 126:1, 402:5
literature/books aspect, 118:5, 119:2
  history books, 128:6
  See also illiteracy/reading, *this section*
local school boards, 130:5
minority culture, study of, 121:3, 126:4
mobility, intellectual, 131:3
music aspect, 401:1, 457:6
"National Merit School," 120:1
New York City schools, 130:2
outcome of product, 123:1
Palestinians aspect, 369:4
parents/home/family aspect, 117:2, 117:5, 118:2, 121:5, 125:3, 131:1
performance of schools, 118:1
poverty, answer to, 119:5, 120:2
private schools, 122:5
quality/excellence, 15:4, 118:7, 125:6, 126:3, 127:5
reading—*see* illiteracy, *this section*
reform, 118:1, 123:1, 123:3, 124:2, 124:3, 129:2
religion aspect:
  prayer in schools, 230:1, 244:6, 484:1
  teaching of, 483:5
Republican Party (U.S.) aspect, 118:6

Education/schools *(continued)*
research, education, 117:4
science/technology, courses in, 126:1, 491:5
spending on—*see* government, *this section*
stage/theatre aspect, 401:1
Star Schools, 122:3
students, 127:3
  background, 118:2
  black/minority, 123:2
  bonding to idea of education, 121:5
  college, 127:3
  desire to learn, 124:5
  disruption by, 118:3
  dropouts, 109:4, 117:6, 119:1, 128:5
  handicaps, 124:5
  learning ability, 129:2
  motivation, 117:2, 131:5
  Pledge of Allegiance, 17:6
  promoting failure/automatic passing, 125:1, 126:5
  slow-learners, 127:2
  teacher demands on, 118:3
  useful subjects, learning of, 119:4
success in valuing of, 124:4
teaching/teachers, 17:6
  blue-collar aspect, 121:6
  dedication, 120:1
  demands on students, 118:3
  experience, 130:4
  incentives, 127:5
  incompetence, 119:3
  motivating students, 131:5
  pay/salary, 120:1, 121:4, 123:4, 125:6, 126:3, 128:5
  perception of profession, 126:3
  quality, 118:5
  standards, 128:5
  tenure, 130:1
  value/importance of, 117:3, 125:2, 125:3
  women on faculty, 23:4
  writing compared with, 416:1
  young teachers, 130:4
uneducated citizenry, 123:5
urban/cities aspect, 119:6
values aspect, 53:4, 119:5, 162:5
valuing education, 117:2
women on faculty, 23:4
college/university/higher education, 125:6, 126:1
  arts aspect, 399:4
  authoritative, 130:3
  baseball, 508:3, 515:2
  basketball—*see* Basketball
  "the best," 128:1

Education/schools *(continued)*
  college/university/higher education (continued)
    blacks/minorities aspect, 27:3, 28:4, 128:3, 131:4
    choice of, 131:2
    co-ed, 123:6
    Commerce/business aspect, 42:3
    contemplation, places of, 130:3
    dissent/disagreement/gentility, 124:1
    education, schools of, 117:3
    elite/majority aspect, 131:3
    football, 127:6, 129:4, 504:6, 506:4, 507:3, 515:2
    hierarchy of courses, 117:3
    Ivy League schools, 125:5
    populism, 121:3
    regional schools, 125:5
    research universities, 129:1
    Soviet-U.S. moral-equivalency aspect, 168:3
    students, 127:3
    tuition/costs/affordability, 98:1, 116:2, 120:5, 122:2, 128:3
      aid/loans, student, 118:6, 118:7, 120:4, 122:3
      salary-withholding payback, 120:3, 122:4
      College Savings Bond, 120:1
    waste, empires of, 130:1
    women's, 123:6
    See also specific colleges and universities
Egypt, 384:3
  Mubarak, Hosni, 383:5, 389:4
  women, 31:5
  foreign relations/policy with:
    Israel, 383:5, 391:1
    Syria, 389:4
Eisenhower, Dwight D., 77:4, 235:5, 241:3
Elections—*see* Politics; *and specific countries*
Elizabeth I, Queen, 340:3
Elizabeth II, Queen, 487:5
Ellington, Duke, 460:4
Ellison, Pervis, 516:2
El Salvador:
  Communism/socialism, 285:2, 307:2
  democracy/elections, 285:2, 307:3
  Duarte, Jose Napoleon, illness, 291:3
  economy, 307:2
  killings, political, 287:4
  rebels/FMLN/insurgency, 285:2, 290:2, 307:2
  foreign relations/policy with:
    Cuba, 285:2
    Nicaragua, 285:2
    Soviet Union, 285:2

El Salvador *(continued)*
  foreign relations/policy with: (continued)
    U.S., 290:2, 307:2, 307:3
Emotions, 473:4, 474:1
Employment—*see* Labor
Energy:
  coal, 134:3, 139:3
  consumption, 135:4
  fossil fuel, 139:3
  glut, 133:5
  methanol, 134:1
  Nuclear power, 134:3, 135:3, 139:3
    accidents/Chernobyl, 136:2, 139:5, 335:1
  oil:
    domestic production, 134:4, 135:4
    drilling, 133:5, 134:1, 134:4
    environmental aspect, 133:5, 134:4
    foreign/imports, dependence on, 133:5, 134:1, 134:3, 135:4
    OPEC, 135:4
    prices, 133:5, 135:4
    Saudi Arabia, 376:4
  Persian Gulf aspect, 363:5
  prices, 133:5, 135:4
  solar, 489:4
England—*see* United Kingdom
Environment/pollution, 18:3, pp. 133-141
  accomplishments, 140:4
  acid rain, 136:4, 138:5, 139:6, 140:4, 140:5, 284:1
  after-the-fact repair, 133:4
  agriculture/farming aspect, 137:7
  air, 18:3, 133:1, 135:2, 137:4, 137:7, 138:2, 139:2, 140:1
  animals/wildlife, 138:1
  architecture, modern, 134:6
  awareness aspect, 133:3
  Bolivia, 140:2
  climate, 135:2
    ozone depletion, 139:6
    warming/"greenhouse effect," 137:4, 137:7, 138:2, 140:4
  color aspect, 137:2
  Congress (U.S.) aspect, 137:4, 137:7
  conservation, 134:5, 140:2
  crisis mentality, 139:4
  Democratic Party (U.S.) aspect, 133:6
  Dukakis, Michael S., aspect, 134:2, 139:1
  economic aspect, 137:4, 140:2
  flowers/plants/trees, 137:1, 137:2, 138:1
  forests, 133:2, 137:7
    rain forests, 133:1, 140:2
  garbage, 140:3
  individual responsibility, 139:2

Environment/pollution *(continued)*
land, unspoiled, 133:6
landscape, nation's, 137:1
life-support system, 138:1
movement, environmental, 137:5
national-security aspect, 133:4, 134:3
oil drilling, 133:5, 134:1, 134:4
one planet, 137:3
Parks, National, 138:3
population aspect, 136:1, 148:4, 489:4
recreation, 134:5
Republican Party (U.S.) aspect, 133:6
resources, consumption of, 136:5, 140:2
response, effective, 133:3
science/technology aspect, 137:5
space aspect, 136:3
Soviet Union, 136:3, 172:5, 357:3
Third World, 135:2
United Nations (UN) aspect, 136:3
waste, toxic, 139:6
water/oceans, 18:3, 135:1, 135:5, 139:6
dumping/sewage, 134:2, 137:6, 138:2, 138:4, 139:1
Equality, 476:5
Estonia—*see* Soviet Union
aEthics—*see* Commerce; Government; Law: lawyers; Politics; Presidency, U.S.
Ethiopia:
civil war/rebellion, 275:6, 277:2, 277:3
Communism, 273:3
Eritrea, 275:6
famine/starvation, 273:3, 275:6, 277:2, 277:3
resettlement of peasants, 276:1
terrorism, 168:4
foreign relations/policy with:
Soviet Union, 158:1, 277:2
U.S., 168:4
Europe, pp. 329-357
Berlin Wall, 333:6, 345:3
cooperation, internal, 346:3
defense/military, 77:4, 80:4, 338:2
conventional aspect, 333:2, 335:1, 341:5, 341:6, 343:3, 349:5, 350:2
INF treaty—*see* Defense: arms control
missiles, 146:1
NATO/Atlantic Alliance, 73:4, 77:5, 77:6, 78:4, 83:5, 88:2, 146:2, 333:2, 333:3, 333:4, 336:1, 343:3, 343:4, 343:5, 346:2, 348:4, 348:5, 353:2, 354:2, 356:5, 394:2
nuclear aspect, 333:2, 335:1, 341:3, 341:5, 343:4, 348:3, 350:2
Soviet threat, 75:2, 345:5

Europe *(continued)*
defense/military *(continued)*
U.S. aspect, 87:5, 336:1, 341:6, 346:2, 348:3, 350:4, 351:6, 353:2, 354:2
troops in Europe, 73:3, 80:5
Warsaw Pact, 77:6, 333:2, 349:5, 394:2
division/partition, 335:6, 341:1
economy, 316:2
Common Market/Community, 304:6, 336:2
internal market, free, 339:4, 346:4, 347:3
nuclear power, 335:1
space aspect, 489:2
trade, foreign, 339:4, 346:4
unification, 336:2
United States of Europe, 353:5
utopianism, 478:5
foreign relations/policy with:
Americas, 304:6
Asia/Pacific, 313:2
China, 320:1
Persian Gulf, 364:2
Soviet Union, 75:2, 146:1, 146:2, 153:1, 336:1, 343:3, 345:5
U.S., 170:1, 339:4, 345:6, 346:4, 347:3, 348:4, 348:5, 350:2, 354:1
Bush, George, 170:1, 354:1
culture, 14:7
economic aspect, 107:3
Marshall Plan, 281:4, 344:1
See also defense, *this section*
See also Europe, Eastern; *and specific European countries*
Europe, Eastern:
freedom, 332:3, 332:4
literature/books, 421:2
reform, 356:4
repression, 331:5
status quo, 335:3
West, relations with, 356:5
foreign relations/policy with:
Soviet Union, 69:1, 85:5, 331:5, 335:3, 341:1, 356:4
U.S., 332:3
Euthanasia—*see* Medicine
Evans, Edith, 465:2
Evert, Chris, 506:5
Existence, 480:7

F

Failure—*see* Success
Fame, 420:3, 479:1, 513:6
Family—*see* Social welfare
Farming—*see* Agriculture
Fascism, 334:2

Faulkner, William, 418:4, 420:1, 424:1
Federal Aviation Administration (FAA), U.S.—
    see Transportation: air
Federal Bureau of Investigation (FBI), U.S.—see
    Crime
Federal Communications Commission (FCC),
    U.S.—see Broadcasting
Federal Express Co., 181:1
Federal Reserve Board, U.S.—see Commerce
Feeling, 472:4
Ferraro, Geraldine, 208:2, 231:6
Fiedler, Arthur, 310:2
Films—see Motion pictures
Finance—see Commerce
First Lady—see Presidency, U.S.
First Nationwide Savings, 182:5
Fischer-Dieskau, Dietrich, 457:1
Fitzgerald, F. Scott, 415:2, 421:2
Flynt, Larry, 408:1
Football:
    agents, 504:6
    baseball compared with, 504:5
    coaching, 507:3
    college, 127;6, 129:4, 504:6, 506:4, 507:3,
        515:2
    defense—see offense, this section
    drugs, 514:1
    make other guys screw up, 499:5
    offense/defense, 510:7, 511:3
    players:
        release of, 501:2
        salaries, 123:4
        specialization, 508:1
    politics compared with, 234:6
    quarterbacks, 512:5
    Super Bowl, 402:5, 499:3, 500:3
    team sport, 504:5
    winning/losing, 504:2, 509:5, 511:3, 516:5
    teams:
        Denver Broncos, 499:3
        Niagara University, 507:3
        Ohio State University, 510:7
        University of Georgia, 510:7
        University of Michigan, 510:7
        Washington Redskins, 123:4, 499:3
Ford, Gerald R., 151:4
Ford, John, 446:3, 447:1, 448:2
Foreign affairs/policy, pp. 142-173
    aid, foreign, 157:2, 165:5, 173:2
    aligned, non-, 151:5, 394:2
    Ambassadorships, 161:2, 170:4
    arms sales—see Defense
    arrogance, 142:2
    beliefs, trumpeting of, 164:5

Foreign affairs/policy (continued)
    black, being, 157:1
    black-and-white aspect, 156:2
    blocs, power, 151:5
    bully on the block, 169:3
    Bush, George, aspect, 150:4, 157:5, 166:7,
        249:2
    buying friends, 160:2
    "Can I help you?", U.S. attitude of, 18:1
    career diplomats, 161:2
    chaos in, 144:1
    cold war, 142:4, 168:5, 170:3
    colonialism, 154:4, 162:3
        See also imperialism, this section
    commitments, foreign, 168:2
    complexity, 166:2
    Congress (U.S.) aspect, 143:3, 144:1, 160:5,
        160:6, 170:5, 176:2
    conservatism/right aspect, 158:4
    covert activities—see intelligence, this section
    crises, 157:4
    decency/values, 75:5
    Democratic Party (U.S.) aspect, 149:3, 149:4,
        151:3, 207:3
    detente, 143:5
    dictating events, 168:1
    diplomacy, 160:5, 167:2, 302:3
    Dukakis, Michael S., aspect, 144:3, 144:5,
        145:2, 145:3, 145:4, 149:3, 149:4, 155:3,
        157:1, 157:5, 158:2, 166:7, 227:1
    Eastern bloc, Western support of, 171:5
    economic aspect, 153:6, 168:5, 169:2
        debt, foreign, 154:4
    enemies, 142:3, 142:4, 149:4, 156:2, 166:2
    forces overseas, commitment of, 157:5, 170:5
    Foreign Service, U.S., 143:1, 167:2, 169:1,
        170:4, 171:2
    getting along with foreigners, 156:4
    good, U.S. as force for, 13:4
    human-rights aspect, 142:1, 147:1, 149:5,
        150:2, 156:3, 162:4, 172:4, 476:5, 484:4
        Helsinki accords, 155:5, 349:1
        torture, 152:3
    imagination/courage/daring, 166:7
    imperialism, 168:2
        See also colonialism, this section
    intelligence/spying/CIA, 176:3, 177:5, 241:3,
        295:4, 308:1
        capabilities, 152:2
        Congress (U.S.) aspect, 172:3
        covert activities, 148:5, 157:5
        drugs, 64:5
        informing public, 147:3
        libraries, Soviet spying in U.S., 418:2

Foreign affairs/policy *(continued)*
  intelligence/spying/CIA *(continued)*
    reform/change, 152:2
    secrecy, 172:3
    Soviet Union, 171:3, 418:2
  isolationism, 144:2, 160:3, 167:1, 167:4
  judging others, 158:5
  leadership/responsibility, U.S., 13:2, 144:2,
    144:6, 145:2, 145:3, 145:4
  liberalism/left aspect, 158:4
  linkage, 155:4
  little countries, 159:4
  loved, U.S. desire to be, 151:2, 153:2
  meetings/talks, 146:4
    summit meetings, 143:5, 147:4, 147:5,
      148:1, 154:1, 154:3, 155:5, 163:5 166:6
  mistakes, 158:3
  mistrust, 166:5
  moral equivalence, U.S.-Soviet, 168:3
  multinational organizations, 144:3, 145:2
  naivete, 158:6
  National Security Council, U.S., 161:4
  overthrowing governments, 149:5
  political prisoners, 152:3
  population aspect, 148:4, 148:6, 160:4
  poverty, 148:6
  power/force, use of, 146:3, 150;2, 154:5,
    155:2, 155:5, 171:1, 302:3, 395:2
  Presidency (U.S.) aspect, 143:3, 146:3, 157:4,
    158:2, 158:3, 159:5, 160:6, 161:3, 161:4,
    163:1, 169:1, 170:5: 176:2, 241:3
  Reagan Doctrine, 164:2
  refugees, 159:6
  respect, 151:1, 151:2, 220:3
  risks, 169:1
  sovereignty, 162:4, 167:5
  State, U.S. Dept. of, 57:8, 59:5, 161:2
  State, U.S. Secretary of, 157:1, 161:3, 169:2
  terrorism/hostages, 143:2, 156:6, 162:3, 165:4,
    167:2, 171:2, 374:5, 388:2
    concessions, 150:5, 367:1, 368:2
    extradition, 168:4
    hijacking of Kuwaiti aircraft, 143:4
    informing public, 147:3
    of the masses, 162:2
    Pan Am plane crash in Scotland, 147:3,
      360:3
  tough talk, 209:1
  treaties, 147:4
  truth, telling of, 163:6
  United Nations (UN):
    aim of, 171:1
    environmental aspect, 136:3
    founding of, 171:1

Foreign affairs/policy *(continued)*
  United Nations (UN) *(continued)*
    importance of, 159:1
    limitations, 144:3
    Middle East—*see* Middle East
    peace-keeping aspect, 159:1, 161:1, 394:5
    Secretary General, 161:1
    Soviet Union, 161:1, 172:5
    UNESCO, 159:3
    U.S., 172:2
  Voice of America, 333:1
  "winning," 169:3
  See also specific countries and areas
Forster, E. M., 414:4
France:
  Catholic/Protestant aspect, 334:6
  defense/military, 345:4
  dynamic power, 334:1
  liberty/equality/fraternity, 346:1, 476:5
  Mitterrand, Francois, 344:5, 350:1
  united/reconciliation, 345:7, 350:1
  foreign relations/policy with:
    Algeria, 363:1
    Germany, West, 345:4
    Palestine Liberation Organization (PLO),
      376:3
Franco, Francisco, 336:4
Franklin, Benjamin, 18:6
Frazier, Joe, 498:1
Freedom—*see* Democracy
Future, the, 470:2

G

Gama, Vasco da, 313:2
General Electric Co. (GE), 42:2
General Motors Corp. (GM), 104:2, 263:5
Genet, Jean, 466:1
Germany, East:
  Berlin Wall, 333:6, 345:3
  Olympic athletes, 503:4
  foreign relations/policy with:
    Germany, West/reunification, 341:1
    Nicaragua, 158:1
Germany, Nazi, 329:3, 344:2
Germany, West:
  defense/military, 80:5, 331:3, 343:5, 345:4
  economy, 90:2, 113:2
  Kohl, Helmut, 279:1
  foreign relations/policy with:
    France, 345:4
    Germany, East, 341:1
    South Africa, 279:1
    Soviet Union, 331:3, 336:3, 341:1
    U.S., 344:1

Gershwin, George, 460:4
Gibson, Althea, 510:3
Gibson, Bob, 505:3
Glass, Phillip, 400:1
Gleason, Jackie, 438:5
God—*see* Religion
Godfrey, Arthur, 438:5
Goldman, William, 449:3
Golf, 508:2, 510:5, 512:3
Gorbachev, Mikhail S.—*see* Soviet Union
Government, pp. 174-198
  accountability, 189:3
  acting swiftly, 190:2
  activist, 180:1
  advancement, opportunity for, 189:4
  affects lives every day, 184:2
  appointees, political, 174:1, 189:4
  bad government, 188:4
  bureaucracy, 184:4, 192:4
  business, private, aspect, 182:5, 186:5, 187:4, 192:6
  complexity, 177:5
  compromise, 181:5
  confidence in, 236:1
  conservatism/right aspect, 176:5
  decision-making, 190:6
  discourse, political, 175:1
  disorderly aspect, 190:5
  divided, politically, 187:1
  done, getting things, 183:2
  employees:
    attracting of, 197:4
    benefits, 195:5
    drug-testing, 194:3, 195:6
    financial disclosure, 194:3
    leaving and arriving, 183:1
    salary/compensation, 197:5
    treatment of, 195:6
  as enemy, 188:4
  equal opportunity, assurance of, 185:5
  ethics/corruption in, 176:6, 177:1, 177:3, 177:6, 180:2, 182:2, 185:2, 185:3, 186:1, 186:4, 186:6, 187:6, 188:1, 189:5, 190:3, 191:7, 195:3, 196:2, 197:6, 199:5, 200:2, 201:6, 202:3, 202:4, 203:6, 204:2, 205:1, 213:4, 226:3
  excellence in, 15:4
  Federal system, 179:2, 189:6, 192:6
  Founding Fathers, 175:1
  growth, public-sector, 191:6
  hearings, 183:3
  independent counsels/special prosecutors, 186:4, 204:5
  influence-peddling, 177:3

Government *(continued)*
  information, freedom of, 179:1
  "iron triangle," 193:1
  "kiss-and-tell' books, 179:6
  law-making, 174:2, 175:2, 188:5
  leadership, 178:1, 183:4, 192:3, 232:4
  leaks, 190:6, 409:2
  liberalism/left aspect, 176:5, 178:1, 193:1
  liking officials, 178:1
  limited, 176:5, 192:2
  lives in balance, holds, 175:6
  lobbying after leaving office, 188:2, 196:4, 197:6
  loyalty, 179:6
  lying by, 174:3
  morality aspect, 193:4
  no, courage to say, 193:3
  overlapping functions, 183:5
  people, confidence in, 178:1
  people tell what powers are, 192:1
  perception of, 188:1
  power, 175:7, 196:5, 480:1
  power is in position, not ideas, 175:2
  press/media aspect, 179:1, 182:1, 183:7, 193:1
  privatization, 181:1, 182:4, 191:1, 191:6, 195:5, 347:1
  public service, 175:3, 177:3, 177:6, 180:1, 180:2, 182:6, 195:1, 197:4
  regulations, 187:4, 192:6
    See also specific enterprises
  Republican Party (U.S.) aspect, 188:4
  revenue-raising, 179:3
  rigidity, 183:4
  selfishness in, 182:6
  separation of powers, 189:3
  sports game compared with, 183:7
  state/local aspect, 179:3, 187:4, 189:6, 192:6
    Governors, state, 163:1, 185:4, 194:4
      Presidency (U.S.) aspect, 180:3
      Republican Party, 235:4
      running for, 207:3, 234:2
    Legislature, 194:4, 195:2
    Mayors, 266:2, 266:4
    power of states, 245:1
  stupidity of, 113:2
  success, reward for, 184:4
  taking over private entities, 185:6
  tripartite aspect, 181:5
  trusting the people, 192:3
  undoing what others have done, 193:5
  Washington, D.C., 183:1, 184:3
  See also Congress, U.S.; Constitution, U.S.; Politics; Presidency, U.S.; Vice-Presidency, U.S.; *and specific countries*

Governors, state—*see* Government: state/local
Graf, Steffi, 510:3
Great men, 477:7
Greece:
    foreign relations/policy with:
        Cyprus, 346:6, 354:5
        Turkey, 346:6
Greed, 17:3, 48:6, 74:3, 177:3, 479:5
Greenspan, Alan, 45:2
Grenada:
    Communism, 244:5, 302:5
    foreign relations/policy with:
        U.S., 169:3, 218:2, 244:5, 273:1, 302:5
Grove City College, 19:5
Guatemala:
    killings, political, 287:4
    violence, 288:4
    foreign relations/policy with:
        Panama, 298:1
Gun control—*see* Crime

H

Haiti:
    democracy/freedom/elections, 283:4, 283:5,
        284:2, 295:3, 297:2, 305:2
    dictatorship, 287:4
    Duvalier, Jean-Claude, 305:2
    social welfare, 297:3
    foreign relations/policy with:
        U.S., 283:5, 295:3
Hamadi, Mohammad Ali, 378:2
Hamilton, Alexander, 182:3
Hand, Learned, 18:5
Hart, Gary, 240:6, 246:5, 251:1, 406:5
Hartford, Conn., 267:2
Harvard University, 127:6, 515:6
Hawks, Howard, 447:1, 448:2
Hayes, Helen, 466:7
Hayes, Woody, 510:7
Health—*see* Medicine
Helms, Jesse, 209:3
Hemingway, Ernest, 415:2, 418:4, 421:2, 423:5
Herblock, 247:1
Heroin—*see* Crime: drugs
Hispanics—*see* Civil rights
History, 128:6, 473:1, 476:4
Hitler, Adolf, 247:5, 291:1
Hobbes, Thomas, 320:2
Hockey:
    Stanley Cup, 509:4
    violence, player, 510:6, 517:3
    winning/losing, 509:4
Hollywood—*see* Motion pictures
Homeles—*see* Social welfare

Homosexuality, 230:1, 427:2, 429:1, 429:2
Honduras:
    foreign relations/policy with:
        Nicaragua, 282:4, 290:5
        U.S., 295:4
Hong Kong, 315:1, 315:5
Horse racing, 502:4, 512:3
Hospitals—*see* Medicine
Housing—*see* Social welfare
Human rights—*see* Foreign affairs
Humor, 443:3, 470:3
Humphrey, Gordon, 209:3
Humphrey, Hubert H., 247:4
Hungary:
    Communism, 149:1, 347:2
    economy, 342:6
    parties, political, 340:1
    reform, 334:4, 347:2
Hunger—*see* Social welfare
Hussein I, King—*see* Jordan
Hussein, Saddam—*see* Iraq
Huston, John, 448:2, 448:7

I

Iacocca, Lee A., 48:6
Idealism, 482:2
Indelicato, Gerald, 213:4
India:
    defense/military, 325:6
    middle class, 313:1
    nuclear energy, 325:6
    poverty, 313:1
    foreign relations/policy with:
        China, 321:6, 326:1
        Indian Ocean, 315:4
        Pakistan, 326:1
        Persian Gulf, 315:4
        Soviet Union, 315:4
        U.S., 312:3, 315:4
Indian Ocean, 315:4
Indians, American—*see* Civil rights
Individualism, 473:5, 475:6
Industry—*see* Commerce
Intellectual ability, 473:4
Intellectuals, 471:5, 484:3
Interest rates—*see* Commerce
Internal Revenue Service (IRS), U.S.—*see* Taxes
Iowa, 237:7, 246:2
Iran:
    defense/military, 373:5
    elections, 374:2
    foreign affairs, 380:5, 381:2
        See also foreign relations, *this section*
    human rights, 378:2

Iran *(continued)*
  Islam, 374:2, 381:2
  isolated, 375:2
  Khomeini, Ayatollah Ruhollah, 80:2, 158:2, 223:4, 244:5, 246:1, 378:2
  Shah, 378:2
  terrorism, 361:6, 378:2, 391:2
  foreign relations/policy with:
    Afghanistan, 315:6
    Iraq/war, 71:5, 145:2, 359::1, 360:4, 364:2, 365:2, 372:6, 373:4, 374:1, 374:3, 381:1, 387:4, 387:5, 392:1, 395:1
    U.S., 244:5, 374:1, 374:2
      arms sales, 143:2, 150:4, 150:5, 165:4, 223;4, 246:1, 291:4, 363:2, 363:3, 365:4, 367:1
      Bush, George, aspect, 143:2, 150:5, 236:1, 246:1, 367:1
      downing of Iran airliner, 145:1, 363:6, 364:3, 365:2, 365:3 365:5, 368:6, 372:6, 375:2, 380:6, 390:5, 392:1
      hostage negotiations, 368:2
      Iran-contra scandal, 150:5, 152:2, 157:3, 165:1, 165:4, 171:4, 179:5, 185:3, 186:1, 236:1, 241:2, 291:4, 295:4
      North, Oliver, 163:2, 201:4, 289:4
      Poindexter, John M., 201:4
Iraq:
  Hussein, Saddam, 374:1, 378:3
  Kurds, 373:1, 378:3
  poison gas, use of, 373:1, 378:3
  foreign relations/policy with:
    Iran/war, 71:5, 145:2, 359:1, 360:4, 364:2, 365:2, 372:6, 373:4, 374:1, 374:3, 381:1, 387:4, 387:5, 392:1, 395:1
Ireland:
  foreign relations/policy with:
    Britain, 162:3
      Northern Ireland, 341:2, 344:4, 482:3
    Libya, 162:1
Islam—*see* Religion
Israel, pp. 358-392
  Arabs aspect—*see* demographics, *this section;* foreign relations, *this section*
  borders (1967), 385:1, 385:4
  defense/military, 379:6, 391:1
  demographics/Arab population, 371:1, 377:4, 377:5, 379:1, 379:6, 387:1, 389:2
  economy, 372:5, 379:5, 384:4
  elections, 379:5, 382:4
  essence of, 361:3
  Gaza—*see* occupied Palestinian territory, *this section*
  Jerusalem, 358:1, 366:3, 373:3, 375:1, 376:5,

Israel *(continued)*
  Jerusalem *(continued)*
    377:3, 377:5, 379:2, 386:1, 387:3
  Jewish aspect, 359:2, 362:3, 368:3, 370:1, 370:2, 371:1, 375:3, 375:4, 376:1, 377:4, 379:1, 379:4, 379:5, 383:1, 383:3, 383:4, 389:1. 390:1, 390:2, 391:3
    "who is a Jew" controversy, 485:3, 486:2, 487:2, 487:3
  "a light unto the nations," 362:4
  Likud Party, 379:5, 382:3, 382:4
  occupied Palestinian territory/West Bank/ Gaza, 162:3, 358:5, 359:2, 359:4, 359:5, 361:4, 370:1, 371:1, 371:3, 372:1, 372:2, 372:5, 375:4, 376:5, 377:3, 377:4, 378:1, 379:5, 379:6, 382:3, 384:2, 384:6, 385:4, 387:1, 388:1, 388:5, 390:2, 390:6, 391:1
    uprising/*intifada* in, 358:1, 358:2, 358:3, 360:2, 362:2, 362:4, 364:5, 365:1, 366:1, 367:2, 368:1, 368:3, 368:4, 369:5, 370:2, 370:6, 374:4, 375:3, 376:1, 376:2, 378:4, 379:2, 380:3, 380:4, 382:1, 382:4, 383:1, 383:2, 383:3, 384:3, 384:5, 385:5, 386:1, 386:2, 386:3, 386:4, 386:5, 389:2, 391:3
  Peres, Shimon, 374:4
  political prisoners, 152:3
  Shamir, Yitzhak, 367:3, 370:6, 374:4, 376:5, 377:1, 379:5
  Sinai, 391:1
  Six Day War, 370:3, 385:4
  small country, 370:1
  socialism, 384:4
  terrorism, 378:1
  West Bank—*see* occupied Palestinian territory, *this section;* Jordan
  Zionism, 162:3, 369:5, 387:2, 390:3
  foreign relations/policy with:
    Arabs, 361:2, 361:3, 379:3, 379:4, 379:5
    Palestinians:
      conference, international, 359:5, 369:2, 370:6, 371:5, 376:5, 377:1, 382:3, 382:4, 383:5
      PLO, 358:4, 359:4, 359:5, 360:1, 363:1, 366:2, 366:5, 367:3, 371:4, 373:3, 374:5, 381:4, 381:5, 382:2, 382:3, 382:5, 384:6, 385:2, 385:3, 385:5, 387:6, 388:4, 388:5, 390:4
      See also occupied Palestinian territory, *this section;* Palestinians: foreign relations
    Egypt, 383:5, 391:1
    Jordan, 371:3, 376:5, 382:3, 385:5, 387:6
    Lebanon, 370:3

Israel *(continued)*
  foreign relations/policy with: (continued)
    Soviet Union, 369:2, 379:6
    Syria, 376:5, 389:4
    U.S., 361:4, 364:1, 364:4, 366:3, 366:4,
      369:2, 370:5, 270:6, 371:2, 371:4,
      372:2, 372:3, 372:5, 375:3, 376:1,
      379:3, 379:6, 381:3, 381:5, 382:5,
      383:1, 383:2, 385:3, 386:3, 386:4,
      387:3, 388:5, 389:1, 390:3, 391:1, 391:4
Italy:
  arts/culture, 459:4
  Fascism, 334:2
  music, 459:4
  foreign relations/policy with:
    U.S., 334:2
Ives, Charles, 460:4

J

Jackson, Michael, 415:5
Jagger, Mick, 457:6
James, Henry, 420:4
Japan:
  defense/military, 327:1, 327:4
    arming, re-, 311:2
    See also U.S., *this section*
  economy, 90:2, 113:2, 115:4, 326:6, 327:1
    See also U.S., *this section*
  education aspect, 117:1, 125:6
  elections, 314:6
  foreign affairs, 311:2, 319:6, 326:2, 327:1
    aid, foreign, 312:1
  investment, foreign, 45:1
  medicine/health aspect, 433:5
  nuclear power, 139:3
  railroads/trains, 264:6
  science/technology aspect, 490:1
  trade, foreign, 304:6, 311:1, 316:5, 319:2,
    326:6, 327:4
    See also U.S., *this section*
  foreign relations/policy with:
    Americas, 304:6, 312:1
    Asia/Pacific, 316:5
    China, 304:6, 320:1, 321:6
    South Africa, 279:1
    U.S., 310:1, 311:1, 311:2, 312:1, 314:6,
      319:2, 319:3, 321:5, 325:7, 326:2,
      326:6, 327:4, 490:1
      an ally, 319:3
      defense/military, 80:5, 87:5
        bases, U.S., 310:1, 325:7
      economy aspect, 311:2
        stock market, U.S., 48:4
      trade, 39:1, 43:3, 101:1

Japan *(continued)*
  foreign relations/policy with: (continued)
    U.S. *(continued)*
      See also Civil rights: Japanese-American
        internment
Jaruzelski, Wojciech—*see* Poland
Jazz—*see* Music
Jefferson, Thomas, 18:6
Jerusalem—*see* Israel
Jews—*see* Religion: Judaism
Jobs—*see* Labor: employment
Joffrey, Robert, 463:4
John, Tommy, 506:3
Johns, Jasper, 402:7
Johnson, Ben, 501:4
Johnson, Lyndon B., 151:4, 251:5, 320:3
Joplin, Janis, 460:2
Jordan, 384:3
  Hussein I, King, 382:3, 387:6
  terrorism, 168:4
  West Bank, 371:3, 377:3
  foreign relations/policy with:
    Israel, 376:5, 382:3, 385:5, 387:6
    Palestinians, 364:1, 371:3
    U.S., 168:4, 364:4
Jordan, Michael, 514:2
Journalism/the press/news media, pp. 406-412
  baseball, 508:4, 512:2
  broadcast/television:
    ABC News Nightline, 406:3
    anchors, 407:3
    Cable News Network (CNN), 406:3
    CBS News, 410:1
    economic aspect, 406:3
    elections/campaigns, coverage of, 411:5
      conventions, political, 409:5, 411:1
      exit polls, 409:5
    Fairness Doctrine, 412:4
    half-truths, 410:2
    ratings, 411:5
    responsibility, 410:5
    U.S. aspect, 410:2
    Washington, D.C., bureaus, 406:4
  celebrities, coverage of, 411:6
  in Communist world, 412:2
  criticism aspect, 412:2
  cynicism, 412:1
  freedom of the press/First Amendment, 408:1,
    411:6
  government aspect, 179:1, 182:1, 183:7, 193:1,
    409:2
  important/exciting things, coverage of, 411:2
  interviews, 410:6
  investigative reporting, 407:1

Journalism/the press/news media *(continued)*
  leaks to the press, government, 409:2
  liberalism/left aspect, 407:5
  magazines:
    literary, 414:7, 419:6
    fiction in, 414:2
    writers' contracts, 414:7, 419:6
    titles:
      Harper's, 419:4
      Hustler, 408:1
      Ploughshares, 414:7
  minorities, treatment of, 25:3, 32:6
  newspapers:
    chains, 406:2
    economic aspect, 406:2
    elections, coverage of, 411:5
    endorsements, political, 411:4
    as history, 411:7
    minorities on staff, 408:2
    publishers/editors, 406:2
    television critics, 439:5
    newspapers:
      The New York Times, 221:1, 411:7
      The Washington Post, 411:7
  Nicaragua, 301:1
  novels compared with, 413:1
  objectivity/bias, 407:5, 410:4
  parody of public figures, 408:1
  politics aspect, 406:1, 407:4
    See also broadcast: elections, *this section;*
      newspapers: elections, *this section;* news-
      papers: endorsements, *this section*
  power, 406:1, 406:2
  Presidency (U.S.) aspect, 176:4
    news conference, 198:2, 408:3, 408:5,
      410:3
  public belief in, 193:1
  Pulitzer Prize, 411:3
  reporters/journalists, 409:4, 410:1, 412:1,
    412:6
  Soviet Union, 344:3, 348:6, 408:4, 409:1,
    412:3
  standards, voluntary, 406:5
  tennis, 506:5
  Washington press corps, 406:4
  women in, 409:3, 412:5
  "write for talking," 407:2
Joyce, James, 423:5
Judges—*see* Judiciary
Judiciary/courts, pp. 199-205
  Appeals, Court of, 200:4
  black aspect, 205:3
  capital cases, 66:4
  circuits, conflict among, 203:3

Judiciary/courts *(continued)*
  counsels, independent—*see* Government: in-
    dependent counsels
  expense of litigation, 201:2
  judges:
    appointment of, 200:1, 201:1, 203:2
      See also Supreme Court, *this section*
    Constitution (U.S.), interpreting of, 200:1
    crime aspect, 53:2, 53:6, 59:6
    death-penalty cases, 203:4
    independence, 201:1, 201:3
    interpret/not legislate, 200:1
    liberalism/left aspect, 200:1
    making law, 53:6
    mind-set, 201:2
    sentencing, 201:5
  Justice, U.S. Dept. of, 59:5
    Attorney General, 20:2, 27:3, 66:2
      Meese, Edwin, III, 190:3, 191:7, 195:3,
        199:4, 199:5, 200:2, 201:6, 202:3,
        202:4, 203:6, 204:2, 213:4, 223:4
    conduct, codes of, 205:1
    jurisdiction, 204:4
    outside-U.S. cases, 204:4
  level playing field, 201:4
  litigious society, 202:5
  packing the courts, 203:2
  precedent, 200:4, 201:2
  scale of justice, accuracy of, 201:3
  Supreme court, U.S.:
    abortion, 30:1
      See also Women: abortion
    appointments/nomination to, 30:1, 199:2,
      200:1
      Bork, Robert H., 19:4
    conferences among Justices, 204:1
    conflict among circuits, 203:3
    financial disclosure, Justices', 194:3
    impact on people's lives, 200:3
    women aspect, 29:4
      women/minorities on Court, 200:3
      See also Women: abortion
  television dramatizations, 205:2
  trials not won by eloquence, 203:1
Judaism—*see* Religion
Justice, U.S. Dept. of—*see* Judiciary

K

Kampuchea (Cambodia)—*see* Cambodia
Kemp, Jack, 90:4, 242:1
Kennedy Center—*see* Arts
Kennedy, Edward M., 19:4, 211:3, 219:5
Kennedy, John F., 15:3, 15:5, 151:1, 209:4, 210:1,

Kennedy, John F. *(continued)*
   214:4, 223:6, 224:3, 235:5, 243:4, 251:5,
   438:1, 473:1
Kennedy, Robert F., 438:1
Kentucky, 49:4
Kenya, 276:3
Khomeini, Ayatollah Ruhollah—*see* Iran
Khrushchev, Nikita S.—*see* Soviet Union
Kim Il Sung—*see* Korea, North
King, Billie Jean, 510:3
King, Martin Luther, Jr.—*see* Civil rights
Kirkland, Lane, 112:1
Kissinger, Henry A., 80:4, 158:4, 320:3, 341:6
Klinghoffer, Leon, 382:5
Koch, Edward I., 329:2
Kohl, Helmut—*see* Germany, West
Korea, North:
   Communism, 322:2
   Kim Il Sung, 317:2
   foreign relations/policy with:
      China, 322:2
      Korea, South, 322:4, 323:2, 325:1
         reunification, 317:2, 322:2, 322:5, 323:1
      Soviet Union, 322:2
Korea, South:
   Chun Doo Hwan, 315:3
   democracy, 311:3, 315:3, 321:7, 322:3, 322:6
   economy, 322:3
   government/politics, 322:1
      abuses, 315:3
      opposition leaders, 315:2
   human rights, 321:7
   leadership, 314:5
   Roh Tae Woo, 314:5
   trade, foreign, 39:5, 311:1, 325:2
   foreign relations/policy with:
      Korea, North, 322:4, 323:2, 325:1
         reunification, 317:2, 322:2, 322:5, 323:1
      U.S., 317:2, 322:3, 323:2, 325:1, 325:2
         economic aspect, 104:2, 311:1
         trade, 39:5
Kosygin, Alexei N., 329:4
Koufax, Sandy, 505:3
Kuwait:
   hijacking of Kuwaiti airliner, 143:4
   foreign relations/policy with:
      U.S., 168:4
         arms sales, 366:4

L

Labor:
   automation, 103:4
   career changes/transition, 90:3, 96:4, 100:4

Labor *(continued)*
   contingent workers, 91:4
   drugs in workplace, 64:3
   employment/unemployment/jobs, 92:2, 95:6,
      96:2, 98:1, 100:3, 103:5, 108:2, 111:5,
      113:3, 114:5, 231:3, 255:4
      blacks, 93:6
      capital-gains aspect, 37:2
      cities, 97:6
      competition for employees by companies,
         106:4
      creation, job, 93:5, 93:7, 94:3, 95:1, 95:4,
         99:1, 100:4, 222:4
      education aspect, 96:4, 119:6, 126:5, 127:1
         dropouts, 109:4
      export of, 42:2, 104:2
      foreign-investment aspect, 49:4, 50:1
      number at work, 93:4, 98:5, 113:4, 116:2
      plant closings, 96:1, 112:2
      pride aspect, 94:2
      protectionism, job, 38:2, 97:5
      women aspect, 31:5, 32:2, 93:6, 106:5,
         112:4
         equal pay/comparable worth, 20:3, 256:3
   future work, 470:2
   hiring people, 44:2
   Labor, U.S. Dept. of, 106:3
   Labor, U.S. Secretary of, 106:3
   manpower crisis, 109:4
   non-traditional groups, 102:2
   Occupational Safety and Health Administra-
      tion (OSHA), U.S., 187:4
   "organization man," 107:5
   performance, job, 103:2, 103:4
   retirement, 472:1
   science/technology aspect, 496:6
   service industry, 97:6
   skilled/qualified/trained workers, 38:3, 96:4,
      101:2, 109:4, 113:5, 115:1, 115:3, 126:5
   strikes—*see* Nicaragua; Poland
   unions, 102:5
      AFL-CIO, 112:1
      busting, union-, 182:4
      crime aspect, 54:5, 58:2, 104:4, 185:6,
         202:3
      government take-over of, 102:6, 115:2,
         185:6
      leaders/hierarchy, 112:1, 114:4
      necessity of, 105:5, 108:2
      representation, poor, 112:1
      Teamsters Union, 114:4
         crime aspect, 54:5, 58:2, 185:6, 202:3
         government control of, 102:6, 115:2
   See also Poland

Labor *(continued)*
vacation time, 91:4, 100:6, 112:4, 116:1
wages/salaries/income, 90:1, 93:7, 96:2, 98:5,
99:4, 104:1, 111:5, 113:4, 116:2, 256:4
minimum wage, 115:5, 256:3
See also employment: women, *this section*
Labor, U.S. Dept. of—*see* Labor
Labor, U.S. Secretary of—*see* Labor
Lancaster, Burt, 444:2
Lang, Fritz, 443:4
Latin America—*see* Americas
Law:
American Bar Association (ABA), 199:6
choosing which to obey, 204:2
conservatism/right, 200:5
intellectual life of, 199:2
lawyers:
case assessment, 202:5
ethics, 204:2
firms, large, 199:3, 202:2
good, do, 199:1
income/fees, 199:3, 202:2, 202:5
pro bono services, 199:6, 200:6
representing all, 202:1
timid in what they say, 199:2
making of—*see* Congress, U.S.; Government;
Judiciary: judges; Presidency, U.S.
poor/Legal Services Corp., 199:6, 200:6
respect for, 186:6, 202:5
rule of, 200:5, 204:3
Law enforcement—*see* Crime
Lawyers—*see* Law
Leadership, 478:2
See also Government; Politics; Presidency,
U.S.
Lebanon:
elections, 368:5
terrorism, 168:4, 365:6
foreign relations/policy with:
Israel, 370:3
Syria, 385:6
U.S., 168:4, 170:5, 365:6
hostages, 143:2, 150:5, 363:2, 363:3
Lenin, Vladimir I.—*see* Soviet Union
Liberalism/left—*see* Politics
Libya:
Qaddafi, Muammar el-, 158:2
terrorism, 391:2
foreign relations/policy with:
Chad, 162:1
Ireland, 162:1
Panama, 162:1, 286:4
U.S., 162:1, 218:2, 273:1, 274:5, 277:1
Life, 470:1, 471:1, 471:7, 472:3, 472:4, 472:5,

Life *(continued)*
477:1, 477:4, 477:6, 478:3, 479:3, 480:7,
481:5
Lincoln, Abraham, 108:7, 212:1
Liston, Sonny, 498:1
Literature/books, pp. 413-424
Canada, 415:3
competition from other media, 419:5
criticism, 418:1
education aspect, 118:5, 119:2, 128:6
ethical impulse, 416:4
history books, 128:6
"kiss-and-tell" books, 179:6, 245:5
lasting, 422:6
libraries, 418:2
light/holiday reading, 421:1, 423:1
magazines:
fiction, 414:2
literary, 414:7, 419:6
music compared with, 414:5
novels, 413:2, 415:3, 415:4, 415:6, 416:1,
417:6, 418:3, 418:4, 419:4, 424:5
journalism compared with, 413:1
motion pictures compared with, 448:5
quality, 413:6
time, defying process of, 413:1
poetry/poets, 480:1
acclaim/wealth, 415:5, 417:6
black, 415:5
conservative (political), 420:6
free verse, 424:2
inspiration, 417:5
language, manipulating, 417:4
Poet Laureate, U.S., 420:2
political, 420:5, 420:6
Soviet Union, 419:3, 423:6
three "nevers," 416:5
success, 416:5, 417:6
writing speed, 424:3
poems:
Comas, 424:3
political aspect, 420:5, 420:6, 424:5
"kiss-and-tell" books, 179:6, 245:5
pornography, 420:1
publishing, 419:2, 419:6
editors, 413:4, 421:3
money aspect, 422:1
multinational, 421:4
quality, 413:6, 420:1
readers, creation of, 416:2
reading:
television's effect on, 437:4
See also Education: illiteracy
Soviet Union/Russia, 408:4, 415:3, 418:1

Literature/books *(continued)*
  Soviet Union/Russia *(continued)*
    Russian, 19th century, 415:3
    See also poetry, *this section*
  speechwriting, 420:6
  stage/theatre compared with, 448:5
  stores, 419:5
  storytelling, 413:2, 415:2, 419:4, 420:4
  thrillers, 413:6
  values, literary, 420:1
  writing/writers, 448:5
    bad/poor, 415:6
    block, writer's, 422:5
    bureaucracy compared with, 416:3
    a catharsis, 413:3
    characters, 416:6
    close to writers, getting, 414:6
    concentration, 416:3, 420:7
    copying successful authors, 415:2
    discipline, 422:5
    ego, 423:2
    English dept., school, 423:5
    entertainers, 415:2
    European aspect, 421:2
    fame, 420:3
    finishing a book, 417:3, 422:2
    greatness, 420:4
    hard work, 417:4
    historians, 422:4
    humble, being, 417:2
    independent, 421:4
    inspiration, 417:5
    invention, 414:3
    language as a tool, 424:1
    last lines, 422:3
    Latin America, 421:4
    literary, 414:7, 415:2, 419:6
    loneliness/isolation, 413:5, 419:1, 421:5
    mechanics, 424:4
    modesty, 423:2
    money, 415:6
      contracts, 414:7, 419:6, 422:2
      royalties, 413:5
    output, 414:4
    place, sense of, 418:4
    plot, 418:3
    political aspect, 424:5
    practice/dedication, 417:7
    prosperity/stability, 423:4
    quitting, never, 417:2
    reader, respect for, 417:1
    rejections, 421:3
    Russian, 19th century, 415:3
    scholarly research about, 414:1

Literature/books *(continued)*
  writing/writers *(continued)*
    speed, 414:4, 424:3
    success, 417:6, 423:2
    talking about writing, 421:5
    teaching compared with, 416:1
    tell a story, 419:4, 420:4, 424:4
    thought clearly expressed, 417:1
    "Three Ps," 417:7
    U.S. aspect, 421:2
    at whim of their talent, 421:2
    women as characters, 423:3
    yourself as audience, 415:1
    See also specific writers
  titles:
    The Invisible Government, 172:3
    Perestroika, 336:1
Lithuania—*see* Soviet Union
Los Angeles, Calif., 263:5
Love, 470:4
Lubitsch, Ernst, 443:4
Lugar, Richard G., 210:1

M

Magazines—*see* Journalism
Mailer, Norman, 404:1, 415:6
Mandela, Nelson, 272:4
Manigat, Leslie F., 295:3
Mann, Thomas, 423:1
Marcos, Ferdinand E.—*see* Philippines
Marijuana—*see* Crime: drugs
Marriage, 470:4, 477:2, 480:6
Marshall, Wilbur, 123:4
Martin, Billy, 512:6
Martin, Peter, 463:4
Marx Brothers, 443:3
Marx, Karl/Marxism, 97:1, 274:2, 282:2, 305:1, 312:4, 473:6, 480:2, 481:6
  See also Communism
Massachusetts:
  crime/furloughs, 56:3, 63:6, 224:2
  Dukakis, Michael S., as Governor, 213:1, 227:1
  health insurance, 427:3
  jobs, 114:5
  racism, 33:1
  sewage, 139:1
  taxes/spending, 109:1, 110:4
Materialism, 14:2, 15:5, 471:2
Mauritius, 275:3
McCarthy, Joseph R., 223:2
McGovern, George S., 219:5, 227:4, 238:2
Medicare—*see* Medicine: insurance
Medicine/health, pp. 425-436

Medicine/health *(continued)*
  abuse of spouse/children, 426:3
  acquired immune deficiency syndrome (AIDS),
    51:1
    Bush, George, aspect, 434:4
    companies/employers aspect, 425:5, 431:5,
      434:1
    confidentiality/discrimination, 434:4, 435:4
    dancers, 468:4
    economic aspect, 429:2
    government aspect, 425:1
    homosexuality aspect, 427:2, 429:1, 429:2
    needles, supply of clean, 427:1, 433:4
    spread of, 428:1
    testing, 435:4
  autopsies, 432:2
  Bush, George, aspect, 427:4, 434:4
  cancer, 425:2, 426:5, 435:5
  costs, 428:6, 429:5, 433:1, 433:5, 434:2,
    435:6
  death, 429:6
    See also euthanasia, *this section*
  deoxyribonucleic acid (DNA), 435:1
  developing countries, 425:4
  diabetes, 428:2
  diet/nutrition, 258:4, 430:6, 431:3
  doctors/physicians:
    choice of, 429:4
    competence of, 429:3, 431:4
    costs/charges, 428:6, 429:5, 433:5
    patients, 425:2, 429:5, 431:4
    psychiatrists, 481:7
    Soviet Union, 481:7
    U.S., 481:7
  drug abuse, 434:3
    AIDS/needles aspect, 427:1, 433:4
    alcohol, 55:5, 428:5, 430:3, 430:6, 431:2
    cocaine, 431:2
    companies/employers aspect, 425:5, 432:5
    dancers, 468:4
    a disease, 432:6
    education/prevention, 432:5
    government spending on fighting, 428:4
    heroin, 431:2
    "just say no," 425:3
    testing, 52:5, 432:5
    treatment, 51:4
    See also Crime: drugs, illegal
  drugs, testing of new, 425:2
  elderly/senior citizens, 426:1, 426:2, 428:3,
    432:4, 433:1, 434:3
  euthanasia, 26:1, 432:1
  exercise, 428:3
  fetal research, 435:3

Medicine/health *(continued)*
  funding, competition for, 430:4
  heart patients, 433:3
  hospitals, 51:1
    choice of, 429:4
    costs, 428:6, 435:6
    death rates, 433:2
    infections contracted in, 432:3
    insurance aspect, 256:3
      Medicare aspect, 432:4
  infant-mortality rates, 425:4
  insurance, 256:3, 434:3
    company/employer aspect, 426:4, 427:5
    Massachusetts, 427:3
    Medicare, 428:6, 432:4, 433:1, 433:2
    South Africa, 427:3
    universal health care, 427:5
  Japan, 433:5
  life extension, 426:1
  mental illness, 258:5, 426:3, 481:7
  natal care, pre-, 427:4
  nursing/nurses, 426:2, 430:1
    education, nursing, 117:3
  nursing homes—*see* Social welfare
  patients—*see* doctors, *this section*
  priorities, 434:2
  prison aspect, 51:1
  quality of care, 429:3
  research, 117:4
  smoking/tobacco, 55:5, 430:3, 430:5, 430:6,
    433:3, 435:2, 435:5
    business' attitude, 425:5
    companies, tobacco, 431:1
  spending on, government, 95:5, 428:4
  technology, advances in, 429:6
  trust, public, 432:2
  unnecessary services, 435:6
Meese, Edwin, III—*see* Judiciary: Justice, U.S.
  Dept. of: Attorney General
Mengistu Haile Mariam, 273:3
Mexico:
  Communism, 291:1
  democracy, 283:6
  economy/debt, 287:3, 296:2, 304:3, 304:4,
    304:5
  elections, 304:2
  drugs, 304:1
  trade, foreign, 289:3
  foreign relations/policy with:
    Nicaragua, 302:4
    U.S., 283:6, 289:3, 291:1, 296:2, 304:1
Mexico City, Mexico, 140:4
Michelangelo, 456:6
Middle East/Arabs, pp. 358-392

Middle East/Arabs *(continued)*
  defense/military:
      advanced weapons, 387:5
      arms sales, 363:4, 365:4, 366:4, 389:3
  peace, opportunities for, 377:2
  Persian Gulf, 387:5
      Asia/Pacific aspect, 365:2
      energy aspect, 363:5
      Europe aspect, 365:2
      India aspect, 315:4
      Soviet Union aspect, 146:2, 153:1, 368:6
      U.S., 80:2, 145:1, 145:2, 150:3, 157:5,
          164:1, 165:4, 359:1, 363:5, 363:6,
          364:2, 365:2, 365:3, 365:5, 368:6,
          372:6, 375:2, 380:6, 387:4, 390:5,
          392:1
  terrorism, 360:3, 361:1
      See also U.S.: hostages, *this section*
  United Nations (UN) aspect, 359:4, 359:5,
      362:1, 362:5, 369:3, 370:5, 371:4, 375:5,
      381:5, 382:2, 382:5, 384:1, 386:3, 388:2,
      388:3, 388:5, 390:3, 391:4
  foreign relations/policy with:
      Soviet Union, 146:2
      U.S., 371:2, 380:2
          arms sales, 363:4, 365:4, 366:4, 389:3
          Camp David accords, 385:5
          hostages, 363:6, 367:1, 368:2
          See also Persian Gulf, *this section*
      See also Palestinians; *and specific Middle
      Eastern countries*
Military—*see* Defense
Milton, John, 416:4
Minorities—*see* Civil rights
Mitterrand, Francois—*see* France
Moderation, 475:3
Mondale, Walter F., 69:5, 178:3, 206:5, 219:5,
  227:4, 231:6, 240:6, 246:2
Money—*see* Affluence; Commerce: monetary
  system
Morality, 476:1
  See also Values
Mostel, Zero, 465:6
Motion pictures/films/cinema, pp. 442-454
  acting in, 446:5
  American Film Institute Life Achievement
      Award, 447:3
  animation, 449:5
  art-form, 449:5, 450:1
  artificiality, 442:1
  audience, 445:4, 445:6, 448:4, 450:1
  auteur theory, 450:2
  black-and-white, 443:2
  business aspect, 454:4

Motion pictures/films/cinema *(continued)*
  characters, 448:2
  collaborative aspect, 449:1, 449:4, 450:2, 453:1
  colorization, 443:2
  commercial success, 444:1, 444:5, 450:1,
      451:5
  commitment aspect, 454:6
  "committee approach," 449:3
  conceit, 445:1
  copying past films, 445:6
  costs/economics, 444:4, 445:5, 450:4, 452:2
  critics, 444:5, 446:3
  curiosity aspect, 448:7
  destroying old material, 452:1
  directing/directors, 443:4, 444:3, 444:4, 445:1,
      446:1, 447:1, 448:2, 448:4, 448:7, 450:1,
      450:2, 450:3, 451:2, 452:3, 453:1, 453:6,
      454:3, 454:6
  editing, 450:2
  emotions, 448:6
  as entertainment, 454:1
  executives/leadership, 445:6, 449:3, 450:4,
      452:2
  historical, 446:3
  Hollywood, 451:4
  humor, 443:3
  ideas/messages, 448:6, 454:1, 454:2
  insecurity of industry, 451:2
  lawyers and accountants, 452:2
  making the film, 449:1
  manipulative, 450:3
  metaphor, 442:6
  moguls, old-time, 449:3
  "movies" (the word), 448:3
  novels compared with, 448:5
  old days, 449:3, 450:4
  "political" films, 454:2
  power of, 451:3, 454:1
  pretend and real, 443:3
  producing/producers, 454:4
  psyche, film lives in, 448:5
  public taste, 451:3
  ratings, 20:6
  serious subjects, 467:1
  sex aspect, 448:1
  "shrinking" medium, 451:1
  Soviet Union, 442:3
  stage/theatre compared with, 465:1, 465:2,
      467:1
  stereotypes, creation of, 454:2
  stories, good, 452:4
  studios, major, 451:5, 452:2
  talent, 451:2
  technique/stylization, 448:4, 454:3

Motion pictures/films/cinema *(continued)*
  television compared with, 437:1, 442:4, 452:3
  theatres, 442:4
  think, helping people, 444:6
  writing/writers, 437:1, 446:1, 448:5, 453:1, 453:2, 454:4, 454:5
    actors also writing, 449:4
    dialogue, 443:1, 452:3
  films:
    Ben Hur, 452:1
    The Dead, 448:7
    Drums Along the Mohawk, 446:3
    Fame, 450:2
    The Graduate, 446:4
    In the Heat of the Night, 453:2
    It's a Wonderful Life, 443:2, 510:5
    Network, 218:2
    Rambo III, 445:6
    Solomon and the Queen of Sheba, 448:1
    Waterloo, 446:3
    The Wizard of Oz, 452:1
  See also Acting
Motivation, 471:6
Mozambique:
  rebels, 272:7
  foreign relations/policy with:
    South Africa, 272:7
    Soviet Union, 157:1, 158:1
    U.S., 157:1
Mubarak, Hosni—*see* Egypt
Mulroney, Brian—*see* Canada
Murdoch, Iris, 414:3
Murnau, F. W., 443:4
Museums—*see* Arts
Musial, Stan, 505:3
Music, pp. 455-462
  classical:
    age of musician, 459:5
    amateur/professional aspect, 461:3
    approach, wrong/right, 461:4
    audience, 458:6, 460:6
    Britain, 460:6
    composing/composers, 455:1, 456:1, 458:6, 460:1, 460:4, 461:4, 462:3
    conducting/music director, 455:1, 456:4
      superstars, 455:4
      women, 458:1
    critics, 456:4
    entertainment vs. art. 456:3
    eternal, 456:6
    government support, U.S., 459:4
    instrument, choice of, 460:5
    low sounds, 459:1
    meaning, 461:1

Music *(continued)*
  classical *(continued)*
    orchestras:
      funding, 459:4
      small-town, 459:4
      See also conducting, *this section*
    piano, 460:3, 462:1
    recordings, 456:1, 460:3
    stage/theatre compared with, 467:3
    "star" performers, 460:1
      See also conducting, *this section*
    U.S. aspect, 459:4, 460:6, 462:3
    violin, 459:6
  confidence aspect, 457:6
  "early music," 460:5
  education/schools aspect, 401:1, 457:6
  electronic, 456:1
  Italy, 459:4
  jazz:
    instruction in, 457:4
    misunderstood, 457:3
  lieder singing, 457:2
  literature/books compared with, 414:5
  musicals—*see* Stage
  opera:
    audience, 462:2
    Augusta (Ga.) Opera, 455:3
    celebrities, 462:2
    composing/composers, 455:1, 457:5, 460:7
    directing/directors, 458:5, 461:2
    Metropolitan Opera (N.Y.), 456:3, 461:6
    singers, 456:5, 457:1, 458:4, 459:2, 459:3, 461:6, 462:2
    small-town companies, 455:3
    stage/theatre compared with, 467:3
    theatrical aspect, 458:5
    time, from another, 460:7
    time periods, 455:1
    words, 457:1
    operas:
      Aknahten, 400:1
      Fidelio, 455:1
      Tristan und Isolde, 400:1
  popular:
    quality, 460:2
    songwriting, 456:2, 461:5
  rock, 457:6
  sensual art, 448:6
  Soviet Union, 458:2
  understanding music, 458:3

N

Nabokov, Vladimir, 414:6
Najibullah—*see* Afghanistan

Namibia/South-West Africa:
  apartheid, 278:5
  independence, 272:5, 276:4, 278:5
  socialism, 271:1
  SWAPO, 271:1, 276:4
  foreign relations/policy with:
    South Africa, 271:1, 272:3, 272:5, 276:4,
     276:6
    Soviet Union, 271:1
    U.S., 278:5
National Broadcasting Co. (NBC)—*see* Broad-
  casting
National Rifle Assn. (NRA)—*see* Crime: gun
  control
Navratilova, Martina, 506:5
Nazi era—*see* Austria; Germany, Nazi
New Jersey, 139:1
New York City, N.Y.:
  dance, 468:4
  life in, 480:5
  poverty, 258:3
    beggars, 256:2
  schools, 130:2
  See also Bronx, N.Y.; Stage: Broadway
New Zealand, 516:3
News media—*see* Journalism
Newspapers—*see* Journalism
Nicaragua:
  civil war/cease-fire/negotiations, 284:5, 285:3,
    285:4, 288:6, 289:1, 289:2, 294:4, 300:7,
    320:3, 363:1
    Arias, Oscar, peace plan, 284:3, 292:1,
     294:2
    See also contras, *this section*
  Communism/Marxism/socialism, 244:5, 282:2,
    291:1, 299:2, 300:4, 301:5, 305:1
  contras/rebels, 145:2, 150:4, 162:1, 165:4,
    278:5, 281:1, 281:2, 282:2, 282:4, 283:1,
    283:2, 284:3, 284:4, 284:5, 285:1, 285:3,
    285:4, 287:1, 287:2, 288:6, 289:2, 289:5,
    290:5, 291:4, 291:5, 292:1, 294:2, 294:3,
    294:4, 295:1, 295:2, 296:4, 297:4, 298:2,
    299:2, 299:6, 300:1, 300:2, 300:7, 301:1,
    301:4, 301:5, 302:2, 302:3, 303:1, 305:1,
    305:4, 307:6, 308:1, 363:1
    drugs aspect, 56:2
    U.S. Iran-contra scandal—*see* Iran: U.S.
  democracy, 282:2, 282:5, 283:1, 284:3, 284:4,
    285:1, 287:1, 288:6, 294:2, 295:2, 296:4,
    298:2, 299:6, 302:1, 302:2, 303:1, 305:1,
    305:4, 306:3
  dictatorship, 164:3, 288:5
  drugs, 56:2
  economy, 288:5, 300:4

Nicaragua *(continued)*
  human rights, 301:1
  hunger, 294:1
  Ortega, Daniel, 155:5, 158:2, 281:1, 282:2,
    287:1, 294:2, 295:2, 301:4
  political opponents, crackdown on, 287:4
  political parties, 306:4
  press freedom, 301:1
  prisoners, political, 285:3
  repression, 305:1
  Sandinistas, 145:2, 281:1, 281:2, 282:2, 282:4,
    282:5, 283:1, 283:2, 284:3, 284:5, 285:1,
    285:3, 285:4, 287:1, 287:2, 288:5, 288:6,
    289:2, 289:5, 290:1, 290:5, 291:1, 291:4,
    291:5, 292:1, 294:2, 294:3, 294:4, 295:1,
    295:2, 297:4, 297:5, 298:2, 299:2, 299:6,
    300:1, 300:2, 300:3, 300:5, 300:6, 300:7,
    301:1, 301:4, 301:5, 302:1, 302:2, 302:3,
    303:1, 305:1, 305:4, 306:3, 307:6, 308:1,
    363:1
  strikes, labor, 307:4
  subvert/attack/threaten neighbors, 292:2, 299:2,
    301:4, 302:4
  foreign relations/policy with:
    Bulgaria, 158:1
    Costa Rica, 301:4
    Cuba, 158:1, 296:4, 302:4
    El Salvador, 285:2
    Germany, East, 158:1
    Honduras, 282:4, 290:5
    Mexico, 302:4
    Palestine Liberation Organization (PLO),
     158:1
    Panama, 299:2, 302:4
    Soviet Union, 158:1, 287:2, 295:2, 299:2,
     301:1, 301:5, 302:2, 302:4
    U.S., 145:2, 162:1, 165:4, 244:5, 281:2,
     282:2, 283:1, 283:2, 284:3, 284:4,
     287:1, 287:2, 288:6, 289:5, 290:1,
     290:3, 290:5, 291:4, 291:5, 292:1,
     292:5, 294:2, 294:3, 294:4, 295:1,
     295:2, 296:4, 297:4, 297:5, 299:2,
     299:5, 300:1, 300:2, 300:5, 300:6,
     301:1, 301:4, 301:5, 302:2, 302:3,
     302:4, 303:1, 305:1, 305:4, 307:6,
     308:1, 380:6
    Democratic Party aspect, 281:1, 291:1,
     300:3
    drugs aspect, 56:2
    Dukakis, Michael S., aspect, 300:3,
     301:5
    Iran-contra scandal—*see* Iran: U.S.
Nigeria:
  defense/military, 271:2

Nigeria *(continued)*
  democracy, 271:2
Nightingale, Florence, 353:4
Nixon, Richard M., 211:3, 214:4
  courts, packing of, 203:2
  ethics, 186:1
  foreign policy, 158:4
  monarch as President, 179:5
Noriega, Manuel Antonio—*see* Panama
North Atlantic Treaty Organization (NATO)—*see*
  Europe: defense
North, Oliver—*see* Iran: U.S.: Iran-contra scandal
Northern Ireland:
  Britain, 329:2, 482:3
  Irish Republican Army (IRA), 343:1
  Protestants, 329:2
  violence, 341:2, 341:4, 343:1
  foreign relations/policy with:
    Ireland, 341:2, 344:4, 482:3
Norway, 340:2
Nuclear power—*see* Energy
Nuclear weapons—*see* Defense
Nursing—*see* Medicine
Nursing homes—*see* Social welfare
Nutrition—*see* Medicine: diet

O

Odom, William, 151:6
Oil—*see* Energy
Olympic Games—*see* Sports
Oman, 168:4
O'Neill, Thomas P., Jr., 219:5, 231:6, 251:2
Ortega, Daniel—*see* Nicaragua

P

Pacific—*see* Asia
Pain, 481:7
Painting—*see* Arts
Pakistan:
  Administration, new, 310:6
  elections, 310:4, 328:4
  poverty, 310:5
  ruler, reluctant, 328:5
  Zia ul-Haq, Mohammed, 310:4, 311:5
  foreign relations/policy with:
    Afghanistan, 311:5, 328:3
    China, 326:1
    India, 326:1
    Soviet Union, 311:5
    U.S., 328:4
Palestine Liberation Organization (PLO)—*see*
  Palestinians
Palestinians, 162:3
  education aspect, 369:4

Palestinians *(continued)*
  Palestine Liberation Organization (PLO)/
  Palestine National Congress (PNC), 360:2,
    362:3, 371:3, 377:3, 380:3
    Arafat, Yasir, 286:1, 358:4, 361:1, 366:2,
      367:3, 373:3, 374:5, 376:3, 381:4
    See also U.S.: Arafat, denial of visa, *this
      section*
    France, 376:3
    Israel—*see* Israel: Arabs: Palestinians
    Nicaragua, 158:1
    Soviet Union, 369:3
    terrorism, 359:4, 360:5, 361:1, 362:5,
      366:2, 366:5, 373:3, 374:5, 375:5,
      376:3, 381:5, 382:5, 383:1, 385:2,
      385:3, 388:2, 388:3, 388:4, 388:5
    U.S., 286:1, 358:1, 360:5, 361:1, 372:1,
      372:3, 372:4, 376:3, 382:2, 382:3,
      385:2, 385:3, 388:4, 388:5
      Arafat, denial of visa to, 362:1, 362:5,
        369:3, 375:5, 381:5, 382:5, 388:2,
        388:3
  role in history, 359:3
  state, independent / sovereignty / homeland,
    358:1, 358:5, 360:1, 360:2, 362:3, 363:4,
    364:1, 366:5, 369:1, 369:2, 371:3, 371:4,
    371:5, 372:3, 373:2, 377:3, 378:1, 381:4,
    382:2, 384:6, 385:1, 385:4, 385:5, 388:1,
    388:5, 390:2, 391:4
  terrorism, 378:1
  See also Palestine Liberation Organization,
    this section
  foreign relations/policy with:
    France, 376:3
    Israel, 358:5, 362:3, 364:1, 369:4, 370:4,
      370:5, 372:3, 378:1, 380:1, 387:2,
      390:2, 390:6, 391:4
      acceptance of Israel, 358:4, 360:1,
        366:2, 367:3, 369:1, 371:5, 373:2, 376:3,
        381:4, 381:5, 382:2, 388:4, 388:5
      See also Israel: foreign affairs:
        Arabs; Israel: occupied Palestinian
        territory
    Jordan, 364:1, 371:3
    Soviet Union, 362:3, 369:2
    U.S., 162:1, 364:1, 366:5, 369:2, 372:2,
      388:1, 391:4
      See also Palestine Liberation Organiza-
        tion, *this section*
Pan American World Airways (Pan Am), 147:3,
  360:3
Panama:
  Canal/treaty, 281:3, 299:2, 302:4
  Communism, 291:1

Panama *(continued)*
  democracy, 281:3, 286:1, 286:4, 293:1
  drugs, 56:2, 64:5, 150:4, 209:1, 212:5, 281:3,
    286:4, 286:6, 292:5, 298:1, 298:3, 299:3,
    299:4, 306:1
  embargo/sanctions, economic, 282:1, 286:4,
    296:1, 296:6, 298:1, 298:3
  Noriega, Manuel Antonio, 56:2, 212:5, 223:4,
    236:1, 281:3, 282:1, 286:1, 286:4, 286:6,
    290:4, 292:5, 293:1, 293:2, 296:1, 296:6,
    298:1, 298:3, 299:3, 299:4, 303:2, 306:1
  political opponents, crackdown on, 287:4
  foreign relations/policy with:
    Argentina, 298:1
    Bolivia, 298:1
    Costa Rica, 298:1
    Guatemala, 298:1
    Libya, 162:1, 286:4
    Nicaragua, 299:2, 302:4
    U.S., 209:1, 212:5, 223:4, 236:1, 281:3,
      282:1, 286:1, 286:4, 286:6, 291:1,
      292:5, 298:1, 298:3, 299:2, 299:3,
      302:4, 303:2, 306:1, 380:6
Paraguay, 306:2
Parents—*see* Education; Social welfare: family
Paris, France, 400:5
Patriotism—*see* America
Peace—*see* War/peace
Peres, Shimon—*see* Israel
Performing arts, pp. 437-469
Perkins, Maxwell, 422:1
Persian Gulf—*see* Middle East
Peru:
  economy, 287:4, 293:4
  political centralization, 293:4
  violence, 296:3
Philip Morris, Inc., 431:1
Philippines:
  Aquino, Corazon C., 158:1, 310:2, 319:4,
    320:2
  Communism, 309:1, 314:3, 319:4
  democracy, 150:4, 309:3, 309:5, 314:4, 320:2,
    324:4
  economy, 309:2, 314:4
  human rights, 309:5, 310:3
  insurgency, 309:1, 309:5, 314:3
  Marcos, Ferdinand E., 150:4, 204:4, 309:3,
    324:4
  foreign relations/policy with:
    Soviet Union, 158:1, 313:5, 314:3
    U.S., 150:4, 314:4, 319:4, 324:4
      bases, military, 309:4, 313:5, 318:4,
        319:1, 323:3, 323:4, 324:3, 380:6
Philosophy, pp. 470-482

Phoenix, Ariz., 266:5
Photography—*see* Arts
Pinochet, Augusto—*see* Chile
Plato, 126:4, 472:3
Pledge of Allegiance—*see* America
Poetry—*see* Literature
Poindexter, John M.—*see* Iran: U.S.: Iran-contra
  scandal
Poland:
  church, 342:2, 347:5
  Communism/socialism, 149:1, 347:5, 354:3,
    355:5, 356:1, 356:2
  democracy/freedom, 332:3, 342:2, 353:7
  dictatorship, 347:5
  economy, 330:3, 330:4, 335:2, 346:5, 347:5,
    347:6, 349:4, 354:3, 354:4, 355:4
  human rights, 335:2
  independence, 342:4
  Jaruzelski, Wojciech, 155:5, 338:3, 353:7
  life, everyday, 330:4
  pluralism, 356:2
  reform, 353:7, 355:4
  strikes, labor, 354:3, 355:4, 356:1
  unions, trade/labor, 346:5, 353:7
    Solidarity union, 335:2, 352:5, 354:3
  West, friendship with, 352:3
  foreign relations/policy with:
    Soviet Union, 342:3
    U.S., 332:3
Police—*see* Crime
Politics/elections/campaigns, pp. 206-252
  activists, ideological, 210:5
  advertising/commercials, TV, 215:4, 216:2,
    218:1, 233:3, 240:7, 248:6, 250:1
  affect lives every day, 184:2
  against things, being, 234:4
  answers, simple, 229:1
  astrology, 241:2
  baby-boomers aspect, 234:3
  blacks/minorities aspect, 21:2, 24:3, 216:4,
    219:2, 227:2, 230:3, 230:5, 230:6, 233:1,
    233:4, 234:2, 244:2, 250:7, 252:3
    See also Jackson, Jesse L., *this section*
  Britain, 225:4
  cattle shows, 207:2
  caucuses, 230:2, 236:4, 237:6, 240:5
  change, people want, 212:6, 249:2
  charisma of candidate, 217:2
  conservatism/right, 209:3, 223:2, 228:3, 232:5,
    234:3, 234:4, 242:1, 244:2, 480:2
  child-care, 260:6
  civil-rights, 30:5
  Dukakis, Michael S., aspect, 223:6
  foreign affairs, 158:4

Politics/elections/campaigns *(continued)*
  conservatism/right *(continued)*
    government aspect, 176:5, 189:3
    Jackson, Jesse L., aspect, 242:1
    law aspect, 200:5
    poets, 420:6
    Quayle, Dan, aspect, 209:3, 244:2
    Republican Party aspect, 206:4, 234:1, 254:4
    static, 234:1
  consistency, candidate, 248:6
  conventions, political, 409:5, 411:1
    anachronistic, 206:1
    blandness/dull/boring, 217:3, 225:2, 409:5, 411:1
    press/TV coverage of, 206:1, 217:3, 225:2
  debates, candidate, 210:4, 236:2, 237:3, 239:3, 314:6, 515:5
  dress, candidate, 206:3, 229:4
  emotional aspect, 247:5
  ethics/morality, 182:1, 226:5
  fears, playing on people's, 218:1
  financial disclosure, candidate, 212:4
  financing/money aspect, elections/campaigns, 208:1, 221:6, 228:2, 229:1, 231:1, 235:2, 238:3, 250:1, 251:3, 251:4
    political action committees (PAC), 221:6, 231:1, 243:3, 251:4
  football compared with, 234:6
  friends, belief in, 248:1
  friendships, ruining of, 216:3
  Governor, running for, 207:3, 234:2
  hunted, candidates, 229:3
  ideology/competence, candidate, 213:5, 222:4
  incentive to participate, 210:5
  incumbents, 237:2, 251:4
  issues, 174:5, 207:3, 208:2, 213:1, 219:3, 221:1, 229:2, 240:6, 247:3, 248:5, 249:4
  Jackson, Jesse L., aspect, 15:1, 21:2, 24:3, 207:1, 207:5, 210:3, 211:3, 211:4, 212:5, 216:4, 217:4, 219:2, 221:5, 222:2, 227:2, 227:4, 230:4, 230:5, 230:6, 231:2, 232:3, 236:5, 237:1, 242:1, 244:4, 250:7, 251:5, 251:6, 252:1, 252:3
  Jewish aspect, 228:3
  leadership, candidate, 217:5, 227:6, 228:1, 228:5
  length, campaign, 225:4, 238:5
  liberalism/left, 216:2, 218:2, 228:3, 234:3, 234:4, 240:5, 242:1, 242:2, 251:2
    ACLU aspect, 221:2
    attacks against, 233:1
    baby-boomers aspect, 206:4
    crime, 53:6, 54:2

Politics/elections/campaigns *(continued)*
  liberalism/left *(continued)*
    defense/military, 69:6, 84:3
    Democratic Party aspect, 215:5, 242:1, 242:2, 251:5
    Dukakis, Michael S., aspect, 206:5, 213:1, 215:3, 223:6, 224:1, 244:1, 244:6, 245:3, 247:4
    economy, 94:3, 102:3, 104:5, 109:1, 110:4, 111:1, 111:3
    foreign affairs, 158:4
    government aspect, 176:5, 178:1, 193:1
    Jackson, Jesse L., aspect, 242:1
    judges, 200:1
    press aspect, 407:5
  libertarianism, 206:4
  literature/books aspect, 424:5
    "kiss-and-tell" books, 245:5
    poetry, 420:5, 420:6
  loyalty, 250:4
  marketing game, 240:3
  mental/physical aspect, candidate, 225:4
  middle ground, candidate in, 248:2
  mistakes, candidate, 249:2
  momentum/marathon theory, 221:4
  monochromatic candidates, 229:4
  motion-pictures aspect, 454:2
  motivation, candidate, 235:1
  negative/nasty campaigns, 206:2, 210:2, 216:2, 218:1, 218:2, 219:1, 222:1, 222:5, 223:2, 224:2, 224:4, 224:7, 232:5, 233:3, 236:5, 237:2, 238:4, 240:7, 241:3, 247:1, 247:3, 251:1
  news coverage—*see* press, *this section*
  nominating process, 236:4
  offending voters, 482:3
  packaged and managed candidates, 239:1, 250:2
  parties, political, 306:4, 328:4
    distinctions, 215:5
    loyalty, 215:5, 248:3
    static aspect, 234:1
  passion, candidate, 225:3
  vs. people, 18:2
  personal aspect of candidates, 229:2, 240:6
  personality, candidate, 212:3, 214:1
  perspective, candidate, 174:4
  poetry in their politics, people want, 211:3
  political action committees (PAC)—*see* financing, *this section*
  polls, 207:4, 211:2, 223:5, 229:1
    exit polls, 409:5
  Presidency (U.S.), running for, 17:4, 207:3, 208:1, 210:4, 225:3

Politics/elections/campaigns *(continued)*
Presidency (U.S.), running for *(continued)*
elected, being, 178:2
press/news coverage, 182:1, 206:2, 215:2,
221:1, 226:5, 229:2, 229:3, 248:5, 406:1,
407:4, 409:5, 411:5
conventions, coverage of, 206:1, 217:3,
225:2
endorsements, newspaper, 411:4
winners, TV early announcing of, 226:1
primaries, 208:1, 217:4, 219:2, 219:3, 221:1,
224:6, 225:4, 231:4, 236:4, 239:1, 240:1,
409:5
promises, candidate, 248:4
reform, campaign, 243:3
registration, immediate, 230:4
religion, 246:4
running for office, 235:2
See also Governor, *this section;* Presidency,
U.S., *this section;* Senate, *this section;*
Vice-Presidency (U.S.), *this section;*
Women, *this section*
Senate (U.S.), running for, 207:3, 238:3
South, the U.S., 231:4, 246:3
special interests, 212:4, 228:4, 243:3, 246:2,
251:3
speeches, candidate, 239:6
talking to voters, 219:3
"Tarmac Campaigns," 219:3
television coverage, 217:3, 225:2, 227:6,
247:4, 248:5
See also press, *this section*
13-year-old level, 211:2
three Ps, 210:5
throwing the rascals out, 229:3
transcendent process, 207:2
Vice-Presidency (U.S.) aspect, 217:4
debates, 515:5
nomination, 231:4, 231:5, 231:6, 232:1
running for, 240:2
Watergate, 239:4
winning/losing elections, 241:1, 248:5, 252:4
women:
running for/elected to public office, 22:4,
30:6, 32:5, 226:5
voters, 233:1, 247:1
League of Women Voters, 239:3
worst in people, brings out, 250:4
elections:
1800s, 247:3
1908, 252:2
1960, 235:5
1964, 233:3, 247:3
1968, 247:4

Politics/elections/campaigns *(continued)*
elections: (continued)
1972, 238:2
1980, 234:1
1984, 206:4, 206:5, 231:6, 246:2
1988, 15:1, 21:2, 24:3, 95:1, 144:5, 157:4,
166:7, pp. 206-252, 404:5, 407:4
See also Democratic Party, U.S.; Government;
Republican Party, U.S.
Pollution—*see* Environment
Polo, Marco, 313:2
Pornography—*see* Civil rights
Postal Service, U.S., 181:1, 182:4, 189:2
Postmaster General, 182:5
Poverty/poor—*see* Social welfare
Presidency, U.S./White House/Executive Branch:
aides, ethics of, 182:2
appointments, 181:3, 197:3
See also judicial, *this section*
arts/culture aspect—*see* Arts
autocracy, 186:1
Cabinet, 178:4, 182:2, 196:2
minorities aspect, 20:1
character, 174:5
Chief of Staff, 196:1
Congress aspect, 72:1, 82:1, 160:6, 170:5,
179:5, 180:1, 186:3 190:4, 194:1
President being in Congress, 176:2
Constitution aspect, 179:5
courage/patriotism, 241:3
creed, gives voice to unifying, 18:4
criticism of, 186:3
decision-making, 177:4
defense/military, 72:1, 82:1
Commander-in-Chief, 71:6, 143:3
War Powers Act/Resolution, 82:1, 82:5,
170:5
delegating, 177:5
Democratic Party aspect, 207:3, 241:4, 244:5,
246:5, 249:5, 250:6
economy, 93:2, 94:5, 111:1
elected, being, 178:2
ethics, 177:1, 188:1
See also aides, *this section*
Federal system, 179:2
First Lady, 178:4, 189:1, 191:5
foreign affairs, 143:3, 146:3, 157:4, 158:2,
158:3, 159:5, 160:6, 161:3, 161:4, 163:1,
169:1, 170:5, 176:2, 241:3
Governorship aspect, state, 180:3
ignorance, 185:3
judicial appointments, 203:2
See also Judiciary: judges
"kiss-and-tell" books by former aides, 179:6

Presidency, U.S./White House/Executive Branch:
  (continued)
  law-making, 174:2
  leadership, 176:3, 180:3, 198:2, 211:5
  mistakes, making, 176:4
  monarch, 179:5
  national interest, 176:3
  orderly minds, 190:5
  outsider, 220:3
  people, belongs to the, 187:5
  perspective, 174:4
  power, 175:7, 179:5
  press/media aspect, 176:4
    news conference, 198:2, 408:3, 408:5, 410:3
  public trust, 192:7
  qualifications/experience, 176:2, 180:3, 243:4
  represents all the people, 184:5
  Republican Party aspect, 187:1, 235:4, 245:4,
    249:2, 249:5, 252:2
  running for, 17:4, 207:3, 208:1, 210:4, 225:3
    See also elected, being, *this section*
  sweeping What House clean, 181:2
  the team, 185:1
  transition after election, 181:3
  two-term amendment, 192:5
  veto, line-item, 93:2, 109:3, 111:1
  Vice-Presidential aspect, 175:4, 177:2, 178:3,
    191:3, 228:1
  weakened, 193:1
  woman as President, 183:6
Press—*see* Journalism
Prison—*see* Crime
Protectionism—*see* Trade, foreign
Proust, Marcel, 420:4
Pulitzer Prize, 411:3
Pushkin, Aleksandr, 472:3

Q

Qaddafi, Muammar el—*see* Libya
Qatar, 168:4
Quayle, Dan, 76:4, 151:4, 178:3, 210:2, 223:3,
  366:4
  cities aspect, 267:4
  conservative/right aspect, 209:3, 244:2
  National Guard aspect, 209:2, 214:2, 235:3,
    242:4
  qualifications/experience/youth, 209:3, 209:4,
    210:1, 214:4, 216:1, 223:4, 232:4, 239:5,
    240:4, 243:1, 243:2, 243:4

R

Racism—*see* Civil rights
Radio—*see* Broadcasting

Railroads—*see* Transportation
Rayburn, Sam, 215:2, 223:2, 246:1
RCA Corp., 42:2
Reading—*see* Education: illiteracy; Literature
Reagan, Ronald, 250:5, 251:1
  astrology aspect, 196:3, 241:2, 245:5, 492:5
  Democrats, Reagan, 233:3
  economics/Reaganomics, 96:5, 100:7
  era, Reagan, 222:3
  foreign affairs, 172:1
    Reagan Doctrine, 164:2
  illusion, creating, 238:1
  Republican Party aspect, 221:3
  scandals, 241:2
    See also specific scandals
  social welfare, 253:3
  tolerant man, 206:4
  vigor, 238:6
  women's rights, 223:4
  See also Civil rights
Reform, 479:6
Relationships, personal, 482:1
Religion/church, 478:6, pp. 483-488
  abortion, 21:3, 22:1
  atheism, 483:3, 485:1
  black aspect, 485:6, 488:4
  Britain, 483:4, 485:5
  Christianity:
    Bible, the, 196:3, 483:1, 488:3
    black aspect, 485:6, 488:4
    "born again" aspect, 487:4
    changes, 486:4
    Christ, Jesus, 483:1, 484:2
    conservatives/moderates, 483:1
    diversity/pluralism, 483:4, 488:2
    evangelists, 484:2, 485:2, 486:5, 486:6
    Poland, 342:2, 347:5
    women, ordination of, 483:4, 486:1, 486:7,
      487:5
    Anglican Church, 483:4, 486:1, 486:7,
      487:5
    Assemblies of God, 484:2
    Baptist Church, 488:3
    Catholicism, 334:6, 485:6, 486:4
      Poland, 342:2
      successful people, attitude toward, 473:3
      tax exemption, 20:6
    Episcopal Church, 486:1
    Lutheran Church, 487:4
    Methodist Church, 488:2
    Protestantism, 334:6
      See also Northern Ireland
  France, 334:6
  freedom of, 217:1

Religion/church *(continued)*
  freedom without domination, 485:4
  God, 474:3, 487:4, 488:1
  intellectuals and, 484:3
  Islam, 156:4, 374:2, 381:2
  Judaism/Jews:
    British House of Lords, rabbi in, 485:5
    Democratic Party (U.S.) aspect, 228:3
    intermarriage, 486:3
    Nazi era, 344:2
    political aspect, 228:3
    Republican Party (U.S.) aspect, 228:3
    Semitism, anti-, 23:2, 390:1
    Soviet Union, 331:4, 487:1
    "who is a Jew," 485:3, 486:2, 487:2, 487:3
    See also Israel
  patriotism aspect, 218:2
  piety, 483:2
  Poland, 342:2, 347:5
  political/elections aspect, 246:4
    See also Judaism, *this section*
  prayer, school, 230:1, 244:6, 484:1
  reactionary force, 483:3
  revival of, 484:3
  schools, teaching in, 483:5
  science aspect, 483:2
  Soviet Union, 349:1, 483:3, 484:5, 485:1
    See also Judaism, *this section*
  state, separation of church and, 21:3, 119:5, 483:6
  studies, religious, 484:3
  tax exemption, 20:6
Republican Party, U.S., 212:6, 223:1, 242:1, 245:1, 245:4, 251:2
  arms sales to Arabs, 366:4
  baby-boomers aspect, 206:4
  campaign tactics/reform, 223:2, 243:3
  child care, 260:6
  civil rights, 22:2, 26:3, 30:5, 206:6, 211:4, 220:2, 220:5, 220:6, 230:4, 233:2, 233:5, 234:5
  Congress:
    House, 187:1, 235:4, 244:3
    Senate, 235:4
  conservatism/right aspect, 206:4, 234:1, 254:4
  defense/military, 76:4
  Democratic Party aspect, 226:2
  drugs, 64:5
  economy, 99:2, 102:3, 105:2, 110:6, 111:5
  education, 118:6
  election, 1988, 222:1, 229:5, 230:3, 237:4
  environment, 133:6
  future, vision of, 237:6
  government aspect, 188:4

Republican Party, U.S. *(continued)*
  Governors, state, 235:4
  issues, speaking out on, 233:6
  Jackson, Jesse L., aspect, 210:3, 211:3, 211:4
  Jewish aspect, 228:3
  mandate, 235:4
  moderate wing, 235:5
  open door, 212:2, 220:5, 220:6
  poverty, 220:2, 261:1
  Presidency (U.S.) aspect, 187:1, 235:4, 245:4, 249:2, 249:5, 252:2
  principles, 215:4
  privilege/class aspect, 220:6
  Reagan, Ronald, aspect, 221:3
  social welfare, 254:4, 257:3
    Social Security, 261:2
  the South, 206:4
  talent, dearth of, 211:1
  time in office, 230:3
  tolerant, 206:4
  women aspect, 19:2, 32:4, 225:1
  youth, 206:4
Retirement, 472:1
Rice, Jim, 505:3
RJR Nabisco, Inc., 35:2, 46:4, 431:1
Robb, Charles S., 242:1
Rockefeller, Nelson A., 178:3
Rockwell, Norman, 262:1
Rogers, Will C., 364:3
Roh Tae Woo—*see* Korea, South
Role models, 471:4
Romanenko, Yuri, 496:2
Romania, 394:7
  Communism, 331:2
Roosevelt, Eleanor, 32:1
Roosevelt, Franklin D., 28:5, 151:1, 171:1, 180:3, 203:2, 221:3, 223:2, 223:6, 224:3, 227:5, 231:3, 245:1, 293:3, 406:4
Roosevelt, Theodore, 180:3, 214:4, 302:3
Rose, Pete, 504:4, 505:3, 507:1
Rossellini, Roberto, 443:4
Rostropovich, Mstislav, 333:1
Running (sport), 516:3
Russia—*see* Soviet Union
Ruth, Babe, 505:3
Ryan, Nolan, 506:3

S

Sadat, Anwar el-, 366:2, 389:4
Salinger, J. D., 418:4
Sao Paulo, Brazil, 140:4
Saudi Arabia:
  defense/military, 376:4
    U.S. arms sales, 365:4, 366:4, 367:4

Saudi Arabia *(continued)*
oil, 376:4
spending, government, 376:4
terrorism, 168:4
welfare of people, 376:4
foreign relations/policy with:
U.S., 168:4, 361:5, 364:4, 365:4, 366:4, 367:4, 376:4
Savimbi, Jonas, 145:2, 273:4
Schembechler, Bo, 510:7
Schoenberg, Arnold, 457:2
Schools—*see* Education
Schweitzer, Albert, 474:4
Science/technology, 476:3, pp. 489-497
Asia, 311:1
astrology aspect, 492:5
biotechnology/genetic engineering, 492:1, 493:3
breakthroughs, 494:4
bureaucracy, 495:3
collider/particle accelerator, super, 494:5
culture, part of, 492:4
economic benefits, 492:1
education/schools aspect, 126:1, 491:5
environmental aspect, 137:5
funding/investment in, 489:5, 490:2, 493:6, 495:2, 495:5, 496:3
knowledge base, 490:1
Japan, 490:1
medicine/health aspect, 429:6
military/civilian aspect, 495:5
Presidency (U.S.) aspect, 495:2
religious aspect, 483:2
scientists, 494:2, 494:3
small firms, 493:3
socially relevant, 494:2
Soviet Union, 329:1, 352:2, 352:4, 491:3, 494:1
See also space, *this section*
strategy, long-term, 492:1
understand, need for public to, 491:6, 492:4, 496:1
U.S., 489:5, 490:1, 490:2, 491:5, 492:1, 494:1, 495:2, 495:5, 496:1
use of, 493:1
work/jobs aspect, 496:6
space:
astronaut/cosmonaut, being an, 493:5, 495:1, 496:2
"brain drain," 496:4
colonization of, 489:4
commitment, 496:3
defense/military aspect, 69:3, 78:1, 496:5
See also Defense: defensive systems
environmental aspect, 136:3

Science/technology *(continued)*
space: (continued)
European launchers, U.S. use of, 489:2
funding, 490:3
future of country, 493:6
goals, 490:4
laboratories in, 263:1
liberations aspect, 494:6
manned aspect, 489:3, 493:4
Mars, 491:1, 493:4, 496:2
National Aeronautics and Space Administration (NASA), U.S., 489:3, 490:4, 491:2, 496:3, 496:4
safety, 491:4, 492:3, 493:2
shuttle:
Challenger disaster, 491:2, 491:4, 492:2, 492:3, 493:2
Discovery, 492:2, 492:3, 493:5
Soviet Union, 495:4
Soviet Union, 489:1, 490:3, 491:1, 495:3, 496:3
shuttle, 495:4
Sputnik, 311:1, 496:5
transportation aspect, 263:1
U.S., 489:1, 489:2, 490:3, 491:1, 493:6, 495:5, 496:3
Self, 478:6
Self-interest, 482:2
Selznick, David O., 450:4
Shakespeare, William, 416:4, 472:3
Shamir, Yitzhak—*see* Israel
Sharah, Farouk, 389:4
Shaw, George Bernard, 472:3
Shevardnadze, Eduard A., 145:5, 145:6
Shostakovich, Dmitri, 461:1
Shubert Organization—*see* Stage
Shultz, George P., 142:2, 143:1, 282:5, 362:2, 374:4
Simon, Paul, 90:4
Simpson, Alan K., 210:1
Sinatra, Frank, 233:5, 400:3
Singapore:
"clean and green," 316:1
economy, 316:2
Smoking—*see* Medicine
Social Security—*see* Social welfare
Social welfare, pp. 253-262
beggars, 256:2, 258:1
child/day care, 99:3, 255:1, 256:3, 261:3
conservatism/right aspect, 260:6
Democratic Party (U.S.) aspect, 253:7, 260:6
Republican Party (U.S.) aspect, 260:6
tax-credit plan, 253:7

Social welfare *(continued)*
  children aspect, 254:3, 261:5
    See also poverty, *this section*
  Democratic Party (U.S.) aspect, 253:3, 257:3
    See also child care, *this section*
  elderly, 256:1, 258:2, 260:1, 261:2, 261:5, 262:3
    See also Medicine
  entitlement programs/benefits, 101:4, 104:3, 253:3, 258:2, 260:3
  family, the, 14:4, 192:2, 260:2, 260:5, 262:1
    single parents, 255:1, 260:2, 262:1
    surrogate parenting, 255:5
    two-income, 262:1
  fortunate, knowng one is, 254:1
  government aspect, 254:4, 257:2
  helping others, 253:5
  homeless, 255:2, 257:6, 258:5, 259:3, 261:4, 262:2, 266:5, 267:3
  housing, 255:2, 256:3, 257:4, 259:3, 266:5
    rent control, 257:5
  hunger, 172:5, 258:4, 259:1, 259:3, 259:4
  nursing homes, 426:1
  nutrition, 258:4
    See also Medicine: diet
  poverty/poor, 80:2, 94:4, 96:2, 104:1, 107:2, 148:6, 218:2, 253:6, 254:5, 255:3, 255:4, 257:1, 257:4, 260:3, 260:4, 261:3, 267:3
    black aspect, 25:5, 255:4, 257:2
    children, 258:2, 258:3, 258:4, 261:6
    education aspect, 119:5, 120:2
    gap between rich and poor, 255:4
    legal services—*see* Law: poor
    Republican Party (U.S.) aspect, 220:2, 261:1
    Third World, 148:4, 153:6, 258:3, 258:6
    war on, 111:1
    working poor, 256:5, 261:1
    world, 148:4, 148:6
  Reagan, Ronald, aspect, 253:3
  Republican Party (U.S.) aspect, 254:4, 257:3
    See also child care, *this section;* poverty, *this section;* Social Security, *this section*
  safety net, 255:3
  Salvation Army, 258:1, 259:3
  Social Security (U.S.), 91:1, 114:3, 258:2, 262:3
    baby-boom generation, 253:1
    Congress, 254:2
    cutting benefits, 253:1
    Democratic Party, 261:2
    earnings limitation, 256:1
    fund/reserves, 254:2, 262:4
    generational equity, 262:4

Social welfare *(continued)*
  Social Security (U.S.) *(continued)*
    information, 259:2
    off-budget aspect, 253:4
    pension system, 253:4
    political aspect, 261:2
    Republican Party, 261:2
    taxes, 253:4
    wealthy, payments to, 260:3
  South, the U.S., 255:3
  Soviet Union, 253:2
  under-class, 131:4
  values, 255:2
  welfare, 255:1, 256:4, 256:5, 261:3
    crime aspect, 60:2
    mentality, welfare, 253:2
    state, welfare, 114:1
    work incentives/programs, 253:3, 256:4, 257:2
  women, 262:2
Socialism—*see* Communism
Society, 473:5
Solis, Manuel, 293:2
South, the U.S., 24:1, 29:1, 32:6, 33:1
  political aspect, 231:4, 246:3
    Democratic Party, 246:3, 252:3
    Republican Party, 206:4
  social welfare, 255:3
  women, Southern, 21:4
South Africa:
  apartheid/blacks, 271:6, 272:1, 272:6, 273:1, 274:1, 275:4, 275:5, 276:6, 278:2, 279:1, 279:2, 279:4, 279:5, 361:4
    African National Congress (ANC), 272:4, 276:2, 278:1
    emergency, state of/violence, 272:2, 274:4, 278:3
    sanctions, foreign, 271:5, 272:3, 274:2, 277:4, 278:4, 280:1
  capitalism, 279:1
  Communism/Marxism, 274:2, 279:1
  Conservative Party, 279:4
  economy, 274:1, 279:2
    See also apartheid: sanctions, foreign, *this section*
  medical insurance, 427:3
  National Party, 279:3, 279:4
  political prisoners, 152:3
  terrorist state, 275:1
  foreign relations/policy with:
    Africa, 276:6
    Angola, 272:5, 276:6, 278:5
    Britain, 279:1
    Germany, West, 279:1

South Africa *(continued)*
  foreign relations/policy with: (continued)
    Japan, 279:1
    Mozambique, 272:7
    Namibia, 271:1, 272:3, 272:5, 276:4, 276:6
    U.S., 271:5, 272:1, 272:3, 273:1, 273:4,
      274:2, 275:5, 277:4, 278:5, 279:1, 280:1
      Democratic Party, 275:1
South-West Africa—*see* Namibia
Soviet Union/Russia/U.S.S.R.:
  art and spirituality, 330:2
  arts, 342:5, 403:3
    cultural exchanges, 399:5, 402:2
  Brezhnev, Leonid I., 347:4
  Communism / Marxism / socialism, 330:5,
    332:1, 332:2, 332:4, 337:1, 337:4, 345:1,
    348:6, 352:4, 354:6, 357:1, 357:2, 408:4,
    485:1
  dance, 463:4
  defense/military, 72:3, 146:5, 164:4, 333:4,
    341:3, 349:5, 351:4, 353:6
    arms control/disarmament/reduction, 69:1,
      71:1, 71:2, 71:4, 73:3, 73:6, 74:2, 74:4,
      75:5, 77:4, 79:1, 81:4, 83:2, 84:3, 85:5,
      87:4, 147:2, 147:5, 155:4, 161:5, 335:5,
      339:1, 345:5
      INF treaty—*see* Defense: arms control
    buildup/modernization, 71:2, 71:4, 82:4,
      162:6, 314:3, 352:4
    defensive/offensive aspect, 68:2, 69:1, 72:5,
      86:4
    NATO, 336:1
    openness, 77:6
    shelters, nuclear, 72:2
    space defense, 83:3
    spending, 71:2
    U.S. aspect, 68:4, 69:3, 69:4, 71:1, 71:2,
      71:3, 71:4, 73:2, 73:3, 73:4, 73:6, 74:2,
      76:1, 76:2, 76:3, 77:4, 77:6, 78:4, 79:1,
      79:4, 82:4, 83:2, 83:4, 83:8, 84:3, 84:5,
      85:2, 85:3, 86:1, 86:2, 86:5, 86:6, 87:4,
      88:2, 147:5, 148:1, 161:5
      equipment comparable, 68:3
      INF treaty—*see* Defense: arms control
  democracy/freedom, 329:4, 332:1, 332:4,
    337:2, 337:4, 337:5, 338:1, 344:6, 349:1,
    354:6, 357:1, 357:3, 357:4, 484:5, 487:1
  dissidents/refuseniks, 331:1, 339:2, 349:2
  doctors, 481:7
  economy, 90:1, 106:1, 146:1, 151:3, 166:3,
    168:5, 329:1, 329:4, 335:5, 336:3, 337:3,
    338:5, 340:5, 345:5, 348:1, 352:3, 352:2,
    352:4
    budget deficits, 339:3

Soviet Union/Russia/U.S.S.R. *(continued)*
  emigration/exit/entry, 339:2, 349:1
  energy, nuclear/Chernobyl accident, 136:2,
    139:5, 335:1
  environment aspect, 136:3, 172:5, 357:3
  Estonia, 329:3, 338:6
  ethnic protests, 333:5
  foreign affairs, 146:1, 151:3, 164:4
    advice, accepting, 154:2
    brink, reaching the, 154:1
    debt owed to it, 154:4
    diplomacy, 142:6
    empire, 334:3
    "evil empire," 150:3
    expansionist / interventionist / aggression/
      domination, 72:3, 148:1, 149:3, 151:6,
      155:4, 155:5, 162:2, 164:7, 165:3,
      171:3
    intelligence/spying, 171:3, 418:2
    niceness/smiles, 166:1, 353:3
    responsible role, 172:5
    settling conflicts, 153:4
    stability in, 153:1
    summit meetings—*see* U.S., *this section*
    troops, commitment of, 152:1
    trustworthiness, 158:6
    United Nations (UN), 161:1, 172:5
    West, relations with, 142:3, 142:6, 161:5,
      169:4, 356:5
  Gorbachev, Mikhail S., 149:2, 160:1, 163:4,
    332:1, 335:4, 340:4, 347:4, 351:1, 351:3,
    353:6, 356:6
  history, falsified, 329:3
  human rights, 72:3, 146:4, 147:2, 148:1, 150:1,
    151:6, 155:4, 155:5, 161:5, 166:4, 348:6,
    349:1, 350:5, 351:1, 351:2
  Jews—*see* religion, *this section*
  KGB, 158:6
  Krushchev, Nikita S., 160:1, 210:1
  Lenin, Vladimir I., 288:3, 330:5, 337:1, 340:4,
    408:4
  literature/books, 408:4, 418:1
    19th-century Russian, 415:3
  Lithuania, 338:6
  living conditions, 342:5, 344:3
  motion pictures, 442:3
  music, 458:2
  one-party system, 288:3
  openness/*glasnost,* 77:6, 145:6, 146:5, 156:1,
    165:2, 171:3, 330:1, 332:2, 333:1, 333:4,
    337:2, 337:4, 338:1, 348:2, 352:1, 357:1,
    409:1
  political prisoners, 351:5
  President/Party chief, power of, 351:3

Soviet Union/Russia/U.S.S.R. *(continued)*
press/news media, 333:1, 344:3, 348:6, 408:9, 409:1, 412:3
reform/change/*perestroika,* 68:2, 71:2, 72:3, 90:1, 142:5, 144:4, 145:5, 145:6, 146:5, 148:1, 149:1, 151:6, 155:5, 156:1, 159:2, 162:6, 165:3, 166:3, 167:3, 169:4, 170:3, 171:3, 253:2, 329:4, 330:5, 331:5, 332:1, 332:2, 333:4, 334:4, 335:4, 335:5, 336:1, 336:5, 337:1, 337:2, 338:4, 338:5, 340:4, 345:2, 345:5, 347:4, 348:2, 351:1, 351:2, 351:3, 351:4, 353:6, 354:6, 356:4, 356:6, 357:1, 442:3, 484:5, 491:3
religion, 349:1, 483:3, 484:5, 485:1
Jews, 331:4, 487:1
rigid system, 352:4
rotten, becoming, 334:3
science/technology, 329:1, 352:2, 352:4, 491:3, 494:1
space, 489:1, 490:3, 491:1, 495:3, 495:4, 496:3, 496:5
shuttle, 495:4
Sputnik, 496:5
Stalin, Josef, 169:4, 171:1, 330:5, 331:2, 345:1, 345:2, 347:4, 351:3
Supreme Soviet, 330:5
television, 440:1
trade, foreign, 172:5, 331:4
welfare, 253:2
foreign relations/policy with:
Afghanistan, 146:1, 146:2, 152:1, 155:5, 158:1, 244:5, 323:6, 328:3, 350:5
troop withdrawal, 311:6, 312:5, 313:3, 315:6, 318:1, 319:5, 320:4, 320:5, 321:1, 321:2, 321:3, 324:1, 324:2
Americas, 146:2, 149:3, 153:1, 155:3, 155:5, 292:2, 292:3, 293:3
Angola, 153:1, 155:5, 157:1, 158:1
Asia/Pacific, 153:1, 313:4, 313:5, 314:3, 322:2
Cambodia, 153:1, 155:5, 158:1
China, 153:1, 321:6, 324:5
Cuba, 151:1, 288:2
Czechoslovakia, 334:5, 350:3
Ethiopia, 158:1, 277:2
Europe, 75:2, 146:1, 146:2, 153:1, 336:1, 343:3, 345:5
Europe, Eastern, 69:1, 85:5, 331:5, 335:3, 341:1, 356:4
Germany, Nazi, 329:3
Germany, West, 331:3, 336:3, 341:1
India, 315:4
Israel, 369:2, 379:6

Soviet Union/Russia/U.S.S.R. *(continued)*
foreign relations/policy with: (continued)
Korea, North, 322:2
Middle East, 146:2, 153:1
Persian Gulf, 146:2, 153:1, 368:6
Mozambique, 157:1, 158:1
Namibia, 271:1
Nicaragua, 158:1, 285:2, 287:2, 295:2, 299:2, 301:1, 301:5, 302:2, 302:4
Pakistan, 311:5
Palestinians, 362:3, 369:2
PLO, 369:3
Philippines, 158:1, 313:5, 314:3
Poland, 342:3
Syria, 389:4
Third World, 172:5
U.S., 142:4, 142:5, 142:6, 145:5, 145:6, 146:4, 147:1, 147:2, 149:2, 150:3, 151:3, 151:6, 153:3, 155:1, 156:1, 156:5, 157:1, 158:1, 158:6, 159:2, 161:5, 163:3, 163:4, 164:1, 164:4, 164:7, 166:1, 166:2, 166:3, 166:4, 166:5, 167:3, 173:1, 286:1, 303:4, 313:4, 331:4, 333:4, 336:1, 341:5, 343:3, 343:4, 343:5, 350:2, 351:6, 399:5, 402:2, 494:1
ideologies, 150:1
intelligence/spying, 171:3, 418:2
moral equivalence, 168:3
negotiations, 151:4
realism, 153:5
summit meetings, 143:5, 147:5, 148:1, 154:1, 154:3, 155:5, 163:5, 166:6
Voice of America, 333:1
Vietnam, 313:5
Space—*see* Science
Spain:
defense/military, 349:3
democracy, 336:4
economy, 336:4
foreign relations/policy with:
U.S., 349:3
Spenser, Edmund, 416:4
Spinks, Michael, 498:1
Sports, pp. 498-517
black/racial aspect, 500:6
champions, 499:6
cheating, 503:3
drug/steroid use, 501:1, 501:4, 506:2, 511:7
fan unruliness, 428:5
fitness, physical, 506:1
government compared with, 183:7
length of seasons, 513:5

Sports *(continued)*
  Olympic Games:
    amateur/professional aspect, 500:1, 510:1, 512:4
    cheating, 503:3
    drug/steroid use, 501:4, 506:2, 511:7
    financial support for athletes, 505:5
    Germany, East, aspect, 503:4
    humanitarian aspect, 514:2
    laziness, athletes', 516:3
    risk-taking, 503:1
    success in, 503:4
    television coverage, 505:1
  players:
    salaries, 500:4, 513:5
    talent/ability, 505:2
  real-life aspect, 500:4
  risk-taking, 503:1
  television coverage, 505:1
  unhappy athletes, 500:4
  winning/losing, 505:2, 516:3
  women, 508:2
  work ethic, 505:2
  See also specific sports
Springsteen, Bruce, 233:5
Stage/theatre, pp. 463-469
  acting, 463:1, 463:3, 464:2, 465:1, 465:2, 465:4, 465:6, 466:2, 466:5, 466:7, 469:4
  Britain, 464:2
  Broadway/New York, 463:3, 463:5, 467:1, 468:2, 469:2
  costs/economics/funding, 465:6, 468:2, 469:1
  diminishment, 463:5
  directing/directors, 463:1
  family turmoil, plays about, 468:3
  future, 463:5
  glamorous side, 466:2
  issues, moral/social, 467:2
  language aspect, 464:2
  literal art-form, 467:3
  minimalism, 468:1
  motion pictures compared with, 465:1, 465:2, 467:1
  music compared with, 467:3
  musicals, 460:2, 467:1, 467:6
  new material/plays, 464:6, 469:1
  novels compared with, 448:5
  opera compared with, 467:3
  plays (non-musical), 467:1
  quality, 466:1
  regional theatre, 469:1
  schools aspect, 401:1
  Shubert Organization, 468:2
  storytelling, 465:3

Stage/theatre *(continued)*
  television compared with, 465:2
  ticket prices, 463:3, 463:5, 468:2, 469:2
  true to oneself, 464:4
  U.S. aspect, 464:2
  writing/playwrights, 448:5, 464:6, 466:1, 466:3, 467:5, 468:1, 468:3, 469:1, 490:4
  titles:
    The Cherry Orchard, 465:1
    King Lear, 465:1
    'night, Mother, 467:5
    Song and Dance, 467:6
    Waiting for Godot, 18:3
Stalin, Josef—*see* Soviet Union
Stanford University, 121:3, 125:5
State, U.S. Dept. of—*see* Foreign affairs
State, U.S. Secretary of—*see* Foreign affairs
States, U.S.—*see* Government: state/local; *and specific states*
Steiger, Rod, 453:2
Steinbeck, John, 418:4
Steinbrenner, George, 508:4
Stendhal, 419:4
Stewart, James, 443:2, 510:5
Stewart, Potter, 420:1
Success/failure, 16:5, 340:2, 473:3, 475:7, 477:2, 477:3, 479:4, 480:4, 481:5, 481:6
Sudan:
  terrorism, 168:4
  foreign relations/policy with:
    U.S., 168:4
Supreme Court, U.S.—*see* Judiciary
Surliness, everyday, 481:4
Surrender, 475:1
Susann, Jacqueline, 420:1
Swaggart, Jimmy, 484:2
Sweden, 97:1
Swimming, 499:6
Switzerland, 505:4
Syria:
  Assad, Hafez al-, 389:4
  economy, 389:4
  Hamra massacre, 384:3
  terrorism, 168:4
  foreign relations/policy with:
    Egypt, 389:4
    Israel, 376:5, 389:4
    Lebanon, 385:6
    Soviet Union, 389:4
    U.S., 168:4, 389:4

T

Taiwan:
  Chiang Ching-kuo, 318:3, 327:5

Taiwan *(continued)*
Communism, 316:4
democracy, 316:4, 318:3
economy, 90:2
Kuomintang, 327:5
trade, foreign, 326:7
foreign relations/policy with:
China/reunification, 316:3, 321:6, 323:5, 327:5, 328:1
U.S., 326:7
Taxes:
capital-gains, 37:2, 92:6, 99:5, 100:3
corporate, 108:4
deduction, mortgage-interest, 91:1
Dukakis, Michael S., aspect, 37:2, 227:3
increase/decrease, 90:4, 91:2, 92:5, 92:6, 93:3, 93:7, 94:1, 94:3, 94:5, 95:2, 95:3, 96:3, 96:5, 97:2, 98:4, 99:3, 99:5, 100:1, 100:2, 100:3, 100:5, 100:7, 104:1, 104:3, 104:5, 106:1, 107:1, 109:1, 110:1, 110:4, 110:5, 111:2, 112:5, 114:1, 114:2, 220:3, 327:4
indexing, 111:2
Internal Revenue Service, U.S. (IRS), 95:3, 108:7, 120:3
rebates, 102:4
religious exemption, 20:6
sales tax, 98:3
shelters, 108:4
Social Security taxes, 253:4
state/local aspect, 179:3
Tax Reform Act of 1986, 108:4, 112:5, 261:1
Tchaikovsky, Piotr Ilich, 458:2, 514:3
Teamsters Union—*see* Labor: unions
Technology—*see* Science
Television—*see* Broadcasting
Tennis:
Australian Open, 501:6
media coverage, 506:5
players:
improvement each generation, 510:3
pressure, 507:6
retirement, 506:5
temperamental, 509:3
U.S. Open, 510:4
Wimbledon, 501:6, 503:2, 506:5, 510:4
winning/losing, 501:6
women, 508:2
Terrorism—*see* Foreign affairs
Thach, Nguyen Co, 310:2
Theatre—*see* Stage
Third World/developing countries:
defense/military, 70:4, 87:1, 387:5
economy/debt/poverty, 107:3, 148:2, 148:4, 153:6, 154:4, 160:4, 173:2, 258:3, 258:6

Third World/developing countries *(continued)*
environmental aspect, 135:2
hunger, 172:5
medicine/health aspect, 425:4
population, 148:4, 160:4
trade, foreign, 160:4
foreign relations/policy with:
Soviet Union, 172:5
U.S., 148:2, 148:3, 157:1, 165:5, 166:2, 258:6
Thorndike, Sybil, 465:2
Thought, rational, 474:1
Tibet—*see* China
Time, 476:2, 479:2
Tolstoy, Leo, 418:4, 420:4, 472:3
Torrijos, Omar, 281:3
Toscanini, Arturo, 459:2
Towne, Robert, 446:1
Toyota Corp., 49:4
Trade, foreign, 34:1
access to markets, 34:6, 39:5, 43:3, 48:3
deficit/balance, 34:6, 37:1, 39:1, 39:2, 43:3, 46:1, 47:5, 48:2, 50:1, 50:5, 95:5, 101:1, 105:1, 105:2, 111:4, 116:2, 121:2, 327:4
imports/exports, 37:1, 46:2, 48:1, 50:1
negotiator, trade, 42:1
policy, 35:1, 43:2
protectionism/tariffs, 38:2, 38:6, 39:5, 41:4, 43:2, 46:1, 46:2, 48:1, 97:5, 101:1, 167:1, 167:4, 291:2, 346:4
Third World, 160:4
Traditions, 476:4, 476:5
Transportation, pp. 263-265
air:
aging of aircraft, 264:5
deregulation, 263:2, 263:3, 264:1
expansion, airline, 265:4
fares, 265:4
Federal Aviation Administration, U.S. (FAA), 263:3, 263:4
manufacturing aspect, 265:3
pilot performance, 263:3
quality of service, 264:1, 265:4
safety, 263:2, 263:3, 263:4, 264:5, 265:4
hijacking of Kuwaiti aircraft, 143:4
Pan Am crash in Scotland, 147:3, 360:3
automobiles/cars:
computers, 263:5
dependability, 264:4
of the future, 264:3
imports, 264:4
right to use, 263:5
deregulation, 263:2, 263:3, 264:1
government aspect, 263:3, 265:1

Transportation *(continued)*
  highways, "smart," 263:5
  mass transit, 263:5, 264:2
  railroads/trains:
    drug-testing, 265:1
    government aspect, 265:1
    high-speed/elevated, 264:6, 265:2
    Japan, 264:6
  space aspect, 263:1
  trucking, 263:2
Trudeau, Gary, 247:1
Truman, Harry S., 54:2, 151:4, 209:3, 223:6, 224:3, 245:1, 251:5, 473:1
Turkey:
  foreign relations/policy with:
    Cyprus, 346:6, 354:5
    Greece, 346:6
Turner, Tina, 457:6
Twain, Mark, 155:2
Tyson, Mike, 498:1

U

Uganda, 152:3
Unemployment—*see* Labor: employment
Union of Soviet Socialist Republics (U.S.S.R.)—*see* Soviet Union
Unions, Labor—*see* Labor
United Arab Emirates, 168:4
United Kingdom/Britain/England:
  coal industry, 347:1
  confidence, 353:1
  democracy, 271:3
  "disease, British," 353:1
  economy, 110:3, 316:2
    privatization, 347:1
  elections, 225:4
  government:
    House of Commons, 353:4
    House of Lords, 485:5
    Prime Minister, woman, 353:4
    privatization, 347:1
  Labor Party, 343:2
  music, 460:6
  Northern Ireland, 329:2, 482:3
  religion, 483:4
    Anglican Church—*see* Religion: Christianity
    Judaism, 485:5
  stage/theatre, 464:2
  television, 437:2, 441:2
  Thatcher, Margaret, 279:1, 340:3, 347:3, 356:3, 487:5
  foreign relations/policy with:
    Africa, 271:3
    Ireland, 162:3

United Kingdom/Britain/England *(continued)*
  foreign relations/policy with: (continued)
    South Africa, 279:1
    U.S., 169:5, 170;2
    See also Northern Ireland
United Nations (UN)—*see* Foreign affairs
United States—*see* America
Universe, the, 474:3
Universities—*see* Education: college
Urban affairs/cities, pp. 266-267
  crime, 50:1, 267:3
  crisis in, 266:5
  economy, 257:2
    development/growth, 267:2
    jobs, 97:6
    zoning, economic, 97:6
  education aspect, 119:6
  flowers/color, 137:2
  gambling, casino, 266:6
  government/Federal aspect, 257:2, 266:3, 266:5, 267:3
  inner city, 267:2
  Mayors, 266:2, 266:4
  Quayle, Dan, aspect, 267:4
  rhythm of life, 266:1
  rural towns, 266:7
  urbanization, 266:7, 267:1

V

Values, 53:4, 56:2, 75:5, 119:5, 162:5, 255:2
Vanderbilt University, 26:6
Van Gogh, Vincent, 401:4
Versatility, 477:6
Vessey, John, 289:4
Vice-Presidency, U.S., 244:2
  abolition of, 187:3
  ceremonies, attending, 191:4
  importance, 178:3
  politics aspect, 217:4
    debates, 515:5
    nomination, 231:4, 231:5, 231:6, 232:1
    running for, 240:2
  Presidential aspect, 175:4, 177:2, 178:3, 191:3, 228:1
  qualifications, 209:2, 209;3, 209;4, 210:1, 214:4, 216:1, 223:3, 231:4, 231:5, 232:4, 239:5, 243:1, 243:2, 243:4
  responsibilities, 219:6
Vietnam:
  capitalism, 312:4, 326:5
  Communism/socialism, 312:4, 317:4, 326:5
  economy, 310:2, 317:4
  "new Vietnam," 310:2

Vietnam *(continued)*
  political prisoners, 152:3
  foreign relations/policy with:
    Cambodia, 310:2, 320:5, 326:4
    China, 321:6
    Soviet Union, 313:5
    U.S., 159:4, 310:2, 313:6, 326:4, 326:5,
      363:1
      war, 79:3, 155:2, 169:3, 313:6, 317:3,
        320:3, 321:4, 326:3
        U.S. veterans, 214:2
Vivaldi, Antonio, 400:3
Vodery, Will, 460:4
Volcker, Paul A., 40:4, 102:4
Volleyball, 507:5

W

Walesa, Lech, 335:2
Wagner, Richard, 461:1
War/peace, pp. 393-395
  peace, 73:6, 79:2, 83:8, 158:4, 213:2, 478:6
    arts aspect, 404:2
    collective responsibility, 394:5
    communications aspect, 393:1
    economic aspect, 393:4
    fraternity and well-being aspect, 394:4
    never-ending process, 393:2
    nuclear aspect, 393:1
    through strength, 69:6, 71:6, 158:3
    United Nations (UN), 159:1, 161:1, 394:5
  war, 82:2, 163:6, 348:3
    absurd, war as, 393:5
    arms, absence of, 394:7
    big/small aspect, 394:6
    confrontation, 395:2
    force, policy of, 395:2
    mistakes made in, 393:3
    television aspect, 394:3
    World War II, 79:2, 151:1, 242:4, 329:3,
      355:2, 355:3
    world-wide problem, 394:2
Washington, D.C., 183:1, 184:3
Washington, George, 99:5, 111:4, 182:3, 328:4,
  359:4, 374:5
Watergate—*see* Politics
Watt, James, 223:4
Wealth—*see* Affluence
Welfare—*see* Social welfare
Wilder, Doug, 242:1
Wilder, Thornton, 466:3
Williams, Ted, 505:3
Wilson, Woodrow, 180:3
Winfield, Dave, 123:4

Wolfe, Thomas, 17:2, 421:2
Women/women's rights:
  abortion, 20:5, 22:3, 25:2, 28:2, 30:1, 30:7,
    136:1, 218:2, 230:1, 244:6
    religious aspect, 21:3, 22:1
    Roe vs. Wade, 20:4, 26:1, 28:1
  acting, 447:2
  baseball umpires, 502:5, 506:6
  British Prime Minister, 353:4
  Bush, George, aspect, 32:4, 225:1, 247:1
  business aspect, 23:1, 23:4
  church ordination, 483:4, 486:1, 486:7, 487:5
  compromise, 21:4
  Congress, U.S., 32:5
  crimes against, sexual, 62:1
  defense/military aspect, 79:5
  education aspect:
    academic faculty, on, 23:4
    college aspect, 123:6
  Egypt, 31:5
  employment/jobs, 31:5, 32:2, 93:6, 106:5,
    112:4
    pay, equal/comparable worth, 20:3, 256:3
  Equal Rights Amendment (ERA), 26:2, 32:4
  familiarity aspect, 30:2
  Federal Bureau of Investigation (FBI) aspect,
    65:5
  fiction, as characters in, 423:3
  golf aspect, 508:2
  journalism aspect, 409:3, 412:5
  men aspect, 19:3, 22:5, 30:4
  more, wanting, 19:3
  nursing, 426:2
  orchestra conductors/music directors, 458:1
  organizing of, 32:1
  politics:
    running for/elected to public office, 22:4,
      30:6, 32:5, 226:5
    voters, women, 233:1, 247:1
      League of Women Voters, 239:3
  prejudice, 25:4
  President, U.S., 183:6
  Reagan, Ronald, aspect, 223:4
  Republican Party (U.S.) aspect, 19:2, 32:4,
    225:1
  social-welfare aspect, 262:2
  Southern women, 21:4
  sports, 508:2
    See also specific sports, this section
  Supreme Court (U.S.) aspect, 29:4
    women on, 200:3
  tennis aspect, 508:2
Worthwhile, anything, 472:6
Wright, Jim, 226:3, 251:2

Writing—*see* Broadcasting; Education: composition; Literature; Motion pictures; Stage

Y

Yale University, 129:4
Yemen, 168:4
Youth—*see* Age

Yugoslavia:
Communism, 149:1
reform, 334:4

Z

Zia ul-Haq, Mohammed—*see* Pakistan